The Juniper Bush

Audrey Howard has her roots in the Merseyside she depicts so well. Although she lived for a year in Sydney, Australia, she is now firmly settled in St Annes on Sea, Lancashire. *The Juniper Bush* won the 1987 Romantic Novelist of the Year Award. Her other novels, also available in Fontana, are *The Skylark's Song*, *The Morning Tide* and *Ambitions*.

AUDREY HOWARD

The Juniper Bush

FONTANA/Collins

*For my son Howard and for Janet,
with my love and thanks for all they have
done for me*

First published in Great Britain by Century Hutchinson Ltd,
1987
First issued in Fontana Paperbacks 1988

Copyright Audrey Howard © 1987

Printed and bound in Great Britain by
William Collins Sons & Co. Ltd, Glasgow

CHAPTER ONE

It was her laugh which drew him to her. It rang out high and clear and he heard it above the sound of the waters of the beck which foamed noisily at his side. The laughter was young and joyous and rich, tugging at the corners of his own mouth and lifting them into a reluctant smile. It seemed to take wing from the densely contrasting foliage of the golden birch which trembled down to the water's edge, erupting from the leaves to swoop like a bird about his ears.

He had ridden along the path from Chapel Stile roughly following the route of the beck, and was approaching the spot where its gleaming ripples ran into the lake when he first heard it and both he, the roan on whose back he rode and the dog running beside him pricked their ears to listen but as quickly as it had come, the lovely sound was gone, silenced suddenly as though with a gag.

He reined in his horse and turned, looking about him and then back in the direction from which he had just come. Though it was a mile away, faintly on the clear air of the settling day he could detect the subdued murmur of the Emmerson Gunpowder Mill as it ground slowly to a halt, for tomorrow was Sunday and this was the end of the last shift, but it was quiet beside the beck and along the track he travelled, the peace disturbed only by the tumbling of the waters.

There was a faint acrid smell on the air. It came from the mill where the timber-burning retorts turned silver birch, alder and the juniper, which flourished on the lower slopes of the fells, into charcoal, one of the three ingredients used in the manufacture of gunpowder. As he looked back he could see the pale blue shreds of vapour from the flues spilling out into the eternal beauty of the Lakeland skies.

The autumn sun had turned to flame as dusk approached and as it dipped behind Tilberthwaite Fell its vivid colours ran into the waters of the lake and the trees along its edge were on fire with it. The flame became pale rose, then apricot. The water held the colours and the earth surrounding it faded to pale green and primrose as darkness began to creep stealthily, blurring the day's brightness to a faded hue and up on the fells purple shadows formed.

An early owl began its hunting and bird-song died away to a soft, fitful murmur, drifting like the sound of the laughter from the trees on his left. The horseman stood for a minute or so, listening intently, but he could hear nothing beside the swirl of the water, the drowsy call of the quietening birds and the heavy breathing of his mount.

The little Lakeland terrier who ran beside him, a rippling streak of black and grey – game and cocky and never more than a foot or two from the dangerous hooves of the roan – stood when he did. He lifted his head and sniffed the air, growling in warning, almost without sound, deep in his throat. He had a torn ear for he was a hunting dog, his enemy the fox, and he was scruffy but his eyes were bright and intelligent and his good ear, the one able to stand up as it was meant, swivelled comically as he tried again to pick up the sound which had stopped his master. The man watched him, wondering at his own curiosity as the terrier darted off the path and into the rustling sea of bright copper bracken which carpeted the floor of the woodland, disappearing between the narrow silver trunks of the birch trees. Their leaves were falling in a bright, twisting spiral as autumn shook them from their summer blooming and the track would soon be a mosaic of gold and copper, bronze and rose and pale yellow.

The man sat and waited, lounging indolently in the saddle. The horse's fine head drooped to crop the grass beside the track and in a moment the terrier reappeared, standing and tossing his ragged head as though to beckon

6

his master to come and see what he had found. He waited silently for a command, one paw raised. The man sighed at his own foolishness but nevertheless, drawn by some impulse – he was never to know what though he often wondered – he dismounted, his booted foot feeling instinctively for a soft and silent place to tread.

He was a tall lean man, with strong-muscled shoulders straining at the seams of his well-cut coat. His hair was thick and ebony black, inclined to a vigorous curl beneath the tall beaver hat. He was clean-shaven, his dark-complexioned face slashed with stark black eyebrows, his chin thrustingly arrogant and his mouth firm – hard even – yet sensual with a lift at its corner which spoke of humour.

But it was his eyes which were his most compelling feature. In the midst of so much uncompromising darkness they were a beautiful vivid blue, the strange evening light placing the brilliance of sapphire in them. Long black lashes framed their vibrant, narrowing depths as he searched for the faint path the dog had followed and though he was too fierce to be considered handsome, emanating an unusual, almost angry vigour, his eyes softened a face which otherwise might have been forbidding. Hidden deep in them was amusement, watchful and mocking as though he found the world an entertaining place to be providing it did not interfere with *him*. It was readily clear by the set of his jaw he was a man with a fine sense of his own infallibility for there was a certain insolence in the lift of his dark head and in the casual stance of his long, lounging body. A man diverse and complex, it seemed to say, with many shades to his nature and much of it hidden!

Despite his obvious and complete masculinity, he was dressed in a way which most of those with whom he associated considered foppish, for this was not London, nor even Carlisle. Homespun was good enough for them, the Hodden grey contrived in the spinning of wool blended from grey and black fleeces. Jacket and breeches should be plain, serviceable and warm. A freshly laundered white

shirt with a neat stock, gaiters and good boots to keep out
the damp which was an integral part of the lakelands, but
this man wore a beautifully fitted plum-coloured coat of
the finest worsted, dove-grey trousers and an exquisitely
pleated and tucked shirt, while a snowy-white waterfall of
fine linen formed his neck-cloth. His black knee-length
boots were polished to a glowing lustre and his hat was
the exact dove-grey of his trousers.

The roan stood where he was left, continuing to crop
delicately at the sweet grasses beside the track.

At a slight gesture of his master's hand, the wiry dog
slipped silently into the undergrowth and the man fol-
lowed. The terrier looked back constantly as though to
reassure himself the man was still there, waiting now and
again for him to catch up, then ran on until he reached a
tiny clearing beneath the brimming canopy of oak and
beech and birch through which the dying rays of the
evening sun glimmered.

The last of the sunlight fell on the young girl and boy as
they lay in a shaft of it, their backs to the gnarled trunk of
an enormous hornbeam tree. The roots formed a deep nest
rising up on either side of them, and mosses created a soft
velvet bed upon which they might lie and when the man
saw what they were about he understood why they had
not heard his approach.

Two horses, one a roan like his own, reddish brown
with a black mane and tail and a white blaze between its
eyes, the other a pretty chestnut mare, were standing
quietly against the far side of the clearing, their reins
looped carelessly about the branch of a holly bush, the
casual manner in which they had been secured by their
riders pointing to an eagerness to be about an activity of
some urgency!

The sun's rays caught the girl's hair. It was thick and
silken, dark, shot through with tones of russet and chest-
nut, and the boy's excited handling must have brought it
down to tumble and drift about her shoulders. It slipped
in a heavy mass, curling loosely at its ends, springing back

8

from her upturned face and the boy's hand caught it, holding its living beauty in fingers which were strong, slender and brown.

His other hand was at the neck of the plain bodice of her riding habit. Quickly, since he was young and eager and so was she, caring nothing for the lingering grace of the experienced lover, he undid each button, pushing the dark material of her gown away from her shoulders and her exposed breasts lifted to his hand. His thumb and forefinger took her ripe, flushed nipple, rolling it enthusiastically and she arched her back, straining up to him as though she could not get enough of his touch. His mouth left hers as he pulled her further down into the depths of the twisting roots, travelling down the curving column of her throat until his lips reached and enfolded the bursting flesh.

She groaned then and her hands flew to the boy's pale golden hair, slipping into the thick, curling depths of it. She gripped it fiercely, bringing his mouth more closely to her own pink-tipped breast, crying out with such passion that the man who watched was frozen to stillness, horrified to be an observer and yet unable to tear himself away. There was beauty here – a young free, loving beauty which in all his years he had never before witnessed, nor known, and for that second which was to alter his life he stayed. His own manhood stirred and he felt the hot, melting fire of it run up into his belly and down his inner thigh ... and still he could not seem able to set his heavy limbs in motion and he was ashamed! They were young, not more than seventeen, probably from a nearby cottage or farm, two youngsters tasting for the first time the deep, possessed madness of love. To stand and watch must surely be the act of a pervert, a peeping Tom, but the pervading aura of sensuality and the beauty of the two youthful lovers rooted him deep in the ferns which grew about his boots.

The dog shifted questioningly beside him and as he felt the movement against his leg the momentary spell was shattered and the man stirred, smiling ruefully to himself.

He would slip away at once, he thought, before they became aware of him. They would not even know he had been here. He would save himself and them the agony of the embarrassment which his presence would bring about. The image of himself caught red-handed gawking like some lustful schoolboy almost had him laughing as he turned cautiously, ready to creep away as quietly as he had come.

The girl lifted her head then, throwing it back into the soft bed of wood anemones which was her pillow as the boy's hand reached now to the hem of her dark blue riding habit. The material, rich and glossy, gleamed in a stray beam of sunlight and perhaps it was this which cleared the watching man's mind, and with clarity came fresh bewilderment. A farm maid did not wear a riding habit made of rich zephyr cloth from beneath which could be seen only too clearly a petticoat trimmed with expensive Valencienne lace, nor did she go about on the good-looking animal which was tethered at the edge of the clearing. And rarely in her busy day had she the time to stop and dally with another servant, male or female! From dawn to dusk and beyond she was beneath the watchful eye and at the beck and call of her mistress!

As she arched her long white neck the girl's mouth, bruised to a deep pink by that of the boy, opened again in a soft cry of need. The thick brown lashes which rested on her heated cheek fluttered rapidly, quivering in her mounting ecstasy, then her eyes flew open to stare sightlessly beyond the tumbled curls of the boy's head into the lattice of golden leaves and the dark-streaked dusk of the sky and as they did so the man who watched knew her!

'My God, it's Christy Emmerson!' he proclaimed out loud, speaking before he had time to consider the effect the sound of his voice would have on this couple who thought themselves to be utterly alone in their enchanted world! He could have bitten his tongue and he wished the words and himself with them on the other side of Skelwith Bridge. To be caught in the act of spying – for that was how it would seem – on a boy and girl fast in the pleasures of love was ridiculous and he felt off-balance, a condition he did not relish. But what was worse – strangely for he was not a man to be impressed with the emotions of romantic love, never having experienced it – was to watch the almost unearthly quality of their rapture dashed away and the emergence of bewildered horror come to take its place. To see what was quite breathtaking become tawdry, to watch the sensuous beauty of two young lovers turn to the scrabbling urgency, the ungainly commonplace foolishness of those caught in an act of veniality.

At the sound of his voice the boy rolled away from the girl, leaving her lovely young body defenceless and exposed. White breasts and thighs. Long slim legs, narrow ankles and feet and a face which, even in its pathetic shock, still contained the lingering softness of her passionate love.

Alexander Buchanan looked at Christina Emmerson and his stomach quivered and his breath was short and hard in his chest. He was a man well used to the charms of women. From the age of fifteen he had sampled them, at first awkwardly when they were offered, then, as experience came, with growing finesse. From Whitehaven to Barrow, from Carlisle to Kendal he had roamed for he had been wild in his youth, drinking and gambling and much involved in the sport of bare-knuckle fighting, and later in the practice of Cumberland wrestling. He had been well-known for his great reserves of strength, his skill and stamina, and had regularly won the leathern belt, the traditional prize which went to the victor. He was admired by the ladies and resented by the men he fought and out-classed. He was favoured by women who liked the dominance of his arrogant ways and there were more than one or two blue-eyed cuckoos in the sparrow nests of the small, sturdy dalesmen who lived and farmed in the valleys of the north!

He studied the awkward return of Christy Emmerson to the conscious world about her. She was the daughter of a wealthy business associate, the man from whom he bought the gunpowder used in his own mines, and with whom he had spoken not more than an hour since, and the boy – though he had seen him gallop his horse through the village with the God-given right of one whose family had once owned it and ride the lower slopes of the fells with the same arrogance – was the privileged son of the local Squire and virtually a stranger to him. He was away at school, or wherever it was these young sprigs of the gentry went, for most of the year, but he evidently came home often enough to acquaint himself with the charms of the delectable Miss Emmerson!

The girl lay flushed and dishevelled, still as a woodland creature caught in the glow of the poacher's lamp. Her eyes stared into his and she made no attempt to cover herself for she was deep in shock and her instinctive woman's reflex to defend herself from a stranger's eyes had not yet sprung into action. She appeared to be mesmerized, scarcely able to comprehend that he was there. An enchanted moment ago, her bemused expression said, she had been held in the eager arms of her love, her flesh wanting his. Entranced and bewitched beneath his long sweeping caresses and now, before she could get a grip on the loss of it and command her urgent body to stillness and modesty, there was only this man's chilly gaze, his stiff-backed hauteur and his voice still echoing her name round the clearing where there should have been silence.

'Mr Buchanan,' the boy stammered, raising himself to a kneeling position. His hands were at his pleated shirt and the belt of his trousers, fumbling in their eagerness to cover his brown chest across which whorls of pale hair lay finely, attempting to conceal the evidence of what he had intended for his companion. There was a crown of wood violets in his blonde curls, put there no doubt by the girl with the high laugh he had heard.

The boy's breeches were of a beige cord, tight and straining across his thighs and buttocks and when he stood his finely drawn body was tall and slender. He was exceedingly handsome with eyes which glowed a deep, chocolate brown in his sun-tinted face and as he spoke his teeth slashed startlingly white against his wide mouth.

Still he did not reach to help the girl.

'Have you no manners at all, boy?' Alex Buchanan said coldly, his eyes flickering to the girl's state of undress.

'I beg your pardon, sir.' The boy's face was flushed with the residue of unfulfilled love and the agony of his embarrassment at being caught out in it. He was young, the dilemma in which he found himself seemed to have robbed him of his senses and he gave the appearance of not knowing quite where he was.

'There is a lady present!' The words were ridiculous in the circumstances, but neither of the men found them unusual and the girl was not yet out of her trance and still unheeding.

'Have you not the decency at least to offer her your coat?'

'Oh . . . of course . . . I beg your pardon . . . we had not heard . . . Christy . . .' The boy's politeness and the inbred courtesy which was directed towards those older than oneself might have amused Alex Buchanan in another time and place, but now he did not smile.

Only then, as the voices penetrated the fog of her bemused senses, did the girl come from the quivering languorous narcosis into which the boy's hands and lips had spun her; and suddenly, before he could move awkwardly to cover her with his jacket, in a neat and contained movement she sat up and deftly pulled her bodice about her. She twisted her legs modestly beneath the full skirt of her riding habit and swiftly did up each button, her eyes cast down, her expression remote and unreadable.

Immediately, but for her rosy face and long-fingered hands, every inch of her flesh was covered. When it was done she stood up, moving to lean protectively beside the boy. She slid her hand into his and then turned to stare, her eyes flashing defiantly at Alex Buchanan! No anxious

13

humility for her! Her head lifted and the softness of that first awkward shock had left her eyes which had turned to flint and her mouth hardened to an unsmiling resentment.

'Good afternoon, Mr Buchanan,' she said boldly. 'We did not hear your horse on the track – did we, Robin? – nor your own approach. Perhaps you and your terrier were careful where you stepped through the trees to this clearing which is, after all, well away from the track. Are you out for a stroll, taking the evening air, or were you looking for something which might be ... of interest to your habits?'

By God, if she wasn't taking the offensive by accusing him of creeping up and spying on them, he had time to consider admiringly, then his own temper took him over and his lean face darkened.

'If I had come with the Grasmere village band I doubt you and ... and ... your friend would have noticed, Miss Emmerson.' His lip curled scornfully across his even white teeth.

The girl's eyes narrowed furiously and Alex saw the boy's hand clench warningly about hers, but she took no notice.

'Robin and I are not just friends, Mr Buchanan. As soon as it can be arranged, we are to be married.'

'And the sooner the better, I would say, Miss Emmerson!'

'Nobody is asking you to say anything, Mr Buchanan, particularly about something which does not concern you.'

'And whom does it concern, Miss Emmerson? Your father possibly?'

She showed the first sign of confusion.

'My father ... when he ... when we have told him of it will be only too pleased.'

'He is not aware then that you and ... and Robin, is it ... ? are to be married?' Alex Buchanan's dark eyebrows arched and his eyes gleamed with sardonic amusement.

'Well ... we have not ... it is only today that ... but as soon ...'

14

'I should advise him of it at once if I were you, Miss Emmerson. In fact I would have supposed a gentleman . . .' He turned his ironic expression on the boy, '. . . would have already done so. Your meeting up here with this young man . . .' He looked again in the direction of the painfully embarrassed boy, '. . . alone, might be miscon-strued, don't you think?'

'We were doing no wrong . . .' she began, then bit her lip and her faced became a vivid scarlet. 'We were doing no wrong,' she repeated more loudly, as though her insistence would convince him of it. Her face assumed an expression which said she seriously believed it and so should he if he knew what was good for him! They were in love, she and Robin, and what could be wrong in the sweet display of it to one another? A love like theirs, her eyes told him stormily, could have no fault in it and she defied him to find one. It was as though she was resolved to justify what they had been about, knowing quite well that if it were to be discovered and advertised in the circle of her family's acquaintances, her reputation would be in shreds. Even were she to merely ride in the same carriage with a gentleman not a relative, she could be ruined for life!

But she threw back her shoulders and lifted her head, the action saying quite clearly that she was *not* ashamed, and again Alex Buchanan felt that stirring of admiration, not just for her fine body which was now as completely and decently covered as society demanded it to be, but for her bold courage. She did not cower behind the shoulder of her lover but lifted her chin and flashed her sparkling eyes and dared him to say more.

He did!

'Come, Miss Emmerson. Do you seriously expect me to believe that your father allows you to be out here alone?'

'I am not alone, Mr Buchanan. Robin is with me!'

Alex Buchanan let his dark amused eyes drift to the boy's flushed face and his cold smile was contemptuous, mocking.

15

'I doubt he would permit you, despite your forthcoming betrothal – which, from what you say, he knows nothing about – to ride out with only this ... gentleman to accompany you. From what I know of Job Emmerson, a gentle stroll in the bright sunshine of the garden with himself at the drawing-room window to oversee it would be all he considered fitting. A proper, a very *proper* gentleman in the true sense of the word ...' here a sneer at poor Robin, '... is your father, Miss Emmerson, and I shudder to think of the consequences to this young man if he were to learn of this ... escapade. Come now, tell us what you did with the groom in whose protection your father must surely have placed you. Job Emmerson is not one to permit such a valuable ... treasure as yourself to blunder the fells unchaperoned.'

His eyes gleamed wickedly, but his face was cool.

The girl faltered then and Alex saw her fingers clench more firmly about those of the boy. She turned to look up into his strained face and as she moved the rippling curtain of her hair swung about her. A strand wisped across her face, caught in the pink moistness of her lips and she reached up a hand to brush it away.

As her hair caught in the golden light of the dying rays of the sun it turned to burnished mahogany, her grey eyes – strange and cat-like – darkened to pewter. The movement of her arm lifted the rounded fullness of her young breast, and she watched as Alexander Buchanan's eyes narrowed in appreciation and she was angry for he had a wife at their home near Skelwith Bridge and within the month she was expected to give birth to their child!

Christy Emmerson lifted her head imperiously, throwing back her hair and Alex Buchanan felt the blood run warm in his veins and the heat of it move again to his belly. Her little chin squared up to him and her eyes changed colour once more, striking like bright steel in her proud challenge of his authority. She was like a kitten spitting and showing its claws to a fully grown panther and the man felt a spurt of envy at the realization that it would never be his task to tame her. Even had she not been mad with love for this squireen, son of Squire Forsythe of Dalebarrow, she was the most cherished child of a respected member of the community, a man with whom he did business and whom he called, if not friend, at least neighbour! She was not a woman to be tumbled in a hayrick, enjoyed and forgotten. If she were it would not take him long to accomplish it and walk away, his emotions intact.

But she was not yet done with him! 'Thank you for your concern, Mr Buchanan.' Her expression dared him to attempt control of either herself or her Robin who still stood wordless before the seniority of the man whom he, in his youthful conceit, considered old enough to be his father. 'It is kind of you to show concern for my safety, but Ned will be along presently and . . .'

'When he catches up with you, you mean?' His smile was icy.

'Can I help it if my mare was fresh and I could not hold her?' she countered.

'And this . . . gentleman . . .' The pause before the word was insulting, '. . . just happened to be here on the very route along which your animal bolted!'

'Sir, I can explain.' The boy, who appeared to have been quite overwhelmed by the older man, spoke at last.

'Aah, you have a tongue then, Mr . . . er . . .'

'Forsythe, sir. My father is . . .'

'Of course, Squire Forsythe's boy. It is a while since we met, Mr Forsythe. You have grown somewhat . . . in more ways than one.'

The boy blushed, the blood running beneath his smooth skin in the painful way it does when one is young, and again Alex Buchanan wondered at his own cruelty in baiting this youth who had done him no harm.

'Thank you sir, but let me explain. Miss Emmerson and I . . .'

'Yes?' Alex Buchanan's voice was silky, but his eyes narrowed in the menacing fashion over which he appeared to have no control and the boy clung more tightly to the girl's hand.

'We . . . well . . . it was my fault. I realize I should not have . . .'

The girl sprang immediately to his defence, her whole body turning to his in a fervour of tenderness. She glowed with that strange fragile beauty of a young woman newly awakened to love as she held his hand with both of hers and gazed up into his face.

'No, Robin, no,' she protested, '. . . it was not entirely your fault . . .' and it was left in no doubt what she meant. If Alexander Buchanan had not come along when he had, she was saying, by now she and her Robin would have been more than a girl and boy on the edge of physical commitment!

The boy put a possessive arm about her and smiled down into her face and his dark brown eyes became even darker with his adoring love for her, and in that moment Alex Buchanan knew he existed for neither of them. Young the boy might be, and gauche with the clumsiness of the untried, but his love for this maid was true!

'Despite your admirable determination to share the blame, Miss Emmerson, I feel you would not care for your father to know of this incident.'

Instantly he was appalled by his own words. What the hell was wrong with him? He sounded petty and mean and as her expression said so clearly, what had it to do with him? He and her father did business together; they were both wealthy landowners, neighbours and occasional dinner guests at one another's table but that still did not give him the right to threaten her with exposure. What she had done today was certainly not the action of the well-brought-up and guarded young girl she was, but then one glance was enough to show even the most naïve that Christy Emmerson was no milk-and-water miss who did exactly as she was bid.

Alex Buchanan bent down and his hand went to his

terrier's head. The dog sat obediently at his feet, his eyes upon his master's face.

'Come, Miss Emmerson,' he said curtly. 'Shall you and I ride back to Hollin House together? I shall say I found you on the Ambleside road where your bolting mare had taken you, and that together we chanced upon young Mr Forsythe here.'

He turned to Robin and his expression was mocking. 'And if I were you, sir, I would do my courting in a more appropriate manner. It is the custom of a gentleman – as you should well know, having been brought up as one – to treat his betrothed as a lady and not as a . . . as a . . .'

'Yes, Mr Buchanan?' Robin Forsythe's voice had become dangerously hard and Alex was surprised. The cub had teeth then, given the right spur.

'She is not a wench to be tumbled behind a haystack, Mr Forsythe.'

'I am well aware of that, sir, and it was not my intention to . . .'

'Your ardour ran away with you? Is that what you are saying?' Alex Buchanan's voice was derisive, cruelly so.

The boy flushed a bright crimson and took a step forward and Alex felt the first thread of respect for him, then wondered again why he was so intent on goading these two children. For that was what they were – two children and nothing to him – so why did he not leave them alone to copulate as they willed and go home to Maude and his unborn child? His words, his foolish words about their morals sounded priggish even to his own ears, and suddenly with a muttered oath he turned away and his long stride took him swiftly to the edge of the almost dark clearing.

He turned again to face them and lifted his hat courteously. Bowing slightly from the waist he said, without looking at them, 'My regards to your father, Miss Emmerson,' and then, with a sharp command to the waiting terrier, disappeared as silently as he had come amongst the tall shadowed trees.

CHAPTER TWO

There is a saying in the north of England. 'From clogs to clogs in three generations', and it had been known to happen, but not to Job Emmerson! True, his grandfather had worn them and even his father in the early days but Job sported fine leather riding boots, supple and polished, with long steel spurs, Wellington dress boots which fitted under his trousers, and 'dress' pumps of Spanish leather with low sides and tied with a small double bow of broad ribbon. His wardrobe was filled with 'jockey' boots in two shades of kid and soft, folded leather gussets, 'hessians' and 'highlows' for country wear and top boots for sporting occasions and he was justly proud of them and of his own promotion to the fortune and respectability which they represented.

By his footwear was his rise from collier's grandson to wealthy manufacturer and mill-owner measured, at least in his own eyes!

He could remember his grandfather clearly.

Jacob Emmerson had been a charcoal burner in the area of the upper Troutbeck valley, working in dirty and arduous conditions to produce the charcoal which was his living, and during 'coaling', when his pits were kindled, work went on day and night for seven days a week without respite, through the late summer and early autumn. The constant attention which the pits required meant the collier must remain in the woods during the whole of this period.

Job could still recall the turf hut in which his grandfather had lived. It was circular and built on a tripod, 'thacked' with sods. It had no windows and the door opening was covered with no more than sacking. He would dearly have loved to stay with his grandfather, sleeping in the comradely fashion of two men without the fuss of a woman's attention but his mother would not hear of it, and each night he was made to trudge off reluctantly to his clean bed and nightly prayers.

Even then there was a sense that the Emmersons were going up in the world and Elly Emmerson would not have her son sleeping rough like a gypsy!

It had been young Job's task – and he no more than a lad of six or seven – to walk the four miles there and the same back, from his mother's kitchen in their cottage at Chapel Stile, to take his grandfather's food, there being no hearth in the sod hut on which to cook. He would stand and watch the old man who was above the age of sixty even then, felling his 'standards', or trees, cutting just above the ground, leaving the bole from which eventually another 'crop' of between ten or twenty new 'poles' would sprout. The coppice wood utilized land which could not be used for any other cultivation and could be harvested every fifteen or sixteen years and the profit made, if managed by a 'canny' man as his grandfather proved to be, could be as much as one hundred per cent on his outlay. On one day, Jacob Emmerson, from his numerous 'pitsteads' had reckoned his expenditure to be £10 14s 3½d and the clear remaining profit a remarkable £21 17s 4¾d!

The process of converting wood to charcoal had fascinated the young boy and when the 'coaling' began at the prescribed time of the year he would help his grandfather to dig the shallow circular pit and set up the stake or 'motty peg' in its centre. These pitsteads were usually in level, sheltered areas with running water close by.

'Get th'wood, lad,' his grandfather would grunt, for living so much alone had made him a man of few words. He was so alone that later, when Job was better able to understand such things, he was to wonder how the begetting of his own father had ever been accomplished.

The wood was piled around the stake until it was shaped like a tall beehive. This was then covered with bracken and upon the beehive Job and his grandfather layered sods so that no air might ignite the wood, rather than 'coal' it. If there should be a wind the young lad would manhandle the interwoven, movable screens made of twigs or bracken to further protect the pit from draughts of air.

When all was ready the central stake was removed and glowing charcoal was placed in the opening which was then sealed with the last special sod. Without a moment's pause the old man, once the pit was kindled, was off to start a second, a third, a fourth and Job's young legs would tremble with weariness for he must constantly be about the important business of checking on each one to ensure that the cone had not collapsed nor a mischievous flame become too fierce and need smothering with wet turf.

'Get off home, lad,' his grandfather would say, probably only the second time he had spoken that day, and the boy would tramp off, conscious of the four miles he must go to his supper and bed.

The 'coaling' took from between twenty-four hours and three days to complete and if he were lucky Job would be there to witness the 'saying' when water was thrown over the pit to create steam and effectively cool the charcoal. It was a special moment for the boy, almost mystical, the climax of days of hard, unrelenting work and his grandfather's laconic 'Aye, it'll do' was the most satisfying of all!

But closely allied to the coppicing of the woodlands of the southern Lake District was the craft of bark-peeling. In early May and again in July, when he was not occupied with his 'coaling', Jacob set about the task of preparing specially chosen 'poles', the bark of which was used in the tanning industry which flourished in the Lakeland.

Slowly, penny by patient penny, Jacob accumulated a 'bob or two', still living rough and spending nothing for his son's wife fed him.

Job's father, Nathaniel, had by this time begun the manufacture of gunpowder on a small site he had purchased close to Chapel Stile, realizing that he had in his own father an unending and cheap source of its main ingredient, charcoal. He did well and he and his family prospered. He bought timber-bearing land and coppice woods, setting men, with Jacob to supervise, in the production of charcoal. When the old man died, still 'coaling' at the age of seventy-seven, Nathaniel reckoned that with what his father brought him, he might call himself a rich man!

But it was Job himself who realized the potential to those of the Westmorland and Cumberland gunpowder manufacturers – for he was not alone in his foresight – who wished to become entrepreneurs. In 1824 he extended his purchase of woodlands in which grew the juniper bushes producing 'savin' coals from which the very best gunpowder is made. There was an abundance of fast flowing Lakeland becks to operate the heavy machinery he would need in the crushing and milling processes; and the other raw materials required, sulphur from Sicily and saltpetre from India, could be readily shipped from Liverpool to Milnthorpe and then by wagon to his mills, and the process reversed to ship back to the port the finished product to be stored in the magazines on the River Mersey.

The range of blasting powder he manufactured was wide. There was the 'Extra Large Coarse Black' used in the quarries and mines which honey-combed the mountains of the Lake District, for since the sixteenth century man had searched for coal, iron ore, lead and graphite. This coarse powder was slow burning and did not shatter the rock into small fragments and Job Emmerson supplied much of the explosives used by the great mine owners in the area.

His 'Extra Fine' was much sought after by those in the sporting world and for military use. He was proud to be able to say that consignments of his product went not only to the collieries in Cumberland, to Glasgow, Wigan, Oldham, Stoke-on-Trent, to the slate quarries of Scotland and Wales, to the limestone quarries in Derbyshire, but to West Africa, to Spain and Brazil, to Portugal and Peru.

Between the two blends he had the markets of all the world and should there be a slump in one, he had the other to fall back on. Canny as his grandfather was Job Emmerson!

His business grew until it covered many acres by the beck from which it got its power, with half a dozen large water-wheels, a fire engine house, a saw mill and joiners shop, a saltpetre house, stores and repair house, cart and wagon sheds, a cooperage, separate changing rooms for the men and women who worked for him — five hundred of them now in two twelve-hour shifts producing one thousand tons of explosive every year. There were stables for his horses and new cottages for his workmen and a watchdog kennel crammed with fierce beasts to guard the lot!

By not only the quantity and quality of his boots was Job Emmerson recognized for a man of substance but by what he had built on, that which his grandfather and father had begun, the only difference being in the old pitstead in which Jacob had once produced his charcoal. Now modern retorts were used and the pale blue smoke drifted across the waters of the mere and on still, overcast days, hung like a veil over the valley.

Now Job was intent on seeing the start of a new generation for he wanted his acres of timber and coppice, his sheds and water-wheels, his saw mill and retorts to pass on into other capable Emmerson hands when he was gone. Indeed before, for though he was in his fifties, he meant not only to see his sons take their place, his place when the time came, but his grandsons sturdily growing and awaiting their turn in the order of things.

Already his sons, Ben and Toby Emmerson, had worked and suffered in every process which made up the manufacture of gunpowder. Each stage must be learned the hard way, Job Emmerson insisted, for a man will only be respected and obeyed when he can do, and be seen to do, what his workmen are employed in and if it was dangerous and complicated, which it was, then all the better for it

24

made men of them and though he still addressed them both as 'lads' he knew them to be men and his pride in them was immense.

He watched them each day donning the protective leather skins and gloves, the special nail-less boots worn by his workers to avoid accidental sparks, preparing to enter the 'corning' house in which was operated the most dangerous process of all. It was here that the compressed aggregate or 'cake' was broken up into the correct sizes so that each grain of explosive would perform its proper task upon firing and this perilous measure was performed by a man striking the 'cake' with a hammer! One wrong blow and the whole lot would be up and over the Old Man of Conistone before you could say 'Now then, lad!' His own self-esteem was enhanced by their dashing disregard for the peril in which they often worked. They were as carelessly courageous as he himself had been and he loved them both beyond all others.

They were alike, the three of them, big and dark and vigorous with enormous enthusiasms and appetites and a total belief in themselves and their future. From the moment grandfather Jacob had built his first pitstead the Emmersons had worked, and prospered as was only right and just, and through his sons Job Emmerson lived again as a young man. He looked ten years younger than his own wife and his faith in himself and their sons was enormous.

'Now then, lad,' he said that morning at breakfast, fixing Ben with a fierce, fond eye, speaking plainly for that was his way. 'When's that lass of yours going to name the day? Six months you've been dancing attendance on her and there's nowt been said to me yet about the wedding. What's she dithering about at, tell me that? You'd think she'd not rest until she'd got you up the aisle, a catch like you. You tell her there's plenty'd take you if she doesn't look sharp!'

He shovelled bacon and eggs into his mouth with the same determined force with which he had been known to feed the furnace in his own engine house and with the same effect! As he fuelled himself up for the morning and he would take another large meal at noon, so did he gather the heat to create the energy which would be needed!

'Hold on, father!' Ben was laughing for he was good-humoured when allowed his own way, quick tempered when he was not, and as yet his father had not touched the spark which would set him alight. At the mill he was 'Maister Benjamin' the owner's son and the future 'Maister' himself, and he let no man trespass on his good nature for it was in such a way that familiarity was bred. The master was the master and his workmen touched their caps respectfully when he crossed the yard, and jocularity between them and himself was frowned upon.

But he could have his temper aroused as easily as any of the Emmersons and there was a flash of blue-grey flame in his smiling eye as he looked across his dish of porridge to his father. 'You know what women are like when it comes to weddings and trousseaux and linen and such,' he continued agreeably enough. 'Everything must be just so. Curtains to be ordered and maids to be employed and the house not half finished yet, but Celia said last night she thought an Easter wedding would suit her fine so that's what . . .'

'Celia said! Celia said! An Easter Wedding! Suit *her* fine! Who the hell does that young lady think she is, I'd like to know? What about us? Have we no say in the matter? We're not some Johnny-cum-latelys with nowt but a farthing in our pockets, Ben Emmerson! And you? What in damnation are you thinking of, letting her dictate to you like that? Don't she know she's getting the best catch in the county? You tell her! Easter indeed! I was looking to a grandson by the end of next summer and another on the way by Christmas.'

'God's teeth, father . . .'

'And don't you swear at me, my lad, for big as you are you'll feel the flat of my hand. It's a wedding before Christmas I'm after or there'll be none at all, that's what I

26

say. It's nowt to me that she's Ira Metcalf's lass' — which was not true for Ira Metcalf was one of the wealthiest manufacturers in south Lakeland. A union between his lad and Ira's lass suited Job admirably for not only did she have money and a claim to gentility but was a plain-spoken, sensible girl and would make a fine mother for Job's grandsons!

Ben's quick temper flared! The Emmersons were famous in the valley for the ease with which their anger was set alight and they were all the same from Ben and Toby — the lads — to young Christina herself. It was undoubtedly inherited from Job's mother who had been Irish and volatile! When they crossed swords with one another sparks would fly and those not involved stepped well back, enjoying it nevertheless for an Emmerson confrontation could be vastly entertaining!

'Well in that case, it's nowt to you when me and Celia get wed then,' Ben said hotly. 'If Ira Metcalf's cash means as little as that we can please ourselves and we bloody well will!'

'It's not his cash I'm interested in, my lad, and watch that mouth of yours. It's how quick that girl of his can put a grandson in my arms and the rate you're going God knows when that'll be!'

Ben's chair crashed backwards to the fine new carpet recently laid in Job's dining room. A source of great pride, it was, to his wife and she winced as heavy boots stamped angrily across it.

'And it's none of your damned business when me and Celia have a child, either. Damnation, you'll be telling me how to go about it next . . .'

'That's enough from you, my lad. There's nowt wrong with a man wanting to see his son set up with a decent girl and a few grandchildren about his knee before he dies!'

'Dies! Goddammit, father, you've years yet! Anyone would think you were to be off within the twelvemonth!'

Job tossed his big, dark head and his shoulders bunched dangerously.

'Now you listen to me, you young puppy. I'm the master in this house and will be until they carry me down that path to the graveyard.' He pointed dramatically to the garden beyond the long window and obediently the whole family and the maid who served them turned their heads to look.

Hollin House was solid stone with a door cut firmly in its middle, a pillared porch, two windows on either side and five above it. Above them, on the second floor were five more, the bedrooms at the back occupied by the maid servants. Built by Job when his first son, little Job, who lay in the graveyard, was born, it had been another symbol of his growing success. There was a large parlour and a larger dining room, all packed with unbreakable, no-nonsense furniture of oak and mahogany. In the stone-flagged kitchen at the back Annie Emmerson still supervised the baking of bread and the making of soap and candles, tasks she had once done herself but which, as the mill-master's wife, it was no longer seemly to perform. Three young maids were worked to a standstill each day, scrubbing and polishing and picking up after Master Ben and Master Toby, keeping immaculate the well-run household.

It was set in a sheltered fold of the lower slopes of Loughrigg Fell with a fine view across Eltermere to the Langdales. Great sweeps of the green valley bottom, bisected irregularly with a cobweb of dry-stone walls, were surrounded by dramatically rising fells, glowing now with the rich red of autumn bracken.

Already the fell farmers, looking towards the coming winter were starting to bring down to the 'in-lands', the small, richer enclosures around the farm buildings, their fine flocks of Herdwick sheep for the conceiving of lambs would take place in November or December, and from the window of the house could be seen the erratic movement of sheep and the dogs which chivvied them here and there and back again!

The house was surrounded by several acres of lawn and flowerbeds, nothing fancy for Annie and Job Emmerson had once lived in a cottage and could not quite come to terms with ornamental gardens and rosebeds and the like! From here Job could look down on his chimneys and his heading mill and the thick stand of trees set between his mill and his house, left there not as decoration but as blast protection. Each morning he would look out and know that everything he saw from his bedroom window belonged to him and each morning he counted his wagons and his horses and his men, making little distinction between them, and watched the smoke curling from his chimney across to the Langdale Fells.

They breakfasted together at six, ready for the twelve-hour shift which began at six-thirty; Job and Annie, his two sons and his daughter, for there was no tom-foolery such as lying in bed till mid-morning in *his* home. His wife and daughter had certain duties; to himself and to his household, to the families of the men who worked for him, for it was his belief that a man will work more readily if his wife and children are well cared for and in her role as the mill-master's wife Annie performed the function scrupulously.

Only when these tasks were done and her visits to poorly children and constantly pregnant wives completed did Job allow his carriage to be got out for the lighter side of his wife's social life. Then she and her daughter might call on other manufacturers' wives or drive to Fellthwaite to shop at Miss Susan Whittam's smart little salon where lace and swan's-down, fans and muffs and mittens might be purchased and a new gown ordered. These goods were brought by carrier wagon from London to Kendal, then from there by coach to outlying towns such as Windermere, Ambleside and Fellthwaite. There was a 'Flying Machine' drawn by six mettlesome horses travelling between Kendal and Carlisle, a journey of six hours which brought passengers, and packages ordered – but soon there would be the splendid London to Carlisle Railway, promising to take even less time to fetch the dress lengths and shawls, the bonnets and stockings so necessary to the ladies of Fellthwaite.

There was the excitement of 'Mr Brownes Coaches', claimed to be late of the Queens Hotel, and the oldest established livery and job master in Ambleside, so he said, who took wide-eyed visitors on tours about the town. On Wednesday it was market day and there was much to be seen in and about the pillared and galleried Market Hall and square. There were two fairs yearly, attended mainly by the country folk who had little else to excite them in their hard lives though Christy herself would dearly have loved to have gone, and in October there was the annual sheep fair.

A thriving market town was Ambleside and Fellthwaite was not far behind, and it was there that Annie and her daughter purchased most of what they needed. Not for Annie, she was quick to remark, for she was a plain woman and past such things anyway, but for Job's daughter who was of marriageable age. He was looking around for someone he considered good enough to be allied with his prospering family and besides, it did no harm to let folk see that Job Emmerson had cash and to spare, not only in his home and in his mill but to adorn frivolously, where there was really no need of it, the person of his lovely daughter.

She and her mother would take a turn or two about the market square on a fine day to let those who were about see what he, Job Emmerson, had in his possession, to watch the coaches come in; and take a stroll to inspect the farm produce on display in the lower half of the Market Hall and from whose stalls Annie chose her eggs and cheese and poultry to be delivered to her back door.

The building was splendid, a recent addition to the small town and on many occasions it was the setting for dances and concerts on its superb upper floor. They would take the carriage about Ambleside to see the grand houses of the newly rich who holidayed there, though none were so grand or so rich as Job Emmerson, or wander up Stock

Ghyll road to view the waterfall, or, if they craved a change from Miss Susan Whittam, to buy a ribbon from Miss Clara Aspin on Smithy Brow, but whatever the jaunt, Annie Emmerson and her daughter were expected to be home and waiting for Job and his 'lads' when they came back from the mill for their dinner.

But this morning which had seemed like any other was getting off to a bad start and Christy sighed in exasperation. She was well used to a 'set-to' between her father and her brothers and had been included in some herself but today she had counted on her father's good humour for she wished to ask his permission to take her mare across the Brathay to visit Emily Dyer, a young lady with whom she had gone to school and whose father supplied timber for the making of the barrels used in the Emmerson Mills. Not that she had any intention of calling on Emily, outside of the few minutes needed to allow Emily's mother to see her and so establish an alibi. The arrangement was well planned and always carefully executed and had been in existence ever since Christy Emmerson had slipped help- lessly into love with Robin Forsythe!

She had first met him in the company of her brother Toby on the occasion of the Grasmere Sports at the beginning of July. Ben had entered himself for the wrest- ling, a sport so popular that crowds had come from as far away as London, Liverpool and Manchester to witness it. It had its heroes and champions and Ben, being a large, well-muscled young man, knowing his own superb strength and eager to impress his Celia had 'tekken hod' a time or two and won a belt and was well pleased with himself. He still wore the distinctive costume, a sleeveless vest, long drawers tucked into stockings and velvet trunks upon which Annie had lovingly embroidered a flower motif with his initials delicately wrought in their centre. He shook the hands of those who congratulated him whilst his mother and father looked on in proud achievement and Celia clung possessively to his arm.

They had all watched the start of the hound trailing in

31

which Job had entered two new dogs but leaving the family to jostle about with the rest of the competitors, Christy and Toby, losing interest, wandered across the damp fields in search of more exciting pleasures. There was a race to the summit of Butter Crag and back, pole vaulting and sprinting and it was in this last that she saw him!

A tall, fair boy, standing out amongst the smaller, sturdier dalesmen with the amused, faintly superior, faintly nervous air of a greyhound amongst a pack of tough little terriers. A gentleman playing a game with his inferiors. A lightweight who was doing this for no other reason than the notion that it might be fun! A small crowd of his privileged contemporaries cheered him on as he ran like some graceful bird, his feet flying across the grass and when he dashed over the finishing line, his elated grin spreading his lips across his white teeth, she was there to see him win and when their eyes met she felt the tedium of her life slip away and an unbelievable excitement take its place.

'Well done, old chap, quite marvellously well done!' she heard Toby drawl and incredibly it seemed they knew one another, perhaps only slightly, but Robin Forsythe made more of it for Toby was the brother of the most beautiful girl he had ever seen!

The next day, how she did not know, he was perched on a delicate chair drinking tea in the drawing room of Mrs Alfred Marsden when Christy and her mother called, and when they were introduced they did no more than bow politely, but when she arrived home the note he had pressed – how again? – into her reticule, begged her to name a place where they might meet alone.

They came regularly after that, those notes, even when he had returned to school, delivered into Ned Roper's hand and from there to her own!

The last one had come in the falling twilight of the previous evening passed from Robin's hand into that of Job's groom, a willing accomplice for he had eyes for Faith who was to be Christy's own maid, and from her to Christy, still warm, it seemed from the fingers of the hand which penned it. She held it now against her heart with a painfully loving hand, the outline of the notepaper a warm, crisp square inside her chemise. The feel of it made her shiver deliciously and the curious and wonderful sensation which started in the deep pit of her belly and always accompanied any thought of Robin, began now, spreading upwards to meet the place where the note lay.

The noise of the argument receded into the grey, misty areas of Christy's mind as it took the well-loved course towards Robin Forsythe. They had met only once since the dreadful day last month when Mr Buchanan had come upon them on the slopes of Birch Hill. She would never forget it, nor the anger he had aroused in her by his interference in what was none of his business. Snooping about the woods, he had been, looking for God knows what, though she was inclined to think the worst of him! He had a wife at home who was said to be a softling with no thought in her head apart from those put there by her husband and did nothing but bear him children, none of whom had lived! What had he been doing, she wondered? What had been the thoughts in his head as he stood and watched herself and Robin . . . herself and Robin . . . Oh Lord . . . ?

The lovely feeling throbbed and spread and she felt her face become rosy as she remembered those moments and hastily she spooned a portion of porridge into her mouth, swallowing it and then another, turning her thoughts from the memory, desperately seeking an escape from it for surely those about her would feel the . . . the heat of her and notice her flushed face and the pulse she could feel beating in the hollow of her throat. They had met in the drawing room of Jonathan Aspin's wife, a friend of her mother, several days later and the tension in the air must have been noticeable for Annie had been curiously uneasy – Christy could see it – and had said her goodbyes to Mrs Aspin exactly within the fifteen minutes politeness

33

required, bearing her daughter away from the hot eyes of the Squire's son for everyone knew where that might lead! The gentry did not stoop to notice the daughter of a manufacturing man, certainly not with marriage in mind and what he was doing in the drawing room of another was an alarming puzzle.

'Now what can that young sprig be doing in Lizzie Aspin's drawing room, I ask myself?' she remarked suspiciously to Christy but of course the reason was not, thankfully, revealed to her and her daughter's lack of interest, which should have warned her for he was an exceedingly attractive young man, lulled her doubts.

Job was now getting up a fair head of steam in the matter of his eldest son's marriage to Ira Metcalf's lass and the house, the gardens about it and the very fells beyond, grew silent as he delivered his opinion to his family. He was looking for good blood and perhaps a bit of breeding in exchange for his cash. He had his eye on a worthy lass for his Toby, though he did not say so; had even had a quiet word in her father's ear and both men were satisfied with their private arrangement and though the girl was not yet old enough for marriage everything was, in Job's mind, settled very nicely in his favour. All tied up neatly and his lads' lives mapped out and his mills waiting and ready to be placed in his two sons' hard and willing hands.

There was just this business of Ben's wedding to be arranged to his liking and he would sleep more easily in his bed. Before Christmas, he was resolved on it and he would tell the lad so, make no mistake.

They were squaring up to one another, pugnacious jaw to pugnacious jaw whilst the others watched with wandering interest. They took these exchanges with one another quite casually for they did not last long and Christy had seen the day when her brothers would go off arm in arm, one nursing a bloody nose the other had given him moments before. They were a close family, fighting each other ferociously, showing every sign of devastating

34

enmity, but they stood as one against outsiders and though demonstrations of affection were rare, it was there nevertheless.

'What in hell's name are you hanging about for?' Job snarled, his face full-blooded in temper. 'When I was a lad I couldn't wait to . . .'

'Job!' his wife said warningly, her well wrinkled face stern beneath her lace and ribbon cap. She was a daleswoman born and bred and used in her younger days to tending to matters of birth and death and was accustomed to rough country ways, but she'd have no low talk at her table, nor indeed, if she knew of it, in her house. She was a strong plain woman who had often wondered what the handsome Job Emmerson had seen in her worth marrying. But it was her very strength which had made him choose her. He meant to get on and needed the support of a woman who thought as he did. He needed strong, healthy children to carry on what he would build and she was the most likely lass to do it for him.

And she had. Twelve children she had borne him, but infant mortality was high and the first four were to die whilst they were still in their cradles, living just long enough to get a good grip on her heart. Nine little graves had fresh flowers put on them every month and no one ever knew of her private grief, but she had given him Ben and Toby, lusty babes and healthy, self-willed boys and he had been satisfied. He was fond of his pretty girl and she would do well for him when the time came, but his lads had first place in his heart. They were set in his mould and he loved them.

'Don't interfere, woman,' he growled, never taking his blazing eyes from those of his son. 'I'll not be told what to do in my own house and I'll have no son of mine answering back neither.' He firmly believed this though there was nothing he liked better, secretly delighting in a stand-up fight for it showed spunk and he loved spunk!

Christy sighed again loudly and immediately he turned on her.

35

'And what's to do with you, miss, may I ask, sighing and fidgeting like a cat on a hot griddle and a face on you as long as the lake at Windermere? Eager to be away to some other engagement, are you?' He was so near the truth she felt her face blaze again but he was merely mouthing the words from habit and scarce looked in her direction. 'Do you want a bray as well, do you? Well, the lot of you will have a right clapperclowe if you're not careful, so think on. You're none of you too old for a clip round the ear, let me tell you!'

He glared around at the assembly looking as though one more word would have him at them with the clouting he threatened but Ben was not finished, not by a long chalk!

'It's nowt to do with you, father.' As their rage boiled nearer to the brim of the pot so did their Westmorland dialect become more pronounced. It was a curious tongue with a variation in pitch which altered from district to district. It had a harsh glottal stop, sing-song, and in females shrill but rhythmic. Now Ben's voice was harsh and strong.

'Me and Celia'll decide.'

'Decide, is it, and what's to decide, I say. There's no need to go "corn-laiting" now, you know,' – an old custom in which couples would go round the district for gifts of corn to set them up – 'nor for a bidden wedding! My sons will be set up in style and want no gifts to . . .'

'Tha's nowt to do wi'it. Celia wants things done right and so do I. How would it look if we were wed within the month as you want? They'll say she's in the family way and that's not . . .'

'What if she were? It would be no bad thing . . .'

'You mind your tongue. You might be my father but if I hear you blacken the name of an innocent lass . . .'

'I'm not blackening her name, blast it, but you're to wed anyway so where would be the harm in . . .'

'Are you saying I should deliberately . . .'

'Was that the works whistle, Job?' The soft voice from the head of the long table split them apart like the stroke

36

of an axe with the only words which would at that moment make any sense to them and immediately the men were striding about the room like caged animals about to be released. Chairs were thrust back as Toby and his sister rose thankfully and Annie smiled complacently.

But Job had to have the last word!

'I've no time to be standing here passing the time of day with you, my lad, whilst the mills grind to a halt for the want of a word from the master. It's gone six-thirty and like as not the day shift men will be gossiping at the gate. We'll deal with this tonight, son Ben, but let me tell you I'm set on my own way. You can let yon lass know she's to be ready to be wed before the year's out or she can start looking for a new groom and she'll not find one as well set up as my son, that's for sure. Now where's my hat? Sally!'

His voice bawled up the long carpeted hallway which led to the kitchen and the maid hurried from the back reaches of the house to possess herself of her master's tall top hat before it was her turn for a clapperclowe.

'Come on, you two,' he shouted and his sons hurried after him. Toby was grinning and careless for what was it to do with him? Unaware of his father's plans in his direction he had a covey of young and pretty farm girls, country lasses, all longing for his kisses and more, if he could persuade them, and the quarrel between his brother and father, echoing still up the slope as he followed behind only made him shake his head and wonder at the folly of settling for one cow when there was a herd still waiting to be milked.

Into the silence their going had left Christy's voice sounded deceptively mild, as though, one way or the other it really made no difference to her.

'Mother, may I go over to Emily Dyer's this morning? Her spaniel has had her pups and they say they are so sweet and I thought . . .'

'You should have asked your father, girl. 'Tis not for me to say.'

37

'But mother, you saw how they were the two of them. I didn't get a chance. Father was in a tantrum.'

'That'll do, Christina! Not another word! I'll not hear you speak of your father like that! Tantrum indeed!'

'Oh please, mother, please. I'll take Ned with me and just go straight there and back. Mrs Dyer did ask me to stay for dinner but if you say so I'll come straight back when I've seen the puppies.'

Christina Emmerson's face was as innocent and guileless as that of a week old babe and her mother hesitated. Christy watched her, trying to still the anticipatory excitement which gathered in her. Of course she would see the puppies and of course she would greet Mrs Dyer most prettily, but afterwards she and Robin would meet and steal away for half an hour alone and with Ned safely occupied by Faith's reluctant presence, no one would know.

Annie Emmerson looked at her daughter, quite fascinated by the bright loveliness of her. Where had it come from, she wondered, that glossy hair, that fine, white skin, the grey velvet of her eyes? Not from her, certainly and not from the Denbys who were her kin and Job was dark of face and eye as were her sons. It was as though she looked at a changeling who had come upon them one day, left by gypsies or the fairy folk, the 'knockers' as they were known, who lived in the mines up Conistone way and were said by their faint tappings to direct the miners to rich ore! Well, Christy Emmerson was rich ore and no mistake, all brilliance, lovely and strong as the juniper bush upon which the family fortune had been founded. With it she would win the heart of some fine gentleman or Job would know the reason why.

'Very well, child, and you may stay to your dinner with the Dyers if they should ask. I will explain to your father that it would be rude to do otherwise. I had intended to take you with me to . . . but never mind.'

'Where, mother?' Christy asked the question politely but she scarcely heard the answer for her mind was busy on what she would wear and the new style she and Faith had devised for her hair and already she was at the door as her mother answered absently.

'Don't worry, lass. I can take Dorcas with me. She's good with . . . It's Alex Buchanan's wife. Her time's come and I said I would go and . . . Off you go, my girl, and give my respects to Mrs Dyer.'

She had turned away and did not see the strange expression on her daughter's face, nor if she had would she have connected it with the name of Alex Buchanan, for her mind was already busy with beef tea and a certain infusion she knew made from marigolds and which was well-known for its relief of pain.

CHAPTER THREE

Alex Buchanan looked down into the applewood cradle and the midwife stepped back respectfully, her face puckering in an expression of sympathy. The doctor stood sadly by, his duty done, and both he and the woman held their breath as the man stared, his face expressionless, at his motherless daughter.

They waited for him to speak, perhaps a word of regret, sorrow, anger even at the fates which had taken so young a wife from him but he said nothing, did nothing, merely gazed with what appeared to be a curious lack of concern at the infant in the cradle.

There was not a lot to see. A fluff of dark whorls on a tiny skull, the satin sheen on the curve of a delicate cheek, a fan of long eyelashes and a bud of a pink mouth which sucked hopefully at nothing.

The four-poster bed stood like a catafalque in the centre of the room, the shrouded form which lay upon it barely raising the white lace edged sheet. A maid, her face wet with tears, was removing the detritus of birth, tip-toeing round the body of Alex Buchanan's wife as if she was afraid she might awaken her. There was a smell in the room, of blood and soap and clean sheets and through the window which the widower had peremptorily flung open, earning a look of reproach from the doctor, drifted the freshness of the last of the summer wild flowers from the orchard which ran at the back of the house.

The doctor cleared his throat before speaking.

'She was not strong, Mr Buchanan. Six pregnancies in as many years, you understand, and then the loss of blood . . .'

He waited for Alexander Buchanan to speak and when there was no response he felt constrained to go on as if to dispel any blame which might be attributed to him. There was none, of course, he knew that. If it was anyone's fault it was this man who looked so incuriously at the infant in the cradle. Five times the poor lady had carried his child and each one lost before it came to term and no sooner was she out of her lying-in-bed than he was at her again, determined, the doctor had heard through the gossip which ran from house to house as servants talked, to get himself a son.

'The child is healthy though, my dear sir, have no fears on that score. I have the wet-nurse standing by.'

'Thank you, doctor, I'm sure you did your best.' Alexander Buchanan did not look up as he spoke and with a sideways glance at the midwife who had helped him, uselessly as it turned out, in his efforts to staunch the flow of blood which had swept away Maude Buchanan's life on its pulsing wave, the doctor turned away, reaching for his greatcoat which, in the urgency of the moment hours before had been flung willy-nilly to the chair in the corner of the room.

'Will I send the nurse in?'

'Thank you, no. I would like to . . . If you would take the child . . .' The man's dark, introspective eyes turned to the midwife, '. . . you say the nursery is prepared . . . a nursemaid is waiting?'

'Of course, sir.'

'I must . . . I believe Mrs Emmerson is waiting?'

'Yes, sir. She is downstairs in the parlour. Shall I ask her to come back later?'

'No . . . no . . . I will see her . . . in a moment.'

'Very well, sir.'

The midwife leaned deferentially across the whipcord stillness of the poor bereaved gentleman and gently lifted the hastily wrapped bundle of his daughter from the cradle, tucking the fine white shawl more closely about the small, puckering face. The baby had been washed roughly about its eyes and mouth and a damp cloth rubbed across the palpitating top of its dark skull; but there was still the stink of violent birth about it and the man turned away as though the blood smell had brought him finally from the trance into which he had fallen when told of his wife's death.

Poor soul, the midwife thought, as she folded the baby in a businesslike fashion into the crook of her arm. Mazed he is by the suddenness of it all and who could blame him? Left at his age with one girl child and no wife to see to the infant's needs and the woman herself only twenty-four at that! Not that he'd be long in getting another, not him! They'd be lining up to take him, child an' all when the news got out of his wife's death. Not only was he one of the wealthiest men in the district of Furness but he was a well set-up chap into the bargain, attractive to women, she'd be bound. A lean and forbidding man with a bleak face set in a cast of lowering adversity just now, but then what else could you expect in the circumstances? He seemed to find little to attract his attention in the child either, but that was men for you! Babies frightened them and ask a father to hold his new-born child in his arms and he would blanche in fear but give him a day or two and the little 'un would become as dear as a jewel.

Alex Buchanan watched the bustling midwife move efficiently about the bedroom. She spoke in a low voice to the chambermaid and they both turned to look at him, understanding, they thought, his need to be alone in his grief. The maid wiped her nose on a scrap of linen, her eyes still brimming over her sad task, then she lifted the large china bowl discreetly covered with a clean white cloth to hide its contents, and moved towards the door. The poor lady was not yet decently, officially laid out but she had been made clean and tidy until the person whose task it was came to make her presentable for those who wished to call and pay their final respects.

The two women left the room followed by the doctor who had been told that food and wine was waiting for him in the dining room and was off to sustain himself after what had really been a most harrowing morning, and Alexander Buchanan was alone with his dead wife.

He did not turn to their bed though. He did not fall to his knees beside her, nor did he bow his head in grief as one would expect of a sorrowing widower. Instead he walked towards the open window and looked across the wind rippled waters of the River Brathay which snaked at the back of his house, like a cord of silver in the noon sunshine. The trees on the lower slope of the fells had turned to that particular blaze of splendour which late autumn brings, a copper fire in which melted every colour from the palest gold to the deepest russet brown. Sunlit trees and glowing heights and the murmur of the breeze whispering through leaves falling in drifts to the damp smelling ground waiting to receive them.

The room was on the corner of the house and moving from where he stood to the window which faced west he leaned his forearm against the low frame and looked in the direction of Colwith woods. The copse of hazel and birch and rowan stretched up from the winding river to the fell top and was so exquisitely lovely that the man, who had felt no pain for the dead woman, harboured it in himself for the beauty which surrounded him. Though he had lived here in this house for most of his life, had been born here and was familiar with the sight which he saw every day, the grandeur overwhelmed him and he stood for a while, studying the shades of the bracken on the mountains which rose steadily before his home. It was beginning to turn from deepest green to the brown of autumn and the heather which was a dense purple coverlet in the summer, was changing to umber. The dry-stone wall which surrounded his garden had, during the summer, become submerged with a burgeoning abundance of growth. Hedge parsley, dock and nettle, meadow cranes-bill, ragwort and foxglove somehow found sustenance amongst the stones themselves and stonecrop and feverfew flourished wildly. Over all lay the tantalizing smell of aniseed from the sweet cecily which grew a foot high almost to the top of the wall.

It was peaceful now that the attendants of birth and death had gone and he felt the gentleness of it enter his mind. His tall frame rested easily and his dark eyes clouded into that unfocused stare of the dreamer. It was as though he was alone in a world of his own shaping, as though the woman on the bed was no more than the beautifully embroidered white quilt which had been removed from it when her labour had begun and which was now folded neatly upon the ottoman. She appeared not to exist for him and should a chambermaid have come upon him she would have been shocked to see the expression which lifted the corners of his strong mouth.

He was shocked himself as he suddenly came to a sense of reality and the manner in which his thoughts had led him. He lifted his dark head and his eyes cleared as he watched a roughly dressed labourer who had wandered into his line of vision beyond the window, ambling slowly along the edge of the orchard towards a small building all set about with fragrant bushes of syringa, lilac and honeysuckle. The man opened a door and went inside, reappearing with a bucket which he carried off in the direction of the rear of the orchard. It was Abel Hodson whose job it was to empty the earth closets which were set some distance from the house. There were two, one for the family, the other for the servants. The sweet smelling bushes helped to disguise the smell with which such necessary places were surrounded but the daily cleaning of the two closets and the twice-daily emptying were something on which Alex insisted. Each hole had a well-fitted white scrubbed lid and seat. The walls were bright with white limestone and the red tiled floors were as clean and polished as those in his own kitchen.

The mundane, everyday activity seemed to bring him back to the reality of what was happening in this, his household. Here he stood, smiling in contemplation of his own future when there were people to see, arrangements to be made, servants who were in confusion and needed steadying with orders, and downstairs, waiting to convey her condolences instead of the beef tea she had brought over, was the mother of the very girl who had been in his thoughts.

He turned and looked about the room. There was a bright cheerful fire in the old, cast iron fireplace, its flickering coals gilding to cream the white lace curtains and the white spotted muslin which draped the dressing table. Though he had shared it with her this had been Maude's room and its white and virginal purity reflected his wife's state despite the six pregnancies she had endured since their marriage seven years ago.

The bed had a white ruffled valance around its base and the mirror which stood on the dressing table was draped in white lace fastened at its centre with a white satin ribbon tied in a bow. There was a white, marble-topped wash stand, the only touch of colour the pink rosebuds which decorated the basin, the ewer and soap dish. Beneath the bed was a chamber pot, empty, in the same pattern.

His gaze was caught suddenly by the small, slender shape beneath the clean linen sheet and he wondered at the complete lack of emotion the sight of it aroused in him. He felt nothing bar a certain surprise that though she had been dead barely an hour he could not even bring to mind the colour of his wife's eyes! He supposed the peace

44

and strange tranquillity in which he found himself was relief. Perhaps he was being unfair to himself for beneath it he felt a prick of pitying sadness for the woman who had tried so hard to give him the son he wanted. She had tried in other ways to please him. There had always been clean, beautifully ironed shirts in his cupboard and his clothes were immaculate, as were the boots she had polished, the state of his home, his well-cooked meals and indeed every aspect of his sterile existence. A good wife, and she would have made a good mother, had she been allowed. But his affection for her had been dictated only by the size of her dowry, the gentility of her upbringing and if he were completely honest with himself and he usually was, the bobbin manufacturing mill, which, as she was an only child, was hers on the death of her father. He had married her for what she would bring him and in the end she had brought him nothing but that mill and one infant daughter. A girl!

'Poor Maude,' he said out loud. 'You did your best and it was not your fault that it was not enough, my dear. The fault was mine in choosing you. Next time I shall do better!'

The words sounded cruel but he did not mean them to be so. He was merely stating the truth. Opening the door he went down the wide, shallow staircase to greet the mother of Christy Emmerson.

Maude Buchanan would have been gratified and quite amazed had she been present – in a manner of speaking – at the number of people who congregated in the chapel where once she had been married and where she was now to be laid to rest. They flocked by the score from as far away as Whitehaven and Cockermouth in the west, where her husband had business dealings, from Milnthorpe in the south and Keswick in the north. Most of the mourners it must be admitted were men with whom he had commerce and their wives. Alex Buchanan had few friends bar those with whom he drank or gambled. He had time for no one who could not be of use to him and those who sat at his dinner table and who now came to see his wife decently buried were men who were connected in some way with his mines.

There was Jonathan Aspin whose ships ran his ore along the coastline and Alfred Marsden whose carters brought it to the ships. Andrew Dyer who supplied him with timber for pit props and Job Emmerson from whom came his blasting powder. They were all wealthy men and their own good clothing and that of their wives declared it.

The little churchyard was quite packed. The road was lined with black draped carriages and the mourners moved between them, making their way up the steep hill to the chapel. Top-hatted gentlemen and ladies in mourning veils, black-edged handkerchiefs to their eyes, who had come to pay homage not to Maude, but to her influential husband, if the truth were admitted. Black silk and bombazine but sprinkled amongst them, or standing deferentially to one side as was their place were plainer folk who had cause to remember Maude Buchanan for her diffident kindness. Shawl-covered heads and cloth caps, wooden-soled clogs, the men's with iron clasps, and the women's made of brass as was the custom.

There were servants from her home, respectable and subdued for she had been a good mistress and what might they expect from the new one, as new one there surely would be? There were several members of her own family, cousins mainly since she had been her father's only child, come to stand and say a prayer and wonder who the widower would take next.

Dancing black plumes on horses' heads, the palely shining sunlight turning the beauty of their black polished coats to ebony. He had done her well, they would say, but the widower moved that day through a hazy-edged blur in which only one figure was clear and sharp in its centre.

Christy Emmerson wore black like the others with veiling on her bonnet for even the death of a woman who

46

was virtually a stranger must be paid the proper respect, but through the fine net he could see the pale grey velvet of her eyes and the slow droop of her thick brown lashes. Though she stood docilely enough beside her mother, her father and two brothers behind her, he was conscious of her impatience, her eagerness to be away and about something more suited to her restless nature. She was young and what was death to do with her, her expression said. She was like a leashed puppy, trained to 'stay' when told but longing only for the moment when the leash would be slipped and the word spoken which would release her from this tedious but necessary situation.

The Squire had come, and his lady, and with them were their three daughters and their son and across the grave of Alexander Buchanan's wife, as the parson spoke the words and the familiar sound of sheep drifted down from Lingmoor Fell, he watched the eyes of the girl and the youth meet, the melting glance they exchanged and his own was speculative.

He allowed a month to go by before he called upon her father!

It was Sunday, cold now as the Lakeland winter approached and in the room which Job Emmerson grandly called his study, a bright applewood fire roared cheerfully up the enormous chimney and its warmth lapped about the legs of the two powerful men as they seated themselves comfortably before it. Job's new trail hounds dozed on the fine rug, nose to tails and Job booted them aside none too gently for though they were both champions and had won him a pursc or two, he held them in no particular sentiment. There was no doubt he prized them. Had he not bred them himself and was he not most particular in the making up of the 'cock-loaf', once fed to cocks before the game became illegal, on which they were fed? It contained eggs, raisins, port wine and another secret ingredient known only to Job, passed on by his father and grandfather before him for the family had all been devotees of the Cumberland sport of 'Hound Trailing'. Yes, he prized them, but he did not love them! They were pampered like the thoroughbreds he had in his stable and which they themselves undoubtedly were but this did not give them the right to keep the fire from their master's feet. They sidled up to his hand, gazing lovingly into his face and as his thoughts pondered on what the widower could want with him, his hand absent-mindedly fondled first one sleek head and then the other.

He and Alex Buchanan had greeted one another cordially enough an hour or two since in the chapel porch. Job had been surprised by the other man's blunt request for a few minutes of his time if he could spare them later in the day and had reflected on the reason for it throughout the heavy Sunday dinner which was customary and which, if he was let, he liked to sleep off before his study fire. To do with business, he supposed but what was it that could not be discussed in his office at the mill?

He waited for the other man to speak first. It was the most important thing he had learned in business. It put the other chap at a disadvantage if he had to 'push the boat out' so to speak.

'It was good of you to see me on a Sunday, Job, but I felt what I have to say should be discussed only in your home. I believe it is customary.' Alex smiled sociably.

'Is it now?' Job answered, but gave away nothing of his mystification.

'Yes. A private matter between gentlemen and one of delicacy.'

'Oh yes?'

Alex did not falter. He had come not to beg for he felt he had no need. What he had to offer was worth any man's consideration and Job Emmerson was not one to turn away a bargain, whether it be in business or in the matter of his daughter's future. Without false modesty he knew himself to be an eligible man in the marriage market. He had already seen the meaningful glances cast in his direction from a dozen mothers with marriageable daughters and had had placed in his path, discreetly of course, for it was only a month since Maude was buried, numerous pretty, smiling young girls. Oh yes, they would all be after him now, longing to comfort and praise and simper and in fact, do anything which might catch his eye and his fancy, his heart and his pocket book, so best get this settled as soon as possible and let them know he was no longer available. Early yet they would say for the period of mourning for a wife should be at least a year but he was a man who cared little for convention and he believed Job Emmerson to be the same.

'This is a . . . ticklish matter, my dear Job, and one which I trust you will treat with respect. I know it has not been long since Maude died but though she was a good wife and we were fond of one another I am a relatively young man and quite simply, I need another! I am aware that folk will tattle but let them, I say. I care nothing for others' opinions bar those I myself respect and I think you know I number you amongst these. I am a well set-up man, Job. I have the means to give a good life to the woman who becomes my wife. I'm healthy and,' he smiled lazily, 'though a bit older I dare say you will agree that is no bad thing. I have a daughter but she is only an infant and would soon grow used to a new mother, would indeed know no difference. She would be little trouble besides for she has a decent girl as a nursemaid. So you see, Job . . .' he grinned engagingly, '. . . I believe I am considered to be what is called "a good catch". I think you know what I am saying, my dear fellow!'

Job did! Instantly!

'You want my girl?'

'I do.'

'You've a bloody cheek.' He beamed delightedly but with no offence.

'I dare say, but that is my way.' Alex returned Job's smile.

'She's young, too young for you.'

49

'She is . . . ?'

'Seventeen.'

'I am twenty-nine. I do not think the difference in age signifies. She will need . . . gentling with a firm hand . . .'

Job snorted with laughter. 'You don't know what the bloody hell you're talking about, lad. And don't stiffen up like that with me. You've not met my lass, have you?'

Alex had for a moment an image in his mind of a soft and rosy face above white shoulders and a thrusting rounded breast. A sighing, bee-stung mouth, a cloud of drifting glossy hair and eyes which burned from beneath heavy, languorous lids. The offence he had taken at Job's words ebbed away and he felt his breath catch sharply in his chest and he thought he might choke. Job was watching him, a smile still lifting the corner of his mouth and he knew he must say something.

'I have not seen as much of her as I would like,' he said carefully and managed to suppress a chuckle, 'but I know she will make a good wife.'

'What makes you say that?'

'She is your daughter, is she not, so she must have a good head on her shoulders!'

'And is that the only consideration, Alex my lad? What about that pretty face of hers? Don't that count?'

'Of course.' Alex shifted uncomfortably in his chair. He was a man well used to dealing with other men but he did not care for the role Job Emmerson had cast him in, that of a man come cap in hand to ask for something Job had which he wanted, and which Job seemed determined to make him grovel for. And there was a brightness in Job Emmerson's eyes and a quizzical smile about his lips which Alex found strange. 'She is a beautiful girl,' he continued carefully, 'and would grace any man's home.'

'And have you heard about her temper, Alex Buchanan?'

'Her temper?' Alex blinked but managed to retain the lounging indolence of his long body.

'Oh yes, she'd take a deal more than – what was the

word you used – "gentling" to tame her! She is a rare bird, that one.'

It was said proudly and Alex began to feel that Job Emmerson was playing some game with him. That he had some private joke which he was not yet willing to share. His eyes gleamed with wicked delight and it seemed he was positively gloating about something.

'Aye, a rare bird and where she came from God only knows. Oh, she's mine, no doubt of that,' he added hastily, 'but she's got summat in her that me and her mother haven't. Don't ask me what it is because I couldn't put a name to it. She's strong, Alex, and won't be put upon. I keep a firm hand on her, make no mistake but sometimes . . . well . . .' he shook his head in wonder '. . . she's as hot-headed as those lads of mine. She'll stand up to me and say her piece but she'll do as she's told, just the same. That's her strength, you see. She knows what she wants but she also knows when to bend. But she's a beauty an' all. A jewel you might say, and precious to me.'

'What d'you want for her, this jewel of yours, Job?'

'Nay lad! Did I say I wanted anything?' Job smiled.

'You don't have to!'

'I was only pointing out, not only her graces, which are many and varied, but her deficiencies as well. She is a competent housekeeper, Alex. Her mother saw to that and she could run this house if she had to. She plays the piano and sings and has all the accomplishments that the academy in Fellthwaite can teach a young lady. She rides and can turn a pretty foot in any ballroom in the county, aye, and keep up with many of them who think themselves above her. She even has a smattering of French! There, what d'you think of that?'

Alex shifted irritably. What the hell was wrong with the man babbling on like some foolishly indulgent father who was trying to sell a piece of goods which, though appearing fine to the casual observer has some flaw in it which must be hidden with a flow of praise? If he didn't know better he would imagine Christy to be the plainest miss between

51

here and the Scottish border with buck teeth and chicken legs. Why did he not come to the nub of the matter which was a simple 'yes' to his request for his daughter in marriage? There would of course be many financial details to be gone into for Job Emmerson would see his daughter well secure before he parted with her, but the heart of it could be settled here and now with no quibbling. A handshake and it would be done, with no one the wiser for a few months but the two of them. He was a wealthy man with property and business in many parts of the Lakeland and beyond. A farm or two up near Ennerdale which he rented. His – once Maude's – bobbin manufacturing mill at Stavely and of course, his copper mines in the Conistone area. The mining fields of the Lakelands – he was not the only man working them – covered an area of ten square miles but the largest copper mine, his own, was situated about a mile north of Conistone and had been worked ever since his father, an engineer, son of a sheep farmer, a 'statesman' and a miner himself, opened it up in 1802 and in the first years of mining speculated every penny he had to make it successful. The mine proved to be of great vigour and with the gains he made he opened up others and within ten years employed several hundred men, women and boys and was making a profit of between thirty and thirty-five thousand pounds a year.

Alex was proud of his forebears and the service they had given succeeding monarchs in the protection of the borders against the unruly Scots. For this service they were given land, a privilege James I of England had tried to take from them, arguing that with the union of England and Scotland there was no further need for their aid. But the dalesmen had clung to their heritage and had threatened a call to arms to protect their 'estates'.

They were allowed to retain their rights and had been called 'Estatesmen' shortened now to 'statesmen'. Not mere farmers were these proud men of Cumberland and Westmorland but statesmen and a true Yeoman class since the days of Elizabeth. They built their farmhouses with thick walls to withstand the harshness of the northern winter, from local stone with heavy slate roofs, protective porch and circular chimneys. The sheep they ran, Herdwicks, were said to have been brought from Scandinavia and they were small, agile and hardy, goat-like in their ability to move about the high fells in summer. Their flesh was sweet and their fleece more suitable to the making of wool for carpets than clothing for it was coarse, but well suited to the climate and conditions of England's highest mountains.

His people had lived in the same farmhouse for three hundred years, adding a bit here and there as the situation demanded or finances allowed and though he did not as a rule boast of it, Alex Buchanan was an enormously wealthy man.

When he was seventeen, being more concerned with his father's mines than the farms he held, Alex was sent to University in Edinburgh where he gained a degree in engineering. He then spent two years doing every job that was done in his father's mines from the joiner's shop, short spells on the dressing floor, the pumping station and a full eighteen months working underground with experienced miners cutting rocks and stoping out the ore. He was familiar with every level of every mine, every course and shaft, vein and string, every fathom and fault and outcrop and when at the age of twenty-five his father died suddenly of a fever, he was perfectly able to continue the working of the Buchanan Mining Company and did so, adding another fortune to the one made by James Buchanan and his grandfather before that.

Oh yes, he was prepared to settle any sum Job Emmerson cared to name on Job Emmerson's daughter, for that was the way of things. A daughter was a valuable commodity to be used in the barter of the marriage market, gaining profit for all those concerned, except perhaps the bride.

'I appreciate Christina is a fine match for any man, Job, and I promise you she will have no cause to complain should you allow her to be my wife. I must confess, for in all things I am a man of business, that your position and wealth have been taken into consideration.' He smiled and Job was quite nonplussed by its sudden warmth. 'And as for her temper, as you call it, well, I must admit I like a woman with spirit. Maude was . . . peaceful and we agreed on everything . . . you are smiling . . . well, I do like my own way and have a strong will when opposed so your Christina and I should have . . .'

'I'm afraid not, Alex.'

'I beg your pardon.' Alex Buchanan's face hardened quite dramatically, still smiling, but no longer warm.

Job Emmerson had the grace to look slightly abashed but the expression did not entirely wipe away the gratified sense of triumph which lit his heavy, jowled face. His eyes were sharp with joy and the hand which had fondled the dogs' heads clenched on the arm of his chair, then went to his neck-cloth to adjust the sudden constriction his mounting pride had brought about.

'I'm sorry lad, but someone's beaten you to it.'

Alex Buchanan's smiling face had set itself fast into the implacable mould which would have been instantly recognized by the men in his mine or his bobbin mill, or in the office where his managers came to consult with him on the growth of his concerns. It was a face which had won him many a hand of cards or game of chance for it showed not a flicker of emotion, nor an inkling of the thoughts in his head. It was cool, self-controlled and as smooth and empty as that of his newly born daughter.

But Job Emmerson was too far gone in the wonder of the honour his lass had brought to him to concern himself with what might be Alex Buchanan's disappointment and when he did he was not unduly concerned for first and last Buchanan was a businessman and would not let such a thing stand in the way of his own business needs. He was a cold man. A man known to have married the first time for money and would do so again, no doubt of it, and his Christy was not the only daughter of a man of wealth in these parts. And most of them were young and capable of bearing the man many fine sons.

'I should have said at once, lad, I'm sorry. I never thought and I wasn't sure at first what it was you were after but there's more fish in the sea than came out of it, as they say and you'll soon find another to suit.'

'They do indeed say that,' Alex replied smoothly, 'and of course, you're right.'

He made no more of it than that and seemed to feel no need to ask Job to keep this to himself. A wise man was Job and knew when to keep his mouth shut. They were business associates again now, no more. They talked of this and that for several minutes, two urbane gentlemen of the world who had discussed what might have turned out to be a decent business transaction but which unfortunately had not met with the agreement of one. It was of no concern. There would be others.

At last Alex Buchanan stood up, his movements, his face, his manner giving no indication of the way he felt. Casually at the door he turned, smiling.

'May I ask to whom congratulations should be directed? Besides yourself, of course.'

Job preened, stretching his already tall frame until his head almost brushed the lamp which hung from the high ceiling.

''Tis the Squire's lad. Yes, you may well look surprised, Alex . . .' though Alex's face had not changed expression, '. . . and so was I. Him and our Christy have met on several occasions in the homes of mutual friends, or so he told me when he came to ask for her. I must admit I was a mite put out at first, him being the Squire's lad and me not even knowing the pair of them had met, but as I said to him, if it was alright with his father it was alright with me! Well, you can imagine the face on the Squire when he called to see me. Yes, *he* called on me and he was none too pleased about it, I can tell you.' Job actually stamped his foot in remembered glee and if Alex had not been frozen in the stillness of the cast which was holding him upright he might have smiled.

'There's tales of the Hall falling down for the want of a bob or two spending on it and the cottages some of those estate workers live in aren't fit to house a pig let alone women and children. Well, he needs some cash and I've got it, Alex, I've got it! That moorland and pasture of his wants some maintaining, you know, and the gentry's tastes are extravagant. Spending money they haven't got on horses and hounds and the like and that lad's education must have cost a pretty penny. Anyway, not to make too long a story of it, that lad of his up and refused to have anyone but my Christy, can you imagine and him with a pedigree which goes back to Elizabeth's day! Said if he couldn't have her he'd have no one and the bloody line could die out for all he cared. The Squire didn't say so but he must have done his best to talk him out of it for he don't like to be associated with the manufacturing classes. He don't know how to treat us, you see. We're neither fish, flesh nor fowl as far as he's concerned. He can't tell us what to do and whip us if we disobey like those he considers his inferiors. We've too much cash for that so the poor sod's in a right fix! Anyway that young Robin's put his foot down, and me and Squire Forsythe made the final arrangements only yesterday – so it's settled. My lass is to wed his lad and one day will be the mistress of Dalebarrow Hall. What d'you think to that, Alex Buchanan?'

'Well done, well done indeed!'

'You'll find another, Alex. A man in your circumstances, well set-up! Why, they'll be clamouring at your gate, man.' Job reached out to shake Alex's hand.

Alex laughed good-humouredly. 'They already are, Job, they already are!'

CHAPTER FOUR

Natty Cooper lived with his wife and three children in the middle cottage of a neat row erected to the south of Job Emmerson's mills, which housed the men he employed and their families. The cottages, two dozen of them, were part of a building which formed an 'L' shape, the horizontal stroke of the letter comprising the stables where the fine Clydesdale horses which pulled Mr Emmerson's wagons were quartered.

There were more cottages across from the stables, all pleasantly situated amongst the alders and birch trees which clustered down to the beck. Opposite the track which led from the cottages to the mill gate was the cooperage and set apart from the rest was the splendid stone-built building housing the offices in which Mr Emmerson and his sons worked.

Natty was a contented man, secure in this age of growing unrest caused by the government's refusal to allow into the country the cheap foreign corn condemned by the landowners who grew it to their own profit. The price of bread was high because of it and there was hunger and poverty in the cities and in rural areas as well but Natty was unconcerned, if he was even aware of it, since he was not hungry and neither were his children. He had a decent job, a roof over his head, a pint of ale and a pipe of tobacco now and again. His children were healthy and his wife warm and amiable in his bed.

He worked in the corning house where one of the most dangerous stages in the making of blasting powder took place and beside it, kept in one designated area to cut down the risk of an explosion spreading, were the other dangerous processes. There was the magazine, the incorporating mill, the pressing house and, in the early days, the stoving processes of preparation.

The 'safe' stages such as the saw-mill, the cooper's shop, the joiner's shop, offices, stores, stables, cottages, the changing houses where the men and women put on their special safety clothing were set well away from the more perilous working area, and all were widely dispersed and protected by earth works and blast screens.

Nevertheless, despite Mr Emmerson's careful and proper precautions, Natty, walking between shifts from the press plate wash house to the corning house, completely uninvolved and minding his own business – as he was to remark bitterly to his patient wife a dozen times a day in later years – was blown from his feet by a small, unexplained explosion in which no one was injured but himself.

He was carried no more than a few yards, merely to the edge of the long riverside shelf along which the headrace flowed, but his right leg was flung willy-nilly amongst the rough boulders which lay there and was shattered so badly he was never able to walk again without a crutch. Of course the doctor, hurriedly summoned from a confinement, set it as best he could but it did no good, and at thirty-four Natty was thrown on the parish with a wife and three children to be looked to.

He understood, though he did not like it, that the tied cottage in which he lived was his no longer, for Job Emmerson had built it to be lived in by his employees and as he impatiently explained to the peevish Natty, he was no longer one of those. It was needed for the man who was to have his job and his two shillings and fourpence a day.

He was found a broken-down cottage which Annie Emmerson ensured was made habitable for his family, on the edge of the village. Here he hopped around all day doing nothing much but wait for his wife to come home from her work in Mrs Buchanan's laundry or Mrs Emmerson's still room and scullery which she scrubbed out each day, or the stone-picking work she undertook before the sowing began or any of the dozen and one jobs she could find to keep them dry and clothed and fed, to cook his dinner and listen to his bitter recriminations against the fates which had put him where he was and to attend his physical need which fortunately did not spring to life often and produced no more children!

His two sons, Dennis and Jack, still too young at ten and eleven to be taken on for the dangerous work in the gunpowder mill went to the mine up at Conistone, to work above ground at the 'grating', picking out saleable ore, and Faith, twelve and as handy as once her mother had been, went to the kitchens of his previous master.

Christy could remember the day young Faith Cooper had come to her notice.

The week before, when the hollow crack had echoed from fell to fell, resounding off each rolling surface of the valley wall, the sound every community dreaded – for most had a son or a husband who worked at the gunpowder mill – her mother's white-faced stiff figure at the kitchen table would always live in her memory. They had been pickling eggs, or was it preserving damsons, she could not remember, she only knew the shattering smack of the preserving jar as it hit the flagged stone floor had sounded as dreadful as the thump of the explosion.

'Dear God,' her mother had whispered, her face turning yellow as the glass scattered about her feet in a hundred dangerous shards and she turned and began to stumble, then, gathering speed, to run, bumping clumsily against the table, the door jamb and, as she left the house, the gatepost which opened from the stable yard on to the drive.

Christy had been twelve, the same age as Faith, and her mother's terror had made a deep impression on her. There had been little damage, a window blown out and a few minor cuts and bruises, one chap with a shattered leg, her mother said when she came back, fretful at her own foolishness, chiding herself for running 'without even stopping to decently put on a bonnet'.

It was a week later that Faith had appeared in the kitchen. Christy had been sprawled in the old rocking chair which was always there beside the glowing fire, two kittens curled in her lap, one of her mother's gingerbread biscuits in her hand – for though Annie was now mistress of several young maids and had a woman whose job it was to do the cooking she still liked to keep her hand in.

'Oh yes, the master said you'd be coming,' she had said and Christy recalled the nervous bob, the quick bright glance from eyes in which brown and green were flecked, before her mother's sharp but kindly voice had brought the young girl to attention.

'How's your father doing, Faith?' she enquired.

'Nicely, thank you, ma'am,' the girl had replied.

'Your mother is managing then?'

'Oh yes, thank you, ma'am.'

'And the boys?'

'They're to go up Conistone way, if you please, Mrs Emmerson. Mr Buchanan is to take them. They're to stay at the old corn mill.'

'Splendid. Now, come this way, child and I'll show you your duties.'

Annie wasted no time in useless sympathy which did no good to anyone, but set about the business of putting back in some order a family whose breadwinner had been cut down, in her own sharp-tongued but sensible way.

Faith did well for she was a sharp little thing and within six months she had worked her way into Annie Emmerson's good graces by being available and willing to tackle any hard and mucky job thrust upon her by those who were at first apt to take advantage of her inexperience, good nature and youth.

But though she was eager to make good and please Mrs Emmerson, for her family really needed the wage she sent home each week, she was not daft and as soon as she learned the routine of the house and which job belonged to whom, she became bold enough to speak up. When Annie Emmerson heard her tell Peg, who was a year older and bigger, that it was not her job to scrub out the dairy but Peg's and she'd clout anyone who tried to make her, Annie began to take more notice of her.

Faith was bright and quick to learn, anxious to better herself and the sad condition of her poor father's life, and she was soon seeing to the bedrooms, allowed to dust the parlour and its dozens of gilt and silver framed pictures, cameos, painted vases, glass domes under which stuffed birds rested and the magnificent ormolu clock on the valanced fireplace. When she was fifteen she was taught the refinements of helping to serve tea to Mrs Emmerson's callers. She wore a smart black dress and a starched muslin apron and cap and could dip a curtsey as gracefully as a debutante and her well-scrubbed, bonny looks earned her Annie's praise and Faith was her devoted slave.

She began to look after Annie's own good clothes, ironing the frilled caps and lace petticoats which Dorcas, willing but heavy-handed, could not seem able to get to grips with and it was but a step to a bit of plain sewing, and the special stitching needed in the fine undergarments Miss Christy was beginning to take an interest in.

One night, as she mended a tear in the fine Honiton lace which frothed about Miss Christy's petticoat, sitting beside Miss Christy's bedroom fire to do it, her young mistress had come into the room and declared herself too tired to brush her hair.

'Let me do it, Miss,' Faith had begged. 'I can sew this later.' And taking the brush in her capable hands she had seated the young girl before the mirror and had begun to do the task which was to change her life.

From then on it became an accepted part of her duties to attend Miss Christy in the choosing of her gowns, the care of them and the dressing of Miss Christy's hair. Between them, studying the London fashion magazines for ideas, they soon produced such a variety of stylish designs for Christy's thick hair, Job declared he was never sure who was going to sit at his table with him, his own daughter or one of the young princesses!

61

They became, if not exactly friends for that would never do, then companions and Christy had been glad of her young maid in the trying times leading up to the day of her betrothal to Robin Forsythe.

It was December now and the days were long and wet and cold and Christy was restless. She and Faith were trapped in the house by the weather and she was bored and frustrated and longing to see Robin and her face was moody as she stared at her own reflection in the mirror. She sighed deeply.

'Will we try the tongs again, Miss Christina?'

'Oh, what's the use, Faith? My hair is too thick and the ringlets just fall straight out again.'

'Well what about the curl papers?'

'It's too heavy. The minute you take them out the curls simply get longer and longer until I look like a spaniel!'

'We could put some bandoline on it. That might keep it in place.'

'But it makes it so greasy and I can't bear the smell of the rum.'

'The essence of almonds should take it away.'

'Well it doesn't and I can't abide the thought of smelling like Edwin when he's been down to The Bear.'

Christy Emmerson stood up abruptly and her maid stepped back, the hair brush still in her hand. She watched calmly as her mistress, sighing as though she had the problems of the whole world on her white and delicate shoulders, walked across the bedroom to stare mutinously from the window.

The garden was bare now as the December 'bottom winds' took away every leaf and petal which had decorated the sloping flowerbeds and hedges and the trees and shrubs during the summer. Only the tall conifers, transferred from the higher slopes of his land by Job when he built the house, had any shape or colour and their leaves were a vivid green with the coming of winter contrasting grandly with the red of the berries which studded the holly bushes.

There was nothing to be seen. Edwin would be in the chimney corner drinking tea for Annie was away for a few days supervising at the birth of a child to her cousin's youngest girl, brought to bed a day or two ago up in Grasmere. Annie liked to keep the old customs, despite her elevation in life, and the child's head would be immediately washed in rum, the ale and spices would be put on the fire and the 'groaning' cheese and bread cut up to be distributed amongst the unmarried women to lay under their pillow at night to dream on. No doubt her mother would bring her a finger of it to put under her own pillow so that she might dream of the child she herself would one day have.

Her eyes became unfocused and her lips curled into a smile. A son she would have first! Robin Forsythe's son! With hair the colour of wheat, thick and curling about his fine head and deep brown eyes to smile at her from his father's face. And then a girl, dainty and spirited with shining silver hair and velvet brown eyes and . . .

Hastily she shook her head and the disobedient mass of her silky dark hair fell about her shoulders.

'Oh God, Faith, will it never be March?' she asked irritably, pushing her hands through the long, heavy curtain of it. 'Three months to wait and I swear I'll go mad if Robin and I don't . . .'

She stopped suddenly and glanced at the maid aware that she had been about to say something the girl might consider improper, that was improper, for how to explain how she felt, how to contain the way she felt about Robin, until their wedding day. But Faith's eyes were sympathetic with none of the usual tendency of a servant to slide away when faced with the eccentricities of a mistress.

They looked at one another, two young girls of a similar age. Christy smiled and sat down in the chair she had left a moment ago, leaning her forearm along its back. She put her chin on it and studied the girl who was being trained now in the serious duties of a ladies' maid. Although for the past year she had been 'looking after' – Mrs Forsythe's own words – Christy and her clothes, and the same for Annie now that she had proved her skill with the goffering iron, she must be properly trained if she was to be the personal maid of the wife of the future Squire of Fellthwaite! Each day she was taken over to Dalebarrow where Mrs Forsythe's own personal maid kept her for two hours, showing her the art of correctly caring for her mistress's clothes, hairdressing, fine sewing, the cleaning of bonnets and boots, the secrets of the ingredients to be made up to wash brushes and combs, pomade and bandoline for the hair and the perfect care of her mistress's boudoir. She must be able to iron her ladies' garments to perfection and should there be an accident to restore whiteness to scorched linen, to preserve furs, for her mistress would surely have them, and feathers and to clean her jewels for she would undoubtedly have those too. Civility to all and servility to none was the maxim she was taught. Deference to the master and mistress, discretion and obedience, and the ability to have no life beyond that of the lady she served.

It was a great chance for Faith Cooper and she meant to make the most of it. Miss Christina had declared she would have a maid of her own choosing, not one picked out for her by her mother-in-law and she wanted Faith to go with her. Job, still bewitched by the idea of his lass being the Squire's lady, could deny her nothing and Faith was suitable. She was quick and clean, handy and young and even before her training with the grand maid of Mrs Forsythe had a knack with their Christina, and Christy, already the Squire's lady, had her way!

Christy yawned widely, then turned her head away to look out of the window. Her eyes were hazed with boredom as she asked plaintively what they should do next.

'I'm sure I don't know, Miss. I've got lots of things I could be doing.'

'I'm sure you have, but please Faith, sit down and entertain me!'

'Me entertain you? How on earth am I to do that?'

'Tell me about yourself?' She demanded regally, determined to be amused on this unexciting day.

The maid smiled placidly and began to put away the brushes, the comb, the curl papers and ribbons with which she and her young mistress had been experimenting.

'What is there to tell? You know all about me.'

'Tell me what you did before your father . . .'

Faith turned and lifted her head to look from the window across the sloping floor of the valley and the lake it contained towards Chapel Stile. She was a bonny young girl, her attraction lying mainly in her look of bounteous good health. Her hair was a shining brown, very neat and tidy beneath her frilled cap and her cheeks were smooth, rounded and rosy. She wore a grey woollen dress and a starched and frilled white apron tied at the back of her small waist in a large and perfect bow.

'Well, nothing really. I helped me Ma at home after I got back from the Dame school in the village. We had a few chickens in those days. I used to collect the eggs and feed them. It was Chapel on Sunday and we would sometimes walk with the hunt.'

'This was before . . .' Christy's face was sympathetically warm as she delicately put the question.

'Mmm. Me Dad was . . . he used to laugh a lot . . . then! He'd put our Dennis on his shoulders and we'd set off across the fells following the hounds as far as we could go. Once we got as far as Heald woods just below Claife Heights and that was going round by Hawkeshead as well! That fox led us a merry dance that day, I can tell you, but me Dad was strong and could walk for miles, even carrying our Dennis.'

Her face clouded and her hands became busy with a tangle of vividly coloured ribbons. Painstakingly she began to unravel them, rolling each bright satin strand into a neat coil. 'Those were good days, Miss Christina, for me Dad and for all of us, but . . . he's changed now. He can't get about and with all of us working he's on his own all day and nobody thinks to visit him. His old workmates used to come by but . . . well . . . he's in pain, you see and when it's bad he loses his temper and shouts and . . . they don't come any more.'

'Do you see him often, Faith?'

'Oh yes, Miss.' Faith's eyes crinkled in a smile. 'Whenever I have a day off I go over to the village and tidy up the place a bit. My Ma gets so tired with all the . . .' She frowned suddenly, looking up at Christy with a bright, false smile, '. . . not that we're complaining, Miss Christy. Your mother's been so good, giving her work in the still room and Mrs Buchanan, God rest her soul, always found her something to do . . . but she's not young. I send all I can manage, and the lads as well but . . . my dad needs medicine for the pain.'

'I'm sorry, Faith, if there was something I could . . .'

'There's nothing, Miss. We've managed nicely all these years and we'll go on managing. Don't you worry about us. Your Ma and the master have seen us right.'

She finished winding the ribbon and closed the drawer and the conversation, it seemed, with a click. Going to the fireplace she carefully selected several juniper sticks to throw upon the fire and fill the room with its lovely, aromatic fragrance, then turned to look about her as though searching out some small task she might have forgotten.

Christy stood up and began to move restlessly about the room. Without her mother here to bully her into doing some household chore or pay an unwilling call on some acquaintance, there seemed little to do but drift about, passing time. Though she had at first blessed the freedom her mother's absence had given her at least the tasks she had been set had been something to do. She had been this way ever since the date had been set for her marriage to Robin. It was as though now they had a day, a goal, an end in sight to the feverish craving, the passionate need they had to be together, the waiting had become the harder. Each time they met now they were hedged about with brothers, sisters, cousins, maiden aunts come from Leicestershire to look her over, chaperones from both families who, now that the contract was signed, were not about to let the substance of it become damaged, or even slightly smirched by a whisper of scandal. No gossip would ever be bandied about concerning the future Squire's lady. She must be above reproach, impeccable, her reputation as white and spotless as the dress in which she would be married.

Christy was on edge, irritable over nothing, bored and inclined to sigh with tedious regularity. She hated sewing and could not settle to play the piano, and without her father's consent Ned would refuse to allow her to take out her mare. Faith did not ride and Ned could not be spared; Robin was away for a few weeks with his Leicestershire cousins and her nervous frustration seemed to get worse and worse as the days dragged on.

If only March would come! If only she could be with Robin! If only . . . If only . . .

She turned feverishly, the weight of her spirits sharpening her face into a fretful frown.

'Oh Faith, for God's sake, let's *do* something. A walk . . . anything!'

'But it's going to rain, Miss Christina. Edwin said . . .'

'Damn Edwin. Let's put on our coats and go up to . . .'

'Where?'

'I don't know . . . anywhere. I know, let's take some fruit or something and go and visit your father. You said he had no callers. I'm sure he would be glad of someone to talk to on a day like this.'

'Well, I don't know.'

'Oh come on, Faith. Are you saying you don't want to see him?'

'No, but . . . !'

'Well get your bonnet on and let's be away!'

They followed the track up to Hill Close turning left to skirt above the mill's perimeter through the browning, waist-high bracken which covered the lower slopes of the

67

fells. The snow had already placed a thin white lace cloth on their peaks but the dry-stone walls were still clearly visible. It was cold and blustery and the low clouds pressed overhead like grey woolsacks draped out to dry.

Sheep called plaintively and higher up the two girls could see small scattered flocks of sheep, and men and dogs gathering them in ready to be brought down. A low musical sound could be heard giving a command to a flashing dog and it dropped immediately to its belly. As far as the eye could see the land undulated fiercely, range upon range of harsh fell land, but down in the dale was a narrow strip of order and fertility skirting the rowan shaded back. Rock ledges, fan-shaped screes, black rocks and ravens contrasting sharply with the green, water-laden lushness of the valley bottom.

The two girls strode out and Christy felt the tension begin to ease from her tight strung body. She lifted her face to the wind which had sneaked up ahead of them, then with a sharp exclamation, snapped the ribbons which were tied under her chin with impatient fingers, pulling the bonnet from her head. She let it swing from her hand and the wind dashed through her glorious hair until it whipped about her head.

'Oh Faith, that's better, that's better! Sometimes I think I'll go mad with being . . . confined! Made to do this and that and never put one foot in front of the other without thinking first that it might be improper. When I'm married it will be different. Robin is like me. He loves to get out, to ride and walk and . . . oh, I don't know . . . do things, not just sit and embroider. Not that he embroiders but he has to help his father with the estate and the accounts. They have no steward at the moment but they are to employ one when . . .'

She stopped speaking abruptly but Faith Cooper was only too well aware, as who in the valley was not, that Christina Emmerson was being married for her money and that her dowry and the allowance settled on her by her father would buy not only a steward but the complete restoration of Dalebarrow Hall and the surrounding estate.

Christy hurried on, speaking quickly to cover the small hesitation. '. . . there will be no need then for him to be occupied with books and he and I will . . .'

'Yes, Miss Christy?' Faith prompted gently.

Christy turned and stopped, then grinned infectiously.

'Never mind me, Faith Cooper. What about you and Ned Roper? Have you what is called an understanding?'

Faith looked shocked. Her rosy mouth became prim and her eyes were stern. She tossed her head in a fair imitation of her mistress.

'Miss Christina! How can you say such a thing? Ned Roper indeed. I've never heard anything so . . .'

'Now Faith Cooper, don't you put that frosty face on for me. I've seen the way he looks at you whenever you put your nose out of doors. Why do you think he was so keen to pass on those notes that Robin wrote? It was only to speak to you and you know it. My God, if my father had found out he'd have lost his job and with no "character" either. You don't suppose he would have chanced that do you, unless he was so besotted . . .'

Faith lifted her nose even higher and began to move ahead. She was immensely affronted and her stiff back showed it.

Christy was delighted. She danced ahead of her maid, her face alight with teasing laughter.

'Come on, Faith, you can tell me. Has he offered to kiss you or have you not got that far yet? Perhaps a little walk in the evening over behind the stables or up the hill beyond the house?'

'Stop it now, Miss Christina! Ned Roper means nothing to me and never will. Just because he passed on those notes from Mr Forsythe, and I was daft enough to oblige by giving them to you, that doesn't mean there was anything between him and me!'

Faith's cheeks were fiery with indignation. She stopped and put her hands on her hips.

'And that's another thing, Christy Emmerson . . .' neither of them noticed the slip, '. . . you'd no right to involve me and Ned in such goings on. I didn't say so at the time . . . well . . . I was new to the job of being your maid and I . . . it wasn't my place, but I didn't like it, I can tell you. Deceiving your Pa like that. It wasn't honest.'

'I see, it wasn't honest, was it? Well it certainly proves then that honesty doesn't pay because look where it got me!'

Christy's face was triumphant and wickedly gleeful and she faced her maid, her feet planted firmly on the flinty track. 'Besides, we're not talking about me and Robin. We're to be married and everything is all settled for us. What I want to know is when you and Ned . . .'

'Ned Roper can go jump in Elterwater for all I care. He can ogle as much as he wants and promise to buy me a . . .'

'Ah ha! So he's promising to buy you things, is he? In exchange for what, may I ask? Now you be careful, my girl . . .' Her voice and expression were a fair imitation of Annie Emmerson, though her eyes gleamed devilishly. She was enjoying herself immensely, some perverse imp in her delighting in her maid's discomfiture. She was not an unkind girl but the frustration she herself felt at her enforced separation from Robin, at the confining of the sexuality which his hands and young man's body had already awakened in her, put the witch in her and she was determined to get a rise out of Faith, Faith being the only person handy.

'. . . that's when you want to watch them, Faith. When they start promising to buy you presents, or take you to the fair! But what do they want in return, answer me that, Faith Cooper, if you can. You get nothing for nothing in this world, my lass.'

She stopped, bewildered suddenly. Now why had she said that, she wondered? Nothing for nothing! What did it mean? Was it her father talking, his manufacturing, working man's blood, which ran in her veins, voicing some

70

subconscious thought which lurked in the back of her mind. Trade! You give me that and I will give you this. My daughter and her money for your son and his name.

Horrified she whirled about, her face becoming still and frozen as though the biting wind had seized her flesh, setting it in ice. What the devil had put that frightening thought in her head? She was well aware — being a girl brought up in a society in which such things were common — that daughters in all classes married where they were told, to gain some advantage for the good of the family, but she and Robin loved one another. Didn't they? They were marrying for love. Weren't they? How could she doubt it? How could she doubt the overflowing feelings which threatened to burst the banks of her heart and mind and drown her in their sweetness each time she saw him? How could she doubt the shining in Robin's eyes whenever they met hers? How could . . . ?

The sound of horse's hooves on the rocky track brought her from her paralysis; that and Faith's anxious hand upon her arm, and the small fell pony was on them before they had time to step aside. There was a great deal of rearing and side-stepping and an oath or two and then the animal was expertly manoeuvred on to the springing turf which lay at the side of the track, its head jerked by the rein in the hand of the young man on its back. Finally he had her under control and he turned then to speak.

'Perhaps it might be as well if you were to look where you were going in future, madam,' he said quietly. 'You nearly had me unseated and yourself trampled on. Walking backwards on a path this wide is surely not wise!'

'This path is not meant to be ridden at breakneck speed by a horse controlled by a madman, sir.'

The man's face tightened. 'I was merely walking her. She is not capable of a full gallop at her age and with a man my size on her back.'

'You must have been going at speed otherwise you would have seen us.'

The young man on the pony had brought her sharply

71

back from the cold place in which her own foolish, yes, foolish – she recognized it now – thoughts had taken her and she squared up to the pony and the man on her back, Faith's hand still firmly upon her arm.

The tall, lanky young man lounged awkwardly in the saddle, his own height and the pony's short and stocky size making it impossible to do anything else; he held the animal in with one hand on the rein, the other resting on his thigh. His long legs were bent almost double in the short stirrup. He was far too tall for the animal and Christy felt the first inclination to laugh and her resentment began to fade away. It really had been her fault and her quick tempered reaction had been caused by her own strange thoughts, not the young man's sudden appearance, startled though she had been by it. She stared at him curiously.

He was about twenty-two or three, decently dressed but rather shabby in Hodden grey, with broad shoulders and big-knuckled hands on the rein. He was not handsome, nor plain for his face was strong, pleasant, now that the quiet anger had gone, and his eyes were intelligent. Into them had come the interest to which she was used, that of a man looking at a pretty woman, but it was not at her that he looked.

She lifted her head haughtily.

'Perhaps you will allow us to move on now,' she demanded, but her eyes were bright with laughter.

'I'm not stopping you,' he answered politely, his eyes resting on the rosy red cheeks of Christy's maid.

'We're off for a walk,' Christy said as though he had asked, 'to see Faith's father.'

'Indeed!' he said, his eyes still on Faith. He raised his hat courteously, as if introductions had been made at the mention of her name, then, aware that it was ungentle-manly to remain seated, even on a horse, when a lady stood, he loosened his feet from the stirrups and put his feet flat on the ground, one on either side of the sturdy animal.

Immediately Christy and Faith began to laugh and after a moment, so did he.

'I know,' he said, throwing his leg over the pony's rump. 'She's far too small for me. I have had her since I was a lad but I intend buying a decent mount as soon as I am settled in my job.'

Their initial animosity was gone and they stood on the windblown hillside, three young people just met with that curiosity a stranger will produce. They eyed one another with interest but as usual Christy was the first to break the silence.

'My name is Christy Emmerson and this is my ... companion, Faith Cooper.'

'How do you do, Miss Emmerson, Miss Cooper. I am David Adams.'

'Mr Adams.' Faith spoke for the first time. 'I am Miss Emmerson's maid whatever she may say. She is being kind when she calls me her companion!'

Christy turned and in a lovely gesture of friendship took Faith's hand earnestly and the tall young man warmed to her though his eyes still lingered about Faith's flushed face.

'You are my companion, Faith, and friend and I shall call you so.'

Faith laughed and shook her head but she was pleased. Pleased with the words Christy spoke and with something else though as yet she had put no name to it.

'And you are to take up employment here then, Mr Adams?' Christy asked with keen attention.

'I am, that is if I can find my way safely to Conistone.' He smiled engagingly. 'I am come from Carlisle but somhow I seem to have strayed from what I am sure is the right track. I stayed overnight at a farm but the directions I was given were a bit vague.'

'Where are you headed then, Mr Adams?'

'To Conistone, as I said. I am to work in the Buchanan Mining Company.'

'Indeed.' Christy's voice was haughty and David Adams

turned his surprised gaze on her. She had more moods than a basketful of kittens.

'You are acquainted with Mr Buchanan, Miss Emmerson?'

'Slightly.'

'And you do not care for him?'

'I did not say that, Mr Adams.'

'But your tone implied it.'

'Please do not find implications where none are meant, sir.'

'Forgive me. I was rude.' The young man looked abashed and Christy relented. It was not his fault that the detestable Mr Buchanan was to employ him, nor that her own antipathy to the man made her sharp.

'So you are to work in the mines, Mr Adams?'

David Adams brightened. Catching Faith's glowing smile his own flashed eagerly.

'Yes. Mr Buchanan engaged me some weeks ago. I am to be his mine engineer but I confess these mountains and the weather I have encountered make me believe that you dalesmen and women are a hardy breed, and I shall have to prove myself if I am to become one of you!'

'You will grow used to it, and us, Mr Adams.'

'I hope so, Miss Emmerson . . . well . . .' He fiddled with his pony's reins, '. . . I must get on. If you would direct me I would be most grateful, and you will wish to continue your walk. Miss Cooper's father will be waiting.'

He stood for a moment, looking from one bright face to the other, like an eager pup who has found two friends and is loth to abandon them.

Faith smiled encouragingly and he smiled back and Christy felt the bubbling happiness well within her, for she recognized that look and knew the fragile budding emotion which shone in her maid's face, answered by the man's.

'Perhaps we might . . . might meet again sometime,' he said hopefully, 'now that we have been introduced.'

Christy doubted her mother and father would consider it an introduction but he was not speaking to her.

'Perhaps we may,' Faith answered, then turned hurriedly to Christy, hot-faced and embarrassed to be seen in what might be called a dalliance in the presence of her mistress.

'I'm sure we shall, Mr Adams,' Christy said. 'In fact I'm absolutely certain that we shall. Now Faith, if you will direct Mr Adams on the path to Conistone – you know the district better than I – I shall continue on our way to Chapel Stile. I'll wait for you by the fell gate. Goodbye, Mr Adams and good luck. I hope next time we meet you have an animal more suited to your size.'

'Thank you, Miss Emmerson and ... well ... thank you.'

She was smiling as she ran down the track in the direction of the village. Her eyes were like stars and her cheeks blazed to rose for she thought the meeting a good omen though she could not have said why, and not only for Faith's future happiness but for her own.

She began to sing, the day's weary beginnings falling away in a sharp thrill of enchantment!

CHAPTER FIVE

Her poise and loveliness were breathtaking as she moved serenely within the group which consisted of Squire Forsythe and his lady, their handsome only son, her betrothed, her Robin and the youngest of Robin's sisters – a dashing young lady who was not, it was whispered, as circumspect as Fellthwaite liked its young ladies to be. There was a Captain Gibson, a cousin of the Squire's lady, and his second wife – his first was lost it was rumoured in bearing his only son who was also present – and half a dozen young gentlemen and ladies too, all, one supposed, friends of the elderly Squire or perhaps his dashing daughter.

The occasion was the Christmas Ball held in the Market Buildings in Fellthwaite, and the party, headed by the manorial lord soon made it plain that they had consented to be present only because of the impending union of one of their number to the daughter of the man whose manufacturing interests had made him increasingly wealthy and, it was assumed, able to purchase the Squire's son because of it. It was well-known that Dalebarrow Hall was simply falling to pieces about the Squire's well-bred ears and that short of selling it – and who would buy it? – he must find someone willing to restore it and the family, to the glory it and they were born to.

The result was Christina Emmerson!

Annie Emmerson was handsome in black satin with little adornment beside her wedding band and a fine gold chain from which hung a beautifully wrought essence bottle, a present from her grateful husband on the occasion of their eldest son's first birthday. Her hair had been arranged by the clever young Faith Cooper into what she was assured was an 'Apollo Knot', consisting of loops of plaited hair, which, like her daughter, she had in abundance, very neat and tidy with a centre parting and a plain tortoiseshell comb to support it.

She felt herself to be exactly as she should be in her role of the wife of one of the leading manufacturers in Furness, dignified and regal, without stepping from her station in life, but despite this her brave heart quailed as she watched the Squire's party approach up the elegant staircase which rose from the ground floor of the Market Building. She and Job were waiting to receive them, and hopefully to be received, with sons Ben and Toby by their side and standing awkwardly, not quite with them and obviously wishing she weren't, was Celia Metcalf, Ben's intended bride. Shy and gauche, pretty enough and confident in her own environment, but in the presence of the gentry inarticulate and breathless, as she was introduced to Ben's sister's future father-in-law.

But Annie had no time for poor Celia. She was the mother of the bride-to-be and as such was to go in on the arm of the Squire, preceding her Job who clung to the

Squire's lady, leading her into the ballroom as though she was his most treasured possession on earth which at that moment she was for she was the crowning symbol of his success.

It was like a vast flower garden with an enormous arrangement of blooms raided from winter gardens for miles around, with twining ivy around each white column and six chandeliers high in the ceiling revealing every blossom and leaf in their summer glory though it was mid-December.

Next in order of distinction came the newly betrothed couple and the room hushed for them for they were a perfectly matched, beautifully matched pair, surely made in heaven just for each other. There were murmurs behind fans, of approval and wonder for Annie and Job Emmerson had certainly done well for this lass of theirs and if the Squire had searched the length and breadth of the land, and him with more than a few to choose from, could he have done better? Where did she get it, they asked themselves, that air of polished graciousness, that lift to her proud head, the straightness of her elegant back, the delicate beauty, the oval-faced, velvet-eyed beauty which had captured the most eligible young bachelor in the district? And yet she had a certain aura of sauciness about her – in the curl of her lip, pink and full; in the suggestion of the dimple in her smooth cheek, and the faint lift of one eyebrow which seemed to indicate that she found the proceedings vastly amusing and not to be taken at all seriously.

But there was no denying the look of melting love in her eyes when they lit upon Robin Forsythe. The joyous blaze in them softened each time they caught his glance, and his were the same for her. As everyone agreed later, when it was over and could be discussed, though it was to be a marriage of convenience for both their fathers, there was no mistaking it for anything but a love match.

She was dressed in white gauze over a skirt and bodice of embroidered white silk with enormous billowing sleeves and a deep, square neckline, tight and cut low to show off the top of her perfect breast. Her hair, also dressed by Faith Cooper, formed a heavy intricate coil, brushed first to a glossy shine and threaded with white rosebuds on velvet ribbon. These had been sent over specially by the Squire's lady from her own hot-house in the carriage which was to take Christy to Dalebarrow Hall to travel with the Squire's party to the ball.

And yet the boy was as beautiful in his masculine way as his bride to be. Almost twenty he was and brought up to do nothing but look after his land and his tenants. Good natured and good looking with nothing to ever upset what he had been taught was his God-given right to expect. Perfect in health and breeding, and in manners too, he was the man Christy Emmerson loved and he appeared to bask in it, to bloom in it even, to become more manly, his slender dove grey shoulders lifting proudly, his white brocaded chest puffed out with pride in the girl on his arm, and his deep love-filled eyes never for a moment leaving her laughing face.

Of course good manners demanded that they dance with others but the first dance was together. Though it was a Christmas Ball and their intention to marry had been publicly announced several weeks ago, somehow it was as if this was their betrothal party and it was treated as though they were the guests of honour.

They sat awkwardly together, the two classes, manufacturing and the gentry, and when Christy and Robin rose to their feet for the first dance, the Squire took Annie Emmerson and the Squire's lady had no choice but to go with Job. For a moment there were just the three couples circling the floor, the rest hanging back hesitantly, reluctant to interfere with what seemed a private family moment, then another couple floated forward. As Robin and Christy turned their gaze momentarily from each other they both looked into the sardonically smiling blue eyes of Alexander Buchanan.

Christy felt the flush start somewhere behind her knees,

rising upwards through the folds of her beautiful ball gown until it reached her breasts. She was sure they had turned a bright, glowing pink and her neck and cheeks and ears, and even, she was certain, the scalp beneath her intricate hair-do. She was positive Robin's hand had become suddenly slippery with sweat, for even through her white gloves the palm of her own was immediately damp where it held his.

Alex bowed in their direction and those of the assembly who saw it thought nothing of it, though Christy Emmerson did not appear to have returned it. Poor man, so young a widower and still in mourning for his wife, dead these three months. The lady with whom he danced was Miss Amelia Whittam, sister of the Miss Susan Whittam who had the smart little dress shop in Howegate and who had designed and made Christina Emmerson's exquisite gown. Miss Amelia was twenty-five years old, everyone knew that for had she not been born and brought up in Fellthwaite, the daughter of Mr Whittam the banker, and no doubt hoping to change her status from 'daughter-at-home' to the privilege of wife. And Alex Buchanan had singled her out for the first dance and what could that mean, Fellthwaite speculated?

The polished floor was filling up now, couples whirling around like dainty, dipping children's tops, the full skirts of the ladies, the huge sleeves and heavily decorated hems on their gowns giving them the momentum to glide in their partners' arms with not the slightest effort to the lilting tune played enthusiastically by the orchestra brought specially from Carlisle.

Ben waltzed by holding in his powerful arms a breathless and exceedingly fretful Celia who appeared to be giving him a side of her tongue which she would have done well to have kept hidden until after they were wed. He scowled down at her, answering sharply, evidently telling her to keep it still. But for the presence of the gentry, who watched with all the interest of spectators at a zoo viewing a form of animal life they had never before seen, she would have burst into tears and demanded to be taken home to her father who was confined to his bed with a cold.

Toby, with the dashing daughter of Squire Forsythe dimpling in his grasp, was whispering in her ear and making her giggle and the assembly watched and whispered too, for if she was 'fast' and he was 'wild', heaven alone knew where the evening might end.

Christy tore her offended gaze from that of Alex Buchanan, lifting her head in that unique way she had. She was not in the least concerned with his arrogant smile, she told herself — despite that dreadful moment in the clearing at Birchwood when he had first laid it about herself and Robin — and she took Robin's hand more firmly in hers. She and Robin had nothing of which to be ashamed! They were an engaged couple now and would be married as soon as Ben and Celia had had their turn. What Alex Buchanan had witnessed had been the exchange of a promise, almost like those of marriage vows, a physical manifestation of their love. It had not been intended to proceed quite as far as it had and there was no doubt that if Mr Buchanan had not come spying it would have gone a great deal further! But nevertheless that moment had been an intensely private and enchanting experience for herself and Robin, an affirmation of their deeply committed love, and she had strongly resented Alex Buchanan's interference and inference that it had been no more than a frivolous bit of fun. But now, here, before the whole of Fellthwaite was the public acknowledgement that they were betrothed, as she had told Alexander Buchanan they were, and he could put that in his 'scouse-tub' and pickle it, her proud bearing seemed to say.

She smiled up into Robin's face and was tempted to place a soft kiss on his lips. What a shock that would be for the watching company. She saw the answering mischief flicker in his eyes and knew he was thinking the same thought and she threw back her head and laughed with joy for where in the world would she ever have found a man whose mind was in such close communion with her own? They shared so much, even what went on inside their own heads, and their lips had no need of words at times for their eyes spoke for them. What did it matter if they scandalized society now? Robin could not compromise her reputation for within three months she was to be his wife.

She had forgotten Alex Buchanan and was conscious only of the lovely lilt of the music, the enchantment of this special moment, the scent of the rosebuds in her hair, the brilliance of the six chandeliers which reflected in the jewellery on so many soft bosoms; of being young and in love and in the arms of Robin Forsythe, the man she was to marry. She saw his mouth move in that achingly familiar way he had when he was about to kiss her. She saw his dark eyes become darker and her heart leaped in delight for she knew absolutely, devastatingly, that he was . . . he was . . . right here before the mesmerized gaze of the whole of Fellthwaite society, high and low . . . he was about to kiss her!

He was bending his laughing head, she was lifting her laughing mouth when the music came to an elegant stop and as it did so the hand of the man who had stopped beside them, one arm still courteously held out to his partner, gripped Christy's elbow. She turned, surprised, her mouth still pouting for Robin's kiss, and looked once more into the mocking, vividly blue eyes of Alexander Buchanan!

'Miss Emmerson,' he said, bowing his dark head politely, 'and Mr Forsythe.'

Miss Amelia Whittam, flushed and almost pretty, was quite bewildered by the expression which came over the face of the beautiful, newly betrothed daughter of Job Emmerson. If she had not known better, or thought she did, she might have believed that Miss Emmerson cordially detested the recently bereaved gentleman with whom she herself had just danced.

Christy Emmerson straightened imperiously and her eyes flashed some warning to the man who addressed her and her fiancé, but with the instinctive reflex of the good manners taught her at the academy, she bobbed her curtsey and returned the formal 'Mr Buchanan', then waited for Robin Forsythe to go through the same charade which society and training demanded.

Alex Buchanan drew Amelia Whittam forward with all the tenderness of a lover though his eyes never once left Christy's. Amelia simpered and confessed she was acquainted with Miss Emmerson but 'No,' she had not had the pleasure of meeting Mr Forsythe. 'What a pleasant . . .'

'I have not yet had the opportunity to congratulate you, Mr Forsythe.' Alex cut through Amelia's pleasantries in a manner which she later confessed tearfully to her sister was decidedly rude but now she stood waiting, as she had been taught, for the gentleman who had taken her on the floor to walk her back across to the group with which she and her sister had come. She could not go alone; it was not proper, but the strange atmosphere which threaded these three handsome people together made her uneasy and she was eager to be got away. It was as tangible as the polished wood beneath her feet and as mysterious as the strange gleam in her partner's eye.

'Thank you, sir,' Robin answered. His hand reached for Christy's and Alex saw it and his mouth tightened ominously.

'And Miss Emmerson. May I wish you every happiness, both of you, in your future life together.'

'Thank you, Mr Buchanan.' Her voice strained itself between her stiff lips.

'You are both recovered?'

'Recovered?' Robin's fingers gripped Christy's until they turned white but she did not wince. This man was saying something to her, to them both, with his brilliant eyes, in the curl of his well-cut lips, in the lounging insolence of his long body which nevertheless was held in that pose with a discipline which revealed itself in the tense muscles at his jaw. The expression on his face was civil enough and those watching would see nothing amiss in what appeared to be two couples chatting amicably between dances. Mr Buchanan, poor man, would be addressing his congratulations and good wishes to the engaged couple, thinking no doubt as he did so of his own dead wife and dashed hopes of a dozen sturdy sons, and he would not get them from Amelia Whittam, that was certain! He needed to find himself some vigorous young daleswoman – there were plenty about, here in this very ballroom – not like the strung out little woman he had taken the first time.

'Recovered from what, Mr Buchanan?' Robin asked defensively.

'Why, from your dilemma the last time we met.'

'And what dilemma was that, sir?'

Christy put her free hand on Robin's arm. It was protective, cautioning and Miss Whittam began to forget her anxiety for it seemed there might be something not only strange, but of a definitely outrageous nature to be divulged here. Though she was not aware of it, Amelia had the reputation of being the biggest gossip in the district of Furness, most of which she picked up in her sister's shop and then spread indiscriminately throughout the town. She pricked her ears eagerly.

'Surely you remember the occasion of our last meeting, Mr Forsythe?' Alex Buchanan's eyes narrowed and his voice was silky.

Beneath Robin Forsythe's skin ran the red blood of intense embarrassment for he was young and had not yet learned the control which comes with age and experience, but his eyes were cool and commanding, as generations of the squirearchy had taught him to be and the knowledge that this man was merely of the new manufacturing classes, a tradesman, stiffened his upper class resolve.

'I do indeed sir, but I would have thought . . .'

'Robin!' Christy pressed his arm, straining it against her breast, her face tense and beginning to be alarmed. 'Mr Buchanan is . . .'

'I am well aware of what Mr Buchanan is, my darling.'

The tone of his voice was deliberately insolent, as deliberate as the endearment he used.

'Come, Mr Forsythe,' Alex's voice was quizzically amused. 'What do you mean, I wonder?' and Miss Whittam edged closer for when it was revealed what Mr Forsythe meant she did not wish to miss it.

'I think that you forget we are gentlemen in the presence of ladies, sir, and to mention . . .'

Robin stopped in confusion for he knew he had stepped into the clever trap Alex Buchanan had set him and like Christy before him his bewildered young mind agonized over why? Why?

'To mention what, Mr Forsythe?' Alex's eyes gleamed wickedly. 'Surely it is not ungentlemanly to speak of the day Miss Emmerson's mare bolted, nor of your gallant . . . er . . . rescue of her. I was most touched to see how . . . grateful she was!'

Miss Whittam's excited face dulled and irritation returned. It seemed they were discussing nothing more shocking than a bolting mare and what scandal could be found in that? She began to glance about her for they were becoming conspicuous standing in the centre of the ballroom floor as they were. The leader of the orchestra was looking fretfully in their direction, eager it seemed to start the next dance and she had promised it to the new curate of the parish church in Fellthwaite and might he not perhaps be a more realistic prospect than Mr Buchanan?

She tapped her foot and looked meaningly at her partner.

Robin Forsythe's crestfallen face took on a youthful dignity. He had in some way, how he did not know, nor why, earned the strange enmity of one of Fellthwaite's wealthiest men and he had just been belittled by him because of it. And yet, had he? What had the man said that years ago, when such things were fashionable and legal, another could take offence at and because of it, have the satisfaction of calling him out? Nothing! He had referred to the event, almost forgotten now, which had been followed by his own determination to overcome his father's aversion to his marriage to a mill-owner's daughter.

Robin loved Christy Emmerson with a young man's intense passion and reverence. She was his first true love. Her beauty and responsive spirit filled him with an emotion he could describe to no one, much less his father who would have told him to quench it in the only sensible way possible for a gentleman of his class. But that would not do for Christy. She was his heart's joy and he would marry her – or no one! He was prepared now to defend her good name with his fists if required though Alexander Buchanan's reputation in bare-knuckle prize-fighting was well-known. It was not the sport of gentlemen, of course, but he would have resorted to it if the man had spoken another word which might have been construed as offensive. Buchanan had not done so but still Robin Forsythe felt that he and Christy Emmerson, his betrothed, had somehow been insulted.

He was young and inexperienced in the world of men but he was ready to bristle up to the older, heavier man should it be required, but Christy's hand was insistent on his arm.

'Come away, my love,' she said clearly as though they were accosted by some riff-raff who was not worth the mentioning and her contemptuous eyes struck like a cobra in Alex Buchanan's. 'I am thirsty and would be glad of a glass of champagne. Come, hold my arm, sweetheart.'

Her smile was brilliant and Robin backed down reluctantly and allowed her to lead him away towards the room where supper was laid out. There was a long table spread with the finest food Fellthwaite could produce. A boar's head garnished with aspic jelly, boiled fowl and bechamel sauce, galantine of veal, chicken pie, prawns and larded capon. Charlotte russe with fruited jelly, custards, Swiss cream, meringues, iced Savoy cake all artfully displayed with bowls of fruit and an epergne filled with hot-house flowers at each end. Small tables and chairs were grouped about the room, and sofas piled with cushions where one might sit and relax from the strain of dancing and enjoy the food brought by one's supper partner.

The room was well-lighted with a hundred candelabra and therefore not suitable for what Christy Emmerson had in mind. She had attended several concerts and dances in the past year and knew the building well; being a pretty girl and of mettlesome and inquisitive nature in the matter of young gentlemen's kisses she knew the secluded corners where an innocent but delightful intrigue might take place.

Holding Robin's hand she went directly across the room and through a curtained recess on to a landing which led away into the darkness. It was enough.

Turning, closing the door in the recess she placed herself before the tall frame of Robin Forsythe and leaning, sighing, languorous and slender as a cat, she wrapped him in her arms and brought his mouth down to hers and in the only way she knew how made him forget Alex Buchanan ever existed.

'Quickly, oh quickly my darling, kiss me for I can't wait another minute.'

'What is wrong with the man?' he would have asked, his face completely mystified, but she would not allow it but opened her lips about his, soft and moist and her tongue touched his and he no longer cared.

'Christy . . . oh dear God, Christy, I love you,' he moaned.

'I know . . . I know . . . oh lord, Robin . . . we can stay but a minute for mother will be looking for me.'

'A minute, my sweet . . . I see you alone so seldom.' His mouth slid easily down her long slender throat until it moved against the soft flesh of her breast and she held his head to her with a passionate, protective love. He would not be hurt, nor insulted by Alex Buchanan, or indeed any man for she would not allow it. She loved him so. She loved him so much it hurt her but they must go back for despite her earlier confident assumption that they could do as they pleased now that she and Robin were engaged, it was not true. Squire Forsythe required the perfect wife for his son, not one whose name was whispered about behind fans.

'Darling . . . sweetheart we must go . . . we must . . .'

'Yes . . . one last kiss . . .'

Later, much later, when the supper table had been cleared and Annie Emmerson was becoming increasingly alarmed and aggravated by her daughter's absence she saw them drift by the group of ladies with whom she chatted, waltzing one supposed, though their closeness would have been better suited to the bedroom. Though Christy was as immaculately turned out as she had been on her glide by the receiving line earlier in the evening, with every strand of her hair and every rosebud in place, there was a certain rumpled look about her, one which her mother did not care for! Robin looked at her with the eyes of a man conquered and glorying in it and as she said grimly to Job later in the privacy of their marriage bed, the sooner that girl had a ring on her finger, the better!

CHAPTER SIX

Christmas came and went and Annie Emmerson thanked God for it since she was of the opinion that no matter how often, nor on what occasion her family and that of Robin Forsythe assembled together they would remain as foreign to one another as if the Forsythes, or the Emmersons, had come from Africa!

They had eaten Christmas dinner at Dalebarrow Hall at the fashionable London time of six o'clock in the evening instead of their own usual late afternoon, in the company of the Squire's house party, numerous splendid high-nosed cousins and persons of quality who were acquainted with the Squire and his wife. Annie, Job, Ben, Toby and Christina had driven over in Job's smart carriage though Ben had argued hotly against it declaring he was damned if he would put up with being condescended to by them as were no better, in fact not as good as the Emmersons who were hard-working, reliable folk, plain, and what was wrong with that, pray? Ben found it hard to accept a man who had never done a hand's turn in his life and besides, if his Celia was not invited then they could do without him as well.

'Oh please, Ben, don't spoil it,' Christy begged him, holding his big, working-man's hand and gazing up into his already well-fleshed young face with the beguiling appeal of a child. 'It's only this once. Next year Robin and I will be married and living at the Hall and everything will have settled down. You and Celia will doubtless have your first . . .'

'Now then, miss, don't you start!' Ben was affronted and turned away but Christy was not to be put off. This was to be her last Christmas as a young 'daughter-at-home'. She had ahead of her a life of rapturous joy, a life to be spent in the adoring arms of her Robin, a married woman with responsibilities to be taken on as she became the Squire's lady in her turn. There would be children. She would no longer be a child, a young girl as she was now and for this last time she wanted to play and dance and giggle as only the young and unmarried are allowed. She and Robin and the cousins were to go carol singing on Christmas Eve and Toby, her merry and amusing younger brother, had amiably agreed to join the festivities since he had been told there would be several pretty and susceptible young ladies in the party.

On Christmas Day, after attending church to hear the Parson's Christmas sermon, when Christmas prayers and hymns and duty was done, there would be presents to be opened, songs to sing, prizes to be won in the games they would play. 'Snapdragon' was her particular favourite. A shallow bowl was filled with spirits and currants. The bowl was placed on the floor and a match put to it. The player must then snatch the currants from the flames and attempt to put them in his or her mouth. It was a game in which a good eye, courage and a quick hand were needed. If one was not lively scorched lips, fingers and tongue were a certainty for the mouth must close over the burning currant to extinguish the flame. To Christy it symbolized the way in which one should grasp life if joy was to be got from it. You must be prepared to take the risk of getting burnt a little if you wanted its good things but if you were willing to chance the danger the reward was the greater and she loved the thrill of it. And the beauty of the dancing azure flames tipped with amber pleased some deep part of her which was stirred by their beauty.

Robin had told her they would play blindman's buff and charades, and sing The Mistletoe Bough and exchange Christmas cards, a new fashion come in only last year. Hers for Robin was made of satin with lace in the shape of a heart with embroidery in its centre declaring the abundance of her esteem.

The great hall would be decorated for the occasion with evergreens, chrysanthemums from Mrs Forsythe's hot-house, holly and many bunches of mistletoe for it was considered quite proper for a gentleman to snatch a kiss from a lady, more than one if they both so desired and could manage it, beneath the tolerant gaze of the young ladies' Mama.

There would be a Christmas tree, a Tree of Love, a young fir cut from the Squire's estate and laden with pretty trifles — crochet purses, bonbons, preserved fruit, alum baskets, charms — and illuminated with small wax tapers. All quite excitingly daring to the young girl brought up in the stricter confines of Methodism, Chapel and a no-nonsense God who frowned upon such frivolities and she wanted to have her family about her, all of them, to share this last enduring moment of change.

'Please say you'll come, Ben,' she implored. 'Celia won't mind. You know she doesn't care for . . . well . . . she's not . . .' How to put tactfully Celia Metcalf's complete inability, despite five years at the academy for young ladies in Fellthwaite, to string together two articulate words in the presence of those she considered her 'betters', and who so totally overawed her she spent most of their visit crying nervously in the larder. A good girl, Celia was capable and well able to cope with any ordinary, familiar eventuality which might occur in her role as Ben Emmerson's wife, but she might have been in the company of the young Queen Victoria herself when Mrs Forsythe pleasantly enquired – with no idea who Celia actually was – of her health, and was able only to bob a curtsey and blush to the roots of her plain brown hair.

'There will be people there, Ben, people of importance who can probably be of use to you in the business. They have connections, people like that, who may well be able to introduce you to others. You know how these things go!'

This was indeed a consideration and one to which young Ben Emmerson, always eager to 'get on', took heed and if she had left it at that her brother would doubtless have gone amiably enough for did not mill matters come before all else? But Christy had not yet learned the art of diplomacy or how to leave well alone when you had already gained what it was you wanted.

'. . . and you can go straight from the Hall to Haverthwaite and be there for tea and then Celia can come over here for . . .'

Ben's handsome face darkened. 'Oh I can, can I? And who d'you think you are, arranging everybody's day for them?' he ejaculated, his reluctant agreement shattered, his eyebrows swooping into a thunderous scowl. 'And their lives as well, I'll be bound if you had your way. You're not the Squire's lady yet, my girl, and I'm not one of your bloody tenants pulling my cap and bending a knee.'

'Nobody's asking you to bend your damn knee though that Celia of yours does enough of it whenever the Forsythes so much as blink an eye.'

'Now then, lass,' Job interjected mildly enough for he was inclined to agree with her. Celia was certainly out of her depth in the society which his own girl had found so easy to conquer. He watched his children bristle up to one another, a dainty Lakeland terrier taking on the might of a bulldog and his pride in them both was immense. Obedient to him they were, often reluctantly so, but his stern discipline had broken neither their spirit nor their opinionated belief that they were always right. Though it made no difference and they must still obey him, he liked to see it in them. He sat back in his chair waiting enjoyably to see how far they would go, ready to intervene, should it be necessary.

'And can't you ask her to try and speak English,' Christy was leaning forward, her face an inch from that of her brother, 'instead of that thick dialect she assumes each time Mrs Forsythe gives her the time of day, and surely she knows there is no need for her to stand up every time the Squire does. I was mortified at the Christmas Ball by the way she acted. They're only people when all's said and done but she acts as though she was with royalty. My God, she's like a damn puppet . . .'

'At least she's got a bit of sense in her! Hellsfire, did you hear that one they call Carolyn, not Caroline, if you please . . .' He put on a shrill falsetto voice and Toby, who cared nought if he went or not, it was all the same to him, began to laugh at Robin Forsythe's sisters; the two eldest, though both married, had none of his charm or beauty and thought themselves to be so far above the manufacturing class into which their brother was marrying they could barely bring themselves to speak to their intended in-laws. Carolyn, Margaret and Elizabeth, and in between them and Robin were numerous little Forsythes lying in the graveyard, for the diseases which carry off infants had no respect for class.

In the end it was Job who had his way as he always did. It suited his purpose to present a united family front to his daughter's future relatives and their friends and so Ben had no choice but to accompany them. Celia, uninvited for the simple reason the Forsythes were unaware, in their high-born state of ignorance of those beneath them, that

Ben was also betrothed, was left behind to have her Christmas dinner without her husband-to-be and her eyes told Christy she had made an enemy and would never be forgiven.

They dined in splendour in the old hall which had seen three hundred years of Forsythes come and go. The Squire's family had owned land in these parts when the Denbys and the Emmersons had been no more than landless peasants, living as gentlemen should off the rents they received from it. The Squire could trace his forebears back to the days before the Civil War but as Annie sat, regal as a duchess with the quiet dignity of her daleswoman's heritage, as gracious in her way as Mrs Forsythe, Job knew he had chosen well all those years ago and he was as proud of her as he was his daughter.

He thought about his grandfather who had been nought but a collier and God alone knew where he came from, and his heart almost burst with the joy of his success. It was going to be difficult adjusting to the realization that he was related to these fine folk when their families were at last united and he debated whether he and Annie would ever become used to it but by God he'd give it a damn good try for none deserved it more than himself.

As the head of his household with the natural right to be obeyed by his wife and children he had brought them to this triumph, despite his eldest son's inclination to dispute almost everything he himself said these days. Though Ben, Toby and the girl had been brought up to honour and obey him and to take pride in the family name, Ben was too like himself to tamely fall into line with what another man decreed, even his own father. But Job found this to be not a bad thing. When he was gone it would need a strong man to take the reins in his hand and continue the proud task of elevating the Emmerson family to its rightful position in the dales, to go even further than he himself had gone. They were part of a community, could consider themselves a middle-class family, soon to be joined to what was an upper-class family, that of a landed gentleman, and it was through a marriage which, as was only right, had been looked upon with an eye to not only financial but social advancement. He had kept a close watch on his young, unmarried daughter, taking elaborate and costly steps to see that she mixed with only those who were socially acceptable and though he had certainly hoped for the son of a banker, perhaps a lawyer, never in his wildest dreams had he considered the son of the Squire. What a reward this was for his assiduous devotion to hard work, his duty to his wife and growing family, his obligation to those in lesser circumstances than himself, to his moral principles and to his own bloody good head for business. His girl, his lass, his Christy was to be the first lady in this community, bringing honour to the man who was the grandson of a collier. He had made it happen, he Job Emmerson and he was to reap his reward!

Pity about Buchanan. It would have been grand to ally his wealth with that of the copper-mining widower but then had he done so he'd bet a cock-penny to a pound he and his family would not have been sitting round the Squire's table nor included in this 'merry-neet'. Christy and the Squire's lad would be married in March, a month after Ben and Celia, it was all agreed and though Celia, who would have her place one day at Hollin House as the wife of his eldest son, was not to be compared with Christina, who was lively — audaciously so at times and often defiant — she was a good lass and would do credit to the Emmersons. He was merely exchanging one daughter for another. Christy would come to live here at Dalebarrow to be trained in the running of the Hall and in the duties expected of the Squire's lady and he, Job Emmerson, would have the advantage of being connected with two prominent families though each was vastly different from the other.

The Metcalfs were mill-owners like himself, being in a fair way of business over Haverthwaite way and there was plenty of money with which to get Celia settled. Ira Metcalf had no sons to carry on his business of manufacturing gunpowder and therefore his three daughters would inherit what he had. Even split three ways it all looked very promising. The absence of a son was the reason Ira had placed his eldest lass in Ben's, and through him, in Job's capable hands since it was only sensible to arrange his daughter's considerable inheritance in the best way he knew how and what better safeguard than to ensure it was in the care of a businessman like himself. Job was well pleased!

And the Forsythes, well, besides being the gentry did they not have connections with persons of quality and breeding up and down the length of the land and though in a business sense they could do him little good for they were not in business, it would suit Job's purpose in certain circumstances to drop, casually, into the pool of conversation, his own firm family involvement with a man who had a seat on the bench, with aristocratic connections, a man to whom other men doffed their caps, a man who was the biggest landowner between here and Whitehaven, even if that man had not one halfpenny to rub against the other.

Pity about Buchanan though!

The next day, Boxing Day, the day on which those with any pretence to wealth gave out Christmas boxes to those who had none, was to be a rare occasion. The Squire and his party, or those amongst them who could be persuaded to it were to attend the Low Garth Farmer's Hunt. A great honour, everyone was agreed, for Lakeland foxhunting was not the sport of the landed gentleman, as it was in the Midlands. Formed by the local farmers with the intention of doing away with the predators which would seize their newly dropped lambs in April and May, the hounds had been purchased and were maintained by wealthy landowners and the subscription of those farmers who could afford it.

There were no well-groomed hunters here; no pink coats bar that worn by the huntsman who led the pack, for even the 'whipper-in' must wear Hodden grey like the most famous huntsman of them all, the great John Peel. Only sturdy boots and a stick were needed for fell packs were followed on foot. Occasionally a fell pony or cob could be seen moving amongst those who strode out but it was rare. The fox and hounds often covered sixty miles in a day for the fell fox was strong and cunning and would hide on the window sill of an isolated cottage, in the roof, or a stream and had even been known to run along a dry-stone wall to throw his pursuers off the scent.

The hounds found the scent just before day broke as the fox returned to the fells after feeding at a lower level during the night. It was a glorious winter morning with the sun rising through a pink mist, delicately tinting the sky, the tops of the fells which were shrouded in snow and the heavy hoar frost which lay thickly upon the ground. The trees were stark and black against the ethereal fantasy of the slowly awakening day. The sun turned to gold as it rose above High Street in the east, lighting the tip of Scafell Pike, the summit of England, as it caught the peak in the distance, and turning the waters of Eltermere to a silent sheet of exquisite gold.

There was suddenly a sense of waiting, a deep stillness like that which must have come about on the first day of life and even the sophisticated and slightly bored group who had come to see the working man at his sport felt a quickening of the pulse as the thrilling notes of the hunting horn rang out to signify that the hounds had found the drag.

Those who felt inclined to it began to follow, their stout boots clinging to the slippery slopes of the shallow gullies, their feet crunching on the crisp, sugar fine frosted grass, their breath wreathing about their heads, their cheeks scarlet with the cold and the exhilarating exercise. The ones who had come to see them away – most on horseback used to the conventional hunt carried on further south and unwilling to chance themselves in this strange custom – watched, cheering on those of their companions who thought it might be amusing to do as their inferiors did.

When the hunt had gone, disappearing into the shredding mist, those who stayed behind turned and walked their mounts away through the brightening dawn towards Dalebarrow, laughing, lounging indolently in the saddle, agreeing it had been vastly entertaining and taking the enormous appetite the morning had given them to the awaiting splendour of their host's breakfast table.

But the terrain on the hillside was difficult, hostile to those unused to it and one by one those of the gentlemen who had started out began to drop away, turning back laughingly, slipping and sliding in the frozen grass, their laughter ringing from fell to fell until the raven, the wild cat and marten and even the fox himself, hesitating on the pitch of the dry-stone wall he ran along, turned his head to listen.

The men of the dales and fells, Ben and Toby and half a dozen of their peers watched them go contemptuously, smiling a little at the sorry state of a man who could not walk a mile or two without a horse beneath him. They strode out just for the hell of it and to boast of it later to any pretty, attentive young lady who would listen. But there were working men: mill lad, miner, factory hand, eager to gain an extra shilling or two on this day when the mill, the mine, the factory were shut and who would earn no wage because of it, for the head of vermin, be it fox or marten, fetched two shillings.

He was a wily creature the fox, taking to the scree to throw off the hounds, hiding in the loose boulders formed there, but one of the lads had a fox-screw, a devilish device on the end of a pole which could be inserted into his hiding place and screwed into his body or into his mouth if he snapped at it. When he was withdrawn from his 'bield' or hiding place, the leading hound would kill him instantly with a snap of his strong jaws for Lakeland hounds do not break up their victims but leave them once they are dead to be hung, as a well-respected, worthy foe on some farmhouse door.

Christy clung to Robin's hand, her skirts hobbling her

as effectively as if she wore leg irons. Given a pair of knee breeches and thick stockings such as the men wore she knew she could keep up and walk the full distance but she was aware that she was holding Robin back. His patience, never strong, was wearing thin as he hauled her over the raise, a heap of stones around which there seemed to be no path. Her skirt tripped her and she fell for the umpteenth time, almost bringing him down with her.

'My darling, it will not do. Can you not see your skirts are just not meant for climbing,' he said at last, his eyes shooting ahead to where the back of his Leicestershire cousins disappeared over the cam of the hill. His deep brown eyes brimming with the eagerness of youth and the need of a man to show his contemporaries, in this case his cousins who thought the whole thing was a huge joke, that he — born and bred amongst the high peaks and fells of this savage country — was as capable of following the hounds even without a mount. He wanted to be up there with the leaders, a leader himself as a Forsythe should be, but his in-bred gallantry demanded he give his arm to his lady.

'Will you not go back, sweetheart? See, if you hurry you will catch Anthony and Daniel. They will be glad to escort you back to Chapel Stile and your carriage.'

His eyes pleaded with her to let him go, to let him join the men, to be a man and not a spiritless runagate who must always go at the speed of his womenfolk. He pointed to where two young men, the sons of one of Squire Forsythe's old friends, were strolling back towards Chapel Stile, down in the valley bottom. The shallow, undulating ridges of frozen ground rolled away down the incline, shadowed on their western side for the sun was still low, and the two young men, the tops of their heads only just visible, moved down until they vanished.

Robin knelt beside her where she sat in a sulk, her soft mouth pouting like that of a child forbidden a jaunt. Her skirts had hitched up to reveal her short, sturdy boots and a slender length of thick, hand knit stockinged leg but

Robin refused to be charmed as she had hoped and suddenly, as her father had seen her do when she knew it was useless to argue, she grinned, admitting defeat. Reaching up behind his head she pulled his face down to hers and just for good measure kissed him lingeringly on the lips.

He began to laugh then and his eyes were bright with his love for her but here merely held out his hands to her and hauled her to her feet, then turning her away from him, pushed her gently in the direction in which the young men had gone.

'Get on with you, Christy Emmerson. You're a witch but you'll not work your spells on me. Run and catch Anthony and Dan and I promise you I'll bring you the brush!'

He was springing away from her, his lithe and healthy body carrying him rapidly up the steepening pitch of the ascent.

'They don't collect the brush up here, you heathen,' she yelled after him. 'Call yourself a dalesman and you don't know that!'

His answer was a careless lift of his hand as he leaped from view over the brow of the hill.

The sun lifted slowly in the sky which began to turn from the pale perse blue of brightening dawn into the achingly beautiful brilliance which heralds a clear midwinter day in the mountains. There were not many such in this land of cloud and rain and storm and soon, before the new year was a few days old, there would be blizzards for January was the month for snow in the land of the lakes. First came the stinging frost with light falls dusting the peaks for Christmas. Blades of grass and bracken would be laced with a hoar fringe. The sun would shine as it did today painting the high peaks to a delicate rose but a sudden dash of low clouds racing across the sky would empty the first flurry of snowflakes and presage the intensity of a briskly falling blanket as violent eddies swept the fell slopes and the full force of the blizzard would strike.

But that was yet to come! Those who were well used to it and the art of reading the weather had ventured themselves out on the treacherous slopes and there was nothing to fear today. The farmers knew well enough the signs and though 'too bright too early' was one of the many maxims by which they lived and might be embraced today, the weather would stay as it was until New Year's Eve. She knew for Edwin, her father's old gardener, had said so and he was seldom wrong. Born sixty years ago not a mile from Hollin House and having been no further than Fellthwaite and seeing no need for it, he had a hundred old sayings on which to draw. 'If Candlemass day be fine and clear, we'll get two winters in one year' was one. 'If the sun shine not on Christmas Day, the apple crop will surely fail' was another and his opinion of 'bottom winds', the sudden gusty winds which swept the valley and plagued his old bones, was rudely expressed and well known in the district.

Christy stood up and shook out her skirt in readiness for the long trudge back to Chapel Stile where the carriage waited. She hummed a little tuneless song under her breath as she stepped out. Her heart was at peace, her pale eyes serene as she watched a curl of silver smoke from a cottager's chimney stand pencil-straight in the clear, windless sky.

It was easier going down though she had to restrain the inclination to gather momentum and run. She dug her heels in, holding up her skirts with both hands and as she went her cottage bonnet -- a smaller and simpler style than the fashionable wide-brimmed shape worn in town -- fell from her head to bang against her shoulder blades, held in place by the ribbons tied beneath her chin. She did not follow the two rather supercilious young men who were guests at the Hall, though she knew Robin would be cross when he heard she had found her way back alone, but took another track which would bring her to Chapel Stile by a different route.

She had reached the lower, more gentle level which

approached the village from the north. 'In-bye' land used at lambing time or when heavy snow threatened, but deserted now, empty of any movement apart from a flock of ravens which had settled on the trees at the far side of the swift flowing beck. Two robins rose suddenly from the branches of a skeleton alder which hung over the water, their red breasts vivid against the black and white beauty of the narrow valley, winging away at her approach.

Her boots were sharp against the frost, crackling the bracken and stiff grasses, snapping the air like dry twigs broken across a man's knee. She reached the water and paused, her heart stirring almost painfully for it was all so perfect, this place in which she lingered, the blue sky which hurt the eyes, the glittering diamond symmetry of the frost-garlanded trees and grass and the sweet wonder of her life which was filled with her love for Robin.

She did not see him at first. Her eyes and brain recognized his presence but her emotions, bemused with happiness, were slow to follow and in that moment he might have been a figment of her imagination for he did not seem real. He had stepped, silently, from a tiny stand of trees which hugged close to the beck, their trunks thick and shielding and as her eyes sharpened with the return of her senses she could make out the shape of his roan, tethered to one of them.

'Mr Buchanan, you . . . you startled me.' Her voice was high, not with fear but with sudden anger for it seemed but a moment since last he had spied upon her and now he was at it again. The last time he had stepped out from the shelter of the spinney to come upon herself and Robin she had been enraged but now she held herself in check for there was an air of something about him to which she could put no name though strangely, sadness came to mind. And yet he could not be sad for he was directing a glance of wry humour at her, his eyes narrowing in the vivid sunshine.

'Miss Emmerson! We seem destined to meet in the most unusual places, do we not, but I'm sorry if I surprised you.

100

I thought you had seen me. I was . . . I had dismounted intending to walk a little. This beautiful day . . .' He looked about him and his face was curiously soft. '. . . it was meant to be savoured slowly. Then I was captured by the . . .' He sighed deeply and looked back at her and she was amazed by the expression in his eyes. It had a yearning quality, nostalgic almost, as if he was crushed by some scarcely supportable distress and had come to this peaceful valley to gain relief from it; from the tranquil and everlasting endurance which, by its very durability gave hope for the future; from the empty stillness which had been here since eternity and would remain forever. Why, he loves this place just as I do, she thought. He is as mesmerized by this moment, this silence and glory as I am. He has allowed the force which makes small our human feelings of petty anger, to slip into his heart and without knowing it he has lost that sharp, sardonic arrogance he usually sports and has now become open, vulnerable and approachable.

She looked away hastily, astonished by her own bewildering thoughts. The dog was with him and it came to sniff at her skirts. Bending thankfully she put a hand to his head and he waved his tail affably for even he seemed to feel the peaceful companionship of the moment and though his eyes turned constantly to the still figure of his master, he stayed by her side.

But the peace was an illusion, and short-lived. His voice was mocking as he spoke again.

'And what are you up to today, Miss Emmerson?' he said, one dark brow arched, his eyes gleaming with derisive humour.

Instantly she was on the defensive.

'I'm not *up* to anything, as you put it, Mr Buchanan. I was merely walking down to Chapel Stile to pick up . . .'

'Walking? Alone? Up here on the fells. Where is the gallant Mr Forsythe? Is he not here to protect you?'

'Against what, Mr Buchanan. I'm perfectly able to walk a few miles without a man to give me his arm, you know. I'm strong and capable and there is nothing to harm me here. I can withstand anything the fells or the people who live on them care to fling in my direction,' you amongst them, her expression seemed to say!

She threw back her head and her hair rippled and lifted in the wind. Her challenge was unmistakable.

'I'm sure you can, Miss Emmerson. Indeed I am sure you can,' Alex Buchanan said and a smile moved across his lean brown face, 'in fact if I may be so bold you seem not only to go looking for danger but to actually thrive on it. Roaming about the hills alone, or if not alone in company which . . .'

'Mr Buchanan, I would be obliged if you would mind your own business and let me mind mine. You seem unable to speak without maligning someone! Is it a habit you feel obliged to encourage?'

Alex Buchanan threw back his head and laughed, then changed the subject, startling her yet again.

'You have been with the hunt, Miss Emmerson?'

'Why yes . . . I . . . my skirts . . . I had to turn back.' She was still angry and yet at the same time tongue-tied and she wondered why for she was always in such command of herself, confident and easy with everyone from old Edwin the gardener to the Squire himself. It must be something to do with this man's determination to insult Robin at every turn, and why should that be, she thought, but his eyes had fallen to the serviceable skirt of Hodden grey she wore and he was smiling again, and again she was confused.

'I have often thought it unfair that men should be so free in their dress and yet a lady is hampered by her clothing. Do you think we gentlemen do it for a reason, Miss Emmerson?' His sharpness was gone. His eyes were gently enquiring.

'Do what, Mr Buchanan?' she asked abruptly.

'Why, insist that our womenfolk dress as they do? It certainly keeps them imprisoned does it not?'

She was quite astounded by this novel idea and she laughed shortly.

'Come now, Mr Buchanan, it is the ladies themselves who decide the fashion, surely?'

'Do you really think so?'

'Of course. Miss Whittam says . . .'

He was grinning now, his mouth wide over his excellent teeth and she felt her own mouth begin to follow. He was wrong, of course, for it was well-known that Miss Susan Whittam had all her most stylish fashions from a London magazine and even from Paris where Monsieur . . .

She saw his eyes grow more vividly blue as he followed her train of thought. The greatest designers themselves were men and were they not perhaps influenced by the very gentlemen who paid for the cumbersome gowns worn by their ladies? The heavy lace trimmed petticoats, the restraining sleeve, immense and distended with stiff linings, the constraining corset, all constructed to keep women tied to their drawing room, their carriage and as much as possible, the nursery!

'Well, Miss Emmerson?' he said and his amazing laughter rang out across the valley and the ravens lifted as one to find more peaceful pastures.

She found herself quite intrigued by this confounding man and her mouth trembled in the start of a grin to match his own, and her antipathy towards him seemed to melt away in the most curious way.

'Do you know, Mr Buchanan, you could be right. I had not thought of it but really, I'm sure you are right.' She dimpled quite deliciously, unconsciously. 'You have a lot to answer for, did you know that?'

'Oh I know it and if I had my way . . .'

'Yes, Mr Buchanan?' She was quite fascinated by this extraordinary conversation and by the very strangeness of having it and she began to walk towards him, her eyes glowing with their interest in his startling opinions. 'If you had your way?'

He put up his hand in mock dismay.

'Please, Miss Emmerson, let us talk of something else for if your father knew I was airing my radical . . .'

'Are you a radical, Mr Buchanan?'

'I would not go as far as to say that.' He became thoughtful, 'But I do have notions which do not always agree with those of my associates.'

'And what are they?'

'Have you a few hours to spare then, Miss Emmerson, whilst I tell you, or does your carriage not wait on you in Chapel Stile? I believe I saw it, and your maid standing before The Fox when I rode through an hour ago.'

'Oh they can wait, Mr Buchanan. It is not often I can . . .' She hesitated and he spoke again.

'Be free, Miss Emmerson?' he said softly.

She was confused again for the words were the very ones she had been about to voice. In all her years from childhood on, through girlhood to the young woman she had become, she had been sheltered, guarded in her father's high-walled garden, escorted wherever she went by grooms, maidservants, her mother, a cousin and only once in all that time had she been given the opportunity to escape.

And this man had found her, doing for her what her father had done since she was born. Protecting her from predatory man. But Robin was not what the word implied. He would not harm her, nor take what she did not freely give and this Alex Buchanan had no right . . . no right to . . .

Suddenly, as the memory of that day flooded back to her mind she flushed and was forced to turn away and the invisible, slender, very fragile thread which had drawn them together for a fraction of a moment, snapped and she lifted her head defensively.

'Are you saying that women may be as free as men in your world, Mr Buchanan?'

'In an ideal world they would be, Miss Emmerson.'

'That is not the question I asked.'

'True, and I am certain that what I say would only relate to some other man's woman, Miss Emmerson, not mine. If I had a woman as beautiful as . . . shall we say . . .

yourself,' his voice was as soft as the finest silk, 'I should keep her so imprisoned no man but myself would ever see her.'

She looked away, hot-faced and perplexed for in all her days she had never known a man so . . . so . . . perplexing! Just when she had decided he was one thing he turned about and became another. She put her hands to the back of her head to retrieve her bonnet, setting it decorously on the sun-lit beauty of her hair.

'I must get on, Mr Buchanan,' she said stiffly. 'My maid will wonder where I am and I am expected at Dalebarrow later. Those who are taking part in the hunt will be back and . . .'

At the mention of her connection with the Hall and those in it, it was as though she had raised a barrier across which he was not allowed to look, let alone wander. She belonged to them now and this man, indeed all men, must know of it.

'Of course.' His face set again in lines which were quite unreadable but his blue eyes danced as though he had found their meeting vastly entertaining.

'Good morning to you, Miss Emmerson, and my regards to Mr Forsythe. May I say he is an extremely lucky young man?' His bold blue eyes raked her quite openly; and Christy caught her breath, convinced that he could see the pink flush which heated her body, moving through the folds of her gown to her neck and cheeks. He bowed impudently, then strode gracefully towards his tethered horse.

CHAPTER SEVEN

It began to snow on the second of January. Violent eddies of air swept the dark fell slopes, throwing great drifts against walls and gates, and around Fellthwaite it gathered and grew and the drifts reached the eaves of cottage and farm and at its lowest level was no less than five feet.

'It'll get worse,' Dorcas said, born in these parts to a farming family. 'I've seen it up to the house-tops afore now and us snowed up for weeks and this'll be the same, you mark my words!'

'Nonsense, girl,' Annie said firmly, though she too had been snow-bound in the cottage in which she had lived with her new husband and it was on one such occasion young Ben had been conceived.

But Dorcas was proved right.

Ned Roper had a dalesman's cottage, the one in which he had dreamed of installing Faith Cooper before his hopes had been dashed by the news of her move to Dalebarrow Hall with Miss Christy. It was no more than fifty yards from the back door of Hollin House and it took him the best part of half an hour to wallow through snowdrifts up to his bum, and even higher in places, to get to the back kitchen door.

He and Cuddy, the second stable boy, called 'boy' though he was a man of fifty-seven, and Mr Emmerson's coachman, Thomas, had had their work cut out to struggle across the yard to the stables to see to the carriage horses and the fine bays ridden by Mr Ben and Mr Toby and to Miss Christy's little mare. Poor old Cuddy, who milked the cows Annie kept, for she had been brought up to believe in the efficacy of her own fresh milk each day, said his fingers damn near froze to their tits and the dark, steaming interior of the barn was positively a hot-house compared to the temperature outside.

Cuddy had been up in the meadow when the blizzard started, repairing the dry-stone wall which surrounded it, replacing the 'cam' stones which had been knocked off when Mr Toby had put his bay to the jump. The stones, all roughly the same size, were stacked on edge and lying at the same angle, their main purpose to discourage the sheep which roamed the fells from getting into Job's fine pasture and to keep Annie's milk cows from getting out.

Cuddy was cursing Mr Toby. His expensively splendid mount should not have been asked to take such a jump. He could have broken both the bay's fragile legs – or his own bloody neck which would have been more to Cuddy's liking – and it would not have been Mr Toby who would have had to shoot the beast. He was an 'animal' man, was Cuddy, hired to help with Mr Emmerson's horses, to milk his cows, not mend the bloody walls, and on top of it all it was beginning to snow.

He was determined to repair the gap that afternoon since he didn't want to come back to it, but the snow had almost reached the top of the wall he mended before he gave up. He had been half-frozen when he finally staggered the length of the field and through the stable yard to the back door. Mrs Emmerson and Dorcas had been forced to beat his top clothes with a stick before they could be removed, so stiff with iced snow were they.

'By God, missis, I've never seen 'owt like it an' I've bin in a few blizzards in me day,' he gasped into the steaming mug of Annie's soup which she had cupped between his stiff fingers as he huddled by the roaring kitchen fire. 'A bloody hour, no more – beggin' your pardon – and yer can't see yer hand afore yer face. I thowt I'd never get back, God's truth. Another ten minutes an' it's bin the end of Cuddy Arkwright.'

'Nonsense, Cuddy, it can't be that bad,' but Annie Emmerson was at the front parlour window for an hour or more peering through the white swirling curtain of snow, watching for Job and her boys to come striding up the path from the mill.

Stride! There was not much chance of that! It was more like the lurching of a troop of drunken sailors! The snow had not yet crusted, cold as it was and the three men had sunk into the drifts to their waists at every step. Their clothes were dragging them slowly down the heavier they became, stiff and wet through, almost frozen upon them with the blinding snow in which they floundered. Their tall black hats were white with snow and it lay inches thick on their shoulders and coated their big, powerful bodies. Their eyebrows bore a shelf-like layer, giving them the appearance of old, white-haired men; their eyelashes were spiked and frozen and they were so weary they were unable to lift an arm to wipe it away.

They were blinded and almost finished when they fell thankfully into Annie's welcoming arms.

The hedges which lined the long drive from the mill-gate to the front door of the house were almost gone, buried beneath a deepening incline of snow and when Annie opened the door the powdery stuff fell in on her, spilling across her lovely carpet and almost burying her as well up to her knees.

'Christ, lass!' Job stumbled across the doorstep and her boys followed, too exhausted to speak. They could do no more than stagger up the long hallway to the kitchen.

'Out, you lot!' Annie said crisply, indicating the hall doorway to the open-mouthed maids and to Christy who was just about to attempt the almost impossible task of removing her brother's overcoat. 'Go on, clear out the lot of you. These lads of mine are to be stripped and they don't want a crowd of giggling lasses about the place.' Even Toby, who under normal circumstances would have liked nothing better, failed to speak up.

'But mother! Can I not . . . ?'

'No you can not, Christy. Get yourself off to your room and none of you show your faces until I shout for you.'

Annie might have been back in her cottage kitchen. The

dignified lady of leisure she had become, or tried to become, was gone with the need to restore these men of hers to warmth and life; and the only way to do that was to remove every stitch of their clothing, rub them down with a rough towel and set them, naked as they were born before the shouting heat of her kitchen fire. She had done it before a dozen or more times. With her own brothers and father when they came in from the fells in weather such as this, facing without embarrassment their nudity in the need to get their blood flowing and the ice from their veins. The land could be cruel to those who were careless with it, to those who did not respect its ferocity or who had wrongly read its warning and many a shepherd had been thawed out in such a way and his dog as well.

The next day they awakened to a white, silent world, the only sound the cry of the ravens upon the crags. Great smooth drifts lay across the valley, concealing walls and gates, tracks and hedges. There was nothing to show where one field ended and another began – only the lacy outline of a denuded tree, or the thick-leafed spread of a conifer standing upright and clothed in snow – through the white and glistening landscape. The sun shone, illuminating brilliantly the high rolling peaks, throwing into black shadow the gullies where it did not reach. The sky was a rich, incredible blue.

'Right lads, let's get down to the mill and see what's what.' Job, fully recovered from his previous day's adventure, and after a peaceful night's sleep and one of Annie's good breakfasts inside him, was ready to tackle anything, even the wall of snow which completely shuttered his breakfast-room window.

'Nay!' Annie was aghast. 'You're not going down there, lad, not in this. You'll not do it, Job!'

Job did not care to be told he could not do *anything*, even by his Annie who had a good head on her. He made his own decisions which she should know by now and besides he had a business to get under way. Most of his labour force lived in the cottages not five paces from the mill-gate so they would not be hard to root out. And someone had to see to the beasts which were stabled in the yard and housed in the kennels nearby.

Cuddy had just returned from his cows and, with Ned and Thomas who had fed and mucked out the horses, was enjoying recuperating by the kitchen fire. They had stepped gratefully over the doorstep, banging the frozen snow from their boots, looking apologetically at the pools of melting mush on Annie's spotless flagged floor before tip-toeing to the warmth of the fire.

'Sorry, missis,' Cuddy said cheerfully, but as Mrs Emmerson philosophically remarked, they'd have a few more puddles before this lot was done.

'Aye, missis,' Cuddy answered comfortably, not much caring how long that would be, as long as his cows were seen to and he could manage that. It looked as though he and Ned and Thomas were in for a pleasurable and peaceful few days for no one would want the carriage horses out in this.

But his complacency was short-lived as Job stamped forcefully into the kitchen and vouchsafed his opinion that it would take him no more than ten minutes or so to get down to the mill. It was then that Annie protested, calling him a fool to endanger himself and her sons in this.

'Give over, woman, we can't sit up here on our backsides until this lot melts next spring. I've orders to get out and them men of mine need directing to it. They'll hang about all day gossiping if me and the lads don't get down to them. See, you . . .'

He turned to the interested Cuddy who nearly choked on the soup he was slurping in reward for his own endeavours. 'You . . . Ned . . . Thomas . . . and you . . . yes, you whatever your name is . . . Cuddy . . . let's be doing something useful, shall we? Have you cleared the yard yet . . . no! . . . well what the bloody hell are you doing here swilling soup? No, don't you argue with me, Annie. I don't care if they have just come in. I want the yard clear or at least paths to the stables and store room and the byre and one down to the mill. Me and the lads will help and when we get down there there's plenty of brawny shoulders to set about the mill yard. We'll have that place going flat out by dinner time!'

'But even if we get down there and the mill is working, how will we move the powder, father? Marsden won't get through this and the roads will be cut off to the coast and even to Buchanan's place. This will mean a big stoppage.'

Ben, as eager as his father not to lose a minute, a second of a good working day, and the profit which would go with it, stood biting his lips, his brow furrowed, his shoulders hunched into the cape of his greatcoat. Toby lounged on the kitchen table, one leg swinging, looking from one face to the other with the greatest interest as though it was merely a fascinating puzzle which was really nothing to do with him.

'Nay lad! Don't let's be beaten before we start. 'Tis not the first time we've had us a bit of snow and it's not stopped us before.'

Fellthwaite was cut off from the rest of the world for almost four weeks. There was another blizzard, the second descending on to the drifts of the first as though the snowflakes were eager to be re-united with those which had fallen before. The drift reached almost to the eaves of the house at the front where it was exposed and Cuddy, Ned and Thomas had to cut holes through to the windows to allow in some light.

Job, his sons and the rest of the men kept a path cut through to the mill and the yard was cleared in order that workmen might move from one building to another so work was kept going much as usual. Job fretted on the enormous amount of black blasting powder which was accumulating in the store houses waiting for the thaw to get it out to customers who were eager for it. He didn't like so much about the place, he muttered on the quiet to son Ben. It was a danger but what else could they do? Until the snows went it must sit where it was. The men must work and of course, looking on the bright side, when

111

they did get it out the shortage which had resulted from the freeze-up would send the price sky high.

Ben's wedding day was set for February the twenty-eighth and the blizzards had kept him and his Celia apart since New Year's day; and the bridesmaids who were to be fitted for the sugar-pink gauzy dresses Celia had decided upon, but Miss Susan Whittam had the measurements of the six young ladies who were to walk behind the bride. She had been making all their gowns since they had left girlhood and knew each one personally, and by a stroke of good fortune the coach bringing the material from Manchester had delivered it before the snows. It needed only one final fitting before the big day and though Celia fretted on it tearfully, wetting the notes her father's groom struggled on foot through the drifts to deliver to Ben, she was assured by everyone who knew the fells that it would be clear for her wedding day.

Christy had not heard from Robin since the day he had accompanied his cousins in their carriage back to Leicestershire just after Christmas, and her anxiety showed in her face. She was quiet and withdrawn for hours at a time, staring off across the everlasting stretch of whiteness towards Fellthwaite and Dalebarrow Hall as though willing the Squire's groom to come stumbling towards her with a note from Robin in his hand. She was jumpy and irritable, her usually merry face almost sullen in its misery. Before he went he had assured her, kissing her passionately and holding her clutching, desperate body to his, that it would be for no more than a week or two. The hunting season was well under way and the Leicestershire cousins were eager to show him their fine new stables, their kennels and to have him look over some land their father had purchased on which they intended to preserve game birds to be shot at the right season. Robin Forsythe was a gentleman and if his lady should ask him not to go he would not, but his eyes beseeched her to understand that this was part of his life as the son of the Squire and that really she must be prepared to accustom herself to it. This time next year, he promised, she would go with him as his wife and he would teach her the joys of the 'real' hunt. He was to ride to hounds as he had always done at this time of the year in the past, staying for a month or two whilst the season lasted, but of course now that he and Christy were engaged and their wedding day approached he would be back before the end of January.

Of course he did not come.

January moved into February and they were about to relax as the snow began to thaw, and movement from house to mill became easier, thinking the worst of the winter was over, when the third and most vicious blizzard hit. It raged for over twenty-four hours and for two whole days they saw no sign of Ned in his dalesman's cottage, nor Cuddy and Thomas who had a snug room above the stables. Job and his lads were caged like animals in the house prowling about from room to room, striding vigorously up and down the stairs to squint through the bedroom windows for some let up in the solid curtain of snow which surrounded the house. It reached above the first floor bedroom windows and Job and Ben were forced to race up to the second floor and the servants' quarters, sending Sally and Dorcas shrieking to their mistress as the master and his sons kept watch from the highest point of the house.

There was no milk to be had and Annie agonized, being a country woman, over the state of the poor beasts which must be milked whatever the weather. She had a storeroom bursting with food, cured hams and bacons, and the enforced stay in the house had produced an abundance of bread, cakes and biscuits for she just couldn't sit about and do nothing she said, so there was no worry that they might starve, but what about the animals?

At last the snowstorm stopped and within two hours Job, Ben and Toby were down at the mill rooting out buried families and directing the men to the 'preparing house' to get the rotary churns under way, the incorporating mills where the large water-wheels were just beginning to go round in the thawing beck, and in an hour the process which would amalgamate the coarse blasting powder had begun. Men were about the yard attacking the drifts with shovels to get through to the horses which had not been fed for almost two days and the kennels where the dogs had become so fierce with hunger that they allowed no one near but Ned's father, Ally Roper.

The thin blue vapour from the flues rose into the still air which hours before had raged like a demon and Job sighed thankfully as he watched it vanish above the roofs of the working mills.

Cuddy, his own version of snowshoes upon his feet, stumbled off across the fields, at Annie Emmerson's insistence, to see how their nearest neighbour fared. He came back with tales of sheep dying in their hundreds – somewhat exaggerated since it had been known for a Herdwick to live for as long as twenty-five days beneath a snow-drift – and the men and dogs were out on the hills, he said, looking for the tiny brown circles in the snow which indicated a buried sheep. The animals, probably several feet below the surface, sweated excessively giving off an acrid odour which the wiry dogs were quick to pick up.

'Farmer Buckly be up there with his men an' their poles an' I said, if it's alright wi' you Missis, seein' as how me an' Ned an' Thomas have got nowt else to do we'd give 'em a hand.'

'Can I go too, mother, please, please?' Christy's face was passionate in her entreaty to be let out of the house, just for a few hours, but Annie was adamant in her refusal.

'Nay! You know your father wouldn't like that, lass. It wouldn't be fitting for you to go traipsing all over the fells with a gang of men.'

Annie Emmerson had been worried about her daughter for weeks. No docile young miss who would sit and embroider and play the piano, she had been used to striding out upon the fells, lately with Faith Cooper to acompany her, or to galloping the lower fells on her little mare with Ned not far behind. She had the blood of farmers, colliers, dalesmen and fellsmen in her veins. Peasant stock used to hard work, hard weather, hard exercise, and the weeks she had been made to wander the rooms of the house with no outlet for her vigorous energy had taken their toll. She was pale, peaky, Annie would call it and she missed that lad of hers. Annie thought he might have taken the trouble to get a note through to her but then men weren't like women. They had so many other vastly entertaining things to occupy their days that, much as they might be in love, they did not give a thought to the woman who waited for her man to remember her. She needed something to take her mind from brooding on it, to take the circles from about her lovely grey eyes, to put the firm, light tread back in her feet which dragged apathetically about the kitchen. A girl for the outdoors was Christy, and Annie understood it, but Job would not allow this. The weeks of being shut in, of having no news of Robin, of watching her father and brothers pacing the house like prisoners incarcerated in a dungeon had set Christy's nerves to flinching at the slightest provocation and this latest fall — just when her longing senses had begun to ease in anticipation of her reunion with her love — had been almost too much for her. She and Ben had snapped at one another for days over trifling matters. Job had had words with them both, telling them to hold their tongues, and Annie had earned herself a private rebuke when she had defended Christy.

'The girl is shut up here with nothing to do, Job. You and the lads are off down to the mill, or engaged in some discussion or other over business, your minds active and busy while she has nothing to think about but that lad of hers.'

'Give her something to do then, woman!' he growled. 'Make sure she's no time to think.'

'Job, we've enough pies and bread and cakes to feed the valley. All the mending is done and the house like a new pin. Besides, she's not domesticated, you know that. She's not been brought up to it like I was, and she'll not do a hand's turn when she's the Squire's lady . . .'

'Well, she's not the Squire's lady yet so see to it she minds her manners and her tongue when she's around me!'

Job, his mind agonizing over loss of production and the vast amounts of blasting powder waiting to be on its way, stored not more than a few hundred yards from his own front door, could not be troubled with the silly mithering of a foolish girl over a lad and he said so forcefully to his daughter. He turned on his youngest son who yawned during the telling and even the good-humoured Toby was jabbed to muttered resentment, earning himself further recriminations.

The maids squabbled ceaselessly, sick to death of one another's company and Mrs Kean boxed Peg's ears and for no other reason than an expression on her face which the cook didn't care for.

They were like prisoners forced to share the same cell, seeing the same faces, hearing the same monotonous conversation over and over again.

When they were awakened at last to the sun which shone so brilliantly it thawed a froth of snow which dripped off the rooftop, though it froze again rapidly in the intense cold, it set them all to bustling around, excited by the prospect of being released.

'I shall go to Dalebarrow at once,' Christy told her mother. 'Robin might have sent a note. Though it has been so bad up here perhaps the roads from the south are clear. He must have sent one and it is probably sitting up at the Hall this minute just waiting for someone to pick it up . . .' Her voice was high and excited, almost hysterically so and Annie was disturbed by it but just the same she knew Job would not care for the idea of his high-bred horses and the carriage being got out in this weather. The very notion was ludicrous but the girl was almost delirious with joy, running here and there gathering her boots and bonnet in the most disjointed fashion, shouting for Faith who must go with her.

116

Catching her daughter's frantic figure as she made ready to gallop the two miles to Dalebarrow Hall in drifts so thick a man six feet tall would be lost in them, she took Christy's hands in hers and looked into the soft, anguished eyes. She wondered not for the first time on the strangeness of loving someone as this girl loved the Squire's boy. She and Job had affection, deep and strong, but what Christy felt for Robin Forsythe, and apparently he was the same, was almost like an obsession. Look at her now, leaping about like a thing demented just in the hope of having a note from the lad who would be back here in a week or two anyway for the wedding.

She soothed her like a child though Christy Emmerson was a woman grown.

'No, lass, no! You can't get those horses out in this. Your father would never allow it, never.'

'Please, mother, Ned can manage them. Father need not know. I'll be there and back before . . .'

'No, lass, it's not right nor sensible.'

'Please mother, let me . . .'

'No!' Annie's voice was firm and she began to move away irritated now by her daughter's foolishness. 'No I say.'

'I *will* go, mother.' Christy's face was white, and set in an expression of mutiny.

'You will *not*, Christina. That is my last word on it.'

Annie left the room, closing the door firmly behind her.

The voices came from the kitchen ten minutes later and Annie raised her head from the plain sewing to which she and Faith had just settled.

'Miss Christy, please,' the first voice entreated, 'beggin' your pardon miss, but it's not possible. T'wouldn't do to expect hosses to get through this lot and say we did, what if we got stuck in a drift? It could come down again soon as look at you and Cuddy says . . .'

The second voice was cool, imperious.

'I do not care to be told what Cuddy says and would be obliged if you would carry out my orders!'

'Nay, Miss Christy . . .' Ned even went as far as to call his master's daughter 'lass', so distressed was he. 'Lass, yer can't take animals out . . .'

'Will you do as you are told . . .' Christy's voice was threatening.

A quiet voice from the door which led from the kitchen into the small back parlour used for a sewing room, turned every head in the kitchen. Annie stood there, red-faced but quite calm.

'Come in and close the door, Ned,' she said to the man who hovered at the kitchen doorway, obviously trying to escape the madness of his young mistress. 'It's too cold to stand about on the step. Come to the fire and get warm. Dorcas, push that pan of soup over the coals and give Ned a drink before he goes up to the byre with Cuddy. A minute or two won't make much difference to the milking though I can hear those cows from here.'

She moved toward the simmering pan which was kept continuously on the fire and had been for weeks now, and like any farmer's wife at home in her own kitchen, ladled him out a brimming mugful of succulently fragrant soup.

Christy pulled her soft woollen shawl more closely about her shoulders and her face became stiff and expressionless. She stood with her back to the dresser and her eyes were like flint, ready to strike sparks off anyone who defied her and her cheeks were aflame.

'Excuse me!' Her voice was dangerously quiet and Annie was reminded of her own husband when he was crossed. Sometimes he shouted and blustered when he was seriously displeased, his voice thundering above those who tried to argue, but it was when it was cold, like iron, as his daughter's was now, that real trouble brewed.

Mrs Kean, Peg and Dorcas – who were mere maids and in awe of the autocratic Mrs Emmerson who had complete dominance over the lives of everyone in the house bar that of Mr Emmerson – stood mesmerized by this defiance and after one horrified stare, kept their eyes respectfully lowered.

Christy did not! Hers were brilliant as stars and as grey as the woodsmoke which rose to them.

'Did you want something, Christina?' her mother asked.

'I was just instructing Ned to get out the horses. I wish to go to Dalebarrow Hall at once.'

Annie's voice was steady but cold as the icicles which formed on the roof above her.

'I have already told you. You may not go.'

Christy sighed as though at the denseness of a particularly stupid child and the room held its breath.

'I must go to Dalebarrow Hall, mother. I wish to ask if they have word of Robin.' Her voice was authoritative, the voice of the lady of the manor she would one day be.

'Have you not seen the snow?' Annie's was equally regal.

'Of course I have seen it.'

'And do you imagine you are able to get through it?'

'Oh for goodness' sake! I cannot stand here arguing.' The room gasped as Christy turned to Ned who stood with his back to the roaring fire, an expression on his face which said he wished he had never bothered to get out of bed this morning.

'Ned, be good enough to get out the carriage and bring it round to the front door.'

The voice of Annie Emmerson was implacable and cold as steel.

'No one but myself has the ordering of my servants, girl.'

They all turned, even the two tabbies who lay wound about one another on the hearthrug. Dorcas put her hand to her mouth whilst Peg, Sally and Faith who had followed Annie from the back parlour, all took a step backwards like three young ladies in a quadrille. Ned cleared his throat and began to edge his way round the perimeter of the room. Bugger the soup, he was off!

'I beg your pardon.' Christy's voice was cutting and Annie felt her strong heart falter a little for the girl must be nearly out of her head to act like this. There was no reasoning with her, but of course she must not be allowed to go on.

'I think I made myself quite clear, Christina. This is my kitchen and these are my servants and you are my daughter who has no control of either. I do not choose to risk the life of one of them, or of the beasts, in the conditions which exist between here and Dalebarrow and if you were in your right senses you would see I am right. I am surprised at you and by the tone of your voice which is rude to say the least. You may be engaged to the son of the Squire, young lady, but that does not give you leave to order the servants in this house. Now get back to the . . .'

'I will leave here at once,' Christy hissed and her eyes dashed fiery venom over all present. 'Can you not see I must get word of Robin? This snow could start again and it could be weeks before . . . Oh God, when shall I see him again?'

'Be quiet, girl! Have you no manners?'

'Dammit mother, let me go before I do you an injury!'

Faith gasped and Ned, who had been just about to let himself quietly out of the kitchen door, turned abruptly.

'I doubt it, Miss. Not while I've breath in my body and strength in my right arm.'

'*I will go, mother. I will and you shall not stop me.* I am to be married to the son of the Squire and you will not stop me. I love him and I must have news of him. *You will not stop me,* you won't . . . you won't . . .'

Her face took on such a look of agony that Annie's softened involuntarily, but it hardened immediately with Christy's next words. 'You are a nobody, d'you hear, a nobody like the Squire says and I am to . . .'

The sentence was never finished for with a resounding slap Annie Emmerson struck her daughter full in the face. Then, as the horrifying noise echoed about the silent room, she clutched the falling girl to her and held her in her arms, stroking her hair and her shoulders and murmuring in a soft meaningless undertone against her cheek.

Christy put her head into her mother's shoulder and

wept. She wept for her own torn heart which throbbed for Robin. She loved him so and needed his arms and his comforting presence and she wept for the woman whom she had just injured with her own dreadful words. In her own pain she had attacked her mother and she did not fully understand why. She was perfectly aware that it was madness to try to get to Dalebarrow, absolute folly and yet her own arrogant will had driven her on.

'Oh mother, I'm sorry . . . I'm sorry . . .'

'I know lass, I know . . . there now . . . there.'

'What have I said . . . oh mother, what have I said to you?'

'Nothing that won't mend, lass, so don't fret. Now sit you down, see Peg . . .' She turned to the silent group of servants who leaped into action with the alacrity of horses put to the spur, 'Put that kettle on and don't stand there with that daft look on your faces and then, perhaps, if it keeps clear we'll see.'

She turned to Christy who had sunk into the kitchen chair. 'Perhaps Ned can get through on foot. Now dry your eyes and wipe your nose.'

The thaw set in two days later, the signs to those dalesmen who had lived with it all their lives very evident. The sheep, brought down from the fells, sniffed the air, their eyes brightening. Clouds streaked the western sky and above the harsh cry of the raven could be heard the sweet dash of water skimming across rocks which had been frozen solid with ice.

The thin yellowed vegetation of the mountains revealed itself and a storm-cock fluted the air at the bottom of the garden with its wild song to the approach of spring. A dipper answered and in the corner of the wall, sheltered from the wind as the snow fell away to reveal the outline of the holly bush, delicate white snowdrops — the fair maids of February — lifted their heads and blinked in the new light.

The next day there was a letter from Robin and Christy Emmerson sang as she walked with her maid on the cleared path which led up the back pasture of the dry-stone wall which Cuddy had begun to mend so many weeks ago. In a few days' time Ben would be married to Celia and though, regretfully, the blizzards which had swept the whole country, blocking all the roads and making them impassable to coaches, would not allow Robin to be there, he was to leave Leicestershire within the week and be home as soon as he could. And on the fifteenth day of March, just three weeks away, Christy Emmerson would go up the aisle on her father's arm and return as Mrs Robin Forsythe.

There were a hundred trifling matters to be got through first but what did they signify compared to the miracle of knowing she was loved. That Robin loved her and that within the month they would be together, alone in that lovely old room at Dalebarrow Hall set aside for them by Mrs Forsythe. In it they would create their own world, shut off each night from the society which at the moment would scarce allow them to sit alone together in an open carriage without damage to her reputation. Their marriage would be for life. Their love would last as long as a month's time they would begin it.

But first there must be visits to Miss Susan Whittam to be fitted into the white dress with the skirt shaped like a bell all trimmed about with orange blossom and lace and swan's-down. The bridesmaids must be organized into the palest of peach gauze, and the bride's mother in dignified royal blue.

The bride's wardrobe must be of the best for Job wanted all of Fellthwaite to see what he could afford for his lass. Feathers and fans, muffs and mittens, brocades and bonnets. An Indian muslin pelisse, carriage costumes, morning dress, evening gowns by the score, close fitting and extremely *decolletté*, ginghams and challis, chintzes and silk, shawls of cashmere, jewelled combs, flowers and ribbons and all befitting the station of Mrs Robin Forsythe.

It seemed she and Celia lived in one another's pockets during those last few days of girlhood, two young brides preparing for marriage to two important young men, their wedding days being so close together, it was as though they were twins and to have a double wedding. Sometimes Christy wished that she and Robin could just slip down to the little church in Ambleside, away from the turmoil which surrounded her, to exchange their vows alone and then drive away on the wedding journey they planned.

Celia loved it, thriving on the importance of being Ben Emmerson's betrothed, on being the centre of the fuss and excitement accorded a young lady about to cross the mysterious threshold into womanhood. Christy's inclination to edge her way from the room and wander off down the thawing garden suited Celia admirably for it meant she had the limelight to herself.

And then it was Friday and tomorrow Ben Emmerson and Celia Metcalf would become man and wife!

CHAPTER EIGHT

The aim in the manufacture of gunpowder is to mix the ingredients evenly in order that the sulphur and charcoal burst into an instantaneous combustion, speeded by the oxidizing effect of the saltpetre. Each grain of the gunpowder must be of an even mixture of all three materials and all the grains must be of the same size, polished, and with no dust or foreign materials adhering to the grain surface. If the grains are packed too tightly an uneven explosion will take place, and if too loosely, full combustion is not achieved.

The Emmerson Gunpowder Mill covered about twenty acres, and the 'fierce' powder manufactured there served mines and quarries throughout the north of England, the mining communities of North Wales and the Crown Agents for the Colonies and West Africa. Powder was delivered to the local slate quarries, to the Buchanan Copper Mines, and taken by horse and cart to the head of

Lake Windermere, by boat to Lakeside and thence to Greenodd for shipment abroad.

Job Emmerson was looking forward eagerly to the coming of the Kendal and Windermere Railway which was to be completed in the next twelve months, for then his wagonloads of powder could be taken each day to the new station which was to open at Windermere, speeding up delivery enormously and providing him with a massive improvement in profit by the time saved.

He had chosen his site carefully. A beck ran down its western boundary fed by the very high rainfall which was a feature of the Lake District, and this provided the water power. There was a large millpond in the centre of the property. The waterways were intricate and power was abundantly furnished by a number of water-wheels. The biggest was over thirty-six feet in diameter and six feet in width and with five others of slightly smaller dimensions, produced a grand total amounting to the power of two hundred horses.

The three basic ingredients of the explosive were ground to a fine powder in the preparing house, mixed by stirring in rotating barrels. Great care was taken to preclude any possible spark or friction as the unwanted grit was swept away, and tools and fitments were made of wood, brass or copper to cut down any possibility of this happening. Once the 'green charge', as it was called, was thoroughly mixed it was moved, carefully again, to one of the incorporating mills, to be amalgamated painstakingly under pressure so that the correct density of powder was produced. It was here that the large water-wheels and heavy runners of limestone were employed, rotating around a tray in which the charge of powder mixture was placed. Several processes later – pressing, corning, glazing, reeling, drying and moulding – the finished product was packed in wooden barrels made on the site in the cooperage from good local timber and transported from there to its destination.

Owing to the unusual weather conditions which had prevailed during January and the first two weeks in

February and the difficulties in moving his finished product to his customers, Job Emmerson had a dangerously large amount of black, coarse powder stored in two sheds in the centre of the site, just below the large millpond.

The men were respectfully chaffing young Master Ben on his forthcoming nuptials and he was taking it good-naturedly enough. Though he was master, or would be one day, he allowed the knowing smiles and leg-pulling, submitting reluctantly to questions on whether there would be 'throwing the stocking' – a subject too delicate to be discussed in the company of a young lady for it entailed a certain amount of the rude simplicity which was dying out amongst those who no longer considered themselves to be of the working class. It was unlikely that young Master Ben and his bride would allow revellers into their bedroom to perform the ritual.

Perhaps the bride was to have the customary 'brides-cake' broken over her head, they quipped, and was there to be a race to the bridal house following the church ceremony, the victor to receive a riband from the bride?

'You'll not win it, Jonty Dow, for you'll trip over them big feet of yours before you get over the threshwood.'

The man who had spoken pointed to the wooden doorstep but Jonty Dow, busy at the tray in the incorporating mill, gently smoothing down the charge of powder over which the heavy runners turned by friction would directly roll, only laughed.

'And neither will you, Willy Wilson, for if I know you, you'll not be out of The Swan till time is called, especially if Master's buying.'

They looked to where Ben and Toby stood by the huge central pillar which bore the whole weight of the edge runners, shouting with laughter at their own wit and the master smiled and nodded for this good-humoured raillery must always be accepted when a man was to be married, be he master or labourer.

In a close-knit community such as existed in the fells and dales, a wedding afforded an opportunity for social contact and though the entire dale had not been 'lated', or invited, as once had been customary, all those who were not on shift and were within walking distance would put on their best 'setting-off' clothes and flock to the church to see the young master wed. The children would tie up the gates of the churchyard when the guests were within the church and the bride and groom, when they emerged as man and wife, must pay their dues, a few pennies, before the gates were released and they were allowed to leave.

'And what about "bidden", master? Will you be riding the fells with your young lady?'

'I don't know about that, Jonty, but if we do can I count on a handsome donation from your pocket?'

Jonty Dow's embarrassed guffaw was joined by the laughter of the rest of his workmates and the simple pleasure shared by these men gave no offence to their master.

The two young men, Job Emmerson's fine sons, were smiling as they walked across the yard towards the glazing house.

'Never mind, brother Ben. You'll only be wed once so all this horseplay will not be endured again.'

'No, I suppose not,' Ben sighed laughingly. 'But just wait until it's your turn, that's all I can say. Perhaps you will not be so complacent. If I've had it said once about a damn bidden wedding, I've had it said a dozen times today and it gets a bit tedious after a while.'

'What does?'

'Oh, the snide remarks.'

'Surely not to the master's son!'

'The bloody master's the worst of all!'

'Well, he is anxious for you to make a grandfather out of him!'

'I know, brother, I damn well know.'

'And you'll do your best on that score, I'll be bound.'

'No better than you from what I hear, and you not even wed yet.'

'Come now, brother, don't try to tell me Miss Celia is the first . . .'

'Watch your mouth, Toby my lad. When my first child is born it will be in wedlock.'

'The first you know of, you mean!'

'Well . . . !'

They were grinning as they approached the doorway to the glazing house where a man was working alone, engaged in cleaning a cylinder. The cylinder in which the powder was glazed had bungs fitted at regular intervals, and, as Ben Emmerson bent his tall frame to step inside the building, the man was in the process of scraping off the powder from one of them, which after being used for some time became clogged up. It was part of his job to go each afternoon at about three o'clock to sweep the floor and prepare the machine for running at night when the second shift came on. Scattered about the wooden floor which had obviously not yet been swept was almost half a hundredweight of powder sweepings. Six cylinders were not working as they had already been discharged and the man was whistling cheerfully as he rasped some tool he held against the bung, working loose the clogged up matter which had collected there.

The whole manufacture of gunpowder is very hazardous but many of the workmen, grown up amidst the danger, had become so familiar, one could almost say indifferent to it, they scarcely recognized it. They wanted no changes to new-fangled equipment or methods of working, perhaps taking them into another class of danger of which they were ignorant and therefore distrustful. This man was apparently one such for what he did was hardly believable and young Ben Emmerson leaped forward to tell him so.

He saw the spark as he moved across the littered wooden floor and spoke the words which were to be his last.

'What the devil are you doing, man? You know the bloody regulations! D'you want us all to . . .'

The 'bottom wind' which was the plague of old Edwin's rheumatism carried the flash like some lively, jumping firework to the granulating house where the explosion lifted the massive head of a hydraulic press, flinging it like a piece of thistledown into the air and carrying it across the river to the other side fifty yards away before leaping on to the second granulating house, where it did the same with a beam thicker than the trunk of a man. Iron cylinders weighing four tons were shattered to pieces, buildings disintegrated like matchsticks and machinery and men flew about the air in every direction. Workmen, enveloped in flames, began to scatter from the wrecked and burning houses, running about blinded, their screams shrill and agonized, crashing into one another as they went, with the instinct of animals, for the mercy of the water in the beck.

One man was actually clinging to part of a wall from the building in which he had been working as it flew over the heads of the stumbling men, and was blown into the beck landing with a loud, maddened splash. Though the man was incredibly not seriously injured the stone held him down until he drowned.

Men, many yards away from the exploding and burning buildings, their clothing saturated with gunpowder dust became ignited by sparks from others and turned themselves into human, screaming torches. They dashed about blindly, beating at their own burning bodies with hands from which the flesh had already gone. Frightfully mutilated bodies tripped them up as they ran and over in the wood, one hundred and fifty yards away, the burning body of Toby Emmerson, lying where it had been flung, set fire to the bark of a tree which, though still laced with snow could not withstand the flames from his rapidly charring flesh.

Splinters of wood were like venomous darts, piercing their way into men's flesh with the force of bullets, and slates from the roofs of exploding buildings sliced cleanly into heads, going through thick caps as easily as butter and decapitating one man with the neatness of a headman's axe.

The fire drew closer to the dust house in which a great

weight of powder was stored. So far thirty-five barrels containing one hundred pounds of powder each had gone up in the space of thirty seconds, and alarmed heads were raised as far away as twenty miles as people looked at one another in wonder for one did not expect to hear thunder at this time of the year.

Job Emmerson was in the 'safe' area, his satisfying weekly balance sheet spread out before him on his large desk when the windows of his office simply flew out, drawn from their frames by the force of the blast, and the five seconds it took for the savage sound of it to follow seemed an eternity as he stared in stupefaction at the space where they had been.

'Jesus,' he whispered, his mind knowing but his big, ageing body slow to react to the horror which his brain told him had come.

'Oh sweet Jesus,' he said again, louder this time and then the screaming began. Men, horses, women, children! Men in agony. Horses in terror and pain as the fire licked at them and a cart loaded with exploding powder lifted the shire which pulled it twenty feet into the air before savagely smashing it against a safety bank. Women and children cried out in fear and dogs barked frantically and all before Job could lift his desperate body from his chair to get to his sons and his smashed mills.

He fell down the stairs, cracking his ankle angonizingly on the last step, unaware he had even broken it as he blundered on despairing feet towards the chaos, and the sound which came from his own mouth was unrecognizable as that of a human being.

The women were in Annie Emmerson's parlour, or drawing room as it was now fashionably called, trying on for the last time before the actual ceremony the gowns they would wear.

Celia's coachman had got her and her sisters across from Haverthwaite, their bridal finery in an enormous packing case, and each of her bridesmaids had done the same, escorted by their Mamas and various relatives to Hollin House which was the most conveniently situated for everyone concerned.

Celia was resolved that hers would be the smartest, most splendid wedding Fellthwaite had ever seen, eclipsing even Christy's forthcoming marriage to the Squire's son. Celia was, if she was honest, a trifle envious of Christy though she could not really have said why. Ben's sister always, without trying, seemed to do or be just a little bit better than Celia! She was prettier, that Celia admitted grudgingly, if you liked a figure so extremely slender, smoothing her own ample curves, but beyond that was not Celia richer, was she not to marry the most handsome, most eligible bachelor in the dales? Was not her own family as well-bred as any of the industrial class hereabouts? Her home was as splendid, her carriage more so, than Christy Emmerson's and yet in a way Celia did not understand her betrothed's sister always managed to outshine Celia at whatever function they attended. She dressed quite plainly, Celia thought, and had been chagrined to hear that plainness described as 'elegance'. She was very outspoken, Celia complained privately to Ben and was mortified to be told that she was 'spirited' with a lively mind and wit, which it seemed Celia was not but would like to be!

But tomorrow was Celia's day and there was nothing more certain than the reality that Celia Metcalf would not be outshone in any way by Christy Emmerson. She stood in her bridal gown of blonde lace over white satin, quite splendid in her healthy, well-endowed young comeliness, her veil held in place with a wreath of orange blossom as Miss Whittam made a last minute adjustment to the train of her skirt for Celia would have nothing less than perfection. Her six young bridesmaids were grouped about her as she instructed them for the fiftieth time on the exact formation she wished them to take as they followed her up, then down the aisle. Miss Whittam flitted here and there, adjusting a flower, a feather, a flounce, hissing out sharp orders to her assistant who knelt at the feet of first one pretty, pink gauzed maiden, then another.

About the large comfortable room, reclining in the warmth and well-fed congeniality which Annie Emmerson, as the chaperone of the motherless Celia, felt obliged to supply, sat the mothers and aunts and cousins of the five other bridesmaids. They drank tea from Annie's delicate bone-china tea cups and sampled her delicious ratafias, macaroons, the superb texture of her pound cake and the lightness of her biscuits; agreeing with one another that never had they seen such a picture as the combined beauty that their daughters, nieces, cousins provided.

There was Emily Dyer, fair and fragile and the perfect complement, they said, for dear Celia's rather majestic darkness. Jane Aspin, daughter of Jonathan Aspin whose ships ran round the coast to Liverpool and beyond, carrying the manufactured goods, the gunpowder, the chemicals, copper, coal the iron, slate and every profit-making commodity to go from Cumberland and Westmorland to the outer world. Jenny Marsden, whose father supplied much of the timber which was used in the mines and mills about the district of Furness, and Celia's own sisters, Sarah and Mary, as dark and handsome as she was herself, both awaiting their turn to be wed to the men of their father's choice.

And Christy Emmerson! No matter which way you looked at her and the girls she stood with, no matter how precious your own child, there was no getting away from it, unfair as it was, particularly to poor Celia, she was like an elegant young swan, pink feathered, amongst a clutch of pretty ducklings. They were attractive, charming even, but Christy Emmerson drew the eye to her like a magnet. Even in the sugar pink confection which Celia had hoped would not suit her she looked, quite simply, stunning!

'I think a fraction lower on the left, Miss Whittam, if you don't mind,' Celia was saying, standing before the cheval mirror which had been brought down from the bedroom for the purpose, her head on one side as she

131

considered the superb fit of her dress and Miss Whittam sprang to obey though she knew perfectly well there was simply nothing further to be done.

'There, that's better.' Celia admired her own image and sighed contentedly and Christy did the same though her sigh was caused by impatience. How much longer were they to fidget about playing handmaiden to Celia Metcalf? An hour they had been tricked up in these ghastly flounces, simpering and posing as a background to Celia's admiration of Celia and if they didn't get a move on she'd damn well scream. The dresses were as good as they would ever be, which when all was said and done wasn't much, and she was longing to get out of the corset Celia insisted upon. They weren't needed, at least she didn't need one though Celia's waist was ample enough, she supposed.

She sighed again and as she did so the mirror before which Celia postured, shivered, cracking into a thousand tiny pieces to fall in a tumbling spray at the astonished feet of the bride. For a second, no more, there was a bewildered silence, then before any of the ladies could register surprise, or even turn their heads to look at one another as they sat, teacups to prim lips and pound cake delicately held in polite fingers, the room was filled with a noise which blasted them to their seats or the piece of carpet on which they stood as firmly as though nails were driven through their flesh.

It was just as though some gigantic hand had executed an enormous burst on a kettle-drum, only one, a thunder-clap of sound slamming the senses, stunning the mind and silencing the ladies' chatter immediately. China ornaments danced and tinkled on tables and shelves and mantelpiece and a fine painting of a country landscape slipped on its hook to hang askew.

'Oh Lord . . . Oh dear Lord!'

Mrs Aspin had time to say no more before the giant struck again and the picture left its hook and fell to the floor and one of the young bridesmaids began to whimper.

'Oh my dear Lord . . .' And again the drumbeat sounded

132

but this time, the third, the giant was furiously angry and the tattoo it beat out on its drum roared about them, pushing against the walls, looking, it seemed, for a way out and finding none, setting about the solid oak furniture, the pretty Wedgwood figurines, the lamps, pictures, the screen and work tables, the ormolu clock, the lacquer work, the silver-mounted ostrich eggs and the ladies themselves as though it would stop at nothing to crush the lot of them in its ferocity.

It was pitiless as it swept dainty Emily Dyer from her feet and slammed her in a crumpled pink heap against the fireplace, uncaring of the dancing flames which leaped merrily to feed upon a delicate flounce. It roared into the midst of Sara and Mary Metcalf and the kneeling assistant of Miss Whittam and lifted them six inches from the floor before tearing Mary's pretty gown from her flaccid form and tossing it up to the ceiling.

Jenny Marsden and Jane Aspin appeared to run backwards with wheels on their feet, their hands reaching instinctively for one another as they went, neat as you please through the drawing room window, taking the glass with them. The noise, the powerful, full-throated bombardment followed them out and all that was left was what, after the tumult, appeared to be no more than a gentle crash or two as every glass pane in every window in the room fell inwards and each and every ornament, mirror and the delicate bric-a-brac followed.

Christy Emmerson felt the bones of her skull grind in agony against one another and she had the distinct impression that two hands had tried to tear her ears from her head. Something had slammed into her, hard as rock, big as a boulder from the fells behind the house, and she was astonished to find that she was no longer standing behind Celia at the looking-glass but that they were both lying full length on the floor beneath the grand piano which her father had bought for her years ago when she had begun to play.

It was quiet then, an unearthly quiet which seemed to

go on and on as lungs which had had the air forced from them struggled to take breath.

No one moved! The ladies who had been seated, remained so. Mrs Aspin still held an unbroken cup to her yellow-white lips though a trickle of blood ran down her cheek from a cut beneath her right eye, and Mrs Marsden had not even turned her head towards the window through which her daughter Jenny had just disappeared. It might have been some grotesque tableau, one of those set up by Madame Tussaud, who travelled about the country and which Christy had paid one shilling to see in the Market Building in Fellthwaite.

Her mother just sat on and on, covered from head to foot in dust, her eyes blank with shock and Mrs Marsden who sat beside her was the same.

It was then Emily Dyer began to scream as the flames from the fire licked the tender white flesh of her arm and the sound, piercing, shrill, agonized, brought to life the nightmare spectacle and the mannequins all jerked and floundered and stumbled and uttered strange noises, none of them making sense. Though it had appeared to last for hours, days even, the whole dreadful catastrophe had taken no more than thirty seconds.

Annie Emmerson was the first to move as the rabbit screams of Emily Dyer ripped through the numbness which held her, and with the instinctive response of a daleswoman to any emergency, she was on her feet and in one competent stride had the rug which lay beneath the screaming girl wrapped around her, effectively putting out the flames. She held her for a minute, comforting as she would any injured animal then thrust her into her mother's arms.

As she took her daughter Mrs Dyer was herself again, her maternal response immediate and with the strength which comes from somewhere when it is needed, she lifted her weeping, full-grown child and placed her on the sofa as though she was no more than an infant.

They all began to cry then except for the two girls

outside in the still snow-covered garden, and they, cut and bruised but miraculously not seriously injured, were deep in shock. There were shouts from the back of the house and cries for help; and in the yard, through the shattered windows Christy could distinctly hear Ned Roper's voice repeating over and over again. 'Oh Jesus . . . oh sweet Jesus . . . oh Jesus . . .'

Her mother's hand dragged at her then, tearing viciously at her flesh as she tried to lift her from beneath the piano.

'It's the mill, girl, the mill! For Christ's sweet sake pull yourself together and come with me. Your father . . . Ben . . . Toby . . . Christy lass, stand up . . .'

Christy dragged herself to her feet. She swayed a little and put her hands to her aching head. Her hair was full of some dry, scratchy stuff and she wondered what it was but her mother gave her no time to dwell on it. Lifting her hand she hit her daughter viciously across her face and Christy's head rocked on her shoulders and the ache which lay in the base of her skull sprang to full life, biting her ferociously, but she was sensible now.

Celia lay as though she were dead but her eyes were open and kept blinking as dust drifted and floated across her vision. Annie ignored her. Taking Christy's hand she began to run across the drawing room, wrenching open the door into the hall.

'Sally!' Her voice was like a scream torn from an injured lioness and in a moment they were all there. Sally, dancing and gibbering about broken windows and burning cats, her voice shrill with terror. Dorcas, strangely quiet and young Peg, eyes blind in shock but in the background, solid, reliable, was Mrs Kean and young Faith Cooper, white-faced but steady. Both daleswomen like herself, useful in the face of any disaster and it was to them Annie turned.

'See to them, Mrs Kean, Faith.' She waved her hand in the direction of the devastated drawing room from which shrill cries were coming and the women nodded.

Annie spun on her heel, still holding Christy by the arm,

ready to open the front door and fly like the wind to her husband, her sons, but it was simply not there. The explosion had taken it, blown it away, but Annie was beyond caring.

'Come on, lass,' she muttered and they went together, Christy in her pretty pink gown, out into the bitter cold February afternoon. As they leaped, light as fawns, even the dignified person of Annie Emmerson, over the doorstep and on to the gravel drive which led down to the mill, the sight which met their eyes brought them both to a shuddering standstill.

There was smoke, billowing and black and threatening, hundreds of feet up into the pastel-blue winter sky and flames deep within it, beginning to roar with the ferocity of an unleashed animal kept too long confined. In the air were a thousand, thousand tiny pieces of debris and ash, floating higher and higher, drifting down when they had reached their peak across the house, the garden, the beck, the lake and a hundred square acres of snow-covered valley bottom.

In the garden, strewn haphazardly like bits of a discarded jig-saw puzzle were dozens and dozens of pieces of unidentifiable objects made from copper, wood, brass, all torn and twisted, some burning and just beyond the snowdrops in the sheltered corner of the summer rosebed was a human hand.

There were screams from somewhere down there, human and animal, and torn shouts echoing up to them. Someone was wielding what sounded like an axe on some solid thing for its noise could plainly be heard above the crackle of the fire. Through the smoke and floating debris they could see men running, their clothing ablaze, bumping into one another, falling down and picking themselves up to knock against someone else. There was the sound of children crying, women keening and the deep, ferocious terrified barking of the guard dogs.

Christy began to shiver and her eyes glazed over as she tried to shut the sight out but Annie would not allow it.

136

'Come on lass, it's not far.' She shouted encouragingly, as though to an uncertain child and began to run down the steep incline which led to her husband's mill, dragging her daughter with her.

It took Alex Buchanan and David Adams, his mine engineer, an hour to reach Job Emmerson's mills from the Buchanan Copper Mines up Conistone way. Only about two miles as the crow flies but they had to travel by the rutted track which led down through Conistone and along the Yewdale Beck and up northwards to Skelwith Bridge and on to Chapel Stile.

The snow was still treacherous on the higher slopes and they dared not risk their horses, even on tracks they knew intimately in the months of summer.

They had felt the blast like the slap of the giant's hand which had destroyed Annie Emmerson's drawing room, as they stood in the little township of sheds, offices, workshops and water-wheels which were the heart of Alex's mining business. He and young David Adams had been about to examine the results of the dressing process and the young man cried out as several women employed above ground sorting the 'knockings', pieces of mixed ore and waste rock, fell to their knees.

'Is it an earthquake, sir?' one gasped, clutching at another convinced the ground was about to split open as she had heard it did in such dreadful events, but Mr Buchanan was already astride his roan which had been tethered nearby, calling over his shoulder to the younger man.

'Saddle up, lad, and follow as soon as you can. Get all the men who are above ground. Put them in a wagon and tell them to get to Emmerson's.'

'What's to do?' David shouted, excited as the young are at any diversion.

'It's the mill . . . explosion . . .' The words only just reached him as Alex Buchanan's horse crashed through the

137

crisp, winter bracken and vanished behind a pile of 'deads' and waste rock and it knocked the light of anticipation from David Adams's eyes. His mouth opened to shout incisive instructions to several men who stood gawping at one another at the top of the engine shaft.

They kept the fire from the two store sheds and the dust house in which the main barrels of blasting powder were stacked and it was Alex Buchanan who held the men together and formed the lines which passed the plentiful supply of water needed to finally extinguish the flames and it was he who sent a messenger to tell the doctors in Fellthwaite and Ambleside to look sharp for the dead and dying were everywhere.

Men buried beneath rubble, calling for help; beneath walls three feet thick which had been pulverized and flung about as easily as the pebbles in the beck when the press and corning houses were completely devastated. Debris lay in all directions to a distance of up to one hundred and fifty yards from the site of the first explosion and bodies, injured and dead, lay like raggedy dolls in heaped bundles of clothing, some charred, against walls and fences and blast screens.

Women called for husbands and sons, followed by clutching, terrified children and others nursed silently those they had found, some beyond help but just as tenderly held.

Jonty Dow, whose feet would never now take him over any threshwood as they lay trapped and mangled in the demolished remains of the wall of the incorporating house, stared in bewilderment at the washed-blue sky, whispering to some unseen wrestling opponent to 'tak hod, lad', unaware that unless someone promptly pulled him from where he lay he would quite soon be consumed by the fire around him.

It had been touch and go! Men risked their lives a dozen times knowing that if the bulk of the powder went up the whole of the valley would go with it. Farms, cottages, animals and all those who lived in the area. They saved

138

the dust house and the explosive within it but despite their efforts and those of a hundred men who came from Fellthwaite, Ambleside, Grasmere and Conistone to help, four of Job Emmerson's mills were destroyed that day and amongst those dead were both his sons.

Job knelt on the ground beside the mutilated body of his beautiful boy and wept. The head of Ben Emmerson had been rammed through the plaster of the building which had been the first to blow and someone mercifully had wrapped a coat about it. The rest of his body was unmarked though his fine suit of clothes was covered in dust.

They would not let his mother and father near Toby!

Job's wife stood beside him, her hand on his shoulder, her eyes unfathomable in her hard-grained face and on a length of charred timber, like a pretty doll which has been left outside in the rain sat his daughter, still dressed in the soaked pink gauze in which she was to have seen her brother married on the following day!

CHAPTER NINE

In the comfortable smoking room of a rather grand house in Leicestershire, before the enormous log fire which roared in the open fireplace two men sat in companionable silence, fragrant cigar smoke wreathing the air about their well-brushed heads. Both wore immaculate evening dress suits of tight black trousers with black pumps, a black double-breasted dress coat, frilled and ruffled shirt and a silk waistcoat. They were rather old-fashioned in their style, with their hair curled and worn quite long and the moustaches and whiskers of the previous decade. One had a gold eyeglass suspended from his neck by a short black ribbon, a gold snuff box from which he had just taken a pinch of snuff before returning it to his pocket and a large diamond pin set in gold glistened in his shirt frill. He exhuded an air of quiet, discreet wealth, wearing nothing ostentatious or showy but the cut of his suit was excellent and the material was of the best. The other was just as faultless in his dress but if one looked closely it was possible to detect an ever so slight fraying, carefully mended, at the cuffs of his jacket and though the quality of the fabric was every bit as good as that of his companion it had been well-worn.

They each held a glass of brandy from which they sipped appreciatively.

'That was an excellent dinner your sister-in-law provided, my dear fellow,' the first remarked amiably.

'Yes, she is a fine hostess but I must admit it is a great help when one has a French chef as she has. She tells me he is a despot in the kitchen and even insists upon his own sitting room if you please but then one must pay for the advantage of his genius I suppose.'

'Quite so. My own cook is competent but I doubt she

could turn out the sauce which accompanied the trout. I could not identify the ingredients but by God I enjoyed it. Superb, really superb!'

'I'm so glad, old chap. My sister-in-law will be most gratified when I tell her.'

'I have already done so and I have also prised out of her where it was she found him.'

'Capital, capital! You will be the envy of Yorkshire!'

'I hope so and may I say I also hope you will be my guest if you can spare the time from that estate of yours. We have some decent shooting which I'm sure you and that splendid boy of yours would enjoy.'

'That is most kind of you, sir, and on his behalf as well as my own I shall be only too pleased to accept.'

There was another pleasant silence as the two gentlemen continued to gaze into the fire, drawing pleasurably on their cigars and sipping their brandy. A gold French clock set with mother-of-pearl ticked on the mantelshelf and a large retriever which lay on the fireside rug sighed in his sleep.

'That was a splendid hunt today, do you not agree?'

'Indeed and your son did well to be the first to reach the kill.'

'Thank you. He is a fair horseman.'

'Come now, sir, you are too modest. He is a fine sportsman, a gentleman and a son of which any man would be proud.'

'You are very kind.'

'I am not being kind, old chap. He is a splendid young man and I merely speak the truth.'

The second gentleman put a hand to the snowy frill of his shirt and smoothed the fabric with a gratified hand. On his face had slipped an expression of alert vigilance as though the first man had revealed something in his words which he had himself only just recognized and he leaned forward an inch or two. His other hand gripped the glass in which the amber glow of the brandy was picked out by the fire's gleam and in his own eyes a prick of light shone.

The silence had become laced with a sliver of tension but both men pretended to be unaware of it and continued to lounge carelessly, at ease with their world and with one another.

But something was in the air and both waited, one for the right moment to bring it forth and the second for the first to do so.

At last he spoke again.

'Where are the youngsters?' he asked carelessly.

'I believe your daughter is playing the piano which, if I may say so, she does beautifully, and my son is turning the pages for her. The company was enthralled as I passed through the drawing room, they made such a pleasing picture – she is a lovely girl – and the music was delightful. Unfortunately I am tone deaf so I can rely only on what others tell me but from the expressions of those listening they were very impressed.'

'Yes.' It was said absently. 'Adele is a fine musician.'

'Indeed she is!'

There was a longish pause and the hushed, almost taut silence stretched on and in it could be heard the faint tinkle of a piano. Again the first man broke it.

'Your son is . . . travelling home with you tomorrow?' It was a statement rather than a question.

'No!'

'But I understood him to say he must get home immediately. The news you brought . . .'

'I . . . shall dissuade him.'

'You are not in favour of . . .'

'No!'

The first man touched the upward curl of his moustache with a steady hand and his eyes looked directly into those of his companion.

'Then I will be direct with you, old chap. In fact I will be blunt. Not to beat about the bush . . .'

'Yes?'

'My girl is . . . very taken with that boy of yours. Indeed she speaks of no one else and her mother and I are quite

142

concerned about her. She has been . . . indulged, I will be honest with you and . . . being an only child – the only one left, that is and no prospect of another, if you understand my meaning – I have been able to deny her nothing.'

His face became fatuous with his fondness for his Adele and he drew on his cigar with the air of a man who owns the most precious jewel from the Orient. His eyes glowed softly and the other man moved impatiently.

'So you see,' the first continued hastily, 'I have been quite at my wit's end as to what to do.'

'How very trying for you. I know how difficult it can be to know what is best for one's child. I have been in the same dilemma myself over my son's future and I freely admit I am . . . I was not at all happy about it.'

'I had heard a rumour that he was to marry a . . .' The man's mouth lifted in an expression of slight distaste and he turned away courteously as though to avoid his companion's obvious and surely justifiable embarrassment.

'Yes, that is so, but I can assure you that if I could find some . . . other course more suitable I would steer him towards it as speedily as possible.'

'He would agree?'

'I would see that he did!'

'My girl will be . . . I hesitate to speak of such things just now but it seems to me it should be said . . . she will be . . . well off. There would be no difficulty there. I have no family, I was an only child and there is money to come from my wife's side. Her father was Sir William Dickinson, you know.'

'Of course. A fine background!'

'Like your own, sir!'

'Thank you.'

'Then we understand one another?'

'We do.'

'Then I shall say no more for the present.'

'My dear chap, I could not be more pleased.'

'Shall we shake hands?'

'Nothing would delight me more.'

143

'There will be no difficulty with the ... the young woman's family?'

'Oh, none at all. They are going through some crisis at this moment and the ... fixing of their daughter's future is the furthest thing from their minds. They will not care unduly. She is a pleasant child and will easily be found another. Think no more of it!'

They exchanged shrewd glances, two gentlemen who had just struck a bargain in the only way a gentleman can. With words which their honour and that of their family would not allow them to break and with a handshake which was all a gentleman needed, surely?

'Splendid, splendid!' They rose to their feet smilingly. 'Now shall we go through and be entertained by my daughter ... and your son!'

The young man, the pale feathers of his curling hair falling about his handsome brow stood up indignantly and began to pace about the elegant drawing room, the tension in him crackling like a living thing as he turned jerkily to face the man who had just spoken to him.

'But surely sir, you cannot mean me to stay away now just when I am most needed. I appreciate the distress ... the grief the family must be suffering but it is my place to be with ...'

'Not necessarily, dear boy. At times like this it is often kinder to leave those who mourn to themselves for a while. Pay one's respects, of course, as is only decent, but no more. A family suffering a loss such as they have known, sharing it, knowing it, as someone who is not a member of the family cannot know it, perhaps would sooner be left alone to ... accept, without an outsider, however well meaning ...'

'But father, I cannot consider myself an outsider. I am to be a part of that family, as Christy will be part of ours.' The young man did not notice the wince of the older. 'Christy and I are to be married. We care about one another more than . . . I feel I could be of some comfort to her at a time like this. Ease her pain. There is nothing else I can do but be there if she should need me and that is what I intend doing. Mr and Mrs Emmerson have one another to take solace from but Christy loved her brothers and will be alone . . .'

'Her mother and father will give her all she needs, Robin. Take my word for it, and take the advice of someone who is older, wiser and, I may say, someone who has experienced what the Emmersons are suffering. Ah yes, you remember I had a brother, your Uncle Roger. He was lost to us fighting Napoleon in the French wars. My mother and father, your grandparents, were quite devastated, as I was myself and though I too was to marry, just as you, I did not want, for a short while, even the company of your dear Mama.'

The young man began to look uncertain. He sank down into a deep, comfortable sofa and leaned back, staring in surprise at his father. His face was drawn and troubled but his eyes were still wary as though he was not at all convinced.

William Matthew Forsythe, Squire of Dalebarrow Hall in Furness and his only son, Robin George Forsythe, were very much alike to look at. Their features were finely chiselled, their bodies delicately balanced on long, well-formed legs. They wore the look of the well-bred of generations, with the accents of privilege when they spoke, and they had the complex charm which thrives in the families of those who are born to govern. Both were tall, fair and slender with an authoritative air of breeding and command, an unconcious swagger of arrogance which spoke of generations of influence, superiority and advantage. It had allowed their forebears to rise above others, giving them perhaps the judgement to always be on the winning side. To choose the way which would lead to benison and favour without relinquishing their right to call themselves gentlemen. It was this which had granted William Forsythe the strength to accept the inevitability of the marriage of his son, his heir, to the daughter of a man of commerce, though it had soured his gentleman's soul to do it.

But he had never given up hope that something better, something more palatable to his well-bred taste but just as wealthy, for that was essential, would come his way, and through him to his son. Robin was a fine fellow. A gentleman in the true sense of the word, he supposed, for he took no account of the financial necessity in marriage. It was considered quite normal, even vital for a young man to marry where money was, but he should always, whenever possible keep within the strict confines of his class.

Squire Forsythe was well aware that his son imagined himself to be in love with Emmerson's girl and would be hard to deflect from his purpose. But then Robin was not a 'clever' man and he, William Forsythe, was and his hope which had almost foundered as the wedding day drew nearer had not let him down.

He sat up in his chair and reached into his pocket for a cigar. He was well aware that his sister-in-law, the wife of his own wife's brother, did not care for cigar smoke in her drawing room but he was a man who gave little thought to the needs or dislikes of others. He lit it and puffed smoke vigorously into the refined air about him.

'I came as soon as I had attended the funeral. There is to be an inquiry, of course, to determine the cause of the explosion and as magistrate I must return for that but you may as well stay on for the Melton Hunt. Your wedding will naturally be postponed for a while. The period of mourning . . .'

'I realize that sir, but really, to talk of staying on for the Melton is out of the question. How would it look . . . oh no . . . I really must insist on returning to Fellthwaite with you.'

Robin stood up as though he would be off immediately but his father put out a restraining hand and, accustomed to instant obedience to his elders, taught him at the Hall and the public school he had attended, he sat down.

'Please my boy, let me finish. I spoke with Mr Emmerson, or rather I attempted to but he is a broken man, Robin. I was forced to discuss the matter with Mrs Emmerson.'

A look, almost of distaste crossed his face as though he had been pressed to communicate with one of his own milk-maids on the home farm.

'She is of the opinion that ... things ... should be temporarily held in abeyance. Only until Emmerson is himself again, you understand, and their period of mourning is over. That would have to be recognized in any case, even should Emmerson recover his ...' He had been about to say 'wits' for really, the man had appeared senseless at the funeral but he changed it crisply to 'health'. 'So you see, my boy, nothing can be done until then.'

'I understand what you are saying, sir,' Robin interrupted and the Squire felt a small twinge of annoyance. Really, the boy was being most stubborn, 'But I must, absolutely *must* go to Christina! We are ... she is very special to me and I know I can bring her ...'

'I understood her mother to say they were going away for a while.'

'Going away? To where?'

'I really didn't like to question the wom ... Mrs Emmerson in her distress,' he lied, 'but I believe they have relatives in ...'

'But what is to become of the mill if Mr Emmerson is to go away?'

'Really Robin! I hardly think that is any concern of ours.'

'It is if I am to marry Christina Emmerson, sir.' Robin Forsythe's voice had become hard and his eyes looked at his father with what appeared to be scorn, as though he knew full well why he had been allowed to choose this particular bride.

William Forsythe realized he had made a slip but he elected not to know what his son meant.

'I believe . . . yes, it was rumoured a fellow manufacturer is to help out.'

There was silence then and the Squire puffed unconcernedly on his cigar waiting for his son's next thrust which he knew he would be well able to parry. When none came he removed his cigar from between his lips.

'I am to return to Fellthwaite this afternoon, my boy, but you might as well stay here for another week or two. It will take your mind from your distress and as Christina and her family will not be at Hollin House until they feel more able to cope with their . . . loss, there is simply no reason for you to accompany me. Your mother is, naturally, upset by the whole dreadful event and I would be immeasurably relieved if you would stay her with her until I return. Why do you not write a letter to Christina and when I get back to Fellthwaite I will make enquiries at the mill where she may be reached and forward it on to her. Tell her how you feel and that you have her in your thoughts. Suggest to her that you are waiting only for her call and you will be immediately by her side. Give her time to heal the wounds of her grief, Robin. Perhaps a month or two and then the moment she feels more herself she has only to write and you can go to her. The wedding can be postponed until the summer, or perhaps autumn for decency's sake, but I really do feel, my boy, that it would be kinder to allow the family their privacy at a time such as this. Mrs Emmerson said . . .'

'Yes?' Robin leaned forward eagerly.

'. . . and I agree with her that only time will help the poor child and you must be prepared to make the sacrifice and give it to her. Will you do that, my boy, for the sake of the girl you love?'

Robin rested his elbows on his knees, his hands hanging down between them and slowly his head sank until his chin was almost on his chest. He felt close to tears in his compassion for Christy but did not want his father to see them. He was aware of the gulf which separated this man whose son he was from himself. The difference in their character was enormous and had always been evident from his being a small boy. His own heart had always been easily moved by suffering, or gladdened by merriment but he had tried to live up to the responsibilities put upon him as the son of the Squire. He had loved Christy Emmerson almost from the first moment he saw her, but he knew he was to marry her only because of her wealth and he thanked God for it, if for no other reason than it had put her within his grasp.

His heart, his every loving instinct told him he should call for the carriage, pack his bag and gallop away up north to help her through her anguish. He longed to feel her against him. To hold her in his arms and guard her from the pain and desolation, share it with her, that which must surely grip her; and yet his father said her own mother had advised him to stay away. 'Give her time,' she had said. 'Leave her for a while,' he could imagine the down-to-earth, commonsense woman who was to be his mother-in-law saying and he knew he must do as she bid him. His father appeared to agree with Annie Emmerson and Robin had no cause to distrust him or either of them.

He stood up painfully.

'I'll go and write the letter at once,' he said.

'Good boy. I'm sure you are doing the best thing for that lovely girl. Now off you go and when you have done, come and have luncheon with me before I leave. Oh, and your Aunt and Uncle tell me they have invited the Kenwoods to dine this evening, you remember them? So with Sir Francis and Lady Mainwood and that charming daughter of theirs . . . what is her name again . . . ah yes, Adele, you should be quite a pleasant dinner party this evening. Your cousins are to put on a charade after dinner.'

'Why does he not come, mother?' The words were spoken dully, hopelessly as though they had been uttered many times before and the answer had always been the same.

'Lass, I wish I knew.'

'It's been a month and still he does not come.'

'I know, I know. There must be some good reason.'

'What, mother? Tell me what reason a man can have that will keep him from the woman he loves when she needs him?' Her voice cracked on the last word and Annie Emmerson felt her heart move in her breast in pity.

'Christy, girl, don't . . . don't hurt yourself like this. Be patient. Men are . . . they are not as . . .'

Annie Emmerson looked sadly at the back of her daughter as she stared sightlessly from the window, and through the torment, angry and bitter, which raged relentlessly in her own heart, she felt the girl's agony. Annie had lost her sons, the handsome, vigorous boys who had been all that were left of the eight she had borne. Though she was not a demonstrative woman she had loved them deeply, choosing to show her devotion in the way in which she prepared the meals they liked best; in the manner in which she turned them out each day dressed in good, serviceable, immaculately pressed shirts and coats; the high shine on their boots, warm, clean, well-shod, the finished product of the loving care and attention she lavished on them. They were healthy young animals, full of energy and high spirits, the pride of her ageing body, the joy of her heart and they had been hideously torn from her and their splendid futures taken from them in the prime of their youth and Annie's anger was ferocious! It kept her strong. It kept her on her feet. It kept her sane enough to deal with the broken man who was her husband and enabled her to hold together the frayed strings of her household. She was dignified in her grief, greeting those who came to pay their respects with the grave face of decency, apologizing for the absence of her husband who was 'indisposed', when Fellthwaite knew Job Emmerson had gone to pieces, shattered and made into an old man by the loss of his lads. He did nought but sit and stare down the hill at the works, uncaring of who was putting the mill together again, or that anybody was! Even the sight of the blue vapour flying for the first time since the explosion and signifying the start of the running of the mill awoke no emotion in him.

But Christy had lost not only her two brothers, the strength and protection of her father but, it seemed, the man she was to marry as well! There was no possibility that he did not know of the explosion. It had been reported not only in the Westmorland Gazette but as far away as Manchester and even, Annie had been told by an acquaintance, in London. Nine dead, amongst them Christy's own brothers, and more than a score injured and still he had not come, nor even sent a note of condolence.

The Squire had attended the funeral and for an instant Christy's dead face had come to life and her eyes had searched beyond the man's shoulder for his son but when they did not find him, they grew cold, like the pale grey ice which coated the frozen ground into which Job's lads, and hopes, were lowered.

It was the first week in April now and the young early lambs were bleating in the 'in-land', the small, rich enclosures around the farm buildings. The wild daffodils around the house were nodding joyously in the bright sunshine which had brought out the green leaf-buds on the trees. On the low-lying, fertile land besides the mere, marsh marigolds and primroses starred the new greening grass and up on the fell the golden gorse and bracken met the blue of the sky in glorious confusion. Wall butterflies hovered in a drift of cloudy bronze and cream, settling to dry their wings in the fragile warmth of the sun and a chiff-chaff pecked vigorously at something on a branch but Christy Emmerson saw none of it.

'I must know what has kept him, mother. He might be ill – an accident. Those animals they use in the hunt can be ... He might have been thrown ... unconscious perhaps and that is why he has not written. Perhaps he is dreadfully injured ...'

As she spoke the last word Christy's face spasmed in pain for it brought back such memories, scarce to be dwelled upon and surely to God there could not be two such crushing blows within the space of a month. The loss of her brothers, her father's complete collapse, the dreadful paralysed grief of Celia Metcalf, her mother's silent, agonized sorrow: she had taken them all, though only God knew how she had done it, but she was not ashamed to admit to herself that it all meant less than nothing to her beside the desolation of Robin Forsythe's desertion when her whole aching anguished heart and body needed him most.

The community had been aghast, shaken to the core of its kindly soul by the tragedy suffered – not only by the Emmerson family but by those of the other men who had been killed and injured in the explosion – and had been swift to rally round, coming at once to offer whatever was needed.

Many of the women had made the 'arvel' bread to be served to the mourners, to save the bother for Annie and the other widows, they said, and a constant sucession of men had sat throughout the days and nights before the funeral beside the bodies of Job's lads as was the custom. They had followed the coffins from the house to the church along the 'corpse-way' for the detour from it would have been regarded as an ill-omen and the bells, the 'passing-bells' had tolled nine times for each man who had died, eighty-one times in all.

And from all this Robin Forsythe had stayed away.

'I shall go to the Hall, mother.'

'Nay lass, you mustn't. You're in mourning and it wouldn't be proper.'

'Do you think I care about that? Do you think I give a damn about the proprieties when Robin might be lying dangerously ill . . . dying . . . for only that would have kept him from me.'

'But surely . . . if there was anything wrong the Squire would have sent word. He said nothing at the funeral and neither did you. Why did you not speak up then?'

'I don't know. There was still . . . hope, I suppose that . . .'

'And is there some now?'

'No!'

'Then there's no use to it, lass.'

'You're right, but still I must go. I must speak to someone, even if it is only to hear he ... he ... no longer ...'

'I can't stop you, girl.'

'No.'

She rode in her black in her father's carriage, no longer compelled to ask his permission for if she had asked to go to London to dance at the Queen's ball her father would merely have nodded his head saying vaguely, 'Aye lass, just as you like.'

Faith went with her, her mourning dress as severe as that of her young mistress for even the servant was expected to show decent respect for the appropriate period.

Mrs Forsythe received her in an unusual state of confusion, ringing for tea though it was not yet five o'clock, the appointed time for it. Fifteen minutes of conversation was all that 'polite' society allowed during the morning and afternoon calls which involved carriage visits from one local hostess to another, but it was very evident from Christy Emmerson's drawn face that this was not one of those. She should not, strictly speaking, have been here at all, not whilst she was in mourning. Mrs Forsythe had only this week returned from Leicestershire and was not yet receiving callers and to be perfectly correct in her society a lady should ask her own manservant to enquire if the lady of the house was 'at home', leaving her card if she was not.

Christina Emmerson had done none of these things and whilst she seated herself in Mrs Forsythe's elegantly shabby drawing room her hostess had a quiet word with her butler as to the whereabouts of the master.

'My dear, I have no need to tell you how ... how sorry

we all were to hear of your dreadful loss. Such fine young men and with their whole lives before them. Your mother must be prostrated with grief, and your father, for I know what store he put in his sons. As we all do.' Her face flushed with some inner anxiety and she went on hurriedly before Christy had time to speak. 'And that fine young woman ... what was her name ... oh yes ... Celia Metcalf ... how is she bearing up under the loss of her betrothed?' Again she appeared to be ill at ease and she bit her lip, '... I had meant to call, naturally, as soon as I felt your mother was ready to receive me but one does not like to intrude on occasions such as this. Tell her, will you not, that she has only to send word and if there is anything I can do ...'

Mrs Forsythe was kind but curiously uneasy.

'Thank you, you are ... but I have come to ... this is not a formal call ... I am not yet out of ... but I was worried and felt ... I had to ask ...?'

'Yes, my dear?' The Squire's lady knew exactly what this lovely tragic girl had come to ask but it was not her place to provide her with an answer. Her eyes wandered anxiously to the closed door but there was no help there and she turned her compassionate gaze back to her visitor.

'I have ... it has been more than a month and I have not heard ... from Robin.' Christy's breath was ragged in her chest and her heart beat painfully in great erratic thumps for it knew so well from Mrs Forsythe's manner, from the way in which she had been received – a casual caller who had come at an inconvenient time and certainly not as the intended bride of the son of the house – that there was something wrong. 'I came to see ... please ... please ma'am ... is he well? I had thought perhaps an accident but then you would have sent word ... surely? I cannot believe that he would not have come unless something, a fall perhaps ... had forced him ...'

The Squire's lady stood up abruptly for she could no longer bear the girl's pain. In her reticule was a note, the fourth or was it the fifth her patient son had written, and his face, as he had pressed it into her hand, had caused her to weep when she was safely in her carriage. On it had been the confusion of youth and the determination of a gentleman to do the right thing, but warring with those expressions had been his utter devotion to this girl and his anguished longing to be with her. Like her husband Rosemary Forsythe had hoped for some wealthy, well-connected young lady for her only son. A healthy, docile young thing who would bring them not only the financial dower so badly needed to inject into the ailing estate – needed if Robin was to keep up his gentleman's role in the community – but the good blood to run in the veins of the dozen spendid children she would provide. A patrician name to be linked with theirs, a pedigree worthy of theirs to carry on the unbroken line of rank which had remained for three hundred years.

And yet she had become fond of Christy Emmerson, the vital and lovely daughter of the millowner, who had caught her son's attention and heart. She had thought she would do very well for Robin for though she was no grand lady she had been well brought up, was mannered and would fit easily into the role of the wife of a landed gentleman. She was not overawed by those who would try to condescend to her with their superiority and had been accepted, somewhat grudgingly, by her own high-ranking relatives for she herself was the great-niece of an Earl. They had been surprised, they had admitted to her, by her son's choice of bride and his father's acceptance of it, but she was not bad, not bad at all, they said. Exceedingly pretty and charmingly mannered and with all that money behind her . . .

The Squire, slightly out of breath as though he had been running, came into the room on a flow of apologies and regrets, his eyes questioningly, warningly on those of his wife and thankfully she let out her breath on a sigh and sat down again.

'My dear Miss Emmerson . . . Christina . . . this is a delightful surprise. How pleasant to see you after all these weeks. I was saying to Mrs Forsythe only the other day that it must be . . . but forgive me, how rude I am not to speak to you of your sad loss. How can we express the depth of our feelings for what you and your family, indeed all the families of the men who died in the accident, have suffered.' In a few words he put Christy and her dead brothers in the same category as the labourers who had died with them. 'And how is your Mama bearing up in the face of your quite dreadful loss? And Mr Emmerson? To lose – well, I must not dwell on it for I am sure you do not wish to be reminded. It is in the past now and I know you will want to forget . . . not your dear brothers . . . but what is gone, and look forward to the future. It does not do to hanker after what can never be brought back, don't you agree? I will have a cup of tea, my dear, if you please,' he said to his wife without looking at her, smiling all the while at Christy as though she was some acquaintance to whom one should extend the politeness afforded a guest in one's own home.

'I had heard you were to go to relatives, my dear,' he continued kindly, leaning back in his chair, sipping his tea as if he was well-used to joining the ladies who called on his wife. 'The very best thing, I always think, after one has suffered a set-back, is to get right away from it. Have a change of scenery. I do hope it has done you all some good. Did you go far?' he asked politely.

'No . . . that is . . . we did not . . .' Christy felt as though she was frozen to her chair, every part of her set in a mould of ice, even her pale lips which refused to form the words she wanted to say, to speak the name which was on the tip of her clumsy tongue.

'Aah, I must have been misinformed,' he said casually and waited.

'We have no relatives other than those who live here-abouts. My mother and father were both born in Furness so there is no-one.' Her voice trailed away, and she blinked her grey eyes as though a curtain had fallen across them, misted and frightening, blinding her to what she must see.

What she had come to discover, for on it her life, her future depended.

'Of course.' The Squire smiled courteously, recognizing with his cool eyes her humble origins, the line from which she had descended, the colliers and farmers and shepherds from whom her family came and who had lived in the same valley for as many years as had his own. Perhaps it was this, his thoroughbred self-confidence in his own power to keep her in her place – in the station in life to which God had put her, as he had put the Squire in his – that untangled her thoughts and loosened her tongue and with a proud lift of her head, a gesture which said that in no way was she here to beg, she said coolly, almost as though it was of little consequence.

'I have come to enquire after Robin.'

'Robin. Why, he is well, is he not, my dear?' The Squire looked at his wife and his face was expressionless. 'We had a note from him the other day, just a note that is all. You know how young men are about writing, do you not? Have you not heard from him yourself?'

Christy indicated with a shake of her head that she had not for she was incapable of forming a coherent answer and he smiled indulgently.

'Well, do not blame him for his thoughtlessness, my dear. I am told none of his friends have heard from him so do not feel slighted. He is very young, you know, and time slips by so quickly when one is below twenty. I know for I was once that age myself and can remember my own lack of thought. Not a moment for anyone but oneself, but he will grow out of it. He is enjoying the hunting season enormously, he says, with his cousins in Leicestershire . . .'

Christy made a small, agonized sound in the back of her throat and Mrs Forsythe lifted a hand for some reason. The Squire took it in his most affectionately and turned again to his guest.

'He has seen a hunter which he seems intent on buying and wanted to ask our permission, did he not, my dear, but I said we must wait and see.'

He smiled at Christy, putting his cup and saucer on the small table at his side. The gesture seemed to signify that the fifteen minutes for her 'call' were almost at an end.

'Did he mention . . . did he say when he would return?' The effort it cost her to say the words put a fine sheen of perspiration down the length of her back and on the palms of her hands, but her voice was steady and Mrs Forsythe's heart almost broke, for this girl was the bravest she had ever known.

'I don't believe he did but I dare say he will come home when he runs out of money. I am to see him next week on my way to London. May I give him a message from you? Or perhaps a note. If you would care to sit down at my wife's writing desk and scribble one out I could deliver it for you.'

The signed contract, drawn up legally by a solicitor in Fellthwaite, between Job Emmerson and William Forsythe on the matter of their children's intention to marry and the exact sums of money involved in the transaction might have never existed, and safe in the knowledge that the man who might have kept him to his bargain was lost in another world of sorrow, and that the girl whom it concerned was too proud to remind him of it, Squire Forsythe smiled peaceably. He was a man who could read character and this girl was not one to lower her head in humility and run weeping to her father to force a match which she believed his son no longer wanted.

'I don't believe so, Mr Forsythe.' She stood up and shook out the full skirts of her black mourning gown. 'I merely wished to know that he was not . . . unwell.'

The Squire too had sprung to his feet, a gentleman in the presence of a lady. She certainly knew how to conduct herself, he considered silently to himself. He gave her full marks for self control and almost had it in his mind to wish that she had been more . . . suitable . . . but it would not do, now that Mainwood was looking so favourably at the Squireen of Dalebarrow Hall. But this one had backbone, he'd give her that, and poise too as she made her farewells, her manner charming, to his wife and himself.

'Give my condolences to your mother and father, my dear,' he said as he helped her into her carriage.

'I will, sir, and thank you.'

He saw her hand clutch that of her maid, who had been collected from the seat in the cold hall where she had waited for her mistress, and the girl winced as she turned, alarmed, to Christina Emmerson; then the coachman urged on the horses and as the carriage drove away from his grand front door he was amazed when his own wife burst into tears.

CHAPTER TEN

Six weeks after the death of his two sons Job Emmerson got up one day and turning to his wife said in the manner of one who has been kept forcibly from it, 'I can't sit about here all day, wife. I'll be off to the mill if I've a clean shirt to put on. See to it, will you?'

They watched him go, his wife and daughter, half the man he once was, shrunken, slower and looking lonely without his two strapping lads beside him and Annie cried for the first time since the day of the accident. Then she had wept in pain, despair and loss, now she cried in relief.

'He'll be alright now, lass. He's over the worst, thank God. It's been a long time coming for I thought those mills would have drawn him down there sooner, healed him like, but still, better late than never. Aye, he'll be alright now!'

But would her daughter, she thought, as she watched her follow her father an hour later, not to the mill, but down the gravel drive towards the road and when she got there she stood with Faith who went everywhere with her.

159

She turned her head this way and that as though she neither knew nor cared in which direction she went.

Her grieving was a terrible thing to see and Annie knew it was not for her brothers she mourned. Fellthwaite was quite astonished by it. Though it was known they had been a close-knit affectionate family, not given to demonstrations of it, mind, but fond nevertheless, it was somehow not quite seemly to grieve so over a brother. Perhaps two brothers doubled the sorrow for the girl was like a wraith, thin as a stick and so withdrawn it was difficult to get two words sensibly strung together out of her. She stood, or sat beside her mother, in church or in her mother's refurbished drawing room when close friends or relatives came to call. When asked about her wedding, which seemed a natural enough question and one likely to take her mind from the death of her brothers, she merely said in a voice which was curiously toneless that she was still in mourning which everyone was well aware of.

She strode the hills with her maid and could be seen sometimes high on the fells above the 'intakes' roaming the heights with the hardy Herdwick sheep. She had taken to running her father's trail hounds with her for he had lost interest in the sport. Her whistle, taught her by her brothers when she was a lass, as she called them in, often disturbed the dogs who worked the sheep.

She had been spotted as far away as Greatrigg Man, sitting in the mouth of the stone cave, the origins of which no one knew though it could have been the workings of an old mine. The shepherd who had seen her said she stared right through him though her maid nodded agreeably enough.

Aye, she was strange alright, Job Emmerson's lass, and it was high time she and the Squire's lad were wed even if the period of mourning was not yet up. A couple of children would see her right and take her mind from morbid thoughts.

Alex Buchanan rode over a week later to see her husband, he told Annie Emmerson courteously, on a personal matter, if he could spare him a moment. He was shown into Job's study where he remained for ten minutes before Job flung open the door and shouted for Annie.

'He wants our Christy,' Job said to his wife when she was seated and for a moment Annie stared, open-mouthed, then over her face came an expression of gladness and she put her hands together and looked to the ceiling and said with a fervency which caused Job to stare in bewilderment, 'Thank you, Lord, thank you!'

'Annie.' Job was fretful. He had hardly come to terms with his own return from the black hole of despair into which the death of both his sons had flung him and though he was getting the feel of running his own business concern again – thanks to this man who had kept it going for him, with the help of his bright young engineer – Job was not the man, nor ever would be, that once he had been and he knew it. He didn't *care* any more, you see, and it frightened him. He went down to the mill, for something must be done with his day, with his life and the business was as good as any to pass the time on. He supposed in a way that was a sign of recovery, to think in such terms, but it did not unduly worry him whether he made a profit or loss any more and he was dismayed by the realization. He knew the dreadful weakness in him and he was afraid. He had clung like a boy lost to his wife's strong hand, feeling safer with her in sight, for six whole weeks, but he had known the time must come when he should go back to . . . to the mill which had killed his lads. It had been his joy, that mill and his pride in it, in himself and his sons had made him a giant, strong and invincible – but they were gone now, the reason for his triumph and only his girl was left and how was *she* to carry on what he had built for *them*? Now, here was Buchanan again, asking for her in marriage when he knew she was promised to the Squire's lad and what was he to do? Buchanan had been told once so what was he doing back here a-begging again?

'It's alright, Job, it's alright!' Annie patted his hand in a way she would not have dared to do a few weeks ago.

161

'What is, for God's sake?'

'You must allow it, husband. It's right for our Christy.'

'Have you gone daft, woman? She's to wed the young Squireen as soon as the . . . the mourning is over.'

'No, she is not, Job.' Annie's voice was quiet.

Alex Buchanan sat across from them, the cheerful little fire spluttering at his feet, the terriers sprawled in a heap of fragile legs and soft eyes about the chair of their master just as they had done over six months ago, and this time he knew he would get her. He had been to see the Squire, demanding to know young Robin Forsythe's intentions as though *he* were Christy Emmerson's kin, with the perfect right to do so, for somebody should. The boy had not been seen since Christmas which, though Fellthwaite had not yet begun to surmise on, Alex Buchanan had.

The Squire had been haughty as only he knew how, asking coldly what the devil it was to do with him, for though Alex Buchanan was a wealthy, respected man he was only two generations from the working class and was certainly not in a position to address himself to his betters as though he was their equal. He might have the influence which came, unfortunately, with hard cash, but what the Squire and his family did, or did not do, was none of his damn business and he told the man so.

But the girl, Mainwood's girl, was not yet in the bag. She wanted to be, oh yes, she wanted to be but Robin was still proving stubborn, determined, he said to go soon to his Christy whether she was ready or not for in six weeks she had surely recovered enough to see *him*. He had given her the time asked for by her mother and though she had not answered the letter forwarded by his father, nor those sent by messenger and his mother, he must go to her, he said.

But when Buchanan told him bluntly his reason for asking, trusting, he said, to the Squire's word as a gentleman to keep it to himself, he had been only too happy to oblige. The sooner Christy Emmerson was wed, the sooner Robin would accept the Mainwood girl!

162

Alex watched Annie and Job Emmerson, and wondered where she was, Job's daughter. Did she sit alone by her mother's drawing room fire indifferent to Annie's sudden departure, not wondering, as young people do, what all the fuss was about, her eyes, soft as grey velvet, looking at nothing? He had seen her above his own house, her maid in tow, the dogs at her heels, walking smoothly as though she was off somewhere, but her eyes had been empty and her direction uncertain and he knew she existed in a world apart from his. She did not see him for her eyes looked into the sky above his head, or through him, searching ever inwards to some pain she bore.

'What are you talking about, woman?' Job was blustering in faint echo of the man he once was. 'In August perhaps . . .?'

'No Job, not in August. Not ever!'

'But they are bespoken . . .'

'He no longer wants her!'

'Wha . . . what are you . . .?'

'He has not come back from Leicestershire, Job. In all this time, this bad time, when she needed him he did not come to her. She went to see the Squire . . .'

'The Squire? When? When was this I'd like to know? A daughter of mine . . .?'

'He had not come. A man would surely come to a woman he loved, wouldn't he, Job? If he loved her he would come to her when she was . . . was in pain.'

'I don't know what the devil . . .'

'Job . . . Job . . . when I was grieving . . . when Ben and Toby . . . you and I, privately, we helped one another . . . comforted . . .'

Alex Buchanan felt he should get up and quietly leave this intimate moment between man and wife for he was intruding. He was immensely moved by the quiet dignity, the deep, voiceless love this woman bore for this man but something kept him fast to his chair.

Job's face had softened and his eyes looked into his wife's in understanding.

163

'Aye lass,' he said and patted her hand.

'So you see . . . she had . . . well, he was not here when she needed him. He had not come. The Squire told her he is . . . concerned with the Hunt and a hunter he was to purchase just as though our girl meant nothing! She cannot forgive it, nor, I fear, forget!'

She looked apologetically at Alex, but she would tell the truth for that was her way.

'She frets for him, Mr Buchanan. I cannot promise she will ever get over it. She's not the same girl . . .'

'I know, I have seen her,' he answered simply, 'but still I wish to marry her. She will be . . . safe with me.'

'Aye, I know that, lad, that's why I thanked the Lord!'

'Marry!' Christy Emmerson spat out the word as though murder had been suggested.

'You must some time, my lass.' Her mother's voice was patient.

'Dear God, mother, it is but seven weeks since . . .!' Her anguish lifted and pierced the air above their heads, breaking the peaceful stillness of the spring afternoon and though her mother winced she held her peace for indeed it seemed indecent to speak of it when the soil on the graves had barely settled. But she knew that Christy had meant not the deaths of her brothers but the living death of her own heart which had been shattered. Christy's face worked jerkily as she strove to compose herself but Annie remained still and silent.

They sat in a sheltered corner of the garden in the wicker chairs Ned had set out for them and the sun was pleasantly warm, though the two women still wore their shawls of deep black cashmere. Annie, who could not abide to do nothing, and unable to force her fingers to the fine embroidery which was all a lady was allowed when callers might come, was quilting a bedspread, putting in the almost invisible stitches she herself had been taught. In her young days she had made all her own household linen and

164

though there was no longer any need she could not rid herself of the habit.

'I know how long it is, child, and your father and I are aware that there will be talk, not only at the suddenness of it for we are still in mourning but it was well known before . . . before the explosion that you were expected to marry the Squire's . . .'

'Don't . . . oh sweet Jesus . . . don't . . .'

'I'm sorry, lass. You know I don't want to remind you, but, well, someone has asked for you.'

'Already!' Christy laughed harshly. 'But of course, I am a prize now, am I not? Job Emmerson's daughter who will have his mills when he goes now that his sons are dead! I should have expected it, I suppose. It's a wonder we have not been overrun with gentlemen who have suddenly become aware of how they do love me. It must be common knowledge that the Squire's son has jilted me so here I am, available again and so much more of a catch. A dowry is one thing, but the whole lot, well, that is a horse of another colour, is it not, mother? I am surprised that the Dyers and the Aspins have not trotted up their doltish sons to be inspected, or is it one of them who has put in the bid? Father would be pleased to have his finger in Aspin's pie, would he not and then . . .'

'Christina!'

Annie's voice cut like a knife through the tormented voice of her daughter. 'You will not speak of your father like that. Has he not suffered enough? You'll do well to remember his heart was nearly broke by his boys' death. He feels, I think, that he could have done something to prevent it, some safety measure he overlooked.'

Her voice became vague, indistinct, as her thoughts rose to her tongue, '. . . and yet all the men had acknowledged the rules he had put up. There were no matches or tobacco or snuff found on any of them and they were all wearing leather and nail-less slippers so . . . it really is . . . They do say that Dunlow had been seen to scrape the bungs on the cylinders in the glazing house and had been told about it but we shall never know . . . not now. Your father says there should have been more space between the buildings, but there is the enquiry to be got through as to how it happened and why. Until he knows he will continue to think it was his doing. He blames himself, you see . . .'

She dropped her needlework into her lap and stared down the hill to the mills which had killed her sons. Already the four which had been destroyed were almost shoulder-high as they were being rebuilt and men moved briskly about the site, shifting timber and bricks, sawing, hammering, laying bricks, mixing mortar, whistling even for it was a fine day and they were alive. It was as busy a scene as it had always been. Her boys were gone but life moved on without them and Christy must be made to see that life went on without Robin Forsythe. Alex Buchanan was exactly the man Annie would have picked for her daughter, even before Robin Forsythe had spoken for her, for he was a *man*, a vigorous, forceful man to keep their Christy well-guarded and safe, especially now. Christy was a girl who needed firmness, a strong hand to guide her, but with care. Robin Forsythe, though a gentleman and mad with love for her, was sweet-natured and kind but a lightweight, a boy who even when he matured would allow Christina to push him wherever she wished him to go, as his father did Annie was shrewdly convinced, and in the end that would do her girl no good. Annie cared nothing for his grand antecedents nor the Squirearchy. She had not been blinded by it as Job had, but he was her husband and would not be denied and she had agreed to it.

Now it was finished, though only God knew why for it was well-known the Squire was still deep in debt, owing money to every tradesman for miles around. The size of Christina's inheritance was enough to tempt not just a Squire, but a Baronet, she would have thought, but there, the boy was gone and that was the end of it.

'The mills will be yours, Christina. Aye, 'tis true and someone must look after them now that . . .'

'So someone has offered his services, is that it?'

'Yes lass, that's it!'

'And who is it to be, mother? Do tell me for I feel I shall have little choice!'

'Your father won't force you, girl.'

'No, I daresay, but if this one is refused another will come to take his place and I must do it in the end. One is much the same as another.' Her face was harrowed, gaunt almost and her mother agonized over where her daughter's beauty had gone. She had been so bonny. Alive with lovely hope and her fervent belief that life was wonderful. Glossy with it, like a well-groomed, healthy young brood mare. Ready for love, ready for marriage and children, glorious in her joy. Glorious to look upon and listen to, with that laugh of hers. It had filled the house, making others want to smile, and now look at her!

'Perhaps it is Ira Metcalf,' she was saying hysterically. 'How it must have irked poor father when he could not have Celia with Ben gone. He really wanted a part of the Metcalf mills, did he not? Now his chance has come again. How would Celia fancy me as her stepmother instead of sister-in-law, d'you think? If I were to take her father what would have been hers will come to me when Ira . . .'

'Stop it, stop it, girl. You go too far. Your father would not even consider . . .'

'So he has asked then? Ira Metcalf?'

'No, of course he has not. He is as old as your father and I would not allow it, even if your father would. You know that! I have done . . . always . . . what my husband has wanted, Christy, helped him to get here, but girl, girl, do you think I would allow . . .?'

'Then who is it, mother, for really it makes no difference. Ira Metcalf, Paul Aspin, they are all the same.'

'It is Alex Buchanan!'

Christy turned her head slowly until she looked directly into her mother's face. It was gentle, understanding, soft as Christy had never before seen it for her mother did not care to show emotion of any kind, but there, plain for her

167

to see was her mother's love for her. She put out her hand and took Christy's, lifting it into her lap, holding it between her own. She stroked it with her thumb and her voice was tired, ragged with her own sorrow, but there was strength in it still, and a sense that what she said was right and true.

'He is a good man, Christy. He will . . .'

'He is an old man. As old as Ira Metcalf!'

'Rubbish! He is not yet thirty!'

'Thirty is old!'

'Don't be silly, girl!'

'He killed his wife!'

'What?'

'She was twenty-three or -four and had been with child six times in as many years and they say he would not let her alone until she gave him . . .'

'Who says?'

'Everybody!'

'Who is everybody, Christy?'

'Sally said . . .'

'Sally is a stupid girl who doesn't know what she's talking about. She shall have a piece of my mind.'

'But it is true that Mrs Buchanan had five miscarriages before she . . .'

'Christy!'

Christy stopped speaking and turned her head away, trying to withdraw her hand from her mother's. She sighed and her shoulders sagged.

'What does it matter, anyway. If he is to have me the sooner I am put in the family way the sooner I will be dead. Within the year . . .'

'Christina Emmerson! How dare you! *How dare you!* I am ashamed! Never did I think to hear a child of mine be so full of her own concerns to the exclusion of all others. So full of self-pity and lamentations for her own plight. For the past seven weeks you have put your own grief above all others, sacrificing others, if I may say so, for your father would have been glad of your comfort . . . and myself. You are our only child now and it might have given your father some hope for the future ... it still would if you take Alex Buchanan. No, don't pull away from me! You are not the first lass to be ... to be ...' she could find no kind word, 'to be jilted nor will you be the last and you have a right to be hurt by it, but to talk as though you cared nought whether you live or die is wicked! Wicked! Do you not think your brothers would have been glad of the choice, or the men who went with them, leaving women grieving as you do but who have pulled themselves together because they have others to see to ... children, to worry how they are to manage without ... Dear God, girl, stop it, stop it! Put it behind you and go on. Take this man if you have no preference for another and make a new life. He will not kill you, my lass, for you will not let him. Maude Buchanan was weakly, a woman with little spirit, and allowed herself to fade away. They say she lay on her couch all day during her pregnancies instead of taking exercise. When I had my babes within me, I worked, ten hours a day and more and they were all born healthy.' Her voice faltered, 'It was afterwards they sickened. Fever. I don't know what it is that attacks them ...' Her voice became staunch again. 'I was a strong woman, and come from a strong family. Look at your father. He has pulled himself together and gone down to that mill though it killed his sons. We are a strong family, Christy, all of us and you are the same. You are like ... like the juniper bushes which grow on the steep slopes. There is little sustenance there but somehow they get nourishment and thrive. The weather shapes them but even the snow and the winds cannot kill them. You've seen them on the bleak mountains, lying the way the winds have swept them, but alive, Christy, and unyielding. They produce the best timber for charcoal and yet the wood gleams when it is polished, lovely and shining! Like all things it has two sides for when the berries are eaten by a pregnant woman they induce an abortion, did you know that? The "bastard-killer", they call it, for it can be destructive, as all life can unless you fight it. A capacity for life or death, and all this from a bush which asks for nothing more than a bit of soil to stand and grow in. That is what Alex Buchanan offers. You will have healthy children, Christy, for you are a healthy girl and Alex Buchanan is a fine, virile man . . .'

'Mother! Dear Christ!' Christy's voice cracked and she snatched her hand away, leaping to her feet. Her tormented heart was bursting in her breast, filling it and herself with such desolation she did not know how to contain it. Her head whipped from side to side on her slender neck in denial and she put up her hands to her face, clutching at her own flesh, the sinews in her neck standing out like rope.

'When . . . when is it to be?'

'Never, if you do not wish it. Next week if you agree.'

'The widower . . . is eager.' Christy's voice was harsh.

'There is no need to wait. He knows his mind and if you know yours the opinions of others do not matter!'

'Yes.' She laughed without humour. 'There will be . . . gossip.'

'Do you care?'

'I just wondered why he is in such a hurry but it does not matter. Now, or next week . . .' She shrugged indifferently, 'What can it matter?'

'You will . . . do it then? Mr Buchanan waits for an answer. He wishes to put up the banns and there is the question of your dress . . .'

Christy Emmerson lifted her hands to her head and dragged them roughly through her hair, scattering pins about the grass and letting it fall to her shoulders in a wild tangle. She looked demented, as though her senses had filled her with pain she could no longer stand and the words, when they came from her mouth, were hoarse, desperate, those of a mad woman!

'*I cannot bear it, Mother. I cannot, simply cannot bear it!* Why did he not come? *Why? Why? Why?* Even for the money? Even for that? Why did he not come?'

'I don't know, lass. I don't know.'

* * *

She stood that night at her window, in darkness but for the glow from the fire in the grate. Down the hill there was light and movement as the night shift swung into action at her father's mill. The reflection of it glimmered in the water of the beck, rippling like grey silk into the shadowed blackness on the far side.

She could see her own pale image in the glass of the window but there was nothing within her to take interest, nor care that her face was thin and hollow-eyed, that her hair hung straight and curiously lifeless across her shoulders; that the white lawn nightdress she wore was barely lifted by the smallness of her breasts; that where once she had been rounded there was flatness and in her neck and shoulders the bones stood out from her fine white flesh.

Her thoughts barely penetrated the mists of her mind. There was a faint, almost painless memory of a girl laughing on a hillside. There was a boy's face, a young man, dead now surely and long ago, for it did no more than shiver the still quiescence of her heart, like a fish dancing beneath the surface of a lake. A beautiful young couple were dancing, round and round in a waltz. There were lights, brilliant, and velvet darkness where a man kissed a girl. Two horses, a roan and a chestnut standing beneath sun-dappled trees and strangely, a terrier with bright, lively eyes. A dress, so beautiful, white and simple and to be worn by a bride. All very lovely but nothing, absolutely nothing, any longer, to do with her. Not with Christy Emmerson!

The door opened and the slim figure of a black gowned maid came into the room, closing the door behind her.

'Miss Christina?' Faith moved quickly across the hooked rug which covered the floor, and stood beside the still girl at the window.

'Miss Christina?' she said again.

'Yes Faith, I am here.'

'Will I brush your hair?'

'If you like. I was just watching the moon lifting across

171

Langdale Fell. See, is it not pretty? A tiny fingernail, no more!'

'A new moon, Miss Christina.'

'A new moon for a new beginning.'

'Miss Christina?'

'You have heard, Faith. About Mr Buchanan?'

'Aye.'

'I can think of nothing else to do, Faith.'

'He is a grand man, Miss Christina.'

'Grand! Do you think so?'

'Oh yes! He is a man of importance, respected in these parts. He will make a good husband!'

'Will he? Will he, Faith?'

'There's no doubt of it, Miss. Now let me brush . . .'

'How do you know?'

'Know what, for goodness sake?'

'That he will make *me* a good husband? What *is* a good husband, Faith? A man who is rich and important? Who can say he owns . . . copper mines . . . land . . . a splendid house? Is that what I want? Is that what I need? How does he know he can give me what makes *me* glad? Does he *know* in his arrogance that I wish to live as he lives?'

'I don't know what you mean.'

'Is that all there is to it, Faith? Is there not a man who takes a wife because he loves her, or a woman who weds a man, not because he is important, grand, but because he has her heart? There must be more to marriage than in those we see about us. Surely? What made my father marry my mother and why did she accept him? Did she love him? Does she love him now? Or is it that money, or gain in some way, is the only consideration? All the women I see, are they happy to be no more than the possession, along with what they bring, of their husband? And the men? Do they require no more than a submissive brood mare, a decorative hostess to sit at their table? Is there no love, no longing for one body to be close to another? Do I shock you, Faith, for if I do I am truly sorry, but I see no sign of it amongst the ladies I meet. There is no . . . contact, no touching of hand on hand, no soft glances, no exchange of affection between man and wife, nor even between those about to get married. Do you think Ben would have considered Celia if it had not been for her mills. Only one ... oh dear God ... only one did not appear to care whether ... and now he is gone for reasons of his own.'

'Miss Christina don't! Let it be, lass, put it behind you and take this new life in your hands. Hold up your head and be brave and show them all that Christy Emmerson is not easily blown away. Take Mr Buchanan and make a marriage, a world ...'

'I do not know if I have the courage, Faith.'

'You do, *you do*, Christy!' The prefacing 'miss' was forgotten as Faith spoke, one friend to another. 'Don't waste your life on wondering about others. Make this decision and hold it to you proudly. Make him love you! You know you can.'

'I don't know if I care to have his love. I have none to give him.'

'Well, love is just one side to a relationship. There is friendship.'

'Friendship with Alex Buchanan!' Her voice was wild and it almost broke on his name. His face floated before her on the pane of glass next to hers and she remembered the moment, months, years ago when he had smiled and told her she, and women like her, were not free to even choose the style of their own gowns. She had laughed at him derisively secure in the knowledge that when she and Robin were married they would both be free to love and ... she must not think ... allow him to come into her mind just now ... not now, please dear sweet Lord ... she would marry ... marry ... and he would be forgotten and the arrogant and assured Mr Buchanan would ... would ... what ...?

'Why not?' Faith was saying. 'He is an intelligent man, I have heard, and who can say what he may give you to replace what ...'

'Oh Jesus, Faith ...'

'Don't look back . . . don't. Forget him . . .'

'If only I could.'

'Try lass, try!'

'You'll help me, Faith?'

'Of course!'

'Come to Howethwaite with me?'

'You know I will.'

They held hands then, and Christy Emmerson gripped tight the life which had slipped sideways and tilted and felt it right itself for a moment in the vast empty tract which was her heart.

CHAPTER ELEVEN

They were married at the end of the following week for Alex Buchanan insisted upon it, and though the whole of Fellthwaite rocked with it, they came, those who were invited for Job Emmerson and Alexander Buchanan were important men. They had expected to see Christy Emmerson wed, of course, for had she not been betrothed before Christmas, but not to Alexander Buchanan.

Now she was standing before the altar, not six months later and only eight weeks after the death of her two brothers which was surely not right, and with no explanation whatsoever was exchanging marriage vows not with Robin Forsythe but another man! The widower, Alexander Buchanan.

Annie Emmerson, when pressed politely by Mrs Jonathan Dyer and Mrs Alfred Marsden, had declined to reply, saying merely that there had been a change of plans which was obvious to anyone with eyes in their head and not just a change of plan but a change of bridegroom too.

Miss Susan Whittam when told that the beautiful white bridal gown she had made for Christy Emmerson would no longer be needed – for Christy had become hysterical when it was suggested she wear the dress in which she was to have married Robin Forsythe – had protested loudly for how was she to sell a wedding dress made for one bride, to another. Her cries had been silenced by the promise that she would naturally be paid for the gown, and also another in a shade of pale apricot Gros de Naples, trimmed with white Honiton lace which must be ready within the week, and a bonnet to match.

Might she be told for what occasion the dress would be worn, she asked, for one could hardly create a morning gown if it was intended for an afternoon? She was informed, shortly, that it was to be for a wedding. 'A wedding? Then surely something in white as was customary?' But she was told the bride preferred not to wear white and the news was soon round the town, advertised by her sister, Miss Amelia Whittam, who had known, positively *known* at Christmas that there was something odd going on. Within the hour and in one day Miss Whittam did more trade than she would normally do in a week as the town's ladies flocked to her salon for news.

Christina Emmerson had an almost ethereal loveliness that day, not quite of this world, pale, slender, breakable and as she moved blindly to stand beside Alexander Buchanan, her hand leaving her father's arm to be placed in his, she felt her mind slip mercifully away to some quiet place where no one could reach her and the words of the ceremony, even her own, were finished and done with when she returned. She had once been a young girl, laughing, loving, warm with a sensuality which had set a man on fire for her. Her eyes had blazed with the brilliance of sunlight on ice, then clouded to the smouldering grey of passion. Her face, now so white, had been rose-petalled, dreaming in contemplation of her love and her full poppy mouth had opened on a sigh of desire and need as she raised it for his kiss. Her hands had been strong, sun-browned as they twined themselves in Robin Forsythe's pale curls and her body had moved and opened in some mysterious way though she had been fully clothed.

She had existed once, but where had she gone now?

They came down the aisle, man and wife, and the church bells pealed across to Skelwith and Tilberthwaite, to Langdale Fell, to Loughrigg and across to Grasmere, echoing on the still, silent air and the fair-haired young man who climbed down stiffly from the back of the tall roan in the stableyard at Dalebarrow Hall, wondered idly who it was who had married.

The wedding party returned to Hollin House. Just a few close friends and relatives of the bride's family for Alex Buchanan had none bar a cousin or two in Carlisle and he did not care to have them come and see him wed for the second time.

Mrs Kean, with Annie's help, had made syllabubs and snow-cake, tipsy cake and vanilla cream and fruit jellies and a rich bride cake with three pounds of best butter, five pounds of currants, sixteen eggs, sugar, flour, sweet almonds, candied citron, orange and lemon peel and a gill of wine and brandy mixed!

Though their Christy stood like a silent, frozen statuette on the arm of her new husband, they must make some concession to the day and what it meant, Annie agonized, as guests stared in bewilderment at the strangeness of the bride and she passed amongst them, with Sally and Dorcas, begging of them to try a little of this and a sip of that and the champagne flowed for it was not every day that one married a daughter, and everyone began to relax. The ladies' cheeks became flushed and their eyes brightened as they speculated amongst themselves on how long it would take Alex Buchanan to get this new one with child.

She changed into her cream printed foulard 'going away' outfit, elegantly simple with no flounces or lace or ribbons, just a plain, full, organ pleated skirt with a bustle, a neat bodice, long-waisted and curved to a point in front, and tight sleeves edged in challis work. Her bonnet was of cream silk with tiny cream rosebuds of tulle beneath its brim and around her neck, her only ornament, was a superb rope of small, perfectly matched, creamy pearls, lustrous and rich, linked with gold, looped in three dainty strands to encircle her white throat, a wedding present from her husband.

Though they were to go straight to her new home for she had streadfastly refused a wedding trip to Italy with this stranger who was her husband, as he had suggested, they climbed into their carriage and were cheered away by the guests as though they were to be gone a thousand miles instead of to Skelwith.

Annie and Job watched the carriage until it was out of sight, standing together with that closeness which had come upon them recently.

'Will she be alright, lass?' he asked softly. 'Have we done the right thing?'

It was a measure of how his sons' deaths had changed him for never had he questioned a decision once he had made it, not in his entire life.

'Oh yes, given time.'

'She thought a lot of the Squire's lad, Annie.'

'Aye, but she'll get over it. With Alex Buchanan she'll have to!'

It was the first time they had ever been alone. She sat beside him quietly and when he spoke she jumped as though she had forgotten his presence.

'Are you tired?' he asked shortly.

'Thank you, Mr Buchanan, I am a little. It has been a long day.'

Her politeness irritated him but he said nothing more.

They reached his home, hers now, and as the carriage stopped before the front door a lad leaped forward to open the carriage door, putting up his hand for her to take, helping her down, his scrubbed face engaged in a grin of huge delight. He was neatly dressed in good corduroy breeches and a brown jacket of serge, the cap on his wiry curls was whisked off, and his boots shone in the pale sunlight.

'Thank you, Jack,' Alex said then turned to Christy. 'This is Jack Hodson. His grandfather is . . . works about the place. Jack is to be trained up by Thaddeus to be your coachman. I need Thaddeus to drive me now and again so you must have your own.'

'Of course. Thank you, and thank you, Jack.' Her eyes became unshuttered for a moment allowing out a candle-flame of brightness to the youth and he grinned more broadly, replacing his cap with a cheery toss before stepping back. It was the first time she had smiled that day.

A woman had opened the door, standing respectfully to one side as her new mistress crossed the threshold. She bobbed a curtsey and smiled and then they were all there, lined up along the length of the wide hallway, a dozen or so men and women; Alex Buchanan's servants, *her* servants!

Alex had taken her arm, no more than a touch as he led her towards the woman who had opened the door, but she shrank from him, holding her arm well into her side and he felt another irritated twinge of impatience. His forbearance, never strong, which he had meant to keep steady this day, was beginning to wear thin. His mouth tightened and his eyes narrowed but he merely indicated where she should step.

'This is Mrs Longworth, my housekeeper.'

'Welcome ma'am.' Mrs Longworth bobbed another curtsey.

'Mrs Avery who will cook for us.'

'Ma'am.' Another curtsey.

'Meg, Lou, Patience . . . er . . .'

'Agnes, sir.

'Agnes, and this is Beth, John, Miles.'

They all dropped their curtseys or touched their brows and as she passed down the line, stared at her curiously, noting her extreme youth, her delicate, drooping head, the paleness of her skin and pondered sagely that this one looked as though she would not be long after the first.

'And this is my daughter, Amy.'

Christy Buchanan, for she was that now, stopped abruptly and swung back again to the last girl in the line. She had been about to go to the foot of the stairs and hopefully, up them to some quiet, private room where she could be alone with Faith – who was following in a second carriage supervising the wagon which was bringing the new Mrs Buchanan's things – but the word 'daughter' caught her blurred attention. The girl was young and buxom with a deep breast against which she held a bundle. The 'bundle' indifferently passed over by Mrs Buchanan, for what was it to her, had begun to squirm and with a determined heave, a small dark head wearing a white frilled bonnet from which lustrous black curls peeped, lifted and turned and two bright blue eyes looked at her solemnly. They blinked and long, silky lashes fanned flushed cheeks. A hand, plump and with questing fingers reached out to Christy's pearls and the blue eyes smiled. They were Alex Buchanan's eyes, so blue as to be almost violet and two tiny teeth, no bigger than the pearls she reached out for shone in the pinkness of her gums.

Christy took a step towards her and a small bud of feeling moved somewhere inside her and she smiled back. A child! A beautiful girl child! She had completely forgotten that Mr Buchanan had a daughter. How strange! During the past few days as he and her father had drawn up contracts, signed scores of papers, made wills she supposed, tying up firmly the future of Christy Emmerson and Job Emmerson's mills – the first null and void now that Ben and Toby, and Robin Forsythe were gone – she had not once thought of the child Maude Buchanan had died giving birth to. Her own mother, her aunts and cousins had been busy with materials and patterns, with peignoirs and fichus, bonnets and parasols and nobody had thought to mention to Christy Emmerson that she would, the moment she became Alex Buchanan's wife, be also mother to his child!

'Amy,' she said and put out her hand to the infant and

179

instantly her finger was gripped by a tiny fist. The nurse-maid preened with as much pride as though the baby was her own, having had her in her care since the day she was born, and was there another quite like her, her expression seemed to ask?

'She is lovely.' The new Mrs Buchanan took the small hand and placed her lips in the baby's palm with such natural delight that Alex, along with the servants, began to smile and look at one another for surely, their faces said, a good start had been made. One heard tales of stepmothers who loathed the very sight of the first wife's offspring, would have nothing to do with them, especially when their own began to arrive. It was early days yet but this one seemed quite taken with their master's baby daughter.

'How old is she . . . er . . . ?'

'I'm Beth, ma'am, and she's a little over seven months.'

'Seven months . . . yes . . .'

A shutter came down over Mrs Buchanan's face then and Beth was shocked as her new mistress turned away sharply, almost flinging her little dear's hand into her face, or so she told Mrs Avery later, aggrieved. You'd have thought the child had the pox or something the way the mistress had scuttled away to the staircase.

'May I be shown my room, Mr Buchanan,' the new Mrs Buchanan said imperiously, her hand on the newel post at its foot, her back to the watching, fascinated line of servants. They cast dumbfounded, sidelong looks at one another and then their heads turned as one as at the door another smartly dressed young lady arrived, as imperious as the mistress, if you please, as she ordered Jack and Miles and the coachman to see to Mrs Buchanan's boxes.

'Ah Faith!' Mrs Buchanan turned with such relief they were confounded all over again. The young woman moved past the lot of them, even the master, as though they were no more than the pictures on the wall and taking the arm of her mistress soothed her, or so it seemed, with a smile and a touch.

'Yes, I have your boxes, Miss Christy,' she murmured and only then turned to bob her curtsey to her new master.

'Sir,' she said, and waited. They both waited, mistress and maid, almost shoulder to shoulder.

Alex Buchanan's face was expressionless but in his eyes a spark flashed, grim and formidable. It seemed to say that he was not used to being ignored in his own house by his own wife's maid but for now, though his chin thrust pugnaciously forward, he would let it be. His voice was quiet as he spoke. He did not look at the line of servants, but at the one at the foot of the stairs.

'Thank you, Mrs Longworth. That will be all. Perhaps you will direct the others back to their work and then show Mrs Buchanan to her room. Miles, John, see to the luggage.' The last was an unnecessary order for they had instinctively jumped to it when directed by Faith, though they were to wonder why afterwards for she was only a servant like themselves.

Compared to Hollin House, Howethwaite was quite enormous. Alex Buchanan's forebears, farmers all of them until his own father, had little desire to improve their land or lay out their money in what they considered unnecessary ways. They were a breed of men content with things as they were. They lived on their own estate, clothed themselves and their families with their own wool, ate oaten and wheaten bread of their own making and grew vegetables for their own table as well as providing their own butter, milk, eggs, cheese, bacon, hams and mutton. Built almost three centuries ago, the original farmhouse was scarce more than a huge kitchen with a scullery off and a bedroom above, but bits and pieces had been added until it had become almost a manor house. A long low sitting room at one side was neatly arranged with country furniture of elm, oak and yew, with chests, footstools, settles, all polished to a mirror gleam by a hundred careful hands. It was dominated by a fireplace in which it was possible to place all the furniture in the room and still have space for a fire. Great logs, six feet long and thick as a woman's

181

waist were burned in it and heavy woollen curtains dyed crimson sheltered the windows.

There were pantries, still rooms, a dairy, a laundry, and there was a study where Alex kept his records which stretched back through generations, telling everything his family had ever done, every transaction they had ever made in the farming of the sheep which had once been their livelihood.

Up the wide staircase which had been put up in his great grandfather's day were two large bedrooms and a warren of small ones, enough in plenty to house all the servants who 'lived-in'. They all bulged with furniture which went back, some of it, to Elizabethan days, stored and forgotten until Mrs Longworth dragged it out to be cleaned and polished and put back again for another year.

The kitchen was a lovely, sweet-smelling world of cleanliness: of bread baking, and meat roasting, of dressers piled with crockery, huge ovens in which there was always something baking or boiling or roasting for there were many servants to feed. Cured hams, rubbed well with salt, then covered with saltpetre, brown sugar, then more salt, hung in muslin bags from the black beams of the ceiling along with bunches of dried herbs. Flour was stacked in bags, waiting for someone to shift them, cats licked their paws before the crackling fire and on the great kitchen table the delicious food demanded by the master was prepared by Mrs Avery. When the kitchen door was open to let out the fierce heat one could look across the paddock to horses dashing their heads in the sunshine and swinging their tails against the flies. Twenty or thirty chickens wandered freely in the stable yard and around the out-buildings with a strong white rooster in charge. It had not been changed for as long as Alex could remember.

The room to which Mrs Longworth showed Christy and Faith was lovely. The house, long, two-storied, plain, with a dozen flat windows on each floor at the front, looked out over Low Park towards High Park Fell, with the River Brathay running at its back. It stood on an elevated piece of ground made over into gardens, orchards, a meadow or two and the paddock for Alex Buchanan's horses to graze in. It was built of silver grey limestone quarried in the district, the roof of Lakeland slate. The hallway which ran from the front to the back of the house split it into two. On one side was the sitting room and the other the dining room, each with three floor-length windows.

Upstairs, across the front of the house was the master's bedroom, a dressing room, once a small bedroom, and a sitting room for the master's wife to use when she was alone. It was an attractive house, sturdy, simple but pleasing to the eye with the typical cylindrical slate chimneys at either end, a porch in the middle and climbing white roses growing almost up to the eaves in the summer.

The lawn before it had yew trees and box-edged walks but that was the limit of Abel Hodson's gardening skill. He kept the wide lawns neatly trimmed, the herbaceous borders weeded, the roses pruned and the rest was left to fend for itself.

Christy stepped across the threshold of the room which was to be hers to sit in and did not even blink at its simple beauty nor at the lovely things which were scattered about. The carpet was of golden wool on which ivory roses swirled. There were butter-yellow curtains in a rich velvet at the window and crisp white net, and on the walls, pale daffodil silk so that the room seemed filled with sunshine. The sofa before the fire was of rich cream velvet with chairs to match picked out in white and gold with tables in polished silkwood beside each one. There were bowls of fruit, out of season, strawberries from Mr Buchanan's hot-house and vases spilling over with spring flowers.

There was a mahogany rocking chair with a canework back, filled with cushions in the palest of pale daffodil yellow silk, to match that on the walls and set before the window so that she might sit and rock, Mrs Longworth said kindly, and watch the endlessly moving tapestry of clouds on the fells and the glittering beauty of the tarns.

On tables and mantelshelf were delicate porcelain,

Sèvres and Meissen. An enormous fire crackled in the grate, smelling of applewood and the room was delightfully warm.

'And this is the bedroom, Ma'am.' Mrs Longworth respectfully led the bemused bride through the dressing room, mahogany wardrobes and drawers, a full length mirror – who was that white-faced girl who crept past it? – placed before the window and into the spacious bedroom she would share with her husband.

The fourposter bed dominated it! It had a canopy of painted silk. There was soft apple green silk on the walls and a carpet the colour of the pale mushrooms Mrs Avery put in her soups, and with a pile thick enough to get lost in. Rosewood tables, dainty with legs like new born lambs, mirrors by the score and wallpaper of handpainted silk. The bedspread was a deep raspberry pink in a lace so fine it was like gossamer and the maids were afraid to touch it, they said. On the walls were lovely watercolours of ballet dancers, so they were told, and women half-clothed and what Fellthwaite would make of it when it heard, as hear it undoubtedly would, God only knew.

There was another huge fire burning in this grate and as the afternoon drew towards its close and the room began to grow dim the glowing topaz of its flames rippled across the shining, silken walls. It was the most beautiful room Faith Cooper had ever seen but all the new Mrs Buchanan could say was:

'And where is my maid to sleep, if you please, Mrs . . . er . . .?'

'Why, with the other maids, Madam.'

'And where is that?'

'Upstairs at the back of the . . .'

'She is to have a room across the hall from mine.'

'Why, Madam, that is where Mrs Avery . . .'

'I don't care! Faith is to be near . . .'

'What is the problem, Mrs Longworth?'

Alex Buchanan stood in the doorway in a misleadingly indolent manner, his arms crossed, leaning carelessly, or

184

so it appeared, against the open doorway. His blue eyes smiled but his face gave away no inkling of his thoughts – as though for all he cared they might have been discussing the placing of a kitten in some corner of the stable – but his smiling eyes had that curious gleam in them which had come when Faith Cooper had laid her hand on his wife's arm in the hall and had been greeted with such sighing relief.

'Oh sir!' Mrs Longworth was quite flustered for she was a good-hearted woman concerned only with the welcoming of this poor little chit of a thing who was to share her master's bed and her expression was compassionate for there was no doubt about it he'd make short work of her.

'It's the . . . the sleeping arrangements, sir.'

Alex raised his eyebrows quizzically for the answer seemed amusing. The sleeping arrangements were so simple how could they possibly cause a disturbance? His wife was to sleep in his bed. Surely she knew that!

'The sleeping arrangements, Mrs Longworth,' he said smilingly.

'Well, sir . . . it be a bit awkward like.'

'Mr Buchanan!' Christy's sharp voice cut through Mrs Longworth's mumble and involuntarily Faith, who had followed her mistress into the bedroom, carrying the box in which Christy's few pieces of jewellery were locked, put up a warning hand.

'Mr Buchanan,' Christy said again. 'There is nothing awkward about it. I wish to have my maid as near to me as possible. There is a room across the landing, round the corner you say, Mrs Longworth, and only a step or two away. That will do very well.'

'But Mrs Avery sleeps there, Christina,' he said smoothly.

'So I believe but one room is very much like an_____ I am sure she will not mind moving.' She t___ Longworth. 'See to it at once, please, M_____ demanded and waited.

Mrs Longworth looked at he____

Alex straightened, his face set in lines of almost smiling challenge. Now it was time to show her who ruled her, and this house and all in it, his expression seemed to say. She must be made aware that though she was now mistress and might have the ruling of the housekeeping arrangements, what went on between them as man and wife was no concern to anyone else, particularly this young girl on whom she seemed to lean. She was a maid and would sleep with the others. It was a small thing but she needed to be shown right from the start that she would not be allowed to play the imperious young miss with him.

His lips curled over his white teeth as he casually reached inside his coat for his cigar case. They watched, the three women as he removed a cigar, placed it between those curling lips and lit it. When it was burning to his satisfaction he blew smoke into the fragrant, rarefied air of his wife's bedroom.

'I'm sorry, Christina. Mrs Avery has been with me and with my mother for many years. She has occupied that room in all that time. Her things are there and it is hardly fair to ask her to move them and herself to another.' His teeth gripped his cigar and he smiled through the drift of smoke.

'Then I will have a . . . a truckle bed brought into the . . . that room between . . .'

'Miss Christy . . . please, I can sleep in the . . .'

'No, Faith, I want you here with me.'

'I don't think so, Christina. That would not do at all, would it?'

Alex Buchanan grinned, while she fought to keep the only friend she had in this strange house, and Mrs Longworth and Faith looked away hastily.

'Mr Buchanan . . .'

But before she could speak again he turned swiftly and with a nod which was completely understood by the two servants, indicated the door and in a moment they were on the other side with it closed between them and their master.

Christy looked properly – perhaps the first time she had ever done so since she had seen him over seven months ago in the clearing above Elterwater – at Alex Buchanan and considered this man who was now her husband. He looked extremely handsome in his light blue dress-coat. It had a velvet collar and beneath it he wore a white satin embroidered waistcoat. His breeches were of cream saxony and his shirt front was a froth of white lace. His ebony hair was smoothly brushed and his white teeth shone in his gypsy brown face. But his eyes, such a pure and vivid blue, had no warmth in them, just a certainty, hard and insolent, that he would have his own way, especially in his bedroom!

In Christy's breast a ripple of something stirred. She didn't know what it was, nor did she care, she only knew that this man, this impudent stranger had taken it into his own hands to dismiss her maid and not only that but was arguing with her as to where Faith should sleep. This was an ordeal for them both, she and Faith. They were visitors almost in this man's house and surely he had the good grace to allow them some time together to accustom themselves to their new environment. If she should need Faith – as she had done so often in the past eight weeks, a comforting hand, a light in the dark, a voice in the night when her stricken soul was at its lowest ebb – she must have her within calling distance and it would hardly do for her to be fumbling at every door along the landing upstairs.

She might have lost her heart, even her will to live at times, but Christy Emmerson had certainly not parted with her temper when Robin Forsythe cast her aside!

'Mr Buchanan,' she said hotly, looking forlorn despite her scowl, in her pretty cream costume and bonnet which she had not yet removed, rather like a guest who is to stay but a minute.

'Mrs Buchanan,' he said mildly, his voice belying the hot breath in his throat, the hammering in his chest, the rushing of blood to his belly for *she was his wife now and he could do with her as he pleased*, 'May I just bring to your notice that not only you, but I am to sleep here tonight and I can assure you, you will have no need of a maid!'

They dined in the pleasant room overlooking the open fells, on vermicelli soup, breast of veal, rolled and stuffed with ham, parsley, sweet herbs and breadcrumbs, followed by a superb transparent jelly inlaid with brandy cherries and topped with whipped cream. A simple meal, excellently cooked and served and Alex sent his compliments to Mrs Avery – and for a moment Christy's dazed mind cleared to speculate on this man's courtesy to his own servant then it blanked again in readiness for what was to come.

But it seemed Alex Buchanan was in no hurry to claim his marital rights and he led her into the sitting room, placing her before the enormous fireplace in which young trees burned, pressing café au lait in a small cup into her hand and she was asked if she would like a liqueur, just as if she was an experienced woman of the world, an event which would have delighted her in normal circumstances, but she declined it with the politeness of a guest at a party.

Alex had a brandy, two or three brandies and several cigars which he lit without asking her permission and chatted quite amiably about the coming of the railway to Windermere and the difference it would make to the many businessmen in the district. He exclaimed on the rapid growth of the Queen's family and the news that she had purchased a holiday home on the Isle of Wight. He asked her opinion on the campaign for the abolition of the Corn Laws, questioning her on whether or not she considered they hindered the expansion of trade and industry by keeping the price of bread artificially high and when she evinced little interest went to great lengths to explain it to her.

He complimented her on her gown of ivory silk, cut low to reveal her white shoulders, decorated only with a spray of enormous ivory tulle roses at her waist. The bodice was pointed at the front, the sleeves short and tight and Faith had brushed her hair until it shone, dressing it simply over her ears and drawing it up into a huge knot at the back of her head. In the knot was a cluster of roses to match those on her dress.

In short, he was the perfect companion!

The coffee cups were gone, the brandy drunk and the grandfather clock, its face painted with shepherdesses and rosebuds, struck ten o'clock and as it did so Alex Buchanan stood up.

'Christina,' he said quite gently. Her face was drawn suddenly into a white cameo, all hollows and shadows and pale trembling lips for she was afraid of this strong and virile man whom she did not love. He held out his hand to her and when she put hers blindly in it, she knew that at last the moment which her mind had forced her heart to forget, that which her mother had tried to warn her of, was here.

'I will be up in a minute,' he said, his eyes looking directly into hers, leaving her in no doubt as to his meaning and intention. Christy Emmerson was to be changed tonight from maid to woman and this man, this husband would do it. There would be no tears, his expression said, no cries of shame nor outraged modesty for he was a man and her husband and whether she considered it duty or pleasure, it would be done!

Faith had gone, quietly, wordlessly, for what was there to say? She knew her mistress loved a man with all her heart and it was not the man who would, in a moment, come into her bed. What was the use in comfort for was there any to be gained, or pity, for what good did it do?

Before she went though she leaned across the huge double bed and kissed the cheek of the lifeless girl who sat in its exact centre. She brushed back the shimmering length of hair without a word. They looked at one another and Christy smiled and shrugged, then resumed her pale staring at the slender fleshed figure of the ballet dancer on the wall.

He strode into the room in a rich velvet robe and his eyes were a fierce, triumphant summer-heat blue.

'Now then, Christy Emmerson,' he declared. 'Let's see what we have here and if you call me Mr Buchanan once more I swear I'll take my horsewhip to you.'

For a moment she shrank back in the bed, her swimming, tender grey eyes darkening in fear and he almost turned away for before God he could not force her. Then, as he had hoped, known she would, her chin came up and she burst into life. He did not care how or why – whether she loved or hated him at that moment – his one need was for her to care, to be alive, to be aware and fighting, involved in what was to happen.

He threw off his robe and his strong, golden, muscular body, eternally masculine, proud, savage and determined, gleamed in the soft light of the candles.

'This is what it's all about, my girl,' he said exultantly. 'A man and a woman alone in a room with no one, and nothing between them. No maidenly blushes, nor lurking in the shadows, nor fumbling with nightdresses so let's have that blasted thing off you and see what I've got. No! You refuse! Then perhaps I can persuade you,' and he began to advance upon the bed, his lips smiling about his white, pirate's teeth.

'Don't you lay a hand on me, Alex Buchanan! Put a finger, come an inch nearer and I'll scream the damn place down!'

She had scrambled to the back of the bed, crouched like a small, wild animal, her hair around her in a curtain of darkness, her arms gripped around her knees and the voluminous white lawn of her nightdress which covered them. Her voice hissed like a serpent's and her eyes flashed iced grey diamonds at him. They eyed his bold, thrusting body with a kind of horrified awe for though she had had two brothers she had never seen a naked man before.

Alex smiled and continued his slow stride towards her.

'Well, that's an improvement on *Mr* Buchanan, I must admit, and as to screaming, my darling, I think not, don't you? You are my wife! A husband may do as he pleases with his wife! Anything he likes or fancies. The law does not care for a man has its permission to treat his own possessions as he wishes, within reason, and believe me, Christy Emmerson ... Christy Buchanan ...' His voice softened until it was almost a whisper, '... you belong to me now and that's an end to it! Now take off that bloody nightdress or I shall tear it from you myself. Come, stand up ...'

Her soft lips tightened and her eyes blazed her defiance but she stood up on the bed and in one careless glorious movement, she drew the nightdress over her head and flung it recklessly to the far corner of the room. Her body, thin still, flat as a boy but as fine as gossamer with pink-tipped breasts, rose before him in the candlelight. Her eyes flashed scorn, daring, challenging as his own and as he put out a hand to lay it on her slender flank she did not flinch, and when he drew her down, down into the softness of the bed and his arms, he thanked God for her spirit for it had given her what she needed to exorcize, at least for this night, the ghost of Robin Forsythe.

He did not love her gently that first time for he knew it must be done, and done at once if she was to be his; but when she cried out in pain, her voice stilled by his mouth, he began again, this time leading her along the sweet, honeyed paths which he knew so well, teaching her the beginnings of the joy of it against her will until, to her surprise, she found herself clinging to him as the only steady thing in a world which rocked in a strange glory.

She slept then, exhausted, close beside him. When she tried to move away he would not allow it, holding her tight against his body, and when she woke in the morning, warm, a soft sighing kitten, surprised to find herself where she was, he turned her at once into a spitting cat and again she followed him and Christy Buchanan's body was very sure that it belonged to no one but Alex Buchanan though her heart remained untouched!

191

CHAPTER TWELVE

Annie Emmerson was in her kitchen when the front door bell rang. On her face was the first expression of peace to lie there since the death of her boys and her stout body had about it somehow the stance of a woman, slippered perhaps, and comfortable in her own environment at a task which suited her. Her hands were tranquil, addressing themselves to the dough she kneaded and flour moved in a shifting mist about her head, settling finely, hardly distinguishable among the grey of her hair.

It was the first time she had known a fragment of content for many weeks and her face had an almost dreaming quality as though the preparing of the dough for the oven, a familiar and well-loved task for as long as she could remember, hypnotized her, bringing her into a state of restfulness after a tiring journey.

Her thoughts lingered about the events of the day before and as her hands moved effortlessly at the smooth dough and her shoulders bunched in rhythmic unison, the picture of her daughter as she had been beside her new husband was clear in her mind.

Oblivious to the maids who worked around and beside her she pursed her lips as though at some faint unease, then shook her head to clear it. She'd looked a treat, there was no doubt about it, their lass, just as a bride should despite her choice of colour for her gown, demure and pale and innocent, but her quietness had worried Annie though why that should surprise her after all the girl had been through, she didn't know! She had appeared not to know what was going on about her and Job had fretted on it in the privacy of their room later, begging her to reassure him that Christy would be alright. Undoubtedly he had imagined her in the bed of Alex Buchanan, as she surely would have been and Annie had consoled him, taking him into her own comforting arms as they lay in their marriage bed.

Why was she so sure, Job had pleaded to know and she could not tell him for she did not know herself; she only knew the idea of Christy in the protective care of Alex Buchanan gave Annie a great deal of comfort.

The last weeks, months, had been got through and though the pain and sense of loss would never leave them, she and Job, they had at least the comfort of knowing their Christy was settled with a good man and the hopeful anticipation of a grandchild to hold within the twelve-month. Alex would see to that. It was a joyous certainty to look forward to, something to fill the great empty hole the death of their lads had left. Perhaps a sturdy boy with the Emmerson dark good looks, spirited and lively to bring pleasure to Job's declining years and give him the satisfaction of knowing his mills, those meant for Ben and Toby, would one day again be in Emmerson hands.

'See who that is, Sal,' she said absently, treating the maid in the manner of the plain daleswoman she was. The pretension to the grand lady which Job had wanted her to assume as their fortune increased, had gone in the more homely atmosphere to which they were both accustomed and which had been resumed lately. It was more – comforting somehow, more comfortable, and with the reason for it gone with his lads, Job had slipped into the role of the plain bourgeois man he really was and she had been relieved to follow.

The little maid settled her frilled cap on her bright head, smoothed down her frilled apron, shook out her pale grey skirts and started for the door. With Miss Christy's wedding, despite the disapproval it aroused in Fellthwaite, they had thrown off the deep black of mourning, thank God, and were to wear half-mourning of grey and lilac and Sally was pleased for she was but seventeen and courting a groom from Dalebarrow Hall, and though she had been upset by the death of Master Ben and especially

Master Toby – who was a great one for a laugh and a stolen kiss if he could coax it from her when the mistress wasn't looking – they were not *her* kin!

Her eyes were brilliant with excited speculation when she came back and her face as red as the geraniums which were just beginning to flower in the window bottom of Annie's kitchen. She could scarce contain herself for not only the polite society of Fellthwaite had conjectured on the sudden switch of Miss Christina Emmerson's bridegroom but their servants as well.

'Oh Ma'am,' she squeaked, 'Oh Ma'am!' and everyone in the room turned to stare at her, mouth agape, eyes agoggle.

'What is it, girl?' Annie felt the first trickle of alarm and had a moment to consider that her peaceful contemplation of the future had not lasted long.

'It's Mr Forsythe, Ma'am.'

'Mr Forsythe!' A picture of the Squire rose to her mind and she wondered what on earth he could want with them. He had made it perfectly plain, at least to her, that he no longer wanted their girl for if he had – no matter what Master Robin had hankered after in the way of a hunter and the excitement of the gentry's affection for the chasing of the fox on its back – the Squire would have trotted him up here as quick as you please, considering nobody's feelings but his own.

''Tis Mr Robin Forsythe, Ma'am! I've put him in the parlour. He asked most particular to see Miss Christy and when I said she wasn't here . . .'

Sally's voice faded away into the far corner of the kitchen as Annie Emmerson turned slowly from the busy table and stared in a kind of horrified fascination towards the door.

'Mr Robin Forsythe?' Her voice sounded hollow to her own ears, booming away down the dread corridors of her mind as her brave heart which had withstood so much crouched fearfully in her breast, afraid of what was surely to come.

'Yes, Mrs Emmerson. He said if Miss Christy wasn't at home he . . .'

Again the maid's voice faded away and Annie felt the trembling begin in her suddenly weakened legs. She tried to still them, reaching for a damp cloth to wipe her fingers, then removed the capacious apron she had put on to perform the pleasantly soothing domestic task she had allowed herself on this first day of content and, yes, relief. Her gaze never once shifted from the door through which she must go.

The kitchen was so quiet she could hear the purring rumble of the cats entwined on the rug before the fire.

'Thank you, Sally,' Annie said at last. She squared her shoulders and straightened her back and moved on unsteady legs towards her own parlour.

He rose to his feet politely when she entered the room, his young face working with a mixture of youthful emotion. It was vivid with hopeful anticipation, shining with some warm feeling only too easy to recognize and yet wary as though it knew it should show sadness for the loss the Emmerson family had suffered, but this joy at the reunion which was surely to come would not allow it. His eyes glowed across the room, such a warm, deep transparent brown, his mouth was forming on a name, his lips trembling about it and his hands and arms were ready to lift, to reach out, to enfold!

The whole became still as those eyes registered who it was who had entered the room and the feet which had been ready to spring across the carpet placed themselves neatly together as he bowed his head respectfully. His acute disappointment filled every corner of the room and Annie felt it wash against her, but still he was the Squire's son, courteous, well-mannered, a gentleman!

'Mrs Emmerson,' he said and smiled tentatively, ready to do, or be whatever she wished. He was young and did not know how to deal with loss or sorrow but his heart was warm and compassionate and if she was recovered enough to smile then so would he, but if not, then he would share her sorrow in any way she chose and show the face of sadness. He had not personally felt it for he had scarce known her sons but he would gladly give anything she might want from him to help her in this awkward moment, his demeanour said.

He waited, his eyes on hers, for her to speak.

'Mr Forsythe . . . how nice . . . it has been so long . . .'

'Mrs Emmerson,' he said again, wanting to say more but not quite certain after all these weeks whether condolences were still expected.

'Won't you . . . sit down?' she asked him and after indicating she must do so first and waiting until she did, he lowered himself reluctantly into the deep plush chair which had replaced the one ruined by the explosion.

'Well . . .' Annie said, certain he must hear the drumbeat of her heart. 'And what . . .?' She had been about to ask him what brought him to her front door but something in the bright expectancy in his face, in the way his eyes strayed constantly to the door told her exactly what he had come for. She agonized on the duplicity of fate which, sneering, teased so carelessly those who seemed to have no control over their own destiny.

A day! Just one simple day. That was all.

'I came as soon as I thought it proper . . . well, that is not true, I thought it proper the day I heard but when my father told me what you had said . . .' His words began to trip stumblingly from his eager lips, as though he wanted her to understand at once that he in no way wished to argue with her opinion though it had differed from his own, but he was anxious for her to know he had tried to abide by it as the properly reared gentleman he was, even if he could do so no longer.

'It has been eight weeks now, Mrs Emmerson, and I have had no word. She has not answered my letters . . . Christy . . .' His face softened on her name, '. . . you know I mean Christy . . . and though I fully understand she has suffered a great sorrow and perhaps felt unable to write for a while . . . well . . . I could wait no longer, Ma'am. If she does not want to see me . . . my father said grief takes some that way for he has known it . . . then I will go away again and wait until she is ready. Not to Leicestershire but at Dalebarrow. I will wait there for really I cannot bring myself to put a great distance between us again.'

He smiled quite shyly with his lovely, trusting brown eyes and Annie was reminded of a Springer spaniel her brother had once owned. The dog had the soft affectionate temperament, the loyalty and enduring devotion this lad was showing, ready to lie down and die for its master, her brother, ready to play or work, or indeed do anything that was asked of it in its steadfast dedication to the man it loved. Its liquid brown eyes had looked at her brother in exactly the same way as Robin Forsythe when he spoke of Christy! Dear God! oh dear Lord in Heaven, how was she to tell him?

'Is she . . . is she at home, Mrs Emmerson?' He looked again at the closed door, the twentieth time he had done so in ten minutes and then to the ceiling as though he would pierce the plaster and wood for a sight of the girl he had come to claim.

'I would keep her but a minute, tell her. I just want her to know . . . I am here. That she is to take all the time she needs to recover. I will wait for her.' He smiled a boyish smile trying to be a man of understanding, '. . . after all we are both young and we have time . . . lots of time . . .' His voice became uncertain and he faltered on the words, 'Mrs Emmerson . . . are you unwell, Ma'am . . . you are quite pale. May I call your maid, Mrs Emmerson? Please, I beg your pardon. I have upset you, I know I have and you must forgive me. To speak of my own . . . when you have so recently . . .'

He stood up jerkily, unused in his young manliness to the upsets of ladies and took a step towards her. As she put out a hand to him, her fingers trembling and as her blank eyes stared at him and her white face quivered he began to sense the strangeness, the tension, the silence after her first words of greeting and into his heart a curious

197

rock formed and began to swell and thump against his breastbone.

'Mrs Emmerson . . . please . . . is there something wrong? Is . . . is Mr Emmerson . . . I had heard he had . . . not been himself since . . . My father said he was . . . unwell . . . at the funeral . . . and that . . . Dear God . . . please Mrs Emmerson, do fetch Christy down to see me since I am strangely afraid . . . there must be something . . . you look so ill . . . is that it . . . there is something wrong with . . . she is not ill, please say she is not ill . . .'

He took a step toward the stiff, silent figure on the sofa and put out an entreating hand to her, begging to be told that after all his strict adherence to the code of honour placed upon him by this woman, the mother of the girl he loved, and his own father that he had done the right thing, that he was to be praised for it and that, because of it the prize he claimed was naturally to be his. That his Christy was upstairs pale perhaps and still grieving, but waiting as he was for the day they would be married.

'Tell me she is not ill, Mrs Emmerson.' He almost went on his knees to her in his desperation. 'She is still away, perhaps . . . with relatives, is that it? She has not yet returned from . . . she will be home soon!'

The staring white face, mutely speaking of all the horrors he had ever dreamed of seemed to send him to the far reaches of his own control and he began to shake.

'Oh Christ . . . tell me she is not dead for I cannot stand it!'

He roared his refusal to believe her when at last she gathered the strength to tell him, standing over her and lifting her bodily to her feet though she was a good deal heavier then himself. He grasped her forearms and shook her forcibly, savagely, until her head lolled on her shoulders like that of a broken doll and she watched his face change before her eyes. The colour had gone, draining away in shock from a healthy bronze to the yellow-pale sweated sheen of a man dangerously ill and his eyes, at

198

first bewildered, disbelieving, almost ready to smile at the ridiculous words she spoke were filled with hatred for her.

'*NO ... NO ... NO ... NO!*' he repeated over and over again and his cries echoed about the room, shattering out into the hallway and along to the kitchen where the servants stood turned to stone, and Sally began to cry for she was in love herself and knew what those despairing sounds signified. Mrs Kean looked out into the yard for Ned since it seemed the Squire's boy could need restraining, as any man might when he has just been told his sweetheart has married another man and it would not do for him to attack the master's wife in her own parlour.

For several minutes he mouthed incomprehensible sounds which fell madly from his mouth, spitting full in Anne's face as his saliva flew. His face changed from white, drawn shock to the suffused red of rage and then back again, and all the while he shook her, needing to hurt something as he hurt, but gradually the words began to take shape, to make sense of a sort.

'Why, why? for Christ's sake, tell me *WHY?*'

He still held her in a ferocious grip, dragging her up to his mad face, his mad eyes, but she was not afraid now.

'She knew I loved her ... she knew I would come ... I waited ... just as you said I must ...!'

'I?'

'You told my father ... I must wait, you said. I did!' His voice rose to a howl and he flung her to the sofa in his demented, frightened, pitiable rage. 'I waited ... I did as you said ...'

It was as though he could not believe that his own exemplary conduct had been so horribly punished and he continued to savage the fact that he had been told, made to stay away when, left to himself, he would have come and by God he would know the reason why.

He turned suddenly, his eyes hot and dry, like brown stones on a dusty desert and his mouth worked in a ferocious grin of agonized frenzy. He strode towards the door, fumbling for the knob and his voice jerked from his mouth in a delirium of pain.

'She is mine, not his . . . I will go to her now and bring her home where she belongs and then when she is ready we will be married just as we planned. How dare that bastard take what is mine . . . He has always wanted her . . . from that first time . . . that's it . . . that first time when he saw us up in the wood.'

His hand seemed unable to perform the function which would turn the doorknob and his words were directed at the panelled door and the delay gave Annie time to gather herself up with one mighty effort from where he had thrown her and get to him.

She grasped his shoulders, shoulders not wide and strong like Alex Buchanan's, or the Emmerson men, but slender, well-proportioned, delicately balanced on his fine body, vulnerable now, and she held on to them and her voice was loud in his face as she turned him about.

'No, no, Robin, you cannot!'

'I will . . . she is mine . . . I love her . . . she is mine . . .'

'*NO SHE IS NOT!*'

'She is . . . we love each other.'

'No, no, she cannot love you now!'

'She does . . . she does, she belongs to me . . .'

'*No! She belongs to Alex Buchanan! Do you not understand! Yesterday she married him! Last night she spent the night with him as his wife! As his wife, Robin! In his bed!*'

She saw it go from him then, the bright and lovely youth of Robin Forsythe, just as she had seen it go from her daughter. Before her eyes he changed from a boy to a man as the truth was accepted by him and the despair, the agony in his eyes matched those of her girl during the last eight weeks. Annie Emmerson and Robin Forsythe looked at one another and he waited quietly enough now, now that he was mortally injured and could fight no more, for her to explain how his own father had cheated him. In that moment they both realized it and were united by the knowledge.

200

'Come and sit down, lad.'

'Tell me.'

'Sit down first.'

'Tell me.'

Annie held on to him still, her face soft with compassion and his was like a rock, old and grey and totally without life.

'You did not come to her, you see.'

'I was told not to.'

'Aye, so it seems, but it did not come from me!'

'I realize that now.'

'So she . . . she fretted . . . she was angry . . .'

'Yes.'

'And when Alex . . .' She saw him flinch and his face become more leaden. 'When he asked for her she took him!'

'So . . . so quickly . . . why?'

'What else was there for her to do. You were . . . lost to her and one seemed as good as another. Her father is not . . . recovered and needed someone to see to the mills. Without his sons . . . there was no one.'

'Of course.'

Annie sighed. He was like a puppet now, moving to the strings which pulled him, only his brain functioning agonizingly inside his handsome head. She felt she could almost see it through the opaque deadness of his eyes, ticking away his life, empty and torpid and yet assimilating her words in the way it was meant.

'Why . . . why did he do it, lad? I thought he wanted Job's cash.'

'He did, but . . . someone else came along. Someone of our – *his* class. A girl, wealthy, whose father is a baronet.'

'Aah!'

The silence settled about them. There was nothing else to say. It was done, finished. Last night Christy Emmerson had become a woman, another man's woman and was now forever out of reach of this man she still loved and who loved her. This time yesterday, even after the wedding, she might have gone with him – would have gone with him Annie knew – but not now. Now she belonged to Alex Buchanan in every way a woman could. Their flesh had 'cleaved', as it said in the Holy Bible. She might even at this moment bear the seed in her body which would become his child and there was nothing Christy Emmerson could do to escape that.

He went then and she watched him walk down the gravelled drive, his horse forgotten in the stable yard. He paused at the gateway into the road, looking from right to left as she had seen Christy do a dozen times as though one direction was as good as another then turned away towards Chapel Stile, away from the Hall and Squire Forsythe, moving like a sleepwalker towards the fells which lay beyond the village.

She began to weep silently for him, for she knew her girl would recover from it one day, but would he?

'Robin, my dear, where have you been? We have been half out of our minds with worry. The Emmerson's groom brought your horse home last night and then your father arrived from Yorkshire and I thought he was about to have a stroke when he learned you had come from Leicestershire; particularly when the man said where you had left the animal and I have been up most of the night at the window thinking you had been thrown. Where have you been? Look at the state of you! Surely you have not slept in the open for by the condition – oh Robin, please darling – you look so dreadful. What is it . . . please!'

'Where is father, Mama?'

'He is in his study, darling, but . . .'

'Thank you. I will see him and then . . . afterwards you and I will talk. I will explain.'

Mrs Forsythe began to cry, knowing of course, but her son just looked at her, quite without interest, for though he was perfectly well aware that she was not in any way to blame for his father was master in this house, she had been well aware of what he was about. She must do as he said, always, as wives did, but he felt the apathy settle about him and her tears, which once would have moved him to passionate sympathy, left him unmoved.

His father stood up jerkily as he entered the study, his face wary, cautious but ready to break into a welcoming, glad smile at the return of his naughty son who had no doubt spent the night in the arms of some woman! That is what he hoped, his expression said, but the incident of the horse and the Emmerson's groom warned him to tread carefully.

'My boy!' he said, falsely cheerful. 'Your mother and I were worried about you. Now I appreciate that you are a man and must find many a diversion,' he almost winked but his son neither smiled nor frowned, 'but your mother was convinced you had taken a tumble from your roan and when it was brought back by some chappie who . . .'

'The Emmerson groom.'

'I beg your pardon, old chap. You said?'

'It was the Emmerson groom who brought my animal back, father, for that was where I left it.'

Squire Forsythe lowered himself gently into his chair and his face became quite expressionless. He would get out of this somehow, he knew that, convince the boy it was all for the best since of course he had been told of the girl's marriage to the Buchanan fellow, but it would be tricky for a while! His son was a good fellow and bright and would realize the uselessness of hankering after a girl who was out of his reach and begin to look with fresh interest at Adele Mainwood. He thanked God only that Robin had not taken it into his head to come home a day sooner. One bloody day. What a narrow squeak that had been, but now, with a bit of careful management he would set the boy in the direction it was right for him to take and within a year perhaps, or even less if he could devise it, they would be married.

Not a glimmer of his thoughts showed in his eyes as he puffed serenely on his expensive cigar.

'You have been to pay your respects to the family then,' he said sympathetically, just as though he was glad his son had been gentleman enough to do, as was only expected of him, the correct and mannerly thing.

'You might say that, father.'

'Good, good, and how did you find them?'

'Mrs Emmerson seemed in good heart and Mr Emmerson has returned to his mills. I did not *find* . . . Miss Emmerson at all.' He could not speak her given name to this man and his face spasmed in anguish for the reason.

'Oh . . . she is . . . away?'

'She is away, father. Away with her new . . . husband!'

The Squire looked at the rigidly controlled man who had once been his cheerful, good-natured, eager to please and pliable son and he felt the first stirrings of unease pluck at his gut. He shifted in his seat, clearing his throat unnecessarily for he must have time to think for a moment, to think of a way to bring that boy back, but Robin Forsythe, the future Squire of Dalebarrow Hall, did not care to wait for his father's quick brain to manipulate his own, should it be able.

'I realize what has been done to us . . . to Miss Emmerson and myself and I know why. You found Adele Mainwood more to your taste, did you not? She was . . . just as wealthy but best of all she was of our . . . class. Her father is a landed gentleman like yourself and no doubt your sudden friendship with him is leading to the betrothal of myself to his daughter. The other . . . arrangement no longer mattered so when the opportunity presented itself you used it to keep . . . to keep us apart. Well, you succeeded, father! She was . . . she was married yesterday . . . Jesus . . . only yesterday!'

For a moment his iron control shattered and he threw back his head, dragging his hands through his hair, pulling at the roots and the flesh of his forehead in despair, then his shoulders slumped wearily and he looked again at the Squire who had become in those few seconds, strangely old, frail almost, as though he knew what was coming.

'So you see ... there is nothing left for me here ... nothing!'

'Robin, please, let us talk. Sit down, old chap and . . .'

'What have we to say to one another? I shall not marry your Adele Mainwood, father, that is all I have to tell you, and nothing you have to tell me is of the slightest interest to me.'

'But surely we can discuss . . .?'

'What?'

'You cannot mean to let this ... girl ... this family stand in the way of your duty . . .'

'My duty? To what?'

The squire stood up fiercely and his anger showed in his heightened colour and the stiff set of his shoulders. His back was straight with the pride of three centuries of service and responsibility to his name, his land, his people, his country and his son's careless unconcern for it inflamed him.

'You have a duty to me, you unlicked cub, and to your inheritance. You are a Forsythe, pledged to carry on the name, and the dynasty, if I may call it that, in the best way you know how. It needs money to continue the line, the growth of the family, and sons to pass it on to as I will pass it to you. And blood counts, sir. Good blood and a good name to ally with ours. One can hardly compare the grand-daughter of a collier to that of a girl whose forebears fought beside Wellington at Waterloo; under the command of Nelson on the *Agamemnon*, and who were great leaders back down the ages, as ours were; who have held the title and the office and the privilege and responsibility of class for as long as we have. They are a fine family, the Mainwoods, and I would be proud to have my name linked with theirs and by God I shall!'

His son stood quietly, saying nothing in his own defence, saying nothing more against his father and the way in which he had twisted two lives, perhaps more, in the cause of his own pride. He waited quite patiently, his face expressionless, weary with the strain of the past twenty-four hours. He had spent them, and himself, on the high fell where he had climbed in his grief and madness and he was empty now, mercifully numb, his weeping done, his boyhood behind him, his belief in the goodness of life gone with the loss of the girl he loved, and the man he had respected.

When his father had finished, the man he had become spoke for the last time to the man who had been his father.

'I'm going away ... abroad ... I don't know where. I might try the Americas, or Australia. They say there are fortunes to be made ...'

'Dear God, Robin ... you cannot mean to turn your back on your inheritance, your name, this place will fall to rack and ruin without ... please ... son ...'

'It's too late ... I cannot ... I must go away. You and I can never be as we were. I can never forgive you, you see, for treating what was the most important thing in my life as though it were nothing. You have ruined our name, if you want to believe it matters, not I, by your contempt for what was good and fine. She can never be replaced, and besides, you surely cannot expect me to live here ... where she is the wife of ...'

'Robin ... you will come home ... you must ...'

'Goodbye, father.'

'Son ...'

But his son had turned and walked away, shutting the door on the Squire of Dalebarrow Hall and on the life which would have been his.

CHAPTER THIRTEEN

He left the house each morning at six to supervise the charge of his mines by the young engineer, David Adams, and his mine foremen. But before he went in those first weeks he drew her into his arms in the lightening spring mornings and to the sound of the cuckoo, the rising larks in the thin, blue sky, the young lambs calling to their mothers on the fells, he made love to her leaving her languidly satiated, smiling, stretching, yawning until Faith came to bring her hot chocolate and fresh buttered toast. Her flesh purred as his hands, lips and eyes took hold of her and she moaned helplessly, wordlessly for him, her skin loving the feel of his, wanting his against it, but when he had gone with a sardonic tilt of his dark eyebrows, a casual kiss dropped on her forehead, she forgot his very existence.

She was maid no longer. She was woman. His woman. He made her so each night in the big bed, showing her what her body needed, showing her what pleasures could be had, showing her how to take it, to please him and herself, but he did not make her love him.

Her day began then when he left her. Her life! What she was, for the woman who lay in his arms each night had a different existence to the girl who, during the daylight hours, was Christy Emmerson. In the candlelight, beneath the caressing boldness of his hands and eyes, she was Alexander Buchanan's woman without the benefit of even her own name, and though she was honest enough to admit her treacherous woman's body came breathlessly alive – not even against her will as it had at first, but willingly – her heart was not touched. Though it fluttered helplessly against her ribs and her breath caught, then exploded from her throat, though her voice called out to him and her arms clung to him in a great desperate yearning; though she was completely aware of who he was when he took her, her heart remained still and unmoved, locked away where she had relentlessly imprisoned it on the day she had accepted Robin Forsythe's rejection of her.

When Alex had gone for the day, on that first day, saying carelessly that he would not be home until six of the clock when they would dine, she lay in the silky tumble of the bed, her naked body achingly fatigued, and yet pleasurably so. She rang for Faith and for the first five minutes could scarce look her in the face for surely she would know, would guess, would smell the very air which seemed to Christy to have an essence of the two bodies which had come so tumultuously together in the night, but Faith had smiled her 'good morning' as she always did, her eyes meeting Christy's with no embarrassment. She had put down the tray of hot chocolate on the table beside the bed and drawn back the curtains.

'It's a lovely day, Mrs Buchanan,' she said dimpling, her eyes cutting to her mistress in mischief.

'Oh Faith, stop it. Mrs Buchanan indeed! It's Miss Christy, just as always,' and she knew then that nothing had changed her. She was exactly as she had always been, Christy Emmerson, untouched by any emotion beyond those she had brought with her to Howethwaite, despite her husband's demanding hands and lips and the passion with which she had met them!

Now, in broad daylight she was herself again. Faith was the same and they would go on as they had done for the past year or so, merely changing houses, the comfort and security of her father's for the comfort and security of her husband's.

For an instant her heart dropped at the thought, plunging despairingly, for what was there to be now, now that there was nothing in her future to stretch out for; then Faith turned and the sunshine touched the beautiful painted silk of the bed canopy and brought to vivid life the raspberry pink of the crumpled bedspread and at the open window the sounds of spring called cheerfully, and she became strong again as she had vowed she would on the night before her wedding.

She sat up in bed, then blushed as Faith quietly handed her her nightgown, but it seemd Faith Cooper did not mean to make anything of her mistress's marital obligations for it was not her place and Christy relaxed and sighed thankfully. Faith poured a cup of steaming chocolate whilst Christy hastily pulled her nightgown over her head, then passed the cup to her, plumping up the pillows behind her to make a cosy nest just as though Christy was an invalid. It seemed Mrs Alexander Buchanan was to have certain privileges not accorded to Miss Christina Emmerson!

'Sit down, Faith, and have a cup with me,' she begged and indicated the velvet chair against the window. 'It seems we have every comfort so let's enjoy it.' She spoke as though she and Faith were guests in another's house.

'I couldn't do that, Miss Christy.'

'Why not? We sat down together at home ... er ... before ...'

'You're the mistress now. It wouldn't be seemly.'

'Rubbish! Who's to know, besides as the mistress I order you to it. Please, Faith. There's a potful of chocolate there. I can't drink it all. Sit down and tell me what they're saying about me in the servants' hall.'

'I'll sit down and drink a cup with you, but I'll not tell you what goes on down there just as I'll not tell them what goes on up here.'

Christy blushed again, thinking Faith was referring to the activities in her bed but her maid looked candidly at her, pouring herself a cup of chocolate, then taking it to the chair by the window. 'I'll not carry tales either way, lass. You know it wouldn't be right but I'll say this. They all think you'll not last the month!'

She began to laugh then, throwing back her head in delight and, startled for a minute since suddenly she felt intensely filled with a sense of well-being and a determination to prove the servants wrong. Christy did the same and so began the pattern of their days together.

They would sit before the bedroom fire, friends, for she had no other, and when they were ready they would idle through Christy's wardrobe and decide what she would wear for whatever the day's occasion demanded and Faith would lay out the costume and help her to dress. Christy would sit in front of the mirror for another drifting hour whilst they tried out a dozen different ways to do her hair, giggling as eighteen-year-olds will; and when it was time

Mrs Longworth would come to her elegant little sitting room to discuss any orders Mrs Buchanan might have for her and her servants. She was indulgent of little Mrs Buchanan now, for hadn't the master put her in her place on their very first night, showing her that routines which had been set up years ago, that rooms allocated to old family servants in his mother's day, were not easily changed. The young mistress was no more than a child, his plaything, the servants had smugly told themselves and would soon have – if she was strong enough, though the look of her that first day had made them doubtful – a child or two to keep her out of mischief.

Mrs Avery was next with the day's menus but after a week she realized that if she'd suggested 'hasty pudding', a kind of porridge made with oatmeal and water, for the master's dinner, young Mrs Buchanan would have carelessly agreed; that the ten minutes' interview was no more than a formality, and that she could carry on with the preparing and cooking as she had done for the past twenty years, pleasing herself as to what it should be. The master had never complained for Mrs Avery knew herself to be a good cook, trained up by the first Mrs Buchanan, the master's mother when mistresses *were* mistresses and knew exactly what went on in their own kitchens. Times had changed since then with the coming of what they called the Industrial Revolution and the elevating of what were really no more than working-class women to the status, or so they liked to think, of the gentry. This one, of course, had been brought up as a young lady, though she was still on the commercial class, and took no interest in what went on, domestically speaking, in her own home.

The new Mrs Buchanan did all the things her mother had not allowed her to do. She lay in her bed for a long as she cared to. She wandered about the garden employed in absolutely nothing but the enjoyment of the sun on her face, the approaching summer's breeze in her loosened hair. She lay on her stomach in the grass, her shoes scattered and lost, and read books of which her mother

210

would not have approved. She did no sewing whatsoever, even the fine embroidery considered lady-like by the better class of Fellthwaite, and all in the company of her own maid which was strange in itself when you considered the many young ladies with whom she might have spent her time.

She and Faith ordered out the carriage whenever they had a mind to, going wherever the fancy took them. To Fellthwaite to Miss Susan Whittam's to order shawls and bonnets, reticulars and fans, muffs and mittens by the score. To Ambleside to the stylish salon of Miss Clara Jenkins to be fitted for a new evening gown of gold broché silk for Alex was to take Christy to a ball at the Market Hall in Fellthwaite in August.

They visited Annie Emmerson once a week to sit and chat about the rebuilding of Job's mills, and the terrible cost to him in new machinery of over six thousand pounds, in which her own husband now had a hand and of Celia Metcalf who had been approached by a wealthy gentleman who owned a coal mine over Whitehaven way and was to take him when her period of mourning was over.

'So soon?' Christy grimaced in distaste.

'A girl must be wed, daughter. There is no other occupation open to her and Celia is a fine girl. She cannot bury her heart in Ben's grave!'

'And of course, she has a few guineas to her name!'

'Now then, Christy Emmerson,' – why was it people still called her that, she wondered idly? – 'that's not a nice thing to say!'

'True though.'

'Aye, but that's the way of it, lass, you should know, and Alex seems well satisfied?' Her voice was mildly inquiring, probing.

'Do you think so?' Christy was astonished for the handsome, smiling stranger who sat across the dining table from her each evening, telling her politely of his day and asking politely of hers; the hard, muscled body in her bed at night, awaking hers to shivering delight, showed no

211

emotion of any kind beyond an indulgent pride in her own, she supposed, growing, maturing beauty and was that not the way of all men when they showed off an expensive possession other men might envy?

She was called upon by Mrs Marsden and her Jenny, recovered now from her dreadful ordeal on the day of the explosion and who was to be married to Paul Aspin in September. Mrs Dyer and her Emily also visited. Her father was in the process of intricate marriage contract settlements, trusts and allowances pending the announcement of her betrothal to a young solicitor, the son of a banker and of a fine family up in Carlisle. Then there was Mrs Aspin and her Jane who, as yet, had not been spoken for, for though she was equally eligible was not quite as pretty. And Christy in her turn, called on them.

They admired her lovely new gowns, the stylish way in which Faith did her hair and the gold and sapphire bracelet – an intricate lacy network of fine chains which her husband had twined about her wrist when she was naked in the candlelight, when he returned from a business trip to St Helens and Swansea – and her horses and carriage and the smartness of her very own coachman, young Jack Hodson.

They were giddy, she and Faith when they were alone and unseen, though Faith was more restrained than her mistress for she was well aware her master would not be best pleased at the way in which Mrs Buchanan encouraged the young man to set the carriage to a mad speed on the dipping, curving country lanes, careering down the hill to Skelwith Bridge with all the careless confidence of youth, risking the animal's fine legs in a way which would have incensed her new husband. Jack was smart as paint in his coachman's cape and breeches, proud of his elevation from groom to coachman and proud too, to be in charge of his master's lovely young wife.

And she *was* lovely again now as July moved into August and the sweet, white rounded flesh settled again on her slender frame. She was a woman made for the sensuality of love, though she was not aware even of the meaning of the word, if her husband was. It suited her. The pleasure of her own sexuality soothed the angry hurt in her. Alex's body fed hers, satisfying some hunger in her which had lain waiting since the moment Robin Forsythe had put his inexperienced hands on her. She became bonny again with health. Warm velvet grey eyes, the iris ringed startlingly in black, the expression in them speaking plainly to those who could read it of her satisfied body. Lustrous dark hair, flushed cheeks and a lively energy which gratified Annie Emmerson enormously for she thought her girl to be happy again as she once had been, not knowing how badly she still grieved for Robin Forsythe. The gauntness had left her face and the haunted look of defeat in her eyes was replaced by an attractive defiance which challenged society to question her ways and because no one could see into the depthless core of her they imagined the smart as a whip Mrs Buchanan to be happy!

She and her husband had their first quarrel over his daughter.

On occasion, when she was bored with Fellthwaite and the constricting, sheltered existence she and those women of her society were expected to live – when the tedious discussions on the problems of servants, the whims of husbands and the waywardness of young, unmarried men was exhausted; and the complexities of how to make a decent syllabub had driven her to leave her hostess's drawing room with more haste than was decent; when the charms of spending her husband's money had become temporarily jaded; when Faith was away over to Chapel Stile to visit her crippled father and Annie was busy with the pickling, or preserving, or jam making in which she became increasingly involved – Christy would take out the doll-like daughter of Alex Buchanan and play with her as though she was a toy. The rug would be spread beneath the shade of the oak tree on the huge, somewhat rough-cut lawn at the front of the house and under the anxious gaze of Beth she would tickle the baby until she screamed

213

with joy, then throw her in the air, careless as though she was a kitten, showing little or no concern for the growing hysteria of the infant – for she knew nothing of children, bidding Beth curtly to mind her business when the nursemaid remonstrated.

'But madam, she will be sick if you fling her about.'

'Have you no other work to see to, Beth? No baby linen to wash or mend?' Christy would say curtly.

'No madam.' Beth was stout in her defence of her little dear, afraid the capricious Mrs Buchanan, as vague about the child as she would be a stray puppy, might wander off and leave her to crawl into God alone knows what danger in the garden. But Christy could be regally, icily authoritative, in the way of a young queen when she chose, as the servants were rapidly learning as her body recovered from its pining for Robin Forsythe, more so now that she was unchecked, and in a voice which would brook no argument told the maid to be off. When the little girl fell asleep from sheer exhaustion, or, as Beth predicted, vomited her breakfast over the mistress's new tarlatan morning gown, she would be dropped unceremoniously into the arms of the nearest servant, once those of the astonished Abel Hodson who had not held a child since the long ago days of his young fatherhood.

'I believe you are upsetting my daughter,' Alex said over his cigar and brandy that night.

Christy looked up from the magazine through which she had been idly flicking, her face comical in its amazement, then it became an indignant red.

'Upsetting your daughter! What the hell does that mean?'

'And I would be obliged if you would not swear. It is not becoming in a lady!'

'Oh for God's sake never mind that. What's this about my upsetting Amy?'

'Just that. I have been told you remove her from her nursemaid's care, even when she is sleeping, and play with her until she becomes so excited she is sick, then throw her back when you are done with her with as much concern . . .'

'Oh, so that's it! The servants spy on me and then tattle to their master . . .'

Alex's face was still, but his eyes were a brilliant, quite dangerous blue. He lounged indolently against the fireplace with the ease of a man discussing no more than the state of the weather but his expression said it would take very little to turn him to black, snarling anger.

'That is not the issue here though they know their place and would naturally report any careless treatment of my child to me. She has had a secure, peaceful unbringing and is happy in the affection of her nursemaid. Now I have no objection to you taking a decent interest in her, in fact I have been waiting for you to do so which would seem desirable in your position as her mother . . .'

'Mother!'

'As my wife and as she is my daughter, yes!'

'Now look here . . .'

'No! You look here, madam. You have certain obligations in this partnership . . .'

'Partnership! Is that how you see it?' Christy's grey eyes had begun to snap and her jaw clenched wilfully.

'That is what marriage is about, I believe. Now in most other . . . quarters . . . you have been most . . . obliging!' He grinned audaciously, his crackling anger forgotten momentarily. His eyes ran over her figure and she felt herself becoming annoyingly warm, 'But in others you have not yet fulfilled my expectations.'

'Your . . .!'

'Yes, my dear. Being my wife does not mean you are merely to warm my bed and, in reward, spend my money, which is all you have done so far, though I must admit I cannot complain about the former.' He grinned again, most intimately, then his face became cool with the compelling arrogance which as yet she had scarcely seen, since up to this incident she had done nothing with which he could find fault.

He was assured, completely certain in his masculine world that he would have his own way in whichever fashion he chose, however painful she might find it. She had been allowed to play at being Mrs Alex Buchanan for a while, whilst it pleased him to let her, but when he was ready, should he want to, he would turn it all about to suit his own purpose and her wishes could go hang for all he cared.

'But she is not my child!'

'She is now.'

'She is a . . . sweet little thing, but she is the child of your first wife and not mine and I cannot think I should be expected . . .'

'But you are, you see. You are expected to do everything I ask of you.'

'I did not ask for this. You did.'

Her eyes hated him then but he merely raised his eyebrows in wry amusement and a smile pulled at the corner of his lips.

'But you accepted, my pet, did you not and does that not constitute a bargain which both sides agree to honour?'

'A bargain between my father and yourself. I was only the goods traded!'

'Goods traded! What a way you do have with words. Goods traded, well now, if that is the case does that not imply your father and I did business? That he sold me something for which I paid a price? But you cost me nothing, my love. Nothing at all. I merely asked Job Emmerson if I might have you and he agreed . . . and so did you!'

'Nevertheless you got a bargain, Alex Buchanan. Besides me you got my father's mills. When he goes you will be the owner of the Emmerson gunpowder mills and everything else my father has. Do you not consider you got the best of the . . . the deal?'

'Well, of course, put like that you are right. I did get the best of the transaction whereas you, you merely got me . . . and my child, which brings us back to our original conversation. I cannot force your affections for an infant who is not your own though I would have been . . . pleased if you could have found some small . . . pleasure in her company.'

His face softened and Christy found herself listening intently to him as he reached out to some quite unknown part of her which she had not been aware she possessed. It touched and lightened a dark corner for a brief instant and something moved in surprise at it then was gone again as he continued.

'She is, as you say . . . a child who . . . she has a certain . . . way with her. I find myself . . . drawn . . . but she is not of your body so . . .' He grew curt then, turning away from her. 'If you can do no more than treat her like some plaything to be brought out and tossed here and there when the feeling takes you, then stowed away until you are bored enough to find time for her again, leave her alone! She is happy in her nursery with her nursemaid. She is . . . only a baby yet and knows no difference.'

He seemed then to forget for a moment that Christy was there, to lose the angry thread of what he was saying and his words were quiet, strange, and the tone of his voice was one she had not heard before.

'. . . it is when she grows, becomes a little girl ready to have other little girls to her home with their mothers. Nursemaids are all very well for infants but for a little girl . . .'

He stopped abruptly, then turned again to her, his face taut with some emotion and she was quite astonished for not once had he shown her the softer side of his nature, only amusement, a certain cynicism, an ironic acceptance of the world as he found it. A long time ago he had spoken to her of the sorry plight of women, she remembered, and his strange belief that they were imprisoned by their menfolk in a male-dominated world and she had laughed at him, and with him, she recalled. He was a curious man and sometimes, when he talked to her she found him quite fascinating but his ideas obviously did

217

not stretch to his own household for he was telling her here that she was expected to act as a kind of nursemaid to Amy when really, the child was nothing to do with her.

His voice was cold as he continued. 'But then that does not concern you, does it, and why should it? You are only a child yourself, so I would be obliged if you would . . .'

'I am no child, Alexander Buchanan.' Christy's voice was steely and her face set itself in the stiff lines of her unsparing will, that which had brought her, sick and trembling, from the pain of losing Robin Forsythe into this man's life. She had made her marriage vows in a twilit haze, not knowing or caring what was done with her. She had become wild and giddy in her freedom from her mother's respectability and her father's rule since Alex Buchanan seemed not to care what she did providing she was at his table and in his bed at night, but beneath it all, beneath the slowly mending pattern of her torn life, was a growing conviction that she could not be expected to be no more than a decorative mistress, in both senses of the word, in her husband's home. It was half a year and more since she had last seen Robin and her heart was buried deep and inviolate, safe now from hurt, and there were so many simple pleasures she had rediscovered and on which she must build a world of her own. She was honest enough, as she looked defiantly at the man who was her husband, to admit he was right about the child. Though she was another woman's, she was no more than a baby and surely easy enough to become fond of, to take more than a passing interest in, without treating her, as Alex Buchanan said, like some doll to play with.

But she was not Job Emmerson's daughter for nothing and however in the wrong she was, she was still not mature enough to admit it.

She tossed her head challengingly and the stubborn set of her mouth gave no clue to her softening attitude but in her eyes Alex saw something move and glow a little and a tiny flame of triumph licked about his heart.

'Well I dare say I can spare some moments each day to spend with the child,' she said loftily. 'She will be walking soon, I suppose, and it would do her good to be taken down to the paddock to see the horses, to get about in the open air . . . and run . . . when she is able for I am a great believer in fresh air and exercise. That Beth has no interest in such things, I'll be bound, and perhaps when you are about your business you might look out for a small pony since I am sure you will wish her to ride in a year or two. Oh, and by the way, whilst we are on the subject I would be glad if you would arrange for my mare to be brought over from Hollins. I have a fancy to go riding again now that summer is here. And perhaps you would inform the servants . . . no, I will do it myself, that I am the mistress in this house and that should there be further running to you on any pretext they care to devise there will be trouble!'

She had the last word and was bold in her certainty that she had won the round but Alex smiled as she swept from the room, her own overweening pride in herself quite insufferable.

But as he had known she would for her heart was not cruel, she had seen the justice of his words and though she had fought the rein, as he had also known she would, she was fair.

That night – though she fought him vigorously in her new found independence, or so she thought of it – he made love to her with almost savage passion, hurting her as she struggled to be free of him. She bit his lip and he laughed out loud, forcing her on to her back and kneeling over her in complete mastery.

'Aah, insolence is it, my sweet, and rebellion?'

'Let me alone,' she shrieked. 'Am I never to have the choice . . .' but his mouth came down on hers and she tasted his blood and as his lips travelled lingeringly with all the night before them to enjoy her in, down the length of her body, she began to sigh and stretch and glow until that sweet, curling filament which began at the centre of her, spread and spread and her hands clung to his dark head and her voice lifted to the silken canopy of the bed in rapture.

CHAPTER FOURTEEN

Her mare came the next week and accompanied either by Miles or John, one of the grooms, she began to ride out again as she had done before her marriage, taking the long winding cart-track which led from the back of the house, across the river by the little bridge Alex had built and up through the woods towards Dun Foot and Crag Head.

The slopes were easy enough for a rider and when they got beyond the line of the trees she could see out over Elterwater towards her old home and beyond to the scattered sheds of her father's works. The pale blue plume of smoke from the flue rose lazily into the sky, drifting whichever way the wind blew and she would dismount, handing the reins to Miles or John, and climb for a while, alone and secret in the loneliness of the memories of young Christy Emmerson and Robin Forsythe who were ghosts now, come only when she allowed them, to haunt her.

But she was irked by the constant though discreet presence of the groom who rode with her and one day, as he held his hands for her to mount in the stable yard she said casually, before he had time to leap into the saddle on his own animal, 'I shall go alone today, Miles. I'm sure you must have plenty to occupy your time without trailing at my mare's tail.'

'But Mrs Buchanan . . .' he shouted after her as she put her mare to a dashing gallop through the stable gateway and across the meadow which led to the track and the little bridge, '. . . I am not to let you go alone . . . wait . . . please . . .'

His raised voice unsettled his own horse and it turned round and round in the stable yard to the vast amusement of several housemaids who, startled by his shouts, peered from the bedroom window as he tried to mount, hopping furiously with one foot on the ground, the other in the stirrup and by the time he was aloft and had gone after her, she had vanished.

Though he rode for several miles in the direction she had always taken she was nowhere in sight. Cursing the flighty Mrs Buchanan beneath his breath and preparing already in his mind the excuses he would give to his master, he turned back, for what was the use. She could be miles away in any direction, following one of any number of tracks which were familiar to her, ones she had ridden since girlhood. It was well-known in the kitchens by now that the second Mrs Buchanan was no milk and water miss as had first been thought and if she had taken it into her head to vanish, vanish she would but by God, he wasn't taking the bloody blame for it!

She rode as high as she could, going carefully in order not to injure her mare's legs, then dismounted, using a rocky outcrop to step on for it was awkward with no one to help her down. There was a stunted tree, a juniper bush with the female cone already beginning to swell to form a hard green berry, the 'bastard killers' which her mother had described, and tying the reins to a branch she left her mare to crop the grass around it.

She climbed then, up beyond Loughrigg Tarn towards Loughrigg Fell, higher and higher, almost hidden in the golden bracken. The track was faint, used by the sheep mostly and a shepherd or two who came to check them and up ahead was a vast sprawling of grey stone and green lichen, patches of tufted green and a hardy tree or two and the grey moving dots which were the sheep.

There was green, grey, golden, and purple where great patches of heather grew. She could hear from somewhere the music of water falling and smell the lovely tang of the air which was filled with nothing but emptiness and solitude, a place for withdrawal from ... from what, she thought?

Why had she decided to run away today, she asked herself and knew the answer and smiled a little for she was not displeased. For the past few weeks since her husband had – surprisingly, for she had not know he cared – asked her to take an interest in his daughter she had gone each day to the nursery, for a short time at first so that she and the child could grow slowly used to one another, and with Beth's permission for she meant to do it properly this time, had taken the little girl on her lap.

Sitting before the nursery fire – with Beth lurking suspiciously in the doorway to the night nursery, not at all convinced that Mrs Buchanan would not drop the baby or, bored suddenly, abandon her on the edge of the sofa where she would undoubtedly fall into the nursery fire – Christy held the little girl carefully, liking the feel of the plump, sweet smelling body against her own, the silken flesh of the child's firm legs and feet in her caressing hand, the kicking toes, the drowsy murmur of her enquiring voice.

Beth was reassured. Mrs Buchanan did no more than nurse Beth's charge, her cheek resting on the child's ebony curls, which in turn rested against Mrs Buchanan's breast. There was no tossing or tickling, just a sense of peace, a snatch or two from some nursery song from her own childhood and as the baby dozed, at peace it appeared and perfectly happy, Beth relaxed and ventured to leave them alone together and when she returned they were both asleep!

'What a change,' she said later, astonished, to Mrs Avery as she fetched Miss Amy's biscuit powder which was soaking in cold water, ready to be boiled in milk and have beaten into it two eggs and sugar. It would then be left to stand and set like a custard. Miss Amy was no longer suckled by the wet nurse being almost twelve months old and Beth was most particular about her diet, giving her the farinaceous foods needed by a growing infant, with semolina, rusks and plenty of milk from the cows Mr Buchanan kept on his land.

'You should have seen her, Mrs Avery, sitting there calm as you please and the little dear loving it. You know how she do like a cuddle, poor motherless mite. Well, you could have knocked me down with a feather. Singing a lullaby she was and whispering to her and you'd have thought Miss Amy was her own child, so careful she was. You know, I think she's losing that wildness she had at first and I reckon we were wrong about her. She'll make a good little mother when the time comes, not that it'll happen if she do go riding that dratted horse of hers. My mother always used to say, and she worked for Lady Andrews up by Cockermouth who had none, that riding was no good for a lady who wanted to breed and Lady Andrews was always in the saddle . . .'

Christy, again with Beth's permission for though she knew there was no need for it now, felt the girl, who had after all cared for the baby from birth, should be given the credit for it, took Alex Buchanan's daughter down the garden paths and round the house to the back in her wicker baby carriage which had wheels and a handle to steer it by. They sat together on the grass, looking through the rails at her husband's horses, the child big-eyed and wondering, and unsure at first how one should address an infant not quite a year old, she talked to the little girl in the way she would an adult.

'That's my mare, Amy, the little one with the lovely mane. Is she not a beautiful colour with the sun on her coat? Of course she is groomed every day and that is the secret of it. See, she is looking at us.'

She pointed through the railing and at the sound of her voice the animal raised its head and began to walk towards them. The child, who had followed her pointing finger began to rock excitedly in her carriage threatening to tip it up as the mare approached so Christy picked her out of it and settled her quite naturally on her hip, pushing up the confining skirt of her little dress. The child's well-fleshed

223

legs were revealed, the sun warming them, straddling Christy's waist and her hand rested companionably on the back of Christy's neck and they stayed that way as the horse nudged her head against them. 'Stroke her nose, Amy, don't be afraid. Watch me, just there.' Taking the child's hand she rested it on the glossy, quivering nose of the animal and the child left it there, completely unafraid in the confident grasp of her new friend, patting clumsily, quite roughly the patient mare, her bright, long-lashed eyes like cornflowers in her laughing face.

Alex Buchanan watched them from the gateway of the stable yard where he had just left his horse and he began to smile for their laughter was infectious. His face was soft and his eyes were warm. He had no particular feeling for his daughter, beyond a strong sense of responsibility for he scarcely knew her. She might have been the attractive child of another man, quite delightful at times and though he had seen her on occasion from his study window crawl about the rug on the lawn and heard her baby laughter, and tears, from far away, she had made no great impression on him. She was his, another of his possessions and therefore treasured, protected but beyond that and a certain pride in her infant beauty, he had no more affection for her than he had for the terrier who was his devoted shadow.

He began to walk across the rough pasture, drawn compulsively to the woman who was his wife and to the enchanted child she was bringing, by her own efforts, to his notice. His footsteps made no sound on the grass and she was speaking, unaware of his approach. He stopped to listen to her, bewitched by his new picture of Christy Emmerson.

'. . . and when you are a little older your father is to get you a pony of your own and I shall teach you to ride and then we will gallop together up to the fells and the wind will blow away our bonnets and we shall be as free as the lark which rides the skies. Would you like that, darling?'

Darling! She had called his child 'darling'! The man

moved closer, mesmerized by the lovely picture the woman and the child created.

The baby looked from the mare to the face of the woman, understanding nothing but a word or two which were familiar to her but responding to the joy in Christy's voice.

'I used to ride up there once, Amy.' Her eyes turned in the direction of Loughrigg Fell and her voice was soft and dreaming. '. . . long ago with . . . with someone. I would escape my jailers and go like the wind, up and up through the trees to the very tops. Ned used to call after me, poor lad, or if we were at Emily's wonder where the dickens I had got to, but I didn't care. I was free of him, of them all . . . It's wild up there and beautiful and there is no one to tell you what you must do or say or think and when you're with someone you . . .'

She stopped abruptly, completely still, a young animal which is aware instinctively of danger, then she turned slowly, the child turning to look with her, into the face of the man. The child was shy, hiding her face in Christy's neck for as her father did not know her, she did not know him.

Christy raised her head boldly.

'Good Heavens, Mr Buchanan, how you do love to creep about,' she said, and instantly Alex's face became shuttered and closed as he was flung back in time to a clearing in which had been this woman and a boy. She had been a girl then, a year ago, and still was for she was barely turned eighteen but she still loved Robin Forsythe for had she not just told his daughter so!

His anger made him cruel and his face became hard with a grinding hostility, as did hers and the child shrank further away, not only from him but from the suddenly rigid arms which held her.

'But is that not how one learns the secrets of others, my dear Mrs Buchanan,' he said, smiling maliciously, 'and sees things which otherwise one might miss. It is quite amazing what one can discover by listening at keyholes, figuratively speaking, that is. If one steps carefully and quietly so that no one can hear or see one's approach the most amusing and enlightening facts are uncovered. Really my sweet, you should try it sometime. It is most rewarding.' He smiled mercilessly.

Her lips tightened and she turned to put the baby in the carriage. 'So it seems, Mr Buchanan, but there is nothing to see here. I was merely telling Amy that she and I will ride . . . but then I doubt if that will interest you, will it? You are only concerned with creeping, not just into a person's private world but into their thoughts as well. How it must irk you not to know what goes on in my head, or indeed in any head. With your penchant for spying you really should be in the pay of some government service, or is it the Army which employs such fellows to find out the opposition's secrets? You would do well in either!'

She turned away contemptuously and as her eyes left his the muscles at the corner of his mouth jumped viciously and his hands clenched with his longing to form themselves into a fist with which to strike her.

'Come Amy,' she said. 'We shall go and have tea in the nursery. Say good afternoon to Mr Buchanan.'

Her mind lingered on that conversation as she sat on the high peak almost touching the clouds which raced above her head, and she wondered why it was they could not speak to one another without the abrasive tongues of enemies. Why did he dislike her so much? Why were his words so cutting always? Why, in fact, had he married her? There were the mills of course, and she supposed she was young and pretty enough and certainly she appeared to . . . to . . . make him happy in their bed. That was the one common ground they had but it was not enough, surely? She had come up here to escape the burden of his constant disapproval, his sardonic, jibing humour, the quizzical curling smile which seemed to say she could do nothing right for him, and yet here she sat with the aura of him filling her thoughts when she had come to get away from them.

She signed and her eyes swept across the craggy beauty which lay all about her, then she rose to her feet and shook out her skirts and began the climb down to where she had left her horse.

She was quiet that night as her husband smiled courteously at her across their dinner table, answering his polite questions on the state of her day and listening equally politely as he told her of his.

The rooms on the lower floor had not been much changed since the days of the first Mrs Buchanan, Mrs James Buchanan, and since she had become the new mistress Alex had told her carelessly she must do as she pleased with them, redecorating if she had a mind to, both the sitting room – the parlour as Mrs Longworth still called it – and the dining room. Christy had little interest for she still did not consider this to be her home. She lived here, true, and would do so until she died, or until her husband decided they would move to another, but she was, in her private mind, a guest here, even if a permanent one. The room was old-fashioned but pleasant and homely and she felt comfortable in it. There were starched white lace curtains, and along each window bottom as was the custom in a farmhouse, pots of red geraniums. Mrs Buchanan had liked them and so, as no one had given orders for the custom to done away with, as soon as they were ready Abel Hodson put them there! The dining table was large, surrounded by a dozen windsor chairs. A stiff white linen cloth was laid on it when they ate their meal and afterwards, when the table was cleared, a heavy green chenille cloth with an ornamental fringe of tassels covered it and on this rested the family Bible.

The table was of polished mahogany, the surface so bright and lovely Christy had idly thought how splendid it would look without either cloth, perhaps with a big copper bowl of chrysanthemums, bronze and gold, but had been too apathetic to bother.

227

Her husband's voice broke the silence.

'Well, my love, it seems you have been misbehaving again,' he said, reaching for his cigars as he rose from the table.

'I dare say.' She sighed as he graciously handed her from her chair and led her in the direction of the sitting room and when he had settled her in another chair and had taken up his customary place with his back to the blazing fire, which was lit in the evening, and his cigar was drawing to his satisfaction he turned and looked at her expectantly.

His face seemed thinner though she could not have said why, but his eyes were just as compellingly flashing with that particularly brilliant blue which was a herald of trouble. His lips smiled though, round his cigar and he waited for her to speak.

'Well my pet! Have you nothing to say?'

'What is there to say? You have, naturally, been told of my "escapade", is that the word, of this morning and no doubt have something to say about it so why don't you say it and have done?'

Her hands were busy at the coffee pot and porcelain cups and saucers, the cream and sugar which Meg had left on the low table at her side and she did not look up at him. She seemed indifferent, careless of what he said, or even why he said it. She looked superb in a dinner gown of amber velvet. Not a gown for guests but one which was to be worn only in the privacy of husband and wife alone and in happier circumstances he would have been enchanted with it. It was, as usual, simple and elegant, plain he would have called it until he saw her in it. The bodice was low, revealing the curve of her white breasts and shoulders and her renewed health showed in the sheen of her skin and the glow of her hair, the clear depths of her eyes and the becoming flesh which had filled out the bones of her neck and wrists.

She was completely female. Not just feminine but womanly, beautiful, and since they had married, sensual, and she was his and yet he did not possess her. Her body, yes, but the sweet, wild essence of her belonged still to the boy. Her vulnerability made him gentle with her for it was none of it her fault. She had been manipulated by four men. By Robin Forsythe in his love for her. By the Squire, Forsythe's father, in greed, by her own father in weakness and by himself and what excuse could he give? She was a woman of her time, put where she was directed by men. She could expect no other treatment and should not be blamed when she rebelled against it.

'You really must not ride alone, Christy,' he said quietly. She looked up, startled for she had expected cold rage. This man who was her husband never failed to surprise her. He seemed to find fault with her in so many ways – which, she supposed by the standards of the day he had a perfect right to do – but sometimes, when she was expecting his disapproval he became instead, quiet, reserved even, almost kind as though there was something in her or in himself which held him back. She was not a conventional woman. She knew that. She railed against the restrictions which held her and always had done. She was not submissive, pliant, willing to be moulded to the whims of whichever man had possession of her, but she certainly realized that what she had done today was well beyond the bounds of propriety. Well, it was too late now and she did not regret it. It would be for the last time and that was why she had done it.

'Christy, I know you despise the rules of our society and really . . .' He smiled and his eyes were suddenly warm with his humour. 'Nature made a sad mistake with you. You would have done far better as a boy!'

'A boy!'

'You have the . . . the recklessness of a young man, Christy. You don't care that you are a woman, my wife, with a position in society, my society which demands that a lady stays at home and sees to her home, her husband and children. That is your function in life, my pet, and you must accept it. If you had been born a man you would have been helping your father to run his mill, riding about as you pleased on a horse as wild as yourself, making love to all the . . .'

'Mr Buchanan!' but she was smiling, quite entranced by the idea and sharing his humour.

'. . . but you are a woman, Christy. Can you not make the most of it? There is so much you can gain from just that. A clever woman can do almost anything she likes if she would go about it . . . as a woman should. If only you would stop getting on my wrong side all the time . . .'

'Arguing, you mean? Demanding my own way?'

'If you like . . .'

'If would be easier for you, wouldn't it, if I shot my mare and sat with my embroidery and took tea with the ladies who came to call.'

The fragile unity they had shared a moment ago began to slide away, as it always did, on the slippery slope of their clashed wills.

'Oh stop it, for God's sake. Anyone would think you were to be asked to live like a . . . a . . .'

'Like a what, Mr Buchanan?' she challenged him.

'Like a wild creature which is kept against its will!'

'And is that not exactly what I am!'

He caught his breath and his jaw clamped with the grinding resolution which had kept him always in control of those with whom he dealt. Show no one your thoughts, had been his rule always.

He managed his usual ironic grin.

'Is that how you see yourself, my sweet? I would have thought you had more freedom than most. I have heard of your madcap races with my carriage horses . . . oh yes . . . I have been spying again.' He laughed. 'I am a well-known gentleman about here, Christy, and you, besides being an extremely beautiful woman which in itself would be cause for gossip, are my wife and as noticeable as a rose amongst nettles. There is always someone to tell me what you are up to so really, if you wish to be indiscreet, to it discreetly.'

'And what the hell does that mean? I do nothing which

could not be seen by the whole of Fellthwaite if it cared to watch.'

'I am sure of that, my dear, or I should not be smiling, but I would like to see you more . . . more concerned with your home, with domestic matters. If you are to ride, do so with John or Miles, but really, my sweet, I do wish you could find it in your defiant heart to be more involved with your household affairs and less with the . . .'

She interrupted him coldly, her head high, her cheeks flushed, her eyes the cloudy grey of a rainswept day.

'Well Mr Buchanan, you are to have your wish it seems!'

He became still then, his face suddenly expectant with, not a knowing perhaps, but a hoping.

'Oh yes,' he said carefully, 'and why is that?'

'Oh nothing much and it won't keep me leashed for longer than is absolutely necessary, I can assure you.'

'Christy?'

His face came alight with an unconcealed joy but she did not see it for she had risen and gone to the window, tweaking aside the curtains, as if she could not bear to look into his eyes as she told him she was to have his child.

Their son was born in May, a little over a year after they were married. Though Christy had chafed and fretted her way through the entire nine months of her pregnancy – telling the patient Faith that she would not suffer this excruciating boredom ever again, longing desperately for it to be over and rid herself of the burden which grew ever more heavy – when he was put in her arms, dark and lusty and yelling his vast anger at being thrust into a world for which it seemed he was not yet ready, she loved him passionately.

'Robert,' said Alex, holding him possessively, adeptly in the crook of his arms as he lounged in a chair by her bedside and was momentarily bewildered by her cry of almost desperate denial.

231

'Benjamin, or Toby, or Nathaniel after my grandfather, please.'

'Nathaniel! My God, poor little blighter! Who the hell wants to be called a name like that? How about John? Johnny Buchanan!'

'Why not Job or . . .'

'Johnny Buchanan. He is not an Emmerson.' He grinned at his son and the bad moment was passed.

'Half of him is!'

'I dare say but he is my son and will be called after my own grandfather.'

He studied the child's sleeping face with the proud arrogance of a king looking down at the heir to the throne. 'Look at that chin. That's my father's chin and the shape of his head . . .'

'Is Amy's!'

He looked up startled, then down again at the infant. He was not yet bathed and still had the smell of blood about him, but Alex Buchanan was not repelled as he had been at the birth of his daughter when his son turned his head into his arm. Christy was right. Though his two children had different mothers their resemblance was quite remarkable, from the dark, curling fluff on their heads to the shape and colouring of their eyes and skin, their small, pouting mouths and starfish hands. And yet this one had a jut to his chin, missing in Amy, which could only have come from Christy Emmerson.

He looked at her now in her nest of pillows, her dark hair still damp with the sweat of her labour, for her son was no more than an hour old, her eyes deep and tired in her pale face and his own softened.

'I'm sorry, my love. You want to sleep and I can do nothing but sit and admire what has come of my own small part in the event.' He grinned wickedly, '. . . though I dare say it could not have been done without me.'

He turned and put the boy in the arms of the discreetly hovering nurse and for a moment as he did so the remembrance came to him of another birth and the death which had followed. Then he knelt carelessly at her bedside, putting out a warm and gentle hand to brush back her hair. He kissed her lightly, his eyes smiling his approval.

'You are pleased then, Alex,' she said, her eyes already drooping and he smiled to himself for it was the first time she had called him by his christian name. Most of the time she called him by no name at all but when forced it was 'Mr Buchanan' or if she was angry, 'Alex Buchanan', as though even yet he was still merely a business associate of her father's.

'You know I am! You know how I've longed for a boy!'

He could have bitten his tongue! He had not meant it as it sounded. He had wanted to say how pleased he was with *her*. How proud she had made him with her strength; the battle she had fought and won against death for it stalked every place in which women struggled to give birth. He had meant to convey to her his joy with their child, irrespective of its gender, but the words he had spoken sounded cool, the words of a man who cares only with the getting of a son to perpetuate himself and what he has created.

Her eyes jerked open and the drowsy warmth vanished.

'Of course! Well, Mr Buchanan, I think I can say I have fulfilled my part of the bargain, don't you? Now, if I have your permission I would like to sleep. It is somewhat tiring producing an heir.'

She recovered quickly and for several months, right through the gentle days of summer she stayed close to her home with her children, seeing no one but Annie Emmerson and Job, who was renewed, as Annie had known he would be, in the birth of his grandson. They came often, Job neglecting his mill, caring nothing for its growth, only that of the boy he swore was the reincarnation of his Ben.

They flourished, her children, for the little girl, Amy, had become very dear to her and she was treated as though she was indeed Christy's own daughter. Throughout the months of her pregnancy the child had been a delight to her and she had spent more and more of her cumbersome time with her. She had learned to walk holding Christy's hand, stumbling over the rich biscuit carpet of the warm bedroom as winter closed in and had played more and more in the rose strewn beauty of Christy's sitting room. Her baby prattle and laughter soothed her stepmother in the long, hard days of imprisonment in the house as Christy settled at last to wait, and her own child kicked inside her.

Amy loved the little boy and, hearing Christy as she kissed her son begging him to 'smile at Mother', Amy did the same, stroking his ebony whorl of curls and without anyone consciously being aware of it, or realizing when it had begun, Amy began to call Christy 'Mother'.

The three of them, the mother and her two children lived for those few months in a small enclosed world of their own and Alex Buchanan scarcely existed for any of them. Christy was slow and content in her new motherhood, engrossed in the nursery, in the small confines of her existence as the creator, the protector of her child and the man who shared that responsibility swam on the edge of her vision, her consciousness like a stranger to whom she had merely to be polite.

She did not know that before she was up he went each morning to the nursery before he set off for the mine and sat for ten minutes, completely alone with his children; tersely dismissing the nursemaid, his son gently held in the crook of his arm, his daughter drowsing against them both, looking into the tiny sleeping face of his son, his own rapt and gentle. He was careful now with Amy, but it was too late to give her the love he gave the boy, but still he was kind with her and she grew to be confident with him.

When he came home at night, sometimes late, after bathing and changing he would go again. Beth learned to slip away at his approach and no one ever knew what he did in those few stolen moments with his children.

'Pity he couldn't have spent a bit more time with Miss Amy before this,' Beth grumbled, resentful on behalf of what the little girl had missed in her early babyhood. 'She's his an' all but for all the notice he took of her she might have been a damn kitten!'

'Well, she's alright now,' Mrs Avery said soothingly, 'with her new Mama and her little brother, and he *does* sit her on his lap now.'

'Aye, you're right. Mrs Buchanan thinks the world of her and she's got a family at last, thank God.'

Alex moved in the shadows of Christy's absorbed world, always there, always polite and bothering no one, it seemed – until the night he strode into their bedroom which he had not shared with her for six months and in the way she had forgotten in her animal-like preoccupation with breeding, made love to her over and over again and the peaceful days were gone!

CHAPTER FIFTEEN

'My pet, why don't you come with me?'

'You know I can't leave the children.'

'Not even for a trip to Europe? Would you not like to see Paris? I daresay I could break my journey for a day or two before travelling on to Germany. Paris in autumn is splendid, Christy. There are those who prefer spring but I have always thought the weather in October to be at its best. And you can order some outfits whilst you are there. What a commotion that would cause in Fellthwaite! Christy Buchanan in a Paris gown! A sensation for the Christmas ball and something for next spring. What d'you say? I'm sure you would enjoy it.'

Alex spoke casually. He was lounging carelessly in the dainty velvet chair in the bedroom he and Christy shared, watching his wife brush the long, heavy swathe of her hair. She had sent Faith away when Alex sauntered in, his cigar clenched between his white teeth, his eyes gleaming appreciatively at the sight of her. She sat before the mirror, sweeping the brush rhythmically from the crown of her head to the curling ends of the dark hair which hung almost to her waist, and at each stroke the snapping tension of it lifted, fine strands shot with gold in the candlelight clinging to the brush and floating in a drift about her cheeks and ears. Her head was thrown back and the mellow softness of the light played about her white throat, throwing deep shadows down into the hollow between her breasts.

She wore a light wrapper of some slipping, cloudy material in a soft, rosy pink. It had ribbons at the waist and wrist in satin and Alex was intrigued as to how the thing stayed on her, vowing to find out in a moment or two but just now he was more concerned with trying to tempt his lovely wife to accompany him on a business trip he was to take to the continent.

He watched her as she turned one of her suspicious looks on him. Oh yes, he knew perfectly well what went on in his wife's cool mind and firmly rooted in it was the belief that, having been married for her inheritance and his need for a son, both of which she had provided, what now did he want with her, particularly on a business trip to Germany?

'It would only be for a fortnight or so,' he continued smoothly. 'Beth is perfectly able to look after Johnny and Amy, particularly now you have engaged that girl who helps her. Good God, Christy, there are more than a dozen servants who would lay down and die for them, to see to the needs of two small children and if you feel anxious, ask your mother to come over each day to keep an eye on things. You know how she and your father dote on Johnny.'

Christy continued to brush her hair, her face inscrutable and Alex felt the familiar feather of irritation slip down his spine. Where the hell had her thoughts gone now? What was behind that calm face which she presented to him each day? They had been married for eighteen months and he knew her body and the sexuality he aroused in it as well as he knew the face he shaved each day in the dressing room mirror, but what was contained beneath the skin and muscle, the flesh and bones of Christy Buchanan?

He knew she tolerated him, sometimes enjoying it, at their dinner table, in the sitting room of an evening when he smoked his cigars and they chatted amiably enough, laughing sometimes when he told her some amusing incident which had occurred in his day. When they walked with the children – Amy's chubby hand gripping his finger, Johnny in the wicker carriage – about the sunny garden and across the grass to the paddock, pausing to admire the fine animals which grazed there, to watch the fat pony which was to be his daughter's. As they rode in their carriage to church each Sunday, presenting a contented picture of a successful marriage to the watching society of Fellthwaite. He knew she came alive to him in their bed at night, her body then, and only then, in complete harmony with his. She called his name, his name in the depthless pool of her rapture but what were her thoughts when it was over and they lay side by side in the darkness, when she stood at the window and stared out over the gardens towards Tilberthwaite Fell on a cool spring morning or when, thinking herself unobserved she dreamily watched the clouds race to the woods above Elterwater where he had first seen her and heard her laugh?

Did she still think of him? Robin Forsythe? In all this time his name had never been mentioned, not by anyone. It was as though the man had never existed. They dined with Annie and Job, with the Aspins, or the Dyers or the Marsdens, men with whom he did business. They gave dinner parties for the commercial men of Westmorland, Cumberland and even on occasion, entertained visitors who came from St Helens, from Swansea or even further to do business with Alex.

They went to concerts and balls and parties, Alex Buchanan and his elegant wife, and had been in the company more than once of the Squire and his wife, though not in Dalebarrow Hall, but not once had the name of Robin Forsythe come up in the conversation.

Was it deliberate, he wondered? Did those who knew perfectly well that his wife had been betrothed to the Squire's son therefore think it expedient, in view of his own standing in the community, to pretend the man had perhaps died, or at least gone to the Americas to get away from her? He had heard a rumour to that effect and certainly the man had not been seen since the Christmas before he and Christy were married.

He stood up smoothly, presenting the perfect picture of a man who offers a gift but is really quite unconcerned with whether the recipient cares for it or not. He moved to the window, his face turned from her, leaning gracefully with his long, hard body against the soft velvet of the curtains which he had pulled back.

Christy watched him through the mirror. The disturbing sensation of hurt resentment his attitude awoke in her was a familiar one now. He cared not a tuppenny damn whether she came or went, stayed here to look after his son or accompanied him to Germany so why did he bother to go through this charade? As long as he had her in his bed, and smiling at the head of his table when he entertained, he seemed perfectly happy to allow her to do whatever she wanted. Providing it was seemly, of course!

He was a handsome man with a sometimes cruel wit which often made her laugh, and had a fascinating store of news, views, gossip, even scandal which he seemed not averse to sharing with her when they were alone. He drove her wild, wanton and fierce in their bedroom and she could not help but enjoy it, but why did he want her *now*? He had all he had aimed for, surely? There must be something to be gained by it, this trip. There must be something he needed which she could provide. Not of the flesh for there must be a dozen women wherever he went to gratify him in that quarter. No, it was to do with business. It must be.

'I don't think I care to leave Johnny so soon. He is only

five months old, after all, and the wet nurse is a simpleton. She has the milk he needs but requires constant supervision or she would nurse him until he is sick! Beth is competent and devoted to both the children but should he be ill . . .'

'Your mother is a capable, sensible woman, Christy. Don't you trust her to care for her grandson?' His voice was mildly enquiring, no more, his back still turned to her. She watched him. His shoulders were relaxed and his hands rose tranquilly to remove the cigar from his mouth.

There was silence. Christy waited. For what, she wondered? To be convinced, persuaded, coaxed perhaps. Given some sign that he really wanted her to go with him for no other reason than he wanted her company.

He turned and smiled good-humouredly, his eyes running across the reflection of her face in the mirror. She swivelled round on the stool and his gaze dropped interestedly to the opening of her wrapper. Her breasts were almost exposed as the soft fabric fell away. Her flushed nipples thrust themselves forward and he began to walk towards her.

'Well my darling,' he said softly, one hand reaching out to push away the garment from her shoulders. 'What shall it be? Yes or no?'

His mouth touched the curve of her breast and his tongue teased her nipple and she sighed in delight.

'No,' she murmured then cried out as his teeth worried her tender flesh for a moment.

'As you like, my pet.' His voice was careless and he was gentle as he lifted her up in his arms and laid her on the bed.

She could not see his eyes in the dim light of the candle, nor did she wonder on the strangeness of how many times they avoided one another's gaze.

The day he left she ordered out her mare for the first time since before Johnny's birth and when the groom would have gone with her she told him curtly to be about his business.

'Mr Buchanan won't . . .'

'Damn Mr Buchanan,' she said fiercely into his shocked face. She kicked her heels into the mare's side and galloped away across the bridge and up the well-known track towards Loughrigg Tarn.

She had gone no more than half a mile, weaving through the tall, almost symmetrically placed silver-grey trunks of the beech trees when she drew her mare into a halt. She stared up into the great limbs spread out above her head forming a complete crown against the arch of the sky. The trunks of the trees stood like the smooth, soaring columns of a cathedral, going up and up in an effort to reach the light. The layer upon layer of leaves cast a deep shade and few plants survived underfoot though the grass was smooth and a cool, thick green. Above her the leaves glowed brilliantly, a mosaic of flaming orange, russet and gold for it was mid-autumn now. A solitary holly bush and a wild cherry grew but the path was clear and unhindered, and for several minutes she let the mare stand whilst she listened to the absolute silence and to the insistent, angry, bewildered beat of her own heart.

She turned then, threading her mare through the trees towards Eltermere, the reins held loosely in her hands, allowing the animal to choose the route, almost as though she was letting the decision be taken from her.

For half an hour she went on, the beck on her left running sweetly from the direction in which she was headed. Her eyes dreamed ahead of her and her breath was slow and steady now. She wore a riding habit she had commissioned Miss Susan Whittam to make especially for her – shocking it had been called – with a split skirt, very full and completely modest but it allowed her to ride astride which no woman of her acquaintance had ever done before. It was the first time she had worn it away from the paddock at the back of Howethwaite and she felt a calm sense of pleasure at the ease with which she could move.

The beech trees began to mingle with others. The quaking aspen so called because its leaves trembled in the

240

slightest breeze; and as she drew nearer the water of the mere there were oak trees, as English as the ground in which they were rooted, towering above her with trunks so thick no man could encircle them with his arms; willow gracefully bending to the water's edge and hornbeam, its fluted trunk covered in smooth, pale grey bark.

And then she was in the clearing.

She dismounted slowly, easily, in her split skirt, putting her booted foot gently to the layer of leaves which carpeted the ground. She was reverent almost, hushed as though she was in a church and on her face was a soft expression of sadness, a shadowed mirage, an inner eye looking at something it saw but was not there.

She tied the mare to the same tree, studying the rich, ruddy gold of the leaves on the branches as though they were something so exquisitely beautiful her eyes could not get their fill.

In the centre of the clearing, leaning towards her in welcome was the fine old hornbeam. It stood with its roots deep in golden leaves and in the hollow made by them was a cushioning pile, brushed there by the wind into a soft bed.

A soft bed where once she had lain with Robin Forsythe!

He was there then. His fine-boned face creased into a slow smile and his deep brown eyes softened with his love for her. His eyelashes drooped along the length of his heavy lids, curling and silken brown and in her memory she kissed them and his eyebrows over which tumbled his pale feathers of hair. She pushed it back from his brow, smilingly reaching up to put her lips to his temple and the line of his hair. Her hands smoothed his young brown cheeks and with a finger she traced the outline of his mouth. He opened it and with his white teeth, a little crooked in the front for he could not be completely perfect, gently bit it, then kissed it . . .

She blinked and her hands left the mare's bridle which she still held and with slow deliberate steps her feet carried her of their own volition across the crisping carpet of fallen leaves towards the tree. Her hand went out to it, her fingers gently tracing the pattern of the bark.

Here they had leaned, her back to the trunk, Robin's weight on hers, his body fitting as neatly, breast to breast, thigh to thigh, knee to knee, as well-balanced as though their bodies had come from the same mould; as complete as two of the buds of the tree itself. Here they had looked into one another's eyes, dreaming, so completely at one, *as* one, thought for thought, sense for sense, pulse for pulse, heartbeat for heartbeat, they had scarce needed to speak. They would gaze, soft, so soft, brown eyes to grey and their lips would form a smile, then kiss, each attuned to the other's love, need fulfilment, and the smile was a declaration of it.

She turned then, leaning where she had leaned before and her heart jolted in anguish, for her thoughts had conjured up his spirit and he was there across the clearing, standing on the rough, tangled path. He looked so real, the fantasy figure her memory had created, with the shaft of sunlight striking gold from his hair, smooth now and short, where once it had tumbled in a profusion of curls.

His ghost had removed his jacket and it was slung over his shoulder carelessly. His plain cambric shirt was open at the neck and his throat was brown as though he had been in foreign parts. His cord breeches were tucked into a pair of fine black riding boots. The vision had another behind it, in the shape of a tall roan with a black mane and tail and a white blaze between its eyes, and they both stood where her imagination had placed them, where a dozen times before she had seen him in the flesh!

She whirled about, her wide skirts disturbing the soft pile of gold leaves which drifted at her feet and her arms went out to encircle painfully the trunk of the hornbeam. Her cheek pressed so hard against it she could feel the bark biting into her flesh but she made no sound.

Then she heard it. No more than a whisper amongst the other whispers which filled the clearing.

'Christy.' A sigh, no more, a wisp of breath on which

her own name floated, unreal, inside her own head, of course.

She did not move. She did not turn. If she did the lovely vision would be gone and she would be alone again, and lonely as she had been for nearly two years. If she stayed as she was – her eyes on the autumn fruit of the hornbeam which nestled like a crouching mouse against the three pointed wings of the leaves – he would stay there, in her mind's eye, but if she turned he would be gone and she could not bear that. Just for a moment, dear Lord, let me pretend. Let me play the game that I am two years younger and that he, Robin, is there, where he always . . .

'Christy, dear God . . . Christy . . .!'

She could hear the jingle of the bridle and the 'hrummph' of the roan as it lifted its head, snorting in eagerness to get at the sweet, juicy grasses beneath the trees. She could hear the swish of booted feet in the leaves behind her. She could hear the swing of his arms and the long stride of his legs, the sound of the coat being dropped, the rustle of the starched fabric of his shirt, the hoarseness of his breath and she groaned in deep pain for it was all so *real* and when she turned it would be gone.

She felt the warmth of him then, the heat of his body behind her and in one blind movement she turned and his arms were about her in desperate strength which took her mind and thoughts and left her only with the feeling, the sense of coming home, home at last! His long, hard body was fused to hers, different to the one she had known but the same, and she was wrapped about in the strong protection of him and his love, and the shuddering of his pain and she clung to it, gripping her hands together behind his back, her face buried in the sweet matt of pale hair on his chest where his shirt had parted. His face thrust itself into the mass of her own hair and she felt his lips on her brow and neck and ears. His hands were at her head, pressing it further into the hollow of his throat, then moving down her back, forcing her body even closer to his.

'Oh God! Oh God! Oh God!' She could hear him cry over and over again and together they began to weep. His tears fell on her hair and soaked through to her scalp and hers wet the front of his shirt and his chest. For ten minutes they stood in the shelter of each other's arms, and the clearing was silent of all the normal woodland rustles of its small animal habitants as the two humans cried for their loss, with anger and bitterness. Their bodies, without words, had spoken to one another as they clung together and Christy knew then that somehow they had been tricked, that a cruel stratagem had been enfolded and that they had been its victims.

'Christy . . . Christy, my lovely girl . . . oh Jesus . . .'

She could not speak, not at all. Her voice had gone, her thoughts spinning it away, only her desperate clutching arms and body telling him wordlessly that it was still the same, still the same and that she was crucified by it.

They were quiet at last. Still wrapped together in one slender column of flesh, but the storm of grief had abated and the silence which follows it came to claim them. It was enough just now to stand in the diffused sunlight and hold each other in famished arms, arms that had hungered for it for two years.

Christy's heart had been filled with angry recriminations, with rancour and coldness, even hatred for she had not understood, or even been aware of what had been done to them. But her flesh had not stopped loving and needing, hankering after what it most desired for the body knows only one thing. It is not concerned with thought or profound speculation on matters of the mind, but with the necessity to be close to the one it most desires.

A deep sigh, a shiver and they stepped reluctantly apart. He kept his hands on her shoulders, she had hers on his upper arm and they looked at last into one another's faces.

He was older, not just in years, but in experience and pain. There were lines about his mouth where it had turned down in bleakness and though his face was still that of a young man, smooth and taut with good health, his eyes were no longer a warm, careless brown. They were wary, the distant clouded hue of sepia as though some of the colour had drained away with his spirit. He was neater with his hair cut short and smoothly brushed and seemed taller, leaner, though his shoulders had broadened. His hands were hard and brown, with callouses on the palm, the hands of a man who did manual work. Yes, he was a man now, bronzed, weathered almost. The boy Robin, the boy she had loved was gone!

He put up a wondering hand and his fingers traced her cheek and lifted to her eyebrows, then pushed back the tumbled, slipping mass of her glossy hair. His eyes wandered across her face, dreaming almost, as though he had done this many times in his own mind and was making sure it was still the same.

On a drifting sigh she spoke his name.

'Robin,' and his eyes smiled into hers, still wet, and it was as though the two years that had gone between had never been and everything vanished but this man.

'Robin . . . how did it happen?' Her voice was filled with pain.

'Come . . . sit down . . . here, where we used to . . .'

'They did it, didn't they?' She didn't know who she meant really, only that someone had.

'Yes . . . oh yes, my darling.'

'Robin . . .' She strained against him, burying her face into his neck and he felt the shudder of her weeping begin again. Gently he put her from him, then led her to a fallen log, knee deep in fern and wood sorrel, sitting her where he could look into her beloved face.

'Sit here.'

'Why . . . why did you not come?' Her voice was as anguished now as it had been when she had asked the question of her mother. Why does he not come, she had said then and now he was here to answer for himself.

'I was . . . prevented.'

'But why?'

'I asked the same question when I heard you had married Buchanan.'

His voice and face had become hard, as bleak as the fells in winter and the words fell between them like a sheet of ice, separating them, cold to the touch and yet invisible.

'Why did you, Christy, and so soon?' Harsh now, his painful anger swaying against his love, pushing it roughly aside. He stared at her, the new Robin Forsythe, the one she did not yet know.

'I . . . don't know now. It has been almost two years. It was . . .'

'*You don't know!*'

'You had not come . . . Why . . . Why? My brothers were dead. I needed you and you stayed away.' Her voice was wild, ragged.

'I wanted to . . . Christy . . . I wanted to. They said you . . . your family needed to be alone in your grief . . . that I would be intruding . . .'

'Intruding! We were to be married . . . Oh God!'

The remembrance of what might have been tore her apart and she fell against him, almost in a swoon. His arms rose to her, holding her protectively, passionately as he rocked her in love, trying to comfort and yet desperately needing it himself. It was like the mighty waters of an ocean, a storm-wracked sea with waves which lifted them up in anger and accusations, then dropped them down into a quiet trough of remorse where they clung together, knowing neither was to blame. They seemed unable to fit their minds together now, now that the first unbelieving joyous enchantment had dribbled away on the pain of remembrance, and their words were halting, muffled with moments of silence into which nothing could be said.

'Who are *they*, Robin?' she said finally, looking down at her hands.

'Oh . . . people about me. Someone who had known grief, it was said and who told me those who suffered it wanted nothing more than to be left alone to it.'

'Your father?'

'I did not say that.'

'No.' Her voice was a tiny sigh of hopelessness.

'I tried to come but the snows . . . you remember . . .'

'Yes . . .'

'I am not making excuses, Christy. Do you believe me? I would have come immediately it was possible but I was . . .'

'Yes?'

'I listened to what was told me. I shouldn't, I know but I was inexperienced in the pain of grief, so I believed what I was told. I should have listened to my heart.'

'They told me you were involved with the hunt.'

'I know . . .'

'That when it was done . . . the season . . .'

He put his head in his hands and groaned.

'That you were to purchase a hunter . . .'

'I know . . . I know . . . it was done by . . .'

'Your father?'

'Yes. I wrote to you but he did not deliver my letters.'

'Robin.' Her cry tore him to pieces.

'Christy . . . Oh God . . . Christy!'

'I went to see him. I thought you had . . . perhaps an accident . . .'

'I know . . . your mother told me . . . she said . . .'

She seemed incapable of listening to him now as she relived those terrible months.

'He said no. You were with your cousins. He offered to take a letter should I care to write one . . .'

'You believed I had deserted you?'

His own voice was like a saw being drawn across a ragged edge of granite.

'Yes . . .'

'So you . . .'

'Alex . . . Alex asked for me. My father couldn't . . . my brother's death unhinged him. He was glad to put my inheritance into the hands of someone who could take care of it, and me . . .'

'So you . . .'

247

'I married him, Robin. We have a son.'

'Yes . . .' He sighed wearily. '. . . I heard . . .'

The clearing was silent again and a tentative bird tried out a call.

'Why did you come today?' It was said with little interest for what difference did it make?

'I have come every day for a week. Ever since I came home . . . back to Fellthwaite.'

She turned, surprised, to look at him and his eyes burned with his love.

'Why Robin?'

'For a week now. I sit for hours . . . I see you here . . . and him . . .'

'Who?'

'The boy who loved you!'

There was nothing more to say then. It was all told, the sadness and the sorrow and the uselessness of it, nothing more to say except one thing.

'Why Robin? Why did he turn against me? I thought my dowry was to restore the estate and with my brothers gone I had more, much more to offer.'

He did not look at her as he spoke and his eyes were clouded.

'He lives in a world where . . . the classes do not mix. It went against everything he had ever been taught to marry his son to a woman from another.'

'But he was willing to put aside his principles for the money.'

'Yes.'

'Then why?'

'Someone . . . better turned up!'

'Better?'

'Yes. Her father is a baronet . . . and wealthy.'

She thought she had known the depths of hell, been to the furthest periphery pain could fling her but she was wrong. The impact of his words sent her spinning down and down into a black chasm of desolation and her hand sprang up involuntarily as though it must have something to cling to or she would never come up again. He took it in his and she looked blindly at the brown strength of it and tried to imagine it doing to another what it had done to her. She pictured the buttons on a dress, white flesh beneath and this beloved hand reaching inside to . . .

But it was too much for her and she understood at last how Robin must feel for she had allowed more than a hand to touch her flesh, more than a kiss. Her body had lain in passionate rapture beneath that of another man, cried out his name in desire, taken into it his seed and borne the fruits of it in a son.

Had he married this suitable young lady his father had placed before him? Perhaps he had a son of his own. She knew nothing of him, nothing, not even that he had been in Fellthwaite for the past week. Why had she not known of that at least? Why had no one warned her? Surely someone had recognized him, the Squire's boy, and remarked on it? To her mother, to Faith, one of the servants . . . to Alex! Did he know? Had he gone away knowing that Robin Forsythe was home again . . . Oh God! . . . Oh God, why had she not stayed at home where she was safe, as Alex had asked her to so many times . . . why . . . why?

The silence stretched on and on but their hands, separate entities, one supposed, from the shuddering pictures in their minds, clung lovingly, familarly together, old friends, parted once but glad to know one another again.

She had to ask it!

'You married her?'

Her heart despaired of the answer.

'No . . . oh no!' Why did she feel so deliriously uplifted for it could mean nothing to her?

'Then where . . .?'

'I have been in America. Working on a ranch . . . a farm . . . it was all I knew . . . horses.'

'And you are home . . . to stay?' Dear God . . . perhaps they might meet . . . with Alex beside her, a sour voice said deep in her confused brain.

249

'No . . . no, I am to return. My mother has been ill . . . she wrote, I could not deny her. It was none of her doing and she did not deserve to be punished like . . .'

'Like your father.'

'I can no longer . . . bear to be in his company. I can never forgive him. I am staying at The Bear. When she is recovered I shall go away again.'

'Robin . . .'

His name was so sweet on her lips after all this time. She tasted it again.

'Robin . . . Robin . . .'

'Yes, my love, I know . . .'

They had been cheated. They had been children, loving one another with growing minds and maturing bodies, ready to become a man and a woman and start their own future. They had been manipulated by two men, three if you counted her father though he had scarcely been aware of what he did. Used by two greedy men then, two unprincipled men who thought nothing of trampling on human lives to gain what they themselves wanted. Squire Forsythe had wanted her money but her breeding had not been as pure as his own, so when another with the good blood of his own class had crossed his path, he had pushed Christy off it without the slightest compunction. And Alex Buchanan! He had taken advantage of her weakness and with it stolen her and her inheritance to add to everything else he possessed. She was trapped. She had his child and soon, by the next spring would bear him another.

She held his arm close to her breast and breathed in the essence of him, drawing it into the centre of her, etching it permanently on her memory. She must go in a little while but first she must have this tiny part of him, this arm, the warmth of it under her hand, this feel of his love about her, the sound of his voice in her ears.

They talked quietly for an hour, their sad voices rising and falling with the softness of the leaves which drifted about their heads. They did not speak of her life but of his. What good would it do to mention her world of

250

domesticity and motherhood, the trivia which formed her days, but he gave her a glimpse of his own to store away for the days and years ahead. She watched the movement of his mouth, grim now where once it had laughed easily and often. Her eyes caressed the bronzed smoothness of his face, and her heart broke at the quietness of him where once he had been a merry, careless boy. He was a man now, harsh perhaps and uncompromising, but the man she loved as she had loved the boy.

Just for a moment he was there again that boy as he asked, diffidently, unsure, and yet knowing her answer – for what else could it be?

'Christy . . . come with me . . .'

They stood up to face one another and she shook her head, unable to speak and gently, oh so gently, for might they not break, their lips brushed and a low sound of pain moved in Robin's throat, then they turned, clumsily, pushing at one another in their agony to have it over.

They did not look back as their horses moved off in different directions. When the clouds which had crept up on her began to empty themselves upon her bare head – where was her hat? – she did not lift her hand to wipe away the rain, nor the tears which washed her face.

CHAPTER SIXTEEN

Christy's second son was born in May 1847, a year almost to the day after the birth of her first and just a month later the railway line came to Windermere, a branch line of the 'Lancaster and Carlisle', from Kendal.

Alex went to the grand opening of the colonnaded railway terminus; standing with other important dignitaries in the booking hall, which was splendid and spacious enough to hold a ball in. They drank champagne and congratulated one another on the ease with which they would now move their timber and iron, their copper and explosives, their piece goods and bobbins for the cotton mills of Lancashire, to a world longing to show them an even healthier profit.

Glasses were raised in Alex's direction and heads nodded agreeably as he was toasted on the birth of another son. She had done well for him, the Emmerson girl, despite her unconventional ways, giving him two lads in just over a year – better than the last one with her one puling girl – and no doubt, if Buchanan had his way and didn't he always, there would be more boys filling the nursery at Howethwaite for Christy Emmerson had proved herself fertile. It was good to have sons, plenty of them to carry on the dynastic line for nature had a way of weeding out infants and the more a man had, the more he could spare.

Job Emmerson was there, smaller now somehow, his clothes awkward on him, not quite hanging as they should no matter how Annie fussed with him. He was hesitant where once he had been decisive, leaning more and more heavily on his son-in-law for advice; his grief for his lads still within him even though he could see them – or so he told Annie – in Christy's bold, sturdy Johnny. The boy was dark and handsome just as his Ben had been but he'd not live to see the lad take over the mills so what was the use of planning for it? Annie liked to think he had accepted his loss so he let her, knowing it alleviated her own grief, but Christy's lad was a Buchanan. Though in his veins ran Job's blood and Alex had promised him – he was a grand chap, Alex, and he thanked God for that blessing since the Forsythe lad would have been hopeless – that the mills would always have the Emmerson name, but it was not the same.

He fretted still on his son's tardiness in marrying Celia Metcalf for might he not have had a chance to get her with child before the explosion which killed him, and the boy – it would have been a boy, there was no doubt of it – would have come under Job's care and guidance, filling Job's empty heart and giving it a purpose in life. An Emmerson not a Buchanan. Direct line from Jacob and Nathaniel to the lad, and it would have kept Job alive – the realization that he must keep going until his grandson was old enough to take up the reins. But it was not meant to be!

The thoughts kept him awake in the night, sleepless and restive beside Annie, and he would get up and stand at the bedroom window and stare out over the long gardens, down the hill to the works where the night shift ran on under the supervision of the efficient manager and foreman Alex had put in for him.

What was the use of it though? It would all go to Alex Buchanan's sons. Not Benjamin not Toby, nor their sons, and Job let the bitterness enter into him and eat slowly at the substance of his life.

Annie began to notice the vagueness which she had thought to be gone with the birth of Christy's boy, and his indifference to the reports Alex put before him. The weekly balance sheets and business accounts which once he had found so absorbing were left to lie on his desk, collecting dust if she had let them.

'What about these papers, husband? Am I to throw them away or will you want to study them?' she would say, knowing that once he would have raised the roof if she so much as breathed on them.

'Just as you like, lass.' His head would not even turn to see what it was she held up to him as he stared vacantly into the fire, and her worry increased.

'Well, I'll just put them into this drawer until you've a moment for them, lad,' and he would nod agreeably which frightened her further.

Then there was their Christy! Like a will o' the wisp she had been again this winter reminding Annie of the days after that lad had supposedly deserted her, silent as the grave for weeks and when she did speak it was to snap your head off. Pregnant again for which Annie was thankful, though she would have liked Alex to have given the girl a bit more time to recover from the last, but she was strong and healthy and would take no harm from it and the more she had the better she would settle herself with her husband and family and forget the Squire's lad.

Annie couldn't shake off the feeling that this last state of depression stemmed somehow from him. She had heard a whisper that he had been seen in Fellthwaite around the time the Squire's lady had been ill at last back end, but she had said nothing to Christy for there was no use in upsetting her, especially when she was in the family way. There was the winter to be got through, the bitter Lakeland winter which could fasten you to your own parlour for weeks and their Christy was hard enough to control in her restlessness during these months without brooding over what might have been. And Alex wouldn't like it if Christy was to be told of it, and Annie had a great deal of respect and yes, affection for her daughter's husband, no matter what Christy might say about him!

But there was no doubt Christy was difficult, awkward and wilful in this second pregnancy and Annie would be glad when it was over, the winter and the birth. Christy was . . . sad, that was the word, though it sounded fanciful, often seeming to be in another world, gazing over towards the fells whenever Annie called, hardly aware, it seemed, that her mother was there.

'What's to do, lass?' she had asked. 'Are you not well? Is this one not lying as easily as your Johnny? Are you sickly in the mornings? If it feels different to the last perhaps it means it will be a girl. Would you like that, Christy?' hoping to cheer her daughter.

'I don't mind, mother.'

'You've no preference then?'

'No, I don't think so.'

Christy's voice was as vague as her manner and Annie tried hard to put the dreadful thought behind her, since it could scarcely even be contemplated, that Christy had not only known of Robin Forsythe's visit to his sick mother's bedside, but had seen him.

She fretted about it, and about Job, as she rode over as often as she could in her carriage to see her lass and her grandson, watching the boy grow stronger and more demanding as Job grew more frail.

Johnny Buchanan, the image of his own father, and grandfather too, Annie thought indulgently, his fists always flailing in his cradle as though at some unseen assailant, his vivid blue eyes staring mutinously at the beautiful brightness of the flames in the fireplace which he could not quite reach. She had seen him crawl at six months, as determined as the men who had shaped him, to be about *something*, even if it was only the flounce on his mother's gown or the patient terrier which was always at his father's heel. He was standing at ten months, pulling himself up against his mother's swollen belly as she rested by her sitting room fire, and walking his first tottering steps into his proud father's arms on his first birthday!

He was a tyrant, ruler of the household, except of course of his parents who would be ruled by no one, not even each other, demanding and getting everyone's attention from Amy who, at two and a half years was his devoted slave, to the ancient odd job man, Abel Hodson, who hovered about the garden during the summer months after the boy's birth, waiting for him to cry in order that he might be the first to poke a gnarled finger into his wicker carriage.

The boy was jealous of his new brother and the sudden swift preoccupation with the intruder rather than himself. At first he was inclined to sulk and throw tantrums but when she was recovered his mother took him off on his own and sat him on her mare before her and rode with him to the woods to show him all manner of wondrous things, and though she and his father made angry words afterwards it made no difference to him, for he had been then and it was too late to take it from him and there was Beth to hold him on her lap and listen to his garbled tale of his adventure. Gradually the new boy was accepted and the time came when Johnny Buchanan forgot he had once not been there at all.

Christy and Alexander Buchanan made angry words

over many things during that winter before the birth of their second son.

'Don't ride alone again, Christy. God knows who you might meet up there in those woods.'

Her heart missed a beat until she realized that he could not possibly know since he had been away for weeks and if he had learned of it, he would not now be speaking in the reasonable manner he showed.

'Why not? No one will harm me.'

'That's not the point though some one could. Suppose your horse shied and you were thrown. You could be injured and lie up there for hours. Apart from that it's not the correct way for a lady to act and you know it. You don't see the new Mrs Paul Aspin riding out alone . . .'

'She's breeding, that's why!'

'Christy! You can be plain spoken when you please but then you always were. But you are still my wife and will act like it, if you please. If you will go riding and I do not complain of that though I don't care for it, you will take Miles or John, though why the hell you can't be satisfied to take your exercise in the carriage like any other woman, God only knows!'

'Because I'm not any other woman.'

'I realize that, my pet, so I'm prepared to allow you marginally more freedom than they have but you will take it circumspectly or it will be denied you.'

'I shall do as I please, Alex Buchanan!'

'Will you indeed! We shall see about that. You will behave properly or you will remain in this house and see to your children.'

'Alex . . . please, Alex, don't stop me . . .'

He had looked at her, surprised then for she had never pleaded with him before and he wondered at her paleness and the soft shadowed circles beneath her eyes.

'Why Christy! Don't tell me my wife is actually asking me for something?' His grin was sardonic but beneath the lightness of his words there was a sudden snapping speculation, for in the five weeks he had been in Germany –

held up longer than he had intended by the pressure of his business – she had grown strange again. She had responded just as eagerly to him in the soft, candle-lit warmth of their bedroom when he returned, desperately he had thought, as though his strength was something to which she must cling and he had been pleased, but her tongue was just as sharp and her face as unreadable in the light of the day, only warming when it studied the face of her baby son or when Amy dozed on her lap in the nursery.

The following week she had told him tersely she was pregnant again, and he believed he knew the reason for her pale listlessness and he was gratified for a man counted sons amongst his wealth. Then realization struck him and his anger exploded and she thought he was going to hit her.

'You knew yesterday . . . last week . . .'

'Yes . . .'

'And yet you still rode out?'

'Yes!'

'How dare you take chances with my child?'

'My child, too.'

'Then one would think you might have more care for it.'

'I shall . . . now.'

'There is no doubt of it, madam! You will go nowhere unless it is in the carriage with Thaddeus. Not Jack! Thaddeus, you understand.'

His face was white with rage and his eyes challenged her dangerously to defy him.

'Yes.' No more.

'Mrs Marsden stopped me today,' he said several weeks later.

'Really.'

'She says you have not been seen for weeks and every time she or one of the other ladies call you are not at home. She realizes you are pregnant, of course, – though that is not the word she used – and will naturally not be quite as active as once you were but she wonders if you are ill and if so, can she be of help?'

'That is most kind of her.'

'What have you been doing?'

'Nothing.'

'Just that.'

'Ask the servants if you do not believe me.'

'Christy . . .'

'Am I to go about or stay at home? You forbade me to ride up into the woods or even walk there one supposes for I might be accosted, saying I must stay at home with my children. When I do so you complain that I am neglecting my duties as . . .'

'For God's sake, woman! Is there no middle road with you? I did not mean you to see no one! Why do you twist everything about? Christy . . .' His voice became surprisingly gentle and he saw the sudden mist of tears — at what? — come to her eyes. He leaned across the candle-lit dinner table and took her hand. It quivered in his, so light and tender and small, its lean brown strength gone now that she no longer rode.

'I don't mean you to . . .'

'Yes, Alex.' She removed her hand and lifted a glass to her lips, sipping the water it contained. His own hand lay, somehow defenceless on the white table cloth and he withdrew it quickly.

'Nothing, nothing,' he sighed, 'but I would be glad if you would have some company, visit your friends when I am at the mine.'

'What the hell for?' He winced at the oath and her savagery as she spoke it. She leaped to her feet, heedlessly knocking over the glass of water she had been holding. 'What the bloody hell for? To listen to them twittering on about babies and servants and the new fans Miss Susan Whittam has in her shop. To share with Jenny Aspin the knowing smiles and whispered enquiries about our "condition". I am . . . smothered by it all. I cannot . . .'

She turned her brilliant, ice-grey eyes from his own startled, then suddenly charged gaze and strode to the window. It was almost December and the stinging rain pattered against the window, running in shining rivulets down each pane of glass. The skeleton of the climbing rose bush trembled against the window frame, swaying and leaning in towards her in the flurry of wind, its loveliness spent with the onset of winter.

'I'm not ... very good at sitting at home with my embroidery, Alex. The children take up some of my time. I like to ... to have them with me. Amy is a ... she gives me a great deal of pleasure. She is bright and loves me and I return her love – for who can resist the appeal of her – but it is not enough. My days are so empty ... so empty! That is why I love to ride, to get out alone on the hills. I know it is impossible now, but when I am able it is hard to abide the constant chiding of John or Miles. "Be careful, Mrs Buchanan", "do not ride at such speed, Mrs Buchanan", "that jump is too high, Mrs Buchanan". I cannot stand it when I am constantly watched and my every word and movement is reported to you. I cannot ... I cannot ... Oh God, Alex, ... I cannot ...'

Her voice rose and her arms lifted in a gesture of defeat, then she was quiet.

Into the silence his voice fell like a falling rock, each word crashing against the walls of the room to echo coldly in their ears.

'It seems you cannot do much at all, my pet. Whatever is asked of you it appears you do not care for it. Well, I for one have had enough so I will leave you to your ... problems and take myself off. There is a meeting at The Bear and some cheerful companions will be a change. Don't wait up for I will probably be late.'

He lit a cigar with a steady hand, bowed mockingly to her back, his eyes hooded and unreadable should she have been interested enough to try, then sauntered from the room. She heard the sound of his voice calling for his carriage and the crunch of the wheels and the horse's hooves on the gravel drive.

She slept alone that night for the first time – bar her pregnancy – since her marriage.

They moved uneasily through the damp winter days, the

steady drizzle keeping Christy and the children indoors; even the placid pleasure of walking up to the paddock to see the horses impossible in the haze of rain which drifted across the mountains, obscuring all but the outline of the trees about the house.

She lived in a daze of pain and renewed grief, mourning all over again – like a widow though she wore no black – the death of her love, dragging herself through the days until it should pass for if it did not she would die of it. The children were peevish, restrained too long in the nursery but she couldn't seem to find it in her heart to care. Alex came and went, a neutral face in a toneless world. She didn't care. Annie drove over, begging her to visit her father who was ailing with a cough and phlegm in his chest you could cut with a knife, but she didn't care.

December was hard, with a frost thick upon the ground; then it snowed and drifts wrapped about each shrub and tree and she ventured out a little but the bright and dazzling winter sun on the frosted snow was cruel and hurt her eyes, and Amy cried with the cold and begged to to taken indoors to the warmth of the nursery – only the baby smiling, in the cocoon of his blankets in the baby carriage as Christy pushed him apathetically about the paths of the beautiful snow-bound gardens.

Christmas came and went, presents under the huge tree Alex brought down from his land across the Brathay; and Annie and Job with a child apiece on their lap, Job content for the moment, recovered from his bronchitis, as he held the wriggling body of his grandson for it took him back to the childhood of his own lads.

Alex gave her a bracelet of seed pearls set in fine gold filigree 'to match her necklace' he said carelessly, a comb for her hair made in ivory and edged with tiny flowers of lapis lazuli, earrings of gold and a length of silk so fine and beautiful in a shade of coral so rich she felt the first stirring of pleasure but when she lifted her face to him, ready to give thanks with a kiss, he had turned away to his daughter and the doll he had given her.

She began to mend as spring came, daffodils and primroses and a tender touch of warmth in the air and a chaffinch challenging her outside her bedroom window. She was heavy now but she and Amy ventured to the edge of the wood at the back of the house and saw a large bush of willow covered all over with great golden catkins and she felt the weight lift suddenly from her, and when Amy ran and jumped and darted about like the swallow which rose from the greening wood she had the delightful sensation of longing to do the same!

The birth of her second son was quick and easy and within an hour of his birth she was sitting up, her hair brushed by Faith and caught with a bright scarlet satin ribbon, her face flushed, her eyes bright, eating the dish of strawberries and cream her husband had produced from somewhere, watching him as he cradled his new son. His eyes moved from the boy to her and she was quite surprised at the warm feeling his approving gaze awoke in her. His eldest son was held protectively against his side, gathered in the circle of his arm. Amy lay on the bed beside Christy's shoulder sharing the strawberries and Alex laughed out loud.

'By God, Christy Buchanan! Was there ever a woman like you?'

'Probably not!'

She grinned and the warm feeling grew pleasurably.

'A son an hour old and you look about fifteen with that blasted ribbon in your hair, no more, and pretty as a picture. And what a boy . . .!'

He turned to Johnny, holding the toddler closer, '. . . but not such a boy as you, son.' He kissed the child's cheek, then lifted him into his lap, passing the baby to the nurse and Christy was again amazed by his sensitivity for the older child.

'Harry,' Alex said.

'Albert,' she countered.

'Albert! Who the hell's Albert?'

'The Queen's husband, of course.'

He threw back his head and laughed and she laughed with him, and the nurse who was new to the district remarked to herself on what a happy, though rather unorthodox couple Mr and Mrs Buchanan were.

Harry was five days old when she insisted on getting up.

'But Mrs Buchanan,' the shocked nurse said, 'You cannot possibly get up. Three full weeks in bed, I insist upon it. My word, whatever next? You will have Mr Buchanan giving me my notice if I don't look after you and the baby in the proper way. He said to me most particularly that I was to pay the utmost attention to your rest and what you ate and to make sure it was the proper food so that you will get your strength back as soon as possible. He was most insistent about it, saying you were to have the very best of everything, and anything you fancied I had only to tell him and he would see you had it.'

Christy was startled.

'He did?'

'Oh yes indeed. Most concerned he was and when you were in labour the doctor had the utmost difficulty in preventing him from coming into your bedroom, especially when you called out for him.'

'I called out for him! Good heavens, Nurse, whenever did I do that?' She was laughing but the nurse was insistent.

'Just towards the end when you were eager to have it done and the doctor had said you must not bear down just yet. Do you not remember?'

'Yes . . .'

'I distinctly heard you call his name and so did he for he sat just outside the door from start to finish. He was most annoyed when the doctor asked him to go downstairs and smoke a cigar and leave it all to us. He was quite . . .' The nurse blushed and smiled a little for Mr Buchanan had a way with him and she was a woman too.

'Well . . .' She almost giggled, '. . . he said . . . oh Mrs Buchanan . . . he said, "I had an important part to play in the making so why may I not be there for the baking?" He is very forceful, is he not?'

'Yes, you might say that.' Christy's face was thoughtful and she lay back on her pillows which the nurse immediately began to plump up about her, then, before the disapproving woman could even so much as put out a restraining hand Christy sprang from the bed and ran to the window.

Ran as the nurse told Mrs Longworth later, like a child and her the mother of two babies, the youngest only five days old!

She was sitting on the garden wall, watching the drift of apple blossom move on the trees in the orchard. Her face was serene, her new son in her arms, Amy, already a little mother of almost three years, guiding the stumbling feet of Johnny Buchanan across the greening grass, when Alex rode up the incline on his roan and in his amazement jerked his hand on the reins and the horse reared then side-stepped fretfully as its rider leaned to quieten him. An expression of immense concern clouded Alex's face, anxious and not at all pleased, then was replaced at once by the one Christy knew so well.

'You can take that look off your face, Alex Buchanan,' she said, smiling impishly. 'I will not stay in bed another moment on such a glorious day. Yes, I know it has been but five days and it is expected of a woman who has just given birth to remain in her bed for three full weeks, then another three on her chaise longue but that is for ladies and I am not a lady. I am a daleswoman, strong and healthy and . . . oh please don't look like that. I really am well enough.'

'I'll flog that bloody woman. How dare she let you up so soon?'

He threw the reins to the running figure of the groom and strode over the rough grass towards Christy. His dismay made him careless in what he said. 'Could you not at least stay near the house instead of romping about here with the children?'

263

'Oh, hardly romping, Alex! I was sitting quite sedately as befits a mother of three, resting on the wall.'

She was smiling, strangely pleased by his solicitude.

'To hell with that. I will not have my son dragged about the gardens before he has barely had time to draw breath. My God, woman, he is five days old. *Five days old* and you have him out here like a bloody doll. You were just the same with Amy. Will you never learn? Will you never grow up, for Christ's sake?'

The sweet, unexpected drift of happiness she had felt on this fine morning shattered away and her heart, that which had been amazed and curiously touched by what the nurse had told her, hardened and her face turned mutinous.

She shrugged her shoulders with cool indifference.

'It seems not, Alex, but then should you have wanted a woman who was *old* why did you not take the Widow Jones from Fellthwaite? She is of your age and capable still of bearing children and had a good portion when her husband left her which must count for something! I must apologize for being young and, and in your eyes as giddy as a March hare. Here, here is your son. Take him before I throw him to the dogs to play with . . .'

She thrust the child into her husband's arms. Amy, eyes huge and brimming with bright blue tears stood directly behind her, her hand still clutching that of Johnny as she restrained him fussily from picking mother's primroses. The boy was trying to shake her off and before Christy could stop herself in her maddened haste to escape the hatred which Alex's words had aroused in her, she crashed into both the small children, knocking them down and falling herself on top of them, her skirts tipping up in a froth of white lace petticoats and drawers.

They were not hurt, any of them for the grass was springy and children can fall a dozen times without mishap. But Amy was frightened, bewildered by the sharp anger of her father and mother and the loud voices they threw at one another, and she cried fiercely and would not be soothed until Beth and Liz came running down the long garden, one for each crying child. She drew away from Christy, thinking she had knocked her down, and Johnny too, whom she adored and mother was naughty to have done it.

For a full five minutes the garden was filled with the voices of crying children, the baby wailing as he was awakened, Christy's voice begging for forgiveness from her small son and daughter, the concerned chirruping of Beth and Liz and Alex's deeper, alarmed voice, with each word growing top-heavy with increasing anger. He was crumbling on the edge of violence, holding his temper whilst he held the child and it was not until they were alone – the babies and nursemaids gone back to the safety of the nursery – that he let it out, but hers was just as hot and virulent and for a full half hour the servants were silent as they listened to Mr and Mrs Buchanan tell each other quite explicitly of their mutual loathing.

'. . . and from now on, madam, you will do exactly, *exactly* as every other lady, though, as you have gone to great lengths to tell me, you are not one, in this community. You will call on them and always be at home when they call on you. I wish to see you visit your mother and father at more frequent intervals since your father would be glad of it in his state of health and at his time of life. He would be glad to see something of his grandsons too, I have no doubt and as they are to inherit his mills . . .'

'Of course, I might have known there were no great philanthropic notions behind your words of honour and duty. The bloody mills that's all it is. Well, they will come to your sons whatever you do . . . or make me do, Alex, for he has nowhere else to leave them . . .'

'. . . and when I come home . . .' She might not have spoken for all the notice he took of her. '. . . I wish to find my children safely in the nursery and you at your sewing . . .'

'You go to hell and take your damn sermons with you.'

'. . . and if I hear one word from anyone, anyone, that I

do not like about your behaviour, as God is my witness I will have you committed or put you in the charge of . . .'

'You can't keep me fastened to your house and your bed as though I was nothing more that your housekeeper and *whore!*'

'Watch your filthy mouth . . .'

'I shall go where I please and now that I am relieved of the burden you forced upon me I shall take my horse . . .'

He was at a point of fury where reason had left him and she knew she was in great peril but she could not stop herself and neither could he. There was a dreadful blankness in his eyes, and his mouth was stretched over his bared teeth.

'You do, lady,' he hissed, 'and I shall shoot the beast.'

'You wouldn't . . .'

'Try me.' His voice was hoarse in his throat as though it strained to get through some barrier and he grasped her arm leaving five finger marks which later would turn into black bruises. 'Try my patience too far and you will learn what I can and cannot do. You are my wife, the mother of my sons and that is your function. Nothing more. If you do not care to be my whore as you so delicately put it, then don't. There are plenty who will . . .'

'Oh yes! Of that I am certain. All those nights you go to The Bear . . .'

'You have noticed then? I thought my absence from your bed . . .'

'I was glad to have you gone,' she lied. 'Glad not to have to suffer . . .'

'Suffer! And there was I thinking those moans and sighs were of pleasure whereas you were hating every minute. You are a consummate actress . . .'

'You bastard! You bastard!'

'No, not that but I can be ugly when I am crossed, Christy. You would do well in future to remember it!'

CHAPTER SEVENTEEN

'What's wrong with father? Does he not go down to the mill in the afternoon any more? He was sitting on the wall with his back to it when I drove up and when I spoke to him he looked at me as though he didn't know who I was. When he finally recognized me he just said, "Christy, is it you, lass?" then went on staring at . . . well, I don't know what he was staring at! Nothing it seemed!'

Christy Buchanan tossed aside the dainty lace parasol she carried, allowing it to land wherever it chanced to fall, careless of its fragile, ivory-mounted handle, the spun delicacy of its fringed border and the froth of satin ribbons and white tulle rosettes which decorated it, her attitude saying quite clearly that its beauty and cost meant nothing to her for had she not plenty more where that came from. It fetched up on her mother's *chaise-longue* from where it slipped to the floor followed by a lozenge-shaped reticule in ivory velvet, the colour matching her gown.

Behind her in an eager rush and tumble of sturdy legs, tousled ebony curls, vivid, bold blue eyes and destructive fingers came her eldest son, his voice demanding immediate attention for was not *he* the most important person in the room? He was followed more decorously by Amy, dainty as a garden daisy in white and yellow, but equally as inquisitive as the two of them began to circle Grandmother's drawing room. It was crammed with so many delightful things, all jostling one another on low tables, just the right height for small persons to reach and small hands to grasp – not placed above their heads as they were at home – and they could not wait to explore.

Their nursemaid, Beth, moved behind them, shepherding them this way and that as she tried to divert their attention from Mrs Emmerson's pretty ornaments, the baby Harry asleep in her arms. Her face was already quite desperate for within two minutes of entering the room the two children had already sampled a silver-mounted ostrich egg, a stuffed bird from beneath a glass dome, a cut-crystal rose vase and a Wedgewood shepherdess, the head of which was placed immediately in Master Johnny's mouth!

Christy appeared not to notice, treating her mother's possessions with the same careless disregard she did her own.

Annie put in several more stitches to the square of bright material she was quilting, her hands, despite years of doing little more than supervise her own servants, still the hands of a working woman. They were square and broad-fingered yet they moved delicately, threading the needle through the cloth to take the almost invisible stitches her own mother had taught her. She was a patient woman, durable and accepting all that life had given and taken from her but her years were beginning to show as she bent her grey head over her needlework.

She put in a last stitch then looked up at her daughter, watching her pace restlessly about the neat drawing room, striding from the window where she had stood for a moment to stare at her father, then back to the sofa to fall impatiently beside her mother.

Christy Buchanan was not a comfortable person to be with any more, Annie thought. Not that she had ever been exactly restful but her energy and dash had been joyful, making those in her company smile however exasperating she might be. They would sit up with expectancy for the bright wit, the blithe, often startling but never malicious gossip she divulged gleefully, the arguments she countered with her own, her fancies, beliefs, ideas, all put forth hotly but with the best of humour.

Annie considered the elegance of her daughter's ivory afternoon gown. It was made of organdy, light and dainty. The bodice was tight, long-waisted to a point at the front, buttoned down the back from the neck to the waist. The sleeves were tight to just below the elbow where a small expansion shaped itself into the fashionable 'bell' finished with white, frilled half sleeves beneath.

Her skirt was just long enough to touch the toe of her white, low-heeled kid shoes, very full and supported by the new 'crinoline', the hem braided in deep flounces of crisp white lace. She wore no bonnet in defiance of her husband, Annie knew, and her hair was held in a riotous tumble of slipping curls threaded with white satin ribbons and rosebuds. She looked magnificent in her careless disregard for neatness but her outfit was completely unsuitable for a respectably married woman on an afternoon call with her daughter and two sons, and she knew it. Her attitude clearly said she cared nought for it, or indeed for anyone bar the two children who sprawled about Annie's drawing room like puppies at play and the infant who still slept in the arms of the nervous nursemaid.

'What is it, mother? Has he abandoned the mills altogether? I had heard he was not as . . . punctual as once he was and that he did not quite give the attention . . .'

'Should not those children be made to sit on a chair and look at a book, Christina?' Annie interrupted mildly. 'Amy has torn the flounce of her dress and if I am not mistaken Johnny is in need of his nursemaid, surely. If his breeches aren't changed he will mark my carpet!'

'Oh, I had not noticed.' Christy turned, distracted as Annie had intended her to be, for she did not wish to discuss her husband's strangeness in front of the interested nursemaid. There was enough gossip about as it was.

'I thought as much, daughter. Perhaps if the girl, see . . . what is your name . . . Beth . . . don't hang about in the doorway like that. Cannot the child be made more comfortable, I would have thought by now he would have . . .'

She was reluctant to appear to question her daughter's upbringing of her own children but surely a child of fifteen months should be more reliable in matters of nature? And they were both so out of hand, rolling now beneath her tables and chairs, and the nursemaid standing confused

269

and uncertain of what to do for lack of an order from her mistress.

There was an outcry from behind the sofa and Amy began to wail for she was easily upset. Her young brother was almost as big as she was and though she loved him dearly if his demands were not met immediately his scowl was enough to reduce her to tears.

Annie tutted in exasperation.

'Really, Christina, if you do not control those children, I will. Does their father allow such behaviour I wonder, for I can't believe it!'

She watched her daughter's face close up at the mention of Alexander Buchanan, and saw her turn away to stare without interest towards the window and the garden where her father still sat, his face turned blankly in the direction of the house. Annie saw the expression cross her face, one of defiance, quite chilling, and her lip curled rebelliously as Annie had seen it do a thousand times, and she sighed.

She was only too sadly aware that Alex Buchanan and his pretty young wife, her daughter, lived in a constant state of anger and dissension, over what she did not know and she wondered sometimes if they knew themselves. Since the birth of their second son they seemed to scarce have a polite word for one another in public and through the servants' grapevine which stretched across the valley and beyond, it was whispered that their quarrels in private could be heard by the horses up in the paddock. Fierce it was and they were often afraid it might come to blows for Mrs Buchanan would not conform to the pattern of wife and mother expected, no, demanded of her, and Mr Buchanan threatened her with . . . well . . . it could not be repeated what Mr Buchanan said to his wife but she no longer rode her mare for fear of the poor beast's life. She defied him in every way she could without hurt to others but she paid for it over and over again, Annie had heard, by her husband's frequent absence from his home . . . and his bed!

He spent much of his time at The Bear and only when

his business interests demanded it did he dine at home, bringing with him gentlemen to be entertained in his now elegant dining room by his always elegant and charming wife.

How much Fellthwaite knew or guessed Annie was never told by the ladies who came to call on her for she did not speak of it, but the servants would gossip and though it would all be politely ignored, or spoken of only in hushed, lady-like whispers, discreet as Alex Buchanan would demand it to be, as he would demand of his wife to be, the sorrow of it, the waste of it on top of the waste of her sons' lives and her husband's health was almost more than Annie could bear. She grieved badly. For her sons and her husband, and for her daughter's unhappiness. She had been so certain that given time and patience and a child or two Christy would grow fond of her husband. He was a good man. Wilful and obstinate, but good. Charming and intelligent, hard-headed and strong, but not patient.

She would sell her soul to give her daughter the peaceful and fulfilling marriage she deserved for the lass had been cheated of it, but in these last months she had grown curiously tired herself. Hopeless and empty! She felt she had had enough and wanted merely to be left in peace with her husband. All her life she had struggled to keep together what they had, what she and Job had created, putting others' needs before her own, and now, quite simply, she wished to withdraw from it and sit in the twilight of her remaining years. But for the pleasure she had from her grandchildren and sometimes, as now, she wished them far enough away, life seemed not to matter much as she watched it drain from her husband.

The children were led away, Johnny complaining bitterly in the muddle of infant babble and the growing number of short sentences he could now form, but he was pacified by the promise of one of Mrs Kean's gingerbread men and the great fuss which would be made of him by the servants in his grandmother's kitchen. Amy clung to Beth's hand, tearful still and glancing backwards to her mother on

271

whose lap she would like to have sat but Christy was, for once, concerned only with her own mother's need rather than those of her step-daughter.

'What is it, mother?' Christy took her hand and Annie turned her head to look at her, surprised by the gentleness in her daughter's voice. 'What is the matter with Father? Is he ill again? I know he still mourns them but I had thought . . . with Johnny and Harry, and the mills going so well he was . . . recovering. Not completely for shall any of us ever do that but . . . better. Is he not?'

'No, lass. He's not over it and I reckon he never will be. Two years now and more and he still blames himself. He won't have it that it wasn't some omission on his part that killed them. The enquiry thought it was the bungs on the cylinders as you know . . . the friction . . . but they weren't sure and we'll never really know and that's what's ailing him. Guilt! I was sure when your lads came he'd be . . . reconciled, and then when Alex promised the name would stay the same when . . . when he took over, but . . .'

'Does he just sit there, then, with his back to it all the time?'

'Oh no! This morning he stumped off down there at the usual time, just as he always did but . . .'

'Yes, mother?' Christy put her slender, organdy-covered arm about Annie's shoulders, stroking her gently, her face warm with concern. Annie was aware in the corner of her mind which was not involved with her own pain, that those who called Christy Buchanan a careless mother, a giddy and irresponsible wife who thought of nothing but her crinolines, her ermine muffs, her silk gowns, her carriage horses and the splendour of the house she was slowly making of Alex Buchanan's home – for how else was she to spend her frivolous time and the enormous amounts of money he allowed her – were quite wrong. There was compassion in her, and warmth and a lively humour which, when allowed, broke free as she romped with her son and with Maude Buchanan's daughter whom she had made her own. They might be given more freedom

272

than most children but was that not because Christy herself had none? She was a loving, caring woman now, despite what Fellthwaite might say but so few saw it, least of all her husband.

'What is it, darling?' Christy pleaded, the endearment by which she called her children coming easily to her lips for this woman she held so dear.

'Yesterday, and many days before that . . . he has taken to hanging about in the hallway . . .'

'Yes mother,' Christy prompted softly.

'And when I ask him why he says . . .'

'Yes?'

Annie's voice sank to a defeated whisper.

'He says he is waiting for . . . for Ben and Toby and if . . . if they don't look lively he will go without them . . . Oh Christy . . .!'

'Oh darling . . . darling . . . why didn't you tell me before? I might have helped . . . spoken to him . . . brought him some . . . some comfort . . .'

'Lass, you have enough problems without mine being added to them!'

'Mother . . .'

'I know, child . . . everyone knows . . .'

Christy held her mother, taking comfort from it, rocking her gently and her face was bleak. Annie did not weep. Annie Emmerson had not wept since the day over two years ago when they had put the last of her sons in the ground. She had shed a tear or two of gladness as her husband went back to his mills after their deaths but she had done with the real business of weeping when her children were taken from her, one by precious one.

'Don't get too fond of them,' her own mother had told her, 'for when they go it will only hurt the more.' But how could a mother prevent the love which insinuated itself into her heart for her child, a son who laughs in her arms, a little girl, sweet and treasured? And they went, until only this lass was left, her ability to weep went with them. Her tears dried up and she was sorry for tears helped to release

273

the hurt. It did not take it away but it eased it at each weeping until the pain was bearable.

'There's nothing to be done, lass,' she said, drawing away from her daughter's comforting arm and straightening her shoulders. 'When you take a man you take the good side and the bad. You laugh with him when he does well and call him clever and watch him strut about like your Johnny, or you comfort the blows and pick him up when he falls. That's what marriage is about, Christy.'

'Yes, I know.'

There was a small silence as Annie waited for the tiny criticism she had hinted at to arouse some response in her daughter but Christy stood up and swayed gracefully to the window, a lovely gauzy flower delicate and fit for nothing but to be beautiful for the adornment of Alex Buchanan's home.

'Yes, I do know that, mother,' she said simply.

Job Emmerson died in his sleep a month later. He lay down beside his wife, turning to kiss her lovingly before he blew out the candle.

'You're a good wife, Annie,' he said, 'and the best thing I ever did was to marry you, lass.'

Annie was the most composed at the funeral though her daughter broke down and wept blindly behind her veil, but her mother comforted her most touchingly as though their roles were reversed.

Job's son-in-law, Alexander Buchanan, now the richest man within a twenty-mile radius of Fellthwaite, held her arm, more in the manner of a gaoler than that of a man supporting a grieving wife but then who could blame him for she was known to be flighty, and it was noted that when the mourners moved back to Hollin House for a sip of wine and a slice of Annie's pound cake – was it only two years since they had done the same for her lads? – husband and wife spoke but once to each other and that was to confirm that Annie must come to Howethwaite to stay with them, an offer she refused.

'No Alex! I must get used to my own company now, lad, but thank you all the same.'

'Please mother, just for a few days.'

'No Christy.'

Squire Forsythe and his lady had been at the graveside but Mrs Alex Buchanan did not greet them though the widow did, thanking them as was her duty, or so they seemed to think, for doing Job the honour. Christy Buchanan did not even glance from behind her veil in their direction; and when her husband would have led her to them, as was only courteous, she shook off his hand and stormed, yes, that was the word Fellthwaite would have used, positively stormed to her carriage.

A week later the Squire was thrown from his horse which had shied as a rabbit ran across its path. He seemed not to be much injured for he joked as they lifted him on to a handy gate to carry him home, showing the careless disregard for pain that countless Forsythes had demonstrated since their ancestor had died in the Civil War – for the King, naturally. But when he took a ferocious fever and began to cough up blood, complaining as he became delirious, of a pain in his chest cutting him in two, the doctor began to show concern. He did not know, he said to the Squire's lady, why her husband had begun to waste away since apart from the bruising on his chest he appeared to be uninjured.

The high fever ate away all the flesh from his bones, but once it broke, the doctor said, and the sweat came, he would be much improved.

The Squire lingered for just over a month, dying on the day his son landed in Liverpool from America, summoned from there by his frantic mother to his father's bedside.

'I will not go to the funeral.'

'You will, Christy, believe me you will!'

'One funeral in a month is enough for anyone, Alex. You go if you feel you must.'

'Common decency demands it.'

'Then go!'

'You are my wife. You will come with me.' His face was obdurate, his voice threatening. There was no more to be said on the subject, his attitude implied, and he turned away from her ready to leave their bedroom. Her maid had been brushing her hair and would have tactfully slipped from the room when her master entered but he signalled to her that his conversation with his wife was ended and she stood obediently, the brush hanging from her limp hand.

Christy stood up and turned to face him and Faith took an involuntary step backwards for the expression of loathing on Christy's face unnerved her. But it was not for her husband, Faith realized, that look of revulsion which spasmed across her mouth, curling her lips back against her teeth and narrowing her eyes to slits but for something else which Faith could only guess at.

'I will not stand at his graveside and pretend to mourn a man I detest, Alex. There are enough hypocrites to do that without my joining them.'

'I cannot imagine why you should detest a man you scarce know but that does not concern me. You will come to his funeral if I have to drag you there!' He was remorseless in his arrogant certainty that she would obey him.

'So be it then!' She lifted her head, flinging back her hair wildly and Faith thought she had never seen her so savagely beautiful.

'You will come?' He was triumphant in his victory.

'No! You will have to drag me there!'

There was a deep and dreadful silence, so threatening, so charged with the unwavering wills of these two people Faith felt the tiny whimper in her throat though she had made no sound.

She took another hesitant step backwards for when they

flew at one another as she was convinced they would she did not want to be between them.

At last Alex Buchanan spoke and when he did his voice grated curiously in his mouth as though his tongue was so dry it could not function as it should.

'It's him, isn't it? Robin bloody Forsythe! It's him you're afraid of, since you know he'll be there, don't you? Be honest, Christy. You were always that whatever else you were. You don't give a damn about the Squire nor the hypocrisy,' his mouth curled in a sneer, 'of standing by his graveside! You're afraid of the *new* Squire, admit it, afraid to stand beside me and see your old lover.'

Christy's face was as white as the turned-down sheet on the bed. As white as the beautiful filmy wrapper which drifted about her but her mouth was red and full of bursting life as she sprang with a scream for her husband's eyes.

'Oh Jesus ... Oh sweet Jesus God!' Faith turned her face to the wall which was suddenly behind her, feeling for the door with a blind crab-like movement but somehow it was not where it usually was and she could not escape the black horror of what was taking place.

Alex Buchanan caught his wife's wrists triumphantly between his strong brown hands, holding them with one whilst the other sank ruthlessly into her silken hair. He dragged her head back so that she was forced to look up at him.

'My word, Christy Buchanan, I never thought to see you afraid to show your pretty face to the interested spectators who will come to stare. For naturally they will remember your betrothal to the lad who is now the Squire!' His eyes were a flashing brilliance of hot blue in his brown face, laughing recklessly, his mouth in a snarling smile across his white teeth. His hair, smoothly brushed in readiness for his usual evening call at The Bear in Fellthwaite, had tumbled over his forehead in a tangle of dark curls and he looked like a gypsy, or a pirate, wild and fierce and incredibly handsome.

277

'What pleasure they will derive in seeing you timidly skulk at my coat-tails, or not there at all which will cause even more speculation!'

You filthy bastard! Let me go . . . let me go or I swear I'll kill you!'

'Kill me, my darling, let me see you try then!' He threw off her hands, laughing wildly, turning in the manner of a wrestler looking for a hold and Faith became still, then turned to look at him, no longer afraid. She could see in his face the savage desire to have his wife strike him so that he might strike her back and her fear was for Christy now. His ugly rage menaced her and she seemed not to care but Faith did and she knew she must stop its pace before it destroyed them.

'Mr Buchanan,' she called imperiously from the doorway which had been there all the time. 'Mr Buchanan, please, you will awaken the children.'

The incongruity of it, the simple homely remark in the midst of such naked hatred and rage brought them both round to stare at her in ludicrous disbelief. The remnants of the killing anger twisted each of their mouths in a straining rictus, but already it was beginning to slip away as the familiarity of their surroundings, of Faith herself, of what she said, of what they had been about to do brought them back to some semblance of normality.

Faith watched Alex Buchanan straighten up slowly and the cold, careless expression, the one he usually fixed on his wife these days come to replace the killing rage which had distorted his features. His hand was unsteady as he dragged it through his hair and his breath left his lungs in a long expulsion of released tension, but he managed a smile, insolent and self-assured.

'My word, what a to-do over nothing,' he said reaching for his cigars.

Christy watched him warily, her breath heaving in her chest, still crouched but like her husband, beginning to regain her composure.

'The funeral is at noon tomorrow, my pet,' he continued

smoothly. 'The carriage will be ready at eleven so I shall expect to see you in it, suitably dressed. I don't imagine I shall see you before then,' he eyes glinted cruelly, 'so I will bid you good-night.'

He lit his cigar in a leisurely fashion and when it was burning to his satisfaction bowed mockingly in her direction and sauntered from the room.

Christy moved sightlessly, tremblingly, her breath leaving her body on long shudders, clinging to the furniture until she reached the bed. She sat stiffly on its edge as though her body hurt from head to toe and she must not jolt it.

'Faith, oh God Faith!' Her whisper reached the woman by the door and Faith's heart moved in pity for she had never seen such desolation.

'What am I to do? I cannot take much more. I have tried ... tried ... after Harry was born I thought ... but he does not ...'

The maid moved swiftly across the room and sat down beside her mistress, taking her hand between her own.

'Does not what, Miss Christy?'

But Christy did not answer for in truth she did not know what it was she had been about to say. Did not want her? Did not need her? Did not love her? She knew all these things, had always known so what had she meant? Did not try, as she tried to make some semblance of peace in their shattered life together? What? What?

They sat in the lovely warm room and slowly, calmed by the serenity of the girl beside her, she began to draw comfort from the hands which held her, which pulled her back from the quaking morass which threatened so often to engulf her; hands which belonged to a woman no older than herself but who was blessed with the gift of saying nothing, not in sympathy, nor recrimination but who was merely there just when she was needed!

'You must go,' she said now, her voice low, soft.

'Yes ...'

'He will make you, you know that.'

279

'I know . . . I know, but how am I to stand beside him and look at . . . after all this time?'

'You will do it.'

'He will see me with . . . with my husband. How will he be able to bear it?'

Faith looked bewildered.

'He has known you are married for over two years. Surely by now he will be . . .'

'No . . . no, he loves me . . . still . . .'

'Miss Christy,' Faith's voice was gentle. 'How can you possibly know that?'

'I do! Don't ask me how.'

'Well, even so, you must stand beside your husband and hold up your head and not disgrace him . . . or yourself!'

'I can't, Faith . . . I simply can't!'

'Yes, oh yes you can, Christy Buchanan, you can!'

And she did.

They stood side by side the next day, Christina and Alexander Buchanan amongst the hundreds who had come to see their manorial lord put respectably to rest, and Alex's hand gripped her arm so tightly she knew she would have bruises to match the ones he had given her the night before. It was not concern for her that gave her his support but the simple determination that the multitude would not have the pleasure of seeing Alex Buchanan's wife slip away at the sight of the man to whom once she had been promised in marriage. She could fall into the grave with the Squire himself for all he cared, she knew that, but he would have her stand proud and unshaken by her husband's side until the last clod of earth had been flung on the coffin. She was Alex Buchanan's wife who cared for no man but himself. He would suppress any whisper or sideways glances with an irrefutable demonstration of their splendid marriage and wedded bliss; and Robin Forsythe would know, *know* unequivocally that Christy Emmerson was the possession of no one but Alex Buchanan.

But he could not control her eyes! He could clasp her to him with the gesture of a devoted husband supporting the frailness of his wife — for women were known to be overcome on such sad occasions and had she not buried her father only the month before — but her eyes flew across the open grave and met those of Robin Forsythe, Squire Forsythe now, as he held the arm of his mother and sister and they spoke from behind her veil and his answered, and though Alex's fingers threatened simply to snap the bone of her arm, she could not look away.

'I love you still,' his said to hers. 'And I you,' hers answered and for an instant as the parson intoned the words and heads were bent, they were alone, not beneath the drifting October leaves of the trees in the graveyard but leaning together against the trunk of the hornbeam. Deep brown, dangerously soft for her were his eyes, and hers a lovely clouded grey and she felt her husband like a strand of tense steel beside her, the snapping compression in him almost visible.

That night, after the silent meal they had taken in the silent dining room of the silent house, a meal in which he never once took his eyes from her as he crumbled a bread roll which he did not eat, added salt to the soup he did not taste, cut a slice of chicken which was left untouched upon his plate, he spoke at last to her. His voice was quiet, conversational, calm with the deadly calm of approaching peril.

'So my love, it is still the same then?'

'What is, Alex?'

'Come, don't let us pretend.'

'Pretend what?' but her eyes slid away and she was busy with the coffee cups, the placing of spoons and the sugar bowl in their precise position on the table.

'Christy, oh Christy.' He lit his cigar, watching her through the smoke. 'This is Alex Buchanan! Your husband! I have not lived with you for over two years without knowing a little about you. Your composure, or lack of it, gives you away.'

'I don't know what you're talking about.' She lifted her head and stared at him haughtily and he felt the anger pound against his temple for she was so lovely, so bravely, defiantly lovely. But she was his, *his* and no one, *no one* interfered with anything that belonged to Alex Buchanan, not even by *look*! Physically she was untouched but his eyes, *his eyes*, that Squireen who had first put his mark on her, had rested on her again today and by God, he was about to take it from her in the only way she understood. In the only way a man can completely dominate a woman, he'd take that look away from her as though it had never been!

He stood up and the chair flew backwards, falling to the floor with a crash which stilled all those in the kitchen. His cigar was flung unsmoked into the fire and he did not even see it go. He grinned and his eyes gleamed cruelly as he walked towards her but she continued to stare at him with the imperious dignity of a young queen.

He stopped then, his mocking smile widening.

'What, my darling! Are you not afraid of your husband? Do you not mean to deny me? I warn you I will not take no for an answer!'

'Go to the devil, Alex Buchanan.'

'Not yet, oh not yet, though I daresay he and I will meet one day!'

'It cannot be too soon for me.' Her voice was as cruel as his.

Something passed over his face then, so quickly she did not even see it.

He stripped her, right there in the dining room and she stood like a marble statue, refusing to be defeated by her very indifference to his hands and his lips and his beautiful masculine body. A servant could enter for the table had not yet been cleared though it was doubtful that any would dare in that house of hopelessness, but he tumbled her to the soft rug before the fire, covering her flame-tinted body with his own and deep inside her, deep, deep where her defying mind could not reach, she began to respond. Her mind fought it, fought him, strained to resist the feel of his hands on her breasts and thighs, the feel of his hot mouth lingering on her belly, but her weak flesh began to purr and stretch and grow languid with sensuality.

Robin ... oh God ... Robin, her soul shrieked as her treacherous woman's body arched to Alex Buchanan's and her bruised mouth whispered her husband's name with such rapture. When he had done he could not stay but flung on his clothes and ran from the house as though the devil had at last called to him.

She was a woman made of stone as Faith propelled her gently about the bedroom later, making no sound nor objection to anything her maid suggested, lifting her arms obediently to be undressed and put into her nightgown, turning this way and that as she was told, sitting to have her hair brushed, and lying neatly in the bed as Faith blew out the candle.

The servants had been afraid to go into the dining room when the master left and it had been Faith who found her staring blindly into the fire, her face quite expressionless. She had fumbled her way into the gown Alex had taken from her but the rest of her clothing still lay where he had flung it. Faith gathered it, and her mistress, quietly leading her upstairs and in her mind was bewilderment and confusion for, here, in her own home with her children upstairs and her servants not more than yards away, Alex Buchanan had treated his wife as though she was a common whore and Faith had seen the marks on her body to prove it!

Would a man subject the woman he cared for to such cruel humiliation, would he? If so Faith wanted none of such caring and neither, it seemed, did Christy Buchanan!

CHAPTER EIGHTEEN

Alexander Buchanan's third son was born on July the thirtieth 1848, in the middle of a summer thunderstorm which threatened to tear the slates from the roof and force in the shuttered windows of the sturdy house. The sky was a violent purple, the colour of a plum, streaking to vivid heliotrope, mulberry and pale lavender as the lightning tore across it. Great jagged forks pierced the very air above the roof, racing angrily to fling sheets of fire behind the peaks. The thunder trumpeted, clashing with a clangour which silenced to heaving terror every animal within its hearing, and the grooms and stable lads worked through the night like madmen calming the beasts in the stable and shippens.

Hour after hour the storm collided about the sky, matching in its strength the labour of the woman on the bed. Its resonance drowned her cries, thunderclaps like shells bursting across the high fells and echoing down into the dales and valleys.

The wind howled about the chimneys as though looking for an entrance to the house, tearing away the threaded smoke which rose from them into the teeth of the storm. Great low clouds whipped across the sky and Tilberthwaite High Fell was hidden in their raging dashing waves. Trees bent low to the ground and the bright peonies, columbines and hollyhocks in the garden were flattened by the wet, lashing rain.

The bedroom was warm though no fire was lit here. The force of the storm had made it necessary to put up the shutters since Alex was afraid for the window panes and the door must be tight closed, said the straining woman on the bed, in order not to frighten the children with her cries.

They grew more shrill as the night wore on and her

senses were lost to her. She was conscious at one point of a hand holding hers and she clung to it gratefully, and a man's voice told her to hang on and not to give in. She supposed it to be the doctor for he was there when she opened her eyes though she was not certain of the shadowy figure who stood behind him.

Faith was there, dear Faith, coming and going, up and down the stairs she was told later a dozen or more times relaying news to the servants who had become fond of their contrary young mistress, and were anxious, sitting about the kitchen, speculating on how much longer it would be, for Mrs Buchanan was having a hard time of it with this one.

Mrs Longworth and Mrs Avery pondered over their umpteenth pot of tea, discussing various remedies which might help poor Mrs Buchanan, until Faith told them sharply to hold their tongues, earning a surprised look for were they not only trying to do a bit of good for the labouring woman.

Jack Hodson had brought the midwife and doctor from Fellthwaite and since then had strode between the kitchen and the stables with a face on him as long as a fiddle and such a frantic air one might have supposed him to be the expectant father!

The storm was at its peak when the child gave its first cry, as triumphant and forceful as though he himself had commanded the thunder and lightning to bring him here and having arrived, ordered them to be gone. His yells were loud and lusty telling those present from the start that nothing would ever frighten him, and his mother turned her head away as they took him from between her thighs. When she looked her son was gone and the storm had died to an intermittent whisper.

An hour later Christina Buchanan lay flat on her back upon the bed, washed and tidy. The doctor would not allow her to sit up and in truth she had not the inclination to do so. The birth of this child, like his conceiving, had been hard. Her face was whiter than the frilled pillow on which her head rested and her dark hair lay in a plait thick as a man's wrist across her shoulder. Her eyes were open, looking beyond the open window to the smashed garden, now bathed in sultry sunshine and her hands were folded upon the turned down sheet which covered her breast.

Alex sat beside her. Faith had gone, drawn irresistibly to the room along the passage where the child was and also the midwife. She was well-pleased with her patient, who, though pushed to the limit of her strength by the strapping boy who had forced his way through the delicate tissues of her body in his eagerness to arrive, was recovering nicely.

Later the woman rested before the fire in the kitchen after seeing the doctor on his way to another confinement, tired after her efforts, sipping tea whilst she waited for Jack to reharness the gig which would take her back to Fellthwaite, exchanging stories of childbirth with Mrs Longworth and Mrs Avery, both childless and likely to remain so but like all women with none, expert on the subject. The midwife did not mind admitting now that she and the doctor had been concerned a time or two during the night. Mrs Buchanan, despite having had two children, both easy births, had had a difficult labour and the boy himself had been so big. What a child! No matter what trick she and the doctor tried to save the mother from damage, he would not be held back but butted his way out into the world like a ram at a wall!

'And what will you call him, your son?' Alex said, his face smoothly polite.

'Job.' The answer was soft and there was no argument this time, laughing or otherwise and the nurse who had cared for Mrs Buchanan after the birth of her second boy wondered at the change in the couple. Of course Mrs Buchanan had not had the easy time she had then but still . . . they were very . . . cool with one another, not like they had been then.

'As you like,' Mr Buchanan said.

'Perhaps you . . .'

'Yes?' his face showed nothing but indifference.

'Nothing.'

Her head was turned listlessly away from him and she seemed to be hardly aware of his presence. He wondered why he stayed but she had just borne him a son and it was expected of him.

'Is there anything you need?'

'Thank you, no.'

'Then I will go. You are tired.'

'Yes, a little.'

'I just came to say I am to go to St Helens. I have been due there these last three weeks but I felt . . .' His words stumbled in his mouth but she did not look round. 'Now that the child is born and . . . everything is . . . you are both . . . well, I must go now. From there I shall go to Swansea and then to the continent. I have left a list of the places where I may be found should you . . . should there be need to reach me.'

'Thank you.'

There was a pause, then he stood up, bending to drop a light kiss on her forehead. 'He is a fine boy, Christy. You have done . . . he is . . . handsome . . .'

'Thank you. I hope your trip is successful.'

'Christy . . .'

'Yes?'

'I shall be gone a month . . . or more. Is there . . .?'

'I am quite well, Alex, and so is your son. You may leave us with an untroubled mind.'

'Christy . . .'

'Goodbye.'

He left her then. Faith stood just beyond the door and he faced her as he closed it behind him.

'Watch her, Faith,' he said. 'See she does not . . .'

'I will, sir.'

'Make her eat . . . and rest. I have not seen her so tired before . . .'

'Yes sir. She'll do fine. He is a lovely boy, sir.'

'Yes.' It was said again with a curious air of unconcern.

287

Christy lay upon the bed like someone prepared to be placed within her coffin. Gone were her pink cheeks, that perfect sheen of health she had carried about with her during her pregnancy. Then her eyes had been clear, her hair glossy but if Robin Forsythe had met her at the lane's end now he would have passed her by without recognition.

'Faith,' she whispered.

'I'm here, lass.'

'Has he gone?'

'Aye, an hour since.'

'Perhaps I will take a sip of broth now.'

She did not get out of her bed in five days this time but sat obediently where the nurse put her, looking to the high fells for hours at a time, doing nothing but what she was told. But she was young, strong, a healthy daleswoman despite her long, hard labour and she recovered slowly.

She began to ask for her children and they came, at first to sit with her, big-eyed and wondering at this quiet mother, but when she laughed and grew stronger and held out her arms to them they became noisy and quarrelsome as they always were.

Amy was four years old now, secure and loved and plumply pretty. A little shy and uncertain, ordered about by her brothers, disappointed that the doctor had not brought her a little sister this time, but happy nevertheless to be allowed to nurse the baby who, for a little while would be as good as having a new doll to play with.

'Mrs Buchanan, should you let her, really, she is only four!'

'Nonsense, nurse. She is quite capable, are you not, my darling, and will be Beth's right hand in looking after her new brother,' and Amy glowed in the praise and held the baby protectively on her lap.

Johnny was as self-willed and audacious as his father at two and a half years old. Ebony curls, rounded glowing cheeks, eyes the colour of turquoise, sturdy brown legs stamping about Mother's bedroom demanding to know when she would get up and take him to the paddock, and

Father had promised him a pony when he came back and he would gallop across the river to see Grandmother, and Harry was not to come, and what was she doing lying in bed at this time of the day anyway ... and on and on in his certain belief that the world revolved about his own perfect self!

Harry was only just on his feet at fourteen months – but as truculent as his brother when Beth tried to stop him from climbing the bed curtains to sit in Mother's bed with her and share her morning chocolate – his grey velvet eyes set in lashes an inch long, his hair a bright chestnut brown, shining and heavy, the child most like his mother.

She had been afraid to look at the new baby, the son created in cruel and angry passion and born in a storm of pain. The son she had carried resentfully, joylessly for nine months, whose father, except in the night, was a polite stranger to her and who merely nodded each morning to her, asking after her health before galloping off. Once he had known she was pregnant, he was not to be seen until the next morning; she was a brood mare chained to the house his manner seemed to imply!

She had been lonely, surprisingly so, missing his biting wit, the keen sense of provocation he aroused in her, bringing her alive; missing his careless, charming compliments and his shrewd observations on the disquieting topics of the day.

The horror of the Irish famine which was bringing the starving men, women and children, even as far north as Westmorland and Cumberland to search for work; the effect the French Revolution might have in England for was there not great privation in this country and might not those who starved follow the lead of the French mob? The sad end of the Chartists who had asked for no more than universal suffrage, a vote by ballot, annual parliaments, payment of salary to its members and the abolition of the hated property qualification which effectively prevented the majority of the population from voting at all. Those who had evinced this sorry idea had been transported for their pains and would trouble their betters no more.

Alex had smiled at her interest, watching her intently through his cigar smoke, talking, explaining where no one else ever had and the evening would go by until it was time for him to take her to their bed.

It had all ended with the death of Squire Forsythe!

And now she had another boy, as dark and handsome as his father and when she looked into his tiny, sleeping face for the first time her own had been tense for surely she could not love a child who had been forced upon her.

Forced! Her mind laughed and her heart shied away from it but her mother's heart recognized her child's blamelessness, his innocent beauty and she smiled at him and loved him as she did the others, cradling him to her in fierce, protective joy.

It was the middle of September when she took her first stroll up to the paddock, a flock of noisy children about her skirts, tumbling like puppies, calling her attention to everything their curious eyes beheld, hands holding out to reach for hers. The baby lay in the wicker baby carriage, the fourth to do so, his plump legs naked to the sun, much to the nurse's horror, but then Mrs Buchanan could be trusted to do the unexpected and besides, she was off tomorrow to another confinement now that Mrs Buchanan was recovered.

An Indian summer they were calling it, as warm as it had been in July, with no need of coats for the children, or shawls, and Christy held her face up to the sun and felt its strength seep into her and knew she was herself again. She breathed in the sharp air, heady as wine, and filled her lungs with it.

Beth and Liz hovered on the perimeter of the busy, darting flock of children, ready to steady the floundering tumbles of Harry, to restrain Johnny from nipping beneath the fence rails in order to get a better view of the horses, to admire Amy's bright, crushed handful of wild flowers and Christy and Faith sauntered side by side, smiling in the peace of the day: smiling to be young and healthy and free for the moment of the tension which predominated when Alex and Christy were under the same roof.

'You're looking particularly pleased with yourself this morning, Faith Cooper,' Christy turned to look at her companion, her smile widening into a grin.

'And why not? Is this not the most beautiful day?'

'It is, but you have a look about you of . . .' She stopped and Faith turned to her, bending her head as though in embarrassment, then lifting it, her cheeks flushed, her eyes bright and shy.

'Give over, Miss Christy,' she protested, though nothing had as yet been said, and her hand went to her already neat head, then fluttered about as though, with no brush or sewing needle to hold it did not quite know where to place itself.

Christy's grin deepened delightedly.

'Now what can it be that has Faith Cooper in such a pother, I wonder? Has Jack Hodson tried to steal a kiss, or Miles?'

'Miss Christy!'

'Abel! It's Abel! He's been chasing you behind the privy! One last fling whilst he can still . . .'

'Miss Christy! Mind what you're saying! The children . . .'

'Come on Faith. Let's have it out. Who has had the cheek to . . .?'

'Don't . . . please . . .'

Christy stopped her teasing and stretched out a hand to the girl who though a servant had been a friend to her without once stepping beyond the bounds demanded of her station in life. She beckoned to Liz to take the baby carriage, then pushing her hand through Faith's stiff arm, drew her away from the children towards the gate which led from the meadow to the gardens at the side of the house. They sat on a bench beneath the shade of a cedar of Lebanon tree and when the silence had become kind and quiet, knowing somehow the answer, Christy asked her question.

'You're going to leave me, aren't you, Faith?' Her voice was sad.

'Aye lass, I'm sorry.' Faith's eyes were bright with tears but they did not fall.

'I'm selfish, Faith, but I really don't know how I shall manage without you.'

It was said simply.

'Fiddlesticks, Miss Christy!'

'I know, fiddlesticks indeed, but there it is. You are my one true friend!'

'Stop it, Miss Christina.' Faith spoke out before she had time to consider, to recall the thoughts she had on the night the master had ... done what he had done ... to her mistress and her own misgivings as to the true state of his feelings for her. She had thought she had seen his pain then, and what of his concern for his wife before he left on this recent business trip. That had been real enough!

Her voice was firm as she went on. 'You have a friend if you would let him!'

Christy turned to stare, her eyes quite bewildered.

'Who?'

'Your husband!'

She began to laugh then, high and fluting and genuinely amused. It pealed about the warm stillness of the garden, disturbing the white doves which dozed on the roof of the dovecot behind them.

'Faith, dear Faith. That is what you always have, just as your name implies, but let us leave this ... this nonscence and tell me quickly who it is that will take you from me.' Her voice broke a little but she kept the bright smile on her face.

Faith did not bob her head now but held it proudly.

'It's David Adams, Miss Christy. We have been walking out for over a year.'

'So that's where you got to on your day off. And I thought you to be with your father.'

292

'We were. David is a respectable man and insisted on meeting my parents but of course afterwards . . .'

'Aah Faith . . . afterwards . . . I know . . .'

'No, you don't. We were . . . very proper . . . always . . .!'

Christy hid her face and looked suitably chastened.

'Of course. Forgive me, Faith. I have always had a humorous turn of mind. It gets me into trouble but I mean no offence. When will you marry?'

'David had spoken to Mr Buchanan . . .'

Christy's face cooled. 'Has he? Mr Buchanan never said, but then . . . he wouldn't, would he?'

'We are to have the manager's house up by Far End.' Faith's face was rapturous.

'When?'

The silence was filled with soft sadness then, regret and yet a joy for Faith Cooper deserved the happiness with this man she so obviously loved and who loved her in return and how could Christy deny her it, or spoil it with her own pain.

'At the end of October.'

'So soon!'

'I did not like to tell you whilst you were . . . before the child was born. Then when you were poorly and slow to recover it seemed . . . but you're strong now, Miss Christy.'

'Strong, Faith . . . Dear God!'

'I shan't be far away . . . if you should need me.'

'Faith.' Her desperate cry was involuntary and she clapped her hand to her mouth to hold it in.

'He's a good man, Miss Christy . . . please don't . . .'

'I know, I'm sorry . . . I'm sorry. Of course he is a good man. I have spoken to him many times when he has come to see my husband. If I had known I would have asked him to dine and you could have been there . . .'

'Miss Christy, how could I? Your maid . . .'

'You are as good as he and would have been with him and you shall in the future.' Her eyes brightened. 'Oh Faith, I have realized, we can be true friends now. You can

293

ride with me in my carriage, not as my maid but my dear friend, call on me and I will have you and your husband . . .'

'Miss Christy,' Faith's voice was patient, 'my husband will be employed by yours. He works for him. He is in his employ and employees do not dine with their employers. You do not have the mine foreman at your table . . .'

'But David is an educated man, a mining engineer as well as manager, Faith, not just a miner, or a foreman . . .'

'It makes no difference!'

'Faith . . .'

'I know, I know, lass . . . how things are, but I'll never be far away, if you need me. You must . . .'

'What Faith? What must I do . . .'

'It's not for me to say . . .'

'Say what, Faith?'

'I cannot interfere between man and wife, Miss Christy . . .'

'No.'

They looked at one another and the barrier between mistress and maid, erected by Faith, was too heavy to lift, for Faith had come from generations of men and women who had served others and the habit was too strong to break through.

Christy rode alone in her carriage to Ambleside the next day and when Jack drew in the horses before St Mary's Church she told him to wait for she had some shopping to do. As soon as she was out of his sight she began to walk in the direction of Grasmere. She left the road beyond The Knoll, striking across the rough pastures until she came to the shallow river. She bent to take off her shoes and stockings, then lifting her skirts, waded across it, the water up to her ankles no more for the summer had been dry, and into the woods on the far side.

The trees closed in on her and her bare feet led her along the dry path, climbing steadily until the trees began to thin out a little and she was in the sunshine. Below her was Rydal Water, the sun touching it with such brilliance it hurt her eyes to look at it. On days of wild weather it would be smudged with swift swirling eddies of wind-blown ripples, but today it was gentle, soft as silk.

She was physically tired. It was but a few weeks since the birth of her son but she felt a great tide of peacefulness wash over her, a gathering of her bruised spirit to the realization that here, or somewhere like it, she could take strength from the mountains about her. The absolute silence entered her soothed heart. She was not allowed to ride out and never would be for the grooms had been told they must not saddle her mare. Round the paddock she could go, Miles had told her apologetically yesterday, or up on the gentle slope behind the house with John or himself but never alone, Mr Buchanan had told him, never alone!

Now she was alone as she needed so desperately to be and she was content. She had found a means to escape in the only way open to her and for a little while only, but it was enough. She would make it enough!

She lay for an hour, her head pillowed on her arm and watched the lake glimmer in the afternoon sunshine, her mind empty of all thoughts but those which drifted pleas-antly, lazily, effortlessly; thoughts which pleased her with their softness as they moved inside her head and her heart. They were without substance, shadows and without form, her eye conveying to her brain the beauty of her surround-ings, the peace, the healing, then she stood up and retraced her steps, picking up her shoes and stockings where she had left them.

She found Jack dozing on the seat of the carriage and laughed when he stared at her for she had been gone for two hours.

'And after all I bought nothing, Jack.'

'I was worried, Mrs Buchanan,' he said defensively, for if anything happened to his mistress his master would flay him alive, he had told him so.

'It looks like it, Jack. Now take me to Hollin House, will you?'

Her mother was at her quilting, sitting in the garden in the late afternoon sun when Jack helped Christy from her carriage. She smiled warmly as she shaded her eyes against the lowering sun.

'Christy, lass. You're looking better. I was wondering when you were going to get out of that bed of yours. A strong girl like you . . .'

'Oh mother,' Christy laughed as she sat down in the chair Ned had brought out for her. 'We're not all made like you, you know. A baby a year and at your kitchen stove the day after the birth.'

'Aye, that's how it was. That's how it always is with a daleswoman and you're one, you know.'

Annie poured the tea she had ordered and which Sally had left on the small table beside her.

'Yes, but Job was . . . not like the others.' A shadow came over Christy's face and Annie waited. She was not one to pry into other folk's concerns, even that of her own daughter, but if Christy wanted to tell her what had caused it Annie was more than willing to listen and to help if she could.

But Christy confided in no one, not even to her own mother the disastrous state of her marriage. Since the night Job was conceived she and Alex had lived the lives of two people stranded by unavoidable circumstances in the same house, strangers who are forced to put on a show of politeness for the sake of others. For the first three or four months Alex had continued to share her bed, taking her body almost nightly as if to reinforce his hold on her, and only when she had confessed her pregnancy did he take to sleeping again in the room at the back of the house which he had turned into a small but comfortable bedroom.

When he returned from his trip abroad she supposed he would resume the sharing of her bed for it was the only place in which they achieved any kind of harmony. Alex had paid for it and was a man who would demand value for his money.

Her mother was looking at her sympathetically.

'I know, lass. Job was harder than the others and . . .'
She had wanted to say she understood how difficult it was
now for her daughter with Robin Forsythe dividing his
time between Fellthwaite and his cousins' fox-hunting
estate in Leicestershire and wherever else it was he got to,
now that he was the Squire of Dalebarrow Hall. The girl
was never certain when she went out in her carriage that
she might not come face to face with him and because of
it would keep even closer to her home.

But Annie was ingrained deep in the habit of 'saying
nowt' and kept her thoughts to herself. Her daughter,
though still young was maturing into a strong woman with
the growing ability to stand up to life's blows, as she
herself had done and she was proud of her. Left to herself
she would accept and live with Robin Forsythe's presence
again in the community.

'Alex is still away?'

'Yes.' Christy sipped her tea, staring down the garden to
the roofs of the mills. The trees between were glorious
with the gold and copper and red of autumn but the sun
was warm on her face in the sheltered corner of the garden.
Her lips trembled a little at what she was about to say and
Annie heard the click of her teeth against the rim of the
teacup and wondered.

At last she spoke.

'Mother! I want no more children.' It was said abruptly.

Annie continued the placid task of pouring herself
another cup of tea though her heart jolted painfully in her
chest, then reached calmly to pass the tartlets she had
herself made that morning.

'Did you hear me?'

'Aye lass, but it seems to me you'll have what God
provides.'

'I think not!'

'And how's that then?'

'You tell me, mother.'

'Nay, how can I interfere with nature, my girl?'

Christy took another sip of her tea and her eyes speared her mother like shining steel.

'I have had three children in as many years, mother. I am almost twenty-one and the mother of four children if you count Amy, and I think it only fair we should. It's enough!'

'And what of your husband? Does he agree?'

'You know he would not. The more I have the more a captive I am!'

'Is that how you look on marriage, daughter?'

'To him, yes!'

'Why do you not ask him his . . . opinion?'

The silence was answer enough. It went on for several minutes.

'There is a way, isn't there, mother. Remember the "bastard killer"?'

'There . . . might be . . .'

'Tell me . . .'

'It has to do with the juniper . . . a woman I know who makes . . . draughts . . . from the berries . . .'

'Tell me, mother . . . please.'

'Child!'

'I must have . . . some time . . .'

Annie stirred her tea, her face sad and wise.

'You are sure of this, Christina!'

'Completely.'

'I don't approve.'

'I know.'

'I had twelve, lass, and never tried to stop one from coming.'

'I know. I could not bear it. Oh God, mother.'

'You're a strong girl. It would not hurt you to have . . . more.'

'No . . . not to . . . not his . . . please.'

'Daughter, he is a . . .'

'I don't care . . . tell me . . . please.'

'I don't approve, lass,' Annie said again.

'I know, but please . . .'

298

CHAPTER NINETEEN

Alex Buchanan took his beautiful wife to the Christmas Ball at the Market Hall in Fellthwaite, and was pleased with the attention she received from the respectfully admiring gentlemen who asked if they might take her on the floor for he knew, was perfectly certain in his arrogance, that though she did not love him she would never dishonour his good name nor deprive him of her loyalty.

Though she might not care too much for him except in their bed which he had taken again to sharing with her since she seemed not to mind, she would always hold honourably the position she held as his wife.

He liked the feeling of satisfaction it gave him to see other men covet her, to watch the appreciation in their eyes as they regarded her lovely laughing face, the slim length of her softly rounded form, the fullness of her breast, the whiteness of her skin and the simple elegance of her silver-tissue ball gown.

He knew they applauded his good fortune in owning her and his good business sense which had brought not only her but her wealth into his hands. A lucky fellow, Alex Buchanan, they said and he smiled as he watched her drift about the floor with this gentleman and that, for he knew they meant nothing to her. She was as she had been when he first met her when they were in the company of others, sharp and bright and flushed with her enjoyment of the dancing. The jewellery he had bought her hung about her neck and flashed in her ears and he looked about him welcoming the envy he saw in other men's eyes.

They were standing by the long buffet when the Squire and his party entered, careless and laughing and completely at their ease as the gentry always are, and he thought for a moment his wife would faint so white did she become. He put out a hand to steady her, thanking God that no one noticed for they were all looking admiringly at the young Squire and the slip of a girl on his arm, pretty and submissive, who, it was whispered, was to be his wife.

'Christina.' His voice hissed warningly in her ear and she felt the sure grip of his hand on her arm and the dreadful emptiness which had taken the place of the bone and muscle, the brain and beating heart of her began slowly to fill again with all the necessary senses which made Christy Buchanan function, screaming in agony as they came back to life. The blessed shock wore off – surely it must have lasted an hour? – though it was no more than thirty seconds and she could hear the music again and the swish of the ladies' gowns and their light feet on the ballroom floor.

There was a soft buzz of speculative conversation amongst the group which surrounded them. Mrs Marsden and Mrs Aspin and Mrs Dyer twittered delightedly for did this mean the young Squire had found his lady; and one or two pairs of eyes turned slyly to look at Christy for Fellthwaite had not forgotten her part in his past, but Alex had her arm in such an excruciating grasp, it held, not only herself in a stiff and upright position, but her head high and her chin set in a thrust of stubborn arrogance which asked quite clearly what was it to her?

'I think I might take my wife on the floor,' she heard Alex say lazily. 'It's high time, I believe, since every gentleman has done so except myself.'

There was polite laughter and Christy's face began to ache, the dull throb caused by the need to smile and smile, replacing the sharp agony which had rippled from one part of her body to another.

Alex put his arm about her waist, steady and firm as a rock and though it seemed to others to be no more than the normal light touch which was all that was required to guide a lady about the floor it was in reality supporting her, almost lifting her feet from the polished wood on which they glided. His left hand clasped her right, holding it in the correct position and he smiled warmly into her eyes, his shining like those of a lover.

'If you faint, my dear,' his tender mouth said to her, 'I shall merely step over your body and walk from the room, this building and your life. You will be discarded, thrown away and your children put under the care of a governess. It will be common knowledge by morning that Alex Buchanan's wife is no fit person to have charge of his home, his children or even herself. I suppose your mother will take you in for mothers are like that as you should know for you are one yourself. Hold your damned head up, my pet, and smile into my eyes and, if you should care to you may even flirt a little, though Fellthwaite would probably be just as shocked for no woman has been known to flirt with her own husband before. Do whatever comes into your head but smile, smile and keep your eyes on me, dammit!'

He got her through the evening by the simple method of never leaving her side, or if he did it was only to put her safely in some other man's arms. He never took his eyes from her, sauntering to be at her side the moment she came from the floor. His business acquaintances – those with whom on an occasion such as this many a transaction was discussed – were quite bewildered by Buchanan's reluctance to be drawn into a discourse on the price of raw copper or the effect on business of this past year of the revolution in France and Germany and the sullen discontent amongst the people; but for once Alex Buchanan refused to be drawn, seemingly more interested in the movement of his young wife than the world of profit or loss.

There was a bad moment when Paul Aspin with whom she was dancing – flushed and quite charmed by Christy Buchanan's flattering attention to his enthusiastic description of a pair of green woodpeckers he had seen in Pull Garth wood, for he had been unaware of her interest, he said, in bird-watching which was his passion – stopped as did the music, immediately beside the new Squire and his partner. It would have been discourteous indeed unusual not to speak for Paul Aspin and Robin Forsythe were of the same age and had ridden together as boys.

'Robin, it's good to see you.'

'Paul.' Paul did not notice the Squire's curious stiffness for though he was good-hearted he was not a young man much gifted with sensitivity.

The Squire, as good manners demanded, could do no less than introduce the young lady with him to his old childhood friend, and his partner.

'May I present Miss Emma Briers? Emma, this is an old boyhood friend of mine, Mr Paul Aspin.'

'I am pleased to make your acquaintance, sir.'

'Miss Briers.'

Their eyes were fixed above the bowing heads and polite hand-kissing of Miss Emma Briers and Mr Paul Aspin. His looked to the left, focusing on a bank of hydrangeas which lined the wall beneath the windows and hers locked themselves, strangely, on her husband who stood, like the marble pillar beside him, rooted to the floor in a position of such rigid intensity that the man to whom he idly chatted turned his head to see what it was Alex Buchanan stared at. The man must be besotted, he thought, for it was only at his own wife who was in conversation with the Squire and one of his party.

'And you know Mrs Alexander Buchanan, do you not, Robin? Christina Emmerson that was,' Paul was saying pleasantly, clearly forgetting their past relationship.

'Indeed, Mrs Buchanan.'

Their eyes were forced to meet for a second before he bent over her hand and the pain in both was exquisite as they stumbled through the polite exchanges. He did not touch the hand she was compelled to hold out to him, merely passing his own fingers close to it, then he turned to his partner.

'Emma, this is . . . Mrs Alexander Buchanan. I . . . she . . . and . . .' In a rush of words which caused Miss Briers to look quite surprised he continued the introduction. Slender hand touched slender hand. Velvet-grey eyes looked into pale, pretty blue and instant recognition, the awareness women have of one another when a man is involved, passed between them.

Miss Emma Briers put her hand possessively through the Squire's arm.

The music began again and they smiled their polite farewells and Paul Aspin put his arm about the arrow straight figure of Christy Buchanan and wondered at her sudden detached impassivity as he waltzed her back to her husband.

'I must go home.'

'You will not.'

'I must leave at once.'

'You will stay to the bloody end and keep *smiling*!'

'Alex, for God's sake . . .'

'Damn your treacherous heart, smile up at me or I'll knock your bloody teeth down your throat.' He grinned engagingly.

They danced and smiled and ate supper with their friends. When the Squire's party was about to leave, duty to the township apparently done, they strolled arm in arm across the shining floor and Alex shook his hand for as he said to him, smiling urbanely – hot blue eyes holding cool brown with memories of four years ago – were they not neighbours now that Robin Forsythe was back at Dalebarrow Hall as its Squire?

At last it was done and when they got home, as the first pink dawn flush brushed the December sky he took her to bed and made love to her with a fervency which left her breathless, putting his masculine mark on what was his. She slept afterwards, unaware that he stared into the dawn, his cheek against her dark tumbled hair, for he had never been so proud of her as he had been that night.

* * *

Faith had been married to David Adams in October, a small tranquil ceremony at the chapel in Chapel Stile with only a handful of guests to wish them well. Her mother in her best 'setting off' clothes, and her brothers the same. Her father gave her away, standing proudly somehow on his shattered legs, held up by *her* arm; for had she not done well, this lass of his and because of it, and the steady hard work of his sons at Mr Buchanan's mine, he and his wife lived now in relative comfort.

Alex and Christy attended and as their wedding gift, beside the delicately lovely porcelain tea service from Mr Buchanan, held a small reception for the couple in their own home.

For the past three months as befitted the mine manager and his wife, Faith and David Adams had occupied a small, ivy-covered house on the edge of Conistone village. It was set in a quarter acre of neat flower and vegetable gardens with its back to a stretch of woodland and had a pretty view from its windows over Conistone Waters.

Further on was the three-storied building, once a corn mill, in which Faith's two unmarried brothers still lived and higher up, closer to the mine was a row of neat cottages which were occupied by those miners who had families. The fell gate opened on to the track up to the mines, on the higher side of which were the steep fells consisting of grey rock alternating with green pasture and on the lower a dry-stone wall which edged the village.

Christy called on Faith at least once a week for though Faith and David Adams might not be invited to dine at Alex Buchanan's table it seemed he had no objection to his wife visiting her former maid.

Mrs Buchanan's carriage had become a familiar sight standing before the newly wed Mrs David Adams's neat little house. She and Christy would take tea in the square parlour from the beautiful teacups Christy had given her, the only time they were taken from the glass fronted cupboard where they safely resided. The room gleamed with sunshine and smelled of beeswax polish and the wild flowers growing in profusion about the walls of the garden surrounding it. Once a small farmhouse with nothing more than a kitchen, a scullery and a bedroom or two above, Alex had turned it into a comfortable home for his mine engineer and manager. The parlour was arranged with many pieces of his mother's old country furniture, all polished by Faith's 'girl', to mirror gleam. There was a square fireplace set with apple logs ready for lighting should the day turn cold and at the window were heavy woollen curtains as was the fashion in these parts for the wind could be vicious in the winter. The house was snug in its gentle fold beneath the soaring heights of the fells but Faith kept to the old ways since they were best she liked to say.

Christy's children loved Faith's kitchen. It had a sweet-smelling neatness which personified Faith herself. A dresser piled with crockery, a glowing oven in which there was always something baking ready for Christy's arrival since Faith took her duties as hostess very seriously, and besides, her man must be well-fed. There were comfortable chairs in which to doze when the excitement became too much; a couple of cats and an odd kitten or two licked their dainty paws before the fire, and the good natured twelve-year-old girl who came down each day from the cottage where she lived with her mining father, mother and eight assorted brothers and sisters, sang cheerfully for she imagined Heaven must be like Mrs Adams's kitchen. She scrubbed and polished and ran about all day, never tiring, not even of the three children of Mrs Buchanan who ran wild about her kitchen and garden, whilst her mistress and the master's wife sat, as ladies should, in the front parlour and drank the tea she made. Linnet, she was called and she sang like one, baked biscuits and macaroons with one hand, or so it seemed, whilst with the other she dandled young Master Job on her hip and when they left, dirty and cheerful as ragamuffins, she would remark cheerfully that it had been a 'treat' to see them.

* * *

The day after the Christmas Ball Alex had left without a word, riding off on his new bay with the ferocious energy which was natural to him, despite the fact that he had danced all night and had made love to his wife until daybreak.

Christy's new personal maid had come from her mother for as Annie said, what did she want with three, besides Mrs Kean the cook, when there was only herself to see to? Sally was fresh and lively and adaptable and under Faith's guidance before she left to be married had been taught how to look after Mrs Buchanan's clothes and jewellery. She was already adept with the needle, the goffering iron and how to keep tidy her mistress's sitting and bedroom and was quick to realize the pleasure of dressing out Mrs Buchanan's beautiful hair. Her romance with the lad from Dalebarrow Hall had come to nought but, both philosophical and pretty, she had recovered from the blow and recognizing where being a maid to Mrs Buchanan had led Faith Cooper, Faith Adams now, Sally was eager to try out her new position and her ideas with Mrs Buchanan's permission, and was soon as capable as Faith.

But she was *not* Faith.

She was kind-hearted, obedient and respectful. She remembered Miss Christy when she lived at Hollin House before her marriage for they were the same age but she could not always identify this quiet woman who sat dreaming before her mirror, or gazing with such deep sadness across the fells with the vibrant, rebellious young girl who had stormed about her father's house four years ago.

She needed cheering up, Sally decided, and so, each day as she laid out Miss Christy's clothes – she could not seem to get into the habit of calling her Mrs Buchanan – or brushed her hair, or made up the sitting room fire whilst her mistress drank her hot chocolate, she prattled on cheerfully about the doings of the kitchen and the garden staff, nothing spiteful for that was not her nature, but irritating nevertheless for her voice was quick and merry.

She was convinced that Miss Christy needed only be chivvied out of her melancholy and she would be herself again.

Only with her children was her mistress high-spirited. They would romp across the garden when the weather was fine, an excited jumble of children and puppies for the two older boys had been given a yellow retriever each for their very own, and Amy's kitten was her dearest possession next to her brother Job. It was a fine autumn, cold but sunny and Christy spent a couple of hours each day, her laughter pure and genuine, in the company of this motley assembly; nursing a child, an over-anxious pup or a wary kitten in turn and her hair would come loose and her cheeks flush, and Sally would say to herself 'there, that's Miss Christy back to herself' but she began to realize it didn't last. With the children went her mistress's bubbling merriment and the docile Mrs Buchanan came to take her place.

'I'm going for a walk, Sally,' she said on the day after the Christmas Ball.

'Shall I come with you, Miss Christy? I'm dying to hear all about the gowns. Did Mrs Paul Aspin wear that . . . ?'

'No . . . no, Sally.' Christy was gentle for she was fond of the girl who did her best. 'No, I'll go alone . . . just up to the paddock and perhaps along to Skelwith Force.'

Sally looked doubtful.

'That's . . . that's off Howethwaite, Miss Christy,' for even she was aware of how close the master liked to keep his wife, though God knew why for what could a respectably married lady like Mrs Buchanan get up to in a small place like Fellthwaite?

'I know, Sally . . . don't say anything, please. I won't be long.'

'Very well, madam.' Sally liked to try out 'madam' now and again for it made her feel grand.

Christy walked up to the paddock and when Jack turned away – losing interest in the still figure of his mistress who was doing nothing but stare at the horses – she slipped quietly into the stand of trees to the right and began to stride out in the direction of Conistone . . . and Faith!

She had put on a pair of stout walking boots, a wide skirt in a dark and sensible blue, discarding her crinoline for several layers of warm petticoats. Her cloak was a thick, lined wool with a deep hood edged in a creamy fur from which her pale face peeped like a spiritless, patient dove and her eyes stared along the track like those of a sleepwalker. Her mind was quite blank for if she allowed in thoughts they would be unbearable!

She took the path through the woods which brought her to the lane going south beyond Low Oxen Fell, Arnside Intake and Tom Heights and which would eventually bring her to Conistone Village. She did not take the lane but walked through the woodland which bordered it, taking the short cut, savouring mindlessly the wine-like texture of the air she breathed, the stiff crackle of the russet carpet of leaves beneath her feet and the growing beat of blood in her veins.

Her back straightened as she walked, mile after mile, and she pushed back the warm hood from her face. A flush of rose pinked her cheek, and her eyes lost their lacklustre mist of despair as she walked steadily on and the life-restoring influence of her mountains moved into her heart.

She stood for several minutes, looking towards Conistone Old Man, realizing, as her brain began to function that she could not possibly get to Faith's house and back without being missed for it would take at least an hour to walk the rambling paths through Tarn How Woods and Low Waterhead, but suddenly she no longer cared!

She had played the submissive wife and mother for so long now – since she had become pregnant with Job – it was almost a natural part of her life but she'd be damned if she would act out the role today. She knew Alex had no objection to her going to Faith's, but in the carriage and with Jack or Miles to drive it, but for once she would be defiant and allow Alex to know she had been defiant. After the performance she had been forced to put on last night and the torment she had suffered in the doing of it for his sake, he could go to the devil and take his rules on conduct fit for a lady with him! He was not aware of her solitary walks up above Rydal Water when it was believed she was 'shopping' at Miss Susan Whittam's, though no doubt someone would see her one day and it would get back to him, but while she could she meant to keep that tiny part of her life secret, even from Faith. It was hers!

But today she would be openly reckless. Last night had been a nightmare of pain but she had got through it. She had been Mrs Alexander Buchanan, acting out the part he had cast her in. She had for the first time been in the same room as Robin and a girl who, it appeared, might become his wife and though her body had ached with the necessity to hold itself straight and steady; with the need to dance gracefully with each man who asked for her; though her eyes had been hot and throbbing with the challenge of keeping back the self-pitying tears and her very teeth had agonized over the compulsion to smile and smile, *she had got through it!* Though she was weak, boneless and trembling with the longing to be, just once, in the arms of Robin Forsythe she had danced lightly through the evening with no apparent thought in her head but the desire to enjoy herself.

She deserved a small rebellion, she told herself, and she would tell Alex so when she saw him at dinner. She was smiling ruefully as she stepped out of the trees just behind the Parsonage, jumping down from the bank quite lightly and on to the lane which led to Faith's house, *and he was there.*

They stood quite still in those first precious moments, savouring them, their eyes seeking one another hungrily. They did not move. It was enough, more than enough, their eyes told each other, to just drift on the enchantment of simply being in the same space, breathing the same air, feeling the same coldness of it, alone, unwatched. To know that in the next moment they would take that magic step towards one another, then the next and the next until their hands would meet and their arms would reach out and both would be home at last, safe and loved where they should always have been.

There was silence and stillness and a great sense of peace, then her heart tripped and began to hammer as her wondering eyes took in the roan, the star blaze between its eyes, tethered to a stunted, leaning hawthorne; the restless hound dog which sniffed at the ditch at the edge of the track; returning to the tall, beloved figure of Robin Forsythe as he waited for her, silently, patiently.

He gave the impression of such remorseless determination she shivered, then her whole body surged and exploded with joy and she smiled in huge delight and his own mouth responded. What might have been a moment of solemn, hushed reverence, such was the nature of their love, became joyous and light, just as it had been when she was seventeen and he but a couple of years older.

'How did you know?' she said simply, making no effort yet to move towards him.

'I knew Faith had married up here.'

'But today? I have never walked here before.'

'I would have come each day until I saw you.'

'How long have you been here?'

'Since . . . since I left the ball. I rode home to change then came here.'

She sighed at the perfection of it, at the timing of it! Their last meeting, up in the clearing above Elterwater, had been too soon for them. They had not been ready in their anguish to take between their hands what was now offered again. Soon, when he married as he surely must, the time for it would be gone, but now, right now, was their moment and it must be seized.

'Will you walk with me?' He held out his hand, his words meaning something else.

'Where?'

'Up in the woods.'

'The horse . . . ?'

'He will follow. He is getting old and will not wander.'

She held out her arms and he walked blindly into them.

They did not become lovers that day. Even should the temperature and situation have allowed it, which it did not, they were not physically ready. It was enough to walk between the trees going higher and higher, away from Alex Buchanan's mines until they reached the snow line which crept down a little further each day. Their hands were clasped, palm to palm, fingers lovingly entwined, thumbs gently caressing.

They stopped a dozen times to place soft kisses upon each other's mouth, savouring the texture of smooth warmth, the taste of sweet breath and sighing delight. There was no passion, merely the thankful meeting of cold, ice-touched flesh to flesh, cheek to cheek, warm lips to cool brow or ear or chin. A pressing together of two bodies long starved of one another. No anguished tears or despairing regret at what might have been. No talk of the future – for what could it hold for them? – nor of the past for that was dead, but of this, *this* which they had now.

'I was afraid last night. I knew you would be there and yet I could not warn you that I was to . . . to . . . play the Squire!' He smiled briefly. 'I considered sending you a note to prepare you but I was not sure of . . . of where he . . . I was ready for it, had steeled myself but I could imagine how you might react . . .'

'It was a . . . shock.'

'You were magnificent. If I had not known I would have believed . . . you no longer cared . . .'

'Oh my darling!'

'You were so beautiful! I have never seen you so lovely and yet so . . . so fierce!'

'Fierce!' She laughed in delight.

'You were like a shimmering ice-maiden in that silver gown. Your head was high and proud, daring anyone to so much as address you, let alone put a hand on you as I longed to do. I was tempted to ask your . . . if I might take you on the floor. It would not have been strange, after all once we were . . . friends. But I knew if I did I would have simply waltzed you out of the door and . . . Oh my lovely girl, do you remember the last time we danced together in that room and you took me to that secret place? I wanted to go again and do what we did then . . .'

'Did you my darling?'

'Oh yes.'

'Show me.'

He took her in his arms and his body was hard and yet tender against hers and his lips smoothed the skin beneath her jawline, like a cat rubbing its face against velvet. He placed her body against the rough trunk of a tree, enclosing it with his own, the trembling of his limbs awakening hers, blending in need until she felt the great oak tremble with them.

'I love you.'

'I love you.'

'The . . . girl . . . ?'

'Yes, my darling?'

'Will she . . . will you . . . ?'

His voice was filled with tenderness. Just one word.

'Yes.'

'When?'

'Next year . . . when she is eighteen.'

'She is . . . well dowered . . . and suitable?' There was no criticism in the question.

'Yes.' His face was suddenly painfully cold. 'I must marry . . . someone and it might as well be someone . . . suitable!'

'Robin!'

'I love *you*, Christy! I love you.'

'I know.'

'Will you . . . can you get away?' No more than that but she understood.

'Yes.'

'When?'

'I don't know but I will.'

'We must find somewhere.'

'Faith will help.'

312

'Will she?'

'We must be alone . . . for as long as we can . . .'

'Ssh, my darling, don't speak of what is to come, only what we have now and be glad of it. I thought to have nothing and now . . . now . . . you are here with me. I am holding you in my arms and can . . . look to tomorrow or the next day and know that you will be there again. Now we must be . . . practical . . . what a nonsensical word . . .' He laughed, his face alive with his love for her. 'We must have a place . . .'

'Yes, but not too far away . . . and *warm*!'

She laughed with him then and it lifted like a strand of music into the air above the fells and several miles away in the big office which served his mines Alex Buchanan lifted his dark head and stood in a listening attitude beside his desk and on his face was a curious expression.

'What is it, sir?' David Adams looked at his employer, his attention taken from the map over which they had been poring.

'I don't know . . . nothing . . . I thought I heard . . .'

'What sir?' for there was nothing to be heard but the heavy clank of the water-wheel at the top of the main shaft as it hoisted 'kibbles' and water to the horse level of the mine.

'Nothing, nothing, Adams. It must be my head! I will admit it is none too clear this morning after a night at the Market Hall. The champagne flowed very freely, I can tell you!'

'Was it a good night, sir?' the young man asked politely.

'Oh yes, yes indeed,' and David Adams was quite taken aback by the sudden savagery which ripped through his employer's voice.

She glowed that night at the dining table and Alex was quite bewitched for he had not seen her so softly, submissively beautiful for a long time.

Bewitched, and vaguely uneasy for he had expected a

313

deathly silence at worst, a cool politeness at best. He watched her as she handed him his coffee, docile as a dove. Her deportment last night had been magnificent. She had danced and smiled and chatted pleasantly to all who addressed her. She had been faultless and yet beneath it all he had known exactly what she had suffered. She had even managed to speak to the man, causing no comment or whispered remarks behind fans, but that had been there, under the watchful eye of the whole of Fellthwaite. This was now with no one but himself to see and yet still she smiled.

She had been acquiescent in their bed but without her usual responsiveness but that was only to be expected and he had not complained. She had accepted his kiss impassively as he left for the mines this morning, agreeing with him that it was a fine day.

What went on behind that gentle smile which reached out to him through the candle flame, behind those soft eyes in which it was reflected? Surely to God she had not become resigned, ready at last to bend her will to his . . . surely? It was what he had always wanted, Christy Buchanan doing exactly as he bid her . . . but then, if that was so, why should he feel this strange . . . regret?

'I had a lovely walk today,' she said before he could speak.

'It seems to have done you good,' he answered warily.

'I went as far as Low Oxen Fell. I could not resist it.'

'You went alone?'

'Yes. You do not mind?' Her face was gently appealing, serene almost, asking not for the previous evening and all that had gone before to be forgotten, but to be laid aside and put away for how else were they to go on together.'

Robin Forsythe's face slipped between them but her eyes were clear, innocent as those of their baby son who had inherited her colouring, and he felt a sudden falling away of suspicion and a strange peace came upon him though he could not have said why. They had fought so long and so hard. Ever since they had married they had sparred about one another, pricking with their cruel tongues, never, it seemed, to have any kind of harmony, even an uneasy one.

He could spoil it now by forbidding her that sliver of freedom she asked for – hopefully, he could see it in her eyes – or he could allow it and go on watching her in the candlelight as she smiled at him.

'No,' he said, 'but don't go too far. The snows will come soon and you will be house-bound then.'

'Yes.' Her eyes thanked him then moved beyond him to stare at the blackness outside the window, the winter blackness which heralded the whiteness of the blizzards to come.

CHAPTER TWENTY

The winter snows were a long time melting and she did not see him from the middle of January when the blizzards began until April but she moved about the house holding the loveliness of what was to come close to her, like a child with a gift it has not yet unwrapped, savouring the coming joy, delighting in the anticipation. They had had only three weeks of fragmented, secret meetings up above Rydal Water, snatched from her 'shopping', meetings in which they did no more than lean into one another's arms, look into one another's eyes, saying little for they had not yet come to terms with the miracle of their being together again and words were difficult.

Then the snows came!

It was beginning to cover the garden when she remarked calmly to Jack that she would be obliged if he would get out her carriage since she had some unexpected shopping she must do in Fellthwaite and was sharp with him when he registered objection.

'Mrs Buchanan! You cannot mean to go out in this?' He

waved his arm distractedly as the huge flakes fell gently, their very gentleness deceiving for within an hour they would become so big, so vicious and blinding it would be impossible to see a yard from the drawing room window.

'And why not?' Mrs Buchanan's voice was cool, the mistress being questioned by a servant and not much liking it, though in her heart she knew he was right and she was unfair to expect it of him. But she must see Robin one last time, if only for a minute before the blizzards came to fasten her to her home for God alone knew how long.

They had devised a method of communicating with one another which was simple but effective. It had long been her practice to walk each day up to the paddock which backed on to the wood, to feed an apple or a carrot to her little mare. No one questioned it. More often than not she took the children and if she were to wander a little way with them into the strip of woodland where the shallow river ran crossed by the small bridge, who was to remark on it? Who would suspect a woman surrounded by four children of being up to 'no good'? There was a tree with a tiny niche, high up where no one would notice, once used by a squirrel perhaps as a store place and in it she would leave, or pick up a note wrapped in waterproof. It was as easy for Robin to come – at night when there was no one about – for the main road into Skelwith, Clappergate and Ambleside ran beyond the woodland.

They barely had time to hold one another in the denuded coppice behind The Bear in Fellthwaite for she had dared go no further and the snow was beginning to drift. Jack had been dissuaded from escorting her to Miss Susan Whittam's shop only by her terse command that if he did not do as he was bid and stay with the horses which were uneasy, she would see that Mr Buchanan fired him. Jack had been amazed for Mrs Buchanan was never less than fair but sullenly he did as he was told.

'A minute, my love, no more or you will never get back to Howethwaite.' Robin's mouth clung to hers, soft as silk but with the demanding need which was growing between them. 'You should not have come, but dear Lord I'm glad you did. Hold me . . .'

'How did you know to come? I had hoped but . . .'

'When I saw the snow I knew.'

'It could be weeks, Robin. I could not stand the thought . . .'

'You're shivering. Come under my cape.'

'Darling . . . kiss me . . . again. I love you so.'

'In the summer . . . when it's warmer . . .'

'I know . . . oh God . . . I know . . .'

'I'll find somewhere . . . a shelter . . .'

'I don't care . . . the heather will make our bed . . .'

'Oh Jesus . . . Christy, you must go, my love. Your man will come looking for you in a minute. At least there is no one about to see. Only fools and those who are in love are out on a day like this and we are both . . .'

'Kiss me . . . it must last us until . . .'

One last despairing embrace, the snow so thick they were coated with it even in the shelter of the trees. He began to brush it from her for she must look as though she had come from the gown shop and his hands lingered at the swell of her breast with the stirring of desire.

'Dear Christ, I love you so . . .'

'Goodbye, my sweet love . . .'

And now in the second week of April the snow was gone and that morning for the first time since it began she was able to walk with the children and the half-grown pups up to the paddock.

Johnny was almost three years old now, sturdy and self-assertive, calling with all his father's arrogance to his bitch as she yelped her delight at the release from their long, enforced months of being housebound. She sniffed the air, ignoring him for she was as yet untrained and began to lope across the pasture and Johnny followed, as happy as she to be cutting capers in the grass which still held little pockets of melting snow.

Harry, a year younger, followed wherever Johnny went and his pup followed him.

She watched them as they lifted their faces, blinking, to the pale spring sunshine, like flowers which have been confined in darkness. They were so beautiful, her sons, so perfect in their flawlessness it struck at her heart and just to look at them was a joy to her. They were dark, like gypsies, like their father, though Harry had the russet streak in his hair and the pearl grey eyes of her own colouring. They each had Alex's curl of humour about their mouths, even the baby, Joby – as Amy had christened him and which had become his name – laughing to show his new teeth in his pink gums. They were as free and careless as the birds in the sky and yet the gleam in their eyes, even at this tender age, and the flash of their spirit showed in their determination to have their own way. They were fearless as they ran to duck under the fence to be amongst the horses and Joby roared his rage not to be with them.

Only Amy was quiet, walking beside Christy, her hand in that of her mother, her kitten, now a full-grown tabby, clasped lovingly to her chest, happy to do nothing but sigh in content at their closeness.

In sudden fearfulness Christy felt her step falter and the child turned to look at her. Big, grave eyes, a lighter blue than her brothers', like her own mother's, Christy supposed, and in them was the trusting faith of a child who loves and is loved, *and expects it to go on forever!*

Dear God, what was she thinking of, playing games with this child's life and with the lives of her own children? To be contemplating, with all the irresponsibility of a sixteen-year-old, the taking as a lover of a man who could be no more to her than an idyllic episode. They could offer one another nothing and for that nothing she was prepared to risk the future of four children. If Alex so much as guessed what she was about his savagery would be so hazardous she would not survive it; nor would her children, for deprived of her protective love they would be put in the care of strangers, brought up by governesses, the

318

boys sent to school, their only affection given by servants, for Alex would be as uncaring of them in his vengefulness as he had been with Amy before they had married. Not deliberately cruel, but neglecting them in his own vindictiveness and hurt. The chances she was taking – had taken in the few short weeks before the snows came – were not to be considered, so dreadful were they and she must cast them aside. She must! She would not see him again . . . she would write a note . . . Her heart crumbled in her breast in agony and she felt the shock of it ripple to the rest of her body.

'Mother!' Amy's voice was anxious and Christy realized she had been standing quite still staring with unseeing eyes at the little girl. In her sudden awareness of the danger she was approaching so recklessly, she had been deaf and blind to the ecstatic wheeling and diving of her sons, the excited yapping of the pups and the determined assault by Joby on the harness which bound him to his wicker baby carriage. He was ordering Beth in his garbled, baby stridency to let him out and join his brothers in the unsteady totter which had developed only this last week. His voice was high and he flung himself about in rage as Beth beseeched him to 'be a good boy'!

'Let him out, Beth,' Christy said in a high, unnatural voice.

Beth looked astounded for the baby was barely walking, in fact he really only stumbled from one piece of nursery furniture to another, covering great distances mainly on his hands and knees.

'Mrs Buchanan, d'you think it wise? The grass is wet and there are patches of snow.'

'Let him out, for God's sake, Beth. He can come to no harm.'

Joby was enchanted and Christy watched him scuttle away in the direction of his two older brothers who were being forcibly restrained by Liz from joining the horses in the paddock; no easy task for Johnny was convinced he had only to jump up into the air and he would be on one of them in a trice. Beth followed, circling Joby like an overanxious duck with a duckling out for its first swim and Amy skipped behind, soothing her tabby.

Oh God, how fragile it all is, Christy thought as she watched them toss and leap from one joy to another, complete in their guarded precious childhood. A moment ago I was bewitched with the prospect of a summer, no more, in the arms of my love and now a child's eyes have turned it off like a beck which has become dammed. I would have asked for no more. Something just for me. Something to call mine. A gift no one has given me but which I have taken because for once, just once, I would be Christy Emmerson again. Not wife nor mother, but the beloved partner of the man I love.

Her serenity was gone and she began to hurry towards the wood where the tree stood in which she would leave the note telling Robin she could not meet him again. She had reached it, blind and senseless with the sudden onset of pain when she stopped. She *had* no note to leave and nothing with which to write one. She must go back to the house and . . .

She had half turned, her thick woollen skirt, plain and sensible for walking, swinging dementedly about her when she heard his whisper.

'Don't turn, sweetheart . . .'

'Robin . . . oh God . . . Robin!'

'Ssh . . . ssh, you can't see me, my love, but I have been watching. I know . . . I know I should not have come in daylight but it has been so long . . .'

'Oh Robin . . .'

'Hush now . . . I heard the children's voices . . . I was passing along the road . . .'

'Dear God . . . you must go . . .'

'I will, sweetheart . . . Christy, you are so . . . lovely . . . I can't wait . . . when . . . ?'

'Robin, I was coming to . . .'

'What, my love? What is it?'

She felt her new-found determination slip away on the

joy of hearing his voice, at his nearness which, though she could not see him she could feel. His words reached out to her, soothing the pain of her flesh, caressing the agony of her nerve ends which had somehow become exposed by the truth of her thoughts. She had felt scarred, battered, wounded by the prospect of never seeing him again and of knowing she would never feel his body in the beauty of their love against hers, but now she was healed again for was not her love here? Her one true love!

'Robin . . .'

'Yes, my darling?'

'I will go to Faith's tomorrow. There are woods at the back of her house . . .'

'I will be there.'

She sighed, exhilarated, and yet sad for there was no choice.

'I love you.' They both spoke together, the words overlapping.

And so it began, that summer of strange enchantment.

Faith was pleased though surprised to see her so early in the morning, she said, but 'come in, come in' and she'd make some tea or would Christy like coffee?

'No . . . no Faith. There is something . . .'

Her eyes went constantly to the kitchen window, across the strip of garden to the woods beyond and Faith looked too, her expression bewildered for what was it Christy saw that was so fascinating in the still bare stand of alder? Though the leaves and flowers had not yet appeared they were covered in catkins, long and yellow, and woody cones and the slight breeze moved them gracefully on the bough.

'What is it?' Her voice had become quiet for she remembered that look, that vibrant, thrilling expectancy which had once gripped her young mistress, and turning for a moment she bade Linnet go and see to the sitting room and leave the baking for now.

'But Mrs Adams, them tarts won't wait.'

'Leave them, Linnet. I will see to them.'

When the girl had gone, Faith turned to Christy.

'What is it?' she repeated.

'Robin!'

Appalled, Faith whirled to stare from the window as though expecting to see the tall graceful figure of the Squire swing down the garden to her kitchen door, then turned back to the held-in excitement which had Christy in a thrall.

'Christy!' It was no more than a whisper.

'Please, Faith, please.'

'No . . . oh no, don't ask me.'

'I will do it some other way if you won't help me.'

'But you can't, lass, you can't!'

'I can, Faith, and I will. With or without your help, but let me say this, if you help me, let me use your house . . . Dear God, Faith, I'm sorry . . . it will be more discreet. I can come here, leave the carriage at the front and slip out the back to . . .'

'No I say . . . No!'

'Then I will do it some other way.'

She began to gather her gloves and bonnet, turning away from the window and calmly, towards the kitchen door and the hallway. She could hear the cheerful hum of Linnet's voice from the sitting room, and at the front of the house the sound of Jack whistling as he took the opportunity to give his horses a bit of a rub down. He knew Mrs Buchanan would be an hour or two and it did no harm to groom them even though their coats already gleamed. When he had done he might go across and talk to the blacksmith whose shop was down at the end of the village street. He could see Mrs Adams's house from there and keep an eye out for the reappearance of his mistress.

'I will call at the end of the week then, Faith, all being well.' Christy said in a light, cool voice. 'The children are longing to see you and show you the pups and how they are grown and Joby is . . .'

'How will you manage?'

'That is no concern of yours.'

'Oh yes it bloody well is and you know it!'

'Faith, if you will not . . . cannot help me it's best you do not know.'

'You don't trust me, is that what you're saying?'

Christy whirled, grasping her friend's upper arms in a grip which made her wince. Her face was but six inches from Faith's.

'I would trust you with my life,' she hissed, 'but he *is* my life and I must see him while I can . . . He is . . . is to marry soon . . . Faith, please . . . He was taken from me nearly five years ago and I was given to another man when I was half out of my mind with . . . I love him, don't you see that? You know what love is now, Faith, but you are married to the man you love. You sleep in his arms at night. You see his face on the pillow beside yours before you fall asleep and when you wake he is still there! Do you know how favoured you are? What a gift you have? Do you? Do you? I must snatch a moment here, a moment there, wondering when the next will be, if there will even be another! Oh Faith, do you think I have not anguished over what I am to do, on the chance I am taking with my children's lives? I care nothing for him . . .' She dismissed Alex Buchanan with a scornful toss of her head and Faith ached for the unknown depths of the man who aroused no more than this in his wife's heart.

Christy released her merciless grip on Faith's arms and turned away blindly. 'But I must have it, Faith. It can go nowhere. We both know it. If it were not for the children . . . my sons . . . we would go away together. Marriage, it would not concern us, if we could live somewhere, anywhere together. *He* would have to let me go and besides, he would not care. He has the mill and my money and would soon get another to warm his bed. We need no one else, Robin and I, but . . .' her voice was muted, far away and pain-filled, '. . . we could not damage the children.'

'Do you not take the chance anyway?'

'Yes.' It was simply said, 'And also the chance that we

will irretrievably damage each other but we can do nothing else.'

'Don't be ridiculous. Of course you can!'

'No Faith, we cannot.'

There was a deep silence broken only by the dragging tick of the clock, the sporadic trill of Linnet's voice in the sitting room as she banged about her vigorous cleaning of the fireplace, and the merry crackle of the fire in the grate. The two women stood side by side looking out over the growing garden towards the strip of woodland which held Robin Forsythe, and the destiny of so many people in its pleasant depths. They were both breathing heavily, flushed with emotion and on Christy's upper lip was a faint sheen of perspiration as though she had run a mile or more to fetch up here in Faith's homely kitchen. Her body trembled with the strength of her emotions and yet her head was held proudly in her love.

'How often?' Faith's voice was painfully harsh.

'I don't know. As often as I can manage.'

'You know that this can lose my husband his job, don't you?'

'Faith . . . oh Faith!'

'I cannot approve but . . .'

'I know, I know my good Faith, but let me have it.'

She ran into his arms and they clung together, every inch of their bodies straining one against the other. His arms crushed her and she felt the agony in them and his strong legs pressed against hers so that she could feel the outline of them against her own even through the layers of clothing which separated them. His face buried itself in her hair, into the hollow of her neck and she pulled it fiercely down, sinking her hands into the softness of his pale hair. He groaned and she whispered his name over and over again and then their mouths found one another and her arms encircled his neck and for seconds, hours, forever, their lips clung together, soft as down, warm, moist, tongue seeking tongue, then hard, almost cruel in the savagery of their need.

They sank slowly down to the cold earth, Robin's back against the broad tree trunk behind which he had waited since dawn for her. He turned her so that she lay across his knees and whilst his mouth still roamed about her eyes, her mouth, beneath her chin to the velvet whiteness of her arched throat his hand was at the buttons of her bodice, undoing them one by one until her breast was in his hand.

'Oh sweet Lord,' he whispered, speaking for the first time. His fingers gently smoothed the full white roundness and his eyes were filled with wondering love. He bent his head and his mouth moved softly on the swelling flesh, tasting first one nipple then the other with his tongue. He pressed his face into the softness, then lifted his head, his lips whispering her name. She looked at him, into his face and felt the tears well to her eyes for surely the sadness she saw there could not be borne. With trembling fingers, no longer able to suffer the beauty and pain of it he covered her sweet flesh, doing up most carefully every tiny button which he had just undone, then he bent his head, putting his cheek against hers and their tears met and mingled.

'I cannot bear it,' he said softly, 'that *he* can do what . . .'

'Don't!' Her voice was fierce. 'Don't say it! Don't think it! We have been together no more than ten minutes and you are . . . please Robin . . . just remember *I love you*. I am his wife, make no mistake about that and have borne him three sons but I love you. If we are to constantly bring him with us we might as well finish it now . . .'

'Christy . . . I'm sorry . . . it is just . . . after so long, all these months, years of wanting you, now that it has come I feel . . . Oh Jesus, is it too late? Tell me it is not too late!'

She held him and rocked him, a mother now to this hurt child and she realized with a faint shock that though she was two years younger than he was, she was much, much older . . . and stronger! And yet he was her love. Her love and how she would love him! How she would love him!

They might have nought but this for even now Alex could be at Faith's gate enquiring of Jack, then Faith, of his wife's whereabouts for her carriage was in full view of the whole village. They might have a day, a week, a year of hiding — and though she knew it was foolish — of hoping, but whatever it might be *she would have it* for, beside that of her children, she had never known love.

They had but half an hour that day but it was the first of many.

Once or twice a week, she would drive over to visit her friend, elegant in her fashionable silk gown and matching bonnet. She would enter Faith's front door, graceful and cool and smiling and within five minutes be hurrying through the gentle, golden-scented afternoon up the strip of garden, dressed in her split riding habit, laughing softly into Robin's arms, breathless and giddy with delight.

He had a big gelding now, strong enough to carry two and in a minute she would be up before him, her back against his hard chest and they would canter, then gallop through the woodland where no one came, round the head of Conistone Water until they reached Monk Conistone moor, high above the lake. They always kept under cover of the trees, going up and up until they came to the mouth of what must once have been a mine working, now deserted but for a timid sheep or two. It was shallow, barely scratching the surface of the boulder-strewn rough ground but it was dry and sheltered, it had a roof and three walls, the fourth, the opening, looking out over the vivid beauty of the lake far below.

The horse was tethered amongst the huge rocks which grew in an outcrop on either side of their small cave, hiding him from all but the birds in the sky. The blankets and pillows Robin had carried up previously were retrieved from their hiding place and spread upon the bed of dried bracken and here, at last, Christy Emmerson and Robin Forsythe loved one another in a way which had been denied them five years ago. They became again those young and innocent lovers they had once been for it was as though neither had known the touch of another in the intervening years.

And in that lovely summer she found the love she had waited for and which moved sweetly now within her, and she forced the treacherous thoughts of her body's delight which she knew in her husband's arms firmly from her, refusing even to acknowledge it, for she loved *this* man and always would. And he loved her! She could not get enough of the love he gave her. Her heart would pound at each sighting of him and her stomach could scarce get over its lurching and her emotions ran away with her as they had done when she was a girl. When she was with him she *was* a girl and his sweet boyish adoration soothed her often-wounded heart. If he could not achieve that brilliance, that vibrant abandonment which Alex awakened in her, did it matter? Was love, after all always to do exclusively with the flesh?

Young and innocent! That was how Robin Forsythe appeared to be in that first moment when his flesh possessed hers, when his body entered her body for the first time, as though he was still a boy and had never known a woman. She wanted to cry out to him to wait for a moment, to wait for her since she was willing, oh so willing and eager but she realized as he fell shuddering upon her breast that she was, surprisingly, out of step with the rhythm of his needs. That honey-sweet kernel of delight which his mouth and his hands had sharpened in her, the enchanted recollection of the young Robin, the unmarried Christy, brought back now as her body responded to the memory, had not yet had time to grow to the explosion of joy she knew with . . . with . . . and as Alex's dark sardonic face glimmered for a fraction of a second against her closed eyelids Robin rolled away from her, sated with the love she had given him – the love her husband took.

For an agonizing moment disappointment shivered in her, stirring her heart to pain. She was confused by her own body's reaction and by the whispering in her brain, stealthy and unwanted which demanded to know why this man she loved and had loved for more than five years, had not filled her to completion – she must be honest – as the man she despised, the man who despised her, was always able to do!

Aah, but your husband has had experience, is older and well taught in the knowledge of how to please a woman's body, her mind whispered. He had known so many whereas Robin has not. Just to look at Alex was to know he delighted in the pleasure a woman could give him, particularly if that woman was well pleased herself. He was a sensualist who knew how to tease and caress, to bring to life her own sensuality, to hold back until she was breathless with the agony of her longing, to smile and kiss and demand her to wait for the exact moment which would bring them both the most satisfaction. Yes, Alex Buchanan could do that, her mind said bitterly, for had he not had more practice in the art than most men, and certainly more, much more than the young and boyish Robin Forsythe who was looking down at her now with all the love and joy their union had at last brought to him. He was waiting, his eyes said, bemused with the delight of it, for her to tell him how wonderful it had been for her, as it had been for him and how could she take that shining warmth from his brown eyes. She could not, she loved him.

They talked later, sitting naturally, arms about one another in the mouth of the cave, the sun touching their naked bodies, no sound but the attractive high song of a meadow pipit as the bird dropped from the sky. They spoke of themselves, their love, of today, of yesterday, of tomorrow and their next meeting. Their thoughts spanned no more than a week, the few days that lay about them, on either side of this one, the weather and the prospect of rain which would prevent their being together, the beauty of this enchanted spot and the joy of living as they did, *now, this moment*.

They would look at one another, quite spellbound, each

of them, by the other's beauty, drawing a tender, reverent finger across a smooth velvet thigh or stomach, the cord-like muscles beneath an arrow-straight back, the delicate arch of a foot, the graceful turn of a neck. A sweep of an eyebrow would be deliberated upon, then kissed and kissed again, toes counted and gently bitten, shoulders, smooth as silk, lips, sweet and tasting of blackberry juice, hair like a living brown cape covering breasts of peach-tipped ivory. The marvel of it, the slow, dream-like quality of it bewitched them and the summer drew on without them being aware of it.

Job was walking steadily now, hurtling to keep up with his brothers, shouting his anger when they left him behind, but she did not tell Robin for it was no part of their world!

The puppies were almost full-grown and beginning to respond to Johnny's patient training, for even at almost four years old he was as single-minded as his father. Job had a fat, tumble-legged labrador pup of his own, at two months as high-spirited and merry as himself, interfering in the seriousness of the training of Johnny and Harry's young dogs, but she did not tell Robin for it was not part of their world!

Amy's tabby had kittens of its own, much to her delighted amazement and the house and garden and paddock spilled over with children and dogs and kittens, with laughter, and Alex's half-hearted, good-humoured grumbling as he removed one or the other from his lap, his carriage or his study, but she did not tell Robin for it was not part of their world.

Her body obliged that of her husband most days of the week for he was still as avid for her as he had always been, eager to put his stamp of masculinity on what he believed to be his, and if he wondered why after a year or more she did not conceive, he said nothing. She responded to him and was not ashamed for her body was no part of her love's secret inner mind.

For his part he was content in the peace they had found, in the joy of her laughter again, in her acceptance of their marriage at last, of her graciousness when they entertained and her readiness to give up the wildness, the rebellion she had shown for so many years. She was mature, and if she cared little for storms any more or the savage arguments which they had barely survived, and if he missed a little that fine spirit, was it not better to live on a plain of concord?

They lived side by side, walked side by side in harmony, or so it seemed, and those about them were unaware that though the paths they travelled were close, they were different paths.

But she said nothing of this to Robin Forsythe as their summer of love drew near to its ending for they were consumed with the problems of the coming coolness of the autumn and the long hard winter ahead. It was inconceivable now that they would be parted and they agonized on how they would meet and where, on the separation which must surely come and the agony of how they would bear it until spring. They certainly did not speak of his forthcoming marriage to Miss Emma Briers, for it was not part of their world!

CHAPTER TWENTY-ONE

Faith's father died suddenly in September and after the funeral Faith brought her mother back to her own home to give the widow a month or two to recover from the shock of it, and Christy and Robin were deprived of the means by which they could ride up to their cave.

The cool days of autumn set in.

They walked hand in hand that day keeping amongst the trees beside the flat smoothness of Rydal Water, their booted feet squishing into the rich quaggy grass which surrounded the lake. Christy's skirt brushed against a massed swathe of bog asphodel, its hem heavy with a ridged circle of moisture but she made no attempt to protect it though it might cause comment from Sally when she got home, striding onwards as though she were a man in trousers.

They did not speak but walked in silence as though the sound of their voices might break the fragile tranquillity in which they were softly enfolded, perhaps to bring a horde of intruders to disperse their solitude. They were dressed in simple country style, Robin in cord breeches, gaiters and a pea jacket over which he had thrown an Inverness cape. He wore no hat and his tumble of fair curls was burnished by the pale sun. Christy wore saxony blue. A woollen dress, warm and serviceable without the vast width of crinoline which was fashionable and a rich blue cloak lined with soft brown fur. Her bonnet hung down her back, the ribbons tied beneath her chin and her hair, as dark and glossy as the fur of her cloak, was arranged carelessly, held in place by a comb and a length of narrow blue ribbon. Great loops of curls hung about her shoulders and fine tendrils clung to her flushed cheek.

She looked about her in dreaming contemplation, her eyes as clear and grey as the water and her hand was soft and trusting like that of a child as it clung to Robin's. It was cool now in the valleys and high on the fells a tablecloth of snow had already been laid, like fluted white lace against the bleak, iron-grey granite peaks. The shaded hostility of Conistone Old Man lifted into the milky blue of the northern sky.

Everywhere was that incredible green brilliance which comes wherever there is an abundance of water and looking across the narrowest part of the lake to the far side they saw fields as smooth as though they had been scythed that day, and even the rocks seemed cast in a patina of viridescence where the moss grew. Scots pines swayed majestically in the small breeze which blew off the lake and beneath them blackberry bushes, laden with unpicked fruit gave off the scent of the summer sunshine which had ripened them.

Moving specks, hundreds and hundreds of them, pierced the high ground over the tops a couple of thousand feet up, sheep and their grown lambs moving slowly from one green pasture to the next. Any day now they would be brought down to the inlands for the farmer would not risk his young stock as the winter approached.

Above the water hung a low lying drift of pale blue mist.

They turned southwards as the roofs of the small village of Rydal appeared briefly beyond the stand of trees which lay along the lake and began to climb up beyond the tree line, confident that they would not meet a living soul beyond a straying sheep or two. Christy seemed not to find it difficult, hampered as she was by her long skirt though Robin had to give her a helping hand now and again up a particularly steep and rocky incline.

They reached the top of the slope and sat down upon a rock to look at the lovely, empty sweep of water and mountain which lay before them. It was bitterly cold up here, away from the shelter of the valley. Now they were higher they could see the smudged yellow of the golden elder growing along the lake, the delicate shadow mirrored in the water.

The drift of thin blue vapour rose above the tops of the trees and Christy lifted a finger to point.

'Look, there is the vapour from the mills. How clear the air is!'

Robin nodded and took her pointing hand as though he could not bear another moment without the feel of it in his.

'It's so . . . so perfect. I don't want to go but it's too cold to sit for long and besides, my darling, it has been two hours. Your coachman . . .'

Christy sighed and her mouth drooped in sadness.

'Yes . . . even I, the spendthrift Mrs Buchanan, cannot pretend to spend more than two hours in Miss Whittam's salon!'

'No, I suppose not.' He smoothed a finger across her cheek, running it down beneath her chin to the fastening of her rich cloak. His hand moved inside it, holding the weight of her breast in the palm. He rubbed his face in the softness of her hair and his voice was rough as he spoke.

'Goddammit, if it were not so deuced wet and cold I would make love to you right here.'

'I know . . . but kiss me anyway.'

He drew her into his arms and kissed her with a thoroughness which brought bright poppies to her cheeks, then stood up and holding out his hand hauled her to her feet.

Hands touching, like two magnets irresistibly drawn together they began the descent, their heels digging into the shifting scree of the slope. For a moment they held back then like two children they began to go faster and faster until they were almost flying, their voices high and pealing with the sheer joy of living. Everything was forgotten, past and future, this moment to be lived, just as it was, effervescent and compelling as the effect of a glass of champagne. *This* was their life and they must taste it and be nourished by it, living each moment as though the next might not happen.

They came to a small stone bridge, rough, grey-hued, but symmetrical. Its arch was simple perfection, its shape blending into the surrounding countryside as though it had grown from the very soil. Beneath it raced a wild swirl of white water, tripping and lurching over stones smooth and gleaming as satin.

They stopped again and looked towards Tilberthwaite, soaring, bleak and beautiful above the big grassy slopes of the intakes, criss-crossed with dry-stone walls and below these, the inlands, smaller and richer, enclosing the haphazard smudges of farm buildings.

She leaned against him comfortably, her back to his chest and he tucked her head beneath his chin. His hands cupped her breasts and she pressed backwards, feeling the male hardness of him, wanting him with a fierceness which surprised her. She turned and kissed him passionately. 'We must . . . must go at once, Robin.' Her voice was urgent.

'I know . . . I know, my love. What the hell are we to do?' His voice was despairing. 'If we could take a room . . . find somewhere . . . discreetly . . . with the winter coming . . . the snows . . . I cannot bear the thought that we might be parted for . . .'

She put a hand gently to his lips.

'Ssh . . . ssh, my love . . . we will manage somehow . . . until . . .'

He looked down into her face and his was bleak for they both knew it would be difficult – even should they overcome the difficulties of the approaching winter – for at the end of October he was to marry Miss Emma Briers!

'And then?' he said harshly.

'I don't know.' There was nothing more to say.

She watched him go, his kiss still warm and desperate on her lips. Her movements were slow and awkward as she turned away wearily, for it was as though he had taken with him the spring of life which welled within her as he rode back to Dalebarrow Hall, leaving her dried up and stiff of limb. It could be weeks, months before she saw him again and she knew with great certainty that she could no longer bear even another day without him, let alone another month, and another beyond that. The weight of it, her love, was almost more than she could bear!

She sometimes wondered in the empty depths of the night if perhaps it would be easier if she were not to see him at all. Was the joy of meeting worth the agony of parting and the uncertainty of when they would hold one another again? Would it not be better if they stayed apart, living their own lives? He with his new wife when he married and the family he would undoubtedly have, she with Alex and her children. At the beginning they had been content with snatched moments for was it not infinitely better than none at all but now, having known what might have been theirs always, she wanted it *always*. It seemed she had just settled down from their meeting, her heart easier and less painful when it would be surging again in anticipation of the joy of their next; yet at the same time, in the midst of that joy was the lurking dread of the parting which would follow.

She shook her head, irritated by her own despondency. Of course it was worth it! Not just the warmth of him in her arms, but his merry humour which laughed her out of her sadness, the sweetness of his love and the patience with which he had learned to confine it in his years of exile. He was her friend and lover, strong and yet dependent on her, the other side of her own nature. Together they were strong, divided would they not surely fall?

Good God, she thought as she dragged along the lane which led to Ambleside and her carriage, where was the Christy Emmerson who had thought nothing of defying the absurd rules and conventions of Fellthwaite's polite society and who had believed in only what she herself devised in her female mind?

She is Christy Buchanan now, a quiet voice answered, wife of Alex Buchanan, an adulteress, and a whore, some would say.

She had reached the smart little shop of Miss Clare Aspin on Smithy Brow, her hand on the doorknob, ready to go in for five minutes to give credence to her alibi, when the thump of booted feet could be heard coming closer and the harsh panting of a man's voice grated on the air and from round the corner, where the carriage waited, Jack Hodson thundered. He waved his hands distractedly, beckoning to her, believing as she stepped away from the doorway that she had been just leaving the salon.

'Mrs Buchanan . . . oh Ma'am . . . thank God . . . Please, you're wanted . . . quick . . . see! I'll fetch the carriage . . . bloody hell . . . I should've brought it . . . I never thought . . .'

'What . . . Jack, for God's sake . . . what is it?'

'Miss Christy, please ma'am, there's been an accident . . .'

* * *

335

Some of the operations in Alex Buchanan's mines were carried out by what are called 'tribute workers', the miners receiving a certain proportion of what they raised. When they were fortunate and a good vein was found, some of them realized a splendid wage under this system, but by far the greater part of the underground work was done by 'bargain', some man, or more frequently, men, undertaking to excavate a given number of fathoms in a certain locality and in an assigned direction, for so much per fathom; the result of their labour was brought out along the levels by wagons, and by 'kibbles', large strong buckets, up the shafts to the surface.

The first intimation of trouble was brought by David Adams to the office where Alex had just arrived from his twice-weekly visit to the Emmerson Gunpowder Mill.

Alex was tired. He had several good men, one in charge of sales, the other in the office, a third who saw to the men, a fourth overseeing the manufacture of the blasting powder – four men to take the place of the father and two sons who had gone, but they in turn must be closely watched for a business which is left to those who are merely employed there will not prosper. He was strong, in the prime of his manhood, but it took time and energy to run two such different enterprises. Job had been dead but two years; Alex had known little about the making of gunpowder and it was only now that it was all beginning to run smoothly.

There was his bobbin mill at Stavely and he must go frequently to St Helens and Swansea – and often abroad – to where much of his raw copper was carried to be smelted and rolled into the sheeting which was used for sheathing the hulls of sailing vessels, and for many other purposes. Mixed with tin it became bronze. Every coin from the bronze farthing to the gold piece had some copper in it and every buyer of it must be personally attended to by himself.

From six in the morning when he left his home, sometimes until midnight, he had worked for almost two years but he needed a rest, a holiday, to get away and leave it now that it was smoothly efficient. Perhaps if Christy . . . France, Italy, sunshine! The children were now old enough to be left in the care of their nursemaids and Annie would keep an eye on them . . .

He smiled grimly at his own foolishness, and yet, why not?

Lately she had been . . . biddable . . . seemingly content with her life. He might suggest in the tranquil moment over their coffee tonight, with the candlelight forming a gentle backdrop to their evening meal, that they take the new railway from Windermere, going to Liverpool, a boat to France, a leisurely trip down to Italy. What would she make of it, he wondered?

'Mr Buchanan, sir. I'm afraid we have some trouble!'

His smiling thoughts winged away and his head shot round to sharply recognize his young manager. His eyes were instantly alert and his expression became obdurate as though trouble had better not dare show itself in Alex Buchanan's mines.

'What sort of trouble?'

'It's the "bargain" men, sir. There is some argument as to the assignment on which they are working.'

'Can you not deal with it, man? That is what I pay you for.'

David Adams's face flushed but his eyes were steady and his jaw was firm. 'I've just come up from the Crossbarrow level, Mr Buchanan, but I intend going down again immediately. I am here only to get the working plan so that I might settle the dispute. There is no need for you to trouble yourself.'

The young man was resentful that his authority had been questioned and it showed in the whiteness about his lips and the truculent set of his shoulders.

I should be the same, Alex thought, smiling inwardly, but he did not apologize.

'I'll come with you, nevertheless!'

'Just as you like, sir.'

337

'I do like, Adams. It *is* my mine.'

It was ninety fathoms down to where the 'bargain' men were working but first the two men must pass along the horse level, ducking their heads at regular intervals beneath the arch of living rock above them for it was too low in many places for a man to walk upright. After walking for about a quarter of a mile they straightened and automatically looked up into the tremendous cathedral-like chasm from which a thick vein of copper, extending to above the huge water-wheel on the hillside, had been blasted. Beneath it began the shaft which reached down and down through all the workings to the deepest level more than one thousand feet below the valley floor. Kibbles containing ore were hoisted here, a few fathoms at a time until they reached the large 'hopper' where they were emptied, and beneath the hopper ran the horse-drawn wagons which waited there to be loaded.

'You go first, Adams, if you please.'

'Yes sir.'

By a series of ladders with wooden sides and iron steps the two men began to descend, coming upon a platform or 'landing' at every few fathoms. They passed beneath short logs of wood, jammed between the two opposite walls of rock, on which men stood to work, barely visible in the intense blackness, only their candles aglow to light the impenetrable dark.

Thundering echoes of distant blasts bellowed from other parts of the mine. The clanking chain of the rapidly descending kibbles resounded close to their ears but they were unperturbed for they both had worked in the underground network of the mines.

The regular thump of the pump which took water out of the mine from the deeper workings sounded reassuringly in Alex's ears, for even as he climbed steadily down the ladder – his mind on the problem he was certainly about to solve one way or the other – his subconscious sense, that which had developed in years underground, took note of every detail which affected the safety of his men, the profitability of his mine which depended upon its efficient running and the possibility of further investment in new machinery which would make it easier to get at the rich ore his mining instincts told him was there.

'This is it, Mr Buchanan,' David Adams said as he stepped from the ladder, his feet splashing in the slick of water which seeped constantly from the walls. He turned to peer into the darkness which revealed the indistinct openings to the levels which had been driven off from this shaft, all going in different directions. Men's voices could be heard along one narrow tunnel, raised in some altercation, and around them several dark shapes loaded the rough ore into the kibbles which rattled continuously up and up on their chain, then back down after they had been emptied at the top of the shaft.

The difficulties and dangers which beset the miner are of no ordinary kind! In some places the rock is so extremely hard that it can scarcely be penetrated and in others so soft it requires considerable skill to prevent it falling down upon the unfortunate man who works it. There is a danger of falling rock, impure and noxious gases, but Alex Buchanan and David Adams gave no thought to these beyond the mining man's normal care in addressing himself to the business of moving through the narrow darkness of the workings towards the 'bunnin' where the men were working.

They crawled past two men, barely visible in the darkness, their only light two twinkling candles plastered against the rock with clay. Each man held and turned a 'jumper' in his left hand whilst in his right he gripped a hammer with which he drove the 'jumper' into the flinty rock. Having bored their holes to a sufficient depth they proceeded to clear them out with a long needle before drying the hole with a wisp of straw until every drop of moisture was completely mopped up.

Each stopped his work for a moment to touch a forefinger respectfully to his brow in recognition of their master's presence, their eyes gleaming wetly in the grey darkness. As Alex watched, each deftly filled a thin tube with gunpowder, placed it in the hole then withdrew the tube leaving the gunpowder within the opening. Carefully they tamped it down and wipe away any stray grains of powder which might possibly have adhered to the sides. An instrument called a 'pricker' was placed gently down one side of the neatly placed blasting powder and the hole was then packed with rotten stone and clay and the pricker withdrawn, an operation of some skill for through the thin passage where it had been must be passed a long straw filled with powder to which was attached a piece of match paper.

'Excuse me, Mr Buchanan, sir,' they said politely, then in voices of piercing clarity shouted 'fire', picked up their tools, lit the touch paper and ran like the devil, accompanied by their employer and his mine manager to be a safe distance from the explosion.

'Nicely done, Matt,' Alex said, brushing down his good suit, and the man grinned, for that was Mr Buchanan for you. A hard master but fair and always willing to give credit where it was due. 'Now, shall we go back to see what your blast has revealed?'

'Mr Buchanan . . .' David Adams sounded exasperated for had he not got half a dozen men sitting about on their arses doing nothing, but Alex had not been down to this level since he had taken over the Emmerson Gunpowder Mill and lack of time had prevented it. His curiosity and the thrill he remembered from the days when he himself had done the self-same job under the supervision of an experienced miner, got the better of him.

'I won't be a moment, Adams,' he said genially. 'You go on ahead and tell them I'm on my way.'

The men had already begun to inspect the effects of the blast, breaking up the larger fragments and beating down any loose pieces that hung about the sides before recommencing boring for a second blast, undeterred by the thick cloud of powder smoke which hung like a fog about the workings.

It was difficult to see and perhaps it was this and his sense of irritation — for after all it was *his* job to see the men did a good day's work for their wages — which made David Adams careless.

The man at the foot of the shaft filling kibbles was adamant that no blame could be attached to himself for he followed faithfully the rules laid down by Mr Buchanan, standing well back as the full and empty kibbles passed him by on their everlasting journeys. It was not his fault, he said later, that Mr Adams stepped too close to the rattling chains and buckets. Mr Adams was the mine manager for Christ's sake, and knew the dangers as well, better, than anyone else and should have kept well clear.

Alex had a piece of rock in his hand, inspecting it in the pale shimmer of the candlelight when the man's voice began to shout. For a second he was disorientated for it sounded so close he thought it was the miner who stood next to him, but from a few feet away the man who had been loading the kibbles was babbling in a high, frantic voice, his pasty face held up to the shaft above him. Others were clustered about him, raising their arms in horrified alarm as they too stared upwards.

Alex turned swiftly and in two strides was at the foot of the dark shaft. Pushing aside the men he peered up it and was just in time to see the struggling figure of David Adams carried rapidly with the kibble up into the blackness of the narrow shaft.

'Hold on to the bucket, for God's sake, lad. Can you climb inside, David ... hold on, lad, hold on ...' His voice was strong and steady giving the young man certainty that there was no peril should he follow exactly Alex Buchanan's careful instructions. A reliable man in an emergency and one to be trusted but the shaft was tortuous and the sides rugged and uneven and as he went up and up into the Stygian blackness, held in its suffocating confines, David Adams was too stricken with terror to hear. He was dragged like a boneless doll, screaming his agony as his clothes were ripped from his body, then his skin from his bones. Both his arms snapped as he took a particularly difficult bend and the lower half of his right leg, caught between wall and bucket was almost torn from the upper, just at the knee, the white bone dragging against the rough-sided wall.

He had stopped screaming by then as the bucket began to fill with his blood and his flaccid dead hands loosened their grip and he began to fall, bouncing from one side of the shaft to the other, his badly mutilated body scarcely recognizable as the pleasant-faced young man he had been.

Alex heard him coming and his breath stopped in his throat with a thud of horror and before the frozen men about him could prevent it he placed himself below the gaping black tunnel, stretching out his arms to catch the falling lad for if he could cushion the fall he might perhaps prevent him suffering further injuries.

'No! No . . . Mr Buchanan . . . no . . .!' but the miner whose skilful work Alex had admired only moments ago was too late as he came to life, springing forward in an attempt to drag his employer from the path of David Adams's already dead body.

'It's too late . . .' he shouted. They were the last words Alex heard as the blackness exploded about him, falling over him like a heavy curtain, trapping his breath in his lungs and flinging him over a precipice in which he could neither see nor hear nor feel.

It took them three long hours to get Alex Buchanan to the surface, dragging him, carefully tied to a rough stretcher, up steep ladders and along low, narrow levels. They were as gentle with him as they knew how, soothing him with soft clucking noises, patting the rough workmen's jackets they had wrapped around him with rough workmen's hands but he said nothing.

As they eased him past candles stuck to the rock face they could see that he had opened his eyes and they were more careful with him still, for if he had regained consciousness they did not want to further aggravate his pain. He noticed how careful they were with him, taking enormous trouble not to jostle the stretcher and he wanted to tell them it was alright. He didn't ache anywhere, he was in no pain and could not understand exactly why they had him fastened to this damned contraption, but there appeared to be something tied about his throat and face and he could not speak.

David Adams came up more swiftly for they could no longer give hurt nor damage to his poor broken body.

They reached the surface and in compassion for the injured man who had been underground in the dark for nearly five hours, covered his eyes from the blinding daylight and he screamed silently within himself in awful fear for he thought he had lost his sight. But then a hand came and took away the blindness and Christy was there bending over him and he knew it was alright.

She put out a hand and touched his face gently, then took a wisp of handkerchief from her pocket and after putting it to her lips, wiped his eyes with it and his mouth, so tenderly he wanted to turn his face into it and just lay his cheek thankfully into her skirt.

He smiled at her and raised his eyebrows in wry humour as though to say what a bloody fuss for he could remember nothing of what had happened. The men, women and children who worked in the 'grating', picking out saleable ore by hand, moved back from the circle they had formed about his stretcher as his eyes roved across them for even now his expression asked what the hell they thought they were doing loafing around the shaft when there was work to be done?

Then it came back to him and he turned a frantic face to his wife.

'David?' he said, his eyes questioning Christy but no sound came from his still lips and he was dismayed when the men picked him up and put him on a wagon, taking him down the steep slope from the big wheel, pulling and pushing, a dozen men, for no horse could manage these slopes.

'Christy,' he called for her face had gone and then all their faces had gone, and the fells and the golden autumn sky, the crushing mill, the spoil tips, the washing plant, all dissolved into a grey mist and were gone.

CHAPTER TWENTY-TWO

The doctor came each day to poke and prod him, throwing back the covers to stare dispassionately at his rigid body, moving his head on his neck, the fingers of his hands and every separate toe on his feet.

Alex was black and blue from his neck to his ankles. The livid discolouration and swellings, the weals and contusions caused by the falling body of David Adams sprang to the surface of his golden skin almost before he had been carried from the mountain, through Conistone and along the road to Howethwaite and placed gently on his own bed.

The doctor was certain of a cure, he said cheerfully after his first careful examination, for there were no broken bones, and lucky indeed had been Mr Buchanan for the poor unfortunate young man had fallen from a good height and things might have been more serious.

Not for David Adams, Alex thought bleakly as the good doctor pronounced on the efficacy of a hot bath, if his men would lift him carefully into the tub before the fire, stressing the importance of keeping Mr Buchanan warm and the avoidance of draughts. The hot water, if he soaked himself in it, would bring out all the bruising and once that was achieved and had died away Mr Buchanan would be as right as ninepence.

'A few weeks, Mrs Buchanan,' he said, addressing Christy, ignoring in the way doctors have the patient on the bed, speaking as though the man was some imbecile who would not understand anyway, but Alex Buchanan had been ignored by no one since he was six years old and was not about to start now and certainly not by some quack who would charge him a guinea for the privilege of having him across his own doorstep.

'Dammit man, I can move no more than my head on my neck and then it is stiff and the pain is severe. I have been lying here like a bloody fallen tree for a week now. Surely to God there should be some movement?'

'Patience, my dear sir, patience,' the doctor murmured, backing away from the dark, angry face which scowled at him from the pillow.

'Never mind bloody patience. I don't feel ill so just get me up from this damned bed!'

The purple weals, the livid bruising faded away to a pale lavender, to washed green and yellow until eventually there was not a mark to be seen on Alex Buchanan's hard, dark body and still he could move neither muscle nor sinew and still the doctor spoke hopefully of Mr Buchanan being on his feet in no time at all.

Christy lived those first few days in a state of frantic, mindless movement, her life reduced to the level where every thought, every decision, every living moment must be considered with Alex in view; his comfort, his discomfort, what he must eat, or *not* eat, persuading him *to* eat; dissuading him from ordering Jack or Miles to put him on his feet for surely if he was upright his damned legs would set themselves in motion!

He was frustrated, evil-tempered, concerned for the tragic death of his young mine manager, for the grieving of the widow, a wife of no more than a year; for the running of his mines, his gunpowder mill, the hundred and one concerns with which he was involved as a business-man. He could not afford, he declared menacingly to the doctor, to lie here and wait for this bloody stiffness to wear off.

Christy bore his raging with blank patience, her mind conditioned by her own will to think no further than this moment, this sickroom, this man. There was a dreadful yet merciful numbness about her, an inability to cast her mind back to yesterday or forward to tomorrow; a state in which she had existed ever since she had flung herself from her carriage and blundered, skirts bunched about her knees, up the track which led from Conistone village to Alex's mines, beyond the neat row of miners' cottages where at every open doorway had stood an aproned woman, those with men above ground and who knew they were safe, and a score of silent children.

The fell gate was open, ready to admit those who went up to wait, ready to pass through those who might, or might not, come down again. The climb was steep and on another day she might have stopped to draw her breath and admire the beauty of the landscape behind her, but not today.

The beck was full of what appeared to be soap suds, brawling and foaming through the deep, ragged ravine and along its jagged course on the bottom. About halfway up the ghyll was a waterfall, the water falling upon a broad ledge which fanned it out like a huge white, lace apron gathered at the waist reminding Christy suddenly of her mother, and as she climbed she was surprised by a strange longing to have her beside her, staunch, steady and infinitely reassuring.

There was another waterfall and another, a mill-race which moved every part of every piece of machinery which worked above and below ground in her husband's mines, until she came – half a dozen men at her heels, those sent down to guide her – to the 'township' of sheds, offices, workshops, and the water-wheels, the biggest of which stood high up the mountain, solitary and splendid, the water which drove it spinning it wildly like a child's toy.

The clatter of machinery from the ore-dressing plant, the crushing and washing plants, the snap of horses' hooves on the roadway as a tram was drawn from the mine contrasted tumultuously with the silent fells and silent water of the lake below, the sudden quiet taste of winter in the air, the bare heights which had been intruded upon by the strident clangour of humanity.

These copper mines had been in existence since before the birth of Christianity, worked by the Romans, it was said, and the Britons before them. Swords were made of copper then and the ore to fashion them was wrested from those mines and others in the Lakeland fells. Save for a few years during the farrago instigated by Oliver Cromwell and his followers, at which time lead and cold iron were more in demand, the mines had never been deserted. Since then mining had continued with great energy and success, worked firstly by a few miners, no more than three or four until James Buchanan had brought his expertise, imagination and capital, turning it into the rapidly increasing concern which his son carried even further. Several hundred men, women and children were employed above and below ground, most of whom appeared to be gathered here today standing in absolute silence as Christy moved up the flinty track.

'This way, Ma'am,' a man said and they continued upwards, slipping and tumbling in their urgency, towards the main shaft where the big wheel was employed in hoisting the kibbles and water to the horse level.

The silence was complete as the crowd parted for her. It had been disclosed that two men had been hurt, already dead perhaps and that one was Mr Buchanan, but what of the other? It could be any one of a hundred miners on shift that day and those women with a man underground waited, patient as dumb animals for the butcher's knife, heads bowed beneath shawls, clogged feet rooted to their bit of ground about the shaft.

Two hours they stood, Christy Buchanan and Faith Adams, and the great crowd of silent men, women and children. The crisp autumn sunshine shone serenely on hollow staring faces, on work-worn hands which folded about one another in grim dread; on Christy's pretty frilled bonnet which she had replaced as Robin left her and the beautiful blue of her gown. It touched Faith's white face, placing deep smudges beneath her unblinking eyes and moved on to hover about the rough springing curls of a miner who knew well the animosity of the deep bowels of the earth. It struck to flame the bracken which glowed on Raven Tor, blazing up and up to the Old Man of Coniston, already wearing a thin cap of white. The sheer magnificence beyond the ravaged level where the mine stood, was, in comparison, multiplied a thousand times by the desecration of man's working.

There was a shout and several hundred heads lifted and turned.

'They're coming. They've got them on a whim.' The sound of the machine which was used for drawing large kibbles out of the shaft, worked by a horse, could be heard faintly coming from along the level. The clip-clop of the horses' hooves on the stone track and then, as they drew nearer, the sound of men's voices speaking softly.

Alex came first. She recognized the fine cut of his trousers and the superb, costly leather of his boots, and she felt the ground tilt beneath her feet and the great golden-blue arch of the sky press down on her in a vast and amazing anguish. She held Faith's arm to steady herself for she must not fall now – and why should she, her confused mind asked – and she felt her heart crash frighteningly in her breast.

He must be blind, disfigured, horribly maimed, *dead* . . . oh God . . . for he was fastened tight to a stretcher and his head was wrapped about with a jacket. She felt the ability to think slip away from her and nausea flooded her throat and as her disordered mind plunged in horror she clung desperately to the hope that he could not be dead, could he? could he? for they were being so careful with him.

Faith led her forward and a miner at the head of the whim shook his head comfortingly, ''Tis only against the light, lass,' he said to the mineowner's wife for were they not all equal now in this moment of tragedy and when the coat was removed, there was Alex, his dirty face creased in his usual sardonic smile and Christy Buchanan was bewildered by the great joyfulness which rippled momentarily along the entire length of her body.

She was almost down to Conistone, her hand on the wagon on which her husband lay, slipped away now to unconsciousness, when the scream rang out – the thin, agonized sound echoing about the fells for several minutes – and she wondered pityingly who it was that was widowed that day.

Since then she had performed automatically the necessary actions and given the necessary directions needed to continue the running of her home, the nursing of her husband whose hazardous temper split the house apart with its ferocity, and the comforting and caring for her children who were apprehensive of the disorder which had come to upset the pattern of their peaceful childhood days.

'What is the matter with father?' Johnny asked when she visited the nursery at teatime as she usually did, on the third day after the accident. His two-fisted courage was temporarily missing in the trembling alarm which had uprooted his young and secure world and he had not objected, despite the startled gaze of his siblings, when his mother took him on her lap and held him close to her.

'Father has had an accident, darling, as I explained to you the other day. He . . . he fell when he was in the mine but the doctor has been to see him and says he will be up and about in no time. He must rest for a while so we must be very quiet and not disturb him. You may take the pups up to the paddock to play and make as much noise as you like up there.'

'Yes, we know that, mother, but why is he so cross? He was shouting at Jack yesterday . . .' Harry, quite tearful, afraid of the sounds which came from the room which his mother and father shared, leaned trustingly against her, a small animal seeking reassurance and shelter, jostling with his brother to share the comfort of their mother's lap.

'I know, sweetheart, but your father is not used to . . . to being kept in his bed and sometimes he loses his . . .' How to explain to two small boys about patience and frustration? 'You know how he loves to ride Duke and stride about and be noisy . . . and do things, just like you both do . . . ?'

Oh yes, Alex Buchanan's sons could understand that for they themselves hated to sit still or stay in their bed once the daylight, or the sunshine, or the snow-filled delights of the garden had called to them, but though they admired their father, even loved him a little despite his being a distant, somewhat forbidding presence in their world of the nursery, he was splendid and strong and could often be persuaded to put one or other of them up before him on Duke and sometimes even have a rough and tumble on the nursery floor. He was not soft and comforting and deeply satisfying as mother was, or Beth, or even Faith, but you knew that whatever came to frighten you father would be there to protect you, and that nothing bad would ever happen, ever *dare* to happen with him to guard your world!

Now that world had turned topsyturvey, filled with doctors and nurses and mother running about with scarce a minute to spare for them, warning them that they had best keep out of their father's way – as if they needed telling in his present fragile state of mind – until he was recovered. Christy looked into their handsome bewildered faces and hugged their soft bodies to her, and turned her mind to the remainder of this household who now, it appeared, all turned to her, dependent upon her, looking to her for comfort, direction and the reassurance that it would all be returned to normal as soon as the master was up and about again.

'Patience, Mr Buchanan, patience and rest. You will do yourself no good by getting upset over it. Just lie still and enjoy the ministrations of your charming wife,' the doctor said at the end of the second week.

Alex glared at his charming wife, the jarring pain in his neck making him wince as he did so.

'Can you not give me some liniment to rub on? Something to unlock this damned paralysis.' He said the word

350

carelessly then! 'I cannot even see to my own bodily needs but must rely on this devil of a woman you brought to clean me up. It is most offensive and I warn you I will not put up with it much longer. *Get me out of this damned bed . . .!*'

'Now Mr Buchanan, please! You are merely exacerbating your condition with this constant worry to be up and about. You must rest . . .'

'It appears I have no bloody option.' Alex said bitterly but he was resigned, it seemed at last, to spending two or three weeks chained to the sickroom. He had sent messages to his managers and foremen and had even gone so far as to request them to advertise in the *Westmorland Gazette* and the *Cumberland Paquet* and even in the *London Times* for a new engineer to take David Adams's place, saying he would be ready to interview the applicants himself when he was on his feet.

Annie came over to sit with him, sending away the stolid nurse who did little but see to his bodily functions. She took out her quilting and settled down in the chair beside his bed with the apparent intention of spending an hour or two in the bad-tempered company of her son-in-law, ignoring his brooding declaration that he was not dead yet! When he insisted that there was absolutely no need for him to be treated like some bloody invalid and she could take herself off and send his wife to him if he *must* have someone spying over his inability to move, he was surprised to be told in a sharp tone that his wife was sleeping and he must make do with her.

'Sleeping! At this time of day? What the hell for?'

'Because she's tired, my lad, that's what for. That girl has been on her feet for nearly twenty hours a day since the accident. There's a lot to do in this house . . .'

'She has a dozen servants to help her, with the children and . . .'

'It's not quite the same thing and you know it. You lying in that bed and demanding her attention every minute of the day could wear out the strongest woman, and that's

351

not the end of it. She must give some time to the children. Oh, I know they're well-cared for and happy enough with that Beth, but they're still needing their mother's notice now and again. This is a big household, Alex, and Christy has a great deal to see to.'

'She didn't say that when she was off traipsing the fells last year looking for mischief. Then she hadn't enough to do, or so she told me.' His confinement made him nasty but Annie Emmerson was used to dealing with peevish masculine tempers and she placidly took a stitch or two, completely unruffled.

'That's as maybe and nothing to do with me in any case, but she's my lass and I'll not see her driven to a standstill with a houseful of servants begging to be directed, four children in the nursery and a bad-tempered husband demanding her constant presence at his sick-bed. She's tired Alex, and worried about you . . .'

And so was Annie for she was a sensible woman and her sense told her that this with Alex was not natural. A man does not lie, his body stranded on his bed with no movement beyond those which nature demanded of it and even those not within his power to control. Not with no good reason, he does not, and what was it that was damaged in Alex Buchanan's body, his mind even, that would not allow him to move it? The doctor was a fool, Annie knew that, but she could not say so to this man, or to her daughter who was his wife. She could only do what she had been doing all her life and that was to stand firmly beside them, ready to give her support if it should be asked for, ready to let it be known if the time should come that she was to be relied on.

'Come now, Annie, *really?*' he was saying, his eyebrow tilted sardonically and his mouth curved in a disbelieving smile.

'Yes really, Alex Buchanan. Your wife holds you in high regard.'

'My bank balance, you mean.'

'No, that is not what I mean.'

'You surprise me, Annie dear,' and she could see he did not believe her.

'Maybe I do but that's beside the point. I'm staying over for a while to see she gets a bit of rest. Faith's no good to her just yet, so until she is, your Mrs Longworth has made up the bedroom at the end of the hall and put me in there, so if you mind that wicked tongue of yours and behave yourself I'll come and pass the time of day with you now and again.'

He grinned and his eyes softened.

'You're a fraud, Annie Emmerson. As big a rogue as I am. Pass the time of day indeed! Before I know where I am you'll be in complete charge, ordering about the blasted woman who hovers over me like a damn vulture. I shall be in your clutches as well and unable to defend myself against being managed as handsomely as you managed Job!'

'Nay lad. Job was the one who . . .'

'Rubbish!'

They smiled companionably in perfect understanding and it crossed Annie's mind that maybe Alex Buchanan understood too much.

She was right about Christy. She had more than the house, the nursery and the sickroom to deal with, for almost before her own husband was safely installed in his clean bed and the doctor beside him, there was the tragedy and pain of Faith Adams to be eased in some way, but how, for her grief was terrible.

Christy made the arrangements, though Faith insisted she could manage, for her husband's funeral, standing beside Faith at the graveside, a rock on which the young widow could lean. She sat beside her at the inquest and held her hand tightly as the accident was described a dozen times – wondering as she heard it at the thoughtless bravery and compassion of her own husband – and then she brought her back to Howethwaite where she had been since the day David Adams was killed, brushing aside Faith's mumbling that she would be alright in her own house. She even broke the news to her that 'her own house' was hers no longer but would be used to accommodate the new mine manager, and his wife if he should have one, when he came.

'You are my friend and shall stay with me as long as I care to have you which is as long as you care to stay.'

'I must work, Christy.'

'And so you shall. My mother is not young and can do no more than sit with Alex. Do you think I can manage all this on my own?' She swept a frantic hand about her to indicate the world in which she was mistress, nurse, wife, mother and even, when Alex would not see them, the decider in some problem at the gunpowder mill, the mine, the factory at Stavely, even if that decision was merely to tell Mr Cartmell, Mr Tate or Mr Dunlop to do what they thought best.

'But what will happen when your husband is recovered? You will have no need of me then. Sally is a competent maid. I cannot be nursery maid, or governess and despite your certainty that you have need of me I will not stay just to make you feel better.'

'Faith . . .'

'I did not mean to be . . . unkind, Christy, but I must go where I can be of use . . . in my way . . .'

'You will, by God you will! Please Faith, stay at least until Alex is better. I am not being kind though I will admit to being glad if I know you are . . . safe, but I need you now more than anyone else. We can . . . help each other, you know we can.'

Faith looked sadly at her friend, understanding, now that she herself had suffered it, the anguish Christy had known over Robin Forsythe. To realize the pain of others, one must bear that pain oneself. She now knew exactly what it was that had driven Christy during the past year in what Faith had considered to be madness, lunacy, and beyond the understanding of those who were steady and sensible, as she had thought herself to be. Steady and sensible, yes, but if she had the chance to see her David, even if it should bring distress to others, would she not take it?

'What about ... Robin?' she asked softly and was moved to pity by the dreadful expression which passed across Christy's face.

Her voice was quite flat as she answered.

'He is to be married quite soon and is, I believe, to go on a wedding journey to Italy ... or thereabouts. These ... these trips ... amongst the gentry who have nothing of urgency to fetch them back often last nine months or a year so you see, Faith, he will not ... trouble us ... either of us ... for a while.'

'I ... I'm sorry, lass.'

'I know. We are sorry for one another, are we not, Faith?'

'We are ...'

Slowly, as Alex Buchanan still fought to lift himself – straining his indomitable mind which would brook no interference from anyone, even his own body, to move his leaden limbs – the dread canker of doubt grew in his intelligent brain which told him this was no ordinary helplessness such as that caused by a fall, by exertion to which one's body was not accustomed, or even by an illness which strikes suddenly.

Annie Emmerson watched compassionately as he began to slip ever so slowly into the pit which his own fertile mind dug for him, his imagination dragging him to the depths of it and filling it in over his still living body. He began to mouth obscenities at the doctor who was clearly mystified and, if he were honest, alarmed by the way in which the hard muscles became slack and flesh and tissue began slowly to melt away from the body which appeared to have absolutely nothing wrong with it. Alex threatened, his fearful dread making him savage, that if the doctor did not get him soon from his bloody bed he'd have him struck off as an incompetent quack and hounded from here to London.

'And you can bugger off as well,' he told the solidly

imposing figure of the woman who, strong as a horse and capable, it seemed, of lifting one, had been engaged to help Mrs Buchanan with the more arduous and delicate aspects of the nursing of him.

'Perhaps . . . er . . . perhaps another opinion,' the doctor had suggested hesitantly at the end of the fourth week when the fine, unmarked body of his patient still appeared disinclined to so much as twitch when he furtively drew his finger-nail across the sole of his left foot. There were other signs he did not like either, signs he had seen in others who had suffered what appeared to be a minor accident and had never walked again, though he kept them to himself.

Mrs Buchanan brought them up!

'Surely my husband should not have this . . .' A delicate subject and one which ladies could not be expected to discuss but Christy plunged on, '. . . this lack of control of . . . of his . . . bladder and . . . I realize that his body has been subjected to a great blow but unless he has some injury within him and you say you can detect none, why does he not *know* when he needs the . . . the commode . . . and ask for it? It is most upsetting for him. For a grown man to foul himself like an infant is humiliating, Doctor, and I wonder if there is perhaps . . . there is something . . . ?'

'I really feel . . .'

'Yes Doctor?'

'I can only say that . . .'

'Yes?'

'He must rest . . .'

'He does nothing else!'

'. . . and eat light, nourishing meals . . .'

'He does so.'

'Well?'

'You are saying you can do nothing more for him?'

'Time is a . . .'

'Please Doctor, I am not a child.'

'I'm sorry, Mrs Buchanan, truly.'

356

She moved blindly, instinctively through those days, an inanimate object which smiled and soothed and comforted, which directed others with a conditioned reflex she was unaware she had gained in her years as Alex's wife and the mistress of his smooth-running home. Her mind was blank, incapable of thought beyond that of the needs of the man who raged in his bed, their bed in which she now no longer slept, and the demands of her children for they must be protected against his bitter anger, their lives sheltered and continuing in the way they had always done.

She was calm as she arranged for her elegant little sitting room to be made into a bedroom for herself where she could watch over her husband as he slept, moving her dainty furniture to a small unused room downstairs making it again into a parlour as it had been in old Mrs Buchanan's day.

'It is only sensible, Alex,' she explained calmly in those first days when he asked suspiciously what the devil she thought she was doing. 'I can't sleep on the sofa, can I, and until you are recovered you must have the bed to yourself.'

'You are expecting a long stay then,' he said dangerously, 'in your own bed?'

'No, I am not but it seems only practical that we should both have as much rest as possible . . .'

'Of course! I see the plan now. It would be most unpleasant to lie beside me as I am at the moment. Offensive even . . .'

'Stop it! You know that is not the reason. We both must have sleep. You so that you may regain your strength and I so that I may keep this house running and give a hand to the nurse.'

'What a perfect opportunity. I had not thought of it but I see it now! You have told me often enough in the past how distasteful you find my embrace. Now you have the best excuse in the world and one which, when it gets around the parish as it surely will, that the Buchanans no longer share a bed, will be fully understood by everyone. Poor Mrs Buchanan, tied to that . . . that . . .'

'Alex . . . don't . . .'

But he turned his head away and still, then, in a shell of shock, a strange pity washed over her for this man, once so strong, powerful and dangerous when his will was blocked but now so helpless, dependent on two women to keep him clean, alive and in good constitution whilst his body healed.

And in all that frozen time she did not allow more than a wisp of a thought of Robin Forsythe to enter her mind for she dare not. She had heard the bells ring out joyously over the brown heights of the fells and across the silk-patterned waters of the lake, down into the green valleys and hidden dales, just as they had done on *her* wedding day and it was then that she switched off her mind to him and turned it to the only thing which was real now in her life. Her husband was held fast to his bed and had been looked over by half a dozen eminent men from London, each one shaking his head and going away again. Into his eyes she saw come the deadness which held his body. It set them into a stare which never wavered from the ceiling and had it not been for her mother, Faith still too deep set in her own grief to care much for Christy's, she would have gone under.

'Hold my hand, child,' her mother said and she did so and it was the line she clung to as she crept to her feet.

'I'm here, lass,' her mother said, 'for whatever you might want of me. Tell me,' and she did so and stood up with her mother's quiet courage to stiffen her, straight-backed and erect.

'Will he recover, mother?' she asked and her mother was the only one who was truthful with her as she had always been.

'No lass, not without a miracle and they're a bit hard to come by.'

'How am I to manage, mother?'

'Just as you have always done, my girl. He's your

358

husband, you know that, and . . . I heard the bells too . . .
the other day . . .'

'Oh Jesus God, mother. I seem to lose him again and
again . . .'

'He's not yours to lose, my lass. He never was, you
know that.'

'And now . . . there's Alex.'

'Aye, there's Alex,' and if she had not had Annie's hand
to hold on to she would have gone under.

CHAPTER TWENTY-THREE

Squire Forsythe brought his new young wife home in
April, already pregnant, it was said, which was altogether
natural for they had been married for six months. It was
not unusual for the gentry and those of the leisured classes
to return from their wedding trip with their first born not
only conceived, but in the arms of its nanny!

They had travelled extensively throughout the cold
winter months which had fallen, as was customary, upon
the north of England, idling luxuriously in the sunshine of
southern Italy until the winter was gone, and spring came
to the Lakeland to place swathes of wild daffodils about
the silver lakes and decorate the wild pear trees in a froth
of blossom. The meadows in the valley bottom were
massed with cranesbill, a shimmering lilac-blue carpet
moving in the breeze off the lake, lady's bedstraw, a
delicate lace of the palest yellow blending with the brilliant
green of the new grasses.

Sycamore and beech and juniper sprang, almost over-
night, fully-leaved into the spring air. In the depths of the
woods yew and ash stood deep in lilies of the valley and
butterfly orchids, and marsh cinquefoil, like purple-red
stars, grew close to the water and there were white water
lilies on the upper tarns.

Duck and geese fluttered their wings as they danced on the surface of the lake, ready to greet the summer ahead, their honking cries mingling with those of the hundreds of plaintive new lambs which would soon be taken up to the fells.

The Squire and his wife were not to stay long in Fellthwaite, gossip had it, for the new Mrs Forsythe – the old one presumably pensioned off to some corner of the Hall where she could trouble no one – was 'delicate' and it was thought best she be placed nearer to the expertise of the fashionable doctors in London, her mamma, whose thought it was, putting little faith in 'country' doctors. A house had been purchased for them in the smart quarter of Mayfair, a wedding present from the bride's very wealthy father, the baronet Sir William Briers and whilst she awaited the – from everyone's viewpoint but her own – happy event, her husband, having done his duty most ably, it was considered, might visit his cousins in Leicestershire to shoot the hand-reared game, to ride and hunt and do whatever young country squires did when they were enormously wealthy and could afford to do it!

But first they must stay for a month or two in the Squire's parish for it was expected that the tenants would consider it only their due to meet their new lady; and there would be, of course, a great deal of entertaining of the Squire's friends and family relatives now that Dalebarrow Hall was restored to its former splendour. All of those in the past who had been sympathetically dismayed by the deterioration of what had once been a fine and honoured old manor, an illustrious estate – those who themselves might, if they had not done as the Squire had done and married wisely and well, have seen their own manors fall about their ears – must stay awhile to admire what the Squire and his wife's money had achieved and to congratulate them on the completion of it!

It was said that Mrs Robin Forsythe, though young, was a splendid match for the new Squire. Fellthwaite had heard she was an excellent hostess, brought up to be one by her own mamma whose reputation for entertaining high-ranking guests in her London home and her Scottish home and her villa in Naples was unsurpassed. Whilst the young Forsythes had wintered in Italy, Dalebarrow Hall had been transformed into the kind of home Lady Briers had envisaged for her daughter. Every room was redecorated, the old wood torn out and new put in. Chimneys which had smoked for years did so no longer. A large and draughty room on the first floor had been made over into a magnificent ballroom with mirrored walls and a dozen chandeliers. There was new plasterwork, curtains and bedcovers, and on every floor were laid rugs and carpets so thick and deep and warm, her child would never, ever feel the cold in this far-flung, barbaric corner of the country where, occasionally, she supposed she must live.

There were new kitchens – and servants – for her daughter was used to French cuisine, and of course the stables must be considered for when the young Forsythes and their guests were in residence a decent mount was expected!

Fellthwaite was agog, positively agog, as it had been on their wedding day in October as news got out of banquets and balls until dawn, dancing on the terrace, if you please and in April, and all the madcap silliness the young gentry get up to. Lights blazed all night up at the Hall; and the village which surrounded it, and even Fellthwaite itself was often awakened as dawn broke, to the mad dashing gallop of horses' hooves and the excited shouts of what one could only assume to be the Squire's guests up to some lark!

Annie Emmerson, though she had been home now at Hollin House these past three months – for she could not live with her daughter forever, the length of time it seemed possible Alex Buchanan would remain in his bed – went over to Howethwaite on most days, doing nothing much but let herself be seen to be there, ready should she be required. She sat with her grandchildren and nursed young Job, the only one who would allow it, and kept an eye on the nursery maids who were inclined, if no one took care, to sit and drink tea and gossip.

She took a turn or two about the kitchen, stately and serene, allowing her daughter's housekeeper to see her run a finger round a saucepan or a milk jug, letting it be known that should Mrs Buchanan have missed it through sheer pressure of work, her mother was on the alert for any slackening.

She sat with Alex on the nurse's day off, allowing her daughter to walk for an hour, wherever she pleased now, or even ride if she wished, as once she had done, as once she had begged to be allowed to do. Strangely, now that she could order the saddling up of her mare, knowing the stable boy or groom would leap to do her bidding, she no longer had the urge to do so.

She would walk through the small but beautiful oak and birch wood at the back of the house, wandering along the grassed-over track between the lichened trunks of the oaks, moving towards the bridge which crossed the river, high now with water from the melted winter snows. Just to sit on a heavy boulder covered with moss, peaceful and so quiet the squirrels would venture to the hem of her skirt. Her spirit, sore and damaged, was soothed in the communion she had always known with this earth which was always steady beneath her feet, this tranquil air which she could breathe, as she could not breathe the air of the sickroom, this isolation which lightened her heart and gave her the courage to stand up and return to what awaited her at home.

No one spoke to her of Robin Forsythe but she had sensed her mother's stillness, a waiting, as though, should she want to speak of him herself, Annie was ready to listen. Faith had held her hand, reaching for it instinctively when Sally, her mind filled with the dazzling splendours of Dalebarrow Hall and all that went on in it since the Squire's return – and which had been passed on to her by

362

her cousin who was newly employed as kitchen maid –
begged Mrs Buchanan to be impressed, as she had been,
by the description of it. She had been affronted when
Faith, only a maid herself once and no better than Sally,
or so she believed, had told her sharply to 'run down to
the kitchen and fetch some coffee' just as though *she* and
not Mrs Buchanan were the mistress.

In her pique she had not noticed her mistress's strange
white face, nor the staring clarity of her grey eyes and had
certainly not heard the moan which escaped Christy Buch-
anan's lips when she left the room. Now she had heard he
was to be off again soon, through Sally again and perhaps
it was best to hear it from someone who had no conception
of what she did, back to London to leave his wife in her
mama's care to await the birth of her child and take
himself God knows where. She was thankful only that he
was not to be here, wondering sadly how he would survive
the life of the fashionable 'man about town' which his
wife's family were determined, it seemed, he was to be!

When his wife was not there Alex Buchanan lay in his
bed and wished that, like David Adams, he had died in the
mine. He was clean, and he supposed, comfortable, though
he did not really know it. His face had been shaved and
his growing hair cut only that morning by the barber from
Fellthwaite. The room was warm. It must be since an
enormous fire roared crisply in the fireplace, its glow
rippling across the white ceiling, turning it to rose and
orange and amber, creating shadows which twisted away
to elude his gaze, into the far corners of the room. He
could smell something fragrant, coming he supposed from
a bowl of flowers on the deep sill of the window, and
another by his bedside and just within the range of his
painfully turning head he could make out a splash of
colour but what the blooms were eluded him.

The woman who looked after him sat in the rocking
chair by the fire. She was doing something with a needle
and some thread. Darning his socks, perhaps, ready for
the next winter for up here in the frozen heights of the

Lakeland warm wool must be worn to keep the feet from the cold. He felt the fierce, bubbling, derisive laughter jerk bitterly in his chest, tearing at his lungs to be free, aching to shout forth the vicious frustration which confined it but, should anyone have been watching, they would have seen nothing but the impassive, expressionless face of Alex Buchanan, pale now against the white pillow on which it had lain for the past six months.

Six months! How had he borne it? Because he had no other choice, a voice answered, and the sour laughter seethed inside him again – for how was a man who could lift nothing but his own eyebrows to raise the gun to his head, the poison to his lips to finish the deed which had begun with the dead weight of David Adams's body smiting his? And if he could do these things there would be no need of it!

The irony of it brought a snarl to his mouth, silent and ferocious and he turned his face slowly to the far window, his eyes shadowed in pain. He had pondered on it, the doing away with himself, hour after hour for what else was his mind to dwell on beyond the escape from his body and it held his thoughts – the bad ones, the really bad ones – from viciously invading his tortured spirit.

Thoughts of . . . of Christy . . . Christy! Of Christy and himself, himself as he once had been. Though his body was dead his imagination and the sense which, wholly masculine, had responded to her female sensuality, was not and he was tormented with visions, dreams, nightmares for that was what they had become, of their bodies, warm, soft, hard and lusty, entering and receiving the secret messages of love in this very bed! Here, where he lay like some loathsome, white-withered creature, the husk of his body holding down, despite its weakness, the soaring of his mind and spirit, perhaps to welcome death, but at least escape. Here, where he and his wife had performed the lovely act which surely must symbolize the very highest peak to which life can climb. Life!

There was a hesitant scratching at the bedroom door

and the woman by the fire lifted her head. She wore a neat mob cap, frilled and spotlessly white. Her dress was a good grey wool and over it she had about her, covering her from her neck to its hem, a starched white apron, tied firmly in a bow at the back. She was a big woman with strong shoulders and a quietly impassive face. Her hands were large and firm as she plied her needle and she smelled strongly of disinfectant and soap. Her cheeks were rounded with good health and good food, and rosy from the warmth of the fire.

'That dratted dog,' she tutted, and would have gone back to her task but the harsh voice from the bed twitched her cap in its direction and she rose from her chair, putting her needlework on the table beside it.

'Let him in, if you please,' the voice said, grating as though from misuse.

'But Mr Buchanan, this is hardly the place for a dog. No doubt he has been out in the stable yard and his paws . . .'

'I don't care where he has been, let the bloody dog in and then go and find something useful to do. Go on, I can be left alone, for God's sake. I'm hardly likely to get up to any mischief! I promise I won't interfere with your knitting or whatever it is you do by the hour. Go on, woman! I pay your wages so I expect to be obeyed!'

'Now then, Mr Buchanan. I am in charge here and I will not have that animal leaping about on the bedcovers. That bed's only just been changed as you well know, and I'm not going to put the maids to the trouble of doing it all again just for the sake of a dog. They have to do it often enough as it is.'

She was a plain-spoken woman with little imagination. She did not mean to be unkind, she was merely stating an obvious fact, but Alex Buchanan clenched his teeth together in a spasm of agony which had nothing to do with physical pain. He closed his eyes and turned his head away, the only movement he could make without the help of others. The reminder of the humiliating exercise he was

365

forced to suffer each time his own useless muscles, those which controlled his bodily functions but failed to do so, brought him close to striking . . . Oh God . . . if only he could . . . if only he could move his arm . . . just his arm . . . no more since with that he could . . . he could . . . he would slap the foolish smile from the damned woman's face . . . Oh God . . . Oh dear Christ, why did you leave me like this? Why did you not take me with the boy . . . *instead* of the boy . . . ?

'Let in the dog, please, Mrs Jackson, and then you may go,' he said through his clenched teeth, his eyes still closed.

'Mr Buchanan, I am afraid . . .'

'*Will you open that bloody door!*'

Mrs Jackson 'tched-tched' angrily, tossing her cap to show she was not at all pleased but moved on majestic feet to the bedroom door which she opened reluctantly. She stepped hastily to one side with such alacrity one might have been forgiven for thinking a bag full of rats had been emptied into the room, and the small Lakeland terrier slipped by her, his torn ear trembling in anticipation.

'I'll leave you then, sir,' the nurse said reproachfully, 'but for no more than five minutes and I would be obliged if you would command that animal to remain on the floor.'

'Get out . . . get out!'

The door closed quietly behind the woman for even in the most trying circumstances one did not bang a door on a patient.

'Come on, boy, come on,' Alex said softly and immediately the rippling streak of black and grey was up beside him. A long pink tongue touched his face, gently going over his cheek, his ear, his suddenly wet eyes, and then with a sigh of sheer content the dog settled his furry side against his master, his wet black nose an inch from Alex face. It was a scene which had been enacted many times in the long, unendurable six months which had gone by since his accident and it followed a familiar, desperate pattern, one in which the dog must play his part.

Alex began to talk to him, saying the urgent, angry words, spewing out in a low, frightened moan all the things he could say to no one and the dog listened gravely, his head on one side, his eyes never leaving those of the man on the bed. The voice droned on and on, hopelessly relinquishing to the dog its message of despair, oppressive in its wretchedness, self-tormenting and overcome by defeat. At last, reaching the far limits of his strength he cried out to the dog.

'. . . lie on my face, boy, come on, good old boy, lie on my face . . .'

The dog had risen to his feet, looking anxiously down into Alex's anguished face, his tail gently moving. He understood his master was telling him to do something, giving him an order but he did not understand what was being asked of him. He would die for him if he could, leap to obey any command he had been trained for, but this was not one of them and though he longed to help he did not know how.

'. . . see, put your head here boy, over here, come on, good boy, now lie down . . .'

The dog obeyed the only words he knew and lay down obediently but by Alex's side and Alex groaned, straining with his teeth against his stretched lips in an attempt to force his own rigid head into the depths of the pillow.

'Oh dear sweet Jesus . . . help me . . . let . . . me . . . out . . . of . . . this . . . body . . . which . . . holds . . . me. Please, oh please . . . someone . . . anyone . . . let me free . . . let me go . . .'

The door opened and immediately the sounds from the bed ceased as footsteps shushed across the deep pile of the carpet. He could not feel the dog against him but he sensed the weight of him go and though he did not turn his head to look he knew who had entered the room. He would have known if he had been deaf and blind as well as paralysed.

'Alex.'

Christy leaned over the bed and looked into the ravaged face of the man who stared somewhere over her left shoulder into a nightmare world in which no one existed but himself. She knew he was aware of her. He knew everyone who came to see him, to stand beside his bed, and express regret and hope and belief that some miracle from God – the parson – would come to bring him back to life. He was polite, indifferent to his children, to the men who came from the mines, from the mill which had been her father's, thanking them for their concern, caring little for the reports they brought him of the state of his businesses, waiting patiently until the time came for them to leave.

With herself he acted as though she did not exist. If a man who has no use in any part of his body can be said to 'stiffen', this is what he did each time she came near him. He rejected her. She knew if he had the means to do away with himself he would do so and the only time he came to life, if it could be called that, was when the dog was with him. She had stood outside the door listening to his voice whisper to the terrier. He appeared to be entreating the animal to do something for him, seemingly something the dog was unable to do for afterwards, when the dog had gone Alex would slip away, almost into what appeared to be an unconscious state, as though the dog's departure took some hope with him, leaving him again to his joyless state of extinction.

Perhaps she should leave the dog with him all the time. It was said that an animal brought a sympathy to those who were afflicted, a sympathy they could not accept from others. The unquestioning devotion this dog gave quite simply to Alex, not caring much how it was received was perhaps all that he could manage of emotion until he came to terms with his disability, grew to accept it and move on as he surely must. The dog might help to achieve it and God knew she was willing to try anything which might bring Alex from the grave he had dug for himself and in which he now lay, refusing any hand which might lift him from it! Mrs Jackson wouldn't like it but if it gave Alex some comfort, brought a fraction of life into his sterile world, she would insist upon it.

'Alex,' she said again, resting a soft hand on his cheek to attract his attention, watching him flinch away from it. 'I saw Mrs Jackson in the kitchen so I came to ask if you wanted some company but I see someone else had the same idea.' She smiled down at the alert animal. 'He is only happy when he is with you, I fear he frets dreadfully when he is shut up in the stable.'

There was no response. The dog looked up at her from the end of the bed where he hovered hopefully and his tail moved gently.

'What a scamp he is! He is only waiting for a word from you and he will be in the bed with you. Why do you not ask him to lie here beside you again. I don't mind even if Mrs Jackson does. In fact I think it would be a good idea if he remained with you all the time. He is a perfect nuisance when he is let out, trying to sneak through the kitchen when no one is looking. He had a maid on her back yesterday and ruined Mrs Avery's sponge pudding which she had on a tray. What a commotion! He could sleep here, beside your bed.'

She was rewarded by the sudden glow of gratitude which shone in his eyes as he looked for a second into hers, then it died again. She watched him for a moment, hopefully, then sighed, her expression one of resignation.

'Shall I read the newspaper to you?' she asked, expecting no answer and getting none. It was a daily occurrence and though he said nothing and appeared not even to listen when she read out loud, she comforted herself with the thought that into his brain went words which told him of events happening beyond these four walls; and though he gave the impression of not caring one way or the other, might it not stimulate something of that which had once been Alex Buchanan?

She pulled the nurse's chair across the room and placed it beside the bed where she knew he could see her. Patting the bed she invited the delighted dog to lie again beside his master and shaking out the *Westmorland Gazette*, studied it, picking out items of news she thought might interest her husband. The dog dozed and the fire crackled and as his wife's voice drifted about him with her perfume, Alex Buchanan felt, for a few moments, the only stirrings of peace he knew.

'It seems that the Sessions is to establish a policy of self-government for our colonies, Alex,' she said, her voice soft, like velvet against his flesh. 'They have become so numerous and so large they can no longer be managed by the centralized system of the Colonial Office, it says. No doubt there will be posts for representatives and Jonathan Aspin will be angling for one for that sorry creature he calls a son. He has tried him in the shipping office but to no avail. Perhaps this is the answer.'

She paused and rustled the pages of the newspaper as she turned them.

'Aah, and Her Majesty has been delivered safely of a third son. Imagine, she is but thirty and has given birth to seven children already. Thank God you are satisfied with the three we have for I swear the idea of having another four by the time I reach that age is quite . . .'

She stopped abruptly, aware that the subject was hardly a suitable one to be discussed in the present circumstances, cruel even, with a husband who was incapable not only of impregnating his wife but of every other function known to man! She glanced at him but his face was as expressionless as always so she continued smoothly, pretending not to have been aware of her own thoughtlessness.

'Oh, and poor Sir Robert Peel has had an accident . . .'

She stopped, appalled and her hand went guiltily to her mouth. Dear Lord, she had done it again. It seemed that whatever she said today led the mind to an immediate connection with the shell of the man on the bed, to his state of inanimation, his inability to do more than lie there fixing his stare on the ceiling above him whilst his once fine masculine body rotted slowly away.

'Alex . . . I'm sorry . . . I did not mean to . . .' She leaned forward to look into his face, her pity for him great, but he turned his head away so that she could see no more

370

than a hollow curve of his gaunt cheek. It was there in the grim set of his mouth, in the strange containment he was able to gather about himself so that though he did not move he gave the appearance of walking away from her.

Another repudiation, a denial of her existence. It was as though he hated her now, could not bear her near him where once she had only to glance at him, smile, to touch his arm and his eyes would be hot for her and his arms reach out possessively to take what was, in his opinion, rightfully his.

'Alex . . .' She leaned back in her chair and the dog watched her as she roughly turned the pages, defiantly almost, determined, her attitude said, to do her duty in the caring for her invalid husband, even if it was against his will! She was allowed to do nothing else for him now, not even feed him, for once it had become apparent the task would need to be done for him for the rest of his days, unless some miraculous cure was engineered, he had told her coldly he would prefer the nurse to do it for him.

Privately, since she felt it was less humiliating for him to be treated by a stranger she was thankful to have the undignified duty of caring for his wasted body taken from her by Mrs Jackson. But surely he could not object to her doing something, *anything* which might ease her conscience a little, to help expunge the knowledge of where she had been and with whom on that day when he was in the accident, which had taken all but the beat of his strong heart from him.

She continued hurriedly, eager, not only to help him in some way, but to take away the memory of that day.

'There has been a proposal to have an Exhibition in London . . .'

Her voice trembled slightly as she went on and the man in the bed felt the despair for her and for himself move in his chest and throat. He was no more than a eunuch, a freak, a log slowly withering and with the strength of his resourceful mind, the only part of him still alive, he meant it to be soon, but as he went he would do it with some

371

dignity, at least before this woman he had once been master of. He had grown old and weary in this bed though he was only thirty-five but she would not share his ageing with him, nor he hers, he'd see to that.

'His Royal Highness has put forward the idea that in this age of modern development in art and science it would be a splendid notion to have a great exhibition to show . . .'

She continued for another half an hour, sending away the nurse who came to sit again with her patient and when eventually she left him he heard her tell the woman the dog was to remain with him

'But Mrs Buchanan, I cannot have that animal in my sickroom. He most likely has fleas and will pass them on . . .'

'Rubbish, Mrs Jackson. I will see he has a bath before the day is out. The groom will come to take him for a walk twice a day. He will be no trouble to anyone.'

'But I cannot work with the beast under my feet, Mrs Buchanan . . .'

'Then you must take your nursing skills elsewhere, Mrs Jackson,' Christy replied coolly, 'for I'm certain there will be someone who will not mind sharing the company of my husband with his dog.'

Alex smiled grudgingly to himself, turning himself stiffly to watch his beautiful wife haughtily dispose of the tyrant who ruled him.

'That Sally of yours is walking out, for want of a better word, with Jack Hodson, did you know?'

'No, I did not realize that they were even . . .'

'Oh aye, and if something's not done soon there'll be a "groaning cheese" being cut up and with no wedding first, or so I'm told.'

Christy looked at her mother, startled, her eyes moving away from their contemplation of her three sons and their dogs running wildly in circles in the garden. It was a

372

pleasantly mild day, the edge of winter gone at last and the primroses were already making a fine show against the garden wall.

'What on earth do you mean?'

'What d'you think I mean?'

'Jack and Sally . . . ?'

'Aye. There's talk they slip away up into the woods at night, or so Faith tells me, and that Mrs Longworth should be doing something about it before it's too late. I could say something but this isn't my house, lass. Now we don't want that girl to get into trouble, do we, if she isn't already in it, which wouldn't surprise me. She always was flighty even when she was up at Hollin House. I remember seeing her hanging about our Toby, and what about the stable lad up at Dalebarrow Hall? What happened to him, d'you suppose?'

'I didn't know she was courting Jack. I've been so . . .'

'Well, I'd hardly call it courting, but it's got to be seen to, Christy. She's your responsibility just as they all are!'

Christy turned her head sharply, irritably away from her mother, then stood up to walk jerkily to the window. She rested her forehead on the glass watching as Job flung himself ecstatically into the soil his young dog had just dug up, clutching great fistfuls in his already filthy hands. Beth was squeaking as she ran across to him and he turned, scowling, his face so completely like that of his father she felt her heart turn over. She began to smile a little for this was how Alex must have looked at the same age, the same pugnacious thrust to his small jaw, the same sudden grin which came to light Job's face as Beth popped a 'sweetie' in his open mouth.

She stood quite still in a small pool of silence, the sound of her mother's voice, the children's high calling, the dog's barking, all receding into the far channels of her mind as she recalled his smile. She had not seen it for a long time now. It had flashed out once or twice in those first weeks in the often quite humorous moments when he laughed at his own 'stiffness' and, as she leaned over him displaying

373

the soft upper curve of her breasts, recounting in detail what he would do to her when he was recovered. Then he still believed he would recover, could indeed see no reason why he should not.

She remembered her own terror on that dreadful day when they had brought him from the mine that he would be blind, or dead, and the sweet surge of relief when his smile had come to reassure her. How strange! How puzzling it was to recall it, and her own feelings, and how puzzling the feelings themselves. Robin had not been married then and if Alex had ... had ... She let the thought lie tantalizingly on the edge of her conscious mind, then pushed it hastily away and her mother's voice slipped back into her awareness.

'Are you listening, girl?'

'Yes mother. You are saying Sally is ... is ...'

'Dallying, let's hope that it's no more, with Jack Hodson.'

'And should be restrained!'

'Aye, or the lad asked his intentions!'

'Surely we know those, mother. They are the same as all men's ...'

'Christy!'

'... and if that is the case we shall have to go to the juniper bush, shall we not, mother, to get Sally out of her fix. But there is one thing we can be certain of, and that is it will not be needed by anyone else in this house again!'

CHAPTER TWENTY-FOUR

She was alone in her parlour the next day for Faith had gone to put flowers on her husband's grave taking Amy with her, and her three sons were out somewhere with Beth and Liz.

The house was quiet without the three robust boys to

shatter its peace — she had long given up demanding their tip-toeing silence around their father — and the pale spring sunshine crept in a soft-hued strip across her carpet, touching with young tender fingers the delicate shade of the cream and pink of its pattern, the rich burnished rosewood of her table, the cream velvet of her elegant little sofa and the great copper bowl spilling over with daffodils and hyacinths which bloomed in the window bottom. The curtains tapped gently against the window which she had opened for it was mild again and the breeze had on it the fragrance of budding leaves, the straining new grass and the sharpness of recently turned soil.

The bright new day had encouraged her to put on a gown she had ordered last summer — the summer of her strange enchantment — a gown she had Miss Susan Whittam design with Robin Forsythe in mind, though of course she had not said so. It was light and immensely feminine, which was how she had been at the time, in a pale peach organdy. The bodice was shaped to the waist, flaring out below it into the fashionable basque. The neckline was high and modest, edged with velvet ribbon in a darker shade of peach, tied in a froth of bows at the back. The skirt was enormous, flounced from waist to hem, each one edged with the same velvet ribbon and the hem twelve to fifteen feet in circumference. The pagoda sleeves were tight at the shoulder, expanding abruptly to a wide opening, slit up the front and falling lower behind. She had pulled her hair into a deep chignon at the back of her neck, tidy and neat but soft curls escaped to cling about her forehead and ears. She had recovered from the shock of Alex's condition but the anxiety had fined her down to a slenderness which gave her the appearance of the girl she had been at seventeen. She looked glossy and well-cared for, like her own little chestnut mare, with a bloom about her which peached her cheeks to match her gown and her eyes were a clear, pale grey, like the waters of Conistone on a rainy day.

She sat in her chair and stared out beyond the half-opened window, her eyes seeing but not absorbing the great sweep of wild daffodils which lay at the bottom of the sloping lawn beneath the spread of oak and sycamore, just beginning to show foliage. Beyond were the unfathomable, endlessly rolling fells, the peaks only just losing their snowcaps but her gaze travelled on, drifting to the clouds, stretched strands of white wool against the pale blue of the sky.

She had just said a polite 'good morning' to Mr Cartmell and Mr Anderson, two of the men who helped to manage the Emmerson Gunpowder Mills, promising to speak to her husband on their behalf for he was unable to see them today, she had told them. What they had said to her had pushed her mind into an uncomfortable awareness, and not for the first time, that unless Alex was forcibly dragged from the semi-comatose state into which he was gradually sinking and made to face up to his disability, made to see what was happening to his mills and his mines, they would slip through his fingers like trickling water. They were held now by hands which had a careless grip on them for no one but the master has full control, the initiative, imagination, the incentive needed to put heart into a concern and without Alex the hearts of his mines and mills were beginning to beat lethargically.

For a while they would go on, the momentum kept rolling by the initial shove they had been given by the man who owned them, but when he was not there, the men who took his orders would become careless and the whole precision-like movement would slow until it came to a halt.

They spoke of orders not being out on time, not their fault, of course, for it was no part of their job to see to the transporting of the finished product from the mill to the new railway station at Windermere, an innovation Mr Buchanan had had in hand just before his unfortunate accident. Mr Pendle, whose job it apparently was, was questioned by Christy when he came to call to make *his* complaint. He said bitterly that those who packed the powder in the wooden barrels ready for transporting were sitting about doing 'damn all if you'll pardon me, Mrs Buchanan,' because someone, presumably Mr Cartmell or Mr Anderson, had overlooked the necessary order to the cooper to pass on to *his* workmen the need for the making of the barrels, in fact the 'damn, pardon me, Mrs Buchanan' wood, dry and well-seasoned, had not even been ordered from Mr Andrew Dyer and they had none with which to make the barrels. How was he to send out orders, backing up now for several weeks, if he had nothing in which to pack the powder? One or two customers were already looking elsewhere for their gunpowder and did Mr Buchanan know that there had been none sent up to his mines for a week now? If he could just have a word with the master, perhaps . . .

But by now, of course, they all knew it did no good to have a word with the master.

Alex was beyond the point where the sound of their voices, their respectful and sympathetic presence beside his bed, the words of pleading to be told what they must do about this or that or the other, mattered to him.

It was the same at the mine. Workmen whistling cheerfully as they went about their work were supervised only by men who knew nothing of mine engineering, of mining as Mr Buchanan and Mr Adams had known it. They were good men, but they were somewhat at a loss when it came to decisions on the quality of the ore they mined and on the selling of it; and as one said to Mrs Buchanan, it was six months now since anyone had been to Swansea or St Helens to visit the firms there which purchased Mr Buchanan's copper. He'd go himself but he really knew nothing about it. He was in charge of the office, of finances, under Mr Buchanan's eye naturally, and he could manage by himself for a while until . . . but someone should go. Goodwill it was called and that was only one aspect of it! Contact must be kept between seller and buyer or the buyer might be distracted by another, particularly if what they ordered failed to arrive when it should. After all they must maintain their contracts to make the copper bottoms for the hulls of sailing ships, barges, and all the other uses to which Mr Buchanan's smelted ore was put, and if they could not rely on him as they always had in the past, there were mine owners in Wales only too eager to replace him in their order books, the buyers were saying!

Her mind was far away, brooding on a fascinating, quite breathless notion which had come to her several weeks ago but which as yet was no more than a tightening of her heartbeat in thrilling anticipation, a quickening of her pulses, a drawing in of her breath in fearful and yet excited dread.

She was bringing it closer to her, reeling it slowly in like a man fishing, with dream-like, hesitant hands, watching it come nearer and nearer, recognizing an idea here, a flash of imagination there, admiring the splendour of it, wondering with burning exhilaration whether she dare grasp it, when there was a knock on her parlour door. Meg opened it, stepping inside and closing it behind her with the air of a conspirator about to disclose some tremendously exciting secret. Her open country face was quite rosy and she dipped and bobbed as though the Queen herself, accompanied by Prince Albert, might be standing in the hall.

Christy had few callers, social callers that is, since Alex's accident. She did no entertaining and those of Fellthwaite's ladies who rode in their carriages from hostess to hostess, taking tea and gossiping the days away, felt quite queasy, they told one another, at the thought of the poor man who lay motionless directly above their heads, doing nothing they had heard but stare at the ceiling, speaking to no one, not even his wife, in the company of his old terrier which lay beside him.

Poor Christy Emmerson, they said. Her father and brothers gone! Jilted by the Squire's son years ago, wed uneasily to the widower who was a hard man to acommodate at the best of times, and now, in the prime of young womanhood forced to live the life of housekeeper and nurse to this invalid. Not a few ladies considered her well out of the nasty business which wives were forced to suffer in their marriage bed, the trials of pregnancy, and were envious of her freedom from it but naturally they did not say so, even to one another. And was she not now in sole charge of his financial affairs for she had no man, no family relative to step in to guide her. With three sons to raise she was almost in the state of widow but without the benefit nor hope of being able to take another husband to care for her frailness.

They stayed away after the first courtesy call and Christy was relieved. Annie came regularly, of course, glad of the excuse to help though she would wish on no one the suffering she saw in her son-in-law's eyes. She still sat with him though she knew he did not care, saying little beyond the everyday things she saw from the windows of her home and the small gossip she heard about Fellthwaite. She and Christy grew closer, more affectionate with one another than they had ever been, for it seemed they had both lost something now.

'Ooh, Mrs Buchanan, ma'am. Are you at home, please?' Meg babbled, clearly overcome by the importance of whoever it was who stood in the hall.

'Who is it, Meg?' she asked irritably for the last thing she wanted at this moment was some well-meaning friend of her mother coming to see how 'poor Mr Buchanan' was progressing. She was surprised they had not been before, since to spread the news that 'the poor man' was still fast in his bed and likely to remain there forever if he did not pull himself into some sort of order, would surely add some small excitement to the bearer's day.

''Tis the Squire, please ma'am, and he asks most particular that you might see him.'

Christy rose instantly to her feet turning that peculiar shade of white which presages a swoon. She felt the blood run from her head and panic freeze it in her veins and she could not move, not even to speak. She was not prepared for it! She had not steeled herself for this moment simply because it had not once occurred to her that it might happen. Six months and the rapture of last summer was firmly locked away in the most secret depths of her heart, kept there for the most part by her twenty-four hours a day commitment to the man who was her husband. Five years she had been married to him and in that time she had jerked and pulled, rearing back on the reins by which he guided her, from the bonds which tied her to him, but now, when he was as sharply cut away from her as though he were in his coffin beneath the ground, he held her to him with a grip of iron.

And her thoughts were held captive too, imprisoned for the most part by her own choice, only becoming free when she slept and dreamed in the uneasy sleep of one who has an ear alert for the cry of the man who never called to her. Though he was within her and always would be, Robin Forsythe had ceased to exist for the conscious Christy Buchanan.

Now he was here to shatter the composure which she had painstakingly built around herself so that she might go on!

'Tell him I'm not at home, Meg,' she said, her mouth stiff and awkward, her lips stumbling over the words. But it was too late for the door opened and there he was filling the doorway, the room, the very house with his masculinity, his shadowed brown eyes, his tall, beloved frame, and Christy was certain that in the room above the man in the bed was aware that Robin Forsythe was here. In this house of sickness there were only women and children – the latter kept well away from the sickroom now for their father frightened them – the doctor and the parson; and the virility which this man brought, the sensual need which was formed in an almost visible aura about him must surely reach every corner of the house.

Or so Christy thought as they looked at one another over Meg's bobbing head. She would have gone on staring and staring, lost in wonderment and love but Robin broke the silence which was beginning to alarm the maid.

'Mrs Buchanan, do forgive my coming unannounced but I felt I must call on your husband to see how he progresses. I have been away for several months, as you may have heard, but as soon as I arrived home and was told he was still in his bed I came to see if there was anything I could do.'

Though his voice had the warmly polite tones of a gentleman calling upon a lady whom he scarcely knew, his brown gaze had acquired the glowing softness of topaz and his attempt at nonchalance put an uncertainty, a vulnerability in his face that pulled at her heart. His hair fell in windblown feathery curls, pale and shining across his brown forehead and he held an armful of hot-house roses out to her.

She stood like a rock, silent, unable to so much as move a muscle to take them from him.

His eyes wavered from hers for a fraction of a second in the direction of the maid who still stood to attention by the half-open door and obeying his silent command Christy turned to her at last, her head moving in a painful jerk upon her shoulders.

'Thank you, Meg. That will be all. You may take the . . . the roses . . . put them in water.'

'Shall I bring tea, madam?'

Christy looked politely at Robin.

'Would you like some tea, Mr Forsythe, or perhaps something . . . ?'

'No, no thank you, Mrs Buchanan.'

The door closed behind the maid and they stood there in the quiet vacuum her going had left, and neither spoke. Far away, Christy heard the excited, delighted yapping of her sons' dogs; the warbling voice of Lou as she 'did' her butter in the dairy and the plaintive call of an early cuckoo as she looked for a suitable nest in which to deposit her egg.

'I came each day to the wood . . . for a month . . . when I returned,' he said without further preamble. 'I left notes . . . looked for them but you did not come. I was afraid

'. . . I asked after you and . . . and your husband, and they said he was still . . . I met your mother and she told me . . .'

'She did not say . . .'

'I expect she thought it best.'

'I expect so.'

'I went away thinking when I returned he would be recovered and we could perhaps . . . There was not a day, an hour when I did not think of you.' His voice was abrupt, harsh, as if he were angry.

'I'm sorry . . .'

'*Sorry!*'

'Yes, what else can I say?'

'Dear Christ . . . it is not your fault . . .'

His despairing cry tore the heart from her and she took an instinctive step towards him, her hands rising to touch him, to convey to him her own pain.

'Robin, there is nothing to be done. We cannot . . .' Her mouth worked painfully and he reached for her and in a blind movement which neither meant to happen they walked into one another's arms.

'Sweetheart . . . Christy . . . oh Christy.' His voice fluttered about her, soft as thistledown, as though he was afraid the man upstairs would hear him. For an exquisite moment they held one another, every nerve and muscle, every square inch of flesh straining to be close, then they moved apart.

He went to stand by the window, his back to her and she sat down, afraid her legs, trembling with the need to run across the room to him, might crumple beneath her.

He spoke to the pane of glass directly in front of his face.

'Will he never walk again?' His voice was bleak.

'They don't know.'

'What is wrong with him?'

'They don't know that either.'

'You have had other doctors? Old Bell is no more than a country quack. There are men in London . . .'

382

'They have been.'

'And they . . . hold out no hope?' For him and for us, his voice asked silently.

'They do not say there is no hope. They say wait, be patient. Given time he might . . . but if he does not recover soon, he will die of it.'

He swung round and for a moment his eyes held a blaze of hope though what could come of it neither knew, then it slithered away in shame. He looked down at his own strong straight body.

'I would die of it too, Christy. Poor bastard, poor bastard.'

'He is shrivelling away, Robin. His flesh is melting from his body. I do not see it for he will not allow me . . . he is a proud man, but the nurse tells me.'

It was as if she must talk of her husband, keep him there between herself and Robin Forsythe like a shield, a wall over which they might peep but must not ever again reach over.

'And his muscles have gone from lack of usage. He is simply . . . shrinking, shrinking to nothing more than a dead face on a pillow . . . oh Robin.'

He looked at her, puzzled by her intensity and his own face became still.

'You . . . care about him, do you not? You show . . . great concern, Christy.'

'Of course I do. Would you not be concerned to see a man who once was strong and arrogant brought down like a fine hunter with a broken leg? We would shoot an animal, Robin, if it were in the pain Alex suffers.'

'He is in pain?'

'Not physically. He has no feeling to realize pain, but in his head he has pain.'

'What will you do, Christy?'

'Do, Robin? What can I do but stay with him?'

'Of course.' His face was like a death mask. 'I expected no other for you are . . . Christy Buchanan.' It was the first time he had called her by her true name.

383

'My darling, I am sorry.' She swallowed the pain in her chest and throat, wishing she could weep.

He shrugged helplessly.

'I could not go away without letting you know . . . that I . . . that I think about you . . .'

'You are to go then?'

'Yes. I . . . we . . . my wife is expecting a child.'

'Yes . . . I had heard.'

'She wishes to be near her mother . . . for the birth. I would have liked . . . my . . . to be born at Dalebarrow as I was but . . . she is frail, I am told and needs . . .'

She looked into his strained face and her heart ached for the engaging youth, the fine good-natured, cheerfully loving man she had known so many years ago; and she realized sadly that he was being slowly manipulated until he had become the man his wife's parents had bought for their daughter. He was a sweet man, eager to please everyone, kind, patient and humorous but his very gentleness had made him easy prey for the subtlety of those who would manoeuvre him to their own way.

'I understand, Robin. You do not have to explain it to me. It is . . . not my concern.'

'No. I just wanted you to be aware that I shall not be here for the summer.'

'It makes no difference. I could not come to meet you, not now.'

It was said without hope.

'Of course . . . I realize that.'

'I'm sorry, Robin.'

He turned to face the window again, afraid of what he might see in her eyes.

'So! He has you now, my love.' His voice was quite expressionless.

'It seems so, Robin.' Hers was the same.

'Does he want you as much as I do?'

'He does not want me at all.'

'Then why . . . ?'

'He does not want me but he needs me.'

384

'In what way is that, Christy?' he asked with little interest, the sag of his proud shoulders dragging at him, pulling his body into an attitude of defeat.

'I'm going to run his business concerns for him, Robin.'

He whirled about, his hand reaching out to the chair-back to steady himself.

'You're . . .'

'Someone must, Robin, for they are grinding slowly to a halt without him.'

'But *you* cannot do it, Christy. You are a woman!'

'I have a brain. A good one!'

'But you know nothing of business.'

'I must do something to try and save the mine and the mill that was my father's for if they go how will my children be fed?'

He moved swiftly towards her, his arms already lifting to hold her to him, his eyes alight with the tender certainty that at last here was his chance to do something for her.

'My darling, do you think I would let you, or your children starve? You have but to ask!'

'And my husband?' She took a step back, away from his arms and they fell helplessly to his side. 'And what of your wife . . . and child? You would let them go?'

'Dear God . . . Christy!'

'Of course you would not, and neither would I.'

He shook his head in bewilderment, still so young, and trusting that if they could only work out the proper way to go about it, everyone could safely be got through this drama and a small, sweet portion be salvaged for himself and his love.

'Christy, I love you. I have loved you for so long I cannot imagine how it would be not to love you.' It was said with such honesty Christy felt the knot at her throat tighten in agony. 'I would take you away now . . . if you would come. Do you think I care about Emma or the child? It will be *her* child, hers and her mama's . . . Christy, Christy. You have only to ring for your maid to fetch your cloak. I would put you up on my horse before me as we have done so many times before and ride away with you, a knight rescuing his damsel in distress.'

He smiled sadly, knowing as he spoke it would never happen, could never happen now. He ran a finger lovingly along her silky eyebrow. 'But I am no knight and you are no damsel though your distress is obvious. You will not come, will you?'

She shook her head.

'No, and neither would you. You speak of caring nothing for your child but wait until he is put into your arms, Robin. He will put his hands about your heart and never let you go. He will be *yours*, Robin. Keep him that way, don't allow others . . .'

'I would not care how we lived, Christy,' he went on hopelessly, not listening to what she said, not knowing yet that it was true. 'Dalebarrow means nothing to me without you in it.'

'Yes it does, my darling. You love it as your father loved it.'

'No.' He sighed. 'No Christy, I love you.'

'I know, I know.'

'But I must . . . leave you?'

'Yes.'

'May I say . . . that it is . . . just for now? I must have some hope that we will meet again . . . up on the fells.'

'I must stay to look after my sons' inheritance. I must take care of it until my husband is able to do so himself. When . . . when . . . if he were ever to . . . to walk again . . .'

'Yes my darling?'

'Dear Christ . . . please go . . . please go . . .'

'Are you awake Alex?' she whispered at the doorway later that day and from the fireside Mrs Jackson rose to her feet moving regally across the bedroom to face her mistress, her starched apron crackling officiously.

386

'He is, Mrs Buchanan, but in a bit of a paddy, if you don't mind my saying so!'

'A bit of a paddy? Mrs Jackson.' Christy's voice was quite bewildered. 'Whatever for?'

'I couldn't say, but I've had my head snapped off . . .'

'Oh for Christ's sake, woman, get the hell out of here and leave me in peace.' The voice from the bed was cold, cold as the ice which formed each winter on the lakes and just as whip-cracking when it snapped, and Mrs Jackson raised her eyebrows and her big-muscled shoulders in the way of someone sorely tried.

Christy stepped into the room, gently pushing the nurse into the hallway, indicating with her head that she might go downstairs and get herself a nice cup of restoring tea. She moved across the carpet to look into the twisted face on the pillow and with a tumbling heart realized that Alex Buchanan knew that Robin Forsythe had been in his house, in his wife's parlour and probably, it was almost certain, in her arms. Someone had told him, most likely the innocent Mrs Jackson, imparting the news that his home had been honoured by a call from the Squire. The kitchen would be humming with it and if Mrs Jackson had been down there . . .

'Alex.' She stood quietly by his bedside and the dog moved his tail on welcome.

'Alex,' she said again.

'You've been whoring again, have you, madam, and in my own house.' His voice was cracked, shrill with outrage, ugly with menace. 'You bitch, you filthy slut. If I could stand I'd knock your teeth down your throat and enjoy doing it, by God. Have you not the decency to take your lovers to some other rendezvous? Must you bring your alley-cat morals into my home, in the place where your own children . . .'

In the dimness of the last of the spring daylight his eyes were hazed with the red blood of madness, glowing like live coals beneath the canopy of the bed.

'Alex . . .'

'Don't expect me to provide cover for your amours, you bitch. I have seen what you can get up to, don't forget, and I want none of it . . .'

'Alex!' Her voice was as icy as his and he turned now to glare at her, the blood running hot beneath his flesh as it had not done for six months.

'Don't you stand there and tell me . . .' he began again, but she put up an imperious hand for silence.

'Alex Buchanan, I am tired of being told what I must and must not do by you. I am bored with the sound of your voice saying "don't do this" and "do that". I find it tedious to listen to you ordering me to be what you consider the perfect wife and mother and I tell you quite frankly I have had enough of it. Yes, the Squire was here but, as you seem to think, we did not fornicate on your carpet. Believe me, if I wished to there has been ample opportunity this past six months. I am hardly likely to carry on beneath the interested eyes of my own servants. The Squire came to ask of your health for he has only just heard you were still in your bed after all this time . . .'

'Lusting after you was what he was doing, lady. Probably offering to do my job for me knowing I am unable to service my . . .'

'By God, Alex, you've a foul mouth and I will not stay to be made filthy by it. I can walk away, unlike you . . .'

Their hoarse breathing ripped through the silence which followed but now she had provoked him from his shell of impassivity she meant to keep him from it. Her voice was careful as she continued.

'He brought you some flowers, roses from his hot-house, God knows why, and informs me that his wife is to have a child and they are off to London where it will be born. We did no more than discuss your health,' she lied without shame, '. . . and then he left. I dare say I shall never see him again but then I shall have no time for socializing at Dalebarrow Hall, should I be invited. Do you want to know why, Alex? No! I shall tell you just the same.' She smiled. 'Are you ready for this since I fear it might shock

388

you. Quite simply, I am going to run your businesses, Alex, that is what I am going to do, so I shall be too busy to concern myself with calls.'

She straightened her shoulders triumphantly, lifting her head like a young goddess about to do battle with some mortal, ready for anything which she was certain her husband would aim at her. But Alex Buchanan's face had lost its livid animation and the raging blood drained away and he became quite, quite still.

'Did you hear me, Alex?' she said. 'I am going to the mining office in the morning and then to the mills to see if I can make some sense of what these men tell me. Will you not ... advise me on what questions I should ask them?' She knelt at the side of the bed, eager, now that he was quiet again to include him in her plans, eager to have the ideas in his head transferred to hers for in her naïvety she was convinced that he would not, could not refuse her. They were *his* concerns and if she were to find out exactly what was needed and bring it back to him, make herself his voice, his messenger, could they not deliver the mines and the mills back to what they were?

'Alex ...'

His thin face turned slowly away from her, the light gone now from his eyes and he resumed his careful contemplation of the ceiling.

She raised herself slowly to her feet and her face became taut and white with her anger. Her lip curled and with a defiant, mocking gesture she put her hands on her hips, throwing back the thick, loosened mane of her hair. Her eyes flashed scornfully.

'Have you nothing to say, husband? Do you not wish to command me to stay at home and do fine embroidery and see to my children, and come up here every half hour to check on your further decline? I am after all only a woman and not capable of anything else beyond this ... oh, except for the yearly task of bearing your child!'

'Dear God ... have you no ...'

'No what, Alex? Pity? Is that what you want from me?

389

Well, you shall find none here. It seems I am to have no more of your children and I cannot say I am sorry. Not now, not to a man who has not the guts to try to save what is rightfully his. No, I want no more but I tell you this. Those I have will not suffer from your refusal to face the fact that you are no longer willing to provide for them. Willing, yes, willing Alex, for if you put your mind to it, if you put your bloody mind to it you could direct your business from this room. With my help and the right men you could do it.'

'Goddammit, woman . . . get out of my room . . . my life . . .'

'Oh no, that's what you would like, wouldn't you? No one to prick that . . . that shell you have built around yourself. No one to disturb the smooth contours of the grave you have dug and buried yourself in. Well, I shan't come to put flowers on it, Alex, for I shall be too busy protecting my sons' future. That mine, my father's gunpowder mill, the factory at Stavely which was once Amy's mother's and which will be hers again one day. I may not succeed but by God I'm going to have a damn good try! Someone has to!'

CHAPTER TWENTY-FIVE

Faith had been, quite simply, appalled and said so unequivocally, repeating again and again that she had never heard anything like it and would have absolutely nothing to do with it. 'No! Don't ask me . . . no! no! Christy . . . stop it . . .' She would *not* do it and neither would Christy! They argued hotly for an hour before she began to see it did no good. She would do it anyway, Christy said, putting someone else, a stranger in charge of her children and that was worse still!

If she was fair Faith would admit that when Christy had

asked her to look after her children because she would no longer be there to do so herself, she had swung from a momentary rapturous delight at the thought of having Christy's four lovely children to herself – particularly the sweet little girl who was her favourite – to direct and nurture as she thought fit, to horror at the reason for it since had not Robin Forsythe been at Howethwaite today? Surely to God?!

'No Faith, not that.' Christy had known what was in Faith's mind. 'He came to . . . to tell me he is to go away, for good I think he meant.' She shivered as though she was suddenly cold though the elegant little parlour in which they sat that night was warm. 'No.' She lifted her head defiantly, already prepared for argument it seemed. 'No, I am going into business, Faith!'

'Business! What business?'

'I am going to manage the Buchanan Copper Mines, the Emmerson Gunpowder Mill and the bobbin factory at Stavely which belonged to the family of my husband's first wife.' It was said with supreme confidence, with the positive belief that there was really nothing to it and what there was she would quickly learn. 'I cannot, of course, run all three at one and the same time so I must go slowly at first, learn what is needed, find the right men to do it, or organize the ones already employed, and ensure that it is done properly.'

'Christy, lass . . . you cannot, you simply cannot . . .'

'Someone must, Faith. That's why I need you to help me. My children need you. It breaks my heart to leave them, they are my treasure on this earth and I have always been here when they needed me but I must do this. Will you take my place here, Faith?'

'You know I will if you must do it, but you cannot move about by yourself going to . . . to mines and mills and factories and God knows where else. Your husband would not allow it.'

'He has no choice. I gave him one and he refused it.' Her face was hard.

'Refused it?'

'Yes. I can't explain but let me just say he will certainly not deny me what I intend to do.'

'Which is?'

'I have told you. I am going to run the . . .'

'Yes, yes!' Faith brusquely waved aside Christy's calm assertion of what she was about to do. 'But what exactly are you going to *do* there?'

'I don't understand.'

'My God, Christy Buchanan, how the dickens do you expect to pick up the reins of your husband's business concerns when you cannot even answer a simple question?'

Christy bridled. 'Don't you speak to me like that, Faith Adams. I intend to . . .'

'What? Go on, what? Tomorrow morning which is when I presume you mean to start, when you climb into your carriage and give directions to Jack to take you to Conistone, or Chapel Stile or Stavely, what will you do *first* when you get there?'

She sat back triumphantly as though to say 'there, answer me that!'

'Well . . .'

'Yes?'

'Give me a moment . . .'

'To do what?'

'Let me think, damn you.'

'Best to do it here then and not at the mine shaft or at the door to the pressing-house.'

'You're right . . . what the devil comes first, Faith?'

They studied one another, the gently-reared, carefully brought-up daughter of a wealthy commercial gentleman and her maid – friend now who though her station in life was considerably lower had been equally sheltered from the harsher aspects of it. They were young women of their age, the product of a world in which men kept their women at home to rear the children they gave them; to care for the homes they put them in; to cook, or see to the cooking, of their meals; the care of their wardrobe, however meagre it might be. In that world women were not expected to recognize a balance sheet, nor how it was balanced, the workings of the machinery, or even that there was such machinery, to run a water-wheel, a lathe, or indeed any of the hundred and one parts of the hundred and one businesses which thrived, not just in Westmorland and the surrounding Lakeland but in the country, in the world! They were taught nothing but how to run a home, how to be *domesticated*! It was as simple as that. They knew no more, any of them, so where was Christy Buchanan to begin? She had never listened, not with any degree of attention to her husband, her father or her brothers, when they spoke of their day, and if she had would it have told her what she must do tomorrow?

'What . . . what would you advise, Faith?'

'Nay lass . . .'

'I cannot just give up. There must be a starting point!'

'Will not Mr Buchanan tell you where . . . ?'

'No, he does not . . . care to.'

'Perhaps Mrs Emmerson might . . . ?'

'I cannot . . . would not like to bother her . . .'

'No . . .'

'Well, this is a fine beginning, I must say.' Christy stood up briskly, shaking out the pretty peach flounces of her dress, looking down at the crisp organdy with a certain astonishment. Was it only a few hours since she had put on this gown with the intention of looking sweetly pretty in order to charm her husband's managers? To charm them with what in mind? In truth she did not know, nor did she know what she would do tomorrow but when she got there she would know and she would damn well do it!

'Good morning, Mr Tate.' She smiled serenely as she was handed by Jack from her carriage the next day, greeting the mine's office manager as he came hurrying down the steep flinty track to meet her. He bowed awkwardly, his feet none too sure on the path, his tongue none too sure on the words, and as he babbled incredulously on this surprise, she had time to consider anxiously the steepness of the path she must take. She had done it the last time in her frantic, bewildered panic to get up to where she had been told Alex was injured, perhaps dead, but she had no recollection now of how she had done it. But climb it she must – and in a copy of what Miss Susan Whittam had assured her was a Paris gown – wondering how on earth she could have forgotten this hill which she must ascend to get to the mine.

She had been determined to look her best in this, one of the most important moments of her life, knowing from past experience that confidence in oneself was vastly improved by the knowledge that one looked poised – even if one wasn't! – so she had put on her newest morning dress of coffee and cream-striped silk. It had an open bodice filled in with cream lace, tight sleeves and a deep flounce on the enormously wide skirt trimmed with the same lace, and with it she wore a saucy bonnet of cream straw. The wide, coffee-coloured velvet ribbons were attached to the brim itself, the very latest style so that when they were tied beneath her chin the brim was drawn inwards towards her cheeks forming a circular frame to her face. The colours suited her, turning the whiteness of her skin to the hue of rich, new cream and shading her clear grey eyes to deep smoke.

'Start as you mean to go on,' Annie had told her a hundred times and that was just what she intended to do. First impressions were important and if she gave off an air of positive belief in herself and her right to be here in Alex's place, a sureness, an unmistakable conviction that no one could possibly question, then she would carry it off. It would all be bluff but they would not know it. They must be made to think she was perfectly at ease. Once she had made that first step, got past their first shocked disapprobation she would continue the illusion of the detached calm she did not feel.

But she had made her first mistake in wearing this

elegant gown! A good sturdy cloth made up into a plain and sensible riding costume in a muted colour, with separate skirt and bodice would be more appropriate. Well-cut, of course, perhaps with a ruffled shirt like those worn by gentlemen and a cravat. Pantaloons beneath for easier walking and climbing, and half boots of good leather and tall riding hat of beaver . . . with a ribbon.

'Mrs Buchanan, ma'am . . .' Mr Tate was saying. 'Is there something wrong? Not Mr Buchanan, surely?'

Mr Tate was quite devastated by her appearance, fumbling with the fell gate to get at her, to hand her back into her carriage which she seemed intent on leaving, to bow and tell her how charming she looked on this bright spring morning, to stand and admire the view with her – anything at all to get her away from the small crowd which was gathering to gawp. They had seen her before, naturally, on the day of their employer's accident but then they had all been drawn together in the comradeship which comes about at times of disaster. She had been one of them on that day for her own husband had been involved but now she was a curiosity, a grand lady, one of the leisured classes in her beautiful silk with her fine carriage and glossy horses. What could she want here with them, their inquisitive expressions asked? The women bobbed a curtsey as she moved beyond the row of cottages in which they lived, undeterred by Mr Tate's hovering anxiety to have her return to her carriage, but the children were inclined to run beside her, darting about like gad-flies, expressing their astonishment and amusement with a cat-call or two.

'Mrs Buchanan.' Mr Tate was almost as nimble as they as he nipped about her skirts like a small terrier. 'To what do we owe this honour? I trust that all is well at home . . . May I ask why you are here . . . yes, it is a fine day, ma'am. . . and Mrs Buchanan, my goodness, those shoes . . . if I may say so, are not really suitable . . . Indeed, it is good to see the end of the winter and . . . Yes, ma'am, I do agree, this is quite a stiff climb, may I offer you my arm?'

When they reached the waterfall he could bear it no longer.

'Mrs Buchanan, please ma'am, I must ask you why you are making this hazardous climb up to the mine. It is really not suitable for a lady. I am afraid you might slip and fall and Mr Buchanan would not be at all pleased . . .'

'I am here on his behalf, Mr Tate.' she interrupted smoothly, bestowing on him a candid, glowing smile, her soft grey eyes like velvet. 'He cannot, at the moment, get up here himself so to put his mind at rest I said I would come up and look around and give him an account of what I saw . . .'

'But I can do that, Mrs Buchanan. You have only to say the word and I can come along to Howethwaite. I should be only too pleased to do so . . . daily if Mr Buchanan wished and give him a full report. He did not appear . . . er . . . concerned the last time I came and I thought . . . well, you spoke of putting another manager, an engineer to replace Mr Adams and I have done my best to keep things going until then. I had no idea, the last time we spoke that you intended . . .'

'Mr Tate, please, no one is blaming you for any . . . problems which may have arisen and indeed, my husband *does* intend putting in a new engineer, someone who can see to the . . . the technical working of the mine until he is able to do so himself.'

'Mr Buchanan is . . . recovering, then?' Mr Tate spoke delicately, no doubt remembering the wasted, still and staring figure of his employer the last time he had seen him.

'It is a slow business, Mr Tate, you understand, but . . .'

'Of course, of course, but if I may say . . .'

'Yes, Mr Tate?'

'Until then I really think it is best to . . .'

'Yes, Mr Tate?'

'Well, Mrs Buchanan, forgive me, but the mine is hardly the place for a lady.'

They had reached the level plateau amongst the hills

which she recalled vaguely seeing six months ago, containing a vast sprawl of sheds and workshops and offices and the hideous clatter of machinery. The noise made any further conversation if not impossible, extremely difficult. Great masses of ore, just come from below ground, were being thrown from the wagons which had brought it out into heaps over which a fast flow of water rushed, cleaning the lumps of ore and quartz to show more clearly what each lump contained. Men were like ants about it, raking it on a grating along which numerous small boys, and some women, were actively engaged in picking out and separating the richest pieces of ore. The boys leaped about the grating like a tribe of small, incredibly agile monkeys, expert even at such a young age in making their selection, sorting and tossing each rock into its proper receptacle. The richest portion was carried at once to the crushing mill and the remainder was thrown into another shed to be broken up and further picked over and what was useless was wheeled off to a rubbish heap.

The ore was passed twice through the crushing mill on an endless chain of iron buckets where it was ground to the size of coarse sand. From there it was carried to the 'jigging' troughs, large square boxes filled with water; and by the process of 'jigging' or agitating the ore-filled boxes under water the grains of pure ore which are heavy, fell through the grating to the bottom of the box. The remainder was carried away for a further pounding and washing or 'buddling', each time drawing off more deposits of ore and separating the impurities. Even the waste water, once it had been used, was collected and the slime from it, looking like bronze, was shipped with all the other ore to Swansea to be smelted.

The din was horrendous. Down on the slope where the miners' cottages were, the sound of the ore-dressing plant addressed the ears in a muted clangour, dulled somewhat by the surrounding hills, but up here it beat against the ear-drums in a wave. There seemed to be hundreds of workers about the site, all intent on some task, and Christy could feel their stares, especially those of the men, as though they had never seen a woman before.

She had never felt so out of place in her life.

'Shall we go into the office?' Mr Tate shouted in her ear and she nodded thankfully, allowing him to lead her across the uneven, worn grass to the brick building which housed the offices. Here, though the explosion of sound could still be heard, it was relatively quiet and she was glad to sit down in Mr Tate's office and accept his offer of tea.

'Where is my husband's office, Mr Tate?' she asked innocently.

'Oh that is on the upper floor, Mrs Buchanan.' He studied her, his expression one of approval for a lovely woman, mixed with displeasure that she should be flaunting her loveliness about in such an unsuitable place. It said he was reluctantly willing to give her tea and a few moments of his valuable time, but the sooner she was on her way back to her own environment the better he would like it. If she felt the need to look over her husband's concerns that was her affair, and there was nothing he could do to stop it. He considered her statement that her husband had *sent* her to be ludicrous, so it must be sheer curiosity that had got her up here – though God knows why any lady should want to see it was beyond him – but he could do no more than offer her tea, then escort her back to her carriage. Wasting a good hour or so of his valuable time, that was all it was, but he could do nothing about it for after all she was his employer's wife.

'I'd like to see it if I may,' she said sweetly, setting her cup and saucer on the desk.

'I beg your pardon?' Mr Tate was clearly bewildered.

'I'd like to see my husband's office.'

'But why . . . ?'

'Mr Tate.' Her voice had become tart. 'Would you direct me to my husband's office.'

'Of course, but . . .'

Alex's office though kept polished and dusted and swept, ready for his return, had obviously not been used since he strode out of it on the heels of David Adams six months ago. It was tidy, without a paper on the desk, the pens and pencils and paper knife all neatly placed by some careful hand, the inkwell dried up, the silver stand cleaned, the chair set in its symmetrical position before the desk, with a faintly musty air about the whole thing. The panelled walls shone dully in the dim light and from them a row of pictured elderly gentlemen – who were they? – looked down at her with what seemed to be hostility in their eyes.

'Hmm,' she said, looking about her speculatively. 'Yes, I think this will do. Does my husband have private . . . er . . . facilities, Mr Tate?'

'Facilities . . . ?'

'Yes, a . . . a dressing room . . . for . . . a room where . . . ?'

'Why, Mrs Buchanan!' Mr Tate was clearly shocked. 'I cannot see . . .'

Christy sighed deeply, looking at Mr Tate as though considering how she was possibly to keep her patience about such a fussy, pedantic little man and yet at the same time she knew he was merely doing his job *and* trying to be a gentleman whilst he did it.

'Mr Tate,' she said briskly now. 'I might as well tell you. I shall be using this office several times a week . . .'

'Using this office! Mrs Buchanan, I cannot . . .'

'If you will allow me to continue.'

'Mrs Buchanan. Does Mr Buchanan know that you are here . . . ?'

'Mr Tate.' Her voice was dangerously soft. 'May we get one thing perfectly clear. If you and I are to have an amicable working relationship . . .'

'A working relationship!' Mr Tate's face was a picture of comic disbelief.

'Yes, then I must insist that you do not dispute every sentence I utter, and I would be obliged if you would not repeat every word I say, either. I am to take my husband's place for a while, that is all, act as his . . . proxy . . . is that the word, and I shall need this office in which to do it. And I shall need a dressing room in which to . . . change.'

'*Change!*'

'There you go again, Mr Tate.' She smiled mischievously. 'I shall want to change from . . . from whatever I am wearing into clothing suitable for going underground . . .'

'*Underground!*'

'Underground, Mr Tate. I feel I must at least go down and see what is taking place and I must rely on you to help me in this. Perhaps you could arrange for one of the mine foremen to accompany me and explain the various processes of mining . . .'

Mr Tate's voice thundered – there could be no other word for it – through Alex Buchanan's office and for several minutes Christy was quite overcome with admiration for her husband's office manager for there was no doubt he was a brave man, believing firmly that right was on his side in denying absolutely Mrs Buchanan's entitlement to go down her husband's mine. It was not only dangerous and filled with every peril which could beset a man, never mind a lady, from falling rock to gunpowder smoke which might damage the lungs, the difficulty in climbing ladders and wading through water, the rats which abounded and which would surely throw her into hysterics, men who might not watch their language or even be . . . in a state of undress! It was highly, *highly* unsuitable for a woman . . . beg pardon . . . a lady to go underground and he could not stress the fact strongly enough. Mr Buchanan – and Mr Tate was not yet convinced he even knew of it – would simply not allow it and Mr Tate was honour bound to do what he believed his employer would want. If Mrs Buchanan felt she must . . . must sit in Mr Buchanan's office and do whatever it was she had come to do, then he, Jasper Tate, could do nothing to prevent it, but he absolutely forbade her to go down the mine unless she had her husband's written permission to do so.

His face was the colour of a ripe plum and she was afraid he was about to have an apoplectic fit!

She had expected it, of course. She had expected disbelief, resentment, incredulity, hostility, even amusement and she knew she would get it wherever she went, but she had made up her mind that if she showed them she had a quick brain, resolve and the strength to use both she would make them accept her. They could not physically bar her from Alex's concerns since without actually hearing it from his own lips, which was unlikely, that they were not to allow her to do it, they would not be altogether sure he had not given his permission, was even enthusiastic about it. There were so many reasons in their minds why she should be persuaded, forced to stay at home and mind the babies. She had not the physical strength of a man; she had not the knowledge though she was prepared to bluff this out somehow; she knew nothing of commerce, the state of the market, profit and trading, balance sheets and accounting – but she could learn. She could learn and she meant to, but she was not going to say so to this man.

She sighed. It would make no difference what she said so she must just bluster her way through. Assume her most regal manner, her most compelling imperious demeanour and challenge them to defy Mrs Alexander Buchanan, the wife of the man who owned these mines, these mills. She must be arrogant, as *he* was, overbearing, as *he* was, demanding their obedience, as *he* did. She could lie until she was old and grey and the mines gone out of business for lack of a hand to control them, *this* man would not believe that Alex Buchanan would place his trust in a wife who looked as though she had not only just come from a Paris fashion design house, but had not a sensible thought in her head! Pretty women were meant merely to decorate. All women had been trained from birth to be able to do nothing but bear a man his children and run his home. The men with whom she was about to do battle would dig in their heels and prove as awkward as they knew how, swearing they could manage until Mr Buchanan was able to take up his duties again. It was not needed for Mrs Buchanan to bother her head about ledgers and sales invoices and production figures, Mr Tate would say firmly, and as for going down the mine, as he was saying firmly, well the men simply would not have it. Now and again Mr Buchanan allowed male visitors, gentlemen interested in his mining methods to venture underground, but a woman, a lady, and his wife! *Never!*

Christy stood quietly at the window, looking out over the busy ore-dressing plant and waited for him to run out of words. Then she turned, walked to the desk and sat down in the chair behind it. She took a deep breath.

'Mr Tate, may we get one thing straight before you refuse me permission to enter the mines. For the want of a better description shall we say that until Mr Buchanan comes up that track to take over what is his, you may assume that I am Mr Buchanan. Anything Mr Buchanan did, I am to do. Did my husband enter the mines . . . yes . . . then I shall do the same.'

'But for what reason, Mrs Buchanan?'

Her face was set in cold, resentful lines now, outrageously annoyed with this servant who questioned her right to go about her own domain.

'My husband wishes me to report on the progress in every stage in the mining of his copper ore, and I can hardly do that sitting taking tea in his office, can I, Mr Tate? I wish to talk with the men on this shift and find out their views on the . . .'

'The *men's* views, Mrs Buchanan?'

'Yes. You have foremen working the mine, I presume, Mr Tate, and at the moment without an engineer such as Mr Adams was, they are the ones best qualified to answer what I want to know.' Whatever that might be, she added silently to herself, praying she could carry on this subterfuge and find some information which might prove useful.

'Now, Mrs Buchanan . . .'

'Have *you* been down Crossbarrow lately?'

'No . . . that is not my job but . . .'

'Or Big Garth, Moordale, Eagle Nest . . .'

'Mrs Buchanan! It is not my job to go underground.'

'Then someone must do it, Mr Tate, and as my husband cannot, I will.'

Mr Tate became quiet then, and his face closed up. His voice was as coolly polite as hers.

'Mrs Buchanan, I cannot stop you working in this office. I cannot stop you from perusing your husband's books nor from studying his balance sheet from as far back as you wish to go but I can prevent you from going underground. I have only to speak to the man who is in charge of the kibbles at the mine shaft, and you would not be allowed to put a foot on the ladder, *and I shall*. If you are to go underground I must either have it from your husband's own lips or a letter written in his own hand. I'm sorry, Mrs Buchanan, but I will not take the responsibility. Now, if you have finished with me I must get back to my work.'

He bowed politely and left the room.

It was precisely the same at the bobbin factory!

An intermediary was the word she confidently used to Mr Dunlop, the manager at the Harkness Bobbin Factory at Stavely when she introduced herself.

'But I am well able to run the factory until Mr Buchanan is on his feet again, Mrs Buchanan,' the man said, quite affronted that his employer should send his own wife, a lady, into the male-dominated, male-operated confinement of the bobbin mill. Christy herself was extremely disconcerted as she stepped from the hansom cab which had brought her from the Stavely railway station, into the inches deep, rutted mud track which led to the bobbin mill, for a sudden downpour of heavy rain had turned the surface of the track into a quagmire. Her stylish shoes, already damaged on the path to the mine, were irretrievably ruined and the hem of her gown was thickly stained with the oozing brown liquid before she had moved more than a yard from the hansom.

A man hurried forward, cap in hand, intent on directing her back into her carriage for surely there must be some mistake, but she brushed him aside, asking to be shown to the office of Mr Dunlop. The mill was set somewhat out of the village hidden away in a damp patch of woodland, sited beside a small, rapidly flowing beck which threaded from the River Gowan. The water-wheel which powered the mill stood tall, going round in a mad whirl of spraying water, behind the clutter of buildings; and in every direction Christy looked the piles of long coppice poles from which the bobbins were made were stacked upright.

As at the mine, men stared curiously, some even with undue familiarity, sturdy dalesmen with brown speculative faces and springing curls on which they carelessly pitched a cloth cap, shirt sleeves rolled up despite the rain. There were carts pulled by horses, all piled with lengths of wood, or empty and on their way back to the coppice woodlands to fetch more supplies, the clatter of machinery coming from the open doorway, and over it all the fragrant tang of new timber.

Mr Dunlop, warned now by some unseen messenger, hastened from the open doorway, his face expressing consternation for what the devil was pretty little Mrs Buchanan doing up to her ankles in the mud, her silk dress already ruined by the look of it, the lovely velvet ribbons on her straw bonnet beginning to wilt in the drizzle which fell about it.

'Mrs Buchanan, good heavens, what can be the matter? I do hope Mr Buchanan has not . . .' He could think of nothing which might have brought his employer's wife all this way to the mill unless some dreadful occurrence? . . . but what? And why?

'No, no, Mr Dunlop. Do not concern yourself. My husband is progressing nicely, but of course he is not yet able to come himself to see to his business so he has sent me instead.'

She smiled gaily and began to walk determinedly in the direction of Mr Dunlop's office taking no heed, it seemed, of the sucking mud which threatened to tear her shoes from her feet, not even waiting for Mr Dunlop to follow and show her the way.

'What a dreadful day it has turned out to be, Mr Dunlop. This weather of ours really cannot be relied upon, can it? I swear the sun was burning my face when I left home and I had to put up my parasol but now I am in dire need of an umbrella. But I had to come for Mr Buchanan was anxious that I make a start . . . oh, and would you ask the driver to wait for me, and indeed, if he could pull a little closer to the doorway I would be most grateful. I should have worn stouter shoes but I shall next time.'

Next time! Mr Dunlop scampered after her, his face scarlet and horribly embarrassed as Mrs Buchanan blundered, not into his office as she intended but directly into the centre of the bobbin-making operation where the eye of every man in the room fell on her; a huge room filled with the harsh grating and clatter and whirr of machinery. There were fan belts and wheels everywhere, machines and cloth-capped men and boys, timber, ladders, shreds and shavings and slivers of wood six inches deep on the floor and a fine film of sawdust hanging like a creamy mist from floor to ceiling and coating every square inch of man and machine alike. There were baskets filled with bobbins in various stages of production, saw-horses, a fine spider's web of ropes and pulleys and such a snarl of activity Christy came to an appalled halt, convinced she had stepped into a madhouse!

Mr Dunlop's hand was on her arm and, quite senseless with the noise, she allowed herself to be drawn away and into a small, quieter room, but just as cluttered, with desks and stools and clerks.

'Sit down, Mrs Buchanan, please and allow me to give you a . . .' A *what*! This was no drawing room in which tea was served nor was it the splendid office Mr Buchanan himself had up at his mines. This was a relatively small business, begun by the father of Mr Buchanan's first wife, a nice steady business making a healthy profit, but not to be compared with his employer's other ventures. The men brought their own food and drink, as he did himself, put up for him by his wife in his manager's house in Stavely.

'No, please, Mr Dunlop. I want nothing to drink.' Christy saved the poor man the embarrassment of agonizing over the producing of a cup of tea and sat down gladly, giving herself a moment or two to recover her senses before she took up the thread of her visit.

'I'm sorry, Mrs Buchanan, if you had only informed me of your . . . your visit I could have had my wife fetch something up.' The manager was stiff, his face set in lines of indignation for he considered Mrs Buchanan to be overstepping, not only the lines of propriety but the bounds of respect which should be shown to him as manager. A spy, that's what he reckoned her to be, though what Mr Buchanan was thinking about sending her along like this he could not imagine. That is if he *had* sent her. His employer had only to summon him and he would go up to Howethwaite and report personally on the progress of the mill which had never faltered, not once, in all the years Mr Dunlop had been manager. No, not even now, with the owner lying ill in his bed, which the accounts books would show. And the last time Mr Dunlop had seen Mr Buchanan, just after Christmas it was, the man had stared through him as though he was a pane of glass. Now he was expected to believe he was himself again and working from his sickroom through this elegantly fashionable lady who knew nowt about the making of bobbins, and if he had her right, couldn't read a balance sheet if her life depended on it!

Christy Buchanan could *not* read a balance sheet *then* but one thing she *could* do and that was to please, charm if you like, those who were determined not to be charmed. She was also a good judge of character and she could see that though Mr Dunlop was quite sure of the ground he stood on in his own domain he was not altogether certain of what to make of *her*. She was the wife of the owner of the mill and could not be ignored, nor forcibly ejected and

Christy smiled to herself as she watched the expression of longing to do just that clench the mouth of Mr Dunlop.

'Mr Dunlop, please.' She smiled winningly and held up a gloved hand. 'Think no more about it. I came merely to see that . . . all is well . . .' The slight hesitation was not lost on Mr Dunlop who was an astute man of business and could also discriminate between strength and weakness – and this woman was strong. 'I shall keep you but half an hour. Will you show me round, if you please.'

'Show you round, Mrs Buchanan?' Mr Dunlop was astounded.

'Yes, if you have a moment. If not . . . perhaps your . . . assistant . . .' She turned her brilliant smile on the young clerk who sat at a high desk, goggle-eyed and open-mouthed.

'But Mrs Buchanan . . .'

'No, Mr Dunlop, I absolutely insist. My husband would go round with you if he were here, would he not, so I must do the same as his . . . agent. I must report to him all that is happening.'

'But will you understand it, Mrs Buchanan?' Mr Dunlop asked drily but in his eyes shone a growing respect for this woman who dared him to defy her.

'Perhaps not, but you shall explain it to me.'

And so the gratified operatives were treated to the sight of the delectable wife of their employer being given a 'grand tour' of the whole of the Harkness Bobbin Mill, shepherded by the expressionless manager who had no option but to stand beside her at every process in the manufacture of bobbin reels – from the sawing of the poles into lengths slightly longer than the finished reels; the 'blocking-out' of the bobbins, to where they were passed into a drying kiln. In the next room the operatives 'wrinced' the size of the holes to the exact specification required, Mr Dunlop explained tonelessly – though he did not say what 'wrinced' meant – and from there they were sent to be 'finished' by hand. Finally the finished bobbins were dyed or waxed by tumbling them in a hand-turned revolving drum containing lumps of wax.

'And they go from here to . . . where, Mr Dunlop?'

'Why, to Lancashire, ma'am, to the cotton industry. The textile plants of south Lancashire are supplied with Lake District bobbins by as much as fifty per cent of their needs. But then Mr Buchanan must have explained that to you when he made you his . . . agent!'

Mr Dunlop could not resist a satisfied smile but Christy wiped it briskly from his face.

'Quite so, Mr Dunlop. Now if you will have your accounts books and ledgers put in the hansom cab I will be on my way. Mr Buchanan intends to study every contract and negotiation you have made in his name over the past six months, and to ascertain the exact profits received. He assures me he will take no longer than necessary and will send them back within the week. Oh, and I will take some samples of your finished bobbins, if I may. Just a few at random so that my husband can compare the quality with those which you turned out before his accident. It is not that he does not trust you, Mr Dunlop, believe me, but a manufacturer has his reputation to keep up and his good name to protect. I'm sure you would agree with me. Thank you, sir, and good day to you!'

CHAPTER TWENTY-SIX

It was one of the wettest summers on record that year and Christy Buchanan felt the damp and the misery and the bleakness which swirled about the fells and the lowlands, enter her soul, falling about her like the low lying clouds which lay across the mountains she rode through.

Each day she dragged herself from the bed into which it seemed she had only just that moment fallen, rising sometimes as the early light of the summer day struck Wansfell Pike in the east, not sunlight for there was very little of that in her life, but the misted gauze of daylight which passed for it.

Sally, her devoted Sally — who it appeared did not sleep much either for she was there each night to put Christy into her bed — was always up to help her with her hair and to see her into one of the elegantly tailored riding habits she would put out for her.

Christy had decided from that first bad start that she would not dress 'suitably' — if there was such a word to describe what the whole of Fellthwaite gossiped about — as she navigated her way carefully through the hazardous journeys of her new life, and so she had designed some outfits which she had taken to Miss Susan Whittam with instructions to have them made up within the week. Good cloth, plain and serviceable, able to withstand the vagaries of the Lakeland weather, but in strong colours. A clear, deep green, another in mulberry, a third in a rich russet brown, one in black, simple and elegant, and the last a lighter, softer flowing voile, shaded a pale silver grey the exact colour of her eyes, for warmer weather. The bodice was cut tight in the style of a man's waist-length jacket, and beneath it she wore a white, pleated and frilled shirt with a waterfall of ruffles at her neck and a crisp flat-bowed cravat. The skirts were full with yards of material gathered at the waist to fall in graceful folds about her feet, but at the side she instructed Miss Whittam to arrange a corded loop which could be contrived to lift up and fasten the hem of the skirt so that walking and climbing was made easier. Beneath it she wore matching pantaloons tucked into black leather boots so that at all times she was completely modest. Her tall top hats, just like those once worn by her husband, were in colours dyed to match each outfil, with a wide ribbon in a contrasting shade about the crown, tied at the back in a dashing bow, the wide ends left to drift down between her shoulder blades.

She looked quite stunning but not at all how Fellthwaite liked its ladies to look! And what she did was worse! Going about completely unescorted in her carriage, riding up to Conistone in all weathers, sitting in her husband's office and dealing with her husband's miners, some of them ... well, one could only call them quite rough, mixing with men one would not allow in one's stable yard; striding about in those unladylike outfits of hers and, one was told, accosting her husband's managers as they tried to go about their work. It was said she commanded to be told every facet of the refining of copper ore, as if that was anything to do with a lady; and on one occasion she had actually donned a working-man's clothes and spent a whole day going through the whole process of the manufacture of gunpowder, from the incorporating house to the dust removal and wax dip houses – though naturally this could not be true for even Christy Buchanan would hardly dare to be so bold, and besides, was it likely Annie Emmerson, her poor mother, would allow it?

And what of the gossip which had blazed throughout the town like raging wildfire when it was learned that she had demanded to be taken *underground* at her husband's mine. A lady – if one could call her that though Fellthwaite seriously doubted it now – to actually go down alone into the depths of the earth in which hundreds of men worked, when it was considered improper to ride alone in a carriage with a male who was not a relative *in broad daylight*! The town rocked with it!

No one said anything of Alex Buchanan, poor man, for it was well-known he was not long for this world and had no control, nor interest, it was rumoured in what his infamous wife did. She traipsed about the countryside in all weathers, urging her coachman to dash at speeds which could only endanger lives if one should meet her, leaping from her carriage to the railway train – on which she travelled quite alone – to Stavely and the bobbin mill which was another of her husband's concerns, and there was even a whisper that she and the manager there, a Mr Dunlop, were more than a little friendly!

One took many of these rumours with a pinch of salt, naturally, for she was the daughter of Annie Emmerson, a truly good woman and a pillar of the community, but, as the saying goes, there is no smoke without fire and Christy Buchanan had always been known for a firebrand. And what of her children? Left in the care of a woman who had been no more than a scullery maid in her mother's kitchen, uneducated and certainly not fit to rear the sons of a gentleman, even if he lay in his bed uncaring.

Fellthwaite shook its head in disbelief!

Christy Buchanan was fully aware of all that was said of her and she was sorry, but as there was simply nothing she could do about it, she put it firmly from her mind and carried on with what she had set herself to do. One day, when she had time – when the mill and the mine and the factory were returned to the healthy state in which they had been under her husband's guidance – then she would make the effort to be the lady her sons would need for a mother, to play the mistress of Howethwaite and do all the things that were expected of her. But until then she was simply too distracted by the urgent obligation of holding her sons' inheritance together to worry about the gossip.

It was three months since she had begun the terrifyingly daunting task of attempting to replace Alex Buchanan in

411

the businesses he operated, and yet when she thought back to the beginning it seemed a lifetime away. And where had it got her! *What* had it got her but the rigid disapproval and resentment of the men with whom she tried to deal. They were sullen, politely so for she *was* the wife of the owner and they were not yet certain she had not got his blessing in this mad scheme of hers; but obviously disbelieving when she implied that Mr Buchanan was intent on continuing to run his concerns from his bed, using herself as messenger. They were patronizing as she flustered her way through 'orders', said to come from Mr Buchanan but agonized over and composed by herself in the long evenings when she pored over the companies' books, weekly reports, audits, accounts and wages books, letters from customers containing orders and complaints, most of which made not a grain of sense to her. She inferred that her husband was in full control of his mind. Though his body was temporarily out of order his brain was not and things would go on just as usual with herself as spokesman, she said, for them and for Mr Buchanan.

They could not believe what was being asked of them, clinging like terriers to the ledgers she demanded to see. They were outraged when she had made it clear that she intended speaking to every man in her husband's employ whether he be miner, cooper, the men and women who worked in the crushing and sorting mills or the smelt mills or the carters who took the ore to Nibthwaite Quay and from there to Greenodd, the major copper port for Westmorland.

In short Mrs Buchanan meant to delve into every brain of every man, woman and child who was employed in the Buchanan Mining Company for it was only in this way that she would learn exactly what was done there. She would go down to each level, she said, despite Mr Tate's refusal to allow it, to see the conditions the miners worked in. 'How many fathoms, two hundred and five, and a fathom was what? Six feet, well there, Mr Tate, I have learned something already. Mr Buchanan? He is progressing nicely, thank you, Mr Tate,' she lied prettily. When she left the site she would fall back in her carriage almost in a swoon, allowing her limbs to tremble and her breathing to sob in her throat, for then there was no one to see her but Jack and he kept his back sympathetically turned towards her.

It was marginally easier for her at the gunpowder mill for here she was on familiar ground for she had been on several occasions, the last on the day her brothers were killed, to the site of the mill. She knew many of the men who touched their caps to her and were prepared to stop and ask how she was, and Mr Buchanan, and would talk if it pleased her to do so.

Mr Cartmell and Mr Anderson and particularly Mr Pendle were not so well disposed and though as their employer's wife they could hardly order her from the site, their expressions said she would be best at home with her children, leaving them to muddle on as best they could until it was decided what was to be done with what had once been her father's pride and joy.

'Does Mr Buchanan intend to sell?' Mr Cartmell asked tentatively, speaking the unspoken thoughts of them all for what else *could* he do, poor devil, and wondering, no doubt, if their jobs could be held on to in the upheaval.

'Sell, Mr Cartmell? Whatever put that in your mind?' Christy laughed. 'Why should my husband sell?' The very idea seemed to amuse her and the gentlemen looked confused for even they knew with no one in charge to hold it all together, no matter how hard they worked, the business would no longer be the profit-making concern it should be.

She worked every day of the week for even on Sunday she spent several hours in Alex's study going over the weekly balance sheets, the company books and accounts, despairing that she would ever convince her husband's managers, foremen and even the nudging, winking ordinary workmen to take her seriously.

Strangely, the only man to recognize and respect the

determined strength of Christy Buchanan was Mr Dunlop at the bobbin factory. He was a man of fifty or so, a blunt man, conscientious and hardworking and he admired it in others. The mill he managed for Mr Buchanan was the only one of his employer's concerns that continued to work, and show profit, as it had done before the day of the accident. Though he had at first resented Mrs Buchanan's intrusion into *his* affairs he found himself forming a regard for her audacious tenacity, her absolute resolution to take up her husband's duties and reluctantly, gruffly he had offered to explain his clerk's neat book-keeping. He pointed out the quickest and most efficient way to balance one row of figures against another, and with this small toe in the door Christy was able to unravel the complexities of his, and through his, the other business methods of accountancy.

Now she could read a balance sheet!

Every morning except Sunday Faith would be in the kitchen waiting for her as the cock began his crowing to rise the rest of the servants, and if Mrs Avery was not yet up would make her a pot of tea, perhaps fry a slice of bacon or coddle an egg to see her on her way.

She would stride forcefully into her husband's bedroom, a dramatically lovely figure bringing life and vigour into the sterile atmosphere of the sickroom for whatever she did to prevent it the odour was always there.

'Good morning, Alex,' she would say, bending over the bed to look into his face, never giving up hope in those first months that she might see a response there – an expression which said that at last he was getting a grip on the hand she held out to him as she recounted her day, what had once been *his* day – but every morning it was the same. A slow turning away of his head, a blank transfer of his gaze towards the open window, or far worse, a stare directed at her with such uncaring deadness her heart cringed in her breast. No matter what she did she could not stop herself from shrinking a little as that coldness fell about her. He repulsed her with it, just as though her life and spirit offended the non-existence of his, as though what she now was had been stolen by her from him, leaving him empty and lifeless and without purpose.

'Share it with me, Alex,' she had begged him night after night. 'Tell me what is in your head. Help me. Let me help you! Let me give you what I have,' and she would sit beside his bed, recounting every moment of her day, telling him what had been told her, describing what she had seen, reading out the columns of figures which danced before her tired eyes, but which she was proud of now being able to understand; ready to discuss with him their meaning in the way of profit or loss. But he said nothing, refusing to answer beyond telling her to do as she pleased as long as she left him alone. He no longer cared what happened, he said tiredly – no, not even to his sons, when she begged him to consider them – and if she would turn down the lamp as she went out he would be obliged for he wished to sleep.

He no longer became angry and it had begun to frighten her. Once he would have railed at her, abused her in a rage of anger and despair, shouting at her in language which offended Mrs Jackson, calling her names, his face livid, his eyes hot and hating her – but now he simply withdrew himself to some mystical plane where she could not reach him.

'What must I do about this letter from Swansea, Alex? They are having some problem with the smelting and are writing to see if you could . . .'

'The wood for the barrels has not yet arrived. Do you advise me to go direct to Andrew Dyer or . . .?'

'The price of saltpetre has gone up, Alex. Shall I cost the rise into the price of the powder or . . .?'

'They say there is a crack in the vein but without a trained man it is hard to . . .'

'Mr Tate has refused to allow me . . .'

'I can find no reason for the answer in this column . . .'

'No matter what I say they will not believe . . .'

'They are asking to see you again. Will you not . . .?'

'Explain this contract, will you, Alex . . .?'

'They say they will cancel this order . . .'

'They are a month behind in their payments. What must I do . . .?'

She might as well have addressed herself, and with as much result to her four-year-old son, and she began to realize finally, that she was, simply, on her own. She must, in fact, make her own decisions and whether they were right or wrong she must stand by them. If he answered at all it was merely to tell her vaguely that she must do as she liked. He was, if possible, thinner than he had been three months ago and his flesh was the colour of damp clay. His thick brown hair had streaks of white in it and his eyes had become cloudy just as though, now that he no longer used them to do anything beyond stare at the ceiling, they had become unfocussed, useless and dead as the rest of him. When he did speak his voice was hesitant, a whisper almost and when he was spoken to he took several long seconds to become aware of it and even more to reply. He was semi-comatose, slipping more and more rapidly towards a completely unconscious state. Nothing roused him. His brain was stimulated by nothing she said or did. Nothing brought him back from the far distant places he roamed when he was alone, and more and more often she could see a strange contentment slip about him as though he knew it would not be for much longer.

That day she was to go to St Helens for the first time. Several purchasers of Alex's ore had written to say they were dissatisfied, not only with the quality they were now receiving, but with deliveries which were not as they had once been, nor with the price which was higher than those of their competitors in Wales. She was going, like a gladiator into the arena, with no weapon, no defence beyond her own quick brain and a *pot-pourri* of knowledge and information she had picked up from reports she had read in Alex's mine office. She had not the slightest idea of how she would conduct her meetings with them,

416

nor of what they would expect of her. She had become somewhat adept in the past three months at sidestepping direct questions, at the mine, at the gunpowder mill, and only in the company of Mr Dunlop was she completely at her ease. She found she had the knack of improvising, waiting until her opponent in the game showed her his hand and then – her quick mind racing like the big water-wheel on the hill above the mine – she would retrieve the answer, or failing that, make a great show of manoeuvring until *they* themselves divulged it.

She hoped to God it would not fail her in St Helens!

She took Sally with her for even she was well aware that no matter how strong-willed and obstinate she might set herself up to be, no lady would travel far without a companion, particularly on the brand new railways which were spreading their tentacles to every part of the country. The men with whom she was to deal would not like it and she must make a favourable impression upon them. And, if she were honest, the step she was about to take away from the familiar surroundings which had been her home for twenty-three years, was one she did not care to make completely alone. She had never been further south than Kendal and Sally not even as far as that, but the mere act of guiding the intimidated maid from one train to another, from one compartment to another, of telling her to pull herself together, to pick up that box, to sit down, to wait there, just as if she had done the journey herself a dozen times before, gave to Christy a feeling of confidence. By the time they had reached Preston, changing at Kendal to the Lancaster and Carlisle line, a journey of no more than two hours, she felt herself to be a seasoned traveller.

Not so Sally! She clung almost tearfully to Mrs Buchanan's skirt, like a child who finds itself in a world of strangers, hanging her head and averting her eyes from the most inoffensive male gaze. Mrs Longworth had warned her not to speak to *any* man, though only God knew what dire straits she might find herself in if she did. Anyway she could not understand a word anyone said so it made no difference.

'Sally, for God's sake girl, will you stop huddling up to me like that. You'll have me on the railway line in a minute.'

This was at Windermere, and when the train exploded into the station Sally let out a shriek to compare with the piercing whistle of the engine itself, and had to be pushed forcibly on to it by the combined efforts of Jack and Miles who had come to see Mrs Buchanan away on her great adventure.

They had travelled in comfort, stowed away carefully by an overawed Jack into a first class compartment. Sally was almost speechless at the sight of so much splendour.

'Why ma'am, we might almost be at home,' she breathed reverently as she walked with her mistress through the dining car which had blinds at the window, fine lawn tablecloths, delicate bone china and cutlery of the highest order.

A hansom cab was hired at St Helens railway station to take them along the length of Church Street to The Kings Head, the post house where they were to put up. Christy had sent a letter ahead, asking for two bedrooms and a sitting room, the best they had to offer she insisted, with no conception of how they would be for she had never been inside an inn in her life.

'What's that smell, Mrs Buchanan?' Sally asked as they stepped across the bustling station yard at St Helens towards the cab, wrinkling her nose and reaching for her handkerchief. The harmful acidic vapour, noxious and foul-smelling, clung to everything it touched, including the elegant travelling outfit – Christy had decided against her mannishly-tailored riding habit for this business trip, guessing instinctively that she might have more effect on gentlemen dressed in her prettiest gowns – of young Mrs Alexander Buchanan and her neatly-dressed maid, causing them to gag palely as they climbed into the cab.

A great yellow pall hung above their heads, drifting

418

slowly with the eddying wind over buildings blackened and dirty and even the cobbles beneath their feet, damp from the grey dizzle which fell from the ragged clouds, were slimed with some sooty mixture from the hundreds of chimneys which stood about the town. There had been rows of them belching forth filthy smoke as the train approached the station and both the young women brought up in the clear air of the Lakeland were appalled by the sulphurous stench.

Christy was aware from her reading that St Helens was a growing industrial area. Factories were everywhere making soap, vitriol, alkali, smelting copper, manufacturing nails and bolts and plate glass; there were wire and rolling mills, brass foundries, candle makers, refining plants and of course the coal mines which were the cause of the industry being there in the first place. They provided the power which fed the furnaces which in their turn produced the merchandise going to every corner of the known world.

A thriving, growing town, filled with hard-headed business men who would do anything to make a profit, who admired a sharp mind and the ability to make one penny into two, but who would, without the slightest compunction, grind under their heels anyone who fell beneath them and take up with any man who would give them a better deal. She had the names of four copper-smelting companies to whom Alex had supplied copper ore and some others as well and meant to call on each one in turn. She must convince them that though there had been a minor hitch or two in the delivery of Buchanan copper to their smelting factories, it was no more than that and with Mr Buchanan well on the road to recovery they need have no fear that it would happen again. She was here merely as an emissary to convey to them her husband's apologies for any delay in deliveries during his illness following the accident, and to assure them that from now on they would receive regular and punctual shipments. The price would for the moment remain the same but with good will on both sides, perhaps if they were willing to purchase a larger amount, it being only common sense to realize that the more one bought the less it cost, she was certain Mr Buchanan would meet them on price.

She had studied every company book going back even as far as the days of Alex's father, reading far into the night about profit and loss, and though she knew nothing about the quality of what she sold – for only a qualified engineer could realize that – she had learned a great deal about the finances of the company. She must bluff her way through the rest!

It seemed Alex had been successful in surviving the price war, with the smelting cartel largely waged at the expense of the Cornish mine adventurers, and due mainly to his efficient, low-cost working of his mines; his ability to stay one step ahead of his competitors in the Welsh fields; and his strict and utter reliability in the dispatch and delivery of his ore to the buyers. He had supported, not just with his ore but with the shares he bought in many of the smelting companies, the experiments which resulted in the perfecting of copper fastenings suitable for sheathing sheets to ships. The practice of copper sheathing the wooden hulls enabled ships to sail faster and to spend less profit-making time in re-fitting. Now ship owners were clamouring for the copper bolts and nails to secure the sheathing. The time was ripe for further expansion but unless Alex Buchanan could keep up with these men – to whom commerce and the profits which came with it were the pivot of their lives – his copper would lie uselessly, either above ground or below for if it were not delivered on time they would go elsewhere for it. Already there was ore coming in from Chile and Cuba and the import duty had been reduced to such a level that the low grade British ore must be competitively priced to remain attractive to the buyer.

It was Christy's task to make it so and if she could renew the confidence these men had in her husband, she was certain she could hold on to what would belong to her three sons until Alex was able to take it from her.

'Come, Sally,' she said crisply as she descended from the hansom cab, sweeping her skirts in a graceful dip across the front steps of The Kings Head, bowing her head pleasantly to the inn-keeper.

'Your rooms are ready, Mrs Buchanan,' he said, touching his forelock to the fine lady who had come on some mysterious errand, no doubt to do with a gentleman of the town. When, the next day, she asked him courteously to call her a cab to take her to the factories of some of the most powerful men in St Helens he was nonplussed. She had not emerged from her rooms once she was in them, sending her maid for everything she needed and no one had called upon her!

As he saw her away on that first morning his curiosity deepened, and on the three successive days on which she stepped gracefully into the hired carriage – her neat maid beside her and all very proper – there was more than one pair of eyes to admire her small waist and soft breast and the intense sparkle of her grey eyes and to wonder where in thunderation she came from, and where she went

In the fading rose-tinted peace of the house near Fellthwaite the evening glory of the setting sun dipped into the bedroom at the front of the house, touching to gold the pale face of the man who lay on the bed.

The dog lay on the floor, well used by now to the routine of the sickroom, his cold black nose resting on his crossed front paws, his bright black eyes dozing in the last bit of sunshine in which he lay. Mrs Jackson dozed with him, her head on the chair back, her thoughts calm and scattered. There was no sound in the house – for the children were all asleep in their beds, thank God, the little scamps – and she slipped easily in and out of a light doze, believing the man across the room was himself asleep. His head was turned to one side and she could not see his face in the growing dusk.

When he spoke she jumped quite dramatically and the dog raised his head for Alex Buchanan had not opened his mouth except to eat since Mrs Buchanan had gone away. Mrs Jackson did not engage him in conversation for what was the use, she asked Mrs Longworth plaintively, when you got no answer.

'Where . . . is . . . my wife?' His throat was rough from disuse.

'My goodness, Mr Buchanan. You didn't half give me a start.' Mrs Jackson put her hand dramatically to her capacious breast. 'I thought you were asleep.'

'Where is . . . my wife?'

'Well I'm sure I couldn't say, sir. Business was all I was told and though I say it myself I'm not one to poke my nose into what doesn't concern me. Back on Friday she said, so there you are. You know as much as me.'

He waited patiently for her to finish speaking for there was no power in him to interrupt her when she got going.

'Friday?'

'That's right, sir.'

'When . . . is . . . that?'

'Why! Tomorrow, sir.'

'Tomorrow . . .'

Mrs Jackson was quite astounded for never in the almost twelve months she had been in his service had Mr Buchanan shown the slightest interest in his wife's whereabouts. But then Mrs Buchanan had never been away overnight before!

CHAPTER TWENTY-SEVEN

She wore a gown of rich, twilled shot silk in a delicate shade of apple green with white lace undersleeves and collar, her crinoline so wide it had required ten yards of material round the hem to cover it. There were seven rows of flounces on the skirt each one edged with dark green velvet ribbon and her silk bonnet was lined with the same material. Her parasol was a froth of white lace and tulle, decorated with lovers' knots of green velvet and pale pink rosebuds.

She looked her best and the knowledge put the stiffness in her straight, slim back and lifted her dark, glossy head to regal heights as she stepped into the hansom cab. Sally moved respectfully a foot or so behind her as a lady's maid should, soberly dressed in plain dove grey. No one could doubt the complete respectability of Mrs Alexander Buchanan nor deny her unquestionable beauty.

The day was warm, sultry, as the sun – which one presumed was moving as usual across the blue bowl of the sky – tried unsuccessfully to penetrate with its rays the yellow, sulphuric pall which rested just above their heads. Christy felt she could stand up in the cab and reaching just a little, touch the heavy, breathless blanket which spread from one end of the town to the other. It did not subside, as she had hoped, when the cab headed out of town towards the open countryside – crossing the wooden bridge over Sankey Canal which brought the coal to the copper and the glass works – but seemed to become even worse as smoke belched from chimneys on either side of them. It poured upwards and southwards as currents of air took it, joining the already heavy pall which hung there. The rain of the day before had done little to clear the air or the dirt which lay upon everything, and Christy could see Sally's face assume a horrified expression as she tried to avoid contact with the grime which had filtered through the window of the cab, settling thickly on its upholstery. She herself sat carefully, afraid to move lest it rubbed off on the soft pastel green of her gown for did she not want to make a good impression, the best she had ever made, when she arrived *unannounced* at the office of Mr Wilton, owner of the Eagles Head Copper Works? The sight of grubby lace and spotted silk was not one likely to impress anyone.

They passed the Navigation Tavern which, she had learned from her careful research into Mr Wilton's affairs, belonged to the copper works and was a social gathering place for the workers; and where, to his credit, Mr Wilton provided newspapers for those of his employers who could read, and a 'sick club' had been organized under his enlightened patronage. From all her studies of the reports of Joseph Wilton it seemed he was not only a far-sighted and shrewd businessman but one who knew the value, like her own father, of well-contented workmen. Eagles Head possessed several subsidiary departments which manufactured brass and included a brass foundry and nailmaking department. Some of the copper nailmaking was put out to local women nailmakers who required, presumably because they had children, to work within their own home. Mr Wilton had built cottages for his workers, dozens of them in neat rows, and because so many of his workforce had come, as the first copper had come, from Wales, one of them was called Welsh Row. Two or three hundred men – many coming from the surrounding district besides those of Welsh origin – worked at the copper smelting, and as Christy stepped down from the cab and shook out the crushed fabric of her elegantly wide shirt, it seemed that most were at that moment gathered in the yard enjoying the first short break of the day. It was eight-thirty. They had been employed since five-thirty and were now allowed ten minutes to eat the breakfast most had brought wrapped up in a scrap of cloth; to relieve themselves in the vast containers in the corner of the yard; and to stretch muscles which had been cramped, or used vigorously for the past three hours and which must be returned to for another nine, or ten, or even eleven! Many of them had faces as bright red as a summer sunset and the sweat stood out on their skin or stained their clothing, and the stink, not just of them but the general all-over pervasive stink of smelting copper had Sally blanching.

There were calciners, earning one and sixpence a day in the burning of the ore, and smelters and roasters, all working in intense and enervating heat and earning the same. There were refiners whose station in life was marginally higher and who received two shillings; charge men and furnace builders who earned three shillings and one and fourpence respectively, and their apprentices who counted themselves lucky to get sevenpence halfpenny. And the whole great assembly stopped as one to stand and stare as Christy Buchanan and her terrified young maid hesitated in their midst.

But Christy remembered those other times, at the bobbin factory and the mines office, when men such as these had gaped and nudged one another, ready to tell her she had no right to interfere with their masculine world, and she had overcome their reluctance to admit her then and she would do the same now.

She lifted a gracious hand, beckoning to one rough fellow who – though he was no different to the rest in his dress or demeanour – had a knowing air about him and he hurried forward, grinning like a 'gay dog' and thinking himself to be one, no doubt, to have been chosen by the gentlelady. Christy smiled politely, her eyes, and those of Sally assiduously averted from the container in the corner where a young boy, quite paralysed by his amazed curiosity, still stood unbuttoned and unabashed.

'Could you direct me to Mr Wilton's office, if you please?' she said pleasantly and when the man, scratching his head which he had relieved of his cloth cap, answered in a northern dialect she found it incomprehensibly different from the Westmorland one to which she was used. She continued to smile and pray to God that help would come from somewhere for how was she to find her way from this vast sprawling yard into, and through, the equally vast sprawling building at her back? Already she felt indescribably filthy and was certain that the fastidiously fashionable Mrs Buchanan who had set out half an hour since had vanished in the noise and filth and heat which surrounded her, her place taken by some wilting drab.

The workman was pointing to a doorway across the yard from which some steps could be seen leading upwards and at the window on the first floor above it several faces appeared, joined by others as men were called to look at the phenomenon in the yard.

Herself and Sally!

'Thank you,' she said graciously, confidently, and with a smiling nod and instructions to 'Follow me, Sally,' she began to walk purposefully towards the steps. She was praying urgently now to some god that she was walking towards Mr Wilton and not some ghastly nightmare of furnaces and heat and near naked men, for in truth she had not the slightest idea what to expect of a smelting works. She remembered her own confusion when she had first gone to Stavely, and the noisy madness of the factory there, and that had been the clean, relatively small industry of bobbin manufacturing!

The men parted before her as she and Sally moved across the yard, the swaying hems of their skirts brushing against God alone knew what filth on the cobblestones. As they approached the doorway a man appeared and by his dress she assumed him to be a gentleman. Or at least not a labouring workman.

'Madam, please, may I ask what is your business here?' he asked brusquely, quite polite but very evidently, as they all did, believing her to be lost, or mad!

'Good morning,' she smiled and watched dispassionately as his eyes warmed with his appreciation of her comeliness. 'I am here to see Mr Wilton.'

'Mr Wilton?' He lifted his eyebrows enquiringly. Admiring of her looks he might be, but he was not about to merely step aside and allow her to walk right in as she had intended and she found herself forced to stop awkwardly, Sally and the interested crowd of men and boys at her back, her face only inches from that of his. He regarded her almost insolently, his eyes touching her face, her breast and hips with the casual certainty that he could do so, since she was not a lady or she would not be here. He had no idea why she was here but his attitude said quite plainly that if she wished to be pleasant, whatever her intention, he would be likewise – indeed, his expression said, he would be delighted to accommodate her at a later date in any way she chose but would it not be simpler if she and her companion climbed back into their cab and took themselves off?

'Is Mr Wilton in his office?' Christy's face was like marble, creamy and smooth and her grey eyes splintered to silvery ice as her voice cut through the strange and definitely prurient atmosphere his manner had brought about. She became, in an instant, the well-bred but autocratic lady she had been taught to be, mistress of her household, director of her servants, well-used in all things to instant obedience; a *lady* who would deal with mutinous ruffians such as he with the ruthless contempt she gave to any who would stand against her and he found himself moving hastily to one side, his back rigid against the wall, allowing her and her companion to move ahead of him up the staircase.

He tried still to force his authority on her saying from behind her that Mr Wilton was extremely busy and that he doubted his master could see anyone, let alone a woman, er . . . lady without an appointment, but she continued to regard him as some underling whose manner she did not care for and whom she was certainly about to put in his place if he continued with this foolish assumption that she could be put in hers!

'I would be obliged if you would announce me,' she said

427

imperiously, turning on her heel to study the row of clerks who stared open-mouthed from the bank of windows where they had watched her every move since the cab had entered the yard. Her chin was high and she raised it higher, her expression enquiring of them whether they had nothing better to do with their time than stare at her? They slunk, as one, back to their desks, bending over them to continue with whatever it was they had been about ten minutes earlier.

'Well!' she said, turning again to the man who had confronted her and who still stood haphazardly at the top of the stairs, uncertain yet of how to deal with this gloriously commanding woman.

Sally looked as though she would be pleased if the floor opened up and swallowed her whole!

'Your name, if you please, ma'am,' he said at last.

'Mrs Alexander Buchanan.'

'Mrs Alexander Buchanan?'

'I am she and I would be glad of ten minutes of Mr Wilton's time if he would be so kind.'

'Mrs . . . Buchanan? The wife of the copper . . .?'

'That is correct.'

'But what the devil can the wife of . . .?' His mouth fell open slackly and his sour expression ebbed away and with it went the almost animal speculation with which he had still been regarding her, and in its place came dismay, appalled and bewildered and an almost fawning air of deference.

Mr Wilton came swiftly from his office to greet her since she was after all, a lady, the wife of one of his most respected business associates and though he was as bewildered as his chief clerk as to exactly why she was here, she must be treated with the respect one gave to the wife of a gentleman.

'Mrs Buchanan! This is indeed a pleasure,' he said as he bowed over her hand, his eyes as approving as those of his clerk, but very respectful. He gave no hint of his confusion though he supposed later, when he thought about it, he should have guessed for why else would she be in his office if it were not on her disabled husband's behalf? He was shocked, and not a little put out that she should have the gall to enter this rude world of men with no more than a maidservant as chaperone but not a hint of his thoughts showed in his smooth, fleshy red face. His blue eyes smiled over her hand and though he was shorter than she was he led her, with Sally tremulously following, into his dark-panelled office with the confidence of one who knows it really did not matter in his case; and so charming and attentive and gentlemanly was he they might have been socializing in his own home, in his wife's drawing room rather than his place of business.

He pressed tea on her and from somewhere biscuits were produced and for quite fifteen minutes they were so civil with one another that Sally, on her discreet chair by the door, began to wonder why she had ever been anxious about accompanying Mrs Buchanan on this strange journey. That was until her mistress put down her cup and saucer on the edge of Mr Wilton's desk and in the deliberately misleading way of a lady about to beg advice of a gentleman, who was after all, her manner seemed to say, a good deal wiser than she, asked if she might consult him on the subject of her husband's copper ore.

Immediately Mr Wilton's courteously admiring benevolence was wiped away and his smiling eyes became cool. He was a businessman, his expression seemed to say, and what was that to do with her? His father had founded this great smelting works fifty years ago, dominating the Lancashire copper industry within ten, and he, his son, was made in the same mould. The site had been well chosen – close to the Sankey Canal just where the coal from the coalfields came down from Ashton and Garswood to the Sankey Canal wharf – and while coal was cheap and the price of pure copper high, his father had built up what Joseph Wilton now carried on. Shrewd, watchful, expedient always, a man to strike a bargain to his own advantage when he could, he had often been exasperated that Alex

Buchanan had never allowed himself to be outwitted. Fair, Buchanan had always been that, and honest, and their business had always been conducted to their mutual self-interest, making them both a profit – but here, out of the blue, fate had presented him, perhaps, with a chance to weigh that benefit in his own favour. She was a woman, and what woman had any head on her for business? Certainly none Mr Wilton knew of, and more to the point she had no experience in the trading world in which he had ruled for the past forty years.

He leaned back in his chair and waited.

'I had meant to travel to St Helens to call on you ever since my husband had his accident,' she was saying sweetly but Mr Wilton had crossed swords with the best – not a woman, mind – the very best in the business and she was not about to get round him by begging for his sympathy.

'It has taken some time to arrange my affairs so that I am free to travel about to our customers . . .' Clever! Mr Wilton had to give her that! She had just told him that he was not the only gentleman in the smelting business to be interested in the good quality ore which the Buchanan Copper Mine produced. '. . . and so it is only now that I have been able to call on you, and the Long Close Works at Windle. I have an appointment to see Mr Barrett directly, but I took the chance you might have time in what I am sure is a very busy day, to see me for a moment or two.'

She smiled and her thick, black lashes fluttered quite devastatingly and her velvet grey eyes warmed to him across his desk. 'I trust you will bear with my ignorance, Mr Wilton, in these matters but I must do my best to repair any . . . strain which has been put on the goodwill the Eagles Head Copper Works and the Buchanan Copper Mines have enjoyed in the past, by my husband's present inability to keep in close touch with his customers.'

'Indeed Mrs Buchanan, that is most . . . commendable.'

She could gain nothing from this courtesy nor from the smilingly expressionless face which rose from the tight stock about Mr Wilton's sturdy neck. She showed no sign, however, of her own unease but continued to sit straight-backed but quite relaxed in the chair in which he had placed her. She might have been taking tea in her mother's drawing room.

'I do understand the pressure which has been put upon your forbearance during these past months with regard to deliveries, Mr Wilton,' she went on. 'For a while I am afraid the mines were somewhat . . . unsupervised and I will be quite honest with you, shipments of ore were held up, but I can guarantee that everything is now completely re-organized. Under my husband's watchful eye . . .' She laughed merrily, the brave little woman struggling to overcome a grave difficulty but not for a moment doing it without a man's ordering,' . . . I am to ensure that not only does every order get away on time but that it arrives at its destination when it should. I can assure you that if you will overlook the . . . misfortune of the past months you will have no further complaints of the service you receive. In short, Mr Wilton . . .' She smiled so stunningly Mr Wilton could not refrain from smiling too, '. . . we are ready to do business in exactly the way you would wish.'

Though she was as straight-backed as ever, she appeared to relax somewhat, smiling disarmingly as though there was not the least doubt in her mind that Alexander Buchanan and Joseph Wilton, through herself – though they might have one or two unimportant difficulties to iron out – were now in perfect agreement on the running, and fusion, of their two ventures. Her confidence was supreme!

Mr Wilton regarded her steadily, then leaned forward, putting his elbows on his desk. He fingered his chin as though considering what he should say but there was no mistaking the curious gleam in his eyes, and her heart thudded against her breastbone in the most alarming way.

'Well now, Mrs Buchanan, it is most kind of you to come all this way to reassure me of your intentions and when you return home do tell Mr Buchanan how much I appreciate the pain it must cause him to be forced to send his lovely young wife to speak for him. I know myself how I should feel if I were compelled to let my wife go about as you are doing, but I shall certainly do all I can to help.'

His voice was silky and to a less astute woman, one who had not for the last few months been made to deal with men just like him, he might have appeared consumed with sympathy, benevolently disposed to remorse for her sad plight but Christy knew he was none of these things. In his way he was telling her that no matter what her circumstances were, being what she was, a lady, she had no right to flaunt herself about as she was doing and in his opinion, her husband had no right to let her. He would not allow *his* wife to do it. No gentleman would. No man would, and if she was insulted, so be it! She had only herself to blame. Nevertheless, now she was here, he meant to make the most of the opportunity of a possible gain to himself.

'You say you are now in a position to guarantee me the two hundred and fifty tons a month I was getting from you before your husband's unfortunate acident, Mrs Buchanan?'

Christy's voice was light, courteous, the voice of a hostess speaking, as one should, to a guest in one's own home. No matter who they were or in what circumstances they had chanced to be together, they were to be treated with the utmost politeness, but without humility.

'That is correct, Mr Wilton. In fact I have been considering sending the ore by train instead of by ship round the coast to Liverpool which would make the enterprise an even more viable prospect for both of us. As it already comes from there to St Helens by rail, a very circuitous route you must agree, it seems that now we have a line right through to Windermere it would be much more economically sound to . . .'

'And what has Mr Buchanan to say to that, Mrs Buchanan?'

Dear Lord! He had nearly caught her out! She was becoming so used to making a decision and carrying out what she had decided, she had quite forgotten the pretence she kept up of Alex being the instigator, the master who still, from his sickbed, controlled the fortunes of his own concerns.

'Those were *his* words I was speaking, Mr Wilton.' She smiled engagingly and Mr Wilton's eyes narrowed suspiciously. He was not at all sure now, what to make of this lovely, self-contained woman who presented herself as the messenger of her husband's goodwill. She brought Alex Buchanan's words, his idea and presumably his business deal with her, and yet behind that smiling face, those appealing eyes, that womanly softness, was there perhaps more than was apparent to his masculine eye?

'Mmm.' He sat back, still fingering his chin reflectively. 'It all sounds most impressive, Mrs Buchanan, but I am still concerned about your ability to produce the amount of ore I need *and* to deliver it when I need it. As your husband knows I turn out one thousand tons of pure copper annually. A sixth of the national production, Mrs Buchanan, so you can understand my reluctance to rely on a source, even for part of it, which has for the past six months or so been so unreliable . . .'

'We have a large quantity of ore – the miners have continued to bring it to the surface, you understand – and it has only to be carted to Windermere and put on a freight train. In view of your . . . need, urgent you say, I am sure you would wish to avail yourself of the slightly lower prices I am offering . . . we are offering to valued customers as a gesture of our goodwill . . .'

'Alexander Buchanan agrees to this . . . offer?' Mr Wilton sat back and smiled.

Christy's face continued to smile too but her eyes were like the ice which forms on Lake Windermere on a clear winter's day, just as the sun catches it at the end of its shining.

'He has left it to my discretion, Mr Wilton.'

'Come now, Mrs Buchanan!'

'Do you want my ore, Mr Wilton?'

'*Your* ore, Mrs Buchanan?'

The game was over. In her chair by the door Sally stared feverishly at the reticule she held in her twisting hands and considered what she should do if Mr Wilton became abusive, a situation which seemed, to her, to be highly likely. Mrs Buchanan was pushing him to it, she could see that. He didn't like to be argued with, by anyone, let alone some upstart young woman who had pretended at first to bow to his greater, masculine knowledge and experience but who was now showing she had not only an inventive mind but a shrewd one.

There was a small silence, then he sighed sadly.

'I'm afraid I have applied to Mona Ores in Anglesey for some parcels of copper ore, Mrs Buchanan . . .'

'Which has been refused, I believe, Mr Wilton, as they had none to spare!'

Joseph Wilton's head snapped sharply and his face became a bright beetroot red. His hand went to his stock this time in an involuntary effort to loose the stricture which had him by his throat and his mouth opened on the words before he could stop himself.

'How the good God did you know that? I have only . . .' He bit back the bellow of outrage but it was too late! He had given himself away immediately for it was the truth. He had been refused but how the hell had she known?

Christy Buchanan smiled forgivingly. She had not known! Quite simply it was the kind of move she herself would have chanced in this devilish manoeuvre for advantage, which was the intrinsic essence of the business world. You watched your opponent and waited for your opportunity. You took chances, especially when you had nothing to lose as she had nothing to lose; for if she let slip this buyer and word got out to the other smelters that Buchanan copper was in the hands of an incompetent woman, she would be their pawn, their malleable tool in the game of profit and loss! She had learned that during the past months and she had also learned that if you could not make your way in one direction you must find another.

She had become rather good at it, she thought, relishing her own talent, undiscovered until recently, of searching out and embarking upon the correct, often different approach, to each gentleman with whom she did business!

'Come, Mr Wilton, don't tell me you would turn down this venture which, if you take it, gives you an enormous advantage. All the ore you need with better deliveries at a cheaper rate, and to convince you of my guarantee I will add the . . . the . . . bonus of deducting a half per cent of your buying price for each late delivery. What could be more attractive than that?'

'Mrs Buchanan, I could get my ore . . .'

'Not with a deal like this you couldn't.'

'You are presumptuous, young woman!'

'Probably, but you are not going to let that stand in your way, are you, Mr Wilton?'

'And if I decide to . . .'

'You are a businessman, Mr Wilton.'

'And by God so are you, Mrs Buchanan!'

Five days from the day she had left Windermere, Christy Buchanan sat beside her maid in the first class compartment of the train which carried them on the second leg of their return journey, from Lancaster to Kendal. They were both quiet, soaking in the soft splendour of the green foothills of south Lakeland as they approached Kendal. Christy had opened the window and the fresh air blew in and unconsciously both women dragged it deep into their lungs, exhaling the last of the noxious fumes of the industrial town in which they had stayed.

'My word, Sally, that does my heart good . . . and my nose!'

Sally laughed and leaned closer to the window, her young face relaxed now that she had become almost a world traveller – for that was how it would seem to those left behind in Fellthwaite – but her eyes were excited as her brain sorted out all the wonders she would have to tell the servants at Howethwaite most of whom had never been beyond Ambleside!

'I know, Mrs Buchanan. I'll have me work cut out getting rid of this old stink from our clothes!'

'We'll get used to it, Sally, for it will be a regular job from now on.'

Sally turned, her expression quite horrified for though the journey had been a big adventure and one, now that it was over, she would not like to have missed, she was not sure she wanted to repeat it.

'Yes, I'm afraid so, Sally. I must go quite regularly to St Helens now that I have had some small success with Mr Buchanan's customers, and in a week or two I shall journey to Swansea to make the acquaintance of those who buy from him there. I must have someone to accompany me, so if you feel unable to continue as my maid you must say so right now.'

Her voice was challenging. It said quite plainly that those who travelled with Christy Buchanan, now that she had found her feet to be relatively steady on the stony path of business, must be as strong as she was. If Sally wanted only to linger in the safe protection of Howethwaite then that was her choice. Another could be found to take her place.

Christy grinned suddenly.

'Come on, Sally. Don't tell me you didn't find it . . . exciting!'

'Well,' Sally giggled, 'I must say the look on that chap's face when you told him you were the rep . . . repre . . . what was it . . .?'

'The representative of the Buchanan Mining Company.'

'Yes . . . well . . . I thought he was going to wet his . . . Oh pardon me, Mrs Buchanan. I didn't mean to . . .'

'I know, Sally, and what about Mr Watson? Did you see his eyes pop out of his face? I though they were going to jump into my lap . . .'

'That was because he couldn't keep them off your . . .' Sally blushed and dropped her gaze to her hands. Really, when Mrs Buchanan got going you forgot she was the mistress of a big house, the wife of one of Fellthwaite's most important men and the mother of four children. Her eyes sparkled quite wickedly and you'd swear she'd enjoyed every minute of it. Sally was not so sure. It was strange sleeping in a bed others had slept in before her, Strangers, and she had been frightened of the train at first but really, when you thought about it, what was there to be frightened of? Mrs Buchanan was so . . . so clever and unafraid. It did you good just to see her squaring up to those chaps in those fine offices, it really did.

'Well, Sally?' Mrs Buchanan asked smilingly.

'I reckon I could manage, ma'am . . . if you want me.'

That night, taking no notice of his averted gaze, the slack indifference in his vacantly staring eyes, Christy sat down beside her husband's bed. Mrs Jackson had given him his bed bath and rearranged him neatly beneath the covers, and disappeared to the kitchen for her supper. The dog lay at his side. The clock ticked and the fire crackled and they were alone.

'Why did you not tell me how exciting it is, Alex?' she said at last. She expected no answer and got none. She really did not know why she was here speaking to him of what had happened during the last few days, since he had no interest and Faith was waiting in the small parlour, positively agog to hear it. She supposed it was because it was a world familiar to him, one he had experienced and would understand where Faith did not and because of that she felt a great need to speak of it to him.

'I had no idea,' she mused, her head resting comfortably on the chair back as she gazed beyond the window to the blurred heights of the Old Man of Conistone. The room was almost dark now as the twilight deepened. She had not yet lit the lamp and the only light came from the glowing fire which was never allowed to go out for Christy believed a constant temperature and fresh air were beneficial to Alex's condition.

Her voice was soft, as though she spoke to herself. 'To feel so marvellously ... victorious when you see the agreement in their faces and know that it is *your* words, *your* daring, your effrontery which has turned them about to believe what you want them to believe. Oh I know that at first they were charming because I am a woman and your wife, which I suppose must account for some of it. They thought in their bewilderment that I was calling on a social visit, can you imagine? They could not believe you had sent me to speak on your behalf but I was able to convince them. They said they were about to make other arrangements since your copper, though of a better quality, was now never reliable in its delivery, so I told them they need have no fear on that score for I mean to hound the foremen at the mine until they are more efficient. They have grown slack, I fear, since your ... since your ... and from now on I mean to freight it by train. There is talk of a line being laid from Conistone to the newly completed Furness Railway at Broughton. Did you know that? But in the meanwhile I think it worth considering taking the ore to Windermere and then on to Kendal by train. That journey could be cut by days, Alex. Instead of carting it to Greenodd to go round the coast to Liverpool by ship, it seems quite logical to take it to Windermere and send it by the direct railway route to St Helens. Do you not think so? And if that is the case and we find it cheaper to freight, could we not sell at a lower price to our buyers and therefore retain their custom, and others besides? Well, I put this to them and they all agreed, except one, a stuffy old devil called Postlethwaite – what a name – that if I ... or rather you ... could prove to them within the next month that deliveries will be punctual and the price right they will continue to trade with us. They hold you in great respect, Alex, and I am inclined to believe that that is one of the reasons they agreed.' She grinned delightedly. 'And my business acumen helped, of course.'

The silence was deep and empty as she stopped speaking but she seemed not to notice it in her satisfaction. She had told him, or what was left of him, of what she had done, proud of it and herself, expecting no answer, nor interest and was not surprised, nor disappointed when none came.

She stood up and taking a taper from the fire lit the lamp. She turned to look at him, holding the lamp up and her cool grey eyes appraised him.

'Well Alex,' she said, her lips curved in a sardonic smile. 'There you have it. The state of your copper business as it is at this moment. Far from being on its feet again but I mean to get it there, and with my efforts in the charming of the smelting gentlemen of St Helens and the browbeating of Mr Tate at the mine, there is hope for it and I intend to keep it. The gunpowder mill is holding its own now that the managers are being made to believe you are keeping a sharp eye on the company's books since I have learned how to read them, and even organize them to a better efficiency. Perhaps with a bit of prodding, or a new manager to be at their backs as you used to be, we will bring it back to what it was in my father's day. Mr Dunlop is the only one I trust to carry on without my constant presence at the bobbin mill for he is honest and hard-working, so he will do. But without you at the mine to search out new sources of ore, new veins, and to assay the percentage of metals in the samples – yes, I have been reading your mining books in the study, so you see I know a little bit of what must be done though not, unfortunately, how to do it – we shall fail. We need an engineer, a mining engineer to show us where the dead ground lies, to locate the counter veins. The men are beginning to encounter barren rock away from the main lode, they tell me, and they are not qualified to know how to take out the water from the deep level which is beginning to be a problem. You see, I have been down there, Alex, and I know what they say is true. Again I had a problem with Mr Tate who refused me permission – me, the owner's wife! – to go down there without a note from you. Quite like a parent sending a note to the teacher it was! Well, I couldn't bother you with it, could I? You have told me often enough you do not *care* to be bothered, so I forged your handwriting and signature and he had to make do with that. There is a way round everything, I find, but we cannot do without a mining engineer. Sadly I can find no way round that! Now, if you cannot, or will not help me, I must find one myself. How I shall tell good from bad I don't know, but there, I dare say I will manage.' She smiled into his passive face. 'Really, I cannot think what men make such a fuss about. It is no more than managing a household. Put in the right people to work it for you and the thing runs smoothly. Well, I will leave you to your thoughts and get to my bed. I am very tired.'

She left the room without looking at him again and as she closed the door he turned his head to where she had stood and the expression in his eyes was agonized.

'Oh Christy . . . Christy, what am I . . . doing to you?' he whispered, and the sound trembled about the hushed room. The dog pricked his ears, then jumped to the bed, settling in his customary place beside his master and when Mrs Jackson returned from her supper it seemed they were both asleep.

CHAPTER TWENTY-EIGHT

It was more than a week since she had seen her mother and so on the following Sunday she packed the children into her carriage, dogs, kittens and all, waving to Faith who stood anxiously on the doorstep as though she did not trust her charges with their own mother. But Christy declared she deserved a rest from this tribe and she should have one, so there was no use in arguing.

Faith was thin, her grief at her husband's death still etched in her face, fine lines of sorrow drooping about her mouth, but she had taken comfort from the homely atmosphere which prevailed in Christy's kitchen. These were her people, people of the dales and fells, used to hardship and blessed with the common bond which rallied round those in trouble. She lost herself in the company of Christy's children. She was neither nanny, nursemaid nor governess and so she was merely their friend. They grew to trust and love her. She tried to be their older sister, on their side most of the time and they all, particularly Amy, whom she loved dearly, searched her out wherever she was, taking their joys and sorrows to her as naturally as they would to their mother. She grieved not only for her husband but for the child she did not bear him and the little girl eased her pain when she nestled on her lap before the nursery fire. In helping Christy, she herself was helped.

'Go and find a sunny corner of the garden to sit in and read for an hour,' Christy told her, 'or take a walk. Be by yourself for a while, dear Faith. I'm sure I would need it if I had this multitude to contend with all week. No, I insist, I shall take them off your hands, besides I shall enjoy it. I do not see enough of them and I want to discover what they have been up to all week and how much Amy has learned since last Sunday.'

Amy had a governess now, interviewed in Christy's absence by her mother, who would not be taken in by a charming manner which might conceal a lack of brains and a careless disregard for her grandchildren's morals. She was a sweet-faced young woman of twenty-two, the daughter of an impoverished parson from Hartsop, now dead, who had herself received a good, sound upbringing and could pass on to the little girl all she had been taught by her father, a well-educated man. She was gentle and quiet and Amy, who was five years old now, had already become extremely attached to her. Miss Crawford was teaching her all that was required of the daughter of a gentleman: to write a beautiful copperplate, to read, to add a few simple figures together and subtract them again, to dance and sing, and play the piano in the back parlour, and to sew a sampler. Though Faith was acting as supervisor in the nursery, making sure that Christy's children were well looked after in her absence, Miss Crawford was to take over the first educational beginnings of each child as she or he became old enough. Of course when the boys were six each would go to the grammar school in Fellthwaite, as their father had done.

It was what old Edwin up at Hollin House – dead now these two years, carried off by the 'bottom' winds he had detested – would have called a day of Indian summer. Warm with a golden blue sky, the land, though still green, thirsty for some rain which had not fallen since the end of the rainy summer. Wild flowers still bloomed in intense patches of colour in the fields and up on the fells the bracken would be crackling underfoot.

The children were excited, jostling for a position next to their mother who was inclined to spoil them a little since she saw them so seldom these days. Amy was fretful and worried for the safety of the latest addition to her family of cats and Beth – brought along to keep some order whilst Christy took tea with Annie – lifted the little girl and her kittens upon her knee, calming her inclination to tears with a fond kiss. Despite her affection for Mrs Buchanan's lusty lads this first child of Alexander Buchanan still had the strongest hold on her heart. It was not often she got a look-in with that new governess taking over her little pet, and Faith moving into the nursery the way she had, and she intended making the most of these few hours with her 'baby'. The poor mite had a hard time of it in the masculine challenge of her brothers' world where she was outnumbered three to one, and Beth was still called upon to protect her from their wildness. They needed the firm hand of their father in her opinion and had been worse since Mrs Buchanan had taken to going off each day to 'business' whatever that was. They had become ill-mannered without their mother's strong will to discipline them and Faith was too soft by half. Without the proper authority to chastise them, by which Beth

442

meant a good smacked bottom, and with no one to provide it during the day, the boys were getting out of control. They were handsome lads with the charm and mischievousness of a cart-load of monkeys but wilful! Well, she had given Master Johnny a clout or two in the past months, and would do so again when Faith was not about no doubt; but she did hope Mrs Buchanan would soon organize whatever it was she did so that she might be at home more often to steady these rowdy boys of hers. They were young yet, granted. Johnny was four and a half, Harry a year younger and Joby a boisterous two and a half, too young all of them for a tutor. What they needed was to go to school but that was a long way off and if Mrs Buchanan didn't look sharp they would grow up wild and wayward. They were so headstrong, quite ungovernable at times, and she for one was ready to tell Mrs Buchanan so if things didn't improve. Look at them now, squabbling over whose dog should sit where, and the three animals leaping everywhere putting their mucky paws on Mrs Buchanan's fine silk gown and she not seeming to care at all. She was laughing and hugging Joby to her, brushing back the ebony curls which lay thick on his forehead to place a kiss there, and Beth could see the glow in her eyes which had been missing for months and wondered what it was that had put it there.

Annie wondered the same thing as she watched them flow from the carriage to pour like a tidal wave of shouting children, barking dogs and darting, clawing kittens, intent on making for the safety of the trees. Amy was immediately at the mignonettes, her fingers eager to pick their yellow-orange brightness so that she might press them between the pages of her book as Miss Crawford had taught her. The two eldest boys followed the kittens, swinging on the low branches of an old oak, Johnny boasting that he would climb to the top. He elbowed aside his younger brother and they fell to the ground, pummelling one another with the ferocity of bare knuckle fighters. Joby was chasing the three dogs, determined to catch them as

443

they made for her shrubbery and in a matter of minutes the garden was a chaotic muddle of children, dogs and kittens, each one intent on making their voice the loudest. In the midst of it all her daughter stood and stretched her arms above her head, gazing with deep pleasure across the valley to the fells beyond, breathing in the warm air with the intensity of a wine drinker. Her eyes shone and the lovely golden smoothness of her skin was flushed with rose-amber at her cheekbones. She had discarded her parasol as frivolous with her new tailored outfits and the sun had tinted her face to a most becoming, though unfashionable hue.

Today she wore a flattering apple green foulard afternoon gown trimmed with multiple rows of small flounces reaching to the hem, each one edged with dark green velvet ribbon. She had removed her feathered bonnet, tossing it carelessly by its brim into the open carriage. She called something to Jack who nodded before taking the carriage round to the stable yard; then laughed at the sight of Beth retrieving the yelling Joby from the shrubbery. Spinning lightly on her heel she caught sight of her mother in the drawing room window and waved, throwing back her head, and her heavy hair fell to her shoulders in an unruly tumble of dark chestnut curls. She looked no more than seventeen.

'You look pleased with yourself, my girl,' Annie remarked as Christy entered the room, two kittens about her shoulders like a demented fur collar, rescued from the playful attention of the dogs. 'And you can put those things in the kitchen, if you don't mind. Your house might be a menagerie but mine certainly isn't. They'll be sharpening their claws on my rosewood sofa the minute you take your eyes from them.'

Her voice was sharp but her eyes smiled welcome, and she moved across the carpet to put her arms about her daughter, hugging her – and the kittens – with a deep fondness she had not revealed to her in her childhood.

'Oh mother, they'll do no harm, poor little things.

444

Between those naughty boys of mine, the puppies' unwelcome affection and Amy's cosseting they get not a minute's peace.' And indeed when she put them on her mother's fireside rug they curled up until they were one indistinguishable fluffy ball before the fire and fell thankfully asleep.

They sat before the small fire and talked idly, companionable, not only in their conversation but in their silences. They listened to the shrieks of the children and the high excited yelps of the young dogs and Beth's distracted voice beseeching each and every one of them to behave.

Amy came in and lay dreaming before the fire, her hands gentle on the purring kittens, her own head nodding in the warmth for despite the lovely welcome sunshine which crowded through the long windows, Annie always had a fire burning. She was feeling her age now, the damp mists and drifting rain, the intense cold of the many Lakeland winters she had seen, creeping into her old bones, making them stiff. Her hands were at her quilting. She was making a coverlet for the cradle of her cousin's daughter's latest baby: delicate shades of pink, lavender and white, and her face was soft with the peace which comes so often with old age. Her daughter was obviously content with her world, accepting at last her place in it, though what she did up there at the mine and here at Job's mill she didn't know, or even care to. It was enough to see the strain, the pain of her youthful years gone from her for a while. She had grown used to her daughter's presence in her home these last few months, and to the many problems she brought with her. Not for Annie to solve for only she herself could shape the pattern of her future, her mother knew that, but just to empty out the words and thoughts which multiplied in her mind over the days. Annie did not force them. She knew Christy was grateful for her own still, incurious quality which asked nothing of her. Though Annie was willing to give her opinion, advice, support, she did not invite confidences unless they were freely given.

'How is Alex?' she asked.

'He . . . is worse, I would say.'

Annie put down her needlework and lifted her head to stare sadly across the long sloping garden to the mill and the lake beyond.

'I can't believe it you know! A strong man brought down until he is no more than a baby. Perhaps it would be . . . better if . . .'

'No!'

'No? Do you not pity his . . .'

'He does not want pity! He wants to be as he was.'

'But . . .'

'Listen to me, mother. I would like to put an idea to you which has been growing in my mind for several weeks now. Might I just . . . place it before you? Your . . . impressions are sound and I value your advice.'

'What is it, lass?'

'Would you say . . .' she paused '. . . Alex is . . . dammit, how can I put this?' She leaned forward, her face peached by the firelight, her eyes clear and steady. 'He is like a . . . skeleton, mother. A living skeleton. His flesh, what there is of it hangs in folds and he has . . . nothing beneath it but bone. No . . . no substance. The doctor explained that muscles not used will naturally wither away.'

There was silence. Christy looked into the fire, her expression reflective.

'It appears to me then if that is the case, the opposite will also be true. That muscle moved daily, or *made* to move will strengthen and become firm again. If that is so, Alex must be made to use his muscles.'

Annie did not gasp or beg to know how this could be done but sat quietly, the sponge to absorb Christy's ideas, the board against which Christy bounced the ball of her thoughts.

'Would it not seem logical that if a man cannot use his legs to walk himself then someone could do it for him? As he lies in his bed his limbs could be lifted and bent, moved as though he was actually walking. His arms too. He has to be constantly turned. You know how he suffers with

446

bedsores, so why do we not make him *sit* when he is stronger, devise some method of strapping him to a chair? He could . . . look out of the window, read. It would take a great deal of time and work, another nurse perhaps, great patience. He could be massaged to put . . . I don't know . . . something back into his flesh. He is dying, mother. He has no will to live so he is dying though the doctors can find nothing wrong with him. I am often amazed that he has lasted as long as he has. There must be a spark . . . hidden . . . which even he is unaware he has, but if we could give him something to live for, even if it is only a hatred of me and what I am forcing on him it might . . . bring him back to life.'

'Have you put it to him?'

'Good God, no! He would refuse.'

'So it will be against his wishes?'

'We would have to fight him every step of the way but at least he would *be* fighting. What d'you think?'

'It would take up a great deal of your time. What about the children, and the businesses?'

'The children are already well cared for, mother. You know that. Amy is devoted to Miss Crawford and she to Amy and she adores Faith. They are virtually inseparable and I think it would do Johnny no harm to spend a few hours a day in the schoolroom with them, though he will not like it. He could learn to cypher, to read and write his name. Beth and Faith are capable women and well able to manage Harry and Joby. As for the businesses, they are . . .' she smiled a mite smugly '. . . coming along. Slowly. I have a lot to learn and a long, long way to go and must watch everything, and everybody, like a hawk but now I am beginning to see the light on the financial, if not the technical side, I think I have it more or less under control. If Mrs Jackson needs help I shall get another nurse.'

'How will you start?'

'I haven't the faintest idea!'

'I wish you well, lass. By God, it's a hard road you've

walked, Christy Emmerson, and if there's anything I can do to help you know you have but to ask.'

She put her gnarled old hand on Christy's smooth one and her face was a mixture of sadness and yet a strong pride in this tenacious daughter of hers.

'I know, mother. You are . . . it sounds strange to say of one's mother, but you are a true friend.'

Annie smiled her kind smile, pleased, then her expression became somewhat strained and she put out her other hand to her girl, holding hers between them.

'Christy, there is . . .'

'Yes mother, what is it?'

'You call me friend so . . . though I don't wish to hurt you, it's best you hear this from . . . from a friend.'

Christy drew back a little, afraid now. She had sheathed herself in a carapace of protection during the past year, guarded herself against the words, the insolent looks, the whispers and smiles which were laid about her in her husband's mills and mines, but this was not one of those. This was something else, something her mother wanted her to know, here in private, so that they might share the pain of it unseen by prying eyes.

'Robin?' she said carefully, holding herself rigidly the better to bear the shock of it.

'Yes.'

'Tell me.'

'He has a son.'

'Aah . . .' the knife slashed the sound from her.

'You knew?'

Her breath was agonized in her chest. 'I knew his . . . wife . . . was . . .'

'I'm sorry, lass. I thought it best you hear it from me.'

She bore the sadness of it, the wound of the past re-awakened with her to her bed that night; unaware that her husband's eyes followed her stiff movements as she bade him a polite goodnight; unaware that his rusty voice whispered to his dog, asking him what it was that had shattered his wife's peace of mind that day.

448

It was several days before she could bring herself to speak to him.

The room was warm that night, a rosy, flower-scented warmth and Christy felt the tiredness lap about her, easing her languidly into a light doze. Her head rested on the padded chair back and she felt it slip sideways as her weary body dragged her longingly towards sleep.

Alex lay unmoving on the bed and the dog was beside him, his nose twitching, his ears pricking, his muffled bark deep in his throat as he chased a rabbit in his dreams.

She turned her head abruptly, then sat up. Mrs Jackson would be back from her supper soon and though Christy had worked for twelve long hours in the office of the gunpowder mill – impatiently being led yet again through the intricacies of the making of powder by Mr Anderson – and was eager to get to her bed, she had made the decision that tonight she must bring Alex from his deep world of mists and face up to him with her plan. *Her plan!* How foolish it all seemed now that she was about to place it before him. She could imagine how he would have treated the idea a year ago if it had been devised to help some other poor soul. He was a realist with no time for wild schemes which had no chance of surviving and yet, surely, some hope, however small, was better than none? And if it did not work, if he was still as helpless when they had done, the mere fact of trying must work to his advantage. He had said a dozen times or more in her hearing that a man was a fool who made no attempt to pit his wits and his strength even against the most appalling odds, and was that not what she was about to ask him to do? She must give him the chance, the hope of living again for no one can live without hope.

'Alex,' she said incisively. 'I want to talk to you. Will you listen?'

The dog lifted his head and looked at her, moving his tail amiably, ready to give his attention, but Alex continued to look in the direction of the glowing fire, his expression quite dreamy and peaceful. Christy sighed for what else had she expected? It was always the way no matter what the subject. A struggle first to capture his attention, then when that was caught, the battle to put into his brain the essence of what she wished him to know, and the last, the answer, not even worth the waiting for! Complete and total indifference most of the time, a whisper of protest at being disturbed was the most she could hope for. She felt the irritation ruffle her breathing.

'Did you hear me, Alex? I want to discuss something with you. It could ... possibly ... I make no promises for I am not a medical man ... could help perhaps to give you ...' She sighed deeply. '... I don't really know what good it will do. I suppose it's just a wild dream but I had this idea ... Will you listen?'

She repeated the conversation she had had with her mother last Sunday; the ideas she had mulled over since the doctor had explained his condition to her, and the hope she had nurtured in her heart during the weeks which followed. Her voice was soft as she explained her conception of how they might try to accomplish what was really no more than a thread of hope, an endeavour which she had no guarantee would not do more harm than good. She was guileless in her sincerity, matter of fact and free from artifice, as she told him honestly what the chances were of success, indeed she said she did not know if there were *any*, but they could try, couldn't they, they could try!

She might have been talking to the bedpost for all the response she got.

'Alex, please ... listen to me. *Dammit*, you *will* listen to me, *and* answer me as well. I know you can hear me. Listen, for God's sake, this might be your last chance ... listen, damn you, you will listen if I have to force you ...' but the soft-scented, fire-crackled peace of the bedroom dragged on and on. At that moment Christy Buchanan tore free from the last bonds which held her, and the hundreds of thousands of other women of her class, and with a soft oath she stood up.

'So! We are to do it the hard way, are we? Well, that

450

suits me fine, Alex Buchanan, for I must admit I have always enjoyed a good fight, as well you know! I have learned during the last months, you see, doing your job! Yes, doing the work you are too ... too afraid to do yourself. You would have loved to tell me to stop, wouldn't you? You would love to tell me *now*, wouldn't you, but you are hoist with your own petard, as they say. You have decided not to speak and so you have not the voice to do it, and even if you should find it you have not the stomach! Have you *nothing* to say, husband? No words with which to put me in my place. The place I am meant to occupy. The role I am meant to fulfil, or will you lie there and say nothing, do nothing, *be* nothing?'

Over the sound of her own heavy breathing she could hear that his had strengthened, her rage breathing something into him, something she had not believed was still alive.

Suddenly she snapped her finger at the dog. 'Get down, boy,' she said positively and after a momentary glance at his master's face the dog reluctantly obeyed, jumping to the floor.

With the gesture like that of a wizard revealing some magical sorcery beneath his cloak of illusion she lifted the light blankets which covered Alex's emaciated body and whipped them away, flinging them as though they were made of swan's-down about her head, then dropped them into a fleecy bundle beside the bewildered dog. He began to bark frantically, not at all sure whether some mischief was about to be done to his master whom he had guarded for months now, but Christy was possessed and with a harsh cry of anger she pointed to the rug before the fire.

'Lie down, sir, lie down,' she commanded and he did as he was told.

There was a hesitant knock at the door and Mrs Jackson's voice asked timidly if there was something wrong ... she'd heard the dog bark ... it was not like him to ... she had wondered ... was Mrs Buchanan perhaps ...?

'No thank you, Mrs Jackson. My husband and I are just having a discussion. I shall call you when I need you.'

The head on the pillow slowly turned towards her, the effort so appalling, even in the savage depths of her anger, Christy felt the agony of it in her own muscles. The dead eyes stared into hers with such hatred she felt the compulsion to recoil but she knew she must not. She must not allow him to see any weakness in her now. She stared back, then allowed her gaze to run down the wasted length of the once hard, proud, beautiful body of her husband and he began to weave his head about on the pillow, his mouth forming a silent scream.

He was wearing a short, snow-white gown, one of the dozen he had for the nurse changed him constantly. They had devised a towelling napkin, somewhat like the ones her own children had worn as infants, and she could see the bulky shape of it standing up about his hips. The rest of him was flat, narrow, skeletal, every bone peaking obscenely through his flesh, through the material of his gown. Her heart plunged and bucked into her throat in fear for in truth she had not been aware of what his body had become since she had last seen it, and her bright, determined spirit quailed, but she would not let him see it. Not if it cost her her life!

The sinews of his neck strained as he spoke.

'You filthy . . . bitch, cover . . . me . . . up . . . damn you . . . to hell . . .' but she continued to appraise him as though he was a leg of mutton on a butcher's slab, one she was not really certain she wished to purchase.

'So this is what you have become, is it, Alex Buchanan? Well, we shall have to see about that, won't we? You think if you lie here long enough in your own filth . . .'

'You bitch . . . let . . . me . . .'

'. . . you will simply fade away and we shall put you in the ground, wiping our hands of you and shaking our heads, duty done, and you can go to your Maker clutching your self-pity about you as you have done for the past year.'

452

She took his foot in her hand and though her heart filled her breast, beating wildly with pity for him, she lifted his leg and then let it fall callously to the bed.

'I can see we shall have our work cut out here, Mrs Jackson and I, but you listen to me, Alex Buchanan, and listen well, for I mean to have my own way in this. You have bullied me for over five years, but now it is my turn. I have danced to your tune but now you shall dance to mine. Aah . . . I actually see you smile! *Is* it a smile or are you merely conveying in that silent way you have, that you wish me to do something for you? Come on, Alex,' she taunted, 'tell me what it is. Speak man, tell me your thoughts!'

'*God . . . damn . . . you . . . to . . . hell, Christy Emmerson.*'

'Bravo!' she clapped her hands. 'Now that is what I call a bloody good start!'

CHAPTER TWENTY-NINE

'We shall begin with the oil, Mrs Jackson. A massage once a day to start with, then, when my husband has become accustomed to it, twice a day. I shall do the evening one myself . . . I'm sorry, Alex, you wished to say something?'

'Go . . . to . . . hell . . . leave me . . . alone.'

'You have already given me that order several times and as you see I am still here.' She turned back to the bemused nurse, and though the man on the bed continued to struggle to use the muscles of his throat and lips which had scarcely been in motion for months, she continued to ignore his efforts as though he were no more than an infant babbling in his cradle.

'But I don't understand, Mrs Buchanan. What is it all for? I don't know how to . . . what d'you call it . . . massage.'

'I shall show you,' Christy said briskly, confidently though her own knowledge was vague. Perhaps in her ignorance she was about to do more harm than good but if so, what had Alex to lose? She could not hurt him for he had no feeling in his body. It was deteriorating so rapidly, kept alive, in all probability and against its will, only by the nourishing food which was stuffed into his flaccid mouth every few hours. He would die soon despite this for he meant to die, so how could she make him worse? She had worried over it in the night, reluctant to inflict more pain, not physical for that was impossible, but with the humiliating indignities she must heap upon him. Perhaps it was kinder to let him sink slowly into death but some instinct – some knowledge which she had gained about him during their five years of marriage – was curiously aware that though he ignored her very existence he was in some mysterious way searching for help. He did not know it himself. He had been an over-bearing, self-willed man with an unshakable belief in his own strong body and mind, incapable of asking any man for help, but in his mind perhaps there was still a tiny portion of his challenging will remaining. Enough to awaken at least his hatred of her and thereby unlock his spirit.

'But Mrs Buchanan, he will not like it,' the nurse said dubiously.

'There is nothing he can do about it, Mrs Jackson.'

'Mrs Buchanan!' The nurse was shocked by Mrs Buchanan's unfeeling disregard for the poor man on the bed. She herself had seen his shame at the indignities she forced upon him but they were necessary. This was not! This was an impetuous whim on the part of his wife and she would speak to the doctor about it. She had no particular medical knowledge herself, being employed merely because she was strong, handy and clean and could do what was needed. If the doctor had wanted massage, would he not have ordered it. But Mrs Buchanan had not yet finished it seemed.

'Now when Mr Buchanan has become used to the

massage and the . . . the handling it entails I intend to start
. . . now what shall we call it?'

'I'm sure I don't know, Mrs Buchanan. I shudder to
think!'

Christy turned to gaze at Alex and his eyes looked back
venomously at her and his mouth worked, a dribble of
saliva escaping to run down his chin. Her heart beat fast,
thudding in compassion for him but she would not be put
off. Already his face had come alive and she had not yet
started the . . .

'. . . manipulation! There, that's what we shall call it.'

'*Manipulation!* I've never heard of it.'

'It means . . . it means . . . to move something . . . handle
something but with . . . with dexterity.'

'*Dexterity!*'

'Yes. With care. Skill. We will learn to be skilful, Mrs
Jackson, you and I, and when we have done . . .'

'Yes, Mrs Buchanan?' The nurse was affronted, her
expression saying she was in serious doubt of Mrs Buch-
anan's sanity.

'Well . . .' For a moment Christy faltered. What *would*
happen when they were done? Would he walk again?
Would he move and speak and be the man he once was?
Would he grin again in that jaunty arrogant way he had,
insolently charming, cruelly witty, strangely gentle as he
sometimes could be and passionate in their bed? Her pulse
beat a curious tattoo in her throat and she felt a tiny
thread of . . . of . . . something so fragile it had gone before
she could grasp it.

She took herself and straightened her back. Lifting her
head she stared defiantly into her husband's haunted eyes.

'Well, we shall see, Mrs Jackson, and so, let us make a
start.'

'Damn you . . . Christy . . . leave . . . me . . . be.'

'Nonsense, Alex!' How else was she to treat him? Pity
would shame him further. She must be brisk, confident,
self-assured. She must make him fight!

'Right, Mrs Jackson, off with the blanket, and Mr

Buchanan's nightshirt and I will help you to turn him on to his face. We shall have to do this together for a day or two and then, when you are more skilful, I shall leave you to it for I shall be away each day at business.'

'You . . . go . . . to the devil . . . Jesus, Christy . . . leave . . . me.'

They stripped him down to his flesh and turned him on his face taking away his pillows, moving his head to one side so that he could breathe, and in the continuous flow of obscenities which dribbled from his mouth Christy Buchanan began her attempt to re-build the life of the man who was her husband.

Strangely she did not question *why* she did it!

'I should begin . . . here, I think,' she murmured thoughtfully to Mrs Jackson, indicating the bony structure of his shoulders. 'Do no more than work your fingers across the skin firmly but gently, for we want no bruising and the skin will be tender. Avoid touching those sore spots at first though I suspect the oil might be beneficial to them, then move across the whole of his body, working gently all the time. When you have done that for ten minutes each side . . .'

'Confound it, Christy, I . . . am not . . . a . . . bloody . . . side of beef . . . goddammit.'

'. . . gently take his feet, one at a time and bend his legs . . . say half a dozen times, then his arms. Tonight we will lift him together into a sitting position which will exercise his . . . his spine, and Mrs Jackson . . .'

'Yes ma'am?'

'Do not let him . . . stop you. You understand?'

'Oh yes, Mrs Buchanan.'

That night before she dined in the solitary elegance to which she had become used, she took her first turn at massaging her husband's body. Mrs Jackson watched her, giving her a tip or two for having done it that morning for the ten minutes stipulated by Mrs Buchanan, she felt herself to be quite the expert.

Alex moaned feebly trying desperately to lift his head,

to turn the malignant loathing he felt for this creature who had decided to make his already miserable existence even more unbearable. But he was trapped, trapped, forced to endure it, forced to endure her gaze upon him, her beautiful grey velvet eyes running across his wretched body and he could scarcely bear the pain. He could hear her voice and by the movement of the bed knew she was bending over him taking her turn at torturing him but he could feel nothing, nothing of the hands which once he had burned to have about him.

'Christy . . . for . . . pity's . . . sake.' He was pleading now but she took no notice, continuing whatever she was about. And there was worse to come for when she and Mrs Jackson heaved together to get him on his back he could see her then, see where her eyes went, see where her hands were directed and he felt the feeble tears of hopelessness, of complete self-loathing fill his eyes. His body was broken and now she was breaking the tiny spark of spirit he had in him, humbling him, scorning his pride as he lay naked and shamed before her.

'A towel, please, Mrs Jackson,' he heard her say and for a second he felt gratitude as she laid it across his shrunken genitals then he turned his head away and let the tears slip into his thick hair.

'What's the matter, Alex?' she said crisply. 'Do you not want to be helped to recover?'

'Go . . . to . . . hell . . . go . . . to hell,' he mumbled.

'It seems that is your stock answer to everything,' she said absently as her fingers moved slowly across his breast and rib cage to his upper arm, feeling the wasted muscle, the bone beneath. She could trace the tendon and the sweep of the top muscle in his forearm, running back to the outside of his upper arm, and as her gentle touch moved down she closed her eyes, 'seeing' with her finger tips where the two crossed each other over the elbow where she could push the top of her fingers between them. Quite fascinated and hardly aware of the man whose body she examined, or of the woman who watched, she ran her hands along his shoulder joint, his collar bone, tracing muscle and bone, sinew and tendon, one leading to another down the length of his arm. His hands were made up of dozens of small bones, and his wrists, all delicately laced together in a precise pattern. She could feel the slack ligaments which must surely hold together the hundreds of bones which formed his skeleton and marvelled at this beautiful but somehow damaged piece of machinery.

'See Mrs Jackson,' she murmured, 'put your hand here, no, just here. Now tell me what you feel.'

'Nothing!'

'No, please, run your fingers across his calf. See, if I bend the knee . . . there, can you feel the contraction of the muscle?'

'Why . . . yes . . . yes, I can feel it pull, Mrs Buchanan.' Mrs Jackson became quite excited and she began enthusiastically to bend poor Mr Buchanan's other leg, his arm, clenching his useless hand with her own strong fingers. 'They all sort of . . . of . . . *move*. Very weak, mind, but there's something there . . .'

'I know . . . I know . . . feel this . . .'

'Here, let me have some of that oil, Mrs Buchanan. You do his arms while I have a go at his legs. Why, we'll have him up and . . .'

'*Mrs Jackson!*'

The words came out like whiplash and poor Mrs Jackson fell back from Mr Buchanan's legs as though they had risen up and kicked her.

'Mrs Jackson.' It was said more quietly now for Christy had the woman's attention before she began to babble of miracle cures, and even of Mr Buchanan being on his feet by morning. 'I think that is enough for now. If you will sponge my husband down I will be back in a minute. I wish to have a word with him.'

Now that her task of discovering how Alex's body was structured had been started – the bone, the sinews, the tendons and ligaments which lay beneath his skin – she moved sensitively away, taking her gaze from him, allowing the indignity he must suffer, of being cleaned up by Mrs Jackson to be done in private. She sat for a moment before her own fire, her hand on the head of the terrier who had been banished to the adjoining room whilst Alex was 'manipulated', then turned as the door opened. The dog slipped silently through it to resume his vigil beside his master.

'Done now, Mrs Buchanan,' the nurse said as she bustled from Alex's bedroom into Christy's. 'He's all done and dusted but he's none too pleased with what you an' me's up to.'

Mrs Buchanan's ally now in this wonder in which she was to take an important part, Mrs Jackson beamed broadly, conspiratorially, for what did it matter what *he* wanted.

Mrs Buchanan was the mistress and *master* in this house.

'Thank you, Mrs Jackson. Come back in an hour to sit with him whilst I have my meal, and then you can finish for the night.'

'Thank you, madam.' It was said with respect for Mrs Jackson had just realized that there was more to the pretty Mrs Buchanan than met the eye. Wayward and wilful, she had heard her called by those who had known her for years but credit where it was due, she had a head on her shoulders!

Christy drew the chair up to the bed on which Alex lay, 'all done and dusted', the sheet drawn neatly up to his chin. He had closed his eyes and the dog stared anxiously into his face waiting for some acknowledgement of his presence.

'Lie . . . down, boy,' and he settled thankfully at his side.

'Alex, look at me Alex.'

'Go . . . away . . . Christy. For God's sake . . . woman . . . have you not . . . done enough . . .'

'I will not go away, Alex, let us make no mistake about that. I am determined on this. I have . . . through ignorance . . . allowed you to lie in this bed for almost a year because

459

I was not aware there was another course open to us. I am not even sure where this will lead us, or indeed if it will lead *anywhere* for I have no medical knowledge, but we can *try*, Alex. We can *hope*. Help me in this, please. Help yourself. Allow Mrs Jackson and I . . . or if you prefer, a second nurse to . . . manipulate your body. Let us try to . . . make it strong again. I don't know why you cannot move . . .'

'Dear . . . God . . . in Heaven. Have . . . you . . . no pity? Is . . . it . . . not enough that I . . . am forced . . . to . . . lie . . . here . . . but you must . . . remind me . . .'

His voice jerked in spasms from his twisted bitter lips and his eyes flew open to turn an expression of such deep despair on her that she felt herself falter.

'Leave . . . me . . . please . . . Christy. Do . . . not . . . torment . . . me . . . with this . . . bloody . . . nonsense. I know . . . have always . . . known you . . . do not . . . care for me . . . but you . . . are . . . not a . . . cruel . . . woman. You show kindness . . . to . . . your children . . . friends. Can . . . you . . . not do the . . . same for . . . for me?'

Her heart surged in pain for him and she felt the most profound urge to lean over and take him in her arms, as she would one of her children when they were hurt. It was the longest sentence he had spoken for many months, and it was said with the simple dignity of a man who could stand little more. His face was haggard and grey and she could see the effort was exhausting him but she was relentless on her resolution. If she gave way now, she would never start again, for she would not have the strength to withstand him.

'No! I cannot.'

'Why . . . why . . . do you . . . hate me?'

'I don't hate you, Alex,' she said crisply, 'and I am not deliberately being cruel. I truly believe this treatment can help you . . .'

'Christ, woman . . . can you not . . . experiment . . . on . . . someone else?'

'I know of no one else who cannot move.'

460

The silence which followed this callous remark stretched on and on, and his blue eyes – once bright and alive, glittering with keen enjoyment of any verbal battle between them – stared curiously into hers.

'You really ... have no ... heart ... at all, have ... you, my dear?' For a fraction of a second the flippant humour which had once been his, lifted his dark eyebrows sardonically and his mouth curled in what was almost a mocking smile.

'If you wish to think so.'

'Oh ... I do ... but let ... us keep ... to ... the subject in hand. You may ... believe ... whatever you wish ... to believe about this ... manipulation ... as you ... so quaintly call it, but I absolutely ... refuse ... to ... be the ... the means of ... your experiment. Do ... you hear ... me? Take ... your bloody nurse ... and your oil ... and ... your ... hare-brained ... ideas and leave ...'

'You see, Alex, already you are more lively ...'

'Goddammit, lady!'

'You are *fighting* me! Your face is *alive* with anger where for months it has done nothing but lie on that pillow and stare at the ceiling. It *must* be progress, Alex. It must be an improvement, even this small start we have made.'

His head began to move ... slowly ... slowly ... from side to side. He had only a fraction of power in his neck muscles and the effort was enormous. His eyes rolled up in their sockets in his frustrated attempt to simply convey to this woman that he wanted nothing more than to be left alone. He strained to force his once formidable will on hers, to dominate her with the only weapon he had, his cruel tongue.

'Get ... out ... of ... here, get out. Go ... and ... amuse yourself in some other ... way. Can you ... not find ... something else ... to divert ... you? Go and ... play with ... the mills ... the mine. You tell ... me how easy ... it is. You ... are ... free ... now, Mrs Buchanan.

461

You . . . may do anything . . . that . . . pleases you . . . for I cannot . . . stop you. Ride . . . your damned . . . mare about the . . . fells, visit whom you please . . . do whatever . . . you . . . have a fancy for . . . take a . . . a lover . . . perhaps . . . the Squire would be . . . glad of . . . some . . . diversion . . . aah . . . I . . . see . . .'

His eyes blazed in his livid, straining face. Christy felt the heat of them sear her, and her own dropped quickly before he could read the expression in them but it was too late!

'. . . so . . . you . . . have already thought of it . . . have you, madam, or . . . perhaps done more than just . . . think about it! There . . . is . . . no one . . . to tell me the . . . news . . . so you are . . . quite safe . . . are you not?' His voice dropped then, exhaustion and . . . and something else she did not recognize stripping away the weapon of his anger.

'You bitch . . . you . . . faithless bitch . . . get out . . . get . . . away from me. I cannot bear . . . your hands . . . on me. Go . . . go and . . . lay them on . . . that spineless boy . . .'

He spoke the vicious words with such quiet force they were more compelling than if he had shouted them.

Christy jumped to her feet and the dog turned to watch her uneasily as she began to stride about the room. The irony of it made her want to smile, and yet the sadness was almost too much to be borne. He was so close to the truth and yet so far away! When she *had* been faithless during that lovely summer, her content had made *him* happy. During the period she and Robin had been lovers, surprisingly she and Alex had been closer than at any time during their marriage. Now, when she was blameless she was to be accused of something for which she was innocent!

Her anger grew until she could scarce contain it. She felt no guilt. She had felt none then and she felt none now, for the love she had for Robin Forsythe rose above guilt or shame. It had been, as she had been, handled carelessly,

462

considered not worth the importance of thought. It had been an integral part of her, as easy and natural and necessary as the breath she drew into her lungs and they had thrown it aside, all of them, with as little compunction as one would a worn shoe. It might so easily have been damaged and yet it was strong, as whole and shining now as it had been then. She had guarded it zealously and it still bloomed, as the fells had bloomed during her summer with Robin Forsythe. She would not have it destroyed. She would not have it ridiculed nor spat upon, made to appear tawdry by this man who had helped to separate her from it. She did not know, even now, what was to happen to it. Perhaps it would die from lack of nourishment for when would she see Robin again? He was married with a son of his own, living in London and Leicestershire, she had heard, and Dalebarrow Hall left, in its new grandeur, in the hands of servants. But it made no difference. The love they had was no small thing to be slung about carelessly or spoken of scathingly. It was the deepest, the most truthful emotion she had ever known apart from the natural mother love she had for her children, and this man who was her husband, because *they* had made him so, *would not destroy it!*

Her anger was ferocious as she whirled to face him and the dog could bear the tension no longer. With a soft moan he slid from the bed and ran to lie beside the closed door.

'So that is the quarrel, is it?' Her voice mocked the man on the bed. 'We are to bring up the past, is that it? Not content to rot away in your self-pity you intend to drag up what has corroded your damn soul ever since we wed. Take a lover! Ha!'

She flung herself about and strode to the window then leaned forward to place a hand on either side of it. She blinked into the rapidly falling darkness, forcing back the tears of rage and bitterness, swallowing the hard knot of pain which lay in her throat. She'd be damned if she'd weep before him since that would give him pleasure but by God, she'd show him what she intended and she'd have no argument either. She had tried to spare his masculine pride, the arrogant maleness of him which had turned to shamed humiliation, for in her compassion she had allowed her antipathy towards him to falter and fade away. She had done her best to spare his feelings, to be gentle in her handling of his wounded self-esteem but it seemed she had wasted herself in the endeavour. She had tried to treat kindly the damaged body and humbled spirit of this strong man, and had received nothing but curses and accusations for her trouble!

So be it! If that was how this drama was to be played, so be it!

Turning, she moved slowly, hazardously across the pretty carpet until she reared over the distorted face which glared at her from the pillow.

Her voice was soft. 'He is married, Alex. Robin Forsythe is married! My *lover* has a wife and a son now, but "give a dog a bad name", I believe that is the expression is it not, and you have given it to me so perhaps I might decide to live up to it. Wife, or husband, what does it matter? They do not present an insurmountable hurdle, do they, Alex . . .?'

'May . . . you . . . rot . . . in . . . hell . . . Christy Buchanan.'

Her voice rose contemptuously. 'And you too, my dear husband, but by God before you get there you will go through it here on earth, because I am going to put you through it, Alex Buchanan. Yes . . . oh, yes, I long to go to my lover . . . aah . . . that caught you where it hurts, did it not, but you . . . *you* have stopped me. This accident of yours, it stopped me, for I do believe I was ready to leave you. Yes, I think I really was. I would have given up . . . everything I hold dear . . . but I cannot go now, can I? I am chained to you by far more than marriage vows. I must protect my sons' legacy for with you intent on staying forever in that bed, someone must see to it. I intend to ensure that the concerns which will one day be theirs are still intact and thriving when they come to them. You do not seem to care whether they have a roof over their heads or even a scrap of food to put in their mouths. Well, I do, Alex, I do. Until you are well enough . . . *be quiet*, damn you, for I will not be stopped, until you are well enough to look to your children's welfare I must do it for you.'

'Can . . . you not . . . get it into . . . your . . . bloody head I shall . . . never . . .'

'Oh yes you will. Be very sure of that. You will leave that bed or I shall die in the attempt. I intend to work your body until it is capable of doing more than lie in its own filth . . .'

'You whore . . . you . . . you . . .' He was almost screaming now in his violent fury but hers was as great.

'Yes, whore, that is what I shall be called but the name for you has not yet been invented. Whore is a good honest name, Alex Buchanan, and this whore has complete control of you. I own you! Everything that was once yours is mine! I can do as I want with it all. Your house and everyone in it all belong to me. Your sons, your servants, your businesses, your money, your horses and carriage, and your body! When I speak my voice is the one listened to, not yours! Think of that, Alex, whilst you lie there, and think of this: you will not be free of me until you are capable of speaking for yourself and you will not do that until I have forced you to it. Now, I shall go and dine and leave you to your thoughts. And I shall continue to do my share of the manipulation and massage even if we do employ another nurse for I want to see for myself what is happening to you.'

Whirling, her skirt billowing in a graceful bell she glided gracefully across the room, opened the connecting door and as she passed through it said graciously over her shoulder. 'Goodnight, husband, sleep well. You have a big day ahead of you tomorrow!'

The first thing she did the next morning was to order the day nursery to be moved into the large room directly above Alex's bedroom, turning out the three maidservants who slept there.

For most of the day the excitement was intense as four rowdy children, plus the usual noisy pack of delighted animals got in the way of Jack and Miles and John as they carted all the old and comfortable nursery furniture from one floor to the next and cleaned the chimney, unused for years. Meanwhile Patience, Meg and Lou scrubbed floors and windows, grumbling that they were not dirty for had they themselves not occupied the room for years, re-hung curtains and laid carpets suitable for destructive children to sprawl on. The big nursery table at which Amy and the reluctant Johnny learned their ABC was thumped down the flight of stairs from the nursery floor and placed in the centre of the room. For most of the day the energetic noise of four children, three dogs and innumerable kittens settling themselves into their usual careless, everyday life sounded clearly to the man who lay beneath it.

'Why Christy?' Faith begged to know. 'I simply cannot keep those imps quiet all day. I thought that was what we agreed, to keep them out of Mr Buchanan's way, and now that the weather has turned cold they do not get out . . .'

'It doesn't matter, Faith. Let them make as much noise as they usually do.'

'Christy! That poor man! He will get no rest . . .'

'Exactly!'

'I don't understand you, Christy, really. How can you be so cruel . . .'

'Listen, Faith. For a year now Alex has lain in a cocoon of near silence. I have deliberately kept the children from him except for a formal "Good morning, father" when I felt he could stand it, but it was a mistake, Faith. He has slipped further and further away from reality, lying there with that old dog and Mrs Jackson for company. He should have more communication with the life of the house about him. It's all he has and I have kept it from him believing it to be for the best. You see what it has done to him. He needs to hear and see the children as they

466

are. This artificial view of his growing sons and daughter, the one I created out of sympathy for him is not enough. I am going up there now to see them, and believe me I intend to stir up such laughter and excitement he will imagine the ceiling is about to fall in on him and be glad to get out of his bed to avoid it.' Her face softened. 'Don't worry, Faith, the children will be out of there by five in the evening and he can rest as much as he wants to then.'

'Oh Christy, do you think . . .?'

'I do, Faith.'

Their clatter, the pipe of their voices, their screams of laughter, or shouts of angry tears were to be a constant reminder to their father of their normal childhood presence. And *her* laughter – that lovely pealing carillon which had first drawn him to her so many years ago – floated down to him and he would turn his head to listen, and his awakened senses fluttered painfully at the disturbance which would not let him slide thankfully into the peace he craved.

Christmas came and went and the house was a blaze of lights and high childish laughter for no one told them to be quiet now; the everlasting yapping of the dogs whom nobody seemed capable, nor even cared supposedly, of training to silence. The Tree of Love was erected in the hall, with Jack to stand on a ladder to place the decorations on branches which the children could not reach. It was laden with fruit and flowers and charms and each night during the twelve days of Christmas fresh wax tapers were lit, each tiny flame reflected in the bright, wondering eyes of Alex Buchanan's children.

Evergreens were brought in from the woods, holly and ivy and mistletoe and with the coloured and gilt paper chains the clumsy fingers of his sons and daughter had fashioned, Alex Buchanan's bedroom was decorated and, at least whilst the children were there, subdued and nervous, he refrained from swearing. It was different when they had scampered gratefully away, still not at ease with the silent figure of their father, for then he raged at Christy to take the blasted stuff away for what had he to celebrate, he asked furiously.

'Oh, don't be such a spoil-sport, Alex,' she answered lightly. 'It is Christmas after all and the children would be heartbroken if the decorations are gone when they come to bring their presents for you. They will be here shortly so you had best put a smile on if you are not to frighten them.'

They were small gifts, chosen by the children themselves for as Christy agonized with Faith, what could possibly be given to a man who did nothing but lie in his bed? But the pictures Joby had painted with violently clashing colours; the perfectly-pressed flower from Amy to lay on his pillow, she said shyly; the cone which Johnny had found which opened, he explained gruffly, when the weather was to be fine; and the lovely big, smooth pebble Harry had discovered in the stream last summer, to be used as a paper-weight, had been given freely.

They sang a piping carol for him – The Mistletoe Bough – all fidgeting and stumbling over the words, Harry out of tune and Joby not even sure what it was. And then they raced noisily, thankfully from the room to erupt above his head, greeting the three dogs as rapturously as if they had been gone for a week and Christy was gratified by the flush of colour which warmed his pale face.

The massage and manipulation continued, at first twice a day, then, as he seemed to take no harm from it, every two hours. A nurse was employed to come in during the day to help Mrs Jackson for it was arduous work, wringing the sweat from her as though she had been in a Turkish bath.

Each morning Christy strode vigorously into his bedroom demanding wickedly to know if he could touch his toes yet. Mrs Jackson would be there, coming from the tiny slip of a room – which, years ago, Christy had wanted to put Faith in on the day she became Alex's wife – just across the landing. She was up before the rest of the servants so that she might have her patient clean and tidy for his morning inspection. She was Mrs Buchanan's devoted slave now in her careful carrying out of the massage and manipulation they had devised between them, and which she had 'trained' the new nurse to do. She and Mrs Buchanan had done it together, exploring his body, feeling with their sensitive fingers which muscles went where and did what, and though his body could not be described as able to move, it shrank away from their touch. In the three months since they had been at it, despite his lack of co-operation Mrs Jackson swore she could see a difference, slight and scarcely noticeable though it was, in the texture of his muscles. They had become firmer, less like threads of old string, she would say cheerfully, though of course he wouldn't have it. Lay there like a bag of old bones, he did, his thin face turned to the ceiling, or staring into that of the dog when he was on his stomach and only when *she* came into the room did he show a spark of anything and then it was only hatred. Molly Jackson had never seen anyone *hate* like Mr Buchanan did and directed at his wife too, the woman who was doing her best to get him out of his bed! She reckoned that was what kept him alive, the way he felt about his wife. He fed on it, she could see it, brooding for hours on what spiteful thing he could say to her when she came home from wherever it was she went all day in her carriage. He had stopped the obscene cursing with which he had greeeted her own massage, or Nurse Livingstone's, but that was because it was them, Molly Jackson decided, but the minute Mrs Buchanan came into the room of an evening – enveloped in the large white apron she wore for her share of the task – he started on her, calling her every filthy name he could put a tongue to. Mrs Jackson had asked her how she stood it, but Mrs Buchanan only laughed and gave him as good as she got and by the dear Lord, did it get his dander up! He came alive then, his head, the muscles of his neck gaining strength now, thrashing about from side to side; and if Mrs Jackson had not felt, actually felt the hatred which spewed from him at every encounter with his wife, she might have gone as far as to say he looked forward to that moment when she came through the door!

'And how are we today, Alex dear?' Mrs Buchanan would say mockingly each morning.

'. . . off, Christy,' he would reply vigorously and so it would go until Mrs Buchanan left the room, the wide hem of her tailored gown whispering on the deep pile of the carpet, the fragrance of her perfume lingering for minutes on the air before it was overlaid by the odour of the sickroom.

Mrs Jackson and the nurse would strip back the bed-clothes, after first ensuring that the room was warm enough, for Mrs Buchanan was very particular about draughts and the possibility of Mr Buchanan catching a chill in his weakened condition. His nightshirt would be next and he would stare indifferently at nothing whilst she worked the oil into his supple skin – the lubricant soaked up and already doing its work, her fingers, sure and knowledgeable now, searching out each flabby muscle, smoothing and kneading, firm, regular, rhythmic. Next would be his legs. Lift and bend, lift and bend, the foot rotated and stretched as though he was walking on air. Back to his chest she would bend them, then pulled to their fullest length, each leg worked in turn. His arms were next. Lift and bend, lift and bend. Above his head and down until his fingers touched his thighs and all the time she could feel the pull of the useless muscles, worked, not by Mr Buchanan, but by the clever hands of Molly Jackson.

Though she and Nurse Livingstone chatted amicably for they got on well, Mr Buchanan spoke not a word until his wife came to bring life to his dead eyes and colour to his pale skin – and Molly Jackson began to see what it was that linked them so fast to one another.

CHAPTER THIRTY

The young man sat opposite the elegantly clad woman in the absolute comfort of the office of the Buchanan Mining Company. There was a large, well-polished desk between them, empty of anything but the papers he himself had handed her and she studied them now with intense concentration.

He glanced about him staring at the sombre paintings on the panelled wall, paintings of elderly gentlemen dressed in the fashions of an earlier decade, of country scenes and pastoral views and his plain, unsmiling face showed no trace of his thoughts. He returned his gaze to the woman, Mrs Buchanan, she had been presented to him as, and his mind conjectured on her presence, on her appearance and on the consideration of her qualifications to judge himself suitable for the post of mining engineer for which he had applied. She was very beautiful, and young too — younger than himself he would have said — so what was she doing here in her gown of tawny grenadine, he wondered, but his face registered nothing more than the respectful regard a man would direct towards his prospective employer.

Christy studied the sheaf of papers Mr Richard Forbes had politely handed to her; turning them over one by one, reading the words, the legal sounding sentences which commanded those who appraised this notice to be quite sure that the gentleman named was not only highly qualified and well able to manage Alex's mine, anybody's mine, but was a conscientious, honest, hard-working, God-fearing gentleman. There were stiff parchment documents from the University of Edinburgh declaring that Richard Forbes was an expert in the science of locating and extracting useful minerals from the crust of the earth; the exploration to determine the extent of a deposit and the development of it and the exploitation of such ore as was found in the mining he undertook. There were references from men under whom he had worked, from a parson, a magistrate, a doctor, all testifying to the fact that this man was the very one for whom she searched, all extremely gratifying and all pointing to him as the new mine manager – so why was it she felt a sense of unease when his flat, cold grey eyes looked unblinkingly into hers? He was extremely polite with the manners of a gentleman, which he undoubtedly was. He was well-dressed, well-spoken and these papers could not be faulted. Out of the five young men she had seen he was the most suitable, or so these papers said, and yet she hesitated. *Why?*

She looked up and smiled coolly and the young man did the same. She knew she should question him, ask him about ... something, but what? What questions would Alex ask if he were sitting here instead of herself? How would he conduct an interview with a man he was considering for employment? Dear Lord, *something* should be said, asked, commented upon, but what? The young man was looking at her enquiringly, as had the other young men who had sat in the same chair, ready to tell her anything she asked but the trouble was she didn't know what to ask beyond the basic questions – the answers to which lay before her in the degree in mining engineering he had gained, the references he had been given by these eminently respectable men and the records of previous employment which reported on how he excelled in his chosen profession. Perhaps that was enough!

But this man was looking at her with the same expression *all* men cast about her; the look which, though on the surface was perfectly respectful, had behind it the faintly withering look of a man who wonders what the devil she thought she was doing playing out this stupid role she had taken on.

Oh, he would mouth the polite questions and answers

they all did, just enough to satisfy her – or so they thought – that they were taking her seriously, but when she was gone they would do exactly as they pleased and when she complained later that her orders had not been carried out, would be most apologetic, saying they must have misunderstood, implying that it was *she* who had misunderstood. She who was therefore to blame for the mishandling of an order, the bungling of an account, the mismanagement of a consignment of gunpowder, which ended up fifty miles from its destination and two days late into the bargain, and she must travel swiftly to the irate customer to smooth his understandable irritation, promising humbly that it would not happen again! She knew that they did it on purpose in order to persuade her that her duty really did lie in her husband's home, not his business, and that if she left them alone to get on with it they would manage perfectly well without her.

And perhaps, in the long run, they might! She had been so naïvely satisfied with her visit to the men in St Helens, and later to those of Alex's customers in Swansea; and yet was it not the truth that if this man, or one of the others she had seen, was put into the mine, visited those same men, production would increase, the ore be delivered on time and the profit lost be recovered since they knew what they were about and were not stumbling in the dark as she still was – but which man to choose?

She had liked the first. He was charming and merry and had made her laugh. She had felt he coud be trusted not to cheat her, but was his very charm, personable and easygoing, the right manner with which to treat the men who would be under him?

The second had been surly, ill at ease with a woman and obviously not happy to even be in the same room with one who would presumably have the right to order him about; and the third, direct from a mining college in Derbyshire, so young and shy, the mere idea of him issuing directions to some of the laconic old miners who had been in Alex's mine since his father's day was quite absurd.

This one appeared to be the most suitable. He had the qualifications and experience and an air of command, of knowing exactly what he was about and that was reassuring but there was something ... some essence of cool assessment, of self-satisfied imperturbability about him which disturbed her. Should he be quite so ... confident? He knew his worth obviously, and had stated himself to be satisfied with the salary he had been offered together with the house which had once been Faith's. No, he was not married he said with a small, puzzling smile but no doubt there would be some woman who could come in and cook and clean for him. Perhaps one of the miner's wives anxious to earn a few shillings a week, that was providing he was offered the position, of course.

Another cool smile and another pause. He crossed the perfectly tailored legs of his pale grey trousers and Christy looked away from his expressionless face and felt the indecision slither through her with the stealth of a snake.

Dear Lord, why did not Alex retain that angry hold on life which sprang so vigorously to his stagnant brain when she went into his room each evening to massage his body? She had thought she had begun to drag him from his passive indifference, jubilantly believing that with his decisive and shrewd mind, the intelligent and imaginative way in which his brain worked that – as he saw his body improving as it had done over the past six months – he would regain his hold on life and would begin to run his business, as she had hoped, from his sickroom. Through her he could pass on his orders, see through the eyes of the mining engineer he chose what was being brought from the mine, assess the methods used, the state of the machinery, the problems which had arisen in the sinking of the new mine shaft begun a month before his accident, the pumping out of the water from the deep level which was becoming increasingly dangerous, all the dozens of anxious concerns for which she had no answer.

With time and ingenuity she was learning to deal with the gentlemen with whom Alex did business. She could, and already did the balancing of the weekly accounts which all three businesses incurred, and was rapidly becoming adept at turning loss into profit, and with the help of the bank manager in Fellthwaite who was only too pleased to come to the aid of a customer – the large proportion of whose funds lay in his hands – she was becoming familiar with the investments and shares Alex had in a score of concerns. On the financial side she could, she knew, take Alex's place in the mine, the gunpowder mill and with the investing of monies in certain new businesses which Mr Mansfield, the shrewd manager at the bank, had recommended to her – but with the best will in the world she could not take over the physical work done by a trained and qualified engineer. She would master the men who worked for her eventually, make them realize that she was now the absolute ruler of her husband's domain, and those who would not bow to it would be replaced – but she could not distinguish copper ore from vein-stone and she desperately needed someone who could. Her father and brothers, and then Alex, who was himself a man who understood machinery, had learned over the years the process of manufacturing gunpowder. They had each been employed on every dirty and dangerous job the mill demanded, except perhaps Alex, who nevertheless knew enough to see that it was done correctly – but Christy Buchanan could not do that. She could only watch and listen and struggle on, take each day as it came, learning a little here, a little there, and pray the whole would come together before it disintegrated about her ears for want of a knowledgeable leader!

She lifted her chin and looked into the inscrutable face of Richard Forbes. First things first! Let her get this problem ironed out, *then* she would turn to the gunpowder mill and the troubled waters there. Thank God for Mr Dunlop. At least the bobbin factory was in good hands and needed no more than a weekly visit from the manager to *her* parlour. He had indicated that he would be better suited to visit her and not the other way around, saying gruffly it was not seemly for a young woman to associate with the rough men he employed. His accounts were immaculate and a steady stream of profit poured weekly into Alex's account at the bank. Not only that but he was also willing to lend a bit of shrewd advice when asked, glad it seemed to be of service to this young woman he had come to respect for the dashing courage and determination she had in grasping the sword her husband had laid down and her ruthless resolve to use it in defence of what was his, and would be his sons' after him. He did not ask to see Mr Buchanan and Christy was grateful for his delicacy in not doing so.

'Well, Mr Forbes,' she said to the colourless, thin-lipped young man who sat opposite her, and as she spoke she noticed absently how his hooded eyes shot open momentarily, the only indication he gave of emotion.

'I will take your documents with me, if I may, for my husband will, of course, want to study them.'

'Of course.'

'He might even require you to come and see him. You are no doubt aware of his ... his condition since the accident at the mine.'

He smiled sympathetically. 'Yes, most unfortunate, Mrs Buchanan.' Everyone knew of his condition, his expression seemed to say and of Mrs Buchanan's foolish pretence that her husband was in full control of his own concerns. No one had seen him – so Mr Forbes had been told by the garrulous Mr Tate in the outer office – since he had been paralysed eighteen months ago and one had to do business with Mrs Buchanan who was her husband's spokesman, or so she would have everyone believe.

'So you would be prepared to ... to take on the complete control of the mine? Do all the surveys necessary, do the sampling and ... and ...'

Oh God, whatever else did a mining engineer do? She tried to remember the things Alex had talked about in their years of dining alone but not one item came back to

476

her as she stared into the neutral face of the man opposite. He seemed to read her mind!

'Don't worry, Mrs Buchanan. I am perfectly capable of doing all that your husband did, as you can see from my qualifications, but there are one or two small conditions I must insist on.'

'Yes Mr Forbes?' Her expression was wary.

'If I am to be in charge . . . complete charge of the mine, taking on responsibilities that would not ordinarily fall on my shoulders I feel, should you decide to employ me, that a slightly higher remuneration would be in order. Do you not agree?' Before she could reply, quite startled by his sudden reversal from polite subservience to challenging command, just as though he knew he had the whip hand, he went on, '. . . and I do think that a . . . a contract should be drawn up stating fully my duties, my authority and my . . . gain from the workings.'

'Gain?'

'My . . . salary!'

She was cool. 'I would have to discuss it with my . . .'

'Of course.' Did his hooded eyes have a touch of . . . insolence in them?

She lifted her head imperiously. 'And the second . . . condition? You did say one or two . . .'

'I have been told you are in the habit of coming to the mine and talking to the men, discussing with them matters . . .'

'Yes, Mr Forbes . . .?' Her voice was quite dangerously soft, somewhat as her husband's would be on such an occasion.

'I'm afraid I could not work in such circumstances. I would not be able to fulfil the terms of my employment with . . .'

'A woman poking her nose where it was not wanted?'

'I did not say that, Mrs Buchanan. I shall be on my own so I must be sure that I am in complete command. I cannot be put in a position where my word is questioned, you do see that, Mrs Buchanan?'

Christy felt her anger flare and with it came the definite inclination to tell this clever young man that he would do exactly as he was told, but then there was no one to tell him, for who at the mines would know more than he? If there was such a person she would not be considering this one. Confound it, perhaps she should take one of the others ... the merry one, or the young graduate who would be more biddable ... but did they have the ability ... the experience?

He saw her indecision and smiled reasssuringly.

'I am a very capable manager, Mrs Buchanan, and a fine engineer. You need have no fear of putting your husband's mine in my charge. I can guarantee I shall double your output within twelve months with my methods.'

'Which are?'

'I doubt you would understand, Mrs Buchanan. I am, after all, an engineer, and you are not.'

'I would have to know exactly ...'

'I'm sorry, Mrs Buchanan, those are my terms. A higher salary and complete control of the mine.' He shrugged lazily. 'If you find you cannot meet them then we must both look elsewhere but if you agree I guarantee you a well-run and profitable mine. Why do you not consult your ... husband? I'm sure he will agree that is fair. Perhaps I might come and ... discuss it with him. Would this evening be convenient?'

Christy stood up and instantly Richard Forbes sprang politely to his feet, the epitome of a young gentleman of quality giving due respect to a lady of similar class, waiting for her to speak – or not. Patiently he stood before her and Christy felt the blood beat in her temples since before God she did not know what to do for the best. Oh Alex, Alex, why have you left this awful choice to me? Her eyes stared into the colourless smile of the young man and she felt the urgent need to look away, to wring her hands and bite her lip, but then that was what women did, the slightly amused expression on his face said and the thought stiffened her spine and she knew she must make this decision alone.

Although her instincts, female again and therefore suspect, told her she did not like him was that a good enough reason not to employ him? It was not unreasonable for a man to wish to run a business which he was to manage without the owner, the man who had employed him to do just that, peering over his shoulder at every turn. He seemed the perfect man for the job, experienced, confident and certainly well able to command a work force. He had almost taken command of *her*.

'Believe me, Mrs Buchanan, I have run a profitable mine before,' he said, smiling politely. 'I could do the same with Mr Buchanan's.'

'Thank you, Mr Forbes. I'm sure you could,' she said calmly. 'Nevertheless I must talk it over with my husband. If he feels up to it I will send word for you to come up to the house to meet him. Now, Mr Tate will see you out. I have other applicants as you must realize.'

Oh yes, he did realize! He had seen them but he merely bowed courteously over her hand.

'The decision lies in my husband's hands. I merely report to him what I have seen.'

'Quite and thank you, Mrs Buchanan.' He bowed again showing no emotion beyond the customary gallantry shown by a gentleman to a lady; and the thought went through her head that he had the speculative gaze of Amy's tabby cat as it watched a sparrow peck at the lawn in search of grubs!

That night – as she worked on her husband's inert arms, bending then stretching the lifeless limbs in the semblance of a man lifting a weight above his head, watching the muscles pull and wondering for the hundredth time why that muscle, stronger now, still refused to work in the involuntary way it once had – she told him of Richard Forbes, as she told him of everything that happened now in her day.

Her fingers smoothed the firming flesh, kneading deeply into the striated muscle fibres beneath the skin. She did not look into his face as her senses concentrated on the task her clever hands undertook and she did not see his eyes slip to hers as she spoke.

'I interviewed another man today, Alex. Very clever, or so he would have me believe and I must say his credentials were flawless but there was something about him . . . don't ask me what . . .' as if he would, her amused mind reminded her, '. . . but I felt uneasy with him. Edinburgh University like yourself and a string of letters after his name as long as my arm but . . . well . . . patronizing is the word which springs to mind. Of course every one of them patronizes me for they all know I am ignorant of but the bare bones of what they do.'

Her face was soft and thoughtful, accepting her own shortcomings but not weighed down with them for she would alter that as her experience grew, and her husband watched her curiously, his usual oppressive hostility to what she did crumbling for a moment in her unflagging will. She had fought him for six months over the treatment of his inert body, though he supposed that was no great feat for he had not the strength to resist hers. He had been forced to it, day in and day out, and now for the most part he allowed the activity to drift about his useless form and clouded mind with as little concern as he would show for a fly buzzing at his window. But now and again, such as now, something would catch at his wandering attention, like a hand pulling in a kite which flew further and further away into the skies. It was not what she said, for did he care what happened at the mine, or the mill, or even in his children's nursery directly above his head, but what she *did* which caught his faded imagination. What she *was*! It was as though the more she was opposed the more ruthlessly determined she became to have her way. He could barely remember what it had been like before the accident for his mind shied away from the thought of himself as once he had been. Best let the wound of the memory scar over and heal, than constantly pick at it, but he did bring back deliberately the remembrance of those hours he had spent in conflict with men who had thought they could defy the fixity of purpose of Alex Buchanan, and *he* had been moving in a familiar world where she was a stranger to it. It was one he had been trained for, one he had lived in for all of his adult life. He had been a man moving amongst men, accepted by his own sex, respected for his strength, his shrewd brain, his knowledge of the business world, a rich and successful man who had proved himself amongst others.

And Christy? He felt the anguish assault him and hated her for it. He tried so hard to force her, and the life she now led to the very edge of his consciousness for in that way the pain became less and for the most part he was succeeding. The anger was going. The hatred was going. The bitterness was going. Each day he withdrew a little further from not only the life he had known but the life he knew now. For hours on end he seemed to exist in limbo, doing nothing, seeing nothing, feeling nothing, a speck of dust floating placidly in a shaft of sunlight, for can a speck of dust hurt, or feel, or care where it might land?

But this woman would keep on swirling the air about him, spiralling him up and up just as he was about to settle, clinging to his tired body with the relentless tenacity of the clambering rose which appeared each summer, despite the hardness of the winter, outside his bedroom window. She demanded his attention, calling out his name in a harsh voice which would not allow him that last drift into peaceful oblivion. He could take little more of this obscene body of his which fastened him so securely to this bed, this very existence, but she would insist on nourishing it, strengthening it, fighting death in just the same way his elderly Lakeland terrier had once fought the fox he had hunted.

Why? he asked himself remorselessly. Why should she care what happened to Alex Buchanan? The Squire, the man she loved was married now, she had told him, and had a son, but in the same breath she had spat out that it did not matter to either of them. If she were free she could go to him, she had implied. Take the money, *his* money and the pair of them could drift indolently about the world in the sunshine, living the Bohemian life, doing just as they pleased whilst he mouldered in his grave and his children were brought up by whoever she paid to do so. She had no need of him. She had no need of his body, of his protection, of his strength for was she not proving, slowly to be sure, that she was as strong as he himself had been?

In a split second of memory he was flung back in time to the day he had first seen her. Strong she was, even then, proud and reckless. Arrogant and fearless in support of her young lover. Hair streaming down her straight back, vivid eyes flashing like jewels in her rosy face. She had laughed at him, scorned him and he had wanted her then as any man will want a desirable woman.

'The others were ... young,' she was saying, her eyes running approvingly over the muscles beneath the skin of his chest, '. . . and they were qualified as he was but to tell you the truth I just could not see any of them showing old Bobber Smithson where to place his "jumper".'

She grinned, still watching her own hands as they continued their work and to Alex's amazement the picture her words painted made his own lips almost tremble into a smile.

'So I told him I would discuss it with you, Alex, as I am doing though I doubt you can hear me.'

Instantly, before her eyes had time to lift and see the amused interest in his, he let them waver into the unfocused state to which she had become accustomed and when her gaze met his he was seen to be staring incuriously at the ceiling above her head.

'Yes, I see I am right,' she went on, her breath escaping on a long sigh. 'You are not listening, are you? You are not even here, are you? But then I am growing used to it though I did hope that you might ... when we began the treatment ... well, never mind! I have this decision to make and hundreds of others, so no doubt the sooner I make up my mind to the fact that you are a coward and a weakling, the better I shall be able to get on with it. Do you know, Alex, years ago, if anyone had asked me who was the most dominant, domineering man amongst all those I knew, the one with the strongest will to survive, to ride roughshod over any other in the sheer determination to have his own way I would have said Alex Buchanan, and do you know, you have proved me right. You are absolutely bound and determined to simply fade away and die, aren't you? To escape from what life has flung at you. Your strength of will is quite amazing for you are killing yourself with it. Mrs Jackson and I have forced you, *forced* you to live a little longer, but beware Alex, we are not miracle workers. Be very careful your will does not turn you to something you might find, when it is too late, you do not really want. Now I must go and have a word with Faith. At least she answers when I speak to her. She doesn't give the right answers since, like myself, she is ignorant of the world of business but by God she tries. She tries, Alex, which is more than can be said for you.'

She slapped his breast quite cheerfully, playfully even, perhaps the most insulting thing she could do, for surely it implied it really did not matter any longer whether he answered her or not, then turned away humming lightly to herself. 'Oh, and by the way,' she turned back to him as though in afterthought, 'we are to have you out of that bed tomorrow . . . ah . . . ha, I see you still have some life in there . . .' He had turned his head swiftly to look at her at last. She grinned, her teeth gleaming wickedly in the soft light from the lamp, her eyes narrowing mockingly as she bent towards him. 'John and Miles are to strap you into a chair I had made in Kendal . . . oh, did I forget to tell you? How very remiss of me. Well, it is very heavy and solid with a padded seat and back, adjustable to allow you to lie or sit, and if the day is fine you will be carried into the garden to watch your sons at play. What d'you make of that, Alex Buchanan, hey?'

She shook her head quite playfully as though she spoke to some child who had just announced foolishly that he did not wish to go out today.

'We'll see if a peck of fresh air and sunshine will put some colour in your cheeks and even a spark in your brain. *That* is not paralysed, you know, Alex, despite your efforts to make me believe it is. It ticks away inside that skull of yours . . . or does it? Perhaps it really is as devoid of life as you would have us believe and if that is so we might as well order your coffin and lower you into the ground within the week.'

His eyes blazed suddenly, springing to the incredible blueness of a sapphire, and she felt the exultation thread through her veins and reach her heart as her goad brought him to renewed birth, to animation and she saw that detestation in him, directed at her but what did it matter. If she could prick him enough, make him jerk his torpid brain to feel something, even if it was only hatred of herself, perhaps he might retain that sensation long enough to take up his life again and allow her to go free.

'Oh no lady,' he snarled and his voice was so strong and vibrant she recoiled from it, almost dropping the lamp. 'You'll not get rid of me so easily. You may think me dead but by God I'll see a bitch like you off before I go. And as for the mines, madam, I'd be obliged if you would keep your clever nose out of them and out of my company books, and as for employing an engineer to exploit what is mine you can think again. Any man who goes in my mine will be chosen by me.' He laughed harshly. 'Just like running a household you said . . . well, we'll see about that, you hell-cat. You think yourself so bloody skilful, charming those wolves up in St Helens, don't you, making them do what you want to do, eating out of your hand like puppy dogs. Don't you realize that they have agreed because it bloody well suits them. Buy in bulk and have the cost reduced! Freight by train!'

His voice mimicked hers and she shrank further back from him, for it seemed he was about to rear from his bed and strike her, so alive was his venom. This was what she had wanted; to incite him to such ferocity he would be unable to withstand her jibes, to rise up in violent protest at her cruelty, her careless disregard for his feelings, her taking from him the masculine pride he had in his own achievements, but never had she expected him to react with the blazing contempt he now directed at her.

'Do you think I have not worked to have a railway line laid from the mines to Broughton? Do you think I have not considered sending the ore by other routes than by sea? Hell's teeth, woman, I have lain here for months listening to you babble on about the gunpowder mill and the bobbin factory and what you were going to do about it, and I despaired for what you might do to my business . . .'

'Then why did you not say so, you bastard?'

'My blood went cold as I heard you go on about prices and costs, just as though you were the only one to have ever thought of them. "Mr Tate says I might not do this . . . or that, Mr Anderson has had the temerity to say I am to . . .".'

'Dammit, Alex Buchanan, I had to do it . . . you know that . . .'

'But at what cost . . . what will be left when . . .?'

'When . . . when what, Alex?'

She felt the elation seethe through her like the swift tumult of the beck as it thunders over the stones on its way to the lake after the spring thaw, and her heart raced in triumph. He had become like that same river, the damned water thawed and pouring from him in a cascade of flooding anger. She had done it! She had unlocked the prison door which had kept Alex Buchanan's spirit captured for eighteen months but as she put out a welcoming hand to him – not caring what he did with it, just as long as he knew it was there waiting for him – the anger drained away from him as suddenly as it had come, leaving his face whiter than the pillow on which it lay. His eyes lost their great burning savagery and the vicious spasm of his face muscles subsided . . . and yet . . . surely . . . there was something there, something remaining after the rest had gone. Something small and quiet and fragile, like a tiny bud on an oak tree and Christy leaned over him passionately, her eyes a brilliant diamond-bright blaze in her face, willing him to cling to it, to allow it to unfurl and become a living green leaf, a great, breathing foliage to shelter them under, for she was so tired, so tired without him.

'Alex, for God's sake, don't go again. Don't go again. You're right, of course you're right. I can't do it alone. I can shout at the men and they listen politely and then go away to tell each other what a shrew Alex Buchanan's wife has become. I can pretend to them, that you have sent me but I don't know the answers to their questions. I have been down the mine, but I was so afraid, Alex, afraid of the dark and the rats and the water and the thought of that . . . that mountain on top of me.'

She was weeping now and her warm hand found his lifeless ones and clung to them like a rope flung from a life-raft. 'I *can* do it, Alex, I can . . . I can, if you show me how and I'll have a damn good try if you don't, but on my own it will be like attempting to hold back the ocean with a picket fence. Tell me what to do! Tell me what to say! Get up off your back and sit in the chair and look through the window at the world out there. Go out in it, Alex. Take it by the scruff of its neck and make it do what you want it to again! Through me! If you never walk again at least *live* again. Please Alex . . . please . . . please . . .'

She laid her head on his chest and wept as though her heart was breaking, and her fragrant hair fell about his face, caressing his cheek as it had done when he had loved her in this very bed and he felt the knife of his own despair, and the aching desperation of memory tear into him but the anger had gone from him leaving only the familiar hopeless apathy.

She lifted her head and turned her brilliant, tear-dewed eyes upon him.

'Help me, Alex. Let me bring the men here to you.' She felt him recoil away from her as his horror of being looked over, pitied by the very men who once had admired his arrogant strength, emptied all but his shadowed fear from his insensible body.

'Question them, Alex, *you* choose the engineer you want to go down your mine. Help me to pick the right man . . . Alex . . . Alex . . .'

Her voice peaked in despair but he turned his head away and sighed, sadly, hopelessly.

'Do as you wish, Christy. Just whatever you wish. I really . . . don't care any more.'

CHAPTER THIRTY-ONE

Richard Forbes took over his new position as mine engineer at the end of April 1851, becoming its complete director from the moment he strode up the flinty path from the house which had once been the home of Faith and David Adams, leaving no doubt that he would brook no interference from anyone in his control of it. He made it quite clear that if Mrs Buchanan so much as put a foot on the site which contained the ore dressing plant, the large spoil heaps, the water-wheels, the engine shafts or even the offices from which her husband's concern was directed he would resign immediately. He would himself deliver the weekly balance sheets and the wages books, already made up naturally, to her home each Thursday evening so that she might study them at her leisure in her own parlour. On Friday, if it was convenient, he said politely, his hooded eyes revealing no inkling of his thoughts, he would call again to collect them, and the men's wages, if Mrs Buchanan would be so kind as to have them ready so that he might pay them on a Saturday morning. This way there would be no need for Mrs Buchanan to bother herself with anything other than the perusal of the company's books whenever she cared to; leaving the management of the men, the completion of the new mine shaft, the prospecting for further mineral deposits in his hands. He had it in mind, he said pleasantly, to purchase a mechanical 'jigger' which would sort grades of ore more accurately and speedily, and which would immediately reduce the cost of the production of Mr Buchanan's copper ore since the work force above ground could then be cut by as much as a third and would pay for itself within twelve months.

'But . . . what of the men . . . miners who can no longer work underground and who have been employed in the "buddling" process?' Christy protested. 'Mr Buchanan will not like to see men who have worked faithfully for him for many years thrown on the . . .'

'Perhaps . . . if I spoke to Mr Buchanan. I am sure I could convince him, if he needs convincing, of the necessity for change. We must keep up with modern innovations, Mrs Buchanan. If I am to increase production and reduce the cost of bringing the ore from the ground, I must keep up with the latest methods of doing so. Mr Buchanan would agree, I am certain. May I go and just have a word with him now? He is an engineer like myself and will be better able to understand what I am about.'

He stood patiently, his narrow head almost touching the low ceiling of her parlour, his eyes smiling their cool smile, his expression clearly mocking since all of Fellthwaite knew by now that Alex Buchanan was no more than a mindless vegetable lying all day and night in a state of silent stagnation. It had been whispered about the town, the mining community, the gunpowder mill, that Mrs Buchanan had begun some kind of new-fangled treatment, guaranteed to have him on his feet in no time but that was over six months ago and he was still fast in his bed. His wife fiercely kept up the pretence that he was as right as ninepence, temporarily incapacitated and perfectly capable of watching over his concerns from his bed, but it had been eighteen months now since any of his managers had seen him. Really, it was about time Christy Buchanan put it all in the hands of a competent man of business and got on with the raising of her children who were, it was rumoured, sadly neglected.

Richard Forbes knew all this, his manner said plainly,

488

and if Mrs Buchanan wished to continue the charade he had no objection, in fact he was quite willing to go along with it but he would have his own way in return.

Christy watched the sardonic tilt of his eyebrow, the slight curl of amusement which moved his thin-lipped mouth and knew she was, for the moment, out-man-oeuvred. She had employed this man because she had no other choice. The others had not been qualified to do what he was already doing, and short of starting all over again – advertising, interviewing men for the post of engineer, and who was to say the man who applied would be any better suited than this one – she must make do. For a while. But when she got herself more organized at the mill and had time to spare for the mine she would quickly let Mr Richard Forbes know where he stood with Christy Buchanan! In the few weeks he had been employed he had already put two per cent on the mines' overall weekly profit though God knows how he had done it, but she meant to find out. His, or rather the new method of bookkeeping he had imposed on Mr Tate was quite new to her and she had not yet unravelled the intricacies of it, but figures could not lie and it was all there in black and white, what he was spending, the turnover, the gross and net takings of the mine.

'I'm afraid my husband is sleeping . . . just at the moment, Mr Forbes. He has had a tiring day. Now that the weather is improving he does like to get out in the garden with the children. You did not know that? Oh yes, he is out there most days in his chair.'

Which was true. He lay in the sunshine which warmed a sheltered corner, lifted there by John and Miles in the chair she had had made for him, wrapped around with thick fleecy rugs and a stone hot water bottle at his feet. His face had taken on colour, and looking at him each night as he lay naked – but for a pair of brief drawers the sewing woman had made up for him – she had thought that apart from his extreme slenderness he looked a normal, healthy man. His flesh had not returned as she had hoped but what there was was quite firm and the skeletal look he had six months ago had gone. His face was drawn about his mouth with deep grooves dissecting his lean cheeks and his eyes drooped listlessly, but he was relaxed, accustomed now to the massage and manipulation she and Mrs Jackson put him through, and he barely seemed to notice it. He looked in whichever direction they placed his head, his eyes staring unflickeringly at the ceiling, the far window or the dog at his side, but she had become aware lately that when he thought himself to be unobserved his eyes would follow her movements, or those of Mrs Jackson as she bustled cheerfully about the room putting it to rights after his treatment. They appeared no brighter but they did at least *look* at something.

When he was placed in the garden for the first time she and Mrs Jackson had watched him for an hour from the drawing room window, waiting for some reaction, some sign that he was aware that for the first time in eighteen months he was in another environment, that he had fresh air on his face, the sunshine warming his thick hair.

'Should he have a hat, d'you think, Mrs Jackson?' Christy had worried. 'The sun is directly in his eyes. It must appear dreadfully bright to him after all these months indoors but I did want it to rest on his face. Give him some colour. I had not realized until we put him outside how pale he is.'

'I don't know, Mrs Buchanan. He's got his eyes shut at the minute so perhaps . . . shall I go and ask him?'

Christy sighed. 'He wouldn't answer, Mrs Jackson. If the sun was burning his eyeballs he wouldn't protest. I don't know! Are we doing the right thing? He doesn't speak to me any more. Do you remember when he used to curse?'

'Aye, but happen the children will liven him up a bit.'

They played at the bottom of the garden, or romped with noisy, quarrelsome energy almost about his chair, becoming used to his silent presence. The dogs, all three of them, lay beside him sometimes, tongues lolling after a particularly exciting game, sprawling with his own who would growl warningly. Only yesterday in a game of hide and seek she had seen Harry actually hide beneath Alex's chair, first asking politely if 'Father minded' and on receiving no reply, took it for assent.

Primroses starred the grass where he lay and a bed of wild daffodils waved their bright golden heads in his direction only a yard from his chair. Above his head the green leaf buds of the sycamore tree popped almost visibly and his eyes seemed to be drawn to them. His face was so unutterably sad she felt her heart move in her breast in deepest compassion and she agonized over whether this was what he needed. Surely this contact she was forcing on him with the world beyond the four walls of his sick-room must stimulate his senses to a moment of pleasure. Even the fragrance of the blossoming spring, the country smells of growing grass, the black, turned soil, the delicate scent of wild anemones must, in time, insinuate themselves into his sluggish reflex; the sight and sound of the stone-chat come down for the first time from the fell; the magnificence of the fells themselves, made up of blue sky and golden gorse could not help but fill, just for a moment, the loneliness in which he dwelled.

She went each day now to the gunpowder mill, sitting with Mr Anderson, Mr Cartmell, Mr Pendle, much to their displeasure, bending over each truculent shoulder as she prised from them exactly what they did from six in the morning until six or seven in the evening. She made sure now that she was often there before them in the mill yard, not exactly holding her watch to time their arrival but letting them see nevertheless that she had her eye on their comings and goings.

When Mr Cartmell let it be known resentfully that he thought it most insulting that he, a manager of his own department, should be checked up on in such a way, she told him curtly that if he objected to his employer getting to the mill before he did, then he must find a position where he could please himself what time he turned up for he could not do so in *her* mill. She prayed as she did so that he would not call her bluff, for he was an experienced man and she would have great difficulty replacing him, but her steely grey eyes had forced his to look unwillingly away and she knew she had, for the moment, the better of him.

And where he led the others followed!

Gradually it was taken for granted she was to be found each day before any of them in the office which had been her father's, and she realized that they had begun to recognize it was as much in their own interest to see the mill flourish as it was hers. She had begun to understand the process of manufacturing gunpowder and what she didn't know she was not afraid to ask. She kept an old gown and some stout boots in a cupboard in the office, and she became a familiar sight to the men as she walked confidently about the glazing house, the press house, the corning house, demanding to know exactly what was taking place, and, to the men's surprise, understanding it.

She learned about over-production, too much gunpowder chasing too few customers, and the simple fact that if she sold cheaper than anyone else she gained more interested buyers. She learned to cut production costs, with Mr Cartmell's help, without accepting a lower pofit margin. She had what she called 'conferences' with her managers, infuriating them when she insisted on bringing in the foremen of each processing mill, saying tartly that as these men were actively taking part in the process, they knew best and they had therefore an important part to play in the running of the mill.

'They can enlighten us on the specific work done, the cost of it in man hours and how it might be cut, or made more efficient. They know exactly what their men are doing, or not as the case may be, and can report far more accurately than you or I who only go in there once a day.'

From behind the wide desk, laden with papers and specifications, plans and processes, accounts and balance sheets, she listened to the men grouped about her office, speaking only to emphasize a point, to question a statement she did not understand. She recognized at last that these men were now turning to her as the master of her father's mill. They had not been aware in the months she moved amongst them, as she herself had not been aware, that her serious, businesslike approach, her increasing understanding of what she was about and her sheer vital force of personality was breaking down the last male reserve. Without the mine at present to concern her – beyond her monthly visit to St Helens and Swansea to check on her customer's satisfaction with the ore she sent and the punctual delivery of it – she had the time now to concern herself, not only with the gunpowder mill and the occasional visit to the bobbin factory at Stavely to assure Mr Dunlop she was completely satisfied with his running of it, but on her children, her home, and on Annie.

Each day, when the noonday whistle sounded for the half hour break the men at the mill were allowed, she would walk up the steep drive as her father and brothers had once done; between the dense rows of rhododendron bushes which lined it, her eyes drawn to the deep, flushed pink of the flower heads and the dark green of their shiny leaves, her nose wrinkling pleasurably in the fragrant air after the stifling fumes she had breathed that morning in her father's mill. Annie would have a simple meal ready. A piece of boiled turbot in oyster sauce, with damson tart to follow. Perhaps a slice of pheasant and one of Annie's baked custard puddings with stewed apples. Cheese and salad and fruit and rolled jam pudding, all served and eaten in the companionable calm of her mother's small parlour.

'And how is he today?' Annie would ask, always.

'The same, though he looks better since he lies in the garden.'

'There is no better medicine than the sunshine, daughter.'

'So I have heard but it makes no great difference to Alex, mother.'

'Does he never ask what you are doing?'

493

'Never!' she laughed, 'but I tell him just the same.'

'You would! Never one to hide your light under a bushel, Christy Emmerson!'

'I know, mother, so you tell me.'

Their friendship was a source of deep pleasure to her and she was startled late one afternoon when Dorcas, her mother's faithful maid for over twenty years, burst into her office, her apron still about her plump waist, her hair tumbling from its neat cap, her distress so great Christy felt her heart leap chokingly to her throat. The woman stood in the doorway, her hand on the doorknob, so out of breath she could not speak.

Christy sprang to her feet, her face blanching in sudden terror.

'It's . . . it's Mrs Emmerson, Miss Christy . . . she's had some sort of . . . attack . . . Mrs Kean has . . . sent . . . for the doctor.'

Annie was on her side of the big, canopied bed she had shared for almost forty years with Job Emmerson. She had never been able to bring herself to spread herself out after his death, and even now as she fought to draw breath, supported by pillows into a sitting position, she kept strictly to a lifetime's habit.

She turned her eyes to Christy as she stumbled across the bedroom, able it seemed to do no more than that and a glimmer of a smile shone there.

'Mother . . . what . . . Dear God, what happened . . .?'

She sank to her knees beside the bed and took hold of one of the old hands which lay crossed on the snow-white crochet-edged sheet over Annie's breast; and into her head came the fragmented thought that this was the first time she had ever seen her mother without a needle, a baking spoon, a duster, a meat chopper or even a flat iron in her hands. She had always been about something, some household task in the service of her family, her neighbours or those in need – from the constantly pregnant wives of her husband's employees to the sick child of a farm labourer she just happened to hear about.

The thought terrified her and she clung to her mother as Joby clung to her in the childish nightmares he had.

'What is it, mother? See, darling, I am here, tell me . . . Oh God, where is that damn doctor?'

Annie shook her head slowly and her mouth worked as she tried to speak through the gasping pain which tore at her chest.

'Calm . . . down, girl . . . it's only a bit of a . . . turn. I fell . . . in the yard . . .'

'What were you doing in the yard, for God's sake?' Her fear made her angry. 'Cannot one of the servants fetch whatever you want?'

'Allow me to . . . walk in my . . . own yard, daughter, if you please. I'm not . . . a child to . . .' but the effort of speaking had weakened her and her face turned pale yellow and she closed her eyes and her voice suddenly disappeared and Christy felt the panic slash at her.

'Mother, please . . . it's Christy . . .'

'I . . . know . . . I . . . know . . .' Her voice was a thread but her blue-tinged lips turned up in a small smile as if to say how could she ignore such a demanding child as this?

The doctor came, old Doctor Bell who attended on Alex once a month, just to ensure his fee was safe and that his patient was not about to slip away without his supervision. He took Annie's wrist in his hand and put his ear to her chest, and whispered to Christy he didn't like the sound of it but to keep her warm and feed her on nourishing broth and custard.

'Give her this draught to help her to sleep. Keep the fire in and the windows closed and I'll call again tomorrow. If she should . . . if you need me, Mrs Buchanan . . . send your man.'

She sent word to Faith that she would remain at Hollin House until Annie was better. Would she see to the children and let the mill managers and Richard Forbes and Mr Dunlop know where she could be found? Dear Faith would see to everything that needed seeing to, she knew that, and she settled down at her mother's side dozing in

495

the chair, eating little, holding Annie's hand, willing her own tenacious strength into her mother's body. Not once did it occur to her that the only person not to know of her whereabouts – for who else but she ever spoke to him – was Alex Buchanan.

The doctor came and went, twice in one day, for Annie's glorious spirit was not up to the battle she was fighting and her damaged heart was slowing painfully, irrevocably to its final beat. Death was staking its claim, stripping her of her will, touching her warningly each time she rallied a little as though to remind her it would have its way.

She wandered a little in those last days, reliving her childhood, the wonder of her own first child and the glory of the joy of being loved by Job Emmerson. She chided Ben and nursed Toby through some childish ailment and worried over her daughter's future with Alex Buchanan. She spoke endlessly to her husband about it, becoming increasingly restless, begging him to reassure her that they had done the right thing.

'. . . he is older . . . but she needs a strong man . . . that boy . . . nice boy, but gentle . . . too soft . . . Alex . . . Alex . . . will protect her . . .'

She became worse that night, worried to death she told Job, that their Christy was not content with Alex Buchanan, even yet. And Christy, in desperation, hardly caring what she said, nor realizing the meaning of it, whispered to her mother that Christy Buchanan *was* happy with Alex Buchanan; and the words comforted the fretful woman in the bed and she became quiet, her face peaceful in the light of the lamp.

She opened her eyes just before dawn on the fourth day and when she saw Christy, her arms resting on the bed, her face no more than a foot from her own, she smiled lovingly.

'I'm glad, child,' she said.

'About what, mother.' Christy put a gentle hand to her mother's cheek.

'That you are happy at last.'

'Mother . . .'

'You must make him well now. You must force him to . . . he is all you have . . .'

She died a few moments later, her hand in that of her daughter's.

The carriage took Christy from Hollin House in the sweet new light of that spring morning, the loveliness of it unobserved for she was encased in a glass dome of grief and shock. The oak trees at the edge of Howethwaite were showing the first signs of golden bronze foliage and the apple orchards at the back of the house were in full blossom, and as she got out of the carriage – handed down by a tearful Thomas for what would they do now, he and the rest of those who had served Mrs Emmerson his face asked – a cluster of wild hyacinths beside the open front door seemed to mock her with their promise of life and hope to come.

'Christy . . . dear.' Faith was there, as she had always been, ready to do whatever was asked of her and Christy stepped into the comforting circle of her arms.

'She is dead, Faith.'

'Oh Christy . . . I'm sorry.'

'She died an hour ago . . .'

'Darling . . . let me get you a drink. See, come into the little parlour. The fire is lit. I have waited for you . . . each day. Come and . . .'

'No. I must go . . .'

'Where? Where, lass?'

'I don't know . . .' but she had moved to the foot of the stairs and her gaze wandered up it. She put a foot on the bottom step, then the next and without conscious thought she began the climb, moving stiffly, one foot in front of the other until she was at the top. Faith watched her go but made no attempt to question her. She was going where she needed to be.

He was alone but for the dog. Mrs Jackson had already washed and shaved him and he was lying, neat and tidy as always, with the dog beside him. They both turned their

497

heads as she entered, and she heard him gasp as he saw her – for in four days she had done no more than rinse her face, not even taking the time to change into the fresh clothes Faith had sent over, afraid to leave her mother for a moment. The dog's tail plumed in welcome and he pricked his ears waiting for her to speak to him. The room was bright, warm, fragrant with the bowls of spring flowers which, even without her presence, were put out each day as she had ordered. The window was open wide to allow in the fresh spring air, again as she had ordered.

'Alex.'

He looked at her and even in the depths of his own, he felt her despair. He had not known where she was and the habit of silence was too heavy on him to ask Mrs Jackson. He had thought her to be on business, if he had thought at all – off to St Helens or Swansea or even abroad if it had taken her fancy for she seemed to have it all in hand now, to be in full control of her destiny, that of his children and the inheritance which would one day be theirs – and yet as she stood stiffly in the doorway, her face haunted, he knew with a sudden stirring of something he had thought long dead, that she had done none of these things, been to none of these places but had come from something which had emptied her, dried her up, sucked the life from her, leaving her as desolate as he once had been.

'Alex,' she said again and her face spasmed in pain and her eyes were lost and lonely, those of a child which finds itself amongst cold strangers. It seemed she was asking something of him, something not to do with the mills, nor the mine, nor any of the hundred and one problems which beset her and which she had begged of him to help.

'Christy?' His voice was soft, questioning.

'Oh God . . . Alex . . .'

'What? What is it?' His eyes had come to glowing life on the pillow.

'Alex, I don't know what to do . . . I don't think I can . . .'

'What . . . tell me what has happened.'

She began to move across the room towards him, her gaze held by his and there was something in them, some miraculous intuition in his compelling blue eyes which drew her to him. It was as though he had put out a hand, taken hers, held it close and was leading her to a comfortable chair, a welcoming fire, telling her to sit, telling her to relax and confide in him.

She did not stop to consider the strangeness of it but sank to her knees beside his bed and she began to tremble, the violence of it shaking the bed against which she leaned.

'Get down boy,' he said quietly to the dog and the animal slipped to the floor and went to lie upon the rug before the fire, keeping his eyes on his master.

'Tell me, Christy. Where have you been? What has happened?'

'My mother is dead, Alex.'

He threw back his head in a rictus of agitation, turning from her for a moment as the shock drove him to angry pain, then he swung his head strongly on the pillow, lifting it a little in her direction.

'When?' His voice was a whisper of compassion.

'An hour ago.'

'Why did no one tell me she was ill?'

'I was at the mill . . . a few days ago. They came for me. I have been with her . . .'

The trembling increased and her teeth chattered violently and Alex Buchanan strained at every tiny shred of his resolve to lift himself to comfort her for he knew that was what she asked of him.

'Alex . . . please . . . Oh, Alex . . .' He saw the great wash of tears spring from her eyes and flow across her bewildered face, and his heart jolted for her pain and he strained again to give her something, anything which might ease her hurt. Dear sweet Christ, he would give his own life just to have ten minutes of the use of his arms. Just ten minutes to hold her and soothe her . . .

'Lie here, Christy . . .' he said gently. 'Lie down beside me and put your head on my shoulder. Put your arms about me. Cry, cry, my sweet and I shall cry with you for I loved your mother as you did. That's right, come close, lie alongside me and hold on to me for I've got you. You're safe. Weep, let it go. Annie was a good woman, a dear friend and her death will be felt and grieved over by many people and she is worth your tears, and mine.'

She wept and wept, her face pressed into the hollow of his neck, her head beneath his chin and he felt her tears wet the top of his nightshirt and the sheet which had been tucked about his shoulders. He felt the bed move with the force of her anguish and her voice was muffled as she cried out the words of love and loss for the woman who had supported, protected, sheltered and loved her. When the weeping was done she slept, her wet face drying against his neck and when Faith crept in, Mrs Jackson being diffident about disturbing her master and mistress in their ... well ... embrace, he whispered to her fiercely to go away.

'But you, Mr Buchanan ... do you not need ... attention ...?'

'Get out, woman ... get out. Can you not see she sleeps? She is exhausted. Go Faith, let her sleep. She will call you when she is ready. Leave us ...'

She had awakened as dusk was slipping into the quiet room, stretching quite naturally against his inert body, yawning, rubbing her eyes in the way he remembered when they had shared this bed in the sweetness of the past. When he turned his head to smile at her dismay as she found herself where she was he said whimsically, a shadow of his old humour in his eyes, 'You were exhausted, Christy, and just fell asleep on the handiest bed, which happened to be mine.'

He saw the amusement warm her eyes and they softened gratefully and she rose from the bed and went to the fire which had almost gone out, throwing on more coal.

Through the return of the pain which came at her as she moved away from him, her mind dwelled wonderingly on the compassion she had seen in his eyes and the consola-

500

tion she had found at his nearness. He had been so tender, so infinitely soothing, comforting her grief. His voice had been devoid of its usual mockery, or more recently, indifference and he had given her a strong and amazing relief from her anguish. She turned back to him and his eyes were gentle, warm, *alive* and she had the most curious feeling that this time the . . . the animation she saw there would not slip away so easily.

Christy attended her mother's funeral with only Faith beside her amongst the hundreds who came to pay their respects. Annie was buried with her husband and the eleven children she had borne him. The one who was left grieved tearlessly, her weeping done on the day her mother had died, and she was comforted by the mistaken belief that it was her death which had given life to Christy's husband.

'What will you do with the house, Christy?' he asked later that night as she sat before his fire sipping hot chocolate. She had finished massaging his fragile arms and legs and Mrs Jackson had helped her to lift him into a sitting position, as they did several times a day hoping that the movement might strengthen the muscles in his back. The nurse had bathed him and put on his nightshirt and he lay, his dog beside him, watching his wife in the firelight.

She turned, sighing, her face rosy in the firelight. Getting up from the chair she walked towards him gracefully, the soft floating mist of her cornflower-blue gown drifting about her in graceful folds. It seemed to be made up of frills and pretty satin ribbons and to be lighter than air, the garment of a woman expecting a lover and he wondered idly why she wore it for there was no one to see it but himself.

She sat down in the chair beside him, leaning her elbows on the bed, cupping her chin in her hands and though she looked at him he knew she did not see him. Her hand reached out to the dog's head, scratching it until he almost smiled in pleasure.

'I suppose I must sell it.' Her face drooped in sadness. 'It will be . . . hard, though. Apart from here I have lived all my life at Hollin House. I had a . . . happy childhood and good memories are there. All the things I associate with my father and brothers . . . they live there and to think of strangers . . .' She bent her head and her hair fell across it in a cascade of russet darkness. 'All my mother's things. What am I to do with them? Where are they to go? There is no room here and I could not bear to sell them but . . .'

'Why don't you keep it?'

She looked at him in astonishment. 'Keep that big house and the servants it would need to maintain it, when I could use the money it fetched to invest . . .'

'Christy!' His voice was reproving.

'Well, it would only be good business sense to . . .'

'Forget business . . . just for once, Christy Buchanan. We are not so beggared we need to part with your . . . childhood, your memories to put food in our mouths. That house was your home. You could use it for . . .'

'What?' She was laughing now.

'For . . . for Amy, when she marries.'

'She is six years old!'

They were both laughing when Mrs Jackson returned, and as she remarked later to Nurse Livingstone you could have knocked her down with a feather, really you could, for she never thought she'd see the day when Mr and Mrs Buchanan could share a joke, not in a million years!

CHAPTER THIRTY-TWO

There were days when he cursed her just as roundly as he had in the first days of his treatment. There were days when he bellowed to the children above his head that if they did not stop that infernal racket he would have their mother give them all a thrashing when she came home. There were days when he longed to be left alone to sink into the apathy he had once found so desirable, and there were days when he did so, but in a way which Christy found oddly heart-warming he began to show a ready attentiveness to what she and the two nurses did for him. He would lift his head from the pillow watching them as they exercised his useless limbs, until he complained that his neck ached. The next day he suggested that a wide collar be made, fitting beneath his chin to support the straining muscles of his neck.

'What kind of collar, Alex?' she asked, 'and how would it help?'

His eyes were alert and he frowned thoughtfully as his brain considered the ideas which now seemed to flood there eagerly. 'Well, some soft but strong material would be needed. Pliable enough so that it did not abrase my skin but strong enough to support my neck. If I had that and a decent pillow I could hold up my head and look about the room. Now in engineering I learned that a weak spot, if supported by the correct prop will act in such a way that . . .'

'Yes, yes, but I am not an engineer. Just tell me what to get and how to make it and we will set about it.'

'Well . . . I know nothing of material, woman, but something . . . padded . . . substantial . . . well-made . . .'

A picture slipped into Christy's mind, a picture of a garden, a pleasant corner where a chair was placed beneath

503

a tree and in the chair a woman sat, her needle flashing in the sunshine and about her knee was a lovely waterfall of material, delicate and soft but as strong as she herself had been.

'Mother,' she said quietly.

He turned his eyes in her direction and his face was perplexed.

'What . . .?'

'Her quilting.'

'Quilting?'

'Yes, she used to make bed coverlets, don't you remember? They were made of padding enclosed between two layers of cloth. It was kept in place by cross lines of stitching. She used to put washed sheep's wool very thinly . . . that was it . . . and then . . . Oh Alex, it would be ideal. She had dozens, all shapes and sizes in a chest. I'll go over immediately and get them. With a bit of chopping about and stitching Mrs Duggan could make up a collar which would not only be as soft and light as swan's down, but strong too. Folded over . . . a few thicknesses . . . I hope it will not be too hot . . .'

It worked beautifully and within the week he was propped up in his bed his neck completely supported and easier, he said, than it had been for months. It no longer ached and he could turn it smoothly, watching without strain what went on about him.

A frame was made, designed by Alex himself, with a sturdy stand so that when he lay in bed it could be propped across his chest, with supports on either side and the newspaper laid upon it, or a book, held in place by a strong piece of cord and his voice became a familiar sound in the house as he roared for someone, anyone to come and turn his page. His bedroom door was left open and a passing maid, Faith or even one of the children if they heard him became used to running breathlessly to do his bidding.

But when his door was closed nobody but Christy and his nurses were allowed to go near him. On bad days he lay as once he had done, his neck collar abandoned, his reading frame rejected to stand on the bedside table, his eyes staring vacantly at the ceiling, his old dog's head close to his own. He would snarl at anyone who spoke to him, hissing venomously that they could take their bloody hands off him and leave him alone, for he wanted none of them and none of their lunatic treatment either.

They took no notice, of course. Mrs Buchanan would not allow them to. She would go about her share of the massage — humming cheerfully or telling him about the increasing production at the mine and the wonders Richard Forbes had achieved since he had taken over the management — and in a few days he would respond and smile ruefully and confess to being a bad-tempered devil.

'You certainly are, Alex Buchanan, and I can't imagine why I bother with you. Do you know how much time I have to give to this massage? Time I could spend more fruitfully at the mill.' But she was smiling and her hands as they fitted the collar about his neck were gentle.

'I know that, my pet.' He had taken to calling her by the wry endearments he had once used, half-affectionate, half-mocking, and certainly not with the insolent spirit he had once shown, but sharp nevertheless and infinitely more welcome than cold apathy. One dark eyebrow arched and his eyes gleamed with sardonic humour. 'Just think how many orders you might have taken whilst you have been concerning yourself with this nonsense you perform!'

'It's not nonsense, Alex. You know that. You are in better shape now than you have been since before the accident. The muscles in your legs, your arms and shoulders are firm now and I can feel those in your back improving each day. Come, why do you not allow me to have a . . . a support made for the bed. Like the one you have in the chair outside, then you can sit up here as well as in the garden, perhaps a similar one . . . by the window so that when the winter comes you will still be able to see the garden and the children . . .'

'Do you not think I see enough of those little monsters

as it is? They were in here this afternoon *and* the blasted dogs leaping about like dervishes and sounding like a troop of cavalry. Miss Crawford brought Amy in to spout that new teaching formula she says is the thing now. The alphabet of flowers it's called. Have you heard it?'

Christy laughed and her eyes were soft as she watched his face.

' "Y is for yellow lily which John with a crook,

Is trying to reach from the bank of the brook!

Z is for Zinnia which has carried away

The prize at the grand show of flowers today. . .!"

Did you ever hear such damned nonsense? She's not teaching Johnny that, is she? My God, when I was five I can remember quite clearly beginning lessons after breakfast. Reading, writing, spelling, history, arithmetic, geography, German, French and Latin, and being firmly rapped over the knuckles until my fingers learned to do the right thing!'

'Well, times have changed since then and Johnny is only just five and will be going to school next year. Harry has started too now, you know, just for an hour or so each morning. You should see the two of them sulking round the nursery table, ferocious as two little caged tiger cubs because Miss Crawford will not allow them to go out and play in the garden until they have learned how to spell "cat" and "mat" and "hat". And naturally, because Johnny and Harry are having lessons Joby cannot understand why he doesn't, as though they are having some treat which he is being denied.'

'Why don't you let him then?'

Christy looked doubtful. 'Do you think he should? He is only three.'

'If he wants to let him. It can do no harm and anyway, it won't last, you know. The moment he sees me out in the chair he will be pestering me to let him loll about with me, or look at his paintings, or watch him whilst he throws a stick for that dratted dog of his.'

He would sit in the garden when it was fine for most of

506

the day now, only being carried in when the last twitch of sunshine lifted above the corner he had made his own. It was sheltered from the wind, facing south, and at his back the wall of the house was invisible behind the curtain of climbing roses which covered it.

It was on such a day that he had his first visitor.

The sun shone on his dark, grey-streaked, neatly brushed hair, turning strands of it to burnished copper in its rays, and Mrs Jackson thought how well he looked now that he had a bit of colour in his cheeks. A tiny breeze disturbed the symmetry of her carefully arranged brushstrokes and an unruly lock fell across his forehead. Leaning forward she put up a hand to brush it back, in the manner of a nanny with an untidy boy and was placidly unconcerned, for was she not used to Mr Buchanan and his sharp tongue when he flinched away from her, saying irritably.

'For God's sake, woman, leave me alone! You would think I was no more than an infant the way you fuss.'

'I'm sorry, sir. I was only making you tidy.'

'I know, but perhaps I do not want to be "tidy" as you so quaintly put it!'

'I'm sorry, Mr Buchanan. It's pure habit, you see. I've been doing it for so long I just find myself . . .'

'Well don't! Now can you take yourself off to wherever it is you go when you are not babying me and leave me to a bit of peace?'

'Well, I don't know about that, sir. Mrs Buchanan said most particular that you were not to be . . .'

'Damn Mrs Buchanan! I can come to no harm, can I, and I am certainly not going anywhere, so go away, woman. Confound it, what do I have to do to be obeyed? I merely want to sit here and look at the garden without you jabbering your damned head off in my ear.'

Mrs Jackson rose uncertainly, biting her lip as she considered the man who lay swathed in rugs on the long, padded chair. It was almost like a bed but the back was raised so that he was nearly sitting up. He had himself devised the leather straps across his ankles, thighs and chest to prevent him slipping down, and the chair was so solid and wide there was no risk that it might be tipped over. He had even had made a sort of canopy which might be moved to protect his head from the sun's rays and he had ordered himself four sturdy wheels so that he might easily be pushed from one level spot to another.

'Well, if you think you'll be alright, sir,' Mrs Jackson was doubtful.

'Dammit woman, I've only to shout if I'm not.'

'Very well sir. I'll only be in the kitchen. Abel is down at the rhododendrons doing a bit of pruning, he said, so he'll come for me if you . . .'

'For God's sake, woman, will you get out of my sight.'

Alex Buchanan's sun-browned face turned a dangerous colour and his eyes snapped furiously. He twisted his head to glare at her and the sinews of his neck stood out as he strained to impose his will on hers. There was nothing he could physically do to make her leave him alone and the knowledge filled him with a single-minded determination to do it all the same. Since he had been lifted from his bed in the strong arms of John and Miles and placed in the movable chair, he had felt for the first time a desire to bellow an order or two in the way he had once done, and when he did so he enjoyed the feeling it gave him. In fact he enjoyed it so much he did it more and more often, for he could feel the effect of it almost tingle in his veins and the sensation of being alive was a good one. And he liked the way the servants jumped to do his bidding, their anxious glances awakening the formidable passion he had known to always have his own way – for the simple reason he could not believe himself to be wrong!

'You will have the servants handing in their notice, Alex,' Christy had told him smilingly. 'You have become such a tyrant they are afraid to so much as blink in your presence.'

'And have I not always been that way?'

'Oh yes.'

'Then what difference do they see in me?'

'None, I suppose, but they have had an easy time of it for almost two years.'

'Well, they will just have to mend their ways then!'

His sons were at their studies, even Joby, and the garden was quiet. He could hear the click of Abel's shears and the drone of a fat bumble bee as it moved, heavily-laden from one flower head to another. The sun was warm on his face, hot even and he considered shouting for the gardener to come and lower the canopy but he liked the idea that at least one part of him looked as it once had done. He had seen his own reflection in the mirror and the sun-bronzed face – thin still and deeply engraved with lines between his eyebrows and at each side of his mouth – was as fierce and compelling as it once was. His eyes were their normal bright blue, he had noted, and quite challenging again and he hoped to God he could hang on to it. It had been a close thing and still was at times when he watched his wife move gracefully about his room, saw the friendliness in her eyes, the concern when he was depressed, the effort she made to include him in the everyday events of the house, the savage ways she fought him to bring him back to her world, and knew that he would never have more of her than this. She was young, beautiful, resourceful and during the last eighteen months had matured from a wilful, headstrong girl, weighed down and sharp with the tedium of playing the role he had forced on her, into a strong, self-assured woman. She was lovelier now than she had ever been as though the battle she had waged, was still waging in many, many ways had stripped away the brittle, restless shell of her to reveal the complete woman beneath. She was still spirited, hot-tempered, but she had the softness now to blur the sharp edges which had once cut not only her, but himself! She had struggled with him for years to allow her some freedom, begged him to let her grow and become what she was certainly capable of becoming and he had forbidden it, cramping her into the mould men had created for women.

Now she was free! Now she had proved her worth. Now

her mind was complete and she was at ease with herself, liking herself, and him. She had given him the chance to live again, but what of her? Would she be content to go on this way, pouring herself into the mills and the mine, bringing up her children with only half her attention. A woman ... but not a woman, for did not he himself know her sensuality? It was tamped down now, submerged beneath her need to be mill-master, mine-owner, manufacturer, nurse, mother, housekeeper, but what of the day when Robin Forsythe would return, as he surely would? What of Christy Buchanan then?

He was kept up to date with the gossip of Fellthwaite now, Mrs Jackson only too pleased to chat amiably to her patient when he asked her haltingly of what went on in the community. The Squire, it seemed, had been back only once to Dalebarrow Hall since the birth of his son; to check on the state of his property, to collect his tenant rents on the due date and to visit his mother who was said to be a bit 'batty' now she rambled about the huge place on her own. He had stayed only a day or so, Mrs Jackson said obligingly, but had been seen by no one other than those of his servants who were still at the Hall and the farmer who rented his land.

Had he seen Christy Buchanan, her husband wondered? She had been no different. He had seen no sign of dreaming distraction, no flushes of guilt or lessening of her attention to himself. She was up before six each morning and always, before she left the house she came to his room, asking how he slept, could she bring him something from the kitchen, should she let the dog out, should she open the window, describing to him the state of the weather – and the room would retain her presence and her perfume for ten minutes after she had gone.

It was the same in the evening. Often now she took her meal with him, setting the small table between them at the side of the bed, or the chair if he was in it, putting a forkful of food into his mouth from one of the two plates set out on the table, then the next in her own from the second, as naturally and casually as though every wife of her acquaintance did the same for her husband. She managed to talk through the whole procedure, describing from the moment she entered the mill yard every moment of her day until she left.

When the meal was finished and cleared away she would pour coffee, even tempting him to a sip of brandy, and they would idle the evening away in pleasant companionship. He had found he was beginning to take a quite fascinated interest now in what went on at the gunpowder mill, and her dominance of his three managers, hard-headed, bull-headed, stubborn men gave him immense satisfaction.

Aye! Her father had said it years ago. A rare bird, Christy Buchanan!

The sound of carriage wheels on the gravel drive at the side of the house brought his head round sharply in that direction. Damn it, someone was coming to the house and here he was caught in a trap of his own making – for it was himself who had banished Mrs Jackson – and if he was to shout for Abel whoever had come would hear him as they drew up to the front door. Sweet Jesus, he hoped it was not one of Christy's simpering female friends – for there was nothing more positive than the certainty he would say the most unforgivable things if one should come sympathizing about his chair. He had seen no one but the servants and his own family for two years and Christy's social life had been non-existent for Fellthwaite was none too sure of a woman who conducted herself as she did. Then who . . .?

The stocky figure who came hesitantly through the French windows on to the rough stone path which led to his chair was not immediately recognized by him, and he felt his heart leap frantically in his chest. His mouth dried up and his senses swam for he was alone . . . alone without Christy . . . even Mrs Jackson to keep away the dangers!

'Mr Buchanan, sir,' the man said quite naturally. 'This is indeed a pleasure. My word, I cannot tell you how grand it is to see you, and looking so well. Mrs Buchanan has told me so often how splendidly you are doing, and I must admit I sometimes thought her to be ... well, wives are loyal creatures, are they not, Mr Buchanan, and will protect their families. I pray I am not intruding, sir, but I had hoped to have a word with Mrs Buchanan ... some small problem ... The young maid seemed a trifle flustered when she left me in the drawing room. She had gone to ask someone ... but when I spied you out here in your chair ... I do hope ...'

Mr Dunlop, for it was he, was quite overcome by the poignancy of the moment. A down to earth man who found it hard to show emotion, nevertheless he was torn between sadness in seeing so strong a man as his employer brought down to this frail, warmly-wrapped figure in the wheelchair, and yet – fed for months on rumours on the state of Alex Buchanan's mind, or lack of it – here he was, obviously in his right senses and as good a colour on his thin cheeks as the polished mahogany of Mr Dunlop's own dining table.

'Mr ... Dunlop ... I had not ... I did not recognize you ...'

'Of course not. It is a while since you and I met, sir.'

'Indeed!'

'And sorry I am too, but your wife has done splendidly in your absence, sir. A fine lady, if I may say so.'

'You ... you may ... Mr Dunlop ... er ...'

Mr Dunlop stood awkwardly for several moments wondering if perhaps he should slip away now that he had paid his respects to his employer. The man seemed ... troubled ... uncertain, perhaps unused to visitors? Or should he squat beside him on the grass for want of a chair, or ... or ...

There was an unwieldy silence, then, so suddenly it made him jump, Mr Buchanan bellowed unceremoniously down the garden to some fellow skulking among the rhododendron bushes – certainly nothing wrong with his voice! – and within minutes he found himself comfortably seated, a steaming cup of coffee in his hand and Mr Buchanan's piercing blue eyes – how could he have forgotten them? – fixed upon him questioningly.

'Now Mr Dunlop, perhaps, in my wife's absence, you could tell *me* what the problem is. She will not be back until this evening. She is a busy woman . . .'

'Oh indeed, Mr Buchanan. No one knows better than I, and so quick to appreciate how precious time is.'

'Quite, and I am sure you have much to concern you at the bobbin factory so if you could get to the point.' His *manner* had not changed either!

'Of course.'

It was quite like old times, Mr Dunlop told his fascinated wife later that evening, and that accident had certainly not dulled Mr Buchanan's wits one fraction; for in no time at all they had located the source of the problem, gone over the order, the account, the customer's specification, the delivery date and the matter was in hand before his coffee had lost its heat!

'Whose figures are these, Mr Dunlop, in this audit of the year's takings?' Mr Buchanan had asked him.

'Why, Mrs Buchanan's, sir, naturally.'

'Do you mean to tell me my wife has . . .?'

'Oh yes sir. Clever with figures is Mrs Buchanan.'

'So it seems!'

Mr Buchanan stared off into the far distance and Mr Dunlop thought he had forgotten he was there. He stood up. His employer was right. He had things to do at the factory and he could not spare the time to stand about chatting. He had lost half a day coming up from Stavely as it was. Time was money, that's what he said, but this had been somewhat of an emergency.

'Well sir, I'd best be off.'

'Of course, Dunlop.'

'May I say how pleased I am . . .'

'Yes . . . yes, thank you . . .'

He has not changed one scrap was Mr Dunlop's pleased conclusion as he climbed into the hansom cab which was to take him back to the railway station at Windermere. At least . . . not in his head!

'I believe you had a visitor this morning, Alex,' Christy said as she stalked into his bedroom that evening. As he watched her come towards him – still dressed in the black tailored riding habit which was her customary outfit now since she was in mourning for her mother – he was quite spellbound by the difference in the way she walked, depending entirely on what she wore! In this outfit she was brisk, decisive, even manly as she moved deliberately about the room, but in the soft feminine gowns she put on when she changed, clinging perhaps, or drifting about her like a pastel shift of mist, she appeared to float, her feet barely touching the ground, to move slowly, delicately, a woman!

'I did! Dear old Dunlop from the bobbin factory and by God, how you manage to deal with that pompous ass is beyond me.'

'Alex, that is most unfair,' but she was smiling for Mr Dunlop did have a certain fussiness which could irritate. 'Of all the men with whom I have dealt he has been the most helpful.'

'*He* likes you, too.' His grin was malicious.

'Don't be ridiculous! Just because he and I . . .'

'Yes, my dear wife? You and he . . .?'

'It was Mr Dunlop who taught me all I know about figures . . . balance sheets and so forth. He taught me the secret of . . .'

'Yes, yes, about what? Did he reveal what wicked things he and Mrs Dunlop got up to in the long cold winter nights? Or the scandals which abound the sedate village of Stavely, or perhaps the romantic aspirations of his spinster daughter for the curate? He can gossip like an old maid when he has a mind to. What rumours has he been spreading? Oh God, Christy, I can scarcely bear the suspense.'

He was laughing out loud now, throwing his head back on the pillow in fierce enjoyment, and his eyes snapped keenly in a way she had not seen for two years. His flippant humour, not as wicked as once it had been, but still biting, had not been able to resist the temptation to poke fun at Mr Dunlop nor to tease her about it and she felt gladness enter her. She resolved as she watched him lift his chin to the ceiling that from now on she would make sure that they all came. Slowly at first, a couple each week to discuss with him what was happening in his mine – especially his mine – and his mills for it was very evident that Mr Dunlop's half hour visit had done more to stimulate his subtle mind than a week with the lively children, the pleasant quiet garden or even his slow reading of the *Westmorland Gazette*.

She was laughing herself now, moving towards him, drawn by his infectious humour, admiring the strong line of his jaw and throat, the gleam of his white teeth in his brown face, thinking bemusedly how attractive he had become since ... since ... when suddenly he froze! Naturally his body was completely motionless, had not moved a fraction even during his hilarious bout of laughter, but his head had, moving on the column of his neck as his vital amusement captured him.

Now it was still, his face locked in an atrophied smile, his mouth wide in an unmoving grip, his throat immobile in an arch of brown, supple flesh. His eyes were locked on the ceiling, unblinking, fixed in a stare which forced to life such terror in her she could not move.

He was the first to speak.

'Did you hear it?' he whispered, still not turning to look at her, afraid it seemed to take his gaze from the ceiling.

'What?' She whispered too as though a loud noise might damage something.

'It was a click.'

'A ... click?'

'Yes ...'

'Where?' She turned her head then, looking about the room, staring at the window, the dressing table, the clock on the mantelshelf, the dog before the fire, even into the fire itself.

'Oh sweet God . . .!' He still had not moved. His chin remained pointed at the ceiling and even his eyes seemed afraid to swivel in her direction. The dog stood up and wandered across the room, laying his nose on the bed to stare into his master's ear, curious as to the sudden tension. His tail moved slowly, warily.

'What is it . . . what is it, for God's sake?' Christy stumbled then, tripping on her skirt in her desperate urge to get to him. She fell on her knees beside the dog, reaching out to touch Alex's face and as she did so he relaxed, allowing his chin to fall, inch by inch until it was resting in its normal position. Slowly he turned his head until he was looking into her face. It was as though he was afraid to move it, afraid somehow that the small amount of movement he had, might have been taken from him.

'What is it, for God's sake tell me? What kind of a click? Do you mean . . .?'

'It came from . . . *me*!'

They looked at one another in appalled silence, their eyes locked in desperate appeal, their faces quite blank for in truth they were frozen in such fear their minds had become numbed, unable to send the messages they so frantically needed. Christy felt cold, so cold she thought she might faint with it, and her hands went out then, looking for something to cling to, but of course there was nothing.

'I can still . . . move my head,' he whispered at last.

'Can you? Show me . . . oh show me.'

He rolled his head from side to side, his face coming back to look into hers.

'Does it hurt anywhere?'

'No . . . Christ, I wish it did.'

'Where . . . where was it . . . do you know?'

'No. I didn't feel it, for God's sake . . . I heard it.'

'What . . .?' She swallowed. 'What can it mean, do you think?'

'Confound it, woman, I don't know! You don't suppose . . .'

'What . . .?'

'That . . , that something . . . has, well, I don't know . . . gone into place or . . .'

'Oh Alex!' Her breath fanned his cheek and her eyes brimmed with desperate hope. 'What shall we do? Shall I . . . will you try and . . .?'

'Jesus . . . I don't know, Christy.' His voice was rough and the words came out in a menacing snarl but his eyes clung to hers in mute appeal.

'Shall . . . do you think I should . . .?' She stood up, fidgeting about from one foot to the other, the quick thinking, incisive Mrs Buchanan vanishing in this bewildering new development. 'Perhaps I should send for the doctor?'

'No! What the hell can he do? What the hell has he done? The only person to do any good is you and you are here so . . . so let's have a . . . a look, shall we. Take off the bedclothes and see if you can turn me over. Have a look at my back. I think . . . I'm almost sure that's where it came from.'

'What shall I look for?' she asked as she hurriedly pushed the dog to one side. Lifting the covers and tossing them to the floor as she had done once before!

'How the bloody hell do I know? Just look, dammit!'

She studied the fine curve of his back, the smooth flow of his buttocks, running her sensitive fingers along the bony ridge of his spine, then down each leg, bending them in turn. She lifted his arms and placed them behind his back, asking anxiously every few seconds if he could feel this or that, but his answer was always the same. When she heaved him on to his back again, and replaced his drawers and nightgown and covered him neatly with the discarded blankets, his face was as smooth as the washed pebble his son had given him as a Christmas gift.

'Are you sure you, heard something?' she said hesitantly after she had finished. 'Perhaps it was . . .?'

'What?'

'I don't know . . . something outside.'

517

There was silence, forbidding, frightening. Loud!

'Can I get . . .?'

'No, thank you.'

'Alex . . .'

'Leave me alone, Christy.'

'Alex, what in damnation did you think it was?'

'I don't know, for Christ's sake!'

'But you must have . . .'

He glared up at her, hating her again, hating her for witnessing his despair, hating her for forcing him to expose the ecstatic hope he had felt that something . . . something in his damaged body had . . . moved . . . been replaced correctly . . . what? . . . and that the miracle he had been promised by the Rector had actually happened, hating her for seeing his bitter disappointment.

'*I don't know, damn you.* I heard . . . and I imagined . . .'

'Oh Alex.' Her face was soft with understanding . . . and pity and he did not want her pity!

His eyes slid away from hers.

'Go away, Christy.'

'Let me stay for a while, Alex. I can . . .'

'*Go away, Christy.*'

'But I feel you would be better if I . . .'

'*Will you leave me alone*, damn you. Can you not get it into that clever head of yours that I don't want you here.'

'I see! I am to be punished, is that it? I am to be the whipping boy again.'

But he turned his face from her in the old familiar way, dismissing her in the surest way he knew how and Christy stood for a moment before walking slowly across the room to the doorway. She turned.

'Alex, please let me . . .'

But there was no response.

She woke in the depths of the black night to a jumble of sounds which for a moment she could make no sense of and she lifted her head, cautiously peering about the dark shadows of her room, identifying gratefully the familiar outlines of her furniture. She sat up, still not sure what had awakened her and then it began again. The dog was barking, Alex's dog, and there was shouting and . . . yes . . . it sounded like someone . . . *singing*! The noise came from beyond the closed door which connected hers with Alex's room and from out in the hallway she could hear Mrs Jackson begging to be told what was to do.

Oh God . . .! What . . .! Was he drunk . . .? But how could he be . . .? Was he deranged at last after bearing the final blow . . .? and the dog . . . he sounded afraid . . .

She leaped from the bed, trailing her foot in the long ruffled hem of her nightgown and her hair fell about her in a tangled drift of sleep-tossed curls, blinding her.

The fire was still burning in the fireplace, the only light in the room, but bright enough – even from the doorway where she stood – to allow her to see the gleam of his teeth, the brilliance of his eyes. He had his head thrown back and he was as neatly placed and tucked in as when she had left him but the *feel* of the room was as untidy and cheerful and rowdy as the nursery filled with her three stalwart boys!

'Sunshine and cloud, love, still there must be,' he was bellowing at the top of his voice and the dog began to howl. Outside the door Mrs Jackson was knocking and insisting that she must go in, to someone who was with her, probably Nurse Livingstone; and down the corridor several housemaids clustered fearfully for surely the master was demented, his poor mind gone over at last!

'Alex.'

Christy stood in her lovely nightgown and whispered his name, no more than a thread of sound in the midst of the hullabaloo but he heard it and turned his head.

He was silent then and as she watched tears formed in the sapphire-blue brilliance of his eyes and slipped into the depths of his pillow.

'Christy . . .'

'What . . . for God's sake . . . what?'

'I've ... I've got ... Oh Jesus ... I hardly dare say it for fear ...'

She moved across the room and sank to her knees beside him. She put her face close to his on the pillow and their eyes met, perhaps for the first time in their entire lives in perfect harmony.

'Tell me ...'

'I can ... I have ... feeling in my ... shoulders ... and arms. They ... prickle ... pins and needles ... you know ...'

'Oh Alex ... oh my darling ...'

He seemed not to notice the endearment.

'Pull back the sheets, Christy ... go on. Look at my hands ... see if ...'

She watched intently as he strained his neck muscles, his face scarlet as he willed his flaccid limbs to answer his unbending mind, and as she looked it happened – and she let out a great thankful cry taking the hand, the hand which had just clenched feebly into a fist, up to her wet face, holding it to her lips in the ecstasy of her joy.

CHAPTER THIRTY-THREE

He would be up and about within the week, he said ... well, alright, laughing into her face ... the month, and Mrs Jackson and Nurse Livingstone must work harder in the massaging and manipulation of his body so that it would strengthen more rapidly and perhaps it would be a good idea, now that the feeling was coming back to his arms, to fetch in a chap he knew, an old bare-knuckle prizefighter to help in some weight-lifting exercises, or even that chap in Fellthwaite who was a champion Cumberland wrestler and would know a thing or two about toughening his arms and shoulders and particularly his back. He longed to sit up, he told her, and move his arms freely, feed himself, shave his own damned face, touch things . . . and here he stopped for what he had in mind was too fragile, too easily damaged, too precious yet to even be allowed to be thought of, let alone spoken out loud. She was as triumphant as he was, he could see that, and her emotion, her overwhelming joy on the night it happened had surprised him but he was not yet sure of it, nor of her. It was too soon. He could not, even now, banish Robin Forsythe from his mind, nor the words Christy had spat at him months ago. She was so different now, so . . . so caring and as eager as he to have him from his bed, but he could not ignore the tiny bud of doubt that it was all in order that she might, once he was well, ask for her freedom! But now, in the first delighted days of holding her hand, gripping it in the strengthening exercises she had devised, feebly yet, but getting firmer each day, he was irresistible in his joy.

His soaring excitement was infectious and the children clustered about him as though he were some new plaything they had just discovered; begging to be allowed to show him every trick they could think of, every treasured object they found on their walks, their scrawled handwriting, to listen to them read; and when he was in the garden, fighting with one another to be allowed to push his heavy chair when he wished to be moved.

Though he was irritated at times with their childish, insistent, squabbling demands for his attention – since his temper was still short and explosive – they had become, whilst he was ill, individual personalities, quite often fascinating as they had grown from babyhood, even unbelievable in their trusting acceptance of him and of his amazing rise from the dead, as it were! He had been no more than a silent stranger lying in his close confined bedroom for most of their young lives. They could not remember him in any other way but now they accepted without question his sudden accessibility, his sudden interest in their lives, his demands to hear their spelling, their songs, their games, and even became resigned to his disciplines. They loved to 'help' in his exercises, lifting his arms and clenching his fists with their own small ones, cheerfully looking forward to the day when he would stand up and stride out into the garden; when he would teach them to ride the ponies he promised them; box and wrestle as he had as a boy, take them to the mine and the mill; up on to the fells where Miss Crawford and Faith declined to go saying it was 'too far for small legs'; and to watch the champion Cumberland wrestler when he fought with others at the Grasmere Sports.

But surprisingly in those first weeks it was with Amy he seemed to have the strongest affinity as he began the slow process of regaining the strength of his body. She was a shy, quiet little girl, completely dominated by her three lively brothers despite the protection she begged from Miss Crawford, from Faith and Beth. She was his daughter. She had his eyes but of a lighter blue. She was dark, her hair in a cloud of soft curls about her head and her skin was smooth and flushed, like his, with amber. A lovely child, as he was a handsome man but she had inherited her mother's sweet-natured timidity and the boisterous behaviour of Johnny, Harry and Joby often upset her. They would tease her and her family of cats, urging on their dogs to 'see 'em off, go on, see 'em off', and her terrified belief that the big, good-tempered animals would rend her delicate feline friends into pieces had her in hysterics and often woke her in nightmares.

On her own with them one day and baited beyond reason by Joby's lofty boast that his 'Scrap' would have her 'Fluff' for breakfast she had run from the nursery, the kitten held frantically to her breast, dashing wildly through the first open door which presented itself to her, and which happened to be her father's bedroom.

'What on earth is the matter with you, young lady?' Alex had asked in amusement. 'And if I were you I shouldn't put that animal too near this lad here,' indicating the lazy terrier who showed not the slightest interest in the kitten, being beyond such nonsensical behaviour. 'He loves the taste of kitten . . .'

It was meant as gentle teasing but her screams of terror could be heard almost to the paddock, and to Alex's astonished embarrassment she had flung herself against him, begging him not to allow it.

'Allow what, child?' His voice was gruff and his hand rose slowly to fumble at her hair for it was not yet positive in its movements, nor sure of where it might land!

'Joby's Scrap is going to . . . and I could not bear it if . . . and that . . .' she pointed wildly at the bewildered terrier, '. . . shall not eat . . .'

Miss Crawford, Faith, Beth and several assorted maids who had come running were all sent away and the door was closed on them. When Christy came home she was amazed to find her step-daughter leaning in companionable comfort against her father's shoulder, the kitten purring between them, the old dog shunted resentfully to the floor whilst they studied a book together.

'Those lads of ours are . . . hard on her,' was all Alex would say, his face awkward, diffident in this new-found, protective fondness for his anxious young daughter. 'They need a good talking to so you can dance them in here later and they shall have it. Young thugs! They have been allowed too much freedom with nothing but women about them, but things will be different from now on. My arm will soon be strong enough to administer a thrashing, let me tell you!'

His face had a self-satisfied look about it and he smiled into the upturned face of his child, his weak arm cradling her clumsily to him. Christy could see that his daughter's need of him as the father she had never really had, the man in her life to protect her against other men — even if at the moment it was merely her brothers — was a role he now relished. It was another small step, a victory, a shoring up of his growing vitality and Amy Buchanan found enormous fulfilment in what she thought of as his need of her. To fetch things for him, to turn his page when his 'poor' arms were tired, to put up or down his canopy in the garden, and their relationship was a source of great pleasure to them both.

Later that night when they had eaten their meal Christy broached the subject which had been in her mind for several weeks now. She had ordered from the same firm in Kendal which had made his garden chair, a similar one for the bedroom. Lighter and made of cane it had a tall, adjustable back and a leg rest, both of which he could arrange himself. The padded seat and back were of thick corded velvet in a deep raspberry pink to match the bedspread, and this one had arms and a tray and book stand which could be attached so that he might read his books, his newspaper without overtiring his arms. He had his meals there, lifted each day from the bed by John and Miles, to sit by the fire or the window with its magnificent view across Tilberthwaite High Fells when the weather did not permit him to go out in the garden.

He could feed himself now, slowly and laboriously, complaining the food was cold before he finished but swearing at anyone who tried to help him, and was even demanding to be allowed to shave himself though Christy was doubtful about this saying she did not want him to cut his own throat at this, late date!

But perhaps the most important result to come from the feeling which was returning to his body was his own control of his natural bodily functions. The transformation in his general appearance, the arrogant lift to his head which was returning, the fierce glow in his eyes, the confident way he awoke to each day, the challenging, impatient manner which was purely his own, was the outcome of this miracle. Perhaps more than any other aspect of his paralysis. For he had been brought to the status of a dumb animal with no care for where it relieved itself and this had been the worst to bear, and the release from it had made him again into a *man*!

The feelings of pins and needles he described had not yet reached his legs and he could still not move them though he insisted on them being exercised several times a day, lying on his back whilst Mrs Jackson performed the treatment which she had become expert at in the eighteen months she had cared for him.

Alex was sipping a brandy that night with undisguised pleasure, his head resting on the padded back of the chair. He watched his wife, his eyes studying the pure line of her profile against the fire's light, the sheen of it in her silky hair, the smoothness of her faintly golden skin and the soft rise and fall of her breast. She rested her cheek on the palm of her hand and her eyes were in shadow as she stared into the heart of the fire. Though it was August it had turned cold and Lou had just piled up the coals on the fire to blazing, leaping flames, the reflections spinning about the silken walls and ceiling in flickering orange and bronze.

'Out with it, my pet,' he said quietly, savouring the flavour of the brandy on his tongue. His eyes travelled, warmly admiring, about her gracefully bent head. 'What are you hatching now?'

She turned sharply and smiled, then shrugged her shoulders.

'Nothing really, just . . .'

'What? Just what? Whenever you have that faraway drift about you, that pensive look of speculation, it spells trouble for someone.'

'No, no trouble. I was just thinking that it is August and it is almost over and I would dearly love to go. October, I believe it ends but with this weather . . .'

'Yes?' The impatience sounded in his voice.

'Well . . .'

'For Heaven's sake woman, get to the point!'

'Very well then! I would like to go to London to see the Exhibition!'

'Aah . . .'

'There is much to see in the way of machinery . . .' Her voice was eager and she leaned forward to look into his face.

'Machinery?' He could not keep the ironic tone from his voice nor resist the tilt of a dark, sardonic eyebrow.

'Yes,' she glowed with enthusiasm, 'of every possible kind from the manufacture of medals, envelopes, knives for all purposes, firescreens, in fact anything you could imagine for use in the factory, mill, or household and I thought . . . as you are unable to go at the moment I should have a look to see if there was something . . . in mining perhaps . . . or machinery for the mill . . .'

'Would you recognize it if you saw it?' His voice was cool, condescending, a man stooping to put a woman in her place.

He watched the eagerness die from her eyes and she drew back from him, her face closing up, a flower from which the sun had gone.

'There are men to explain them, Alex, and if you think me unqualified I could take Richard Forbes with me. I am sure he would know how a new pumping system would work and whether or not it would benefit the mine. I have heard the water in the deep level is fast becoming . . .'

Sensing his interest she leaned forward again in her chair and he saw her relax. She took a deep breath, like a child about to divulge some great secret, then expelled it in an enthusiastic puff of energy, her eyes bright in anticipation.

'You have read about it in the newspapers, Alex, the building of the Crystal Palace and the size of it, the sheer enormity of the glass walls, the height of the columns and the nave but all that is just statistics. I met Emily Aspin this morning and she and Paul have been and she said it is quite breathtaking. Beautiful is the word she used. She said she felt she had entered a fairy-like scene of enchantment, can you imagine! There are trees inside, with real birds flying about and flowers and banners, and the number of exhibitors exceeds seventeen thousand and she said that Paul had told her that at least forty-two thousand people go each day . . .'

'Sounds a bit crowded to me!'

'. . . and there are excursions by train from all over the

country, particularly the industrial towns who would naturally show more interest. Most of the exhibits are British but there are some from abroad and I thought if I were to take Faith . . .'

'Not Richard Forbes . . .?' He was smiling now.

'Good God, no . . .!'

'Well . . .' He hesitated. 'I have no right to stop you, my pet, none at all, but I cannot pretend to like the idea of my wife . . .'

'Alex . . . don't. Please don't speak as once you used . . . please . . .' Her face showed her distress for she did not wish to disturb the harmony in which they had lived these last weeks, but at the same time he must be made to realize that she was no longer the girl she had been before his accident. These past months she had been used to making her own decisions, pleasing herself as to her own move-ments and would not take kindly, now that he was recovering, to being dictated to.

'Christy, I am . . . I am not, believe me, asserting my rights as a husband. I will try not to do that again, my sweet, though it will . . . be hard. You know what a devilish temper I have and can believe no one knows better than I on any subject from . . .' he laughed grimly. 'I would be an ungrateful bastard if I did after all you have achieved. You have proved your skill . . . and intelligence . . . good God . . . in these, what is it, almost two years, but I cannot . . . not all at once . . . become accustomed to . . . Be patient with me, my love, until I am more used to . . .'

'*My* doing what *you* would like to do, is that it?'

'Yes, that is part of it . . .'

'What is the rest?'

'Dammit Christy, I . . . do not like to think of you . . .'

'What, Alex?' Her voice was cool.

'Jesus, Christy.' His face was truculent. 'I am a man after all and you are my wife. You're a damned attractive woman and a man does not take kindly to the idea of . . .'

She began to laugh. 'Oh Alex Buchanan, stop it. I am going to look at *machinery*. That is all that interests me and I can promise you I shall have Faith at my heels like my own shadow. I shall collect all the information and bring it back for you to study and you shall decide what to do about it. I am well able to do all that is necessary in the mine and the mills but the technical aspect of the machinery is . . . I would admit this to no one else . . . it is beyond me.' She smiled at him, again the appealing child who has stumbled into an adult world and finds it quite fascinating. 'Now . . .' she went on, 'let us say no more except this . . .'

'Yes?'

'Whilst I am away you will have to deal with the managers at the mill, and possibly Forbes, if he comes . . .'

He was instantly alert. 'I shall enjoy meeting that young man. I was going to ask you to send a message requesting his presence. I think it is about time he and I sized one another up!'

'Would you, Alex?' Her face was alight with relief. 'Would you see him if I send Jack over to fetch him? He won't come without being summoned unless there is an emergency. He sends up the weekly accounts by messenger now and Mr Tate calls for the wages so I haven't seen him for weeks. I worry so about the . . .'

'Well, you can stop worrying, my pet. I would have liked to be somewhat more active than I am before I challenged him to report the state of the mines but I dare say I can hold my own.'

He smiled jauntily and his eyes were fierce with anticipation.

'Well, before you leap on to your roan and go racing off to Conistone, do you not think it would be a good idea if you were to have your massage?'

She rang for Mrs Jackson and Miles, for since Alex had become more active he had recaptured his appetite – and fed now on Mrs Avery's game soup, vegetable soup, rich calf's head soup, roast sucking pig, quarter of lamb, rib of beef, fillets of chicken, trout, roast fowl and tongue, greengage tart, whipped cream, vol-au-vent of plums –

and the weight was settling on his large frame. It was firm, made so by exercise, particularly in his arms and shoulders, and he was heavy and Christy and the nurse could no longer lift him alone.

When they had left she began the half hour massage, pouring the oil gently across his back, smoothing her hands over it and down to his flaring buttocks and legs until the whole surface of his flesh was shining a pale golden brown in the firelight. She worked her fingers back up again and across the broad stretch of his shoulders, gratified by the hard bunching of his muscles, easing her fingers along each silken inch of tissues lingering on the strengthening firmness of the flesh down his spine and into the small of his back. Her knuckles kneaded gently into his buttocks and for some strange reason she felt her breath quicken and her hands moved to smooth the soft brown fuzz of the body hair which ran from them down to his legs. The oil clung to it, catching the light and quite fascinated she stroked her hands down the length of his thighs, across each slender calf and to the frail boniness of each useless foot. She felt her heart contract painfully in her breast at the sight of those awkward, vulnerable limbs, still so fragile compared to the already powerful build of his arms and shoulders.

She held his foot gently between her hands, looking at it and felt a compelling need to put her lips to it.

'What the devil are you doing down there, woman?' he said lazily and she looked up hastily, almost with guilt. His face was buried in his folded arms and his voice was muffled. 'I'm almost asleep up at this end. Just give my shoulders another rub, will you, my sweet and then we'll call it a day.'

She moved to the head of the bed, her limbs strangely languorous and as she did so her eyes met his. In them was no laziness, nor inclination to sleep, but the fierce, vital glow she had not seen for two years. He held her gaze, his mouth moving in an elusive smile, almost flippant but with a firmness which showed assurance and some other emotion she had seen so many times before but could not recognize. His teeth gleamed whitely in the dim light and he lifted himself up on to his elbows, watching her.

She stood, mesmerized.

'My word, I feel fit, Christy,' he said softly. 'I feel as though I could do almost anything. My arms are becoming strong again and before much longer I should not be surprised to find myself doing all the things I used to do two years ago. Do you know, my sweet, I do believe I could turn myself over without too much trouble if you would care to . . . massage . . . my shoulders and forearms . . . and perhaps my chest. It is only a question of turning my top half and then lifting one leg at a time with my own hands. Shall I try, Christy? Would you like me to see if I can do it? Do you think I am strong enough yet?'

She cleared her throat and put up her hand to it, feeling the rosy flush spread from her hairline right down to her toes. There was no mistaking his meaning. She could respond by smiling just as engagingly, by kneeling beside him, putting out a hand to touch the one he offered; oblige him by following wherever he found he could go and she felt herself begin to take that step, to move sensuously in the way he had always made her feel, in his direction but at the last moment she drew back. For some unaccountable reason she felt constrained to step away from this moment, not yet ready for whatever it was he offered.

The silence was warm, a breathless expectancy thudded in her throat and she moved her hand so that he could not see the pulse which beat erratically there. It seemed to stretch on forever and she began to agonize on how she was to end it. He still smiled at her quizzically, half turned, resting now on one elbow and the strong line of his naked chest, waist and hip glowed amber in the lamplight, his long hard body, despite the extreme slenderness of his legs, immensely masculine and attractive. His hair curled vigorously about his head, falling across his brow so that he looked as bold and flamboyant as a gypsy and his eyes were narrowed to slits of vital, vivid blue as he waited for her reaction.

'Christy,' he said, no more, but his smile was wickedly delighted and his mouth curved challengingly and he watched her; his wry humour restraining the moment from becoming too unwieldy, saying that whatever she wished to make of it, whichever course she took he was only too happy to oblige.

The fire hummed gently in the grate. A rush of air from some soft breeze off the fells lifted the curtain at the window and it tapped gently as though to remind them that time was passing. She could hear footsteps on the path which led round the house and a girl laughed, the sound hastily muffled against something . . . a man's shoulder, perhaps, or lips!

The grandmother clock at the foot of the stairs sounded the notes of nine o'clock and a door opened somewhere at the back of the house and a voice said something indistinguishable. All the sounds with which she was completely familiar, sounds she heard every evening but scarcely noticed. The girl laughing would be Sally slipping out unobserved by her mistress to meet Jack whom she was to marry next month; and the servants would be about their duties in the relaxed atmosphere which prevailed at the end of the day when bedtime was almost upon them.

She could not move. She was fixed forever, it seemed, in this state of mindless paralysis which allowed her no movement and no thought beyond the recognition that she had never seen her husband so pleasing to her eye and to her senses, and that within the next moment she would be drawn towards the bed with no perception of how it had come about.

With a prodigious yawn that cracked his jaws the dog at the fireside rose to his feet and stretched, arching his back, extending each leg in turn, shaking himself with the ferocity of a swimmer just come from the water. He ambled across the carpet to lay his muzzle on Alex's pillow, staring unblinkingly but with utter devotion up into his master's face.

The spell was broken and Christy laughed, the sound no more than a tremulous vibrating in her throat. She stepped back from that high strung moment with relief . . . was that it . . . or was it . . . regret and began to busy herself with Alex's nightshirt, throwing it to him almost carelessly, coming no nearer to the bed than was absolutely necessary.

'Shall I call Mrs Jackson, Alex?' her voice was a husky quiver, the words thick and awkward on her tongue. 'Perhaps you would like a hot drink, and that oil must be sponged off.'

'I would have no objection to *you* sponging off the oil, sweetheart,' he said smilingly, 'that is if you have time. Mrs Jackson might be glad of an early night.' His grin was quite wicked and he made no move to reach for his nightshirt.

'No . . . really . . . I am very tired, Alex.'

'Of course, my pet.'

'I must make an early start in the morning. There are a lot of arrangements to be made if I am to be away for a few days . . .' She knew she was babbling but could not seem to stop as she felt his eyes on her and his smile caress her. 'I must get word to the managers that they must come to you if they have any problems and I shall take the train to Stavely, I think, to see Mr Dunlop. He will be pleased to deal with you again. Despite his help I always felt he was glad to see me in my parlour . . . or the . . . well . . . I had best get a letter off to some hotel in London to reserve some rooms. Perhaps you could recommend somewhere suitable for myself and Faith. Quiet but close to the Exhibition. I had better do that now so that it can go first thing tomorrow . . .'

The whole time she was speaking she moved about the room, picking things up and putting them down again, moving the brandy glass from the table beside his chair to the mantelshelf, and was quite tempted to pour down her throat the half inch which remained in it to steady herself. 'My word, what a lot to do and such excitement . . .'

'Indeed!' His voice was lazily smiling.

'. . . and the children will have to be told and made to . . .'

'Of course!'

'. . . and I think I must, absolutely must go up to the mine before I leave and see for myself what has been done . . .'

'Christy, there is no need. Just send a note by Jack that Forbes is to come . . .'

'Oh no, Alex, I really think I should go myself and . . .'

'Girl, slow down, slow down, you are making me feel quite exhausted! Perhaps it might be as well if you pressed the bell for Mrs Jackson.' He grinned impishly. 'I swear I shall have a relapse if you do not stop pacing about and wringing your hands. You look like some actress in a drama about to be thrown out into the cold, cold snow. Calm down, my sweet. There is no urgency. The Exhibition does not end until October as you remarked, so you can spare a day or two to organize your husband, your family and your business into a shape which pleases you before you go.'

He appeared to be immensely pleased about something and his good humour mystified her. Once upon a time she might have expected to see his temper, always on a short fuse, explode at any refusal on her part to do as he wished, whatever it might be. Perhaps she had been mistaken by what she had seen in his eyes. Perhaps the tension, soft and familiar once, had been imagination, or felt only by herself? Had she herself created that speculative gleam in his vibrant eyes and had she dreamed the strength of her own sexuality and enchantment in the beauty of his masculine nakedness?

He grinned infectiously, then leaned back, his folded hands beneath his head and his dog leaped up to lie beside him, licking his face with familiar concern, watching him as he had watched for two years. He began to move his tail slowly, then more quickly as though, just as positively as his master, he knew that things were about to change round here!

CHAPTER THIRTY-FOUR

Christy and Faith travelled on the Lancaster and Carlisle Railway by first class compartment as far as Warrington, where they changed to the London and North West arriving in Euston just thirteen hours after they had left Howethwaite.

Though Faith was not so intimidated as Sally had been on her first railway journey, being a more composed young lady – not given to shrillness at the sound of an engine's whistle or the admiring though polite glance of a gentleman – she was inclined as Christy had promised Alex she would be to walk a scant inch from Christy's heels so that every time Christy turned unexpectedly they were in danger of a collision. She was quite speechless, of course, for the first few hours of the journey, watching the landscape hurtle past the window at a frightening speed. They were in Warrington, a journey of some four or five hours, before she opened her mouth and that was to ask, pleadingly, if this was London!

They were suitably dressed for the occasion in travelling outfits of black Pekin silk since Christy was still in mourning for her mother, the dresses plain with a jacket bodice under which Christy wore a 'gilet' shaped to her figure. At her neck and sleeves to relieve the severity of the gown, she had a stylish froth of white lace and the half dozen petticoats she wore held out the wide, black lace trimmed mass of her skirt. Her bonnet was small, set back from her face, the inside of the brim trimmed with black tulle. In her luggage were half a dozen dresses, all black but extremely elegant and a rather daring evening gown, stark and simple of deep, black panne velvet with two enormous satin roses, also in black, at her waist though she really could not imagine when she would wear it.

Her hair was brushed to a burnished chestnut, her grey eyes were like new-minted silver in her face. Enhanced by the severe black of her outfit her skin was like cream touched only at the cheekbones with rose-amber, put there by excitement.

'Take care, my love,' Alex said carelessly from his chair by the window, 'and if you should meet up with Prince Albert give him my congratulations. He had done us proud I hear and perhaps his German origins will be forgiven him now. They said he was a madman with his exhibition but he has proved them wrong. Oh, and if you should feel the need to hurry back a day or two earlier I shall not object though I daresay I shall be kept busy by Cartmell, Anderson and Pendle who have all promised to call. You did send that message to Forbes, did you not? Well, he has not answered, which I might say does not please me, so if Miss Crawford would come up here she can write me another – I really must employ myself a secretary – and Jack can take it over. Now, off you go, though I must say I do not care to see you looking quite so elegant in your mourning. Why do most women look like crows in black and yet you look quite stunning?'

They were both laughing when she waved from the carriage to where he sat in the bedroom window and her smile was still warming her face as she and Faith boarded the train at Windermere.

The hotel was small, quiet and extremely comfortable, suitable in Alex's opinion for a lady and her maid travelling alone – if such a place existed which was doubtful – but the Grosvenor in Knightsbridge came the closest to fitting the bill. They could dine in the privacy of their own sitting room, situated between their two bedrooms, he had said, which was appropriate for no lady could eat in a public place unescorted and they had really no need to leave the seclusion of their rooms except to go to the Exhibition.

'Perhaps I could take a spyglass and see it from the hotel window, Alex,' she had remarked pertly. 'That way I shall have no need to go out at all. Or perhaps Faith could go along and bring back twice daily reports.'

Her tone had been humorous but there had been a glint in her eye which said she did not care for this arranging of things on her behalf, unasked that is, when she had travelled to Swansea, to St Helens and back many times, and without him to tell her how to do it!

He had laughed, half apologetically, but there had also been a glint in his eye which said that he did not care for the whole thing!

The landlord of the hotel and his bustling staff of obliging chambermaids, and Faith herself, soon had Mrs Buchanan settled before a brightly burning fire in her cosy sitting room with white towels and hot water in abundance and as comfortable, Faith said, as they were at home.

'Is this not exciting, Faith?' Christy said later as they dined on clear vermicelli soup, fillets of whiting, filet de boeuf and sauce piquante, followed by charlotte aux pommes, mince pies, lemon cream, café noir and, at Christy's insistence, a glass of brandy each.

'Oh no, Christy, please. I can't drink brandy,' Faith had said, 'it will only go to my head,' and it did and they both had another and went to their separate rooms giggling.

As a result they both overslept and were late to cross Rotten Row and catch their first glimpse of the fabled Crystal Palace.

The sight, quite simply, took their breath away!

The canopy of glass had been erected over and around the trees which grew there, occupying a site of twenty-six acres or so in Hyde Park, combining engineering, utility and a strange delicate beauty in one staggering whole. It was based on the glasshouses at Chatsworth, home of the Duke of Devonshire and designed by the Duke's own gardener. The effect was stupendous, not only on the people of London and the middle classes but on the working men of Great Britain. They had come in their thousands, in their millions, pouring into the capital on excursion trains from the provinces and industrial towns of the north. From the eighteen million population of Great Britain it was estimated that six million of them had seen Prince Albert's Great Exhibition, his coming of age party for the new Industrial Britain, and it was considered to be no less than a huge shop window for the products of the new industry.

Christy and Faith went only on the exclusive Friday and Saturday, paying half a crown each, overcome by the traffic jams, overwhelmed by the hordes of sightseers who came on the 'shilling days'. The sun shone hotly on the giant crystal mansion, like a many sided diamond sparkling in the clear air. The park itself was lush with sweet-smelling grass and heavy, pollen-laden flowers. There were beautiful things to see; clever and mysterious things to see! Carpets so exquisite and fine it seemed a sacrilege to set one's boots upon them, bedsteads carved so daintily in walnut wood, silken hangings from China, papier mâché firescreens, gold inlaid knives, mother of pearl tie pins, a twenty-four ton block of solid coal, crystal fountains, Indian pearls, tapestries and an amazing model of the dockland of Liverpool with a thousand rigged ships upon it. Foreigners, dark eyes flashing, quick strange tongues falling beside the broad vowels of Lancashire and amidst it all the formidable Machinery Court where there were machines of every conceivable size and shape none of which made the slightest sense to Christy. Hundreds of them all performing some mystical function she could not even guess at until at last, escorted by a most attentive, one might even say persistent young gentleman, she and Faith were directed to a section which dealt exclusively with mining; coal, iron and copper and the machinery which had come to facilitate the easier removal of it from the earth.

'Dear Lord, Christy! How on earth are you to remember

all this?' Faith whispered in consternation. The gentlemen themselves, who were on hand to explain to any other *gentleman* who might be concerned, were themselves quite bewildered, even hostile when Christy evinced interest, believing her to be deranged and in need of a man to control her. But she had not dealt exclusively with gentlemen such as these for almost two years for nothing and her charm and quiet indomitable determination to be not only heard, but given an explanation and indeed specifications on the very latest machine which could benefit *her* business concerns, she said arrogantly, soon had them in their proper place which was to listen to what she needed and give it to her at once with as little fuss as possible. They wilted beneath her scathing comments, her quick-witted grasp of what she was told, her intelligent questions and the incredible flashing brilliance of her eyes which one gentleman, when she had departed, likened to the magnificence of the Crystal Palace itself!

They were to travel home on Monday, spending Sunday, Christy declared, seeing a little of London. They had exhausted themselves, she said as they sauntered slowly through the crowds which thronged the main transept of the Exhibition Hall, in the pursuance of business for two whole wearying days and they were entitled to a little leisure time. She had not come all this way, she argued, to miss the splendid sights which surely must abound in this capital city and tomorrow she meant to see them! Besides, the trains were unreliable on a Sunday!

She stopped to stare in wonder at the great glass fountain which stood in the centre of the hall, and Faith stopped beside her, since it never failed to elicit, not only from them but from the other millions who saw it, a kind of awed rapture. It was twenty-seven feet high and was so contrived that the whole metal structure which supported the glass was invisible. Water gushed from three tiers of fluted basins of decreasing size and descended in a transparent curtain into the pool from which the fountain rose. It was truly magnificent, the showpiece of the Exhibition, the opulent, overdecorated pinnacle of the opulent and overdecorated objects, hundreds of thousands of them, which crammed the enormity of the Hall and there was always a dense crowd about it.

'Your husband will not like it, Christy. He is expecting you home tomorrow,' Faith said half-heartedly for though she was the not challenging Mrs Buchanan, who loved the excitement and glitter of what she had seen at the Exhibition and the stir Christy herself had made in the Machinery Court, she had enjoyed this momentary upheaval in the calm of her days at Howethwaite. Though she still mourned her young husband and the children she had been denied by his death she was content sharing the lives of those born to Christy and Alex Buchanan. She was more companion than maid to Christy though she had offered to take over again Sally's job of personal maid when the girl married Jack. There were rumours that a speedy wedding was called for, Mrs Longworth blaming the laxity, she said in private to Mrs Avery, of her commercial mistress in the over-looking of young maidservants away from home, not considering that this young maidservant was no younger than Mrs Buchanan herself!

'But will you have time to look after me as well as your other duties, Faith?' Christy had asked when Faith made the offer.

'Come now, Christy! Miss Crawford has all four children for the whole of the morning and Amy and Johnny all day. Beth and Liz have scarce enough to do in the nursery now and Mr Buchanan has the children in there with him for at least an hour each day. I need something else to occupy myself so I can quite easily see to you.'

'Oh Faith, I would like nothing better. As soon as Sally is wed you shall be my . . . not maid . . . assistant . . . or better yet . . . companion! How does that sound?'

They were silent now, as were the rest of the crowd still surging about the Exhibition for the awe-inspiring magnificence of the fountain had the effect of quietening even the most raucous voice. It was humid in the hall as it held the heat of the day. The sun was low as the evening drew on, casting long shadows across the grass and the mock Italian garden which surrounded the Crystal Palace, and the copper glow of it, reflected through a thousand square panes of glass to touch the frill of the water turned it to a sheer net of spun gold.

'Your husband will not like it,' Faith said again when Christy did not answer, touching her arm to draw her away for really it would be dark soon and he would like it even less should he learn his wife had been out accompanied by only her maid after night had fallen – but Christy refused to be led away and indeed appeared to be rooted to the spot on which she stood beside the fountain. Her body had become quite rigid and the muscles in her arm beneath Faith's fingers were hard as coiled springs of steel. There was an absolute stillness about her, fixed and unnatural. Her arms were at her side and her gloved hands were clenched into tight fists held against her wide skirt as though, should she relax them for even a moment she might begin to shake and tremble and fall apart before the interested gaze of the assembly who stood about them.

'Christy . . .?' Faith's voice was anxious and she gave the arm she held a little shake, or tried to for it was still locked into the unyielding quality of rock.

'Christy, what is it?' she asked, but Christy did not answer, nor even turn her head but continued to stare through the golden flow of water to the other side of the wide transept. Her lips parted slowly on a silent murmur. Her eyes were wide and shocked but brilliant in a face from which every scrap of colour had fled and Faith could feel the urgent stirring of the tremor in the arm she held.

'Christy?' she said for the third time, staring into her friend's face but still Christy did not answer. Faith felt the tremor move the arm she held and with the jerky action of a puppet on a string Christy took a step forward, then another, closer to the fountain and the fine spray from it drifted a little, settling in tiny diamonds about the hem of her black skirt.

Faith turned to look then, following where Christy's eyes went and he was there, just inside the doorway, the sun catching the feathered layers of his pale golden hair. It outlined the erect and proud angle of his head from which he had removed his hat, the graceful lounging of his tall, arrow straight body as he stood waiting, waiting she knew, for Christina Buchanan – Christy Emmerson – to come to him.

It was as though a lamp had been lit in her eyes, its radiance shining out from between her thick lashes flowing across the fashionable, expensively gowned and suited multitude, across the swaying curtain of water, and her face began to glow. Faith's hand tried to stop her, absurdly for how to stop a whirlwind she asked herself later, but Christy threw it off, moving beyond her.

'It's Robin, you fool,' she hissed and her face was illuminated by the flame of her love.

'Christy . . . don't . . .' Faith whispered deep in her throat, not even sure what it was she asked but desperate to stop the bewitched woman from taking those few destructive steps towards the man who had begun, as jerkily as she, to reduce the distance between them. There were top-hatted, frock-coated gentlemen in sombre hues of black and grey with elegant wide-crinolined, fashionably bonneted ladies clinging to their arms. There was colour and laughter and the polite, well-bred murmur of the upper class who had come like themselves, on the exclusive 'half a crown' day, not caring to hazard themselves with the common man on the 'shilling' days, and miraculously they appeared to part, to drift away leaving a clear passage for the man and woman who moved mindlessly toward one another. Faith, though she still stood where Christy had left her, her hand outstretched in a last despairing plea to her to . . . what . . . have the sense to turn away, to ignore the beseeching urgency which held her, could see the hot brown sweetness in Robin Forsythe's eyes and knew, knew though her back was to her, that it was answered in Christy's.

541

He had her hand to his lips when Faith at last found the strength to move, his eyes warm and sweet as honey. It was there for anyone to see, the love, the hunger, the need, all the emotions which had lain dormant, she supposed, in both of them since their last meeting two years ago. For a dreadful moment Faith thought that beneath the interested gaze of several hundred or so fascinated onlookers he was about to embrace her. His hand rose to her cheek and as it cupped it, hers reached to clasp his and Faith could see the enchantment fall about the woman she loved, cloaking her in the familiar bemusement she had known for seven years.

The paralysis left her then. It had lasted for only as long as it had taken Christy Buchanan and Robin Forsythe to walk the few yards to one another, but it had held her far too long, her anxious mind told her. People were beginning to stop, to turn and stare, murmuring to one another, whispering, smiling at the romantic picture the young couple made, but really, was it decent to stand like that in a public place, she knew they were saying. One might expect it from the lower classes but it was not the behaviour of a lady and gentleman as these two obviously were! The gentry, perhaps even the aristocracy, stared curiously, their eyes warm with speculation, and Faith was aware that the report of it would be passed, if he was recognized since he was one of their own, from them to others and, in the close-knit structure which formed the upper echelon of London society, the news of it would be in the Squire's own home and his wife's drawing room before morning.

But that was not her concern. She cared not a whit for Robin Forsythe's good name nor for the gossip which might run rife of his romantic episode with a beautiful unknown woman beside the fountain at the Great Exhibition. She cared only for Christy . . . and Alex Buchanan.

'Mr Forsythe,' she said boldy at his elbow. 'How nice to see you after all this time. I do believe we have not met since before your marriage. I trust you are well, and Mrs Forsythe.'

542

She might have been some friend greeting another in the casual warmth of her greeting instead of the once scullery maid of Annie Emmerson. She had never spoken before to the man. She was a working-class girl, he was of the landed gentry and under normal circumstances she would have done no more than bob her curtsey and lower her eyes, but this moment called for desperate measures and Faith took them. She must get Christy back from the dazed delight into which Robin Forsythe had flung her. Even her own presence making a questionable twosome into an acceptable threesome might send on their way those who had stopped to stare and wonder!

They both turned to look at her in amazement, Christy's face slack still in her rejoicing, but Robin Forsythe dropped his hand from where it touched her cheek and hers fell limply to her side and they stepped back at once from one another's closeness.

'Miss . . .?' Robin bowed politely, automatically but in Christy's face there was a flare of anger. Her eyes still contained the lambent light of deep emotion and her cheeks the flush which had come from Robin's hand, but the snatching of it from her by Faith Adams filled her with confusion for in truth she was not yet aware of where she was. Her mind was dazed, bewitched by Robin's sudden appearance, the sight of his beloved face and from the love which burned in his eyes still, and she longed for the closeness of him. She had been oblivious to everything but the leaning of his tall frame to hers, the gleam of the sun in his golden hair, the deep hot brown of his eyes, his hand reaching out to her, the curling shape of his smiling lips, the brown flush of his skin and now, now Faith had come to take it from her.

'My goodness, look at the time. Had we not best be on our way?' Faith was saying forcefully. 'You know Mr Buchanan would not like you to be out after dark, Christy. He was most insistent that we be back at the hotel before night fell, was he not, when he bade us goodbye and I do believe the sun is about to set.' She turned winningly towards the young Squire. 'You have no idea how protective he is, Mr Forsythe, towards his wife.'

She could not have done better if she had hit the pair of them full in the face!

The light died from Christy's eyes then, the lovely light kindled only moments ago but he was the first to regain his composure. He eyed Faith coolly.

'Miss . . .? I am sorry, you will think me no gentleman, but your name escapes me . . .' He was as well-mannered as any member of his class was bred to be but Faith could see the small angry cloud in his beautiful eyes, put there by her own interference, his expression seemed to say. Quite devastated that he had forgotten the name of a lady who evidently knew his but scowling and displeased nevertheless. She cared not a fig for his resentment.

'*Mrs* Adams, Mr Forsythe.'

He bowed over her hand, still not knowing her, of course, but willing to be polite about it.

'Mrs Adams.' The silence which followed was deep and long. Their eyes were drawn back to one another of their own volition and Faith agonized over what she must do next. They were at least apart! They looked to the casual observer like any other small group of friends discoursing on the splendour of the Exhibition, the fineness of the evening, the possibility of the weather breaking, only their total silence separating them from the rest of the crowd.

Faith tried again.

'We have been viewing the marvels of the Exhibition, have we not, Christina? Have you been to inspect it yet, Mr Forsythe?'

Again he dragged his gaze away from Christy. Who was this persistent woman who had insinuated herself between his love and him, his expression seemed to say and his answer was sharp.

'No. I do not care for . . . for such things, Mrs Adams.' They are for the likes of the manufacturing classes, his pained countenance informed her.

'Do you not?' Her face and voice were equally cool. 'I

am surprised to find you here then. Mrs Buchanan and I have spent two whole days in the Machinery Court!'

'The Machinery Court?'

'Oh yes indeed. Mrs Buchanan's husband, Mr Alexander Buchanan, you understand, asked us particularly to look out for . . .' What the devil would Alex Buchanan have asked his wife to look out for, her mind despaired but what did it matter as long as she could prise this man from Alex Buchanan's wife? It was immaterial what she said or did to achieve it but she must get Christy away, back to the hotel, back to Fellthwaite before the life she and Mr Buchanan were slowly rebuilding was shattered by this gentleman. Oh yes, a gentleman who would not deliberately set out to destroy the woman he so manifestly wanted but would nevertheless – if this meeting was to lead to others, to a repetition of the summer of two years ago when Faith's home had been used to deceive Alex Buchanan – effectively overwhelm the lives of the Buchanan family. They could not conceal it as they had then and the scandal would devastate them, their world and all the people who lived in it with them. She felt enormous admiration for her master. She had seen him defeated, brought down to the level of a wounded animal dying in its dark lair and she had seen him crawl from it and look up to the light and force himself to recover. She had watched Christy Buchanan help to drag him towards it. She had sensed the slow awareness of their conciliation, the understanding which was blending them into an assurance, a fragile trust of one another that might, if left alone to grow, become worthwhile to them both and this man must not be allowed to interfere with it, not if she could prevent it.

'Oh yes,' she said loudly, rudely she supposed. 'Christy and I have come to see the machinery which might help in the running of the mines. Mr Buchanan's mines you know. Christy has been managing them, and the mills and now that Mr Buchanan is recovering . . .'

He had been listening again with only half his attention,

not even that, his eyes wandering back to rest worshipfully on Christy's face, his expression soft, reaching out to meet the one she directed towards him, but Faith's words captured his notice again and his head snapped eagerly to her.

'He is recovering?' The question was tense, breathless.

'Oh yes, he has the use of his arms now and we are expecting him to be walking soon.' An exaggeration but something must be said to make this man believe that Christy Buchanan's husband was well able to hold what was his.

He brushed her off like some dogged butterfly which would keep alighting on his hand, turning to Christy, taking her hands in his.

'Is this true, my darling?' he pleaded and Faith felt the blood leave her head.

'Oh yes!' Christy's voice, the first words she had spoken, was a soft dreaming chant of love.

'He will . . . will be himself again soon?'

'I believe so.'

'And able to care for . . . for himself?'

She sighed deeply in the ecstacy of their reunion. 'Yes, Robin.'

'Then . . .?'

'Yes?' She swayed towards him and Faith felt the despair move in her heart and she wanted to weep for the brave man who in trying to save her huband had crippled himself. His body was recovering but the crippling of his heart and mind would be far, far worse!

Still she would not let go. *She would not.* She loved this woman who was her friend and respected the man who was her friend's husband, and if it cost her her job, her home she would do all in her power to preserve what she felt was growing between them and *this* man must not be allowed to damage it *again*.

But they were speaking and she might have been one of the drifting assembly which milled about them for all the notice they took of her.

'We cannot talk here,' he was saying, ardour thickening his voice.

'No.' Christy seemed to watch his moving lips as though she was already imagining them against hers.

'Will you meet me . . .?'

'Oh yes . . . where . . .?'

'Christy, really, do you not think it time we returned to the hotel?' Faith's voice was high and desperate, ignored!

'Wherever you wish . . . but somewhere . . . private!'

'We could . . .'

'Yes my darling?' He reached for her hand again and it was there for him.

'We are staying at the Grosvenor . . .'

'In Kensington? I know it . . .'

'Robin!'

'Eight o'clock.'

They were to dine in the intimacy of the small fire-lit sitting room, Christy told Faith, she would wear the black velvet evening gown and Faith thought hopelessly that she had never seen her look more magnificent. Her hair was brushed until it gleamed, pulled into a loose knot at the back of her neck and a single rose of scarlet silk placed in its centre. She wore a black velvet ribbon around her throat and long drops of jet from her ears. Her shoulders rose from the deep décolletage of the bodice and the unusually plain wide skirt was held out by six flounced black petticoats.

'I shall not leave you alone,' she said quietly as Christy waited for him to arrive.

'Very well, we shall go out to dine. There are . . . I believe . . . places where one can find . . . seclusion!'

'Christy, for God's sake, you cannot mean to go . . . where men take women . . . of . . . of loose . . .'

'I shall go if I am forced,' Christy's voice was like ice, like steel in her determination and yet beneath it she was on fire, consumed with her need, desperate enough to do anything to fulfil it.

'But lass . . . listen to me . . .'

'Do not "lass" me, Faith Adams. You are in my employ and will do as I tell you!'

'Christy . . .' Faith was appalled, shaken to the core by Christy's arrogant dismissal of their friendship but she would not give in, not then.

'Please Christy . . . Mrs Buchanan, if you prefer. Do not do this thing.'

'What thing? We are merely dining together.' She stood at the window looking down into the courtyard at the front of the hotel, waiting, watching for the carriage which would bring her love. She was alternately white with anticipation, then flushed with longing, and her fingers beat a rapid tattoo on the windowsill and her feet tapped impatiently beneath the wide skirt of her exquisite gown. Her eyes were like blazing diamonds, huge and glittering between the long, nervously fluttering fans of her eyelashes.

'Don't . . . don't treat me like a child, Christy.' Faith stood behind her, then reached to grip her arm but Christy threw her off, avoiding her eyes, her own unable it appeared to leave the spot where Robin Forsythe would appear.

'Christy, let me stay, at least. Don't be alone with him. If you must . . . dine with him, but let me stay . . .'

Christy whirled round and the lovely fragrance of her French perfume, obtained at great expense for her by Miss Susan Whittam, drifted on the air. She looked fiercely at Faith, then imperceptibly her expression softened and she put out a hand to her friend.

'I'm sorry, Faith but I must . . . must . . . be alone with him. Let me have this, my friend. Go to your room. I will have something sent to you but please, please, if you value our friendship, do not interfere . . .'

'It is because I *am* your friend . . .'

'It is no use, Faith. You will go to your room and stay there, or you may take the train to wherever you wish . . . but not to Howethwaite!'

'Christy!'

'I'm sorry . . . I'm sorry, Faith, but I will not let you

stand in my way. All my life since I was a child I have been sent here and there at everyone's bidding. As a child, a young girl I accepted it. As a wife I was made to conform but I am my own woman now and I will do as I please. I do not know what it is that pleases me as yet but I intend to find out . . . but now . . . this moment . . . it pleases me to dine alone . . . alone, with Robin Forsythe.'

'And where do you think that will lead? Surely you know he has other commitments, *as you do*. Let go of him. Christy. You cannot keep him in your heart forever. Let him go to his wife and child. Allow him to be free . . .'

'No . . . no dammit . . . he is mine . . . I love him! Always . . . always I have been made . . . forced by others . . . by our circumstances . . . to watch him walk away from me. Now . . . now . . . for a few hours, he is mine . . . Faith . . . please . . . leave us alone . . . Let me have it . . .'

Faith Adams felt the violence and the pain and the anger of Christy Buchanan's love for Robin Forsythe dash against her recoiling flesh and she wondered at it, at its fury and the devastation it would cause, and her heart remembered and grew gentle with the memory of her own love. *That* she understood. Her young husband, the clean sweetness of their few months together, the deep, strong bond which lasted yet despite its difference to this passion Christy Buchanan displayed. Yes, that she understood, this she did not!

She turned away and her voice shook a little but her back was pencil straight.

'I will not disturb you, Christy, but tomorrow, whatever you decide to do, I shall return to Howethwaite.'

CHAPTER THIRTY-FIVE

They looked at one another across the lamplit dining table, and across the divide of two years and there was no need to speak. He was the same, now that she had the leisure to study him properly. His finely chiselled face was a little older, his delicately balanced, slender body in his immaculate evening dress coat and trousers was as gracefully lounging but the tension in him, the whipcord leaning of his shoulders towards her seemed to plead that nothing had changed between them. A word, a lift of her eyebrow and she would be in his arms surely, and it would be just as it had always been.

'Robin,' she whispered, her voice low and sweet and she heard him draw in his breath. He put out his brown hand to her, laying it on the smooth damask of the tablecloth and she placed hers in it as naturally as though they were the young lovers of seven years ago.

She sighed and her eyes narrowed to long, smoky curves of love for him and he stood up, moving round the small table, the good food placed upon it left untouched. He drew her to her feet and trembling, a groan of deep need in his voice he pulled her gently into his arms. He did not kiss her, merely held her body along the length of his, her face in the hollow of his neck.

She rested comfortably against his long, hard, familiar body, feeling the warmth of him, the gentleness, the sweet goodness of this man who had held her heart since she was a girl. They were a man and a woman now and no longer loved as they had done then. They had been innocent, ignorant, wanting each other as naturally as young animals, but still their love had been deep. It was just as strong, even yet, but now, now their bodies had changed, both of them were experienced in the way of the flesh and their needs were deeper, more subtle.

'I have lived here in London, and in Leicestershire in the hunting season, for two years and not a day has gone by without my thinking of you.' His voice was gently musing and his cheek rested on her shining hair. 'I often imagined us here, like this, in some room alone with no one to interrupt and now it has happened and I cannot believe it. Tell me that it is real. Tell me that I am not imagining it, dreaming . . .'

She raised her head to smile at him and he looked down into her face and his expression changed from one of dreaming contemplation of his past hopes to sensuality. The glow of melting ice in the depths of her eyes, the poppy-red invitation of her moist lips floated beneath his own and he bent his head and his mouth brushed hers; lightly at first, sweetly, then deeper, harder, desperate to feel, to have, to take and their mouths clung, tongues touching and exploring and they felt themselves sinking down to the soft carpet for if they stood a moment longer they knew they would fall.

'Christy . . . sweetheart, it has been so long . . . so long. Do you remember . . . the cave up on the fells and the sunshine on us . . . you were so beautiful . . . beautiful . . .'

His voice was urgent and his hands were at her face, her hair, pulling out the knot of it, gripping it in desperate, loving fingers. It lay in a glorious mass about her head, moving in ripples as she lifted her mouth to find his. She gripped the soft, gilt streaked curls of his head and drew him down to her, opening his mouth with her tongue, moving sensuously beneath him. His hands smoothed the creamy softness of her shoulder, trembling in their need. His face burrowed beneath her chin and she arched her back and his lips slid, warm and moist along the line of her throat to the full curve of her breast. She felt the warmth of his lips and his tongue as it slipped along the low neckline of her bodice, settling for a delicious moment in the hollow between her breasts.

'Oh dear God . . . my love . . . my love . . .' He reached to the neckline of her gown, easing it away from her, pulling down the soft velvet until the glory of her naked breasts was revealed, and he pressed his face to her soft sweet-smelling flesh, rubbing his cheek across each peaked nipple. He was desperate to have her long, white, lovely body naked against his own and she lifted her hands to help him, slipping her arms from the small sleeves of the gown, pulling it down, down to her waist, as fervent in her need as he and as she moved, smiling a little, his breath was warm against her skin, murmuring softly.

'Dear sweet God but you're beautiful . . . beautiful, Christy, my sweet lovely Christy. There is no one like you . . . no one . . . I could not wait . . . not another week nor even a day, an hour when I heard . . .'

His mouth slid down the silken glide of her white skin to the full nipple of her breast and he took it between his lips and as yet she was not aware, not quite, in her rapturous delight, of what he was saying.

'. . . I could not believe our luck, my darling, when my mother told me you were here. It was like a sign from the gods that we were meant . . . oh Christy, you are so sweet . . . so sweet . . . !'

His mother!

'. . . you have no idea . . . I searched that damn place for hours before I found you . . . you were like a vision . . . the water about you . . . in your black dress against that golden scene.'

He groaned and his lips reached down to beneath her breasts and his hands went to the voluminous width of her skirts, pulling urgently in his need to feel, to see the rest of her body – and as he did so she felt the sudden cold touch of something at the back of her neck and she gasped with the shock of it. It was like ice, a glacial sliver which struck with the force of stinging hailstones bringing a shudder to her flesh and an ache to her bones and the agonizing, overwhelming awareness that there was a *wrongness* here, a contradiction which she could not yet understand but whatever it was when she had unravelled it, she must not, must not do this thing!

It was as though a net had been thrown over her, holding her rigid, captured, unable now to move in the joy of loving this man. A sudden deadening, a numbing of her mind from which the conceiving of the fantasies of sexual love came; from which ardour is born. She felt cold, icy cold and yet the fire was warm on her naked breasts and she could see the flames burnish the pale gold hair of her love. She could feel her jaw begin to clench in an effort to stop her teeth from chattering and her flesh froze and every hair on her arms and legs and the back of her neck rose in extinguished hope.

She became quite still, lying back in Robin's arms, lifeless, her eyes looking somewhere over his shoulder and he raised himself slowly to his elbows, his hair tumbled about his forehead, his face flushed and she thought in her despair that he had never looked more beautiful as she turned her sad, clouded eyes upon him. He looked down into her face and knew immediately what he had done and his face lost its colour and his warm brown eyes became flat and dead.

'What is it?' he said though he really had no need to ask.

'You knew I was here?' she whispered.

'Well, I . . .' His voice was unsteady and she noticed his lips trembled somewhat in the fashion of a child who has been caught red-handed at some mischief.

'You knew I would be here . . . you discussed me with your *mother?* You planned this . . . ?'

'Christy.' His voice was anguished now and she felt her heart move, as it always had, with pity for his defenceless-ness. 'I was at Dalebarrow for the weekend . . . Emma had stayed in London . . . she does not care for . . . I wanted Mama to see her grandson. She does not often have the chance.'

His eyes looked away from her now and he sat up slowly, his naked amber-polished back to the fire. 'We

553

were speaking of . . . things . . . the past . . . I do not have the chance with . . .' He shrugged and she felt the pain of him, of his own willingness to allow others to manipulate him but she did not speak. 'We talked of . . . you . . . and what you do now. My mother said you were the . . . talk of Fellthwaite. She admired you she said, for what you were attempting to do.'

He turned to look at her and his eyes ran swiftly across the gold-tinted beauty of her upper body and she saw the desire flare in them and his breath quickened.

'She said it was whispered about the town that . . . that your husband was . . . no husband to you. You understand what . . . ?'

'Oh yes, Robin, I understand.'

'. . . and that you had been compelled to travel to London to . . .'

'So you came to look for me? To help me out, so to speak?' Her voice was cool.

'Was that wrong? I love you. I had not seen you . . . I wanted to . . . to . . .'

'Do what you have just attempted!'

His voice became ragged and if he had not been Robin, her Robin, she would have said surly!

'You were willing, Christy. You love me . . . ?'

'Yes.'

'Well then?' He turned to her eagerly but it was too late now. The moment, the moment when it might have been possible was gone!

She sat up and her loveliness struck him. Her flame tinted hair tumbled about the weight of her round, peaked breasts and her graceful shoulders and back, and he reached out a hand, a *greedy* hand, she realized it now, towards her and in that moment she knew it was finished, and so did he.

Without a word he helped her to her feet, turning to the fire, fumbling with his own clothes as she pulled her gown into place, smoothing back her flowing hair to grip it with a comb, waiting until she was seated before he spoke.

'It cannot be done, can it?' He turned his back on her awkwardly.

'No Robin. Not any more.'

'Can you tell me why?'

'I do not think I know why.' Her voice was no more than a whisper.

'You . . . you love him then?'

'I could not even tell you that.'

'Then what?'

'I do not know. Something in me, in you, prevents me. Perhaps it is our life, Alex's and mine. We have fought so long together, with one another, against one another, to build it into something . . . our children. I cannot bring myself to throw it away. I cannot allow it . . . all to be wasted.'

'*Wasted!* On me? Sweet Jesus! I thought you loved me.'

His angry pain almost overwhelmed her and she half rose from her chair ready to go to him, to comfort him but she sank back aware that she must not touch him again. Her heart ached with the desolation of it and with her loss, the loss of her girlhood dream for that was what it was, she knew now. Her eyes were brilliant with tears but she remained composed.

'There are . . . too many people involved, Robin. It is not just Alex but my children, and your son . . . your wife. And there are . . . others I cannot bring myself to desert.'

'And us, Christy? We are to be sacrificed then?'

'We were sacrificed many years ago, Robin. Your father . . . mine . . .'

'I cannot . . . will not survive without you . . . some hope of . . .'

'You will . . . you must . . . !' The words hurt her throat, burning it, flaying her tongue with the pain of speaking them since she had loved a boy, a young man for so long, and now, he was gone! She bent her head beneath the weight of her loss.

'And you?' His voice was harsh. 'You will . . . recover . . . ?'

'Yes.'

'Christy ... please ... if I should come to ... to Fellthwaite, would you ... meet me ... sometime ... an hour ... ?'

'No.'

'Christy ...'

'Turn round, Robin, look at me.'

'I cannot.'

The silence settled then about them, sorrowful and spent at last, and Christy looked at the tense, hopeless back, the bent head of Robin Forsythe and finally recognized what she had failed to see before. He was still a boy! A handsome boy with the fine, steel-tempered strength of generations of well-bred gentlemen of the land behind him but he was still ... still *young*! He had not grown as she had! He was acting as a boy would now, a boy thwarted in his attempt to repossess something which had been taken from him. As a boy, he had planned this scene, this ... this seduction, thrilling to his own ingenuity, to the knowledge that he had outwitted them all, even her, to have what he wanted. His fatherhood, his years as a husband had not matured him. He had not become a man, as she had, at last, become a woman! He had allowed himself to be manipulated, as she had as a girl; but she had fought it, spat at it, caught and twisted life to the shape she desired. He had simply moved with it, causing no ripple allowing no waves to dash against him, to harden him into a fully grown complete man.

She felt the ache of it clutch at her heart, squeezing it in a clenched hand for she saw that in the past two years though he was still young Squire Forsythe, in other disturbing ways, he had changed. He was no longer the trusting youth who had so easily been diverted from his pursuit of his true love by a scheming father. He was no longer the eager, loving young man who had held so firmly to Christy Emmerson's, Christy Buchanan's compassionate heart during the spring of their love. It was in his eyes and about his drooping mouth, in his very stance, that which said that for the past two years he had done, and had, everything his wife's money could buy and now he did not care to be denied something which was rightfully his!

'You have a wife, Robin. Do you not care for her?'

'I love you, Christy.'

She sighed sadly, wise now in her new maturity. She spoke even more gently.

'And ... your son, Robin? What of him?' She saw his stiff shoulders relax a little and his breath escape on a long drawn out sound. He turned then and his face was soft with an emotion which she knew had nothing to do with her.

'Marcus?'

'Yes ... Marcus.'

His sullen pain appeared to ease a little and his face grew softer as memories crowded at the corner of his mind. He even smiled a little.

'I always remember what you said, Christy, whenever I hold him in my arms.'

'I ...?'

'Yes. Do you not remember saying to me that he would put his hands about my heart and never let me go?'

'And of course, he has ...?'

'Yes!'

'And can *you* let that go, Robin?' She must give him something to which he could hold, cling to at the moment of their parting.

'Christy!'

'Can you?'

His shoulders sagged and he shook his head and when he looked up at her there were tears in his eyes. She had spoken softly, carefully, afraid now to break the slight grip she had on the real world, the world which moments ago she had almost thrown away.

'No ... I cannot ...'

'I'm glad, Robin.'

'Christy ... if only I were like you ... strong and wise.

All these years I have dreamed of a life together for us and now . . .'

'Don't Robin, please . . .'

'I cannot stop myself. I will always . . . always . . .'

'I know . . .'

'And you, you will remain with him?'

'I must!'

'I love you Christy!' It was the cry of a child who has been denied access to its dearest possession. She felt her heart move with pity, no more and knew it was time to go home!

She was triumphant, glorious, indestructible when she strode into her husband's bedroom on the evening of her return home. She tossed her bonnet on to his bed, swirling in a graceful dip and sway of her wide silk skirt to face him, as he sat propped in his chair. All the lamps were lit and the room was bright with firelight though the last of the long summer's day had not yet drifted from the garden.

He turned his head, his shoulders, lifting himself with his hands pushed against the arms of the chair, his dark hair brushed smoothly and gleaming in the lamplight. His eyes challenged her and his lips curved in a good-humoured smile as he watched her turn in the circle of her own enchantment.

'Well, the voyager home, I see, and in fine fettle.' His eyes glowed approvingly.

'Oh Alex, Alex, it was splendid!'

'So I see! It appears to have met with your approval.'

'It did! I cannot begin to tell you . . .'

'Try!'

'The things we saw, magnificent things . . .'

'Magnificent things? And what about the man who sits before you? Is he not magnificent?' He was grinning wickedly now, his head on one side and she stopped, confused, her eyes scanning his face, running down the length of his body to his feet.

'Well . . .?' he said, then it struck her and her mouth opened and her eyes widened, and her face beamed in huge delight and she put her hands to her cheeks in wonderment – for sitting before her was the Alex Buchanan she had not seen for two years. Gone were his nightshirt, his quilted dressing gown, the warm, fleece-lined slippers, the rug and all the paraphernalia of sickness, and in their place was the immaculately dressed, beautifully tailored, expensive figure of Alexander Buchanan, gentleman, businessman and person of repute.

He had on a swallow-tail dress coat of rich brown lined with silk, beneath which he wore a watered silk waistcoat of pale beige and twill trousers to match. His shirt was white, pin-tucked and frilled and his cravat was tied in a flat bow at his neck. All slightly too large for him since he had not yet regained his full weight but nevertheless impeccable and handsomely elegant as he had always been. Someone had even crossed his useless legs giving him the appearance of a gentleman enjoying the relaxed, after dinner comfort of his own fireside.

'Well?' he said again, his manner tense and yet longing to smile and show his approval of his own appearance.

'Oh Alex,' she breathed, 'Oh Alex . . .'

'Is that all you have to say, woman?' His eyes were a bright sapphire blue in his dark brown face and his eyebrows lifted in quizzical amusement.

'Oh my dear . . . I am . . . without words . . .'

'And that is not like you, Christy Buchanan, so you must be impressed!'

'Oh Alex!'

'If you say "Oh Alex" once more I shall don my nightgown and retire to my bed. Now, since you have admired my elegant self to my complete satisfaction, sit down and tell me all you have seen up in London. And if you say you did not understand, or that some smooth-talking gentleman lured you away to dinner at the Saville, I shall thrash you within an inch of your life and enjoy it immensely!'

He smiled quite lazily, putting out a hand to her but there was a certain tone in his voice, a hidden peril that told her that though he joked about it there was no doubt that he meant it.

She knelt down spontaneously at his feet. 'Well, you can try, Alex Buchanan.' She grinned impishly and surprising them both with it, dropped a quick, butterfly kiss on his lips, a warm brushing of her mouth against his. Her skirt formed a circle about her and taking his hand in hers she looked up into his smiling eyes. Her hair was pulled softly back into a chignon from a centre parting but as she had thrown off her bonnet tendrils had come loose, drifting about her forehead and ears in shining strands. He lifted his other hand and brushed them back from her face, his own eyes dreaming and soft.

'Look at you,' he said. 'Like a child just come from the schoolroom. Your hair in disarray and if your mother were to see you she would send you back to nanny to be put together again neatly – and anytime you wish to repeat that last small gesture of goodwill I would have no objection.'

She blushed quite unexpectedly, quite delightfully and her eyes glowed into his but she stood up and moved away from him. She did not see the tiny, deep-rooted spark which lay hidden in the vivid, alert blueness of his eyes as he continued.

'But I had expected you home yesterday, my pet. The children and I were quite inconsolable when you did not arrive, the five of us continually peeping from the window to see if your carriage was in the drive. Did you find something . . . diverting to keep you in London, or was it merely the pull of the new machinery which charmed you into staying for another day?'

Though his voice was casual, disinterested even, she recognized the arrogant need to be told that there had been nothing, nothing of any importance to her, to either of them which had kept her away from her home for an extra day; and her heart hammered sickeningly for surely he could not know?

She turned, then moved back to his chair and knelt again at his knee, recognizing that this might be, would be, one of the most important moments of her life. She could not tell him in so many words that what she had for Robin Forsythe was no more than the pain one feels for a hurt friend. That the young girl's love for a boy had grown up leaving him behind, but she must make him understand, somehow, that, amazingly, there was no other man beside himself, her husband in her life.

She smiled and in it was the steadfast direct look of truth, her promise of trust, truth and honesty between them.

'There is nothing in London, or indeed anywhere which could keep me for a moment longer than is absolutely necessary from . . . from my world here.'

She did not say 'with you'. It was not yet time. She must empty completely her sad heart of the ashes of her old love before risking – dare she? – a new, but he would know what she meant. Didn't he always?

'So you see, I came as soon as I was able, but never mind that, tell me how *you* are!' she said. She stood up and her voice trembled somewhat and so did his as he answered.

'As you see, in the pink, my love and longing to hear how you have done. Have you come home with plans for the most devilishly fiendish machines ready to revolutionize my mines and my mill, and am I to be beseiged to spend my money on the very latest . . .'

My mines! *My* mills! *My* money! The sudden small twinge of resentment alarmed her but she smiled and the feeling receded as the words fell over one another, tumbling from her lips, as she described all that she had seen in London and not once did she hesitate over the memory of Robin Forsythe.

'. . . so just wait until I show Richard Forbes what I have brought back. There is enough literature in my case to keep him busy until . . .'

'Which reminds me, my darling. That young man has ignored my note delivered into his own hand by Jack asking him to come and see me. I shall have something to say to him when I finally get him up here, probably on the lines of looking for another job. We shall not need him in any case when I am on my feet but I am quite intrigued, really, as to what he thinks he is about.'

'He probably imagines it is a ruse on my part and that you are still fast to your bed. With him I never gave up the charade that you were running the business. I am sure he did not believe me, but he was never quite game to call my bluff. I felt it safer to pretend you were behind me.'

'Well, it is no charade now, Christy, so I would be obliged if you would get up to Conistone tomorrow and fetch that young man to see me.'

'Ah ha, it's errand boy I am now, is it, Alex Buchanan? What happened to my efforts on your behalf whilst you lolled in your bed for two years, tell me that?' Her face moved in an engaging smile but there was a shadow behind it, warning him that though she was willing to joke about it, there was a fragment of truth in her words.

He grinned and his eyes glinted wickedly.

'Well, I'm up and about now, my girl, and would be glad of some company . . . and help . . . pax . . . pax . . . I'm sorry . . . some help until I get on my feet.'

'Some help! I like that and after all I have done!' She smiled too but a tiny bud of caution flickered in her breast. She moved to the window to stare out over the garden, dark now, towards the faint outline of the mountains against the dark blue of the sky.

'Oh and by the way, I had a look at the books whilst you were gone,' he said. 'Anderson brought them over. You've done well, Christy. I could hardly have done better myself.' He did not recognize the faintly patronizing note in his voice. You have done well, Christy, *for a woman*! it said.

She turned quietly, her face calm, withdrawn and he was startled by the sudden change in her. Her kiss, warm and affectionate had astonished and pleased him for it had promised something – delicate yet and to be treated with gentleness, caution even – but a move towards – surely – a new beginning for them both. She was alive with some inner tension, an excitement which intrigued him, but there had been no doubt of the warmth of her greeting nor that she was pleased to see him. He had counted the hours of this day, sending Jack to the station at Windermere to meet the train long before it was due and now she was here.

But suddenly with the unpredictability of all women she had gone from him again, drawn back from the soft intimacy which their reunion promised.

'I know,' she said, 'and one more thing before you start ordering me around, Alex Buchanan, I am having a holiday tomorrow and I intend to go walking, or even take my mare out with Joby.'

'Indeed . . . !'

'Yes, indeed, so if you will excuse me I shall get to my bed. I am tired!'

She left the room, closing the door behind her with a soft click.

'Well!' he said to the dog. 'What the hell d'you make of that!'

CHAPTER THIRTY-SIX

It began to rain the next day, a floating, drifting, persistent drizzle which laced the hills like the net curtains Annie had once had to her windows; tweaked aside for an hour or so now and again by a fitful sun, and Christy knew that the gold-filled euphoric days of summer were done with.

She stood at the window of her bedroom and watched the clouds hover above the fells, trailing like fat grey sheep across the tops and she shivered. Behind her Faith put down the armful of dainty underclothes she was collecting for washing and mending, and moved to stand beside her saying nothing, just waiting in her own quiet way for Christy to speak, or not!

'Well, it looks as though Joby and I will have to postpone our walk, Faith. I cannot take him out in this. He will be in such a tear. What on earth can we do to make it up to him?'

'What do you suggest?'

'Really, I don't know. What are you going to do?'

'I thought I would go over to Hollin House and see to the cleaning. Mrs Kean and Thomas do very well as caretakers but they are both getting on. Dorcas is not much younger so I shall take Meg and Patience and have a good set-to.'

'How exciting! Can I fetch a duster and come too?' she said derisively, then she turned suddenly and put her arms about Faith, hugging her to her then just as suddenly she pushed her away awkwardly, turning again to the rain-drenched window, her eyes unfocused.

'I am . . . forgive me, Faith. You must needs be patient with me for a while. If I am sharp . . . forgive me.'

'I understand, Christy.' Faith's voice was soft.

'Do you? Do you, Faith? It is over. I am not to see him again, ever. Do you understand what that means, Faith?'

'Oh yes, Christy, I understand.'

Christy turned again and her face clouded with concern, with anger at her own thoughtlessness for who more than Faith knew the meaning of loss? She put her arms around her once more drawing her lovingly into her arms, and this time she held her close for several moments before releasing her, then kissed her cheek in an unusual show of affection.

'Of course you do so you will know . . . but I am not yet able to talk about it, dear Faith. You will understand that too, I think.' She whirled about striding in her black draped riding habit and high-topped boots, restless as a caged beast, unable to contain her unfulfilled energy; that which had been released by Robin Forsythe's hands and lips and body and which badly needed some action to suppress it. A walk up to the fells with her young son or a mad gallop on her little mare with him up in front of her, his own stamina and young vigour matching her own. But the weather forbade it.

Alex was exercising and completely naked when she walked into his room, and the enormous man who was with him, lifting the useless weight of his slender legs into what seemed impossibly awkward angles was considerably startled, his embarrassed gaze unable to settle anywhere.

'Christy, this is most agreeable but really, for the sake of poor Jacky here, do you not think you might first knock?' Alex grinned amiably, reaching carelessly for a towel, draping it across his thighs and the old prizefighter mumbled something in his direction before moving towards the door.

'I'm sorry, Alex. I had forgotten Jacky would be here. I came to tell you that as it is raining I cannot take Joby out as I had planned, so I think I will drive up to Conistone and see if I can get hold of Forbes. Shall I tell him to come and see you immediately?'

'What a splendid idea but ask him to make it after lunch. I am seeing Pendle this morning about a shipment of saltpetre which is coming from Chile so it might be . . .'

'Chile?' Her voice registered surprise and he stopped, looking at her questioningly almost as though he had been waiting for this moment.

'Yes.' He smiled engagingly and reaching with his strong arms to the bedhead pulled himself into a sitting position. He leaned across to the table beside his bed and taking a cigar from the box on it he lit it, drawing in the smoke with sensuous pleasure.

'But we always purchase our stock from India.' She was not yet aware of what was happening and her voice was bewildered.

'Not any more, my darling. It is more economical to

565

fetch it from Chile, and so I asked Pendle to make the necessary arrangements to have it shipped from there.'

'When?' Her voice was dangerously soft.

'I beg your pardon?'

'When did you order the saltpetre to be brought from Chile?'

'Why, several weeks ago now. I cannot remember the exact date.'

'Without consulting me?'

'Consulting you, Christy! Why should I do that?'

'Well, perhaps "consulting" is not quite the right word. "Discussing" it with me would perhaps be more suitable.'

'My pet. It did not occur to me that you would care *where* I got my saltpetre, after all if I can . . .'

'*Your* saltpetre, Alex?'

'Why yes.' His eyes gleamed through the haze of cigar smoke which wreathed about his head and his expression was amiable, willing, if she was, to treat this as quite the most natural thing in the world; but there was a certain tension in him, a feeling that he held his breath, an air of waiting.

'I was under the impression that . . .'

'Yes my sweet . . .?'

'That I was the . . .'

'What Christy?'

'Alex . . .' Her voice had taken on a tone of uncertainty for she was not quite clear what it was she wished to complain of. Had she not known, once Alex was recovered, that he would wish to take over again the running of his own business concerns? Had she not been working in the past two years to get him back on his feet to do just that, and had she not told him time and again that she was resolved to keep it all together to hold her sons' inheritance intact until he was again able to take control? Now, he was starting to pick up the threads of his life again. He was doing – from this room and, he said, when he was able to have it fitted out into an office, his study downstairs – all that it was possible to do without

566

physically going to the mine and the mills. When his legs were strong and the feeling returned and he was able to walk again, as he was convinced and determined he would do, he would be in complete control again. He would have no need of her, none at all! He had begun already it seemed, to make decisions, to change things without telling her. She had been overjoyed when the men came up to the house and sat about his chair and had seen his face become positive, confident in his handling of the problems they brought to him, problems they had once discussed with her, and though this was what she had fought for, had she expected quite such a . . . an . . . exclusion from it immediately Alex began to take over again? She had, naturally, foreseen a lessening of the time she herself would spend in the managing of the business, but not for a moment had she even considered that she must go back to the useless social butterfly existence the wives of other commercial gentlemen endured. What had she foreseen, she wondered? What had she visualized her role would be when her husband took the reins from her, and with growing horror she realized that she had given it no thought at all. She had gone no further than this moment, the moment when she would see her husband just as he was now. Indomitable, and unafraid of the future. In complete control of his own and his sons' lives . . . and Christy Buchanan . . . what of her . . . Dear God, what of her?

She felt the anger move in her, simmering like milk in a saucepan before it comes to the boil. Was she to be pushed gently, albeit positively, to one side? Given back to the nursery, the care of her household duties, the social calls, the carriage drives from nowhere to nowhere? No! by God she was not! Had she not only yesterday come from London where she had made a study of the lastest machinery on display at the Exhibition! Had she not made copious, concise notes, and memorized even more, on their workings and cost and production, and brought it all back to this man, and done it as well as *he* would. Damnation, she was as good as he was in matters of business. Only in the area of mine engineering could he defeat her and she would not be discarded now like some useless bit of spoil!

'What exactly is happening, Alex?' she said abruptly. What is it you wish me to do?'

'To do, my sweet, about what?' He puffed on his cigar and his smile was pleasantly polite.

'About . . . about my future? I do feel that what I have done in the past two years cannot be overlooked as though it was . . . was nothing. You might have had the courtesy to tell me about this saltpetre business. We have always purchased it from India and now, without a word you tell me you have decided to bring it from Chile!'

Oh God, that sounded so stupid! Silly! What a woman would say! Querulous . . . like some petulant child who has been left out of adult plans!

'I'm sorry, Christy. I really did not think you would be concerned. In fact, if the honest truth were to be told I imagined that as you are at the gunpowder mill most days you would have known about it. It is no secret.'

'Pendle did not tell me!'

'Well . . .' he smiled, a cat lapping cream from a saucer, '. . . he is, shall we say, old-fashioned and I do believe he would prefer to concern himself with another gentleman. No offence, my love, but you ought to know that by now. Awkward so-and-so and a firm believer in women being kept in their place. He has held on because he has had no alternative but now, with myself back at the helm so to speak, he is only too anxious to bring his problems to me. Now the other two are . . .'

'*You smug bastard!*'

'I beg your pardon!'

'You smug, pompous, insufferable bastard.' She could feel the seething rise in her, overflowing and white hot and she took a step towards him, her face crimson with rage. 'So I am to be tossed aside now, am I? Now that you are back in the saddle and have a firm hand on the reins Pendle is to run up here whenever he feels like it, and I am to sit in my office at the mill and twiddle my thumbs! Are they all to come to see you now, Alex, the foremen who have consulted me for the past year or so, the men who stop me in the yard to offer help and advice, and those whom I have stood beside in the gloom house? It is dangerous in there, Alex, when they remove the remaining water from the product, as you well know, but I have been there when the process is carried out. I have been through them all, even the one which killed my brothers. I was afraid, Alex, I am not ashamed to admit it, but I damn well did it whilst you lay here not caring whether any of us lived or died. Now, whilst you still lie there, even before you are fully on your feet, you have the nerve to tell me in that patronizing way of yours that already changes have been made and that I must accept it, and accept that the men will no longer concern themselves with me because I am a woman. Well, you can go to hell, Alex Buchanan. I mean to carry on as I am doing. I can be a bloody nuisance when I have a mind to be. Ask any of the men. They will tell you and I have no intention of being . . . being captured again and stuffed into a cage with all the other pretty birds of Fellthwaite . . .'

'Christy . . .'

'I will not do it, Alex! I refuse! Those mills have been my life . . . my saviour during these past terrible years. In them I found something I have never had before and I will not give them up . . .'

She could feel the mortifying tears gathering at the back of her eyes and she cursed the afflication of being an emotional woman but at the same time she held her pride about her for – despite being a woman, with a woman's inclination for weeping at times like this – she was not ashamed for she had done well, she knew she had and no one, no one was going to take it from her.

'. . . so you can go to hell and as far as I'm concerned . . .'

'Christy . . .'

'No Alex . . . I will not . . .'

'Christy . . . for God's sake, woman, will you be quiet

and let me speak. My word, what a virago it is when it is roused . . .'

'. . . and don't you speak to me in that condescending tone, you bastard . . .'

'Please, Christy . . . come here . . . be quiet and sit beside me.'

'I will not be changed, Alex. I mean to . . .'

'Sit down . . . please . . . please . . .'

'I will stand here, thank you!' Her head was held high but her mouth had a vulnerable tremble about it, and her eyes were suspiciously bright.

'Very well, if you prefer it.'

'I do!'

He turned to stub out his cigar, then reached for his quilted dressing gown, flinging it about his shoulders, and when he turned to look at her again the expression in his eyes was complex, unreadable, the eyes of a man who knows exactly what he is about but is not prepared to allow it to be seen. It was a look she knew well. His smile was engaging, his demeanour quite unruffled. He was relaxed, reasonable, a man not about to argue for he was a man who had no need of it since no one stood against him.

'Christy, I am the last man in the world to disparage what you have done in the past months, not only the manner in which you have kept the mines and the mill and all my other holdings together, but in the way you have helped to restore me to . . . well, not exactly full health yet, but to the extent where I am able to resume where I left off two years ago. I fully appreciate what you have done, my pet, but do you not think that I am now able to make decisions for myself about . . .'

'This is not about decision-making, Alex, and you know it! It is about your high-handed attitude that says I am no longer needed and therefore I must gracefully step aside, rewarded perhaps with a diamond bracelet, or emerald ear-rings – is that not the usual gift for a favoured wife – and make no more trouble for . . .'

'I did not say that!' His face was fast losing the reasonable calm with which he had seemed determined to address her and the familiar truculence, an expression she had seen only on his sons' faces for the past year or so, took its place. 'I am making the point that a business can have only one master, one man in charge, one man to take responsibility, to make decisions and I am that man. I am not asking you to step aside, though I am not quite certain what you *will* do when I am fully recovered, but just remember that it is I who will say where we buy our raw materials and . . .'

'So I am to be relegated to the nursery then?' Her eyes were narrowed to brilliant slits of outraged anger and the high colour stood out vividly on her cheeks in two round spots.

'If that is where I can get you, yes! Is there something wrong with a man wishing to increase his family?'

'Increase his . . . !' The meaning of his words hit her like a blow and she felt the blood swell in her veins and rush madly to her head, so that it took all her self-control – or what was left of it – not to leap forward and strike him about his challenging face. Not only did he intend her to keep her foolish, female nose out of his business, now that he was able to arrange it to his own satisfaction, but the moment he was able, the moment the senses, the capability returned to the remainder of his body he intended saddling her with another child, children, and to keep her, return her firmly to the place where God intended females to be. Goddammit! God damn him, she'd see him in hell first!

'I see! So that is the way of it! You are telling me that, as soon as . . . as you are able, or I am willing, don't forget that, Alex, I am to resume my duties as the mistress of this house, the hostess at your dinner table and the mother of not only the children we have but the ones you intend to foist on me in the future!'

'I would hardly use the word "foist", Christina, but that is the general idea and one to which I am looking forward with a great deal of pleasure. I admit to putting some thought into our future life together and I had hoped you would agree with me. You seemed not averse to . . . well . . . you were . . .' he seemed to stumble over the word, '. . . affectionate last night and it led me to believe that you were amenable to returning to a life for which you are well suited. Motherhood is . . .'

Motherhood was flung aside disparagingly! 'And what of the life I have lived for the past two years?' she shrieked, unable any longer to contain it. 'Has that not been of use? Where would your precious future be now, would you have one? Would I or the children, if I had resigned myself to the kitchen and the nursery and allowed the men – men, Alex – who were under you in your mines and mills and the factory, to let the whole structure become unmanageable as they squabbled amongst themselves, as to who should do this, order that, supply the other, each man blaming the next man for the disorder?'

'I am well aware of what you have done, Christina, and if you will lower your voice for a moment . . .'

'. . . and I might say the same of this house, this room and the man in it! Yourself, Alex Buchanan. Left to yourself you would still be mouldering in that damned bed staring at the ceiling, or dead!'

'I am denying nothing you say, Christina, and believe me your efforts on my behalf have not gone unappreciated . . .' He was glaring balefully at her now, strong in his mind as once he had been, strengthening in his body and hating her for reminding him of his past weakness, '. . . but they are no longer needed. Can you not see it, woman? I am ready to run my own concerns. There is really nothing for you to do and I can see no reason why you cannot take up your life again as it was before.'

'You cannot mean that, Alex.'

'Why not?'

'You would toss me aside like . . .'

'Shall we leave out the dramatics?'

'You are making a dreadful mistake, Alex. Can you not remember how . . . how we were before? Can you not realize that I am not the same woman as I was then? I must have more in my life than . . . than household duties.' Her voice was desperate and for a moment he felt the familiar urge to reach out for her and soothe her, as he had done when her mother died. She had been soft and fragile then, vulnerable, a woman as he wanted her to be, needing his strength to protect her as all men long to be the protector of their woman. Last night she had seemed to offer something, a promise of companionship, perhaps, the support, the dependence he needed from her, dependence on him! He had been exultant, jubilant with the hope that at last, at last Christy Buchanan was to become, now that he was almost recovered, the woman, the wife, he had always wanted her to be. Now, in five angry minutes she had told him she was to fight him as she had always done. And for what? For the dubious satisfaction of remaining in his business world, sharing his problems, his decisions, arguing as they were doing now, fighting him, no doubt, on every point of company policy.

His disappointment made him carelessly cruel.

'You would do well to remember, madam, whose business this is and the sooner you accept it the better it will be for us all. There is no place in it for two masters and I would be obliged . . .'

'You can go to hell, Alex Buchanan,' she hissed, turning on her heel abruptly and striding to the door. She flung it open then turned, her face as uncompromisingly challenging as his, '. . . and the sooner the better and may I say that *you* would do well to remember that though your mind is returned to you it is still fastened to that bed, whereas I can go to the mine and the mill just as I please, and, if I please, countermand any order you might give. The men respect me now, Alex, strange and incomprehensible as that may seem to you and until you get out of this room and ride up to Conistone or Elterwater, I am in charge there!'

She was halfway to the mine at Conistone before she remembered Joby but it was too late to turn back. She would see him tonight, she told herself, see all of her children, and on the first fine day she would promise them a picnic up on the fells. Take the dogs and go walking. She had neglected them so often during their growing young days and she needed to spend some time with them. To let them see that their mother was not just some busy person who rushed through their lives, amiable certainly for she never allowed her problems to slip into the nursery with her, but unavailable nevertheless when they might need her. She would persuade Miss Crawford to let them play truant and run away from the confines of the garden and the paddock and surprise them with some fun, some childish adventure. It would not only do them good, but herself. She needed to get away from the conflict she seemed to be stirring up again with Alex, to view it from another aspect, to stand back and try to see it from his point of view. Not to give in to him, certainly, but to try and find the words, the logical arguments which would allow him to see it from hers. She had the will, she knew, but she needed the renewed strength to enforce it. She could not let him take it from her. She would not let him, or anyone, send her back to that half existence she had known two years ago. Why? Dear God why did all men think, even now when she had proved again and again that her brain was as capable as theirs of thought, that only babies and menus should concern women? Why did they still insist on treating her as though she was some precocious wilful child who could not be trusted out of the schoolroom? Damn Alex Buchanan! Damn him and all men! They would not get the better of Christy Buchanan and the first one she would get her teeth into this morning would be Richard Forbes!

Mr Forbes was underground, Mr Tate told her, running through the misted rain from the office to meet her as she climbed up the muddy track from the village.

'Then I will wait in the office if I may, Mr Tate, and perhaps you will offer me a cup of coffee.'

'Oh of course, Mrs Buchanan, but Mr Forbes might be some time. A problem with the water in the deep level, I believe.'

She frowned. 'Is that not yet resolved, Mr Tate? It is some months since it was first reported to me.'

'Apparently a spring of water was cut when one of the men was "heading" out a vein and there is some difficulty in pumping it out. I believe he mentioned a quantity of quartz deposited so loosely it will not support itself . . .'

'It sounds as though Mr Forbes has a few problems on his hands, Mr Tate, and if that is the case why has he not been up to the house?'

She shook out the wet length of her sodden skirt before the generous fire in what had once been Alex's office, and where she herself had interviewed Richard Forbes. It looked much the same but for the rows of neatly stacked paperwork which covered the big desk. She moved nearer to the fire, standing in front of it in an attempt to dry her wet skirts and the steam rose in small eddies about her.

'I am sure I cannot speak for Mr Forbes, Mrs Buchanan, except to say that perhaps he thought you yourself would not be experienced enough to . . .'

'And he would be correct, Mr Tate, but my husband is more than able to advise him. He is after all a mining engineer *and* the owner of the mine.' It galled her to say it but she knew she must.

'Oh indeed, Mrs Buchanan, but in his present state of health . . .' Mr Tate's wrinkled face fell into deeper lines of sympathy for the poor unfortunate Mr Buchanan.

'There is nothing wrong with my husband's state of health, Mr Tate. Indeed he has not been so fit for years.' It was not quite true but again it must be said!

Mr Tate looked a trifle confused then his face cleared and his eyes shone in compassion for this loyal woman who still would keep up the pretence that her husband was recovering. There had been rumours, of course, gossip in

Mr Tate's opinion, that Mr Buchanan had been blessed with a miracle but naturally one discounted such tittle-tattle, spread about by those who knew no better, and Mr Forbes had dismissed it as rubbish! Why, Mr Tate himself had been up several times to the house near Fellthwaite and not once had he been permitted to speak to his employer!

'Well, I'm certainly glad to hear it, Mrs Buchanan, very glad indeed. Now, if you will excuse me I must get on. Mr Forbes would not like me to stand about ... er ... chatting. I will send the clerk with your coffee if you would care to make yourself comfortable by the fire.'

When he had gone, bowing and bobbing, hurrying back as his new master would wish him to do, to his desk, Christy moved to stand at the window which looked out over the level site containing the crushing mills, the stamping sheds, the tanks in which the water used in the dressing processes was stored.

The new mechanical 'jigger' had been set up and the raw material from the screen — at which several men, women and children worked, picking out the saleable ore — went into the sophisticated machinery with such speed and accuracy Christy was quite fascinated, remembering the cumbersome grated boxes she had last seen here only months ago. The whole place had an air of efficiency about it with no man or woman lingering a moment longer than was necessary as they went about their work. There seemed to be less workmen actually labouring than usual, almost a feeling of desertion about the place with none of the energetic brimming bustle she remembered. Not that those who worked had no energy, they did. She had never seen them go at such a pace, everybody in sight from the oldest man to the youngest boy working like ten men put together!

Wagons came regularly from the direction of the mine shaft, dumping the ore just brought from underground on to the heap. Here young barefoot boys leaped about like small, drab frogs in their Hodden grey, sorting the richer pieces from the poorer and her heart bled for them. It was cold, the rain slanting in a fine needling chill about their agile, thin-legged figures and for a horrified moment she had a vivid picture of her own sturdy, well-fleshed, well-shod, well-clothed sons clambering about the rough piles as these did, their ebony curls plastered to the shape of their skulls, their jackets wet and clinging to their as yet unformed backs, their trouser legs wet and abrasive against their chapped skins.

It was an hour before Richard Forbes came into the office, his wet hair brushed severely back from his colour-less face, his thin-lipped mouth set in a line of grim disapproval. His clothing was damp about the legs and he moved at once to stand before the fire, stamping his feet and bending his legs as the warmth lapped at him. His pale eyes looked at her with a quite disturbing lack of curiosity.

'Mrs Buchanan,' he said coolly.

'Mr Forbes.'

'It is kind of you to call, ma'am, but I thought I made it quite plain when you employed me that I needed no help, nor, I do not wish to be rude, interference!'

'I have not come to . . . interfere, as you put it, Mr Forbes, merely to ask why you have ignored the notes I have sent you asking you to call at the house. Our agreement was, I believe, that you should bring the account books, call for the wages and at that time I was "allowed" to ask for your report. In six months I have not been once to the mines, but it is at least two since you sent me any sort of report . . .'

'Surely the weekly accounts report our progress, Mrs Buchanan.'

'Oh, I cannot find fault with the profit you are making, Mr Forbes, but wonder how you are making it!'

Richard Forbes's passionless face quivered and his eyes flew open in the way she remembered from their few meetings. It was the only way in which his emotions showed and she knew she had flicked some nerve which lay near the surface of his neutral façade.

'I do not think I care for that remark, Mrs Buchanan. It seems to me you are implying my methods of extracting the ore from the ground are not to your liking . . .'

'I know nothing about it, Mr Forbes.'

'Then you are not qualified to judge, are you, madam?'

'I agree, but my husband is!'

'Aah . . . yes . . .' If Richard Forbes could be said to smile, he did so then. 'Your . . . husband! How is Mr Buchanan? Improving, I hope!'

'Oh, quite spectacularly, thank you, Mr Forbes. He is looking forward to meeting you, that is if you can find a moment to spare in your busy day!'

'Yes, I had his . . . note.' His mouth stretched across his teeth and he moved a little closer to the cosy fire he had built up in the grate. Outside the noon day whistle sounded and for a fraction of a second Christy was diverted as she glanced from the window, her eyes drawn to the source of it, by the sight of every woman and boy sinking in one boneless movement to the ground, drawn there thankfully by the simple need to lay their bodies to some kind of temporary rest. The rain beat down on them but they seemed not to care until, after a moment or two, a man put out a hand to a woman, a woman to a boy and the whole group moved off to shelter in one of the sheds, presumably to eat their clap bread or 'taties', whatever they had brought from home that morning, in the half hour allowed them.

'Those women and children seem quite exhausted, Mr Forbes,' she said sharply. 'How long have they been working? Those young boys are supposed to labour no longer than . . .'

'Mrs Buchanan, I would be obliged if you would . . .'

'No Mr Forbes, I would be obliged if you would answer my question.'

His face was stiff with rage but he had no choice but to reply.

'I have devised a new method of shift working, Mrs Buchanan, which means I am able to run my . . . the mine

578

on a much more profitable basis. Some of the . . . work force have not yet become used to it and . . .'

'What are these new shifts, Mr Forbes?'

He drew himself up, affronted, not only by her question but by her presence in his office.

'Madam. I must insist that you allow me to manage this mine as I see fit. I told you when you employed me that I would stand for no meddling in the way I ran it and you agreed. Since I began here production has risen and you show a healthy profit which, I might add, was not the case in the previous twelve months. Now if you would oblige me by collecting the accounts, which is, I presume, the reason for your presence here, and leaving, I would take it as a favour. This is really no place for a lady, you know, Mrs Buchanan. Some of these people are . . . rough, and quite ready to shout abuse . . .'

'Why should they do that, Mr Forbes? They gave no abuse to my husband as far as I am aware, and none has ever been shown me.'

'I had to fire one or two, Mrs Buchanan, and take on others. Some Cornishmen out of work since their mines failed.'

'And what is wrong in employing dalesmen, Mr Forbes? Men who have lived and worked here all their lives?'

His face showed not the slightest expression now. It was as blank as the smooth, rain-flattened water of the lake she had just passed in her carriage, but his anger showed nevertheless in the rigid line of his jaw, in the strange wide stare of his eyes and the bleached white spots which had appeared on his cheekbone.

'I am sorry, Mrs Buchanan. I obviously seem not to be what you need here at the Buchanan Mining Company. I had mistakenly believed you wished to run a profitable business but your presence here makes it impossible for me to do so . . .'

'Then you must resign, Mr Forbes!' Her eyes flashed silver bright defiance at him.

'I beg your pardon?' His voice hissed, snake-like.

'I said, Mr Forbes, that if you are not prepared to work under supervision you had better hand in your notice now!' To hell with caution and the sham that Alex was in command. *She* was the master here and this bastard must be made to realize it!

His smile was no more than a curl of his upper lip!

'Really Mrs Buchanan, shall we drop this pretence?' he said. 'I am quite prepared to go on managing the mine for as long as you care to employ me but I cannot have you coming here and . . .'

She stood up then and began to walk towards the door, throwing her thick cloak about her shoulders in a graceful swirl and he moved politely to open it for her, believing he had won, smiling his wolf's smile, showing his teeth and gums.

'Mr Forbes,' she said, turning to look imperiously at him as though he had been some servant who had been caught with the silver, the passion of her conflict with Alex still flowing madly in her veins. 'Either you present a full report of your activities, including your new shift system, to my husband this very afternoon, or you will present your resignation, whichever you choose! Good day to you!'

CHAPTER THIRTY-SEVEN

The rain let up at lunchtime and a pale, fitful sun peeked from behind thin cloud and though he had spent the better part of the morning brooding dangerously on the clash of wills which had exploded between himself and Christy, Alex had recovered sufficiently by noon to greet his children amiably enough. He even agreed when they begged him to 'walk' up to the paddock to watch them ride the small cob which Miles was teaching them to mount. Mr Pendle had ridden up from Elterwater, and he and Alex had calculated the saving and profit they would make on the purchase of saltpetre from Chile, which had given him a great deal of satisfaction, and with a delicious lunch, a glass of fine wine and the feeling of well-being the two had brought about he was almost cheerful as Miles and John lifted him into his outdoor chair. He had exercised with Jacky for a couple of hours, which had helped to work off most of his aggression, ignited by his battle with Christy and he smiled inwardly at the remembrance of it.

Really, Christy could be bloody awkward at times, he admitted to himself but by God, you couldn't help but admire the spirit of her, nor her waywardness! He didn't know why he allowed her to get under his skin the way she did, for was that not one of the many facets of her nature he had first admired and he would not suppress it if he could. Nevertheless she must be persuaded to come round to his way of thinking when he was on his feet again. She would damn well have to! It really was foolish of her to imagine she could go on working, trying to share his business with him when she would be far better employed in their home. He'd not deny, as he had told her, that she had done wonders with his arms, returning them to their former strength and making it possible for him to leave his bed and the sick-room. Really, he should not have spoken to her as he had but she would argue and though he had not meant to, since he was grateful for what she had done, before he knew it that uncompromising part of him which would not let anyone best him, nor even equal him, had rushed madly to his brain, and his tongue, and the words had been out before he could stop them. Not that they weren't true, they were, but he could have arranged them in a more kindly, gentler fashion. And she really did run his home superbly and look at the way she had children, sons, and what a joy they were to him. She was made for love and babies and everything else husband and wife could contrive in a successful marriage, and he'd make sure she saw the sense of it. He'd be gentle with her tonight and perhaps with a little candlelight, a glass of champagne and that way he knew he had with a pretty woman — a bit out of practice certainly but never forgotten — they might recapture that breathlessly warm promise that had so enchanted him when she had returned from London yesterday evening. He would be his most charming, beguile her as he used to and who knew where the evening might lead!

His blue eyes grew speculative and he felt the blood warm his flesh as it had not done for a long time and his breath quickened in his throat quite delightfully. His sensual mouth curved in a dreaming smile and he leaned back in his chair agreeing with John that it really was grand to see the sun after so much rain and it certainly had made the grass grow, and they'd best get Abel up here with his scythe.

'No, this will do, John. Set me down here. You can leave me and get back to the stables. Miles will see to the children and the cob, will you not, Miles? It doesn't need two of you, man! I'll send Amy down when we're ready to come back. No, for God's sake, I won't be left alone, Miles is only in the bloody paddock and can see my every move.' He was always irritable when any of them 'fussed' him.

John was reluctant to go for those imps were just as likely to run off, cob an' all, and lead Miles a right merry chase. Fine with horses was Miles as long as there was someone to tell him exactly what to do, like himself who was head groom, but those lads of the master's were little hellions and would have Miles in circles before he knew where he was. Now Miss Amy was sensible enough, docile as one of the kittens she invariably cradled to her. She was almost seven years old now, always anxious to please, loving and bright but still shy. But she'd run a message if the master or Miles needed owt and could be trusted to get it right, which was more than could be said for them impudent cubs who raced round their father's chair like young animals let out of a cage. Even the three-year-old Master Joby could go like the wind, loving freedom as it did, already as tall as Master Harry who was a year older. Since the master's youngest son had been able to heave himself to his feet his determination to do exactly as his older brothers had made him as tough and obdurate as a young bullock, hazardous if crossed by either of the other two. If they could do it, whatever it was, then so could he and he would tackle either of them, or both together; it was all the same to him in his resolution to be included in whatever dare-devil scheme they might get up to. There was no doubt as to who had fathered them, that was for sure and Mr Buchanan was as proud as punch of the three of them even if they were as swaggering as peacocks and audacious as a cartload of monkeys. He was hard with them at times for didn't they need a firm hand but you could see him glory in their fearless effrontery in every boyish pastime they tackled.

The little girl had clambered on her father's lap as she did at every opportunity and though his eyes followed his sons as they darted about Miles's legs when he opened the paddock gate, his arms held her lovingly, and her kitten, and she lay against him sighing her content.

'Well . . . if you're sure you don't need me, Mr Buchanan . . . ?'

'Get off with you, man. I've got my eye on those three and by God they'll jump to it if I raise my voice and between the two of us Miles and I can keep them in hand.'

'But that there pony's a mite skittish when he's fresh, sir, and there are three of them.' His tone said one of them would be enough for any ordinary man and Miles, as undergroom, had not the authority he himself had.

'Oh stop it, man. You're worse than Mrs Jackson. We'll all be fine, won't we, sweetheart?' and the child murmured against his shoulder and John was dismissed.

Miles had a long rein on the sturdy, short-legged little horse and Johnny, as the eldest, was the first to be lifted into the saddle. They had been doing this for two months now, taking turn and turn about, and whilst one rode the other two were expected to stand quietly and watch and

583

listen and learn. Amy might have a 'go' too, her father had told her when the cob arrived but the little girl had soon given up; driven to it not only by her own disinclination for bumping about on the cob's back, but by her brothers' impatient demands to 'hurry up and let them have a turn'! Besides it was much nicer to cuddle up to father now that he was better. He often gave her an affectionate kiss and called her 'puss' which pleased her inordinately. Kittens were much nicer than horses in her opinion anyway, and when father bought them a pony each as he had promised when they could ride well enough, she would ask him if she might have another kitten instead!

The patient little horse, not a bit 'skittish' today, trotted round and round in a growing circle, held to his course by the guiding hand of the groom. The other mounts, Christy's mare, Alex's old roan and the bay, and a couple of hacks they kept for guests – in the days when they had them – had been put in the second field, well away from the riding lesson and for half an hour, ten minutes each on the cob's back Alex Buchanan's sons behaved impeccably. The last one to ride was Joby and he sighed impatiently as he was lifted down and Johnny was put up again. He was sure he could have climbed down himself. Flame was such a little horse but Miles would insist that none of them were yet big enough – and father agreed – to put their foot in the stirrup and get up, and down, unaided. He would have a try next time, he told himself confidently but that would be ages away for there was Johnny, then Harry again before it was his turn. He kicked the long grass irritably, then looked about him for something of interest with which to occupy himself until Miles called to him.

His attention was caught by the sight of Mrs Longworth, the housekeeper, her face screwed up quite fastidiously as she stepped carefully across the rough grass which led up to the paddock. What might have walked there, or done something worse, her expression said, and she did not want to step in it! Following her, almost overtaking her was a gentleman, his long thin legs eating up the distance between the house and the paddock like a darting spider, Joby thought. He and Harry stared curiously.

'Mr Buchanan, sir,' Mrs Longworth panted, quite incensed that the gentleman had followed her. She had told him to wait in the drawing room whilst Meg ran up to the paddock to enquire if the master was at home, but before she had eased him into the drawing room and herself out of it he had been on her heels, most insistent that he see Mr Buchanan. Short of calling John to physically restrain him she had had no option but to run, run mind you, up here and him no more than a foot behind her!

'Please sir, this gentleman was most particular that he wished to see you and when I told him I would see if you were home he just . . .'

The man stepped forward positively, cutting through Mrs Longworth's wordy outrage, bowing most politely as he removed his hat. He held out his hand to the man in the chair despite the child who was on his lap and Alex Buchanan felt the first twinge of annoyance as he was put instantly at a disadvantage.

'Richard Forbes, sir, at your service,' the man said, then turned most officiously to Mrs Longworth, his manner dismissing her as though she was no more than a scullery maid, she told Mrs Avery resentfully!

'Aah, Forbes, so we meet at last,' Alex said, looking up at the tall, fine-boned slenderness, the gaunt thin-lipped face, the cold clear eyes of the man who was in charge of his mine. He knew instantly that his wife was right in her judgement that he was not to be trusted. He smiled dangerously, lifting himself and the child a little higher in the chair.

'Indeed sir, as you remark, at last,' Forbes was saying. 'Forgive my calling unannounced but I was hoping you might spare me a moment, that is if you are . . . well enough!'

Alex felt the irritation grow in him and his brows curved in a scowl. He did not savour Forbes's impudence in

585

implying that he himself was an elderly invalid only able to be seen when he was 'well'. Neither did he care to spend an uncomfortable five minutes – that was how long he was prepared to allow him – straining his neck to look up at him. Five minutes! That was all it would take to put the insolent dog in his place and if he uttered one more word Alex Buchanan did not like he would fire him on the spot! Only the fact that he could not himself, as yet, get underground held him back from doing it now. He fully intended ordering out his carriage in a day or two and with John and Miles's help, surprising them, not only at the gunpowder mill, but at the mine, with his presence. It needed only a minor adjustment to one of his chairs and a couple of hefty men to lift him and he could be fully in charge again at the mine surface!

'I am perfectly well, Forbes, as you can see. A slight incapacity in my legs which will be overcome within the month.' His self-confidence was overwhelming, as was his arrogant belief in his own strength. 'So you will forgive me if I do not stand. Perhaps you would care to sit.'

'Sit?' Richard Forbes looked about him perplexedly, and the three watching children shrank back a little, sensing the malice in him.

'Why not, Forbes? We are all very casual here. The grass is a trifle damp but then you are well used to it underground, are you not?' He grinned maliciously then turned to the two boys lifting Amy to stand beside them.

'Go and wait by the fence, boys, and you too Amy and watch Johnny. Not inside, d'you hear. Just stand quietly and wait your turn. Do you understand?'

'Yes father.'

Obediently they trailed away to stand by the paddock fence, their high spirits strangely dampened, all three looking back to watch the tall thin man squat uncomfortably at their father's feet. His face was quite blank but his eyes were filled with a venom which was not hard to recognize. Alex Buchanan saw it and he smiled lazily, at ease and casually lounging in the comfort of his chair.

'Now then Forbes, shall we have that little chat I have been looking forward to ever since I sent you that first note several weeks ago, and which you chose to ignore?'

'I do apologize, sir, but Mrs Buchanan led me to believe that you were not well enough to receive . . .'

'Do you know, Forbes, I do believe I could smoke a cigar but I quite forgot to bring them with me. Would you be so kind, my dear fellow . . .'

He shrugged amiably, still smiling pleasantly. 'My man would get them for you if you were to ask at the kitchen door.'

'At the . . .'

'Yes, it is quicker than going round to the front. Just ask one of the servants to go up to my room and get my case from the bedside table.' He grinned and his ice-blue eyes crinkled in his brown face, and Richard Forbes had no option but to scramble to his feet, his mouth clamped in a line of bitter outrage, his own eyes saying just as clearly that he did not care to be used as an errand boy.

Alex's cigar was drawing smoothly, the fragrance of the smoke scenting the air, mixing with the heady scent of the climbing roses on the wall of the house before he spoke again.

'You were saying something about my wife I believe, Forbes?' His voice was perilously soft.

'Yes sir. Each time I informed her that I thought it expedient that you and I discussed the mines and the problems that arise from time to time she put me off . . .'

'Put you off?'

'I am only trying to do my job, Mr Buchanan, in the best way I know how and you, as an engineer, can understand what that entails but I am afraid Mrs Buchanan, as a lady, and of course without the understanding and knowledge of mine engineering, appears to think I am remiss in the way in which I manage the men. You have seen the accounts, Mr Buchanan?'

'I have.' Alex Buchanan's face was set in lines of misleading good humour, but his eyes were narrowed and the blueness of them was as bright and cold as a winter sky. He had his back to the pale sunshine which shone directly into Richard Forbes's eyes and the man was forced to put up his hand to shade them.

'And what do you think, sir? Do they not show a healthy profit?'

'They do indeed Forbes, a very handsome profit!'

'Then what can Mrs Buchanan complain of, if I may be so bold, sir? Surely a business showing growth can only benefit . . .'

'I suppose how that growth is gained must be taken into account, Forbes, if I might be so bold. If Mrs Buchanan has laid a charge that you are mismanaging the workmen we really must look into it.' His voice was as smooth as velvet and his lips curved in a supple smile over his strong white teeth.

'Really, Mr Buchanan, I must protest . . .'

'Must you?'

'Indeed I must! I was employed by your wife who could find no fault with me then to run your mine whilst you were . . . incapacitated. She gave me a free hand to do as I thought fit and I have introduced some modern labour saving methods, which surely you must see can only make you a greater gain, then what can she say I have done wrong?' He smiled condescendingly at the idea of a scatter-brained woman querying anything superior man might do, still smarting badly on the errand he had been forced to run, just like some lackey. 'I was under the impression that was what running a business was about but it seems Mrs Buchanan thinks otherwise. She is constantly up at the mine,' he exaggerated wildy, 'and really, it is not easy to carry on the day to day running if she . . . if she encroaches on my authority as mine manager.'

Richard Forbes stood up abruptly, no longer able to sit like a child it seemed to him, at his employer's feet. His face was a mask of barely suppressed fury and a white line had appeared about his thin-lipped mouth. He appeared to tower, a thin thread of malevolence over the man in the chair, and neither of them noticed the three children ease themselves anxiously along the paddock fence to where it met the edge of the spinney. Miles was imploring young Master Johnny to draw the small cob into a walk, turning to look anxiously, hopefully at Mr Buchanan, wishing his master would bellow a word of caution to the boy who really should not be going at such a pace, but Mr Buchanan seemed to be deep in conversation with his visitor and was taking no notice of his son's daring.

'You are here to complain of my wife, are you, Mr Forbes?' Alex said, his voice top heavy with quiet menace but Richard Forbes was too far gone on his maddened path which had begun that morning and he did not hear it. She, that . . . that woman had caused all this with her interference. She had had the audacity to tell him – a qualified mining engineer, well used to managing not only a large mining company but the men employed in it – that he was to give her a full report of his activities, of everything he had re-organized since he had taken up his employment with her, and if he refused he was to be given notice to leave. She would no doubt, at this very moment be questioning the men who came up from underground, enquiring of them his methods of wringing every last halfpenny of profit from their labours, particularly the bargain men, those who mined a certain number of fathoms and were paid only for what they brought out. Many of them, though they were experienced miners, had not the qualifications to assay the quality of the ore they excavated and it had been simplicity itself to gull them into believing that they had hit a poor vein. If she were to find out, tell this man, Richard Forbes would lose not only his job and the profit he took from it, but his reputation. She must be stopped and the only way to do it was to encourage her husband to restrain her. He made a great effort to control the vitriolic words which longed to stream from his mouth.

'I am, sir, but with all due respect to her as your wife. I am sure you would not like to see the way in which she

... associates with the miners, mixing freely with rough common fellows who stare and – I am sorry to have to say this since I am certain she is not aware of the effect she has on them – make unsavoury remarks as she passes by. I have done my best to shield her, to discourage her but she will not listen to me. She is undermining my authority and I beg of you to put a stop to it. I cannot work as I should unless I have the power . . .'

'You have no power in my mine, Forbes. None at all, and as for the men showing disrespect for my wife, may I say that I know, personally, every man who works in my mine and not one would dare to so much as glance impolitely at her! They are decent and hardworking, or I should not employ them and not one of them has showed the slightest discontent with his lot, and if they are doing so now the blame can only be laid at your door.'

Richard Forbes wheeled about and his face was a study of inflexible loathing, suppressed only by the knowledge that though this man was crippled, fastened to his chair and his home and was therefore unable to see what went on at his mine, what he spoke was the truth. Unless he, Richard Forbes, stepped back a little, pretended caution, showed respect, difficult as it would be, Buchanan could be pushed into firing him without the slightest compunction. His smile was barely perceptible as he strained to get control of himself.

'I really must disagree with you, sir, on that point. Whilst I am in charge . . .'

'My wife is in charge, not you! I have given her full power to do as she thinks fit!'

'What . . . !'

'So you see, Forbes, you will do exactly as she tells you until I return, and if you do not care for it then of course you must take your no doubt considerable skills elsewhere!'

'Now see here . . .'

'No, you see here. I may be unable to walk at this precise moment but I can still use my brain and I can recognize when a man is trying to pull the wool over my eyes. Really Forbes, do you imagine I was born yesterday! I was mining when you were at your mother's knee, man.' His voice filled with his contempt, withering in its implications and Forbes took a step forward, provoked beyond restraint, violence in his face and in the fists he clenched at his side.

'And I would not advise you to come any closer since I was well used to bare-knuckle prize fighting in my youth, and even sitting in this chair could dispose of a mannikin such as yourself in short order!'

'I would not stoop to hit a cripple, Buchanan . . .'

'Maybe not but you are not averse to blackening a lady's name with your insinuations, nor to stealing a few coppers from a working man's pocket!'

'Watch your tongue, you . . . you . . .' Richard Forbes's face was suffused now with the rage, the violent temper, hot and terrible which can erupt from a cold-hearted man. 'You cannot . . .'

Whatever it was Alex Buchanan 'could not' do was never revealed for as the two men glared with mutual antipathy at one another – Alex cool and arrogant and perfectly certain that by the end of the day this man would be out of his valley forever – a shrill cry rose from somewhere beyond the paddock. It came again and a flock of starlings rose into the air from the stand of trees. The cry was frightened, that of a child in distress. Both men turned towards the spinney, even Forbes distracted from his purpose of doing some damage to the insolent face of his employer and Alex lifted himself by his arms to a higher position in his chair. The cob continued to gallop in wildly confused circles, egged on by his excited rider and as Miles stopped his turning to stare like his master in the direction from which the cry had come the rein wound round him once, effectively fastening his arms to his sides.

'Miles!' Alex's voice was sharp and his expression of snarling anger was replaced by concern. 'Miles, where the devil are the children?'

'I don't know, sir. I thought they was with you. I haven't took me eyes off Master Johnny . . .'

The pony went round again, becoming 'skittish' now as the child on his back begged him to go faster and another loop of rein imprisoned the groom even further.

'For God's sake, man, get up into that wood and look for them. They must have slipped off whilst . . . hurry man, hurry . . .'

'Sir . . . yes sir, but . . . Master Johnny . . . will you stop . . . give over . . . sir . . . please, the lad won't stop and I can't . . .'

Alex stared in growing horror at the pony which was a fraction away from bolting and at the boy on his back who seemed completely unaware of his own danger. The groom was being dragged against his will towards the far corner of the paddock, unable to leave go of the rein nor even to pull at it to halt the frightened animal's flight.

'Oh sweet Jesus . . . !' Alex's voice whispered a frantic prayer in his throat and he turned, confused in that moment for he was confronted by the awful need to be in two places at the same time, and was powerless to be in either!

'Miles . . . damnation man, what the bloody hell d'you think you're doing? John . . . John, Abel . . .' he turned in the direction of the house and his voice rose in a cry of frenzied entreaty, down the long grassy slope, to the garden where the old man would be pottering with his roses, to the stable yard and the groom. He turned again, his face white as marble, his eyes anguished. 'Johnny . . . Johnny, pull that pony in at once, *at once* d'you hear me, *now, now* dammit . . .' But the boy and the animal were out of control, both frightened now, of each other and of the stout wooden fence which was barring their way and of the frantic voice which bellowed from somewhere behind them.

Alex lifted his head then, looking in appalled terror at the man who stood beside his chair, and in his eyes was the silent appeal which he knew he must formulate into words, a pleading to him to run – where? – to save his son who was at this moment about to be tossed carelessly to a most probable injury; to the wood to see what danger had befallen the other three. His beloved children, for they were that now, counted amongst his most precious treasures and their fate, their lives perhaps, were in the hands of the man who stood smiling pleasantly at him, with all the time in the world his expression seemed to say, in which to saunter in one direction or the other.

'For God's sake, man, do something! The boy . . .'

'Yes Mr Buchanan?' Richard Forbes's voice was soft. 'The boy . . . ?'

'Run man, stop that pony. It will crash the fence, or try to take it . . .'

'And does that concern me? You have just given me notice, I believe.'

'Please . . . he's a child . . . five years old . . . please . . .'

'Well . . . perhaps it might be possible . . . if we were to solve our little differences.'

'Please . . . Forbes, for God's sake . . .' but Richard Forbes merely lounged carelessly, his manner implying he really could not see what all the fuss was about. He seemed to find the moment sweet indeed!

Alex threw off the rug which covered his frail legs and with an oath reached down, lifting each one in turn, his breathing hoarse in his throat. Each foot was placed awkwardly on the rough grass and with a mighty heave he braced himself with his strong arms, ready, if it was the last thing he ever did to stand, to walk, to run to his son, his children who needed him, and Richard Forbes smiled as he turned away.

'Perhaps not, Buchanan. I do not think I could work again for a man who is dominated by a woman. You must find someone else to run your mine for I am afraid I can no longer bring myself to do so. Nor will I run after your foolish brat. Good day to you.'

'Christ! You cannot mean to turn your back on the boy.

For God's sake . . . please do this for me. There is still time if you run . . . I beg you . . .'

But Richard Forbes turned and began to saunter down the wet grass — on which he had been forced to squat, toward the house where he had been forced to demean himself on an errand — settling his hat with a great deal of satisfaction on his head.

He heard Alex Buchanan fall but he did not turn nor did he falter as the terrified pony plunged headlong into the fence. He was halfway to his own horse as the boy screamed shrilly; and the sound of the fence splintering, the voice of the hoarsely shouting groom, the high whinny of the injured cob and the desperate pleading of his employer faded away as he rode carelessly down the gravel path to the gate which led to the road.

She felt absurdly light-hearted as she drove through the thickening, swirling mist of rain which had begun again in mid-afternoon, filled with an anticipatory flurry of excitement for the evening ahead. The day had been a good one, bursting with vigorous challenge despite her exchange with Alex that morning and she meant to continue it just as soon as she arrived home. And her conflict with Forbes had exhilarated her! What joy it had been to fight with him, to order him coolly to do as he was told, to put on his hat and get down to the house and to look sharp about it! It really had been the highlight of her day and she could not wait to get home and tell Alex about it. The man must make up his mind that from now on his instructions would come from Howethwaite, from her and her husband; not only on the system of shifts but on every aspect of the working of the mine, right down to the making of the candles which the miners used. He would be advised that in future she would overlook everything Mr Richard Forbes did, and that his six months of complete control of the Buchanan Mining Company were over and by God the first thing she had in mind was an investigation into the state of those she had seen working on the surface that morning. She had not liked the look of those children, not one bit, and the difference in six months from the cheerful little monkeys she remembered scampering about the piles of ore to the whey-faced, mechanical stick-like figures she had seen today was quite unbelievable. What was he doing up there to change the always hard-worked, but fairly treated, good humoured work force to the woebegone assembly she had witnessed today? She and Alex would soon find the cause and put it right.

She had spent a lively hour with Mr Pendle too, which had put a flush, not only in her cheeks but in his, when she informed him coolly that in future any decisions made by herself or Mr Buchanan would be joint ones. Would he please ensure that a full report of the contract with the mines in Chile, from where they were now to purchase their saltpetre, was on her desk within fifteen minutes. She had enjoyed that and the pale gleaming of respect in Mr Pendle's eyes as he stumped from the office.

There were lights burning in every window as the carriage drove up the gravelled driveway to the front door, and for a moment she felt the soft delight of homecoming, of knowing that behind those brightly lit windows were her children, her friends, her husband, all bustling cheerfully about in preparation for her arrival. There would be delicious food cooking in the kitchen, the fragrance drifting to the front door in welcome. Maids would be making up fires in rooms in which probably no one would sit but obeying her orders – her home – that everywhere should be warm and cheerful. The children would have taken nursery tea, noisy, happy, guarded and precious, ready to overwhelm her when she went up, with the events of their day, the problems of their young, safe lives, their joys and woes and love of her, their disappointments and enchantments. She would be surrounded, immersed in their high spirits, the romping dogs, the dainty arching kittens, in light and laughter and warm young bodies pressing against hers.

And in their room would be Alex, waiting with his infectious, eager grin, waiting to tell her uncompromisingly of the way in which he had dealt with Richard Forbes, waiting to be told of how she had dealt with Pendle, waiting to show her the growing strength of his handsome body. His eyes would be warm and wicked and his hand would reach out to hers as it had begun to do lately and hers would fall into it as naturally as a flower reaches to the sun.

The gladness which filled her heart lasted no longer than a moment for as Jack handed her from her carriage, the front door opened and Faith stood there, the lamplight outlining her neat figure, her face in shadow – and Christy knew that the gladness she felt was but a transitory emotion, a bubble which some demon had come along to prick and she waited hopelessly for the blow to strike her!

CHAPTER THIRTY-EIGHT

She sat beside her son's bed, moistening his lips as the doctor had instructed her, replacing the covers he threw off, leaning over him, her eyes never leaving his painfully small face, watching as the fever he had taken, come from the injury to his head the doctor said, burned him up, swallowed his firm, rounded flesh and pushed the fragile bones of him through his fine baby skin.

'Let me sit with him,' Faith said on the second day, the third day, the fourth. 'I will call you if it is . . . needed and you really should go and see Mr Buchanan. He is demented, Christy. He blames himself and will not be calmed. Really, he will do himself further injury if he is not restrained. He has already struck Jack because he refused to bring him up here and Jack is only acting under the doctor's orders. He says he is not to be moved and that . . .'

'I shall stay here.'

'Please darling, go and sleep a little. It has been twenty-four hours, thirty-six, forty-eight and . . .'

'I shall stay here.'

'Do you not trust me? You know I love the boy like my own.'

'I shall stay here.'

It was as though she was afraid to take her eyes from him, afraid that during that hour of sleep Faith had begged her to take, in the few minutes she might spend reassuring her husband that it was not due to him that their son lay – don't say it, don't think it – that whilst she moved away from him for only a moment a fierce and jealous God might steal him away. She was frantic and blind with a panic which gripped her paralysingly and only here, with her eyes upon him, with her hand hovering above his brightly burning cheek could she contain it. She was only too frighteningly aware that no woman could hope to raise all her children unless she was exceedingly lucky. Her own mother had buried half a dozen and more, and Alex was the sole survivor of innumerable brothers and sisters, but she had loved this mischievously brave son of hers for over five years and it seemed to her that she simply could not bear to lose him, to lean beside a small grave and have them lower him into it and the only way to avert it was to stand guard over him, to protect him with every ounce of her mother's will, with every drop of her mother's blood, with every muscle and sinew and with every light breath she took!

He had been almost totally insensible when they had found him, his movements slow, his breathing weak. The pupils of his eyes had been enormous and when they had begged him to tell them where it hurt he had seemed confused and unable to answer. The doctor had scurried between Alex's bedside where he had endeavoured to set the arm he had broken in his fall, and the room where the boy lay in a daze, the man's elderly face doing its best to convey an optimism he did not feel. He had given Johnny laudanum, to make him sleep, he said and to allow him the rest in which to heal what he was certain was only a mild concussion of the brain. He had made up a mixture consisting of sal-ammoniac, vinegar, whiskey and water and applied it to the lint with which her son's bruised and swollen head was covered and told her to replace it hourly.

'I really must get this splint on Mr Buchanan's arm, dear lady, or he will do it irreparable damage he is thrashing about so. He is in a great deal of pain, not helped I must say by the recriminations he heaps upon himself due to his inability to prevent his son's accident, but the boy is resting now and will continue to do so. If I might suggest you leave him in this young woman's care . . .' he indicated Faith hovering anxiously at her back, '. . . and come and speak to your husband. Your son will take no harm . . .'

'But he is . . . so cold, so white and his breathing is . . . is weak.' She seemed not to be concerned with the doctor's words about Alex.

'That is only to be expected, Mrs Buchanan. He has been stunned and is in a state of shock. You can see that by his inability to move or even to speak properly. Now you must keep him warm and when he is himself not allow him to move. I shall leave you some fever mixture to give him since I must warn you his skin will become hot, his pulse will be full and he will be feverish. There is nothing to be alarmed over. It is quite customary in cases such as this but I feel you should be prepared for it.'

He did not tell her that as a last resort he may have to apply leeches to her son's small head to draw off the blood should there be violent inflammation of the boy's brain!

'Now will you not come and speak to your husband, Mrs Buchanan?'

'I cannot leave my son.'

'You *can* Mrs Buchanan. At the moment he is asleep and in no danger.'

'And I am here, Christy. I will not leave him.' Faith spoke from the shadows for it was night now and the fire's glow and the lamplight shed their illumination only around the still form of the boy on the bed. Christy still wore the severe black outfit, and even the tall, rakish top hat in which she had set out that morning and Faith watched compassionately as she bent in her anguish over the boy. Faith could scarce remember the sequence of events which had begun that afternoon with the arrival of Richard Forbes demanding peremptorily of Mrs Longworth that he be taken at once to the master. She herself had been in the kitchen when the good woman had returned burning with resentment at his uncivil treatment of her, and for ten minutes she and Mrs Avery had shared her anger for after all she was the housekeeper and due some respect.

It had been the sound of horse's hooves on the drive which had drawn them curiously to the window since they had not expected Mr Buchanan's visitor to leave so soon. He had been harsh-faced and short-tempered when he had come to the back kitchen door to ask for the master's cigars, just like a servant himself and badly affronted by it. As they watched him ride away Mrs Longworth had been quite fulsome in the rejoinders she had heaped upon the retreating back of Richard Forbes, and it was several moments before they heard the hoarse shouting which came from the crown of the long slope to the paddock. John was halfway up there, and old Abel Hodson, before Faith was out of the kitchen door, and as she caught up with the old man – his wheezing lungs tearing the frantic breath from him – the groom was bending over Mr Buchanan who was trying to stand, *stand*, his one good arm gripping the heavy chair which he had pulled on top of himself – the other hanging stangely askew.

'The boy!' he was shouting in a deranged voice. 'Never mind me, damn you . . . the boy . . . and the children . . .'

At first they had not known what he had meant for there was nothing to be seen amongst the tall grasses and scattered clumps of wildflowers which grew about the paddock. No sound to be heard but the swelling flight of the late bumble bee at the rich carpet of buttercups about their feet and a linnet singing her heart out somewhere in the depths of the wood, but suddenly there was movement from the paddock and Miles struggled slowly to his feet, his face strangely crumpled, his manner confused and uncertain. They saw it then. The broken fence and the group of horses beyond it and amongst them was the cob, still saddled and flighty in his distress, kicking his heels and snorting angrily.

Faith had screamed. She remembered that quite plainly for just beneath the smashed fence lay Johnny Buchanan.

'Leave me . . . for Christ's sake . . . see to the boy,' the man had said and she and John had run to him and his stillness had terrified her and as they bent over him she remembered, or had she imagined it in her terror, the sound of three small voices piping up in a nursery song and three small figures idling out of the wood in their direction. Joby and Harry had been laughing, scuffling as they always did, companionably this time it appeared, thumping one another on the back in congratulation for the brave manner in which they had rescued Amy's silly kitten from a tree which the foolish creature had climbed, and Amy was smiling as she held it consolingly to her chest.

Now they were asleep in their beds. Fearful and afraid they had been, white-faced and trembling at their father's fury, believing in their childish innocence that he was hurt again and Johnny's poor head was smashed because they had been disobedient and gone into the forbidden spinney. Their mother had brushed aside their need to be comforted in her need to be with her injured son and it had been up to Faith to kiss and console them to sleep. She felt as though she was being torn into several pieces, each one trying to give of her full self to every one of these people she loved. She yearned to be with Johnny, to hover over him as Christy did. She felt the need to cling to the night nursery where Amy, Joby and Harry slept fitfully since they might call for her though Beth and Liz were there, and she was quite desperate to approach poor Mr Buchanan who was almost out of his mind with worry and guilt. They all required something of her but most of all there was Christy!

'Go and see your husband, Christy.' Perhaps they could lean on one another. Draw comfort and a measure of peace from one another. Take hope and strength and reassurance as they shared the anguish of the days that must be got through before their son was out of danger . . . or . . . or . . . but no . . . not that . . . *not that*!

He was lying in the centre of the bed, his old dog beside him exactly as Christy had seen him a thousand times in the past two years. His head turned fiercely to her as she moved across the room and sank to the floor beside the bed. The dog thumped his tail in welcome, turning a mournful eye as though in sympathy, and she put a hand to his head before indicating that he must get down and lie on the floor. Mrs Jackson sat in her old position by the fire, a bit of something in her fingers, some needlework she always did as she watched over Mr Buchanan, brought from the warm corner of the chimney she had found in the kitchen to the task she had thought to be done with. Her strong face was sad for she too felt the pain of this setback. Without a word she got up and moved quietly from the room.

'How is he . . . for Christ's sake, woman, tell me how he really is.' His voice was threatening in its lacerating fear. He tried to raise himself on his good elbow and the sweat stood out on his face with the effort and the pain. 'That bloody doctor bleats on about a mild concussion and rest and not to worry myself but how can I lie here and not worry? Let me go up to him, Christy. Get the men to lift me into my chair and take me up to him. I beg you! I saw him as John carried him from the paddock . . . so white and . . . sort of . . . smaller . . . crumpled . . . dear God, I shall have that picture with me for the rest of my days . . . please . . .'

Christy leaned her elbows on the bed careful not to touch the splinted arm which was strapped across Alex's chest and looked into his glazed, demented eyes and her

601

heart wrenched in her breast for his fearful dread. She could barely restrain herself from leaping up and hurrying back to her small and silent son, and in a moment or two she could do it, but his father was forced to lie here and wonder and wait, filled with self-recrimination, for someone to come and tell him his son was . . . was . . . ! At this very moment, whilst she knelt here Johnny might have . . . have . . . and her not there to hold him in her arms. And Alex must contain his desperate need, the need she had to be with her son, his son, and remain here, paralysed and in pain, his head filled with pictures he could scarcely bear to think about. It was small comfort to sit beside the bed on which a child was ill but at least she could be there to watch over him, whilst for Alex there was only the frustration of second-hand reports brought him by servants or herself when she could tear her mother's anxiety away from her son.

'Alex . . . sweetheart, let me . . .'

'For God's sake, Christy, what did the doctor tell you? He seems to consider I am some idiot cripple . . .' his face twisted in anguished bitterness, '. . . who must be protected from himself, but he is my son and I am . . . able . . . able to . . . to bear the worst . . .'

'There is nothing to tell, Alex. He is . . . stunned, the doctor says and . . .' She must be truthful. Johnny was his son just as he was hers and he had the right to know, even in his weakened condition. 'He will . . . perhaps . . . have a fever . . .'

'Fever!' Alex's white face became even whiter for the word was filled with the horrid spectre of death. For the young and the old, and even for those who were healthy and lived in conditions in which it seemed it could not possibly tip-toe. Fever! It had no name really, just an ailment which could decimate a whole family within hours, stealing about them as rapidly as the mist which floated above the waters of the lakes and disappearing just as abruptly.

'No . . . Alex . . . a high fever brought on by the . . . the blow to his head . . . not . . . not like . . .'

'Oh Jesus . . . !' His voice sank to a whisper. 'Dear sweet Jesus, Christy . . . it is all my fault . . .'

'No . . . no Alex! How could it be your fault?'

'It is . . . it is, believe me . . .'

'No no, my darling!'

'If I had not . . .'

'What Alex?'

'I goaded him . . .'

'Who?'

'Richard Forbes . . .'

'Forbes? He was here? How could he . . . ?'

'I was maddened, you see . . . his attitude towards you . . .'

'Me?'

'Yes. He insinuated . . . implied . . .' His voice rose in a demented frenzy and Christy was appalled by his agony. 'You know my humour when it is roused. I was so enraged I humiliated him, belittled him and when Johnny . . . when Johnny fell . . . he refused . . . he just walked away . . . smiling.'

'Dear God . . .' Her face blanched and her eyes filled with tears and they fell in great crystal droplets on to his hand, as she held it passionately to her face.

'He . . . he laughed, Christy . . . and just . . . walked away! I tried to stand. Dear sweet Lord, for the first time in two years I actually stood up, Christy . . . then I fell down . . . like a bloody infant . . . I fell down.' His voice became vague, haunted by the memory of that moment. 'I fell down and my son . . . my son lay injured . . . dying . . . perhaps dead and I could not even . . .'

'Oh Alex, don't torture yourself so. You are not to blame. Neither for Johnny's accident, nor your own. How could you possibly . . . ?'

'My son . . . and I could not go to him. But for these damn legs of mine I could have run . . . run to him . . . It would not have happened for if I had been a man, a true

603

man it would have been my hand on the rein, my protection for my own children. Miles was . . . it was not his fault . . . only mine . . .'

'No! No, I will not have it!'

'Yes . . .'

'Alex, oh Alex . . .' She leaned towards his wildly thrashing head, smoothing back the thick ebony tumble of his hair from his brow, as she would one of her sons; sensing now with the new instinctive reflex which had triggered inside her, this strong man's strange vulnerability. His pain overwhelmed her. It was almost visible and violent, filled with bitterness and though he fought it, for her sake, she thought, she was afraid of the damage such pain and fury might inflict. Holding his face gently between her two hands she placed her lips on his, moving them sweetly, softly, warmly, breathing her own smooth textured strength into his open mouth, letting them wander intuitively about his jawline and cheek and – despite her own fretting need to be away to her son – her heart sighed in thankfulness as he quietened and a measure of calm took hold of him, his good arm clinging to her gratefully as she whispered against his ashen cheek.

'Don't Alex. Don't do this to yourself. Rest . . . don't snarl at me like that . . . you know you must and I promise I will be down to see you regularly . . .'

'Let me come up . . . please . . .'

'Later . . . when you have slept.'

'Slept! Ha! How the hell can I sleep?'

'Try! I shall be down to see you in a little while.'

But is was not a 'little while' for during the night the fever came, and Christy Buchanan had no thought for her husband's suffering as she watched her son burn up with it, and though she heard him on the fringe of her conscious mind from the room below where her boy lay, shouting and raging, imploring those about him to carry him up, her mind scarcely registered it.

He began to sweat, her lovely child, on the third day, melting away as she watched over him and the full horror of his loss entered her soul and her heart wept with it and she began to pray then, to beg God to let her son live, to take her if He would but to let her son live. She promised Him in her despair that she would stay by her children's side, by her husband's side, she would bear him another child, if it was possible, children! She would never flaunt herself, as they said she did, up at the mine, or the mill, never interfere in the business which she had loved and which had become a part of her. She bargained with Him to spare her son's life and in return she would give her life to her family, to being exactly as she should, to doing exactly as she should, to leading the life the wives of her husband's business associates lived, the wives of all the husbands of Fellthwaite!

'Go to Mr Buchanan, Christy,' Faith begged, 'or I swear he will kill himself. Can you not hear him? He is out of his mind and he is frightening the children. For a moment only, just to reassure him that his son is still alive. He will not listen to any of us!'

But the sight of his wife would hardly comfort his agony, Faith thought as she ran her eyes over Christy Buchanan. She had not removed her clothes in three days! The boy had sweated in her cradling arms and her black gown was stained. Her hair hung about her shoulders in lank disarray, pushed this way and that by her distraught hands. She had dozed a little in the chair with Faith beside her, only allowing it on the strict promise that she was to sleep for no longer than ten minutes and when Faith had let it stretch to an hour she had been menacing in her anger.

'He might have . . . might have . . .' She was perilous in her fury and would not agree to it again, saying she could trust no one. Her face was gaunt and thin. Her eyes had fallen into deep purple sockets and but for a forkful of Mrs Avery's chicken and a spoonful of broth had eaten nothing.

She was alone, her elbows on the bed, her eyes fiercely locked to the tiny emaciated sliver of flesh and bone which had once been her lively, rosy, beautiful son, when the sound at the door, hovering on the edge of her concentration, became more obtrusive and she raised her head though not for a second did she take her eyes from her child. It came again! A scratching like that made by Alex's dog when he wanted to be let in. The dog! Up here?

'Christy . . .' She could barely hear the murmur of her name but she stood up and moved uncertainly towards the door. It was Alex's voice but where . . . how foolish . . . it could not be . . . she was dreaming . . . her mind slipping away to the mindless sleep it so badly needed . . . it could not be . . . ! She had turned back to her boy, her aching eyes reaching for him, her hands lifting to him in desperate motherhood when she heard it plainly this time.

'Christy . . . open . . . the . . . door.'

He was there, on the floor, his face like death, his eyes hollow and staring, the blue of them faded in his agony to the paleness of a robin's egg. He leaned wearily against the door frame, supporting himself on his good arm, the broken limb still strapped firmly to his chest. His useless legs had arranged themselves in a disjointed jumble, it seemed, as though he was some stuffed doll which had been flung there by a careless child.

'Dear God . . . Alex . . . how . . . ?' She knelt beside him, clumsy in her compassion, her own body cramped and aching, nevertheless ready to hold his in any way it could, and on her face was an expression he had never seen before but at that moment he cared nought for it, or her.

'He is my son too, dammit,' he whispered fiercely. 'My son!'

'Oh my God, Alex, how did you . . . ?'

'I crawled, confound you, crawled like a bloody infant. Dragged myself up those bloody stairs one at a time . . .'

'Up the . . . !'

'Yes, up the stairs! No one would bring me . . . so I came myself!'

The servant brought his chair when she called them, and they sat together. When he insisted she slept, for her son would be safe with his father, she knew. She ate a little and washed her face trusting Alex as she had trusted no one, ever, in her life – not even Annie Emmerson – and when the fever broke and their son slept peacefully, miraculously, their hands were clasped tightly together and their tears mingled as she put her face against his.

It rained without stopping for the next two weeks, the hills vanishing in the smoke-like spindrift which eddied, grey and haunted, across Lingmoor Fell, south to Tilberthwaite and the Old Man of Conistone, presenting its drab face to her each morning as she watched her son thrive and become again the engaging, audacious, noisy imp he had been. He wore his bandage at a jaunty angle, like a brigand, his ebony curls escaping in springing, returning health. His blue eyes snapped again, just like those of his father, as he demanded Mrs Avery's gingerbread men, the constant attention of everyone in the house, his dog and the promise of a pony of his own, making an enormous fuss until he got it. Christy marvelled at his resilience, remembering the flickering scrap he had become as the fire almost consumed him. She gloried in him and her bargain with God was forgotten. Her husband argued with her as fiercely as he had ever done, and with everyone who came within his reach, threatening that if the bloody doctor would not let him up soon he would lose his mind instead of merely driving everyone else to lose theirs!

It was time now for her to get back to work, Christy told him decisively, daring him to try and stop her. The memory of those pathetic young boys and stooped, exhausted women she had seen on her last day at the mine still haunted her, and she was determined to find out what Richard Forbes had done to reduce them to their pitiful state. No word naturally, had been received from the man himself, nor had she had word of him. A clerk had brought the weekly balance sheet and the September audit to her with a forecast from Mr Tate, drawn up, no doubt before Forbes's departure, of his production and profit figures for October. The same man called for the men's wages the following day bringing a polite note from the head clerk hoping these positive, indeed splendid, figures were to Mrs Buchanan's liking, and a wish for her son's speedy restoration to full health.

Alex lay in his bed demanding ominously that he be lifted from it to his chair in the corner by the window, but really, Christy said, when one considered the melancholy scene beyond the streaming panes of glass was there any need of it; and was he not better resting in his bed, and until his broken arm had healed did he not feel it would be wiser to avoid the exercises with Jacky which he was threatening to begin again, and really, he was the worst patient she had ever known, more fretful even than his own son!

He grinned reluctantly, then cursed her vigorously as she laughingly declined to 'give him a hand' to get out of his bed, but his eyes were warm as they followed her about the room. He turned awkwardly to stub out his cigar and when he looked at her again the expression in his eyes confused her. They were very clear and direct. Blue, such a deep and lovely blue and he held out his good hand to her.

'Thank you,' he said simply.

'For what?' she miled.

'For . . . for my son,' he said but she had the strangest feeling he meant something she not quite understand, something which had nothing at all to do with Johnny. She moved hesitatingly to him, holding out her hand to his and he took it and bending his head put his lips to the back of it, warm, firm, caressing, then turned it over and dropped a light kiss in the palm and she felt it pull surprisingly at her heart. When he raised his eyes they were smiling in wry humour. He shook his head, still holding her hand.

'So that is how you did it,' he said. 'I wondered!'

'Wondered what?' Her smile was easy now though the curiously delightful feeling still lingered in her breast.

'How you managed all these years to make those men

608

dance to your tune. You are quite a woman, Christy Buchanan.'

'And a busy one as well,' she said quickly, sliding her hand out from his. 'If I don't go to the mine God knows what mischief Mr Tate will have got up to all by himself.'

She was laughing as she left the room, and the small glow of pleasure bought about by his unaccustomed praise spread through her body and she was humming lightly as she stepped into her carriage. She decided to go first to Elterwater to look in on Mr Pendle before taking the road to Conistone and the mine.

She was busy at her desk at the gunpowder mill when the clever young man she had employed to be her personal clerk knocked at her door, asking politely if she could spare a moment. She did not lift her head from the long column of figures she was adding but held up her hand for silence, her voice murmuring in the quietness until she had finished. She made a note at the bottom of the column, then looked up sighing.

'Yes, Peters, what is it?'

'Well . . . there's a man here to see you, Mrs Buchanan.'

'What man?'

'He wouldn't give his name, ma'am. Just said it was urgent.'

'I have no time for a gentleman who will not give his name, Peters! Tell him that.'

'Oh, this is no gentleman, Mrs Buchanan.'

'What do you mean?'

The young clerk tipped his nose slightly in the direction of the ceiling. 'He is a workman, ma'am. Indeed I told him he could not see you and that if he had a problem he must discuss it with his foreman, but he says he does not work here.'

'Where does he work?'

'He wouldn't say, Mrs Buchanan.'

She sighed deeply and the clever young man was quite fascinated by her lovely, lifting breast. He was more than a little in love with the beautiful Mrs Buchanan, wondering gallantly – as many gentlemen of her acquaintance did – if he could possibly give comfort to her in any way, as compensation for the lack of a man in her life and one supposed, in her bed, but of course she was so far above him he had done no more than work himself to a standstill on her behalf as was only proper, and would continue to do so as long as her soft smoky eyes rested on him as they did now. He waited for her decision, glad of the chance to stand and gaze at the glossy thickness of her dark hair, at the rebellious tendrils which wisped about her ears, at the creamy whiteness of her skin and the raspberry pink fullness of the lips she chewed thoughtfully.

'Oh Lord, send him in then, Peters, but tell him I can spare him only five minutes, no more!'

The stocky young man who entered her office, cap respectfully in his hand, not humble but as though he was well aware of his own worth, looked strangely familiar though she knew quite positively that she had never seen him before. It was in the eyes really. They were a curious mixture of brown and green, long-lashed and with a clear, direct gaze and they looked at her as someone else looked at her, but she could not for the life of her decide who it was. He was neatly dressed in Hodden grey jacket and trousers, good sturdy boots and a decent flannel shirt, obviously his 'setting off' clothes worn only on Sunday or a special occasion such as this appeared to be. His hands were covered by the marks of healed scars, splay fingered, big and calloused, the hands of a man who did heavy, manual work.

'Good morning, Mr . . .' Her voice was coolly polite.

He turned before he answered, looking at Peters who still stood by the door, and Christy realized that this man was here on some errand of secrecy though God knows what it could be, but he would not even give his name until Peters was gone.

'Thank you, Peters. I will call you when I want you.'

'Yes, ma'am.' He closed the door quietly behind him.

'Now Mr . . . ?'

'Cooper, Mrs Buchanan. Denny Cooper.'

'Cooper?'

'Faith's brother, ma'am. Faith Adams.'

Her face broke into a delighted smile and so did the face of the young man, and there it was, Faith's smile with Faith's eyes and Christy stood up behind her desk and reached over to take his hand, hers disappearing into his like a little white mouse down a large hole!

'Mr Cooper, how could I mistake you . . .'

'Denny, please ma'am. I work for you at the mine.'

'Do you indeed . . . well, of course you do. I remember Faith speaking of it, years ago when your father had his accident. You went to live at the old corn mill with your brother . . . ?'

'Jack, ma'am.'

'Well, sit down, Denny, please, and tell me what I can do for you.'

'I was going to ask Faith if she would pass on a message, Mrs Buchanan, but then I thought "No, I must go direct to Mr Buchanan" but we heard he . . . well, Faith told us he wasn't . . . himself lately so I came to you as you're the master's wife.'

'Why didn't you come to the house, Denny, instead of walking all this way up to Chapel Stile?'

'Well, as it's business, I thought it was best to come here . . . and . . . well . . . I can mix in here with the rest of the lads but up at the house I'd stand out like a sore thumb, and I didn't want him to know just in case nothing was done if you understand my meaning. We don't want to lose our jobs, Mrs Buchanan, but he . . .'

'Who is *he*, Denny?' she said curiously.

'Forbes.' It was said with a coldness which, if the man had been there would have frozen the marrow in his bones.

'*Forbes*!' She felt the blood run cold in her veins. 'Do you mean the man is still . . .'

'Still what, ma'am?'

'You are saying that Richard Forbes is still in charge at the mine?' Her voice was flat, without expression and her eyes had taken on the still, fixed stare of an animal which has been caught off guard by another.

The man looked puzzled. 'Yes, ma'am.'

'Dear God!'

'I beg your pardon, Mrs Buchanan?'

'Never mind, Denny, go on.'

'He's a bad sort, Mrs Buchanan.'

'A bad sort, Denny?' Her voice was so soft now Denny could hardly hear it and he began to wonder at her strangeness.

'Yes Mrs Buchanan, he's stealing you blind, and treating them bairns like they were animals . . .'

'Stealing me blind, Denny?' It seemed she was capable only of repeating everything he himself said, and Denny Cooper looked even more confused.

'Well, if he isn't, Mrs Buchanan, me an' Jack and a lot of the miners who've worked – and been decently treated for many a long year – by Mr Buchanan, don't feel we can work for *you* any more!'

'Me! What I have to do with it?'

'It started when you hired Forbes, ma'am, so if it isn't him who's stealing food from our bairns' mouth, 'tis you. Nay lass . . .' His honest face softened and he leaned forward to look into her horrified eyes. 'We know it's not you who's putting the lives of good men in danger; who's cutting our wages to the bone so our children are living on oats and taties; who's altered the shifts so we're forced to work one and a half, two men doing the work of three, the same with the women and kids and him pocketing the third wage. He's clever, I'll give him that. Not greedy enough so's you'd notice the difference but the last two weeks or so he's been worse. The drainage is bad, Mrs Buchanan, and needs seeing to. He uses the cheapest timber, so rotten it wouldn't hold up a bit of turf let alone the bloody – pardon me – mountain on top of us . . .'

He saw her shudder for she had been underground.

'. . . aye lass, and that water's coming in so fast the pumps won't take it and if summat's not done soon there'll be deaths on his hands . . . and yours! There's dozens have been sacked for speaking up. Some wanted to come up to the house but with Mr Buchanan so ill, and then the bairn, they felt it wasn't right. He brought in anybody who would work for a pittance, Mrs Buchanan. The Irish . . . they'll do owt to put a bit of food in their children's mouths. Me and Jack have stuck it out on account of ours, but it's no good, Mrs Buchanan . . . so . . . well, they asked me to come . . . all of them, before someone gets killed what with this rain an' all. It's not fit for men to work in the depths, it's not safe, Mrs Buchanan. *You run a dangerous mine, ma'am, and I've come to tell you so!*'

There was an appalled silence for the space of a minute and Christy's dark eyebrows, her silver grey eyes, her red mouth stood out sharply in the clay white horror of her face.

Abruptly she stood up.

'Be good enough to ask Peters to call my carriage, Denny. We are going up to the mine!'

'Aye lass.'

CHAPTER THIRTY-NINE

She was wet through to her underclothes in the time it took her to climb, clinging to Denny Cooper's hand, from the village where she left the carriage to the mine; and her frightened mind considered how the pumps could possibly cope with the vast amount of rain water which poured in a thick, mud-slicked torrent down the flinty track, and which was just as surely pouring through every crack and crevice and spring into her husband's mine.

And it had been doing so for over a fortnight now!

Jack came with them saying it would be more than his life was worth if the master heard he had allowed Mrs Buchanan to come up here on her own and in this weather an' all. Old Sammy at the forge would manage the horses and he'd just come along and see Mrs Buchanan safe into the office.

'I'm going into the mine, Jack.'

They had both turned then to stare at her, Denny's hand pulling her upright, steadying her on a slice of level ground. Jack took hold of her other arm, his expression saying that over his dead body she was going into the mine, and they both shook her a little, a drooping, saturated rag doll which had evidently lost its mind and needed restraining.

'Oh no, Mrs Buchanan . . . oh no!' Jack was adamant and his young face became stern and so did Denny Cooper's and they both turned, vigorous in their determination to take her down the hill again.

'I would never have come for you if I'd known, Mrs Buchanan,' Denny said in an aggrieved voice, and the rain was so driving it ran across his face and into his mouth so that in order to speak clearly he had to swallow it. 'I thought you'd do no more than speak to the men at the shaft head, or in the office, then take it up with him . . .'

'But I must see for myself, Denny. Can you not understand that? There is no one else to check on what you have told me and I must have proof.' And she must be able to describe it to Alex as she herself had seen it, she told herself.

'I am not doubting the truth of what you say, Denny,' she went on, 'but I must make absolutely sure before I can face Forbes with it. Now let go of my arms, both of you. I am going up to the mine.'

She slipped on the wet, plastered grass and her full riding habit, weighted down with rain water became coated with mud. Her top hat kept collecting the rain in its brim and every time she bent her head it poured off like a small waterfall. It was hard to see more than a few yards ahead and the village below had disappeared in the vast, shifting curtain of rain.

They helped her to her feet, still holding her arms but

she shook them off and so ingrained in them was the habit of obedience to the master – or mistress – they allowed it.

'Now then, both of you take my hands and help me up this damned mountain!'

Mr Tate was simply speechless. At first he was not sure who she was. He could not take his eyes from the wet plastered outline of her breasts and the sharp peaks of her nipples beneath the black fitted bodice, and it took a while for his gratified eyes to raise themselves to her wet, staring face.

'Mrs Buchanan!' His mouth fell slackly open on her name and he put out a hand, palm facing her, as though to deny her presence here on a day such as this.

'Where is Mr Forbes, Mr Tate?' she said briskly, doing away with the niceties of greetings. She unpinned her hat and shook it forcefully, splattering water everywhere, then placed it on Mr Tate's mantleshelf above the pleasingly large fire he had, standing before it, her clothes steaming in the warmth.

'Mr Forbes, ma'am?' he said as if she had asked for the Prince Consort.

'You heard me, Mr Tate, fetch him out and whilst you are about it send one of your men down to Denny Cooper's cottage with a message that Mr Cooper requires a spare set of clothing. You don't mind if I borrow a pair of trousers and a shirt, do you Denny? I can hardly go underground like this.' She turned to smile brilliantly at Faith's brother and he shook his head slowly, almost as much at a loss for words as Mr Tate.

'Mrs Buchanan, please, you can't mean to do it.'

'Oh but I do, Denny, so best oblige me with some sensible clothing. I should imagine the . . . the inconvenience will be lessened if I do away with these cumbersome skirts.'

Jack had gone by the time Hetty Cooper had blundered up the hill from the small cottage where she, Denny and their two small children lived, with her husband's working trousers, boots and a shirt wrapped in an old piece of blanket to keep them dry. She bobbed a curtsey wonderingly to Mrs Buchanan, clutching the neat bundle beneath her wet shawl and was astonished when the mine owner's wife took it from her, thanking her warmly, saying she would return them washed and pressed the very next day. She was further bewildered when the quite amazingly elegant Mrs Buchanan, even in the bedraggled condition to which the weather had transformed her, begged her politely to accompany her to Mr Forbes's office.

'I fear I cannot manage the buttons on this gown, Mrs Cooper, so if you would oblige me by giving me a hand.'

Hetty Cooper had never met anyone who could not undress themselves, beyond the age of two years that is, and she turned her confused expression on her husband, her eyes asking him to explain what Mrs Buchanan was up to. But Mrs Buchanan was not inclined to stand about wasting time in explanation, and with the manner of a lady well used to giving orders and having them obeyed instantly, she climbed the stairs to Richard Forbes's office, Alex's office, her office, with the anxious Hetty Cooper on her heels.

Both Denny and Mr Tate hastily averted their eyes when Mrs Buchanan clattered down the stairs for neither had ever seen a lady, a woman in trousers before and though she was as modestly clad as in her full riding habit, she was certainly not decent! She had kept on her own riding boots, tucking the legs of the trousers into the tops. The flowing ribbon from her top hat had been tied about her waist to hold up the trousers, and on top of Denny's soft flannel shirt she had put her 'gilet', the waistcoat-like garment she wore under her open jacket on occasion, considered a trifle 'fast', but smart! She had tied back her thick, wet hair with a piece of the same ribbon and twisted it up into an untidy chignon to keep it away from her face.

She looked like a pirate, bold and quite impudently magnificent. The Hodden grey and white, the jaunty waistcoat, the tightly clasped waist of the trousers and the high leather boots gave her the air of a young gentleman, strutting and arrogant, only the sweet swell of her breasts and the soft line of her creamy throat giving it the lie.

'Well gentlemen, I'm ready,' she said defiantly but her eyes were dark, misted with her fear.

Denny did not look at her as he spoke.

'I'm coming with you, Mrs Buchanan.'

'Thank you, Denny. I would be . . . obliged.' There was a tremor in her voice and her eyes widened, bright with some other emotion she did not care to reveal, but flinging her wet cape carelessly about her shoulders to protect herself to the head of the shaft, she strode out as though she was off for no more than a pleasant walk on the sun-flecked fells which had surrounded this place only a short while since.

Faith was sitting before the parlour fire mending a tear in the delicate lace of Christy's petticoat when Meg popped her head round the door asking if she could see Jack for a minute. He was in a right state about something to do with Mrs Buchanan and . . .

'Mrs Buchanan?' Faith rose to her feet warily for it was not like Jack to come home without his mistress. He took her everywhere, waiting patiently hour after hour whilst she went about her business day, bringing her home safely each evening – as he had done ever since she had come as a bride to Howethwaite over six years ago and he had been appointed her coachman. Young he was but completely dependable and now that he and Sally were wed and to be parents in the new year, he took his duties even more seriously.

'What . . .'

But she had got no further than that when Jack himself burst into the room, brushing past the affronted Meg who was after all a parlour maid and the only one to be allowed in the front of the house, without so much as a by your leave.

'Mrs Adams . . . Oh thank the dear Lord . . . I must

speak to Mr Buchanan at once though what the devil he'll say to me God only knows. Fire me on the spot I shouldn't wonder but there was nothing I could do short of tying her up and you know what she's like when she gets an idea in her head. 'Twas that damn fool who came for her and on a day like this . . . I ask you. 'Tis not fit for man nor beast . . .'

'Jack . . . Jack, will you calm down and tell me what it's all about.' Faith put out an appalled hand to him, her face as white as the lace she mended on Mrs Buchanan's fine petticoat. 'For God's sake, lad . . .'

'I told her, Mrs Adams . . . I tried but she wouldn't listen . . .'

'What . . . oh dear God, Jack . . . where is she . . . ?'

'She's up at the mine, Mrs Adams. There's something wrong up there and she would go and see and I don't know what to do. He should be told though what he can do, I can't imagine. But he should know, Mrs Adams . . .'

'Know *what*, for Heaven's sake?'

'She's going underground, Mrs Adams!'

Alex was reading the *Westmorland Gazette* absorbed by the bulletin of the Government's Annual Budget containing the unpopular proposal for the substitution of the window tax, imposed in 1697 on houses with more than six windows, with a duty of a shilling in the pound on all houses, windows or not and ninepence on shops! Since the introduction of the window act houses had been built with less windows but with each one of a bigger area of glass as the tax was on the number of windows, not the size. What the government was now proposing would effectively gain them more income and confound those who had avoided the hated window tax. Alex turned the page, scanning the reports of rumours abounding in France of another bloody revolution impending and that the conviction was gaining ground that, after all, a monarchial regime was best fitted for the Frenchman! He snorted irritably. Damn French! They didn't know what they did want, that was their trouble!

Throwing down the newspaper which was difficult to manage with one hand anyway, he sighed and turned to look through the rain-spattered window, staring out at the dismal scene beyond it. The trees were swaying, sodden and leafless in the heavy drenching rain, bending away from the force of it and the whole valley was a vague, grey-misted shadow, dark patches merging with pale; the garden, the fells and the sky absorbed into one another with no line to say where one ended and another began. He could hear the children above him, bickering fiercely over some childish grudge, their restless energy compelled to quietness, as they had been for more than two weeks now, in the tedious routine into which they were forced by the weather. There was a crash and a howl of rage and the quick footsteps of Miss Crawford, or was it Faith as they raced to separate the bored and fretful, no doubt battling figures of his sons, and he vowed impatiently that he would see to it that Christy moved them all back to the room they had occupied when he had first become incapacitated. He had no need of livening up now!

He sighed again, bored himself and filled with the same energy, the edgy restive need to be up and doing something which had assailed him ever since he had regained the use of his arms. He had savoured it then, spending it in the strenuous exercises he and Jacky McCabe had devised to strengthen his shoulders and back – but now, again, he was compelled to loll about and do nothing but read and look out of the window at the damned rain. He remembered his plans just before he broke his arm to get up the carriage and have himself lifted into it, and be taken up to Conistone to see what the devil had been done with his mine, and to Elterwater and the gunpowder mill beside it. He smiled grimly at his own eternal confidence and at the devilish fate which would keep coming at him just when it appeared he was regaining his equilibrium, knocking him sideways again with a gleeful grin.

There was another shout of rage from upstairs and both he and his old dog which dozed at his side looked up at the ceiling. What in damnation were those young hellions doing up here, and why was not that woman who was supposed to have them under control rousing herself to stop them doing it? They had spent an exhausting half hour with him that morning, one which he had been happy to see ended, for it seemed the boys were like live firecrackers with the unconsumed buoyancy which had no outlet but in shouting and fighting and teasing one another – and him – to distraction! Johnny was still confined to his own room, deemed not yet strong enough to mix freely with his two boisterous younger brothers, but John carried him down to see his father and the two 'invalids', as Alex sardonically called them, had read the boy's books for a while and chatted amicably man to man, on Johnny's future guardianship, with his brothers, naturally, of his father's business.

'But I will be the master, won't I, father?' the boy asked forcefully, his eyebrows drawn together fiercely at the foolishness of Joby or Harry arguing the point.

'You are the eldest, Johnny, but you and your brothers will share equally what will one day be yours. That is only fair.'

'But they are smaller than me!' the boy said indignantly. Mutinous lips pouted, blue eyes glowed wilfully and the jaunty white bandage was pushed to the back of his black curls. He was the eldest and the biggest and had he not been poorly and must be treated with due care and consideration, his expression said; but when his father drew him on to his lap – and with none to observe it for he was five now – he relaxed peacefully enough in the circle of the strong arm, careful not to hurt the damaged one. He had fallen into the deep, child-like sleep of the very young shortly afterwards and had not awakened when John came to carry him back to his own bed.

Alex sighed again, watching the rain run down the window. 'What a bloody miserable day,' he said out loud and as he spoke they burst into the room with the force of a small explosion, a dozen or so it seemed, filling it with a milling, murmuring urgency of people all intent on speaking at once, and without the decency to warn him of their entrance with even the most perfunctory knock on his door! The dog leaped instantly to his feet, his fur bristling, his tail drooping between his legs and began to bark nervously.

'What the devil . . . ?' he began indignantly, his heart already leaping in his chest in the most alarming way. 'What in God's name are you about, the lot of you? Has the world come to an end? Bursting in here without so much as a . . .' Faith was there and Mrs Longworth. John with his face all agog and Jack . . . Jack, hovering on the threshold, and water from his greatcoat which he had not thought to remove dripping all over Mrs Buchanan's beautiful pale mushroom carpet, his face working fearfully, his eyes filled with something Alex did not care for!

Faith, now that she was in, seemed unable to speak though her mouth opened and closed in an effort to, and behind her, Jack . . . sweet Jesus . . . *Jack* who never left Christy's side . . . never . . . never . . . dear God . . . surely not . . . ?

His brain refused to function at all as his senses told him something was badly wrong and he was afraid to let it try, afraid to word the question he knew he must ask, for he was terrified of the answer they would give him. He was not awfully certain he could stand another body blow. Not after . . . not after Johnny.

'Johnny . . . ?' he said though he knew, of course, that it was not his son. His voice cracked and he had to swallow hard to bring a drop of moisture to his tongue. 'Not . . . not . . . Johnny . . . ?'

No, not Johnny . . . then . . . Oh dear God, let it not be . . . he could not bear it . . . could not bear it if . . .

Faith came to life then and ran across the room, kneeling down beside his chair. She could see in his face the desire to relapse into the shrinking shell of protection in which he had dwelled for so many months. Christy had dragged him from it and he had fought it himself, like a tiger he had fought the crippling blows which had felled him but if he was to slip away from them now, weakened as he had been by his son's injury and what he considered his own blame for it, might they ever get him out of it again? And what of Christy then?

Casting class and respect for one's betters to the wind she took his uninjured hand in hers, clutching it desperately, looking up into his stricken face, her own a pure alabaster white, her eyes wide, moist, staring in horror at the pictures which were in her mind. She had two brothers who were miners. Though she did not see them often she was well aware of the dangers in which they worked, and when the rains came as they had done for the past fortnight the danger was increased a hundredfold!

'Mr Buchanan, listen to me, please sir.'

Alex Buchanan stared at her wordlessly, his eyes a pale, misted blue.

'Sir, it's Mrs Buchanan ... Christy ... oh please listen ...'

'Christy ...' His voice was agonized.

'Yes sir, we don't know what to do ...' And what can he do, her anguished heart asked as she looked into his ravaged face. He cannot stand, nor can he dash up to the mine and give the necessary orders which would bring his wife from her strong-headed wilfulness, from the peril her own determination had put her in, bring her home, safe and unbroken. She bent her head to his flaccid hand and her tears fell warmly across it and she felt a sudden rigidity stiffen his fingers. They flickered spasmodically, like a man with cramp, or pins and needles stretching to ease it and his blue eyes blinked several times as she looked up into his face.

'Sir ...' She tried again. 'It's Mrs Buchanan ... Christy. She's up at the mine, sir. Some chap fetched her from the mill saying there was danger and Jack drove her there, but he didn't know she was going underground or he wouldn't have taken her up there, would you, Jack?'

Jack sprang forward darting to his master's side, not

really caring if he should be blamed as long as *someone* did *something* about his mistress. He wished now he had used force to restrain her. He and that young miner could have held her back but she was so ... so ... well, the word that came to mind was masterful, if you could describe a lady as masterful!

'Sir ... I'm sorry, but I had to come ... I had to leave her ... up there ... I didn't know what else to do. If you could just tell me ... tell me how to go about it, I'll take Miles and John ...' He turned to the groom who nodded vigorously, certain that if Mr Buchanan would just give them the word, tell them the action needed, he and the other two would have her out in a trice. 'We've never been underground, have we, John, but we'll do it if you'll tell us how.'

'Mr Buchanan!' Faith's voice was frantic. 'Your wife is in great danger! Christy has gone below at the mine! Look out of the window.' She turned his head roughly between her two hands. 'Look at the rain. You are a miner, sir, an engineer. It has been raining like that for two weeks! Can you not imagine what it will be like underground? They say there is danger. I don't know what unless it is the pumps but you are needed, Mr Buchanan. Christy needs you!'

'Christy is underground.' His voice began to vibrate about the room, hurtling itself quite violently against the walls as his formidable anger began to grow.

'Yes sir.' Faith's voice said she was willing to be blamed if he should care to accuse her but for God's sake, do something!

He turned again to look out of the window and his eyes wandered about the misted valley as though to find some landmark he could recognize. Suddenly his eyes sprang to vivid life, to the deep sapphire blue of life and his face became contorted as he saw, *really saw* the lashing rain which flung itself at his window.

'Dear God, what ... what the bloody hell is she ...

thinking of? Who . . . who allowed her to do this insane thing . . . ?'

'*You did, Alex Buchanan!*' Faith's voice was hard, like a steel sword and the words cut away the remainder of Alex Buchanan's confusion, and Mrs Jackson was treated to a roar which lifted her a foot in the air, and down in the kitchen the maids cowered back against walls and tables for they all knew Alex Buchanan as once he had been, and Jack's garbled tale of Mrs Buchanan being underground which he had flung at them as he raced across the kitchen had brought their master back again it seemed.

The children heard it and as one they edged nearer to Miss Crawford and she gathered them about her knee at the nursery fire not knowing what had happened in this unconventional household, but determined at all costs to protect her young charges from it, encouraging them brightly to raise their voices in 'Three blind mice' and 'Jack be nimble, Jack be quick', straining her ears for signs of further commotion.

He was in the carriage within half an hour, his face white with pain, his bottom lip bitten through and bleeding as Jack and Miles, clumsy in their haste – in his haste – knocked his broken arm against the carriage door as they lifted him in.

Though he blanched in agony he had insisted on being warmly dressed for he knew he would be no good to anyone if he froze to death on the mountain side. His trousers and boots were easy enough though his lifeless legs and feet had shrunk somewhat, and the tearful Mrs Jackson had been compelled to put two pairs of thick socks inside his boots to hold them on his feet.

'Strap my arm across my chest,' he commanded Jack through gritted teeth, 'then put on my warmest shirt and a thick coat. No, leave the bloody shirt sleeve to hang down, man. I cannot get me arm in it can I? And the same with the coat. Now, my big greatcoat, Mrs Jackson. Which big greatcoat? The one I wear for riding, you fool! Oh, of course, you have never seen me ride, have you?' He snarled

624

ominously and Faith ran to get it for his temper was ugly. He looked as though he would strike anyone who might hold him up for one moment longer than necessary, and the bleached look of pain was washed with the red tone of his desperation to be dressed and on his way. His head turned constantly to the window, watching the rain whipping against it.

The dog shrank back behind his chair, terrified to mute silence by the unaccustomed multitude which surged about the room, and modesty and embarrassment were cast aside as they all ran hither and thither to their master's orders, eager to help at this moment of crisis.

'Warm blankets,' he bellowed, 'and tell Mrs Avery I want plenty of her good hot soup made up, and one of you is to fetch it up to the mine every hour. There will be men who need it. When you have got me up there -- how? -- I'll tell you how, boy, when the time comes . . . but for now you concentrate on getting me to Conistone.'

Jack stood up bravely to Mr Buchanan's snarling venom for was it not all his fault? His master put out his good hand to his and grasped it fiercely, and though he said nothing Jack knew he was being told he had done the right thing and was being thanked.

'Now take one of the horses for I shall need a messenger. You ride it over and Miles can drive me with John. You might be able to get across country on the roan. He was a good animal . . . still is, is he? Good!' He grinned without humour. 'Good lad and we shall need ropes to get me up and a pulley. We must have the carriage up there as well to bring Mrs Buchanan back in . . . oh and put in some warm clothes for her, will you Faith . . . you have done . . . good lass. Now fetch the horse to the front and ride beside me, Jack. I might have some instructions and I shall need you to get about . . . we don't know who we might need. No, you cannot come, Faith . . .'

'I shall walk over then, sir.'

'Dammit woman, you cannot hang about at the mine in this. It's no fit place for a female.'

'No sir, but Christy might need me.' Faith's expression was patiently respectful, but determined.

He was curiously gentle as he put out a hand to her.

'You were right, you know, Faith. It is my fault and you shall ride in the carriage with me. We *all* need you! Now fetch that chair, Miles,' he shouted to the groom, 'and put it in the carriage. No, not that one you damned fool, my chair, with the straps, I shall need it at the mine. Yes, the one I use in the garden with the canopy and wheels. My God, man, are you deaf or something?'

They were gone, disappearing into the shadow of the rain before Mrs Jackson allowed herself the release of a good cry. She drank a cup of tea and her hand fondled the head of the dog, his dog, and she spoke through her tears to him for it was the first time he had been parted from him for two years and he, like her, could hardly make top nor tail of it!

There was no lack of strong, willing arms from those men who were not on shift, to help him up the mountain. They were rooted from their cottages, their faces comic in their amazement for many of them had begun to believe he was dead not having seen him for two years and here he was, unchanged, as overbearing as he had always been.

'Carry Mr Buchanan up the hill! Bloody hell, is this some kind of a joke?' they asked one another, eyeing his useless legs and the chair he sat in; but their eyes gleamed in satisfaction through the curtain of rain when they saw him strapped in it for there was nothing more certain from the look in his eye than that Mr Richard Forbes was going to get his 'come-uppance' and by gum, they wouldn't miss that for the world. They almost fought with one another for the privilege of lifting him on to the wagon, chair an' all and there were dozens of pairs of brawny shoulders to push and pull it up the rain-soaked, slippery track which led to the mine. He was overwhelmed with offers of blankets from women who probably owned no more than one or two to keep their children warn – and but for the danger his own wife was in he would have enjoyed every spirited, energy-filled moment of it. When he had got her out and safe by his side, he told them, for by now word was everywhere of Mrs Buchanan's foolhardy but brave attempt to champion their cause, he would stop by and have a cup of tea with them so best keep the kettle boiling!

They cheered him as the wagon began its perilous journey to the top.

It took almost an hour to manhandle it to the level site where the mine was situated. One man slipped and almost certainly broke his ankle and was carried down the hill again – complaining fretfully that he was going to miss it all – by two reluctant miners, disinclined to forfeit the fun when Mr Forbes came face to face with his employer. There were steep, wet-slicked ridges of rock to traverse. The slope was so slippery that Mr Buchanan devised a clever system of rope and pulley, using the rocks as a fulcrum to heave up the wagon since there was no purchase for the men's boots on the glass-like slope. Half of them pushed, the other half pulled and Alex could feel the jagged pain of his broken arm slice through the top half of his body and knew that the half-healed fragile bone had snapped again. His face was white but the rain washed the sweat away from it as rapidly as it formed.

The box which contained the blankets fell off the wagon at one dramatic moment, tipping over and over as it fell down the slope on which they had just come and two men were forced to go down again to fetch it.

Along their route were men and children, all heaving and pushing in unison though none actually touched the wagon as Mr Buchanan was inched up the mountain side. They shouted encouragement, instructions, all eager to help, all wet through to their skins, their faces shining with the rain, their eyes blinking rapidly in order to be able to see through it, their rough caps plastered to their skulls. Many of the children were without shoes, a sight Alex had never seen in his mine, and he felt the rage boil steadily in the centre of his body at what had been done to his mine and his people – and most of it was directed at himself!

The great resounding cheer which echoed ringingly about the dressing sheds, the crushing and stamping mills, flinging itself from felltop to felltop, as the cavalcade reached the office brought Mr Tate scurrying across the threshold, a vast umbrella held over his head, his face a mask of consternation for this was twice in one day he had been surprised by a visitor and what was afoot now, his doubtful expression said.

His eyes rose to the king-like figure on the wagon. Though he was wet through, like all the other men who had borne him and the weight of the wagon up the hill, there was no mistaking the imposing, vigorous full-blooded man who glared down at him from his throne-like chair, and Mr Tate's voice came out in no more than a squeak.

'Mr Buchanan, sir!'

'Aye,' his employer growled, 'the same and I'd be obliged if you would direct me to the mine shaft, and arrange for some experienced men to go below and fetch up my wife. I believe she has gone in search of Richard Forbes so he can come up as well while they are about it!'

Alex Buchanan's coal black hair, the streak of grey darkened by the rain, curling in a thick, wet mass above his fiercely blue eyes, was brushed back with an impatient hand and none saw the arrow of pain pierce him as the movement jolted his broken arm. His uncompromising jaw was set hard as granite, and his shoulders were hunched powerfully beneath the double caped greatcoat he wore and Mr Tate wondered agonizingly on how he could have been so misinformed on the state of his employer's health.

'Oh indeed sir.' He turned to the group of men who stood in an admiring circle about their master. 'See, you . . . Barnes, Sharples, Watson, get your gear and go down to Crossbarrow . . .'

'*Crossbarrow!*' Alex Buchanan's voice was top heavy with danger. 'Do you mean to say you have allowed my wife to go down to one of the lowest levels in the bloody mine on a day like this? Good God, man, if it's not already flooded it soon will be. Quick . . . quick . . . men . . .' his voice became urgent, '. . . get down there . . .'

'She's been gone two hours, sir. They'll not catch her now but she's got Denny and Jack Cooper with her so she'll be safe enough.'

A slight, well-shawled figure stepped up to the wagon and raising her voice to be heard above the drumming of the rain on the wagon bottom she shouted up to Alex Buchanan.

'They are my brothers, sir. She'll be safe with them.'

Alex Buchanan looked down into Faith Adams's face and their eyes linked in a passionate prayer to some unknown god that she was right.

CHAPTER FORTY

They were down to the fifty fathom level, three hundred feet below the surface when Christy became aware of the bent, stumbling figure of the miner who came hurrying along the tunnel towards them, the tiny star of his candle travelling ahead of him in the thick grey murk of the darkness. There were other candles plastered at intervals to the rock face along the level, dim flickers which hardly broke the gloom, beckoning to her to quicken her pace and she felt a breathless urge to run and when she reached the pale pool of light, the same anxious compulsion to linger there before hurrying through the stretch of inky blackness to the next. She could feel the earth above her press down menacingly to her bent head and defenceless back. The walls of the tunnel swayed inwards with a definite lurch the further she moved along it and the small pinpricks of reflected light in the eyes of the unseen creatures which hovered at the edge of her vision and rustled, angrily she thought, about her booted feet brought a silent moan of thankfulness to her throat that she was not wearing a skirt!

The man stopped in surprise when he saw them.

'Denny! Jack! What the bloody hell are you two doing down here? I thought you were on the next shift and who's this lad with you?' He peered for a second into Christy's face then turned back to the two men, too concerned with his own problem to wonder at the oddness of it and did not even wait for Denny's answer.

'I'm away up top to find Forbes. There's water coming through the shot holes at the sixty fathom level, Denny. That's only ten fathoms below this so I'm off to tell that bugger that if he doesn't . . .'

'Mind your language, Pat,' Denny said abruptly and Christy had to smile at his insistence upon the niceties even in these strange circumstances. The miner stopped, surprised and turned to look at their three faces in turn.

'This is Mrs Buchanan I have with me, Pat,' Denny said awkwardly.

'Mrs Buchanan! Aah, give over, Denny. This is no time for bloody jokes, man. You didn't see Forbes as you came down did you? If water's breaking through, them poor bastards below must come up or they'll be done for, but I'll have to get his bloody permission to fetch them up. Them pumps'll not take the added strain with all this rain we've had. It's beginning to back up the shaft and if that happens it'll spread along the levels and the drainage adit on this tunnel is not enough. We're three hundred feet below the surface here but them on Winderbank and Crossbarrow are lower still, and must be brought up and I'll bloody well tell him so an' all. He looked at them an hour ago and said they were safe and we'd to get on with heading out. A bit of "leakage", he said, and it would be safe to blast but I tell you, lad, I don't like it and I shall tell him to his face. I'm foreman of the gang and . . . well . . . I thought I might find him along here. Geordie Perkins said he heard him say he was to take some "bargain" men up to the horse level. Did you see him?'

'No, he's not gone by us, Pat. Mrs Buchanan wants a word with him and I brought her along to show her the state of the timber he bought to build the "bunnin" . . .'

The miner tilted his candle in the direction of Christy's face, but his eyes were captured suddenly by the rounded curve of her breast, and neat waist above the soft flare of her hips, eternally female even when dressed in Denny Cooper's clothes and he fell back awkwardly, touching the peak of his cap. His face, already strained, became grim and it was very evident that on top of the worrying problem he had to carry to Richard Forbes, the idea of a woman below ground did not appeal to him. Some of the men considered it to be bad luck, but even the less doubtful knew it would do no good to have to deal with the feminine inclination to faint or have hysterics, when the bloody mine was in such a state of disorder. There were men falling through their own 'bunnins', the structure on which they stood to 'head out' the roof above their heads and which must be strong enough not only to support the man's weight but the debris which accumulated upon it. There were men up to the tops of their boots in water at the Winderbank level and God alone knew what depths they worked in at Crossbarrow.

'Mrs Buchanan,' he mumbled disapprovingly, his face truculent and Christy was tempted to draw him on one side and question him on the state of the levels he had climbed to get here, but he had an important message to deliver and he could not stop to talk to her.

'Good day, Mr . . . er . . .' she said and her teeth were all he could see in the pasty blur of her face.

'Todd, ma'am,' he said.

'. . . Mr Todd. Please, go on and find Mr Forbes and if you do, tell him Mrs Buchanan is going down to the Crossbarrow level to see for herself the conditions the men are working in and . . .'

'Bloody hell, Mrs Buchanan . . . I'm sorry, ma'am . . . but you can't do that!'

Pat Todd's face was almost invisible in the gloom,

nevertheless it expressed his horror that a lady, the owner's wife even if she was dressed like a 'navvy', should go down to the lower workings when the mine was so dangerously near to flooding. It was unthinkable and he said so forcibly. He was an older man, almost forty and had worked in the Buchanan Mine for twenty-eight years of his life. He knew every adit and arch, every branch and cross course and fathom of these workings as well, if not better than Mr Buchanan himself. He was down here every day, unlike Mr Buchanan who only went below to do sampling or in an ermergency, and his memory was constantly fortified as he moved to his bunnin and he did not need to rely on plans of the workings as his employer did. His father had been a 'pit man', looking after the pumps and shafts and Pat Todd knew these as well. He had heard the 'Old Men', all the miners of former times who had died and were supposed now to live in this ground they once had worked.

But Mrs Buchanan, it seemed, though extremely polite, cared nought for this, turning away in the direction of the shaft and the iron ladder which would allow her to climb down to the next level.

'I must, Mr Todd. There is no one else to report to my . . . my husband.'

'I can do that, Mrs Buchanan. I can tell Mr Buchanan exactly what is going on in these mines, but first, let me find Mr Forbes and let him know about the increase in the amount of water coming in. He must get those men to the surface before . . .'

'Is there real danger, Mr Todd? In the workings?'

'Indeed, ma'am. In fact I've half a mind to go back and fetch the men out and Forbes can fire me if he must . . .'

'I have the authority, Mr Todd, and you must go back and bring those men out and you shall not be fired!'

'You, ma'am?' Clearly Pat Todd was bewildered for like all the men with whom she had done business or come across in her working day – whether they were at managerial level or the lowest labourer in her father's mill –

they just could not take seriously the order given by a woman.

'Yes, Mr Todd. In the absence of my husband, I am in charge!'

'Well . . .' Pat Todd was dubious and Denny Cooper took her arm, shaking it quite roughly in his agitation.

'Come on, Pat, let's get those men out. Jack can take Mrs Buchanan back to the engine shaft and lead her up. Look man, if it's as bad as you say it is the sooner we . . .' He stopped suddenly and with the exact same turn of their heads the three men froze in a listening attitude. From somewhere below came the sound of a faint thump and in the strangest way the air about them lurched, moving in a manner which took Christy by surprise. It was as though it had reversed, moving away from her in the direction of the shaft down which they must go to reach the lower levels.

She turned to look enquiringly at Denny, the small flicker of fear the noise had aroused in her quivering like a feather at the base of her spine.

The three men stood like rocks, rigid, held in a dreadful paralysis.

'Oh dear sweet Jesus . . . oh Jesus . . . Denny . . . Jack . . . Dear God . . .' Pat's voice was barely audible.

'What is it, Mr Todd? What was that noise?' but Mr Todd took her so savagely by the arm she was almost dragged from her feet. He began to run with her, his back bent double to avoid the low roof and she was forced to do the same followed close on her heels by Denny and Jack, the latter repeating the whole time he ran, again and again and again, 'Oh God! Oh God! Oh God!'

'Run lass . . . for God's sake . . . run . . .' Pat Todd screamed and over the high-pitched terror of his voice and the rattling thud of their feet on the rocky ground; over the rustling, squeaking swarm which ran with them, Christy could hear a great swell of sound growing louder and louder. She thought she heard men's voices crying out a long way off but it was only for a second, then all she knew was the terrible approach of something at her back, the clatter of their feet echoing about the tunnel, the great panting, tearing breaths in the agonized throats of the men who forced her along and the excruciating thumping of her own heart. She ran instinctively with her head low, still attached by the arm to Pat Todd's frantic hand but her chest was on fire. The almost total darkness in which they ran – lit only by the occasional glimmer of a candle, their own dropped in the frenzy of panic – frightened her so much she could feel her brain begin to lose its reasoning power, and she was nothing more than a crouching mindless animal, running – as the rats ran, animals too with their instincts for survival far sharper than hers – away from whatever it was that was coming for her. She had only one coherent thought in her head and that was that she was about to fall and drag everyone down with her.

Ahead of them a small group of 'bargain' men were standing indecisively, young miners without Pat Todd's experience and the sixth sense which he had developed in the Buchanan Mine. Even before he and Christy, Denny and Jack reached them he was shouting his warning in a hoarse voice, desperate to get them on the move so that they would not get in the way of himself and his employer's wife. To be held up for a split second might mean the difference between life or death.

'Run lads . . . run, for God's sake. Get going, damn you . . .' as one or two would have begun to question him. 'Get on . . . Mick . . . Ally . . . run . . . run . . . fast as you can . . . run for Christ's sake . . . run . . .'

'But the shaft's the other way, Pat . . . where . . . ?'

'Don't bloody argue . . . we'll not reach it in time, damn you . . . get going . . . run . . .'

Instantly, now that someone was telling them what to do they began to run ahead of Pat Todd but one, a young boy no more than twelve or so, looked back for reassurance to the strong voice of authority, his young unformed face no more than a white shadow amongst the others.

'Run . . . keep going . . . not far . . . run, lads . . . run,' and the boy, his youthful heart filled with thankfulness that God had sent them this leader to tell them what they should do, looked back again and his feet still in the gangling stages of adolescence tripped over one another and he fell with a great cry.

At once, with that inner spark of humanity which divides man from the rats which scuttled along with them, they all stopped to give him a hand up and the first slick of water ran at their feet and in a minute, less, it was up to their knees and they could no longer run but only wade.

'Keep going . . . for Christ's sake . . . keep going, lads, . . . don't stop . . .' Pat Todd's voice urged them on. 'There's a . . . an adit . . . drainage . . . ahead . . . Mick . . . on your right . . . watch out for . . . it.' His voice grated harshly in his throat and his breath came out in agonized gasps as he tried to speak. 'Keep going . . . run . . . Christ, lass, can't . . . you go . . . any faster . . . you're . . . holding up the rest . . .'

Christy could not answer. Her breath rasped in her chest which felt as though a rough, red hot stick was being drawn through it. Every drop of saliva had dried up in her mouth and her heart pumped so furiously she could feel the blood throb in her head, dazing her, beginning to black out the already black density she ran in. But Pat Todd dragged her along and she had no choice but to keep up!

'We're . . . running . . . towards the . . . end of the . . . workings . . . Pat.' Denny gasped. 'There's . . . no . . . way . . . out . . . man.'

'No . . . a rise . . . along . . . adit . . . keep moving . . . lads.'

The water was swirling about their thighs now and the young lad, so full of hope only moments ago when Pat Todd's voice had come to carry him along, began to cry for his Mam, stumbling against the back of the man in front of him.

'Help him . . . keep . . . going . . . here . . . Mick . . . Denny, on your right . . . man.'

'It's an old . . . adit . . . Pat . . . it goes nowhere.'

'There's . . . a . . . rise . . . an old . . . shaft . . . small . . .'

'Oh Jesus . . .'

'Mam . . . Mam . . .'

'Stop talking . . . damn you . . . save your . . . strength . . .'

There were no candles here and Pat Todd took the lead now moving more slowly as he felt his way in the inky blackness towards what it was he sought. He still gripped Christy's numb hand with a ferocity which, had it had any feeling in it, would have caused her to cry out. Her other was in the grasp of Denny Cooper and his stretched to another and in the form of a human chain they stumbled ahead of the water which was rippling smoothly up their bodies.

Christy felt quite detached as shock took over her senses, holding to the one sure thing in a mindless world, Pat Todd's hand, wading much more slowly now as the water, also slower as it began to find its level, but still rising, inched up her thighs.

'Hold on . . . to each other, for God's sake. Don't leave . . . go . . . Denny . . . ?'

'Aye Pat . . .'

'Jack . . . you there . . . ?'

'Yes . . .'

'The rest hang on . . . in a line . . . Is the lad . . . there . . . ?'

'Aye Pat . . .'

'Keep going . . .'

'Mam . . . oh Mam . . . it's so dark . . .'

'Shut up lad, there's a brave boy. You'll . . . see . . . your Mam . . . soon enough.'

The water was up to their shoulders and they could barely struggle against it when Pat found the rise, a shaft driven upwards for some purpose, probably ventilation, sloping away from one blackness into another.

'Here it is . . . lads . . . stand together now . . . Mick, you there?'

636

'Aye Pat . . .'

'Denny, Jack?'

'Aye Pat.'

'Hold the others together. I'm going up. There should be . . . some . . . handholds . . . something to stand on . . .'

'Oh please Mr Todd . . . please . . .'

The boy began to weep dementedly and Christy could feel the line, the hands which held hers, shake like a rope, one end of which is being vigorously twitched, as the boy lost control and made a heave towards the voice of Pat Todd, the only bond he had to the sane world he had known minutes before. He was drowning. The water was up to his chin and the rats, as terror stricken as he and swimming on the surface of the water, brushed against his face and ears, and between the two horrors his young mind began to snap. He struggled, for what he did not know, his mother's arms, the sunlight which he was sure shone above, the safety of his own Mam's kitchen. The hands which held his, wet and slippery in the thick water began to lose their grip and he knew he was beginning to drown, or the rats would get him, and quite simply he recognized that he would only find safety with Mr Todd.

'For Christ's sake, Will . . . hang on. You'll have us all under . . .'

The voice of the man, older but just as afraid, beseeched the youngster to be still, '. . . see I'll put my arm round you, lad . . .'

'Mr Todd . . .'

'I'm here, Will . . . we're all here . . . hang on, hang on and I'll have you out of this water . . .'

'It's the rats, Mr Todd!'

'I know, but they can't follow us up here, lad,' Pat Todd said and the boy believed him, standing quietly now, bravely as the water lapped about his nose. They were all forced to crouch forward, the low roof about them forcing them into positions of supplicants at an altar. Christy stood, her hand still clasped in that of Denny Cooper, the other stretched out to the space where Pat Todd had gone.

Vanished, she might have said, but it takes a visible presence to go about the process of vanishing, and Pat Todd had simply been a hand, an invisible but comfortingly strong awareness that was no longer there at the end of her arm.

After what seemed an eternity but was no more than half a minute Pat Todd's voice sounded hollowly from above her head. She and Denny were in a better position than the others for they stood rather than crouched, cramped together at the foot of the rise but with their heads inside the aperture up which Pat had climbed.

'Come on Mrs Buchanan, step up slowly . . .'

'Never mind bloody slowly, Pat,' a frantic voice gasped. 'For God's sake go on. The lads are about done and . . .' There was a gasp and a blubbering gurgle as water evidently entered the mouth of the speaker and the rest began to surge towards the spot where Christy and Denny stood, pressing her against the rough, slimy surface of the rock face. 'Pat . . . let us get up . . . Oh Jesus . . . Ally!' A man screamed, the scream becoming a strange bubbling sound, like something boiling fiercely in a pot then the scream rang out further away before disappearing, cut off abruptly as Ally sank below the surface of the water.

Christy could feel the panic strike through her numbed terror and like the rest she fought now to escape the confines of the almost flooded drift. There seemed to be a vast multitude at her back, fingers clutching at her clothing, pulling her away from her handhold in the vertical shaft, then strong arms lifted her, pushed her upwards, slamming her against the raw wall of the rise and a hand came down and fastened urgently in her hair. She was dragged upwards, her own hands clawing at the rough flint, her feet desperately toeing the wall for purchase, her hair, she was convinced in her agony, tearing slowly from her scalp, then she was out of the water and pressed close to Pat Todd.

'Come on, lass . . . keep going alongside me. Put your

hands on either side of you to hold yourself steady and feel with your feet for a hold. Denny . . .'

'Aye Pat?'

'You coming up?'

'Aye . . .'

'And the rest . . .'

'Following . . .'

Inch by inch, her face pressed close to that of Pat Todd, her breast to his chest, their legs moving together, their feet finding the same small, thankfully dry ledges to step on, they moved up through the Stygian darkness. From below came the sounds of men struggling to escape the rising water, scrambling to find a foothold, a handhold in the narrow cramped enclosure, their hands torn and bleeding, their faces grazed against the jagged, broken surface of the adit. There were curses and weak tears and Will called constantly for his Mam, out of his head now with shock and fear.

Up and up they went and Christy could feel the cold and tremors of utter exhaustion ripple through her body. Pat Todd could feel it too and his voice murmured on and on, like a mother comforting a sick child.

'There now . . . that's right, lass . . . just a bit more . . . put your foot next to mine . . . feel around . . . there . . . your hands here . . . feel my arm and follow it along with your hand . . . there see . . . can you lean back a bit . . . good lass . . . I've got you . . . just a bit more . . . lean back again or you'll have me down . . . another step . . .'

He was quite astonished when she asked him very politely, just as though they strolled together in a grassy park, where they were going and if they were nearly there, Mr Todd? He wondered himself, for in truth as far as he knew this rise had been abandoned after being stoped out for a length of about thirty feet, but if they could find a working where the vein had been cut away between levels, or a natural cavity with a bit of level ground off the rise they could at least get out of this narrow shaft and rest and when the water subsided as it should when the rain stopped, and surely to God it must soon, they might then get down again to the adit and find their way out. The level they had come along was a drainage level so it followed that it emerged somewhere on the mountain side. None of them would survive for long clinging to the sides of this shaft for as tiredness overcame them they would simply drop off, probably taking other men with them, and drown.

Pat Todd could feel the difference around him even before his head rose above the lip of the ledge – it could be no more than that – to his right and he breathed a thankful sigh of relief. Please God it was big enough and flat enough to allow them to get out of the rise and rest themselves. It was black as hell. He could feel the darkness press against his straining eyes but all they needed for the moment was to be able to sit, or lie, to huddle any way they could in a bit of flat space until he had time to work out in his mind where they were and how to get out of it.

'Here we are, lass,' he said cheerfully.

'What is it, Mr Todd?' she asked, polite as a young matron at afternoon tea and he knew she was deep in shock.

'It's a bit of a rest for us, that's what it is, so if you lift yourself up over my shoulders . . . that's right . . . I've got you. Put your hands on the ledge . . . can you feel it . . . good . . . good . . . now . . . can you get on to it?'

'Yes, thank you, Mr Todd. What should I do now?'

'Don't move, lass. Just stay there until I'm up beside you and I'll have a look . . . or rather a feel . . .' he laughed quite merrily, '. . . a feel around.'

'Very well, Mr Todd.'

By God, she's a rare one, Pat Todd had time to think as he levered his way up beside her. She was not used to underground as were the rest of the men with the exception of young Will, and yet not a bloody peep out of her apart from 'Yes Mr Todd, no Mr Todd', and to thank him for his help and all in a darkness which would frighten the strongest man. He was preoccupied with discovering how wide the ledge was, would it hold all the men? . . . how many were there? . . . he had been running too fast before the candles went out to count, and if it would not, how was he to arrange the men who would be forced to remain jammed in the rise?

'Are you there, Denny?'

'Aye Pat.' And there was another steady one! Always just there, making no fuss, waiting for orders and carrying them out with the calmness of a man digging his own vegetable plot.

'Everybody in the rise?'

'All except Ally.'

'Aah . . . yes.' He cleared his throat. 'How many, lad?'

'I don't know Pat. Mick's the last one and he's still got his legs in the water.'

'Ask them to shout out their names will you, Denny?'

There were eight men, now that Ally had drowned, and the boy, Will, and they were hanging quite literally by their fingernails to a sloping rise no more than three feet in diameter. They had a slight advantage in that the shaft was on a slight incline and Pat Todd thanked the miners who had stoped it out for had it been perfectly vertical the men could not have climbed it without a ladder, nor clung on as they were doing.

He made a great effort to sound quite ordinary, matter of fact, as though this happened every day of his working life and it would all be over at the end of the shift.

'Right, I'll just have a look round here, Denny, then you can start bringing them up.'

'As quick as you like, Pat,' a voice gasped from the darkness. 'Bloody rats have taken a fancy to my boots and if they get those off me . . .'

'Now then, lad . . . we'll have none of that . . .' Pat said sternly for the voice of young Will began to shout even louder for his Mam. 'Just a few more minutes and then we'll all be tucked up snug as you please.'

Christy felt the man beside her move away and the sudden space he left behind terrified her. She wanted to

641

shout for her Mam, as Will was doing. She had nothing with which to identify. She was like an unborn child in a womb, attached not even to the umbilical cord. There was darkness, a murmur or two from the rise but she felt as though she was in an empty void, a space which had no roof, no sides, only the square scrap of rock on which she knelt. Her eyes stared into the blackness, blinking rapidly, instinctively, in an effort to pierce it but there was nothing, nothing!

It did not take Pat Todd long to explore their tiny island of refuge and in a matter of seconds he was back at her side, a warm, living, solid mass, giving her a sense of being Christy Buchanan again, a vulnerable piece of flesh but there nevertheless.

'It's only small, lad,' Pat said cheerfully, 'so we'll have to take turns. You come up, Will, and sit beside Mrs Buchanan here and keep her company while the rest of us sort out this . . . this shift' – they'd understand that – 'that's what it'll have to be, four of us on and four off, an hour at a time. We'll easily manage that, won't we, and then when that bloody water . . . beg pardon, Mrs Buchanan . . . has gone down we'll be away to a good hot bowl of "crowdy" and what a tale you'll have to tell your Mam, then, eh Will?'

The boy was brought up by means of passing him over the precariously balanced bodies of his mates until he reached the ledge. He hitched up eagerly beside Christy, like one small animal to another, or perhaps with that instinctive childlike need which reaches out for what is female, mother, woman, and she put her arm about him without thinking, as he accepted it without thinking. It seemed that none of them had as yet become aware that they were in the strange company of Mrs Alexander Buchanan!

Jack Cooper, Christy, Will, Pat and a man called Alfie Kitchen were able to sit with their backs to the rock face, shoulder to shoulder, their feet hanging over the rim of the narrow shaft. The remaining four men, Denny, Mick

Ramsgill, Freddie Bull and Peter Whittam inched their way up the rise laying their backs on the sloping side and clinging like terriers with their knees, their elbows, their shoulders, their very eyelashes to stay where they were above the swirling water beneath. Pat prayed that it would come no higher for if it started to rise up the shaft he knew he could not steady the panic which would start for there was nowhere else to go and they would all perish.

'When will they come for us, Mr Todd?' Will asked presently, calm now with the feeling of security the soft arm of the lady gave to him, not even wondering on who she was or how she came to be here to comfort him.

'When they can, lad.'

'Should we not make some noise so that they know where we are, Mr Todd?' Christy asked with her scrupulous politeness and Pat Todd was again astonished.

'You're right, lass. You begin and then Will can carry on and we'll take it in turns. Feel around for a bit of rock and knock it against another. That's right, good lass.'

'This will do. Put me down here, Miles, just by that engine shaft.'

'Shall I get something to cover your head, Mr Buchanan?' Jack said anxiously as he and Miles lowered the chair to the bedded down spoil which had been spread about the mine head to soak up the water and mud which surrounded it. The rain had not let up in the ten minutes it had taken them to manhandle his chair across the quaggy track from the office to the pit shaft, and it fell now on to Alex Buchanan's bare head, on to the caped shoulders of his greatcoat and the rugs which had been spread uselessly it seemed across his legs. He could feel it gather and trickle down inside the neck of his shirt and run from his dripping hair and into his eyes – but nothing on God's earth would make him leave this spot where he would see her come from the mine and walk towards him. Dressed in Denny Cooper's working clothes, he had been told, God damn her for a rebellious, awkward bitch and if it was the last thing he did he would tie her to his chair and never let her out of his sight again for he loved her, adored her, worshipped her – and he'd fight her lovely spirit with everything he had to offer of himself until she loved him in return, for without her he could not live.

'They won't be long now, Mr Buchanan,' an old miner said to him and he turned, surprised to see there was a crowd, getting on for a hundred or so men, women and children, to share his vigil at the back of his chair. Waiting, it appeared, to see this extraordinary woman who had put on the working clothes of one of their own and gone down into their environment to tackle the man who had for the past six months slowly ground them down to the status of slaves in his obsession to get as much ore as possible out of the ground to line his own pockets. The multitude grew all the time and beside him Faith put out a hand to his shoulder and smiled, and he felt her comfortable presence soothe him as it had soothed his wife and his sons.

There seemed to be some kind of a commotion coming from the horse level entrance and he felt a warning prickle at the back of his neck. The hair rose there slowly and he lifted himself up in his chair by his arms, ready if it was necessary to spring up and run to his love and then a man erupted from the mine, his mouth a great gaping hole from which words poured, his eyes great staring pits of horror, his arms reaching out, his legs pumping frantically as he rushed – where? – he did not know or care as long as someone took the dreadful message from him.

The crowd stilled for an anguished moment, its breath held on a dread which always lives in the hearts and minds of those who send their men into the dangerous passages of the earth, and above that horrified calm came the word to devastate them.

'*Flood.*'

Alex distinctly felt his heart stop in his chest and for one devastating moment he was tortured by the consciousness that he was about to have a seizure and because of it his

Christy would die too; for he knew unequivocally that there was only one man amongst this assembly who could bring her out and that man was himself. It was but a fraction of aching desolation as his heart missed its beat and then it surged again, banging and heaving against his ribs and it sent ripples of terror through his entire body and he wanted to cry out, as Faith was doing and all the other women who were milling about and clutching at one another, for not only he had someone who was loved in the mine. Christy, his Christy was there. Christy who had admitted to him that she was afraid of the subterranean honeycomb of tunnels which lay beneath the huge mass of mountain, afraid of the dark and the rats, and yet had put on a miner's outfit and bravely gone down in his place to investigate what had been reported to her. She was there now, struggling perhaps in the torrent of water which would fill the labyrinth below with the force and speed of the surging waters which came down from the hills each year when the spring thaw unlocked the winter snows; perhaps already dead, her fiery spirit quenched, her lovely body still and lifeless and if it was so he simply could not bear it. If it was so he would die as well for what was there left?

Alex Buchanan's voice exploded over all other sounds.

'Where?'

The man turned to him, tripping, falling on his knees in the mud, picking himself up and flinging himself to the foot of Alex Buchanan's chair. He seemed to find nothing unusual in seeing his employer, after two years, sitting at his ease at the head of the mine shaft, and with the intuitive reaction of one who knows he is speaking to the right man began to tell him what was happening in his mines. Other men flung themselves from the shaft, hurtling up the iron ladder and into the open air like jack in the boxes, making just as instinctively for the man in the chair, their mouths working on the narrow escape they had had, on the swift and horrifying rise of the water, on the explosion which surely must have triggered it off in view of what Richard

Forbes had been told. They all spoke at once. Alex's eyes leaped from one to the other and he was surrounded and it was only his ferocious bellow which stopped them.

'Jack!'

'Yes sir?'

'Get some rope and a pulley.'

'A rope and . . .'

'Get me the man who knows what they are if you don't!'

'I know, Mr Buchanan.' A man stepped out of the crowd, an older man similar in strength and demeanour to the trapped Pat Todd.

'Your name?'

'Bobby Fenton, sir.'

'Get what I want and then you and you and . . .' Alex Buchanan turned swiftly, looking round the circle of eager faces, looking for what he needed in the men who would bring his wife back to him. '. . . and you, we're going down . . .'

They fell back then and their glances dropped awkwardly — not from fear or sudden disinclination to risk their lives again for their comrades — but because they had become aware in that moment that the man who ordered them around with all the assurance they once remembered of him was a cripple in a wheelchair.

'What the hell's the matter, damn you, are you afraid to go back?'

Instantly they were bristling up to him and the first man, Bob Fenton, spoke up bravely.

''Tisn't that, master, We'll go, all of us, damn quick but there's no way we can take you!'

'Then I'll go myself! I may not be able to walk but I can climb and crawl!'

Horrified, those about him, including Faith, gasped and fell back further, but he caught Bob Fenton's arm in a grip which made him wince and his eyes were a hot blue flame and his mouth snarled like that of a wolf in a trap.

'My wife is down there, Goddammit, and dozens of your workmates, and if you think I'm going to sit up here on my arse and wait for someone to fetch them out you're mistaken, my friend. I know the bloody mine as well as I know my own home and I was born there! I know just what has happened, so I'm going now and I'd be glad of some help but if you won't come with me I'll go alone and you can all go to hell!'

'It's not that we won't come, Mr Buchanan, sir, it's we cannot take you!'

'Is that so!' His voice was poisonous with menace and those who stood near swore flames came from his eyes. 'Well, we'll see about that! Faith . . .'

'Yes sir?'

'Will you help me?' He never took his eyes from Bob Fenton.

'Yes sir, I'll come down with you.'

'I knew you would, lass. I can count on my womenfolk.'

'Nay, Mr Buchanan, that's not fair. You can't take a lass into the mine and you know it.'

'Very well. *You* come.'

'How are we to get you down, sir?'

'My arms are strong. A rope and a few willing men to lower me down . . .'

'And at the bottom?'

'A set of wheels to run on the track. A man to pull it.'

'Well . . .'

'I'm not sitting here arguing with you, man. I know that bloody mine.'

'We all do, master.'

'Then stop blethering and let's get on.'

Bobby Fenton's steady grey eyes looked for a moment longer into Alexander Buchanan's face and saw the raw, naked pain there, and a look passed between them which each understood, then his quiet voice rang out above the crowd.

'Seth, run to the workshop and get a rope and tackle and fetch that set of old wheels.'

'Lift me across to the shaft, Jack . . . Miles . . .'

And Alex Buchanan prepared to go down into his mine for the first time since he had come out of it two years ago, crippled then and crippled now, to fetch his beloved wife.

CHAPTER FORTY-ONE

Peter Whittam was the first to die.

On the first day Pat Todd had wracked his brains on how to stop those men forced to cling in the rise with nothing to support them, from either falling asleep and slipping down into the water below, or simply letting go in sheer exhaustion. The utter darkness, black and impenetrable, had the effect of disorientating them and without their being aware of it their minds slid off into an almost drugged sleep; or their fingers – as if they also could not become used to clinging to something their eyes could not see – simply let go lifelessly and the men dropped like stones, taking others with them. Their terror was heartrending, the strain even in the first few hours almost more than they could bear and though none was lost, the bottom man on the slope each time having the presence of mind to cling to the one who fell, the toll it took on their already stretched nerves was dreadful.

Pat conceived the idea of every man removing his braces and fastening them to his belt, each set of braces attached then to the man above, and one of those 'resting' on the narrow edge gripped those of the highest man in the shaft giving those in it at least an illusion of security, but the problem was that even the men on the ledge were strained to breaking point, inclined to doze off in the solid blackness which held them severed from reality by the lack of sight, of sound, of smell. With only their sense of hearing and touch left to them, they were lost in the clothing darkness, afraid of it, it hid them from each other and the light doze they fell into was a refuge from it.

The water had risen another foot or so and the bottom man on the shaft had the added horror of resting his feet in it and of knowing that, since he had no sense of feeling in them the starving rats could be nibbling his toes and he would be unaware of it. It began to drive them to the edge of madness and they quarrelled violently as to whose turn it was to be there. Pat rotated them meticulously at first, trying to create a sense of fairness but the difficulty in bringing the top man up and sending one down to the bottom, past three others in the narrow space, began to take its toll even on his determined cheerfulness.

The first day, though they of course did not recognize the passing of time, they spent rapping out their whereabouts to their rescuers who they knew would come the moment the level of water began to fall. For a wildly exultant few hours they thought this had begun to happen when Denny noticed that his feet were no longer in the water when he was low man in the tunnel, but it only receded a mere six inches, not enough to allow them to try for the opening of the drainage adit. But, as Pat told them when their spirits sank again, it did mean they had a measure of fresh air.

'It's coming from the opening on the side of the fell, lads. Just think of that! Fresh air coming from the outside! It only needs to fall another foot and we'll be able to swim out,' he rejoiced.

'What about them rats, Mr Todd?' Will asked anxiously.

'They'll be first out, lad, and'll not bother with us.'

They began to shout when the water receded and Will shouted as well, convinced his Mam could hear him somewhere up there where it was bright and sunny. He was cold down here, though the lady held on to him and stroked his hair just like his Mam did when he was poorly. Mr Todd had said she was Mrs Buchanan but Will had not believed him for what would Mrs Buchanan be doing down here with the likes of Will Johnson. A joke, that was what Mr Todd was playing on him, though he admitted to himself he didn't feel much like laughing.

Their clothes would not dry but just the same when he first felt the need to relieve his bladder and had whispered of it to Mr Todd he had been most distressed when he was told to go ahead and get on with it.

'Here?' he whispered.

'Where else, lad?' his leader told him and after that, until his bladder no longer had anything much to empty it didn't seem to matter.

It was Peter Whittam's braces which killed him. It was the end of the second day and he was bottom man in the shaft when it happened. Not surprisingly he had fallen asleep, almost senseless with the cold and with physical and mental fatigue. Those who were in the shaft were already at the limit of their endurance. They were too spent to hold on, too weary to steady themselves and too exhausted to perform the arduous toil of climbing up and down the rise for their spell on the ledge. The weakened leather of his braces was strained beyond the limit of what they had been created for, merely to hold up the weight of his trousers, and when they snapped he was in the water and drowned so silently, only the sudden loss of his weight warned the others.

They did not grieve him, nor even seem to care much now for they were becoming dulled to everything beyond the relief that it was one less weight on the end of the human chain.

'Shall we say a prayer, Mrs Buchanan?' Pat Todd asked politely as though, perhaps as the wife of the owner of the mine in which Peter Whittam had died, she might have some ideas on the procedures of convention at a time like this.

'As you like, Mr Todd,' she answered in the dulled insensibility into which they were slipping.

'I think he was a Methodist.' Perhaps there was a special prayer?

'Was he really?'

'Yes,' and they fell back into the apathy which was only broken now as the bottom man begged to be allowed up and the quite dreadful conjuring with men and belts and braces must be gone through.

Christy stared into the now familiar blackness and tried to create the faces of her children but no matter how much effort she put into it she could not form them properly. She would see a twinkle of shining, glorious blue as Joby's eyes lit up for some anticipated treat and Harry's ebony curls glowed as though burnished by the sun. The cleft in Johnny's chin emerged from the darkness and his audacious grin and now and again she would hear them all laugh, the sound bringing her trembling from the icy cat nap in which she seemed to exist. She would fall back into a troubled state of half awareness and Amy's gentle blue eyes, soft with childish love, smiled at her from her pillow and her sweet rosebud mouth lifted itself for a goodnight kiss and she could feel her boy – which one? – rest against her breast. She stroked his smooth young cheek and her hand brushed back the straight fine hair from the brow of Will Johnson and she jerked awake from her dream again to the nightmare of wakefulness.

They were not thirsty for a small slip of water bled down the rock to Pat's shoulder and they took it in turns to suck at the handkerchief which Mrs Buchanan had kindly provided and which was soaked in the moisture. They were quite incurious as to her presence here with them now, in the time of their greatest drama, too concerned with themselves and how they were to survive, to ponder over the strangeness of this lady in their midst. She was just another human being, another body to be accommodated on the slip of shelf which was their sanctuary.

She dreamed of Alex on the third day, dreamed that he was close, coming closer to hold her safe in his arms and she cried out and wept for him, longing to sink against his strength, to be warm in that safe assurance only he knew how to give her. She sobbed quite despairingly as his quizzical blue eyes surveyed the dilemma she was in, as though to say that it was all her own fault and she had only herself to blame for her folly. Had he not told her a hundred times not to go out alone on the fells, to ride her mare without John or Miles to escort her, and now look where her rebelliousness had landed her, his humorous blue eyes seemed to say. Why had she not stayed at home where she belonged, where he had commanded her to stay, where her children were, where her duty lay? She would not be in this quandary now if she had listened to him and really, could she blame him, he asked mockingly, if he left her to lie in this bed she had made for herself?

'Oh Alex, please don't leave me,' she cried for him, jerking from her delirium to stare widely into the eternal blackness.

'What is it, lass?' the weak voice of Pat Todd asked her and she felt his shoulder against hers. It was just an added pressure really for her body was numbed, still damp from the immersion in the flood water yesterday . . . or was it the day before . . . or . . . a week, perhaps? She had no idea!

'I . . . was dreaming, Mr Todd.'

'Aye . . . me too!' He coughed dryly, the earthy cough with which all men who worked underground were afflicted. 'I was . . . at The . . . Bear . . . having a pint with . . . my lad . . .'

'You . . . have a . . . boy, Mr Todd?' It was no more than the polite rejoinder which she had been brought up to make in conversation, for her mind still seemed to be functioning at one level automatically, even here.

'Aye . . .' but his voice died away as he slipped into the semi-comatose state in which they all dwelled now.

They had been there four days then!

Two more died that day, from exhaustion, starvation, the cold, who was to tell, hanging on their braces like limp dolls. Pat Todd managed somehow to cut them loose with his penknife, letting them splash quite unfeelingly into the water below before settling down to sleep once more against Mrs Buchanan's shoulder. There were only two left in the rise now, Alfie and Jack Cooper, and within the hour they too slipped silently away, for by now Pat Todd was beyond remembering to change the 'shifts' he had devised and the men were too weak to beg to be brought up, too weak to get themselves up. The fragile link they had with the four on the ledge detached itself from Denny Cooper's slack hand as he fell deeper into the unconscious state they drifted in and out of, and those who remained did not even notice.

She saw Robin then, his brown eyes fixed lovingly on hers, his mouth curling in that way it had when it was about to kiss her and she was a girl again, running through the wood above Elterwater, her hand in his, warm, so warm. He called her name over and over again but somehow her hand slipped out of his, reaching for another, warm as his had been but brown and lean and infinitely stronger. If she could reach it she would be safe, she knew that but tantalizingly it moved away from her stretching fingers and she cried broken-heartedly, tasting the salt lick of her own tears on her dry lips.

It was the sixth time they had lowered him down the endless series of ladders which led past the now unmoving and silent kibbles, to each level as it became accessible and Alex Buchanan knew despairingly that it would be the last. Six days and though the faces of the men about him changed as miners fell exhausted and others came to take their place – except for an occasional hour of nervous sleep snatched when his trembling body could stand no more – he had never stopped, staying at the top of the mine shaft; directing the working of the pump, being lowered into the shaft, being pulled on the small trolley, or carried between two men, up and down each tortuous level and drift, up each shaft and down again, each rise and sole, waiting agonizingly as the water slowly receded from each level, knowing, even as they reached one that those in it must be drowned. They found dozens of men, Richard Forbes amongst them, who had been too late, or too slow, or too dazed by the suddenness of it to escape, bringing them up to the surface where a hundred silent men, women and children waited to claim them.

He had posted a man at every drainage adit on the hillside to watch as the water from the mines poured out with instructions to fetch the rest as soon as it was safe, but though several bodies had been found, trapped as they ran for safety, or carried there by the immense force of flood water, she had not been amongst them. He wanted to be everywhere at once, trusting no one to be as alert as he was, but he knew he was being unfair to them. Many of them had brothers, sons, still underground and were as desperate as himself but still he raged, longing to be in the mine, on the hills, anywhere she might be.

It had stopped raining at last, and he had ordered a huge fire to be lit in the centre of the flat space to the side of the engine shaft. The crowd huddled about it, taking it in turns to watch, sending home an exhausted woman who still waited for the man who did not come, promising they would send for her if . . .

The pumps brought out hundreds of thousands of gallons of water, pouring it down the hillside, manned by a series of pit men, one of them Pat Todd's old father who came creaking up the hill to offer his expertise, for there was none who had known pumps and the shaft which brought out the excess water as he did. Miners came from miles away, from other mines, iron and coal and lead, to offer their help and the numbers swelled and those who watched Alex Buchanan slowly killing himself shook their heads and sorrowed for him – for how could the woman he searched for still be alive, and what kind of woman was she who could kindle such devotion, such agony of spirit in a man like Alex Buchanan. It was two days since they had last found anyone, drowned, of course and that man had been Jack Cooper, poor Mrs Adams's own brother and her already a widow, made so by the mine. He had been caught in a cleft of rock on the fifty fathom level, still half-submerged and today they hoped to search the tunnel, even if they had to wade it but the lower levels were still flooded no matter how fast the water was pumped out.

The crowds had begun to drift away on the fifth day,

women comforting other women whose men were still not found, and only Faith and a handful of men, miners, and Jack Hodson who refused to leave Mr Buchanan's side — no, not even for a rest in the office, he said — remained with him. Bobby Fenton was one.

'Mr Buchanan, sir,' he said gently, looking into the grey, taut, face of his employer and was not surprised when Mr Buchanan failed to respond. Though he had been made to change regularly, irritably, saying he had no time, by Faith who had insisted upon it by the simple expedient of shrieking that if he died of pneumonia none of them would see Christy again, he was dirty, unshaven, his clothes creased and disordered. The man was dreadfully weakened, Bobby Fenton knew, disorientated from lack of sleep, not enough food though the constant supply of Mrs Avery's good hot soup had sustained him somewhat.

'Mr Buchanan, we must give up now,' Bobby Fenton said compassionately.

The piercing, blazing eyes glared up at him then, the flame in them shrivelling him and he fell back alarmed for it was very evident Mr Buchanan was losing his mind. What kind of woman was she, he wondered, that could render a man to such a passion, to such a grinding hazardous belief in his own conviction that she was still alive; that would not let him rest until he had seen her body, that would keep him searching for six days and nights with little rest and go on, even yet, until he had found her? Men who were able-bodied had fallen and still this man who could not even stand up, let alone walk, kept on!

'Give up,' he snarled. 'You give up if you must, Fenton. If you have no stomach to come down again you can fix me up with that hand operated pulley and I'll lower myself into the bloody mine.'

'Mr Buchanan . . .'

Instantly his employer's hand shot out and grasped his, and his face contorted in shame and an expression Bobby Fenton could not identify.

'I'm sorry . . . sorry, man. Forgive me. I . . . you have
. . .' He could not go on for a moment and his hand fell
away to his lap where it clutched desperately on the wool
of the rug which covered his legs. He looked away to the
lightening fells, to where the pale, yellow-gold wash of the
rising sun outlined the great water-wheel, the untidy
sprawl of black rock which would turn to grey in a
moment or two, the lemon-hazed clearness of the fine
autumn morning.

'I cannot believe, you see, that she is dead. That all the
life and vigour, that . . . that passionate conviction, that
hot-headed, warm-hearted emotion is . . . gone. She was
. . . *is* so vital . . . so bloody high-handed she would not
allow herself to be . . . to be . . .'

He turned his head and held out his hand and she was
there, his wife's friend, his friend as she had been for six
days, but for an hour or two of snatched sleep in the office.
She put her hand in his and it was warm and she smiled at
him, the only one who understood though her heart was
filled with sadness.

'She is waiting for me, Faith . . . somewhere. I cannot let
her down. You believe that, don't you?'

'Yes sir.'

'I must go . . . just once more . . .'

'Yes sir.'

'You'll wait here?'

Bobby Fenton lowered his eyes, embarrassed and
strangely moved by such emotion, then he cleared his
throat.

'Very well, Mr Buchanan. We will take you down one
last time. It's nearly a week, sir and we . . . we must come
to a point where it . . . where we know . . . you understand,
sir. The men are experienced miners . . . as you are . . .
and it must be faced.'

His face was pitying and he turned away to hide the
surprising tears which came to his own eyes.

They were down for eight hours, going over every inch
of every level, the twenty fathom, the thirty fathom, the

forty fathom, right down to Winderbank where the water had settled. Scores of men went down that day, more than had ever done so for they had been told that it was to be for the last time until the mine was completely pumped out. They all knew that nothing would be found for where else was there to look? They had searched everywhere, going deeper and deeper, even beyond the horse level where the lowest drainage adit was and under that the mine was below the valley floor and still flooded until the pumps could clear it. They did it in sympathy for the dead-eyed man they brought out as the beautiful October evening fell softly about them. They had found no one. Not even a dead rat and they left him in his chair beside the engine shaft, moving away slowly, looking back over their shoulders, not speaking, their tired grey faces moving awkwardly at the sight of so much pain.

Faith stood beside him, grieving quite terribly for the four people she had now lost in this mine, then she moved away, following the miners, leaving him alone to mourn the woman he loved.

When he was completely alone in the falling dusk he began to weep, putting his good hand to his face, holding the flood of tears in its palm until the sheer force of them washed through his fingers and ran down his wrist, dripping to the rug they had tucked tenderly about him. He rocked back and forth, his grief too great to be borne, his mind bursting in its agony, and yet empty and stagnant for what had he left now to put in it, and her name came to his lips, whispered at first, over and over again, then louder and louder until he threw back his head, the line of his throat arching in torment as he cried out her name.

'*Christy*! *Christy*! CHRISTY!' and his voice echoed about the fells and the men who waited at the office shivered for it was the tortured cry of a lost soul.

She knew she was the only one alive when her senses drifted slowly to the surface of the merciful narcosis into which she fell more and more often as the end drew near. The weight which leaned on her on both sides was heavier somehow, a dead weight and her thoughts wandered a little on the strangeness that she should be the last to die. She sat in the middle with Will on one side of her, the boy who had called out only minutes before – or was it hours, perhaps days – for his mother and on the other was Denny Cooper, drawn up from the rise as the need to stay there was no longer necessary. Four of them there had been left in her last conscious moment, Denny wandering in hallucinations of his baby son, the others quiet, perhaps slipping into death even then and now they were gone.

She spoke their names in the darkness.

'Will?' Her voice was no more than a grating whisper.

'Denny?' There was no answer.

What was the name of the last man? She could not remember and she wept a little for him, for surely it was not right for a man to die with his name forgotten.

Putting out a faltering hand she touched each face in turn, gasping in shock at the icy, rigid flesh which met her trembling fingers and it was then that her numbed brain surged to life, and she began to cry hoarsely for she did not want to die here, alone, already in her tomb. She had tightened the rein on her terror and the paralysing numbness of the horror which had clutched at her in the company of the men, held up by the need to show courage for the boy, the boy who had for a few hours, days, been her boy. She had comforted him, being herself comforted by the performance of it. She had sat shoulder to shoulder with Denny Cooper and Pat Todd and had heard them reassure one another, and her, that when the water went down they would be found and drawn up into the sweet light of day and she had believed them. Two of the men had grappled with one another at the foot of the rise, driven to it by their maddened horror of the rats and the still rising water but they could not be blamed for would she not have done the same if she had been made to hang in space as they had done?

Her harsh weeping seemed to waken Will and he flopped his head into her lap and she began to scream, to edge away from these dead and nestling bodies which surrounded her but panic grew and she beat her fists against the silent stone face of the rock and several pieces fell over the edge of the rim to clatter down its side and crash to the level below.

'Alex!' she screamed. 'Alex . . . Alex . . .' and for a second a breath fanned her cheek, warm and sweet smelling of . . . what was it . . . lavender, verbena? Oh God she was going out of her mind now and she prayed for it to happen quickly so that she was not lucid and could no longer be aware of where she was. If not death then madness for the insane do not know they are insane, nor are they aware of where they are!

She began to scrabble about in the darkness, trying to escape the horror of the three stiffening corpses which leaned so confidingly against her, and her screams grew louder and more anguished and she felt her senses reel and knew that in a moment she would follow the other men into the swirling water at the bottom of the rise.

'Mother . . .' It was the cry all children make as they awake in the terror-filled darkness of the night and as her voice peaked again on the edge of maddened, uncontrollable frenzy, Annie Emmerson touched her gently again on the cheek, her hand warm in the cold darkness and her voice was calm, steadfast, a little impatient with this wayward child of hers, as it had always been.

'Christina . . . stop it, child . . .'

'Mother?'

'It's no good lolling about crying for me, lass. You've only yourself to get you out of this . . .'

'How?'

'Nay, girl, that's for you to find out . . .'

'Mother?'

'Strong you are, Christina . . . remember . . . like the juniper bush? Surviving on the bleak hillside where all the other trees die!'

'Mother . . .'

But there was no one there, of course, only the men who had suffered and died, not as strong as she was, though she could not understand why.

She sat quietly for several minutes and the dead no longer troubled her, only the living called to her from somewhere far off and she knew she must try to get to them. She might die in the waters below but she would die if she remained on this shelf. Before he died Pat Todd had said the flood would recede, that the pumps would slowly take it out, that if the rains stopped the men who manned them would beat the rise of it and that one by one the levels would be exposed. He had gone down a time or two to check, each time returning to say that the water was still up to the roof of the adit and that he would try again but that had been . . . when . . . ? hours ago . . . ? And he had not gone again. They had lost track of time within hours of the flood and she had no idea how long she had been here. She was not hungry so perhaps it had not been long. But then why had all the men died . . . ?

She shook her head in wonderment and felt the apathy creep over her again. It didn't matter really. They were dead and she was alive and . . . and . . . She sighed for she had lost the thread of her thought, regretfully, for it had seemed worthwhile, but really did it matter? She felt quite warm now and sleepy so she would just put her head on Will's shoulder, he would not mind, and go to sleep for a while. Perhaps when she woke up she would remember what it was she had been going to do.

The sound of her own name, harsh and tortured, brought her bolt upright and she felt her heart thump in her breast.

'*Christy . . . Christy . . . Christy . . .*'

'Alex . . . Oh God Alex . . . I'm here . . . here darling . . . Alex . . .'

She sat up eagerly, moving around dangerously to feel the rim of the ledge, dislodging some more small rocks which fell with an echoing clatter to the level below, almost overbalancing herself to peer excitedly down the shaft, looking for the light which would be coming up the adit but there was nothing, only blackness, blackness pressing on her eyeballs . . . and silence!

'Alex,' she screamed again and her voice echoed as the rocks had done as they fell . . . fell . . . fell . . .

She felt the stillness which had settled on her sluggish mind struggle to part the curtain of torpor which veiled it, for there was something there, some memory which demanded to be recalled, something important, vital, if only she could decipher it, a tangible reality which she knew she must recognize if she was to . . . what . . . what was it she wished to do . . . oh God . . . if you are there, her rambling mind begged, help me to fight this dreadful numbness which is preventing me from thinking . . . from . . .

She sat back slowly and her hand fell limply to the rough, rock-strewn edge on which she had lain for all of her lifetime, it seemed, and a tiny pebble was dislodged, chinking down the side of the incline, falling with a sound almost musical as it hit the ground below and it was as if it had rebounded to come flying back to strike her in the face, for in a blinding revelation it came to her!

There was no longer any water in the adit below!

She felt the sickly lurch of her heart and she began to shake so dreadfully she thought she would fall, but she clenched her teeth and gripped her hands into fists and controlled herself somehow as she began to turn in readiness for the climb down. Alone and to what, her frightened mind asked, down the rise which she had come up so long ago, and if she got down without falling in her weakened state, what would be at the bottom, and if there was nothing more alarming than the steady solid darkness she now knew, where would she go from there?

A voice whispered in her ear, a voice she had heard in these very mines, a voice panting and breathless in its terror and she held on to it fiercely. It was a man's voice, a man who had run with her, her hand in his and the words he gasped then had held no sense, no reason for her.

'*There's an adit*,' he had said, speaking to someone else, '*. . . an old drainage adit . . .*'

An old drainage adit! An old drainage adit and drainage tunnels must lead *out* of a mine. That was what Pat Todd had been aiming for when he ran with the bewildered, terrified men away from the ladder and the shaft which would lead to escape. He had known the waters were too fast for them to reach that shaft so he had brought them here. Even so the flood had raced ahead of them and but for the rise and the natural cavity he had found they would all have drowned.

Her mind was sharp now. An old drainage adit, it kept repeating. She was no mining engineer but the words were as clear as the bright, strong hope which illuminated her mind; and she felt the strength move in her weak limbs and bravely she put her back to the circle of the shaft, kneeling on its rim as she began to inch her way in the darkness down the rise.

It took her two hours for several times in that solid darkness she froze in terror as she heard the squeaks and rustling sounds of the creatures who had returned. When she reached the bottom, standing upright for the first time in six days her legs would not support her and she fell to her hands and knees and something skittered over her back and she screamed and screamed, striking at the furry body with a frantic hand and the creatures backed away.

She could not remember which way to go for in truth her dazed mind could not recall which way they had come and for several minutes she sat in the wet pools which covered the rock and wept heartbreakingly. Then the thought came to her that it did not really matter. Whichever way she went she would find her way to the surface for both ways led to it.

On her hands and knees she began to crawl, shouting weakly to discourage the stealthy creeping bodies which moved about her. Her hands were warm now with some sticky wet substance, and her knees, and something dripped down her face from her forehead where she had knocked it against a rock.

On one occasion when she stopped to rest she must have dropped off to sleep, leaning like a weary horse, still on her hands and knees against the rock wall, and only the sharp pain from vicious teeth on her thumb brought her to screaming reality.

'Alex,' she cried out then. 'Please Alex, I can't manage any more. Please . . . please come and . . . get me . . . please . . .'

Her eyes began to trouble her, with blurred shadows which came and went shifting and moving in a way which hurt them and she felt the need to cover them, to protect them. If only she had a scarf to wrap around them, something to stop the . . . the . . . *the light*! It was light . . . oh God . . . sweet, sweet Jesus . . . the blackness was lessening . . . she could *see* a patch of something ahead, a patch that was paler than the rest, a blur, a fuzziness which seemed to shimmer, to shade at the edges, confusing, half glimpsed . . . dear sweet JESUS in heaven . . .

She crawled on, her head up, her eyes staring, concentrating, impervious to the pain in her head, dragging her suddenly weightless body behind her dazzled mind and the sweet, fresh, cold air swept about her, caressing her face and she wept as she reached the overgrown tangle of bracken which covered the opening of the drainage adit, parting the undergrowth with shaking hands until she could see . . . *see* . . . the dark blue, night sky and the drift of stars which lit it. She could smell the cool night tang of fading heather, fading yes, but to be re-born again when the time came, as she was. She could hear the sigh of the wind passing through the waist-high bracken and taste it on her parted lips; and every sense which had been annihilated during her incarceration in the earth's crust sprang to life joyously. She lifted her head and her pulses leapt to the knowledge that another feeling had been born in the horror she had survived and she must hurry to present it to the man she knew waited!

She stood up and put her hand to her blinded eyes, protecting them for even this Cimmerian darkness seared them in agony, then, her legs strong now as the fresh night air of the autumn fells came to nourish her, she shouted his name for she was going home to the man she loved!

He was sitting where she knew he would be, just at the head of the mine shaft. There was no one near him though several figures moved about the site since the work of pumping out the water and getting ready the mine for its re-opening must still go on.

She had crawled a good part of the way, over half a mile down the rock incline from the opening of the adit, moving slowly, painstakingly, a foot at a time towards the huddle of lights where the site was down the hillside.

She rose to her feet to walk that last fifty yards. He did not see her for a moment for his blank eyes stared from beneath lowered brows, at the arched opening of the mine, and when she spoke his name he seemed not to hear, or to believe that he had not heard. 'Alex,' she said again, her voice dwelling on his name with a sense of lovely wonder, a lilting, knowing wonder that this was the name of the man where love dwelled, that this was the man who had cloaked her in it for as long as she had known him. She stood quite still, unrecognizable if she had known it, to anyone but him who knew her with his heart as well as his senses.

'I've come home to you, Alex,' she said softly and her body began to tremble with longing to be where it belonged, where it had *always* belonged.

He lifted his head then and saw her, and his face was like death, the life gone from it, drained empty, the flesh already sunken into the shape of his skull. She put out her hands, lifting them to him and her tears washed away the last of the blindness and she saw that skull come to life, to lighten like the slow turning up of a lamp, the glow at last reaching his sunken eyes, illuminating them to shining, brimming, disbelieving love and his mouth opened wide as he shouted her name.

Heads lifted and stared in astonishment, watching as she began to run – *run* – after six days in the mine, they said afterwards, and his uninjured arm lifted to her, and life flowed into him and blazed into the rest of his dead body, as she placed herself in his safe refuge and the length of her body clung to his and they did not speak for there was no need of it now.

Rhanna
Christine Marion Fraser

A rich, romantic, Scottish saga set
on the Hebridean island of Rhanna

Rhanna

The poignant story of life on the rugged and tranquil island
of Rhanna, and of the close-knit community for whom it
is home.

Rhanna at War

Rhanna's lonely beauty is no protection against the horrors
of war. But Shona Mackenzie, home on leave, discovers
that the fiercest battles are those between lovers.

Children of Rhanna

The four island children, inseparable since childhood, find
that growing up also means growing apart.

Return to Rhanna

Shona and Niall Mackenzie come home to find Rhanna
unspoilt by the onslaught of tourism. But then tragedy
strikes at the heart of their marriage.

Song of Rhanna

Ruth is happily married to Lorn. But the return to Rhanna
of her now famous friend Rachel threatens Ruth's
happiness.

'Full-blooded romance, a strong, authentic setting'
Scotsman

FONTANA PAPERBACKS

ALSO AVAILABLE BY BELVA PLAIN

Evergreen

A rich, romantic, powerful epic of a woman's loves and her family's fortunes against this century's hopes and tragedies.

Crescent City

A sprawling epic of love and war, betrayal and hidden passions, set in the plush mansions and plantations of New Orleans during the Civil War era.

Eden Burning

Set on a Caribbean island, *Eden Burning* is a rich, romantic saga of the great estate of Eleuthera and the flamboyant complex family who owned it.

Random Winds

The absoring, poignant, wonderfully rich story of a family of doctors and a love nothing could suppress.

FONTANA PAPERBACKS

Susannah Kells

The superb, dramatic chronicles of the Lazender dynasty, set against a brilliant picture of England through the centuries. Susannah Kells is a major new British talent, writing in the great storytelling tradition of Daphne du Maurier.

A Crowning Mercy

Four intricately wrought seals – each owned by a stranger, each holding a secret within. These are Campion Slythe's key to the inheritance from her unknown father – her chance to escape from the worthy marriage which awaits her. But to claim her inheritance, and to find again the love she discovered on one golden summer afternoon, Campion must follow the course her father's legacy charts for her. And it is a road full of both peril and enchantment.

The Fallen Angels

Secure beneath the prosperous English sun, the 'little kingdom' of Lazen is unaware it is a house under siege. From the heart of Revolutionary France, the Fallen Angels · the most dangerous men in Europe – spin their web of intrigue, seeking the fall and the fortune of the Lazender family. Only the beautiful Lady Campion Lazender can save the great estate. But one man stands between Campion and disaster – Gitan, the mysterious gypsy – a man who could as easily be her enemy as her lover . . .

'Excellently done . . . Susannah Kells is a natural storyteller' *Catherine Gaskin*

FONTANA PAPERBACKS

Fontana Paperbacks
Fiction

Fontana is a leading paperback publisher of both non-fiction, popular and academic, and fiction. Below are some recent fiction titles.

- ☐ FIRST LADY Erin Pizzey £3.95
- ☐ A WOMAN INVOLVED John Gordon Davis £3.95
- ☐ COLD NEW DAWN Ian St James £3.95
- ☐ A CLASS APART Susan Lewis £3.95
- ☐ WEEP NO MORE, MY LADY Mary Higgins Clark £2.95
- ☐ COP OUT R.W. Jones £2.95
- ☐ WOLF'S HEAD J.K. Mayo £2.95
- ☐ GARDEN OF SHADOWS Virginia Andrews £3.50
- ☐ WINGS OF THE WIND Ronald Hardy £3.50
- ☐ SWEET SONGBIRD Teresa Crane £3.95
- ☐ EMMERDALE FARM BOOK 23 James Ferguson £2.95
- ☐ ARMADA Charles Gidley £3.95

You can buy Fontana paperbacks at your local bookshop or newsagent. Or you can order them from Fontana Paperbacks, Cash Sales Department, Box 29, Douglas, Isle of Man. Please send a cheque, postal or money order (not currency) worth the purchase price plus 22p per book for postage (maximum postage required is £3.00 for orders within the UK).

NAME (Block letters) _____

ADDRESS _____

_____

_____

While every effort is made to keep prices low, it is sometimes necessary to increase them at short notice. Fontana Paperbacks reserve the right to show new retail prices on covers which may differ from these previously advertised in the text or elsewhere.